Child sexual abuse and false
 memory syndrome

CHILD SEXUAL ABUSE AND FALSE MEMORY SYNDROME

CHILD SEXUAL ABUSE AND FALSE MEMORY SYNDROME

EDITED BY ROBERT A. BAKER

 Prometheus Books

59 John Glenn Drive
Amherst, New York 14228-2197

Published 1998 by Prometheus Books

02 01 00 99 98   5 4 3 2 1

Library of Congress Cataloging-in-Publication Data

Child sexual abuse and false memory syndrome / edited by Robert A. Baker.
    p.   cm.
    Includes bibliographical references.
    ISBN 1–57392–182–3 (cloth : alk. paper)
    1. False memory syndrome. 2. Recovered memory. 3. Adult child sexual abuse victims. 4. Autobiographical memory. 5. Psychic trauma in children. 6. Child sexual abuse—Investigation. I. Baker, Robert A. (Robert Allen), 1921–   .
RC455.2.F35C47   1998
616.85′8369—dc21   97–40899
                                          CIP

Printed in the United States of America on acid-free paper

CONTENTS

Preface: The Statement of the Problem
Robert A. Baker   9

Introduction: Hidden Memories: Fact or Fancy?
Barry L. Beyerstein and James R. P. Ogloff   15

PART ONE: MEMORY AND ITS RECOVERY

1. Remembering Dangerously
   Elizabeth F. Loftus   31

2. The Shadow of a Doubt
   Mary Sykes Wylie   49

3. The Seductions of Memory
   Michael D. Yapko   76

4. Facing the Truth about False Memory
   David Calof   87

5. Children's Memories for Stressful Events
   Gail S. Goodman, Jodi E. Hirschman,
   Debra Hepps McKee, and Leslie Rudy   97

PART TWO: REPRESSION AND AMNESIA

6. The Evidence for Repression:
   An Examination of Sixty Years of Research
   David S. Holmes   149

7. Can Memories of Childhood Sexual Abuse Be Repressed?
   Harrison G. Pope Jr. and James I. Hudson   169

8. Forgetting Sexual Trauma: What Does It Mean
   When 38% Forget?
   *Elizabeth F. Loftus, Maryanne Garry,
   and Julie Feldman*   181

9. Repressed Memories: True and False
   Andrew D. Reisner   193

PART THREE: HYPNOSIS, SUGGESTION, AND IATROGENESIS

10. Suggestibility and Repressed Memories of Abuse:
    A Survey of Psychotherapists' Beliefs
    Michael D. Yapko   215

11. Making Monsters
    Richard Ofshe and Ethan Watters   227

12. The Validity of Repressed Memories and the
    Accuracy of Their Recall Through Hypnosis:
    A Case Study from the Courtroom
    Donald R. Tayloe   250

13. The Memory Retrieval Process in Incest Survivor Therapy
    Christine A. Courtois   259

PART FOUR: PROFESSIONAL PROBLEMS AND ETHICAL ISSUES

14. The Professional Response to Child Sexual Abuse:
    Whose Interests Are Served?
    *Frank D. Fincham, Steven R. H. Beach,
    Thom Moore, and Carol Diener*   279

15. How Reliable Are Children's Statements? . . . It Depends
   Stephen J. Ceci and Maggie Bruck   309

16. Avoiding False Claims of Child Sexual Abuse:
   Empty Promises
   Kathy Pezdek   318

17. Child Sexual Abuse: Finding Common Ground
   Frank D. Fincham, Steven R. H. Beach,
   Thom Moore, and Carol Diener   327

18. Child Sexual Abuse: Ethical Issues for the Family Therapist
   Beth Haverkamp and Judith C. Daniluk   335

PART FIVE: RESEARCH, NEEDED RESEARCH, AND LEGAL IMPLICATIONS

19. The Impact of Child Sexual Abuse:
   A Review of the Research
   Angela Browne and David Finkelhor   355

20. Child Witnesses: Translating Research into Policy
   Stephen J. Ceci and Maggie Bruck   384

21. Recovered Memories of Alleged Sexual Abuse:
   Lawsuits against Parents
   Hollida Wakefield and Ralph Underwager   425

PART SIX: SUMMARY AND CONCLUSIONS

22. Where Do We Go from Here?
   Robert A. Baker   461

Recommended Readings   469

Contributors   473

Index   477

PREFACE

THE STATEMENT
OF THE PROBLEM

ROBERT A. BAKER

One of the more serious—if not the most serious—social psychological problems of our time is that of child sexual molestation and
abuse. Nearly three million allegedly abused or neglected children were
turned in to social-service agencies in 1993 according to the National
Committee for the Prevention of Child Abuse. Although there is good
reason to question exactly how many of these charges are valid, undoubtedly, too many of them are factually based and, even if only a few
children are neglected and abused, it is still too many! According to
Frank Putnam, M.D., senior clinical investigator at the National Institute of Mental Health's Developmental Psychology Laboratory, recent
research shows sexual molestation and abuse has powerful and far-
reaching deleterious effects on the growing child: first, while four times
as many girls are sexually abused the abuse of young boys is increasing;
abused young children also have many more physical complaints, e.g.,
headaches, stomachaches, anxieties, nightmares, bedwetting, and withdrawal symptoms than the nonabused; in the mid-childhood range the
abused show more somatic symptoms, poor school performance, dissociative behavior, lack of emotional control, attention disorders, and
sexual misbehavior; next, sexually abused teenagers are also more likely
to be sexually active, delinquent, and suicidal; and, finally, children sexually penetrated and abused by fathers and father figures are considerably
more emotionally and behaviorally disturbed than the nonabused.

Since the issue of childhood sexual molestation and abuse is extraor-
dinarily complex, multifaceted, and so emotion-arousing, any and all

9

efforts toward its solution or resolution no matter how herculean in retrospect today seem both impotent and trivial. Yet, with each day that
passes this problem becomes more pressing, more painful, and more
demanding. Everywhere we look we see the day-to-day fabric of human
lives being ripped and shredded: innocent men and women are being
jailed for crimes they did not commit; teachers and child-care workers no
longer dare hug or comfort a hurting child; therapists are anxious, bewil-
dered, and afraid to ply their trade—they are also afraid of their clients;
our courts are increasingly clogged with false claims and charges and
countercharges of abuse and neglect; every parent is increasingly fearful
for the safety and well-being of their children, so fearful they are at the
point of pathological paranoia; every celebrity and would-be celebrity in
the land now comb their childhood for possible instances of sexual and
other sorts of abuse that can be used to cast them in the role of victim
and converted into sympathetic publicity. Conspiracy theorists are
having a field day finding satanists and sex-maniacs behind every bush
and under every boulder. TV talk shows with their hordes of allegedly
abused limelight-lovers clog the channels while the so-called psychological and behavioral "experts" endlessly pose, prate, and pontificate.
Meanwhile, truth has fled and the children—the true victims—are again
neglected and mistreated. "Neglected" in that they no longer receive the
loving human care they need and deserve and "mistreated" in that they
are propagandized, prompted, and pushed by zealous parents and social
workers on both sides of the legal barricade into various perversions of
the facts. Most disturbing of all is the widespread distribution of the poi-
sons: fear, mistrust, and suspicion. Even the most innocent and gentle
young male is perceived as a rapist and any friendly gestures toward the
young are misperceived as predatory. The results are clear: our freedom
from fear is gone; panic and terror are now pervasive. Any threat to our
children and grandchildren, those we love more than life itself, cannot
be endured; our righteous anger is aroused and protection of the innocent becomes paramount. The mother's primal instinct to protect her
young is unquestionably endorsed and universally understood. Nothing
is more heinous than harm to the young and innocent. Society's outrage
at poor Susan Smith is a classic example. Even the most vicious felon in
a maximum security prison looks with disgust at the pedophile.

In spite of these facts we cannot, in the heat of passion, rush to an
inconsiderate judgment and make the unwarranted assumption that
every child showing any sort of deviancy whatsoever is automatically
therefore a victim of molestation. Similarly, and particularly, whenever an
adult shows up in the office of a psychotherapist we must not therefore
conclude that their psychological or behavioral problem is due to sexual

molestation in their childhood and that it is now our therapeutic duty to root out this maltreatment and its perpetrators and bring them to justice in a court of law. Again, this has been done, and not just once or twice but so many times and so often that it has now become a national scandal. One of the most knowledgeable and respected of experts on human memory, Dr. Elizabeth Loftus, notes that the controversy surrounding repressed memories has been called "the greatest scandal of the century in American psychiatry," and repressed memory therapy "the thalidomide of the mental health industry." These highly critical labels are well made and they are deserved. Within the last decade too many false memories of childhood sexual molestation have been created in the minds of vulnerable and suffering people. False memories aroused through the use of such therapeutic techniques as hypnotic age regression, drugs, dream interpretation, and guided and unguided imagery are common and easily created. They are also antitherapeutic.

On the other hand many cautious, careful, experienced, and dedicated psychotherapists reject with both anger and dismay the claims that they are injecting these ideas and beliefs of early sexual molestation into the minds of their clients. They insist such ideas and notions and beliefs were there to begin with and it was these horrors that brought the client to their doorstep. Undoubtedly, they are correct. Clients differ and so do therapists. Experienced therapists argue that in most of their clients who suffered from sexual mistreatment and abuse as a child, their problem is not in being able to recall or remember the abuse, rather it is in not being able to forget it or to come to terms with it. Whether there is such a thing as true "repression" in the Freudian sense is now being hotly debated with compelling arguments on both sides. Whether our memories can or cannot be trusted is also vigorously disputed with authorities marshaling evidence on both sides. Particularly crucial is the problem of how much children's memory can be trusted when one takes into consideration how easy it is to warp and manipulate their belief and recall. Although it is true that too many clinicians and psychotherapists have ignored the scientific literature that bears on their daily practice, it is also true that all of the needed scientific data to support and assist the practicing clinician in his daily ministrations is not yet available.

Moreover, anyone reading the daily newspapers or watching public-interest programs on the small screen are acutely aware of the terrible complexities underlying the legal and judicial confrontations that occur when parents and children face each other in custody cases and when children allege that they have been abused and mistreated by adults years and years before. How can both the rights and interests of the innocent and the guilty be protected and insured as well as the rights and best interests of society? Such questions are not easy to answer. What sort of research should be undertaken by those dedicated clinicians and social scientists concerned about this complex problem and how should they best go about their work? These are good questions and it would be comforting to say that this book will answer such questions as these and many more. Unfortunately, it will not. It will, however, provide you with a much better understanding of the extent of the problem of sexual molestation and the problem that psychotherapists and scientific psychologists have in trying to meet it, deal with it fairly and squarely, and provide a solution to the problem so that neither victim—be it child or adult—is denied justice or is unjustly treated. Justice is always and uppermost the desideratum when this problem rears its ugly head.

A HISTORICAL LOOK AT SEXUAL MOLESTATION

The problem of sexual molestation of the weak and the young by the strong and the mature is as old as man. Fortunately, as we have become more civilized some of the more flagrant sexual atrocities of the past have receded in both intensity and number across the spectrum of human behavior. Unfortunately, like war, genocide, and other atavistic aspects of human behavior, we have not been able to eliminate or eradicate the neglect, mistreatment, and abuse—particularly sexual abuse—of our children even in the most enlightened and highly educated nation in the world: the United States of America.

Recent reports from such monitoring agencies as the U.S. Advisory Board of Child Abuse and Neglect and the National Resource Center on Child Sexual Abuse are in full agreement that the level of violence aimed at young children—the most vulnerable members of our society—has reached public health crisis proportions. A two-and-one-half-year study by the USABCAN for the U.S. Congress found a level of fatal abuse and neglect far greater than even experts in the field had realized.

Not only is the vast majority of neglected and abused children under four years of age but the homicide rate among children in this age group is higher than it has ever been. Moreover, the nation's assumed protective system has largely failed. Not only are many cases of molestation and child-abuse fatalities never reported but even those most responsible— parents and caretakers—seem unconcerned and callous. As one investigator stated, "The true numbers and exact nature of the problem remain unknown and the troubling fact of abuse or neglect often remains a terrible secret that is buried with the child" (J. D. Rivera, *Los Angeles Times*, April 26, 1995). A report to Congress titled "A Nation's Shame: Fatal

Child Abuse and Neglect in the United States" stresses the difficulty of discovering the extent of sexual molestation because this is even more difficult to determine than simple physical mistreatment or neglect simply because parents and caretakers make major efforts to cover it up.

Despite the horror of its existence today, it apparently is insignificant in light of past historical practices. Students of the history of child abuse, for example, Dr. Lloyd DeMause, are appalled at what they have found. DeMause, who has spent over twenty years examining thousands of original sources such as diaries, autobiographies, letters, doctor's reports, and historical studies in trying to determine how children were treated in the past, has provided us with a very unsettling picture. What DeMause reveals in his definitive book *Foundations of Psychohistory* (Creative Roots, 1982) is a humanist's worst nightmare. According to DeMause, "the further back in history one goes, the lower the level of child care, and the more likely children are to have been killed, abandoned, beaten, terrorized and sexually abused. Growing up in Greece and Rome often included being used sexually. Boy brothels flourished in every city, and one could even contract for the use of a rent-a-boy service in Athens. Adults were instructed by doctors to masturbate their children from infancy. Petronius loves depicting adults feeling the 'immature little tool' of boys, and his description of the rape of a seven-year-old girl with men clapping in a long line around the bed suggests that women were not exempt from playing a role in the process. Castrated boys in particular turned on Roman men, with infants being castrated in the cradle to be later used in brothels . . ."

DeMause also argues that "rather than the incest taboo being universal as it is commonly held, it is incest itself—direct and indirect—that is universal for children in most cultures throughout history. A childhood more or less free from adult sexual abuse is, in fact, a rather late historical achievement limited to a few fortunate children in a few modern nations, many in the West"(Lloyd DeMause, "The Universality of Incest," *Journal of Psychohistory* 19 [1991]: 123–64). DeMause also maintains that sexual molestation outside the Western world is a routine practice in most families—particularly in India, China, and Japan. In India, for example, very few female children over ten years of age are virgins and here also "incest is often the rule rather than the exception." Only recently, DeMause claims, have we moved the evolution of childhood from incest to love and from abuse to empathy. If all of the recent reports are correct, we still have a long way to go.

One of the things we cannot afford, however, in making this trip is the mistake of savagely punishing innocent adults in our zeal to punish those guilty of sexual crimes against children. The argument that so many molesters and pedophiles have gotten off scot-free in the past is not a sufficient rationale for punishing the innocent today. Not even the fact that child abuse may be on the increase is justification for any unjust prosecution of the innocent. Justice for all—both the innocent children and the innocent adults—is the desideratum and it is also one that is attainable if reason, patience, and competent investigation on all sides and from all angles persist.

INTRODUCTION

HIDDEN MEMORIES:
FACT OR FANCY?

BARRY L. BEYERSTEIN
AND JAMES R. P. OGLOFF

The Beyerstein and Ogloff article provides an excellent summary and overview of the problem of so-called hidden memories and it also emphasizes the extreme emotional reactions that have much too frequently accompanied any and all open discussions of these issues in the past.

It has been estimated that, annually in Canada, as many as 20,000 children are sexually abused. Concern about child abuse began to grow in the early 1960s when the groundbreaking work of Dr. Kempe and his colleagues first came to the public's attention. Since that time, every jurisdiction in North America has adopted statutes for mandatory reporting of child abuse. Substantive, evidentiary, and procedural changes have been made to the legal system to improve how the courts and the justice system work with children who have been abused. Social workers, teachers, and medical staff have been taught to look for signs. Sadly, child abuse remains a pressing national problem.

In the vast majority of cases of child abuse and child sexual abuse that are reported and result in prosecution the victims vividly remember the brutalities they endured (even if, for any of a number of understandable reasons, they choose not to make a public accusation for a long time thereafter). Like many Holocaust survivors, torture victims, or those who have witnessed gruesome deaths of loved ones, these adult

This article originally appeared in *The Rational Enquirer* 6, no. 2 (1993), newsletter of the British Columbia Skeptics, and reprinted in the *Georgia Skeptic* (Fall 1994).

victims of childhood abuse often wish they could forget the horrible experiences that intrude mercilessly on their everyday thoughts. In contrast to these cases where obsessive ruminations about past traumas cannot be put aside, a relatively new problem has recently come to the fore. It has begun to affect the legal system and has piqued the curiosity and concern of the media and the public.

The issue is that of allegedly "hidden" or "repressed" memories of child abuse or child sexual abuse. In cases of this sort, the victim reports no awareness of the abuse until long after it supposedly occurred. Often, this newfound knowledge only surfaces in early or middle adulthood when recollection is triggered during therapy for other problems or after the individual has read one of a spate of "pop-psychology" books on the topic (e.g., Ellen Bass and Laura Davis's *Courage to Heal*). Only then does he or she suddenly become aware of the traumatic episodes. Such cases present a dilemma for the legal system and they have engendered heated controversy among memory researchers as well as psychologists, psychiatrists, and other mental health professionals who work with victims of abuse.

Once again we are faced with the age-old enigma of how to decide whether any memory is accurate or not. In cases of allegedly reinstated hidden memories, several additional difficulties arise. A scenario that has been reported to us several times is one where a client contacts a therapist seeking help for feelings of general unhappiness, depression, or anxiety, or for other problems of living. If the therapist happens to believe that ill-focused malaise of this sort is frequently due to childhood sexual abuse, this possibility might be suggested to the client who is likely to be in a vulnerable and suggestible state at the time. Given the usual ways that clients become paired with a particular therapist, it is unlikely that many would be aware in advance of this theoretical orientation on the part of the therapist or that it is not shared by all in the helping professions (some therapists have acquired a reputation for such leanings, however, and self-diagnosed clients are increasingly beginning to seek them out to validate their suspicions). The client who arrives with no inkling that he or she could have been abused may well reject the therapist's suggestion at first, especially in light of the realization of who the perpetrators would need to have been. In the topsy-turvey world of hidden memories this refusal actually becomes evidence for the hypothesized abuse rather than a reason to question it—denial is considered further proof that the memories have been repressed. Several videotapes we have seen of therapists of this bent in action show that they can be very insistent indeed. Former clients who have contacted us tell of concerted efforts by their ex-therapists to convince them that they must have been molested and of how, in the process of counseling, they came to believe that they had been. They also recall their satisfaction at the time at finally arriving at an all-encompassing explanation for their despondency and having someone other than themselves or "fate" to blame, as well as having a target for the negative flood of emotions that ensues.

A variation on the theme, familiar to readers of the *Skeptical Inquirer*, is the related brand of therapist who is inclined to interpret psychological symptoms as evidence of alien abduction. With similar encouragements, alleged abductees can also supply detailed recollections of their capture, the extraterrestrials who snatched them, and the indignities they suffered. Interestingly, the tales abductees relate often have a theme of sexual violation to them as well. The belief that abductees have been rendered amnesic for their period of confinement and that this wall can only be breached by specially trained counselors who know what to look for sounds eerily like the received wisdom among those whose mission is to reveal hidden memories of child sexual abuse. If one has talked for any length of time with an alleged abductee, it is quite apparent that they fervently believe their stories. Unfortunately, obvious sincerity and commitment to an account are not particularly good indicators of its believability.

It is likely that abductees did have an experience, just as they describe it, but this by itself does not prove that it occurred outside of the theatre of their own minds. Recent research on so-called fantasy-prone personalities has shown that there is a small proportion of the nonpsychiatric population whose mental imagery is so vivid and invasive that they frequently generate compellingly real subjective experiences that are mixtures of real percepts and detailed hallucinations. Because they cope well enough in family, social, and work settings, such individuals rarely come to the attention of psychiatrists or psychologists. They seem quite normal to all outward appearances. Fantasy-prone individuals were only discovered because they appeared in large numbers in a research study that actively sought those with the very highest degree of hypnotic susceptibility.

An important difference between the alien abduction and child sexual abuse cases is that aliens, if they exist, are not close friends or family of the victims—and at any rate they are, at least for the time being, beyond the insufficiently long arm of the earthbound law. This difference makes the stakes much higher in the latter cases, for both the accuser and the accused. As one might expect, emotions run very high— not a situation well-suited to dispassionate search for the truth. This was quite evident recently when Harold Lief, a psychiatrist critical of the hidden memory concept, was shouted down and prevented from giving a scholarly address on the subject at McGill University's Department of Psychiatry. The angry demonstrators who disrupted this lecture were activists committed to helping victims of sexual abuse. They came equipped with party noisemakers to drown out the proceedings. This unruly mob refused even to hear the speaker's evidence, accusing him in advance of merely wanting to help perverts escape justice. It was even reported that death threats had been uttered.

The issue which so often gets lost in this inflamed rhetoric is not whether adults sexually abuse children. Sadly, it happens. Rather it is whether coaxing out supposedly hidden memories from adults who were previously unaware of such abuse is a sound basis on which to lay one of the most serious charges that can be leveled against an individual in our society. To help us unravel such a thorny issue, it would be well to consider what the last hundred years of research has taught us about the nature of human memory.

HUMAN MEMORY FOR PERSONAL HISTORIES

The veracity of autobiographical memories is a perennial problem in criminal and accident investigations, court proceedings, historical research, psychotherapy, and everyday life. Skeptical researchers are rarely surprised to find that the recollections of responsible, well-educated people who have no intent to deceive can still be glaringly inaccurate when they try to remember exactly what they saw during a UFO sighting or the precise details of a self-professed psychic's performance. On the other hand, as was demonstrated by the testimony of the Watergate witness John Dean (when Richard Nixon's tapes were finally released), human memory is also capable of great precision and accuracy under the right conditions. Note, however, that the events Dean recounted were relatively recent and he never claimed to have been amnesic for them at any time. Generalizations about such abilities are made difficult by the fact that individuals vary greatly in this regard, as they do in athletic prowess or any other trait. Given the major penalties and payoffs that society apportions on the basis of believability of people's recollections, it is not surprising that the search for an understanding of what promotes accuracy or failure of memory has long attracted many of the best minds in experimental psychology.

Following the pioneering research of the Cambridge psychologist Sir Frederick Bartlett, in the early part of this century, experts have come to accept that human memory is more reconstructive than previously thought. In other words, memory is not simply a perfect echo of past experience. What seems to be an unadorned replay of past events (often complete with detailed visual imagery) has, in fact, a substantial inferential component which has been shown to be affected by cognitive biases, shortcuts in reasoning strategies, social and contextual processes, and even personality factors. Unfortunately, by mid-century, the competing "videotape" theory of memory came, temporarily, to overshadow Bartlett's more valid conceptualizations. This was largely due to misinterpretations and exaggerations of some dramatic demonstrations by the Montreal neurosurgeon Wilder Penfield. Penfield found that vivid, almost hallucinatory memories can be elicited by stimulating the temporal lobes of patients' brains with weak electrical currents during brain surgery. While the results of this procedure made it appear to some that everything a person ever experiences might be recorded in minute detail in the brain (and thus be waiting to be triggered by the right stimulus), this interpretation has since given way under a barrage of logical as well as empirical attacks. Nonetheless, holdovers from Penfield's conception of memory continue to influence the thinking of those who espouse the notion of hidden memories. In recent years, it has been the work of Elizabeth Loftus and her colleagues at the University of Washington that has done the most to cast doubt on this "store everything verbatim" school of memory and to demonstrate the superiority of Bartlett's reconstructive approach.

Since it is clearly impossible, even for the truly astonishing capacities of the human brain, to store every detail of a complex situation, memory must select and compress. Thus, it registers a few salient features of each episode, along with a label for what Bartlett called a "schema." A schema is a body of knowledge, acquired in the process of acculturation, that summarizes what typically occurs in events of various sorts. Which label is attached to the skeleton event stored in memory is a function of the meaning initially ascribed to the episode. Upon recall, the outline is "filled in" from data contained in the appropriate schema. Because these inferential and reconstructive processes are largely unconscious, this creative aspect of memory generally escapes our notice. Inasmuch as daily life does include many repetitious, role-governed situations, this way of storing autobiographical memories is economical of our limited capacity to handle information and, most often, leads to a sufficiently accurate account of what transpired. It can, however, also generate egregious errors on occasion, even among highly intelligent and honest individuals.

Potential sources of distorted memories have been discovered at all stages of memory processing. During the initial experience, one's beliefs, wishes, and expectations can direct attention toward certain features of the situation and away from others. This affects how the event is classified from the outset. Because this interpretation influences the label attached to the event in memory, it can bias the selection of the schema that will be engaged to flesh out any later recollection. Significant omissions or insertions can result. Errors can also be introduced at the recall stage when an interrogator's leading questions invite unsound inferences that seem to arise spontaneously from the recaller's own memory. These misinterpretations can then feed back into the system as this modified version of the event reenters memory to become part of the "recollection" on subsequent attempts. Such tactics, known to stage magicians as "the invited inference," are used very effectively in various mentalist routines and are often copied by charlatans who wish to impress people with apparent psychic powers.

CRYPTOMNESIA

Confusions also arise from the fact that we frequently retain factual information while forgetting how and when it was learned. The anomalous memory phenomena known as paramnesia and cryptomnesia have been studied extensively by psychologists interested [in] personal memories. They contribute to many ostensibly paranormal experiences, including the occultists' old standby déjà vu. It is common for people to experience (during dreams, meditation, free association, daydreams, or hypnosis, for instance) detailed images of places and events that they feel certain they have never learned about or observed in person. Because they honestly cannot recall having been exposed to the information, they jump to the conclusion that it must have been fed to them in a supernatural way. The strong desire to believe in telepathy, aliens, or previous incarnations makes them seem more plausible sources than forgotten personal experiences or books, TV programs, or movies seen long ago. The BBC investigative reporter Melvin Harris presents a beautiful example of this in his book, *Sorry—You've Been Duped*. Jane Evans's "astonishing hypnotic remembrances" of her previous life in ancient France—widely touted as some of the best-ever evidence for reincarnation—turned out to have an uncanny resemblance to events in a historical novel that was very popular at the time she attended grammar school. Evans's accounts contained a mixture of accurate and inaccurate depictions of the time and place that just happened to parallel the artistic licenses taken by the novelist. Evans was thoroughly convinced, as were the researchers who were avidly seeking evidence for reincarnation, that she was recalling true memories of her previous life.

The inadvisability of concluding that just because you can't recall learning about something, your present knowledge of it must have supernatural origins will be obvious from the following example. Ask yourself, "Where is the Eiffel Tower?" Most likely, you instantly replied, "Paris." Can you now recall when and from whom you first learned the site of this famous landmark? Chances are you cannot, despite the fact that you would have been willing to place a very large wager on the veracity of your recollection. This is an example of "source amnesia" and it demonstrates that factual information is somehow stored separately from the autobiographical data concerned with how we came to know it. In such cases, we know something but not how we acquired it.

It is also possible to "know" things in our personal histories that aren't so. CSICOP Executive Council member James Alcock relates the story of reminiscing with old college chums about a fracas in a waterfront bar that had occurred back in their undergraduate days. At some point, Alcock chimed in, "And then remember when . . . ?" only to be met with stunned silence, followed by a friend's retort, "But Jim, you weren't there!" On reflection, Alcock realized that he had heard this story so many times at previous reunions with his college buddies that he had unconsciously "written himself into" the stored scenario for this event that he now realized he could not possibly have witnessed in person. He was amazed to find that the "memory" of the brawl he dredged up included vivid visual images, complete with himself at the scene.

The late developmental psychologist Jean Piaget described a similar experience. As an adult, he was sure that his earliest childhood memory was that of being rescued from a kidnapper by his brave nanny. Only many years later did the repentant nanny come to visit her former charge and confess that she had made up the story to avoid the censure of Jean's parents for bringing him home late. Piaget too had "memories," complete with detailed visual images of the nonexistent attacker and his nanny's stalwart defense. Similar to Alcock's "memories" of the barroom melee, this event had become part of Piaget's family history, retold to the point that it acquired the status of a real event in his mind. It is phenomena such as these that continue to make the study of memory one of the most active areas of experimental psychology.

REPRESSED MEMORIES AND MOTIVATED FORGETTING

Returning to the issue of "hidden memories," an intense controversy has surfaced concerning the concept of "repression" or motivated forgetting of traumatic events. Also known as "inhibition," "dissociation," or a kind of "defense mechanism," repression denotes amnesia for certain distressing experiences, usually without any conscious effort to forget them. Believers in hidden memories contend that the reason there has been no recent awareness of the abuse is that the victim has repressed it to spare him- or herself the pain of reminiscence.

A heated debate exists in the professional literature concerning the very existence of repression. Those who accept the notion are largely therapists with a psychoanalytic (i.e., Freudian) bent. Experimental psychologists, by and large, tend to have more doubts about the idea of repression. They note, for instance, how many people fervently wish they could repress terrible scenes from their childhood. Even among those who accept the reality of repression, there are still disagreements about how extensive it is and what techniques, if any, might bring repressed memories to light. Various clinicians have advocated free-association, dream analysis, hypnosis, dissociative drugs, and guided imagery in a trancelike reverie as ways to revive these hidden memories. Critics contend that these procedures are as likely to produce fantasy and confabulations that feel like valid recollections as they are to expose true hidden memories.

CAN HYPNOSIS OR RELATED TECHNIQUES DO THE TRICK?

Hypnosis researchers such as Ernest Hilgard, Martin Orne, Nicholas Spanos, and Robert Baker have shown numerous times how easy it is to produce pseudomemories in experimental subjects who will state with great conviction that the suggested events actually occurred. Another respected researcher, Kenneth Bowers, has shown that when people are required to identify previously seen objects in a group that contains a mixture of new and old items, hypnosis can slightly improve their hit rate in correctly identifying the previously shown stimuli. However, it also raises the false alarm rate—i.e., hypnotized subjects were also more likely to label as repeats stimuli that they had not been shown before. Hypnosis, in general, is more likely to raise the person's confidence that his or her recollections are true than the actual probability of their being true.

There is a voluminous literature on so-called demand characteristics that shows that overt suggestions are not necessary to create pseudomemories—hypnotic subjects are adept at picking up and complying with very subtle cues as to what the hypnotist wants or expects. Two of the world's leading hypnosis researchers, Martin Orne and Nicholas Spanos, have become convinced, in addition, that formal hypnotic procedures are not required to produce such compliance effects. For instance, the Berkeley researcher Richard Ofshe, in an article entitled "Inadvertent Hypnosis During Interrogation," demonstrated how repeated suggestions by insistent interrogators can elicit admissions to nonexistent crimes. The foregoing kinds of research support the contention that many of the techniques used by poorly trained therapists to ferret out possible histories of abuse are quite capable of producing what Orne has dubbed a "false memory syndrome." A foundation by that name has been founded by Orne and others who feel that at least some of the allegations based on hidden memory enhancement are being generated by sincere but deluded clients of questionably qualified therapists.

Predictably, the False Memory Syndrome Foundation (FMSF) has become the lightning rod for victims' rights groups protesting that the organization is merely giving aid and comfort to those seeking to evade punishment for their actions. On a recent CBC radio program, the foundation was accused of being part of a well-funded right-wing fascist conspiracy! These critics tend to forget that, although members of the FMSF do say that accusations based on hidden memories should not be granted automatic credence just because they seem so real to the percipient, they also freely admit that they cannot rule out, in any given case, the possibility that abuse did take place. The point is that there is no royal road to the truth and in the current climate that sometimes verges on hysteria, we need to be reminded that the possibility exists for unfairly convicting the accused as well as for denying justice to the alleged victim. One of the researchers (not connected with the FMSF) who has demonstrated under controlled conditions how unreliable children's apparently heartfelt recollections can be, Stephen Ceci of Cornell University, refuses to testify as an expert witness on behalf of either the prosecution or the defense in such cases because he feels, quite rightly, that showing how inaccurate memories can be in no way speaks to the truth or falsity of any particular accusation.

In an excellent article in the Fall 1993 issue of the *Skeptical Inquirer*, Scott Lilienfeld details the shortcomings of polygraphs, "honesty tests," hypnosis, and other techniques touted as surefire arbiters of the truth. As one might expect, none of these quick fixes lives up to its advance billing. Unfortunately, assessing witness credibility in the absence of corroborative evidence remains an exact process. The dilemma is not helped by crackpot schemes such as a recent seminar, advertised for continuing education credit for registered psychologists, that offered to teach therapists to diagnose repressed memories of childhood abuse from clients' handwriting!

The time-honored rules of evidence and other due process requirements that have come down to us through English Common Law are far from perfect, but throwing them away because it is very hard to prove certain kinds of guilt is fraught with far greater perils in the long run. The old adage that it is better for a dozen guilty men to walk free than for a single innocent one to be convicted is in danger of being stood on its head in the rush to make amends for our culture's belated recognition of the problem of child sexual abuse. We do not serve the cause of justice by abandoning the demand for "proof beyond a reasonable doubt."

THE THERAPIST'S BURDEN

When apparent memories, elicited by the "enhancement" techniques discussed earlier, generate allegations of abuse suffered long ago, but for which there has been no awareness in the interim, the courts, clinicians, researchers, and various advocacy groups are forced to wrestle with the ethics of acting on accusations based solely on this kind of evidence. This is especially so if the newly convinced victim initially entered psychotherapy to deal with different complaints and the therapist happens to have a strong commitment to the theory that early sexual abuse underlies many, if not most, adult psychological problems.

A further source of worry stems from the fact that many (but by no means all) practitioners who advocate uncritical acceptance of hidden memories are essentially self-taught counselors with little formal training in psychology or psychiatry. In the time-honored New Age tradition, many of them have "graduated" from a narrow apprenticeship in the one and only technique they know. "Watch one, do one, teach one" is their modus operandi. It is significant that those least skeptical of the hidden memory concept are often the least well informed about the relevant data in the scientific literature on human memory. Be that as it may, having talked to many of these counselors, we would be the last to question their sincerity and their caring. They empathize deeply with their clients who are clearly suffering from something and who, on that basis alone, deserve our sympathy and our help. The question is not, "Should we try to help them rebuild their lives?"—of course we should. On the other hand, basic fairness dictates that we should demand reasonable confirmation before conceding that their very real malaise necessarily arises from past sexual abuse for which somebody deserves to be punished.

To muddy the waters further, there is often a considerable power differential between the accused and the accuser, and consciously or not, the temptation to bring down those in authority or to settle past scores must play a part in at least some accusations. In recent years, allegations of sexual abuse have been increasingly used, fairly or not, as leverage in child custody disputes. This has added to public confusion over just what the real incidence of abuse might be and fed suspicion in some quarters that many allegations are self-serving. The recent mistrials and acquittals in several cases involving daycare workers accused of ritually abusing children have revealed many shoddy interviewing practices on the part of overzealous investigators. Moreover, certain tenets of the radical feminist movement also dovetail with the agenda of the hidden memory camp to introduce another explosive element into the mix. Despite these reasons for caution, however, it must be emphasized yet again that sexual abuse and sexual harassment do occur, more often than many of us like to think. We must be careful not to let legitimate doubts about some accusations based solely on supposedly reinstated hidden memories lead us to discount other accusations where large amounts of time have not intervened, the victims never had any difficulty recalling their victimization, and where, ideally, there would be some corroborative evidence to bolster the charges.

THE LEGAL CLIMATE

Traditionally, the justice system has been wary of accepting unsupported memories as evidence if the disputed events are remote in time and/or the recaller stands to gain from the recollections. However, the tide seems to have been turning of late. Increasingly, criminal prosecutions and civil cases have been allowed to proceed, based solely on "recalled" events that have not only been quite old but which also surfaced only after therapists had made concerted attempts to "reveal" early memories. The vast majority of Crown prosecutors are conscientious professionals who want to do the right thing. Many have contacted us seeking guidance—they are caught in an unenviable squeeze between alleged victims of the hidden memory type, clamoring for prosecution of their accused molesters, and the best traditions of their profession that say one does not lay extremely serious charges without sufficient evidence. Though the public does see some prosecutions that should never have gone to court, we do not see the larger number that prosecutors decline to pursue.

The admission that mental health professionals, the media, and the public have been unconscionably tardy in acknowledging that sexual and other abuse of youngsters is more prevalent than any of us wanted to believe has prompted a rebound and with it a growing public willingness to credit, uncritically, any accusation based on hidden memories. Some experts think, though, that the incidence of abuse, tragic as it is, has come to be exaggerated, and that the pendulum has swung from undue skepticism in the past all the way to today's overly credulous acceptance of allegations based on uncorroborated hidden memories. In other words, their worry is that the unfairness may have shifted from that of allowing perpetrators to go unpunished and their victims to be further victimized to the other extreme where an increasing number of innocent people are being denounced by sincere but mistaken accusers.

A PROPOSED CONFERENCE

The Psychology Department at Simon Fraser University has proposed a symposium that will assemble a group of noted experts to investigate the scholarly and practical issues raised by the hidden memory controversy. Several of the best researchers in relevant fields have already expressed an interest in participating if money can be found to stage the conference. The authors of this article are among the program planners; they have raised some of the necessary funds and are awaiting the outcome of other pending requests. If they are successful, the conference will most likely be held in March of 1994. Part of the proceedings will be academic papers and discussions, for which, unfortunately, there will have to be a registration fee and perhaps some restriction on admission, based on professional credentials, in order to allow for fruitful discussions among the experts. Other parts of the conference will be open to the public and a serious effort will be made to give advocacy groups on all sides an opportunity to present their case. In this way, we hope to minimize the likelihood of another debacle such as the recent near riot at McGill's Psychiatry Department.

The SFU program intends to place the various positions in context by beginning with authorities on the basic mechanisms of memory and on autobiographical memory and eyewitness testimony. This will be followed by specialists in the ethical and legal implications of this research. In addition, the organizers intend to invite presentations from clinicians experienced in dealing with abuse victims who will discuss how they assess the believability of accusations of abuse that arise during psychotherapy. They will interact with academic researchers interested in areas such as hypnosis and social demand characteristics. And finally, advocacy groups on both sides of the controversy will be allowed to interact with the invited experts—i.e., spokespersons for those who believe that "enhancement" reliably exposes real abuse, and for those who doubt this is possible. Responsible and fair-minded advocates will be sought to represent the views of the allegedly abused as well as those claiming they were falsely accused. As mentioned above, supporters of the latter argue that at least some accusations are derived from flawed methods that can produce a "false memory syndrome." They assert that such illusory but sincerely believed "memories" frequently result in undeserved loss of reputations, family relationships, friendships, and livelihoods. Their opponents, on the other hand, accuse them of providing shelter for felons.

AID AND COMFORT TO THE ABUSERS?

The organizers of the proposed symposium are well aware of the trauma that surrounds child abuse and child sexual abuse. Obviously, they do not wish to compound the suffering of those who have been mistreated. Rather, their intention is to examine, in an objective and scholarly forum, the theoretical, practical, legal, and ethical issues raised by the hidden memory controversy. The sponsors wish to restrict discussion to cases where the claimant professed no recollection of maltreatment until memory enhancement was attempted. They agree that all accusations of sexual abuse should be thoroughly investigated, first by competent clinicians working with the accuser and, if indicated, by the best methods of police procedure and forensic science. The actual incidence of such molestations is a matter for careful research—it is not the intention of this symposium to question a priori whether popular estimates accurately reflect the real prevalence.

The organizers believe that, ultimately, it is in the best interests of real survivors of abuse for the hidden memory issue to be explored dispassionately and in detail. It would be most unfortunate for real victims if the growing public awareness of some demonstrably false accusations and of the existence of a false memory syndrome were to engender another backlash that would hinder their efforts to achieve justice and to alleviate their suffering. There is a danger that, left exclusively to debate in the media, the high academic credentials of those who can demonstrate that false memories are possible and the questionable behavior of some therapists of the opposite persuasion will lead the public to conclude, quite unfairly, that most accusations of child molestation are bogus. It is also hoped that out of the conference will come a greater public understanding and compassion for those who feel, even if mistakenly, that they were victims of abuse. Like so many of us, they are searching for solutions to their very real unhappiness. Sexual abuse has become a trendy explanation for all sorts of ills and these people should not be castigated if the suggestion rings true for them, even if it is not. If, in trying to spare other innocent parties the horrors of false accusation, we deny these troubled souls this rationale and course of action, we owe them no less compassionate and competent help to discover and deal with the real causes of their distress. It is our hope that the proposed symposium will produce a reliable guide for researchers, practitioners, the media, and policy makers who must deal with this pressing social issue.

SPECIAL TO THE GEORGIA SKEPTIC

The conference referred to in the foregoing article (first published in the November 1993 issue of the *Rational Enquirer*) did take place in May of 1994. To our surprise, many of the funding agencies we approached turned us down, despite the all-star cast of speakers we had assembled. The topic was apparently too hot to handle. Nonetheless, registrants filled the largest lecture hall at the Simon Fraser University downtown campus, as well as an overflow room equipped with an audio-video feed. The conference culminated in a debate between Elizabeth Loftus and Linda Williams, a leading proponent of the hidden memory concept. Another key speaker was Nicholas Spanos who, sad to say, was killed shortly afterward in a plane crash. Nick was slated to speak the following month at the CSICOP conference in Seattle, which also featured a panel on the hidden memories controversy.

The SFU conference included leading academics, jurists, civil libertarians, and a panel comprised of therapists, some of whom attempt to recover memories in the ways questioned by many of the academic speakers. It was hoped that by including these therapists, as well as a number of victims' rights activists, on the program, we could avoid the near riots that have disrupted other forums on this issue.

We succeeded in that all the worst altercations were verbal, with several speakers such as Elizabeth Loftus and Nick Spanos being subjected to insults hurled by a few irate registrants. Rude and uncalled for, but better than what has happened elsewhere. Nick Spanos's careful comparisons of memories of alleged ritual satanic abuse with alleged memories of being abducted by aliens and Elizabeth Loftus's showing, with commentary, of a surreptitiously taped video of one of the Bass and Davis-style "recovered memory therapists" in action aroused the most ire. One telephone death threat was made toward one of the conference organizers, but no physical altercations of any kind ensued.

Despite the attempt to give the proponents of hidden memories a chance to state their case, we were still criticized in some quarters for bias, misogyny, harboring abusers, and adding to victims' burdens.

MEMORY AND ITS RECOVERY

Part One is devoted to the nature of human memory and what we know and don't know about it today.

Elizabeth F. Loftus's article on the dangers of uncritical acceptance of recovered memories and the filing of false charges based upon them is both important and significant. Yet, as Mary S. Wylie cautions, child abuse is widespread, pervasive, and some of the memories are based on fact, and for much too long, widespread sexual abuse has been ignored. Yet Yapko, an experienced therapist, shows vividly how easy it is for therapists to wreak havoc in their clients' lives and how powerful and subtle suggestion can be. Calof insists that few therapists implant false memories and those who are cited are only a few examples of bad therapy and bad therapists. Calof also argues that most stories that he hears of childhood sexual abuse are true.

Childhood trauma can be a crucial etiological factor in the development of a number of disorders both in childhood and adulthood. Dr. Goodman's work on children's memory for stressful events reveals that children's memory is not affected by stress until a very high level of stress is reached. At this point stress does improve free recall and resistance to suggestion. Nevertheless, forgetting clearly occurs and children's memory for stressful events fades just as it does for nonstressful events. In general, stress does not have a decremental effect on memory and both the quantity and quality of emotion play important roles in regulating memory. Though age differences in memory appear, stress does not differentially affect memory as a function of age.

1

REMEMBERING DANGEROUSLY

ELIZABETH F. LOFTUS

We live in a strange and precarious time that resembles at its heart the hysteria and superstitious fervor of the witch trials of the sixteenth and seventeenth centuries. Men and women are being accused, tried, and convicted with no proof or evidence of guilt other than the word of the accuser. Even when the accusations involve numerous perpetrators, inflicting grievous wounds over many years, even decades, the accuser's pointing finger of blame is enough to make believers of judges and juries. Individuals are being imprisoned on the "evidence" provided by memories that come back in dreams and flashbacks—memories that did not exist until a person wandered into therapy and was asked point-blank, "Were you ever sexually abused as a child?" And then begins the process of excavating the "repressed" memories through invasive therapeutic techniques, such as age regression, guided visualization, trance writing, dream work, body work, and hypnosis.

One case that seems to fit the mold led to highly bizarre satanic-abuse memories. An account of the case is described in detail by one of the expert witnesses (Rogers 1992) and is briefly reviewed by Loftus and Ketcham (1994).

A woman in her mid-seventies and her recently deceased husband were accused by their two adult daughters of rape, sodomy, forced oral sex, torture by electric shock, and the ritualistic murder of babies. The

From *Skeptical Inquirer* (March/April 1995): 20–29. Reprinted by permission of the author and publisher.

older daughter, 48 years old at the time of the lawsuit, testified that she was abused from infancy until age 25. The younger daughter alleged abuse from infancy to age 15. A granddaughter also claimed that she was abused by her grandmother from infancy to age 8.

The memories were recovered when the adult daughters went into therapy in 1987 and 1988. After the breakup of her third marriage, the older daughter started psychotherapy, eventually diagnosing herself as a victim of multiple-personality disorder and satanic ritual abuse. She convinced her sister and her niece to begin therapy and joined in their therapy sessions for the first year. The two sisters also attended group therapy with ocher multiple-personality-disorder patients who claimed to be victims of satanic ritual abuse.

In therapy the older sister recalled a horrifying incident that occurred when she was four or five years old. Her mother caught a rabbit, chopped off one of its ears, smeared the blood over her body, and then handed the knife to her, expecting her to kill the animal. When she refused, her mother poured scalding water over her arms. When she was 13 and her sister was still in diapers, a group of Satanists demanded that the sisters disembowel a dog with a knife. She remembered being forced to watch as a man who threatened to divulge the secrets of the cult was burned with a torch. Other members of the cult were subjected to electric shocks in rituals that took place in a cave. The cult even made her murder her own newborn baby. When asked for more details about these horrific events, she testified in court that her memory was impaired because she was frequently drugged by the cult members.

The younger sister remembered being molested on a piano bench by her father while his friends watched. She recalled being impregnated by members of the cult at ages 14 and 16, and both pregnancies were ritually aborted. She remembered one incident in the library where she had to eat a jar of pus and another jar of scabs. Her daughter remembered seeing her grandmother in a black robe carrying a candle and being drugged on two occasions and forced to ride in a limousine with several prostitutes.

The jury found the accused woman guilty of neglect. It did not find any intent to harm and thus refused to award monetary damages. Attempts to appeal the decision have failed.

Are the women's memories authentic? The "infancy" memories are almost certainly false memories given the scientific literature on childhood amnesia. Moreover, no evidence in the form of bones or dead bodies was ever produced that might have corroborated the human-sacrifice memories. If these memories are indeed false, as they appear to be, where would they come from? George Ganaway, a clinical assistant professor of psychiatry at the Emory University School of Medicine, has proposed that unwitting suggestions from therapy play an important role in the development of false satanic memories.

WHAT GOES ON IN THERAPY?

Since therapy is done in private, it is not particularly easy to find out what really goes on behind that closed door. But there are clues that can be derived from various sources. Therapists' accounts, patients' accounts, and sworn statements from litigation have revealed that highly suggestive techniques go on in some therapists' offices (Lindsay and Read 1994; Lotus 1993; Yapko 1994).

Other evidence of misguided if not reckless beliefs and practices comes from several cases in which private investigators, posing as patients, have gone undercover into therapists' offices. In one case, the pseudopatient visited the therapist complaining about nightmares and trouble sleeping. On the third visit to the therapist, the investigator was told that she was an incest survivor (Loftus 1993). In another case, Cable News Network (CNN 1993) sent an employee undercover to the offices of an Ohio psychotherapist (who was supervised by a psychologist) wired with a hidden video camera. The pseudopatient complained of feeling depressed and having recent relationship problems with her husband. In the first session, the therapist diagnosed "incest survivor," telling the pseudopatient she was a "classic case." When the pseudopatient returned for her second session, puzzled about her lack of memory, the therapist told her that her reaction was typical and that she had repressed the memory because the trauma was so awful. A third case, based on surreptitious recordings of a therapist from the Southwestern region of the United States, was inspired by the previous efforts.

INSIDE A SOUTHWESTERN
THERAPIST'S OFFICE

In the summer of 1993, a woman (call her "Willa") had a serious problem. Her older sister, a struggling artist, had a dream that she reported to her therapist. The dream got interpreted as evidence of a history of sexual abuse. Ultimately the sister confronted the parents in a videotaped session at the therapist's office. The parents were mortified; the family was wrenched irreparably apart.

Willa tried desperately to find out more about the sister's therapy.

On her own initiative, Willa hired a private investigator to pose as a patient and seek therapy from the sister's therapist. The private investigator called herself Ruth. She twice visited the therapist, an M.A. in counseling and guidance who was supervised by a Ph.D., and secretly tape-recorded both of the sessions.

In the first session, Ruth told the therapist that she had been rear-ended in an auto accident a few months earlier and was having trouble getting over it. Ruth said that she would just sit for weeks and cry for no apparent reason. The therapist seemed totally disinterested in getting any history regarding the accident, but instead wanted to talk about Ruth's childhood. While discussing her early life, Ruth volunteered a recurring dream that she had had in childhood and said the dream had now returned. In the dream she is 4 or 5 years old and there is a massive white bull after her that catches her and gores her somewhere in the upper thigh area, leaving her covered with blood.

The therapist decided that the stress and sadness that Ruth was currently experiencing was tied to her childhood, since she'd had the same dream as a child. She decided the "night terrors" (as she called them) were evidence that Ruth was suffering from post-traumatic-stress disorder (PTSD). They would use guided imagery to find the source of the childhood trauma. Before actually launching this approach, the therapist informed her patient that she, the therapist, was an incest survivor: "I was incested by my grandfather."

During the guided imagery, Ruth was asked to imagine herself as a little child. She then talked about the trauma of her parents' divorce and of her father's remarriage to a younger woman who resembled Ruth herself. The therapist wanted to know if Ruth's father had had affairs, and she told Ruth that hers had, and that this was a "generational" thing that came from the grandfathers. The therapist led Ruth through confusing/suggestive/manipulative imagery involving a man holding down a little girl somewhere in a bedroom. The therapist decided that Ruth was suffering from a "major grief issue" and told her it was sexual: "I don't think, with the imagery and his marrying someone who looks like you, that it could be anything else."

The second session, two days later, began:

Pseudopatient: You think I am quite possibly a victim of sexual abuse?
    Therapist: Um-huh. Quite possibly. It's how I would put it. You know, you don't have the real definitive data that says that but, um, the first thing that made me think about that was the blood on your thighs. You know, I just wonder, like where would that come from in a child's reality. And, um, the fact that in the imagery the child took you or the

child showed you the bedroom and your father holding you down in
the bedroom . . . it would be really hard for me to think otherwise. . . .
Something would have to come up in your work to really prove that it
really wasn't about sexual abuse.

Ruth said she had no memory of such abuse but that didn't dissuade the
therapist for a minute.

> Pseudopatient: . . . I can remember a lot of anger and fear associated
> with him, bur I can't recall physical sexual abuse. Do people always
> remember?
> Therapist: No. . . . Hardly ever. . . . It happened to you a long
> time ago and your body holds on to the memory and that's why being
> in something like a car accident might trigger memories. . . .

The therapist shared her own experiences of abuse, now by her father,
which supposedly led to anorexia, bulimia, overspending, excessive
drinking, and other destructive behaviors from which the therapist had
presumably now recovered. For long sections of the tape it was hard to
tell who was the patient and who was the therapist.

Later the therapist offered these bits of wisdom:

> I don't know how many people I think are really in psychiatric hospitals
> who are really just incest survivors or, um, have repressed memories.
> It will be a grief issue that your father was—sexualized you—and
> was not an appropriate father.
> You need to take that image of yourself as an infant, with the hand
> over, somebody's trying to stifle your crying, and feeling pain some-
> where as a memory.

The therapist encouraged Ruth to read two books: *The Courage to Heal,*
which she called the "bible of healing from childhood sexual abuse," and
the workbook that goes with it. She made a special point of talking about
the section on confrontation with the perpetrator. Confrontation, she
said, wasn't necessarily for everyone. Some don't want to do it if it will
jeopardize their inheritance, in which case, the therapist said, you can do
it after the person is dead—you can do eulogies. But confrontation is
empowering, she told Ruth.

Then to Ruth's surprise, the therapist described the recent confrontation she had done with Willa's sister (providing sufficient detail
about the unnamed patient that there could be little doubt about who it
was).

Therapist: I just worked with someone who did do it with her parents. Called both of her parents in and we did it in here. . . . It's empowering because you're stepping out on your own. She said she felt like she was 21, and going out on her own for the first time, you know, that's what she felt like. . . .

Pseudopatient: And, did her parents deny or—

Therapist: Oh, they certainly did—

Pseudopatient: Did she remember, that she—she wasn't groping like me?

Therapist: She groped a lot in the beginning. But it sort of, you know, just like pieces of a puzzle, you know, you start to get them and then eventually you can make a picture with it. And she was able to do that. And memory is a funny thing. It's not always really accurate in terms of ages, and times and places and that kind of thing. Like you may have any variable superimposed on another. Like I have a friend who had an ongoing sexual abuse and she would have a memory of, say, being on this couch when she was seven and being abused there, but they didn't have that couch when she was seven, they had it when she was five. . . . It doesn't discount the memory, it just means that it probably went on more than once and so those memories overlap. . . .

Pseudopatient: This woman who did the confrontation, is she free now? Does she feel freed over it?

Therapist: Well, she doesn't feel free from her history . . . but she does feel like she owns it now and it doesn't own her . . . and she has gotten another memory since the confrontation. . . .

The therapist told Ruth all about the "new memory" of her other patient, Willa's sister:

Therapist: [It was in] the early-morning hours and she was just lying awake, and she started just having this feeling of, it was like her hands became uncontrollable and it was like she was masturbating someone. She was like going faster than she could have, even in real life, so that she knew, it was familiar enough to her as it will be to you, that she knew what it was, and it really did not freak her out at all. . . . She knew there was a memory there she was sitting on.

Before Ruth's second therapy session had ended, Ruth's mother was brought into the picture—guilty, at least, of betrayal by neglect:

Therapist: Well, you don't have to have rational reasons, either, to feel betrayed. The only thing that a child needs to feel is that there was prob-ably a part of you that was just yearning for your mother and that she wasn't there. And whether she wasn't there because she didn't know and was off doing something else, or whether she was there and she knew and she didn't do anything about it. It doesn't matter. All the child knew was that Mom wasn't there. And, in that way she was betrayed, you know, whether it was through imperfection on your mother's part or not, and you have to give yourself permission to feel that way without justification, or without rationalization because you were.

Ruth tried again to broach the subject of imagination versus memory:

Pseudopatient: How do we know, when the memories come, what are symbols, that it's not our imagination or something?
    Therapist: Why would you image this, of all things. If it were your imagination, you'd be imaging how warm and loving he was. . . . I have a therapist friend who says that the only proof she needs to know that something happened is if you think it might have.

At the doorway as Ruth was leaving, her therapist asked if she could hug her, then did so while telling Ruth how brave she was. A few weeks later, Ruth got a bill. She was charged $65 for each session.

Rabinowitz (1993) put it well: "The beauty of the repressed incest explanation is that, to enjoy its victim benefits, and the distinction of being associated with a survivor group, it isn't even necessary to have any recollection that such abuse took place." Actually, being a victim of abuse without any memories does not sit well, especially when group therapy comes into play and women without memories interact with those who do have memories. The pressure to find memories can be very great.

Chu (1992, 7) pointed out one of the dangers of pursuing a fruitless search (for memories): it masks the real issues from therapeutic exploration. Sometimes patients produce "ever more grotesque and increasingly unbelievable stories in an effort to discredit the material and break the cycle. Unfortunately, some therapists can't take the hint!"

The Southwestern therapist who treated Ruth diagnosed sexual trauma in the first session. She pursued her sex-abuse agenda in the questions she asked, in the answers she interpreted, in the way she discussed dreams, in the books she recommended. An important question remains as to how common these activities might be. Some clinicians would like to believe that the problem of overzealous psychotherapists is on a "very small" scale (Cronin 1994, 31). A recent survey of doctoral-level psychologists indicates that as many as a quarter may harbor beliefs and engage in practices that are questionable (Poole and Lindsay 1994).

That these kinds of activities can and do sometimes lead to false memories seems now to be beyond dispute (Goldstein and Farmer

1993). That these kinds of activities can create false victims, as well as hurt true ones, also seems now to be beyond dispute.

THE PLACE OF REPRESSED MEMORIES IN MODERN SOCIETY

Why at this time in our society is there such an interest in "repression" and the uncovering of repressed memories? Why is it that almost everyone you talk to either knows someone with a "repressed memory" or knows someone who's being accused, or is just plain interested in the issue? Why do so many individuals believe these stories, even the more bizarre, outlandish, and outrageous ones? Why is the cry of "witch hunt" now so loud (Baker 1992, 48; Gardner 1991)? *Witch hunt* is, of course, a term that gets used by lots of people who have been faced by a pack of accusers (Watson 1992).

"Witch hunt" stems from an analogy between the current allegations and the witch-craze of the sixteenth and seventeenth centuries, an analogy that several analysts have drawn (McHugh 1992; Trott 1991; Victor 1991). As the preeminent British historian Hugh Trevor-Roper (1967) has noted, the European witch-craze was a perplexing phenomenon. By some estimates, a half-million people were convicted of witchcraft and burned to death in Europe alone between the fifteenth and seventeenth centuries (Harris 1974, 207–58). How did this happen?

It is a dazzling experience to step back in time, as Trevor-Roper guides his readers, first to the eighth century, when the belief in witches was thought to be "unchristian" and in some places the death penalty was decreed for anyone who burnt supposed witches. In the ninth century, almost no one believed that witches could make bad weather, and almost everyone believed that night-flying was a hallucination. But by the beginning of the sixteenth century, there was a complete reversal of these views. "The monks of the late Middle Ages sowed: the lawyers of the sixteenth century reaped; and what a harvest of witches they gathered in!" (Trevor-Roper 1967, 93). Countries that had never known witches were now found to be swarming with them. Thousands of old women (and some young ones) began confessing to being witches who had made secret pacts with the Devil. At night, they said, they anointed themselves with "devil's grease" (made from the fat of murdered infants), and thus lubricated they slipped up chimneys, mounted broomsticks, and flew off on long journeys to a rendezvous called the witches' sabbat. Once they reached the sabbat, they saw their friends and neighbors all worshipping the Devil himself. The Devil sometimes appeared as a big, black, bearded man, sometimes as a stinking goat, and sometimes as a great toad. However he looked, the witches threw themselves into promiscuous sexual orgies with him. While the story might vary from witch to witch, at the core was the Devil, and the witches were thought to be his earth agents in the struggle for control of the spiritual world.

Throughout the sixteenth century, people believed in the general theory, even if they did not accept all of the esoteric details. For two centuries, the clergy preached against the witches. Lawyers sentenced them. Books and sermons warned of their danger. Torture was used to extract confessions. The agents of Satan were soon found to be everywhere. Skeptics, whether in universities, in judges' seats, or on the royal throne, were denounced as witches themselves, and joined the old women at the burning stake. In the absence of physical evidence (such as a pot full of human limbs, or a written pact with the Devil), circumstantial evidence was sufficient. Such evidence did not need to be very cogent (a wart, an insensitive spot that did not bleed when pricked, a capacity to float when thrown in water, an incapacity to shed tears, a tendency to look down when accused). Any of these "indicia" might justify the use of torture to produce a confession (which was proof) or the refusal to confess (which was also proof) and justified even more ferocious tortures and ultimately death.

When did it end? In the middle of the seventeenth century the basis of the craze began to dissolve. As Trevor-Roper (1967, 97) put it, "The rubbish of the human mind, which for two centuries, by some process of intellectual alchemy and social pressure, had become fused together in a coherent, explosive system, has disintegrated. It is rubbish again."

Various interpretations of this period in social history can be found. Trevor-Roper argued that during periods of intolerance any society looks for scapegoats. For the Catholic church of that period, and in particular their most active members, the Dominicans, the witches were perfect as scapegoats; and so, with relentless propaganda, they created a hatred of witches. The first individuals to be so labeled were the innocently nonconforming social groups. Sometimes they were induced to confess by torture too terrible to bear (e.g., the "leg screw" squeezed the calf and broke the shinbone in pieces; the "lift" hoisted the arms fiercely behind and back; the "ram" or "witch-chair" provided a heated seat of spikes for the witch to sit on). But sometimes confessions came about spontaneously, making their truth even more convincing to others. Gradually laws changed to meet the growth of witches—including laws permitting judicial torture.

There were skeptics, but many of them did not survive. Generally they tried to question the plausibility of the confessions, or the efficacy of torture, or the identification of particular witches. They had little impact, Trevor-Roper claims, because they danced around the edges rather than tackling the core: the concept of Satan. With the mythology intact, it creates its own evidence that is very difficult to disprove. So how did the mythology that had lasted for two centuries lose its force? Finally, challenges against the whole idea of Satan's kingdom were launched. The stereotype of the witch would soon be gone, but not before tens of thousands of witches had been burned or hanged, or both (Watson 1992).

Trevor-Roper saw the witch-craze as a social movement, but with individual extensions. Witch accusations could be used to destroy powerful enemies or dangerous persons. When a "great fear" grips a society, that society looks to the stereotype of the enemy in its midst and points the finger of accusation. In times of panic, he argued, the persecution extends from the weak (the old women who were ordinarily the victims of village hatred) to the strong (the educated judges and clergy who resisted the craze). One indicia of "great fear" is when the elite of society are accused of being in league with the enemies.

Is it fair to compare the modern cases of "de-repressed memory" of child sexual trauma to the witch-crazes of several centuries ago? There are some parallels, but the differences are just as striking. In terms of similarities, some of the modern stories actually resemble the stories of earlier times (e.g., witches flying into bedrooms). Sometimes the stories encompass past-life memories (Stevenson 1994) or take on an even more bizarre, alien twist (Mack 1994).[1] In terms of differences, take a look at the accused and the accusers. In the most infamous witch hunt in North America, 300 years ago in Salem, Massachusetts, three-fourths of the accused were women (Watson 1992). Today, they are predominantly (but not all) men. Witches in New England were mostly poor women over 40 who were misfits, although later the set of witches included men (often the witches' husbands or sons), and still later the set expanded to include clergy, prominent merchants, or anyone who had dared to make an enemy. Today, the accused are often men of power and success. The witch accusations of past times were more often leveled by men, but today the accusations are predominantly leveled by women. Today's phenomenon is more than anything a movement of the weak against the strong. There is today a "great fear" that grips our society, and that is fear of child abuse. Rightfully we wish to ferret out these genuine "enemies" and point every finger of accusation at them. But this does not mean, of course, that every perceived enemy, every person with whom we may have feuded, should be labeled in this same way.

Trevor-Roper persuasively argued that the skeptics during the witch-craze did not make much of a dent in the frequency of bonfires and burnings until they challenged the core belief in Satan. What is the analogy to that core today? It may be some of the widely cherished beliefs of psychotherapists, such as the belief in the repressed-memory folklore. The repression theory is well articulated by Steele (1994, 41). It is the theory "that we forget events because they are too horrible to contemplate; that we cannot remember these forgotten events by any normal process of casting our minds back but can reliably retrieve them by special techniques; that these forgotten events, banished from consciousness, strive to enter it in disguised forms; that forgotten events have the power to cause apparently unrelated problems in our lives, which can be cured by excavating and reliving the forgotten event."

Is it time to admit that the repression folklore is simply a fairy tale? The tale may be appealing, but what of its relationship to science? Unfortunately, it is partly refuted, partly untested, and partly untestable. This is not to say that all recovered memories are thus false. Responsible skepticism is skepticism about some claims of recovered memory. It is not blanket rejection of all claims. People sometimes remember what was once forgotten; such forgetting and remembering does not mean repression and de-repression, but it does mean that some recently remembered events might reflect authentic memories. Each case must be examined on its merits to explore the credibility, the timing, the motives, the potential for suggestion, the corroboration, and other features to make an intelligent assessment of what any mental product means.

THE CASE OF JENNIFER H.

Some writers have offered individual cases as proof that a stream of traumas can be massively repressed. Readers must beware that these case "proofs" may leave out critical information. Consider the supposedly ironclad case of Jennifer H. offered by Kandel and Kandel (1994) to readers of *Discover* magazine as an example of a corroborated de-repressed memory. According to the *Discover* account, Jennifer was a 23-year-old musician who recovered memories in therapy of her father raping her from the time she was 4 until she was 17. As her memories resurfaced, her panic attacks and other symptoms receded. Her father, a mechanical-engineering professor, denied any abuse. According to the *Discover* account, Jennifer sued her father, and at trial "corroboration" was produced: Jennifer's mother testified that she had seen the father lying on top of Jennifer's 14-year-old sister and that he had once fondled a baby-sitter in her early teens. The defendant's sister recalled his making passes at young girls. Before this case becomes urban legend and is used as proof of something that it might not be proof of, readers are entitled to know more.

Jennifer's case against her father went to trial in June 1993 in the U.S. District Court for the District of Massachusetts (*Hoult* v. *Hoult*, 1993). The case received considerable media attention (e.g., Kessler 1993). From the trial transcript, we learn that Jennifer, the oldest of four children, began therapy in the fall of 1984 with an unlicensed New York psychotherapist for problems with her boyfriend and divided loyalties surrounding her parents' divorce. Over the next year or so she experienced recurring nightmares with violent themes, and waking terrors. Her therapist practiced a "Gestalt" method of therapy; Jennifer describes one session: "I started the same thing of shutting my eyes and just trying to feel the feelings and not let them go away really fast. And [my therapist] just said 'Can you see anything?' . . . I couldn't see anything . . . and then all of a sudden I saw this carved bedpost from my room when I was a child. . . . And then I saw my father, and I could feel him sitting on the bed next to me, and he was pushing me down, and I was saying, 'No.' And he started pushing up my nightgown and . . . was touching me with his hands on my breast, and then between my legs, and then he was touching me with his mouth . . . and then it just all like went away. It was like . . . on TV if there is all static. . . . It was, all of a sudden it was plusssssh, all stopped. And then I slowly opened my eyes in the session and I said, 'I never knew that happened to me' " (pp. 58–59).

Later Jennifer would have flashbacks that were so vivid that she could feel the lumpy blankets in her childhood bed. She remembered her father choking her and raping her in her parents' bedroom when she was about 12 or 13 (p. 91). She remembered her father threatening to rape her with a fishing pole in the den when she was about 6 or 7. She remembers her father raping her in the basement when she was in high school. The rape stopped just as her mother called down for them to come to dinner. She remembered her father raping her at her grandparents' home when she was in high school, while the large family were cooking and kids were playing. She remembered her father threatening to cut her with a letter opener, holding a kitchen knife to her throat (p. 113). She remembered him chasing her through the house with knives, trying to kill her, when she was about 13 years old (p. 283).

Jennifer also remembered a couple of incidents involving her mother. She remembered one time when she was raped in the bathroom and went to her mother wrapped in a towel with blood dripping. She remembered another incident, in which her father was raping her in her parents' bedroom and her mother came to the door and said, "David." The father then stopped raping her and went out to talk to the mother.

Jennifer's mother said she had no recollection of these events, or of any sexual abuse. An expert witness testifying for Jennifer said it is common in cases of incest that mothers ignore the signs of abuse.

During the course of her memory development, Jennifer joined numerous sexual-abuse survivor groups. She read books about sexual abuse. She wrote columns. She contacted legislators. Jennifer was involved in years of therapy. She wrote letters about her abuse. In one letter, written to the president of Bernard College on February 7, 1987, she said "I am a victim of incestuous abuse by my father and physical abuse by my mother" (p. 175). In another letter to her friend Jane, written in January 1988, she talked about her therapy: "Well, my memories came out . . . when I would sit and focus on my feelings which I believe I call visualization exercises because I would try to visualize what I was feeling or be able to bring into my eyes what I could see" (pp. 247–48). She told Jane about her Gestalt therapy: "In Gestalt therapy, the sub-personalities are allowed to take over and converse with one another and hopefully resolve their conflicts. Each personality gets a different chair, and when one new one starts to speak, the individual changes into that personality's seat. It sounds weird, and it is. But it is also an amazing journey into one's self. I've come to recognize untold universes within myself. It feels often very much like a cosmic battle when they are all warring with one another" (pp. 287–88; see also p. 249).

In one letter, written on January 11, 1989, to another rape survivor, she said that her father had raped her approximately 3,000 times. In another letter, dated January 30, 1989, she wrote: "Underneath all the tinsel and glitter was my father raping me every two days. My mother smiling and pretending not to know what the hell was going on, and probably Dad abusing my siblings as well" (pp. 244–45). In a letter written on April 24, 1989, to *Mother Jones* magazine she said that she had survived hundreds of rapes by her father (p. 231).

Before October 1985, Jennifer testified, she didn't "know" that her father had ever put his penis in her vagina, or that he had put his penis in her mouth, or that he put his mouth on her vagina (p. 290). She paid her therapist $19,329.59 (p. 155) to acquire that knowledge.

In sum, Jennifer reported that she had been molested by her father from the ages of 4 to 17 (p. 239); that she was molested hundreds if not thousands of times, even if she could not remember all of the incidents; that this sometimes happened with many family members nearby, and with her mother's "involvement" in some instances; and that she buried these memories until she was 24, at which time they purportedly began to return to her. No one saw.

These are a few of the facts that the Kandels left out of their article.

Jennifer was on the stand for nearly three days. She had "experts" to say they believed her memories were real. These experts were apparently unaware of, or unwilling to heed, Yapko's (1994) warnings about the impossibility, without independent corroboration, of distinguishing reality from invention and his urgings that symptoms by themselves cannot establish the existence of past abuse. At trial, Jennifer's father testified for about a half-hour (Kessler 1993b). How long does it take to say, "I didn't do it"? Oddly, his attorneys put on no character witnesses or expert testimony of their own, apparently believing—wrongly—that the implausibility of the "memories" would be enough. A Massachusetts jury awarded Jennifer $500,000.

GOOD AND BAD ADVICE

Many of us would have serious reservations about the kinds of therapy activities engaged in by Jennifer H. and the kind of therapy practiced by the Southwestern therapist who treated pseudopatient Ruth. Even recovered-memory supporters like Briere (1992) might agree. He did, after all, say quite clearly: "Unfortunately, a number of clients and therapists appear driven to expose and confront every possible traumatic memory" (p. 136). Briere notes that extended and intense effort to make a client uncover all traumatic material is not a good idea since this is often to the detriment of other therapeutic tasks, such as support, consolidation, desensitization, and emotional insight.

Some will argue that the vigorous exploration of buried sex-abuse memories is acceptable because it has been going on for a long time. In fact, to think it is fine to do things the way they've always been done is to have a mind that is as closed and dangerous as a malfunctioning parachute. It is time to recognize that the dangers of false-memory creation are endemic to psychotherapy (Lynn and Nash 1994). Campbell (1994) makes reference to Thomas Kuhn as he argues that the existing paradigm (the theories, methods, procedures) of psychotherapy may no longer be viable. When this happens in other professions, a crisis prevails and the profession must undertake a paradigm shift.

It may be time for that paradigm shift and for an exploration of new techniques. At the very least, therapists should not let sexual trauma overshadow all other important events in a patient's life (Campbell 1994). Perhaps there are other explanations for the patient's current symptoms and problems. Good therapists remain open to alternative hypotheses. Andreasen (1988), for example, urges practitioners to be open to the hypothesis of metabolic or neurochemical abnormalities as cause of a wide range of mental disorders. Even pharmacologically sophisticated psychiatrists sometimes refer their patients to neurologists, endocrinologists, and urologists. For less serious mental problems we may find, as physicians did before the advent of powerful antibiotics, that they are like many infections—self-limiting, running their course and then ending on their own (Adler 1994).

When it comes to serious diseases, a question that many people ask of their physicians is "How long have I got?" As Buckman and Sabbagh (1993) have aptly pointed out, this is a difficult question to answer. Patients who get a "statistical" answer often feel angry and frustrated. Yet an uncertain answer is often the truthful answer. When a psychotherapy patient asks, "Why am I depressed?" the therapist who refrains from giving an erroneous answer, however frustrating silence might be, is probably operating closer to the patient's best interests. Likewise, nonconventional "healers" who, relative to conventional physicians, give their patients unwarranted certainty and excess attention, may make the patients temporarily feel better, but in the end may not be helping them at all.

Bad therapy based on bad theory is like a too-heavy oil that, instead of lubricating, can gum up the works—slowing everything down and heating everything up. When the mental works are slowed down and heated up, stray particles of false memory can, unfortunately, get stuck in it.

To avoid mucking up the works, constructive advice has been offered by Byrd (1994) and by Gold, Hughes, and Hohnecker (1994): Focus on enhancement of functioning rather than uncovering buried memories. If it is necessary to recover memories, do not contaminate the process with suggestions. Guard against personal biases. Be cautious about the use of hypnosis in the recovery of memories. Bibliotherapeutic and group therapy should not be encouraged until the patient has reasonable certainty that the sex abuse really happened. Development and evaluation of other behavioral and pharmacological therapies that minimize the possibility of false memories and false diagnoses should be encouraged.

Instead of dwelling on the misery of childhood and digging for childhood sexual trauma as its cause, why not spend some time doing something completely different. Borrowing from John Gottman's (1994) excellent advice on how to make your marriage succeed, patients might be reminded that negative events in their lives do not completely cancel out all the positives (p. 182). Encourage the patient to think about the positive aspects of life—even to look through picture albums from vacations and birthdays. Think of patients as the architects of their thoughts, and guide them to build a few happy rooms. The glass that's half empty is also half full. Gottman recognized the need for some real basis for positive thoughts, but in many families, as in many marriages, the basis does exist. Campbell (1994) offers, similar advice. Therapists, he believes, should encourage their clients to recall some positive things about their families. A competent therapist will help others support and assist the client, and help the client direct feelings of gratitude toward those significant others.

FINAL REMARKS

We live in a culture of accusation. When it comes to molestation, the accused is almost always considered guilty as charged. Some claims of sexual abuse are as believable as any other reports based on memory, but others may not be. However, not all claims are true. As Reich (1994) has argued: "When we uncritically embrace reports of recovered memories of sexual abuse, and when we nonchalantly assume that they must be as good as our ordinary memories, we debase the coinage of memory altogether" (p. 38). Uncritical acceptance of every single claim of a recovered memory of sexual abuse, no matter how bizarre, is not good for anyone—not the client, not the family, not the mental-health profession, not the precious human faculty of memory. And let us not forget one final tragic consequence of overenthusiastic embracing of every supposedly de-repressed memory; these activities are sure to trivialize the genuine memories of abuse and increase the suffering of real victims who wish and deserve, more than anything else, just to be believed.

We need to find ways of educating people who presume to know the truth. We particularly need to reach those individuals who, for some reason, feel better after they have led their clients—probably unwittingly—to falsely believe that family members have committed some terrible evil. If "truth" is our goal, then the search for evil must go beyond "feeling good" to include standards of fairness, burdens of proof, and presumptions of innocence. When we loosen our hold on these ideals, we risk a return to those times when good and moral human beings convinced themselves that a belief in the Devil meant proof of his existence. Instead, we should be marshaling all the science we can find to stop the modern-day Reverend Hale (from *The Crucible*), who, if he lived today, would still be telling anyone who would listen that he had seen "frightful proofs" that the Devil was alive. He would still be urging that we follow wherever "the accusing finger points"!

NOTE

1. John Mack details the kidnappings of 13 individuals by aliens, some of whom were experimented upon sexually. Mack believes their stories, and has impressed some journalists with his sincerity and depth of concern for the abductees (Neimark 1994). Carl Sagan's (1993, 7) comment on UFO memories: "There is genuine scientific paydirt in UFO's and alien abductions—but it is, I think, of distinctly terrestrial origin."

REFERENCES

Adler, J. 1994. The age before miracles. *Newsweek,* March 28, 44.

Andreasen, N. C. 1988. Brain imaging: Applications in psychiatry. *Science* 239: 1381–88.

Baker, R. A. 1992. *Hidden memories.* Amherst, N.Y.: Prometheus Books.

Briere, John N. 1992. *Child abuse trauma.* Newbury Park, Calif.: Sage Publications.

Buckman, R., and K. Sabbagh. 1993. *Magic or medicine? An investigation into healing.* London: Macmillan.

Byrd, K. R. 1994. The narrative reconstructions of incest survivors. *American Psychologist* 49: 439–40.

Campbell, T. W. 1994. *Beware the talking cure.* Boca Raton, Fla.: Social Issues Resources Service (SirS).

Chu, J. A. 1992. The critical issues task force report: The role of hypnosis and amytal interviews in the recovery of traumatic memories. *International Society for the Study of Multiple Personality and Dissociation News,* June, 6–9.

CNN. 1993. "Guilt by Memory." Broadcast on May 3.

Cronin, J. 1994. False memory. *Z Magazine,* April, 31–37.

Gardner, R. A. 1991. *Sex abuse hysteria.* Creskill, N.J.: Creative Therapeutics.

Gold, S. N., D. Hughes, and L. Hohnecker. 1994. Degrees of repression of sexual-abuse memories. *American Psychologist* 49: 441–42.

Goldstein, E., and K. Farmer, eds. 1994. *True stories of false memories.* Boca Raton, Fla.: Social Issues Resources Service (SirS).

Gottman, J. 1994. *Why marriages succeed or fail.* New York: Simon & Schuster.

Harris, M. 1974. *Cows, pigs, wars, and witches: The riddles of culture.* New York: Vintage Books.

Hoult v. *Hoult.* 1993. Trial testimony. U.S. District Court for District of Massachusetts. Civil Action No 88-1738.

Kandel, M., and E. Kandel. 1994. Flights of memory. *Discover* 15 (May): 32–37.

Kessler, G. 1993a. Memories of abuse. *Newsday,* November 28, 1, 5, 54–55.

———. 1993b. Personal communication. *Newsday,* letter to EL dated December 13, 1993.

Lindsay, D. S., and J. D. Read. 1994. Psychotherapy and memories of childhood sexual abuse: A cognitive perspective. *Applied Cognitive Psychology* 8: 281–338.

Loftus, E. F. 1993. The reality of repressed memories. *American Psychologist* 48: 518–37.

Loftus, E. F., and K. Ketcham. 1994. *The myth of repressed memory.* New York: St. Martin's Press.

Lynn, S. J., and M. R. Nash. 1994. Truth in memory. *American Journal of Clinical Hypnosis* 36: 194–208.

Mack, J. 1994. *Abduction.* New York: Scribner's.

McHugh, P. R. 1992. Psychiatric misadventures. *American Scholar* 61: 497–510.

Neimark, J. 1994. The Harvard professor and the UFOs. *Psychology Today,* March-April, 44–48, 74–90.

Poole, D., and D. S. Lindsay. 1994. Psychotherapy and the recovery of memories of childhood sexual abuse. Unpublished manuscript, Central Michigan University.

Rabinowitz, Dorothy. 1993. Deception: In the movies, on the news. *Wall Street Journal,* February 22. Review of television show "Not in My Family."

Reich, W. 1994. The monster in the mists. *New York Times Book Review,* May 15, 1, 33–38.

Rogers, M. L. 1992. A case of alleged satanic ritualistic abuse. Paper presented at the American Psychology-Law Society meeting, San Diego, March.

Sagan, C. 1993. What's really going on? *Parade Magazine,* March 7, 4–7.

Stevenson, I. 1994. A case of the psychotherapist's fallacy: Hypnotic regression to "previous lives." *American Journal of Clinical Hypnosis* 36: 188–93.

Steele, D. R. 1994. Partial recall. *Liberty,* March, 37–47.

Trevor-Roper, H. R. 1967. *Religion, the Reformation, and social change.* London: Macmillan.

Trott, J. 1991. Satanic panic. *Cornerstone* 20: 9–12.

Victor, J. S. 1991. Satanic cult "survivor" stories. *Skeptical Inquirer* 15: 274–80.

Watson, B. 1992. Salem's dark hour: Did the devil make them do it? *Smithsonian* 23: 117–31.

Yapko, M. 1994. *Suggestions of abuse.* New York: Simon & Schuster.

2

THE SHADOW OF A DOUBT

MARY SYKES WYLIE

O n a pleasant Friday morning in early spring, a group of well-dressed, prosperous-looking men and women, most in their fifties and sixties, gather for a conference at a large convention hotel in the manicured suburbs of Philadelphia, not far from the rolling greensward of Valley Forge Historical Park. From the subdued, convivial roar of the 600-plus voices, these people sipping coffee and peering at one another's name badges might be here for a conference of senior sales representatives or real estate agents.

That is, until unnerving snatches of their conversation are overheard. "My daughter has accused me of raping her from the time she was 7 until the time she was 14," says one grey-haired man from Wisconsin, in the slightly amazed tone of someone who cannot get used to making this statement. In another small group, an Ohio woman, about 50, reports that her daughter—a Harvard M.A. in public policy—convinced the state police to dig up a public park in search of the bodies of many young boys that, the young woman claimed, her father and mother had sexually abused, murdered, and buried there. A woman in her seventies, standing in line to register, tells a companion that her 46-year-old daughter has cut off all family contact with her parents, charging that during her childhood they had engaged in satanic ritual abuse that included rape, murder, torture, and mutilation. "We wanted her to go

---

This article first appeared in the *Family Therapy Networker* (September/October 1993): 18–29, and is copied here with permission.

to the Mayo Clinic for psychiatric testing," said the woman, "but she said her therapist had told her that the Mayo staff was made up of satanists who would get control of her mind." Across the room, a Minnesota woman, elegantly dressed in a tweed suit and looking younger than her 61 years, starts weeping quietly as she talks about her 33-year-old son, who has accused his father of sodomizing him when he was a child. One sister believes him; the other has not taken a stand. "At least one is neutral," she says forlornly. She looks around, suddenly embarrassed. "Am I the only one here crying?" she asks.

Every one of the parents gathered here can tell a similar story of adult children suddenly and without warning turning on them with accusations as horrible and fantastic as they are incomprehensible. Every parent here talks about the absolute shock and horror of hearing their children make these accusations, and every parent here vehemently denies the charges. Often, they say they do not even know what the alleged details are, or exactly when and where the abuse was supposed to have occurred—the son or daughter levels general allegations and then refuses to disclose particulars, saying something like, "You know what you did. I don't have to tell you." It is not hard to identify with these parents—in this post-Kafkaesque era, who cannot imagine the helpless bafflement of being charged with terrible but unremembered crimes, assumed guilty and condemned without hearing? Furthermore, in a psychotherapeutically inspired double-bind typical of our times, denial itself is evidence of . . . *denial,* the pathological indicator that makes declarations of innocence virtual proof of guilt.

It is this strange commonality of experience that brings these families together for the first meeting of the False Memory Syndrome Foundation (FMSF), a support and advocacy organization formed in March 1992, and comprised of the parents of 4,000 families who say they have been falsely accused of sexually abusing their children. Some stand accused of committing even more heinous and sadistic acts—engaging in cultish orgies of animal sacrifice, rape, torture, mutilation, forced abortions on pre-adolescent girls, murder, and cannibalism. As a result of these charges, many parents here have lost all contact not only with their accusing children, but with their grandchildren, if the accuser is also a parent. Furthermore, if the charges become publicly known, and in small communities they typically do, the parents find themselves ostracized by old friends and neighbors, and pilloried in the local press.

The costs are not only social and emotional, however, as many now find themselves waging expensive battles against criminal and/or civil charges for abuses they are accused of committing a decade or two or three earlier, which their adult daughters or sons have only recently remembered. That these parents can be sued or prosecuted at all reflects the astonishing impact of the incest-recovery movement on the law itself. During the 1980s, in order to accommodate the theory of repressed memories, 21 states altered their laws to allow an extension of the statute of limitations, which normally sets a time limit—usually seven years—following the alleged offense, after which a lawsuit or criminal charges cannot be brought. Now, in a movement that appears to be spreading to other states, a plaintiff may bring legal actions against alleged sex-abuse perpetrators up to two or three years after he or she recovers memories of the abuse, which may be decades after the actual events.

So, parents in their late fifties, sixties, and seventies, caught in a bizarre, historically unprecedented struggle with their own children, find themselves engaged in that typically American pursuit: forming a volunteer advocacy organization to lobby public opinion on behalf of their cause. And they go about it much the way every other such special-interest group does—by getting for themselves and their stories as much media attention as possible. There are more than 30 members of the press here—from numerous magazines, newspapers and broadcast networks—all welcomed with open arms and a striking willingness among organizers and attendees to tell their stories to anyone wearing a press pass and holding a pad of paper or a tape recorder. "We will talk to anybody," one father says, before tugging at a journalist to come sit down in a corner and listen to *his* tale.

Every member of the FMSF has a similar story to tell, and it has been told so many times that it now has the ritualized quality of an ancient archetype, repeated generation after generation. As the story goes, the charges against the parents usually come without warning from adult daughters and sons who had apparently been living normal, reasonably happy, and successful lives, until suddenly, often during their thirties and forties, usually while they were going through some temporary crisis, they began having horrifying flashbacks, body memories, nightmares, or vague images. These odd occurrences triggered memories of parental abuse from decades earlier—or at least the certainty that abuse had happened, even in the absence of exact memories of specific events. However vague the details are now, the abuse then had been so terrible and traumatic, the accusers claim, that in psychic self-defense they repressed and buried the memories from conscious knowledge. Years later, these archived images emerged unexpectedly during therapy which the client had sought for what seemed like more ordinary problems—a divorce, eating disorder, mid-life depression, child-raising issues. Sometimes, the flashbacks and body memories occurred while the accusers were reading about the symptoms of childhood incest in popular recovery books (the book, *The Courage to Heal*, by Ellen Bass and Laura Davis, is this weekend's particular *bête noir*) or while they were attending a self-help meeting or workshop for adult children of alcoholic or otherwise dysfunctional families.

The Kelly family, for example, was always a "normal Irish family," says Mr. Kelly as he sits with his wife and two adult daughters at lunch during the first day of the FMSF conference. The family had generally "lived a pretty happy life," Mr. Kelly thought, though he guessed he had gone through a period when he was drinking too much. He and his wife had raised six kids, three boys and three girls; they had been very active in the local Catholic parish and Mr. Kelly had coached Little League baseball. He loved all his children, he says, but Lili, the oldest and the one making the accusations, had really been his favorite. When Lili was a little girl, the two of them had gone horseback riding together every week, and one summer, when he was just getting his business started, he had scraped enough money together to send her to a riding camp. "She never seemed to have one problem," he says. "She never got in trouble, laughed her way through high school. She was happy and beautiful, like a little Shirley Temple."

Lili married when she was 22 and divorced two years later. "I found out then that she had never had any sex with her husband. No sex!" Mr. Kelly says, slapping his forehead. " 'Holy Mackerel!' I thought to myself. 'What does that mean?' " But Lili soon remarried—a man Mr. Kelly likes very much—and had "two beautiful children, outstanding kids." After her second baby though, she began "acting odd," he remembers. "She became very pensive and evasive, and couldn't handle her work very well, or her kids—she would bring them to our house and stay for days." She also started intensely questioning her father about his family, and "picking on her grandparents a little too much," he thought, carping on their drinking. This hurt him because he was proud of them—his hardworking father and mother who had lost everything in the depression, but still managed to raise 12 children. Meanwhile, Lili was reading *The Courage to Heal* and watching John Bradshaw, the popular guru of the inner-child movement, on television. "She told me that there was incest in every family and the Irish were particularly prone to both drinking and incest," says Mr. Kelly. "I said, 'I have to admit to the drinking, but not to the incest.' "

Lili began therapy with a young therapist Mr. Kelly remembers as "a very nice girl." One day, she asked her parents to come to a session with her where the therapist told them that Lili had been sexually abused. She didn't yet know who had done it, but the identity of the abuser would "come out" in time. "My wife and I were horrified," remembers Lili's father. "We said to each other, 'My God, that's awful. Who could have done it?' and we started going over the past, every vacation we had taken—'How about that summer at the shore? Could it have been the lifeguard? What about the vacation in the mountains? Could it have been the boys in the next cabin?' "

At 2:30 A.M. one morning, Mr. Kelly was awakened by the phone. It was Lili, sobbing hysterically. "You did it, Daddy! It was you! You *did* do it, didn't you! Didn't you!" After a sleepless night, the Kellys met with the therapist in a family session that also included Lili, her brother, and her husband, where Lili made her charges again with the family present. "Then, she flew across the room screaming, and started beating on my chest, tearing at my face," Mr. Kelly remembers. "It was the saddest shock I've ever had." Eventually, Lili accused not only her father, but her mother, and thought that friends her parents had invited over to the house when the children were small had also been involved. Later, in a private session with the therapist, Mr. Kelly wondered aloud how his daughter could come to believe all this. "These stories are always true," the therapist solemnly intoned.

At the FMSF conference, the Kelly family is now caught between glum depression and wild hope. Lili still refuses to talk to her parents, but she did show up briefly this morning for one of the sessions. Persuaded by a sister acting as go-between, Lili agreed to come only on the condition that her parents *not* be present at the conference when she was, so they had dutifully stayed hidden in the vicinity during that time. Will she come back to her family? Nobody knows. One of the odd quirks in the plot line of some of these stories is that children do occasionally reestablish contact with their parents, rejoin family life as if nothing had interrupted it, and never mention the issue that caused the break in the first place.

To the conference attendees, these adult children have been hurt all right, but not by child abuse, and certainly not by their parents. Parents and children, they believe, are the innocent pawns in a hysterical crusade against an "epidemic" of sex crimes against children, which is ravaging lives and destroying families across the country. The FMSF thinks it is a witch hunt, engineered by a large, amorphous, profit-oriented "sex abuse industry," a conglomerate of New-Age healers, self-help movement promoters, political activists, radical feminists, social service providers, and mental health professionals.

One of the speakers is Margaret Singer, a psychology professor at the University of California at Berkeley, who compares the individual and group psychotherapy that evokes false memories of abuse to a kind of parent-bashing cult that uses mind-altering techniques—dream work, meditation, guided imagery, and hypnosis, most notably—to suck apparently self-reliant adults into a sinkhole of dependency and self-sustaining pathology. Richard Ofshe, a sociology professor at Berkeley and the first presenter on Friday morning, agrees. "These therapies damage first . . . the trusting, vulnerable, usually distressed, and sometimes seriously ill patients. If there is a perpetrator, it is not the evil monsters the patient comes to see in their families," he says grimly. "The perpetrator is the kindly therapist," guilty of "fobbing off the wild, untested, unsubstantiated speculations [of] a small group of professionals . . . trading on the status and authority of modern medicine to unwittingly press their personal, professional, and political values on persons who have made one mistake: seeking out the wrong practitioner for treatment."

Therapy bashing or not, these words are a bracing *cri de coeur* to parents who feet stunned, horrified, overwhelmed, and helpless, as much betrayed by the healing professions as by their own misled children. During an intense two days, conference attendees listen to experts from a variety of disciplines—psychiatry, psychology, sociology, and law—give substance to the claim that a "malpractice epidemic" is sweeping the therapeutic community. They hear, for example, that "robust repression" of trauma, including the belief that long-term, severe childhood abuse is often obliterated from conscious memory for decades, is a gross pseudo-scientific error, without grounding in substantial empirical evidence. People *remember* their traumas, speakers point out again and again; their problem is not that they've lost their memories, but that they can't get rid of them—they intrude relentlessly into their daily lives, and always have. "Victims of real emotional trauma, whether of child abuse . . . or life in Hitler's concentration camps, or Vietnam-related post-traumatic stress disorder, have very vivid memories," says Harold Lief, a psychiatrist on the advisory board of FMSF, in an interview published recently in the magazine *Addiction and Recovery.* "And I have seen no evidence of repressed memories in these cases."

Not only do skeptics doubt the validity of repressed memories of abuse, they tend to suspect that current incidence rates of childhood sex abuse are highly inflated, and the impact on adult psychopathology greatly exaggerated. FMSF devotes a good deal of time, talk, and typeface to denying that its members doubt the reality of child abuse, its power to damage its victims and the need to prosecute perpetrators. At the meeting, a statement to this effect is a virtually obligatory mantra recited before every session. At the same time, they note the wildly disparate current statistical estimates for child abuse (ranging from less than 1% in some studies to 62% in others) to suggest that none of the figures are worth much, and that with relentless pressure on teachers and social-services staff to report even the merest suspicion of abuse, the cards have now been stacked in favor of overreporting. And furthermore, some people associated with FMSF argue, even if there is a lot of child abuse, it is far from being the automatic sentence to lifelong psychological infirmity it is generally reputed to be. "There is little or no evidence for the idea that sex abuse causes mental illness," says Ofshe. "The data suggest that while sex abuse may be widespread, it is not particularly strongly correlated with the symptoms [associated with it]." Another FMSF ally, Richard Gardner, professor of child psychiatry at Columbia University, is a prominent critic of what he calls "the child-abuse establishment." Gardner argues that social *attitudes* toward adult-child sexual encounters (including incest), rather than the sexual contact per se, make the experience traumatic. "Studies of our culture—which do not start with the bias that they must be psychologically damaging—provide clear demonstration of this," Gardner writes for the Fall 1992 *Issues in Child Abuse Accusations,* a journal edited and published by Hollida Wakefield and Ralph Underwager, founding members of FMSF. While there are women who have been "seriously damaged by these encounters," Gardner continues, "there are many women who have had sexual encounters with their fathers who do not consider them to have affected their lives detrimentally."

This is not a line pursued by FMSF speakers or organizers, who are clearly anxious to avoid being branded as perpetrator protectors, but there is a low, growling undercurrent to many of the presentations that alleged sex abuse is just another handy excuse allowing spoiled kids to evade adult responsibility for their own problems. More than once it is suggested that the child abuse "industry" is simply one more opportunistic infection feeding on the metastasizing culture of victimization in America. "We live in the age of the victim," says Martin Seligman, a cognitive psychologist from the University of Pennsylvania, who speaks at the meeting.

Several times during the weekend, speakers have made a point of emphasizing just how "normal" and solid most of the FMSF families are, how bright, happy and successful most of the children were before their inexplicable fall from grace. At this meeting, the FMSF presents a self-administered survey sent to member parents, which demonstrates, not too surprisingly, that on the whole these are models of wholesome family life: middle- to upper-middle class, educated, unlikely to have been split by divorce, active in their churches, staunch advocates of family togetherness. The children too had been, on the whole, not only reassuringly normal, but even superior. Though some had suffered periods of depression or other emotional disturbances before making their accusations, most were bright, accomplished, dependable, high academic and athletic achievers who had never given their parents any trouble at all. Indeed, several speakers pointed out, adults who recover memories of abuse seem to have been exceptionally well-adjusted children who had had some of the best parenting available.

Surveys like this cannot be intended to convince the opposition that the group is not made up of perverts and fellow-travelers, but [are] probably meant to reassure the members themselves about one another, and to send a signal to potential joiners that the organization really is for "people like us," not deviants and criminals. In response to a rhetorical question they raise in their newsletter, "How do we know we are not representing pedophiles," the editors answer ingenuously, "We are a good looking bunch of people, graying hair, well-dressed, healthy, smiling . . . just about every person who has attended is someone you would likely find interesting and want to count as a friend." They also plan, the piece continues, to encourage all their members to take lie-detector tests. Then, "We will have a powerful statement that we are not in the business of representing pedophiles."

So, if the parents were so exemplary, why are their children now saying such terrible things about them? And why are such accomplished, successful, apparently happy off-spring more likely to go off the deep end with false memories than troublesome, rebellious, surly, under-achieving kids? Even if the abuse never happened, how were their children so easily led into this vicious morass? These nagging questions undoubtedly haunt the FMSF members, in spite of all the purported evidence for family normality and soundness. One pet theory in FMSF circles is that the very stability and closeness of the families, the apparent happiness, good behavior, and high performance of the children were themselves somehow perversely related to the sudden explosion of bizarre accusations. These children were so used to living up to and beyond expectations, a 1992 FMSF newsletter editorial suggests, that when they did seek out therapy for current difficulties in their lives, they carried their drive to achieve with them and became the "best" patients the therapist ever had—the ones most likely to produce exactly what was wanted. "If an expectation that sexual abuse is the cause of every ailment is embedded in that setting, then these children become the most abused," says the editorial. "They are the best students the therapist has and so recover not only the most memories but also the most bizarre memories. They are great students."

There is another, harsher theory espoused by Richard Gardner, who implies that the women making false allegations of sex abuse are, in effect, angry paranoids, as are their therapists, who are, in addition, incompetent fanatics. Over the past few years, Gardner writes in the Fall 1992 issue of *Issues in Child Abuse Accusations,* "many women have found that men can serve as useful targets for their hostility. . . . In other cases of false accusations of sexual abuse, a woman may release her anger via the sex-abuse accusation against a separated husband. Here, the adult woman vents this rage on her own father, who, for many women was once the most important person in their lives. . . ." Gardner believes the woman may have projected onto her father her own unacceptable sexual desires for him and later built around these projected wishes an entire fantasy of abuse. Such a woman enters a *folie à deux* with a therapist, who may have been sexually abused herself and wants to "wreak vengeance on all *man*kind (not *woman*kind). What better way to wreak vengeance on men than to become a therapist and use one's patients to act out one's morbid hostility."

But except for a few grumbles heard at the conference about "man-hating feminists," most attendees appear no more anxious to blame their daughters than to see themselves blamed (though therapists remain a handy target). They are much more taken by George Ganaway's theory, which provides a kinder, gentler psychoanalytic view of the daughter's intrapsychic dynamics. According to Ganaway, psychiatry professor at Emory University in Atlanta and specialist in dissociative disorders, the accusers who make such outstanding therapy clients aren't playing out a compliant, good-child role *in extremis,* but finally getting around to a long-delayed adolescent rebellion against their parents. In this view, the accuser, usually a woman, may never have separated emotionally from her family. On the one hand, she deeply desires to break away, while on the other hand, she feels intense guilt about doing so, fear of standing alone and anger at her parents, whom she unconsciously blames for keeping her tied to them. The conflict, dating to early childhood, has "left her with a feeling of hostile dependency on [her parents], hostility she can't tolerate, a love-hate relationship she can't acknowledge." Without much self-confidence (though a high achiever), always in need of approval, the woman, says Ganaway, "displaces her dependency onto the therapist. He or she becomes the ideal substitute mother figure, who will be all-accepting, all-believing, all-approving, who will offer the patient a mechanism by which she can finally separate from her parents." Instead of working through the underlying unconscious conflict, the therapist offers "symptom relief" by implicitly encouraging her to develop a "new symptom . . . the belief that her parents committed such heinous crimes that her previously unacceptable and troublesome anger toward them is now explained and is totally justifiable. Also, she has an excuse to cut the umbilical cord. . . . The therapist has given her a face-saving reason for making the separation and individuation she could not make otherwise."

At this last point, the audience responds with loud, gratified applause. A theory that may sound to FMSF opponents like a self-serving rationalization provides a plausible escape from a profound sense of cognitive dissonance. It offers the parents answers to otherwise unanswerable questions: How can I have been a good parent and still have a child who truly believes I am a monster? How can I believe in my own innocence without hating my child? How could this terrible thing happen? The theory takes the sting out of the child's *j'accuse* by making it both comprehensible and more benign. It is even more plausible because it doesn't entirely let the parents off the hook, but places responsibility for the accusations in some vague, murky, psychodynamic territory between them and their child. Ganaway's theory brings the problem into the range of complex and problematic, but not too abnormal, family dynamics. Furthermore, it allows for an ultimately more satisfying life narrative, replete with the hope for the return of the prodigal child, penitence, forgiveness, and mutual reconciliation.

It is not surprising, therefore, that one of the most emotionally satisfying sessions of the conference is the appearance of a panel of five "recanters"—women who have taken back their original accusations of abuse. These women, who appear to be in their late twenties to late thirties, tell stories about irresponsible and unethical therapists steamrolling them—using hypnotism, "truth serum" (sodium amytal), and group pressure—into telling the kinds of melodramatic stories they wanted to hear. Interestingly, four of the five recanters are, in fact, survivors of child abuse—some by family members, some by outsiders—who sought out therapy because they couldn't conquer their depression or control their eating or keep their marriages together. One attractive, articulate woman on the panel says that both her father and brother had abused her, but that this was not nearly enough for her therapist, a psychiatrist in a private hospital. The psychiatrist, this woman says, drugged and hypnotized her to "remember" that not only her father and brother, but aunts, uncles, cousins, and kindergarten teachers had also ritually abused her. She was told that she had multiple personality disorder and would not recover until all the personalities had surfaced, and she was not allowed to leave until she had produced a large and varied cast of alters—a characteristic feature of multiple personality disorder.

Each recanter gives a ringing denunciation of a horrific therapy experience, and one tearfully explains that while it is too late for her to tell her own father how sorry she is—he died before she came to realize that her memories were false—she can still help other parents and get the chance to be the good daughter she had not been in her own family. At each awful revelation of appalling therapy from the panel members, the audience gasps. There are tears on many faces during the presentations and extended applause when the women finish. These are the heroines of the conference, the symbolic embodiment of the entire FMSF cause, and their stories are a kind of balm to the flayed feelings of the parents; their recitations are morality tales of contrite children returning home, repenting the harm they have done, however inadvertently, to their own parents. And there is not one parent here who does not yearn for just this kind of ending to his or her own unhappy tale.

Finally, the conference provides strategies for fighting back. "This problem is not going to be solved by education, or better [therapist] training or scientific work," says sociologist Jeffrey Victor, a professor at a branch of the State University of New York. "It is going to be solved by political confrontation—that's the only way massive social movements are changed. And that political confrontation is going to involve suing people who are charlatans." Clearly, like so many other American social controversies, this one seems fated to be fought out by lawyers. "Ultimately, everything in America ends up in a courtroom," says Judge Lisa Richette, a Philadelphia jurist with expertise in child-abuse cases, before introducing one of two main sessions devoted to legal issues. How should parents defend themselves against lawsuits and criminal actions instigated by their children? What are the grounds for bringing suit against the accusing child's therapist or psychotherapy clinic? How do you find admissible expert witnesses for the defense? What about a counter-suit against the accusing child who is withholding visitation rights to see grandchildren? How much will it cost? Can a class action suit be brought against the authors of a book like *The Courage to Heal*?

Many of the parents apparently consider these two sessions the most absorbing of the conference; they take copious notes and ask many detailed questions on abstruse points of law. Ironically, the long social and political campaign to provide beefed-up legal remedies for adult survivors of childhood molestation has come full circle: Many parents seem more than willing to make use of the same adversarial legal weapons that have been leveled against some of them. As one man says, his voice raw with grief and anger, "I'm not going to lie down like a dog and accept this!"

About two months later, now early summer, it is another lovely day the opening of another conference—this one much bigger, clearly better funded and directed to professional therapists. The Fifth Anniversary Eastern Regional Conference on Abuse and Multiple Personality has begun, an intensive, six-day training meeting for professional therapists, with workshops and day-long courses conducted by mental health experts at the very center of the dark star that FMSF families see dimming their own light. Here are the captains of the "child abuse industry" decried by the FMSF, the very people whose "radical and untested" therapies have been accused of casting such a blight over so many American families. And yet, from the inside, nothing could appear to be farther from the stereotypes of bizarre theory, loose-cannon clinical techniques and mutual delusion than the material presented at this conference, the accounts of these therapists' own clients, their conclusions about what they are seeing. Sitting in workshops at this meeting, while remembering therapeutic abuses described at the FMSF conference, evokes a weirdly dissociative feeling, as if trying to match up a photographic positive with a negative and finding that though the two bear a ghostly resemblance to each other, they are still utterly different. Indeed, the FMSF and this conference on multiple personality disorder (MPD), and probably much of the abuse-treatment community generally, might occupy separate, but parallel universes, so close and yet so far apart are their respective worldviews.

At the same time, however, there is an oddly similar complementarity within both camps about each other. Certainly, FMSF and its advocates are not alone in feeling on the defensive. If the false-memory people are deeply suspicious of the motives and modus operandi of the abuse-treatment community, the latter feels the same way. Judith Herman, for example, a psychiatry professor at Harvard and one of the country's foremost and earliest researchers on the impact of incest and trauma, has generally not endeared herself to the opposition. She was recently quoted in the *San Francisco Chronicle* (a quote picked up and published in the FMSF Newsletter) suggesting that, using proven standards for measuring false allegations, probably only about 10% of FMSF members could possibly be innocent of what they are accused of doing. At this year's MPD conference, audience members attending a "town meeting" to discuss the false-memory controversy speculate darkly about mysterious funding sources for the FMSF (which is widely and probably erroneously supposed by the abuse recovery movement to have access to deep, but unspecified, pockets somewhere). Possible CIA connections are mentioned, and it is implied that FMSF advisory-board members are on the take, dishonest, and bigoted. One panel member, Richard Loewenstein, a psychiatry professor at the University of Maryland Medical School and a noted MPD researcher, remarks that he certainly doesn't see the FMSF as a "spontaneous coming together of aggrieved families," but as a "media-directed organization," manipulating its member families and "dedicated to putting out disinformation."

And the inevitable suggestion is made again that the FMSF has more to hide than a secret money pipeline. To a plea on behalf of the FMSF parents by George Ganaway (representing the FMSF on the panel of speakers) that he had found them both credible and anguished, fellow panelist Richard Kluft, director of the Dissociative Disorders Program at the Institute of Pennsylvania Hospital and one of the country's foremost MPD experts, responded that he believed they probably were "genuinely anguished." But, Kluft continued, "I will point out that if you punch a sociopath in the stomach, he is as anguished as if you punch a nonsociopath in the stomach. Anguish is no more convincing from a parent than it is from an abused child. I think Dr. Ganaway should have interviewed the children."

But this is exactly the nub of the issue. Skeptics of the truth of formerly dissociated, now retrieved, memories doubt, first of all, the methods of manipulative and/or gullible therapists, but they also most seriously doubt the credibility of the very same clients that therapists who treat abuse are most inclined to believe. At a panel discussion of false memories at the annual conference of the American Psychiatric Association last June, Samuel Guze, a psychiatrist at Washington University in St. Louis and an eminent diagnostic theoretician, suggested that the testimony of abuse by certain kinds of patients, particularly those diagnosed with borderline personality disorder, just couldn't be trusted. "These people are unreliable, inconsistent reporters," he said. "They will deny having said things in the past when there are lengthy notes [made by the therapist]. . . . There are gross inconsistencies in what they say. . . . They are characterized by frequent criminal and antisocial behavior, impulsive lifestyles, unstable and conflictual personal relationships. It's all part of a pattern."

To members of the angry audience, this sounded like the old canard that you couldn't trust women's reports of sexual abuse or rape because the women making such claims were obviously irrational, hysterical, overwrought, not in their right minds. As John Briere, a leading trauma researcher and professor of psychiatry at the University of Southern California Medical School, pointed out, if therapists assume that severe child abuse hurts people and produces massive psychiatric symptoms, Guze, in effect, was using those same symptoms as evidence for disbelieving their stories about how they got that way. Richard Kluft made a related point even more succinctly in an interview in *Clinical Psychiatry News*: "In situations where it's a parent's word against an adult daughter's, it may be easier to believe the adult who appears to be a normal, upstanding citizen, compared with a distraught woman in therapy. Perpetrators almost always look better than victims because they are the ones dishing it out, not the ones who are taking it."

As if looking into distorted mirrors, each side gazes distastefully at the other and sees a warped and perverted vision of their true selves. Each vision contains the same basic components—usually an unhappy woman or, less often, a man, a therapist, and emerging memories of child abuse. There, the visions diverge radically. To FMSF, women who were unhappy but rational when they first sought treatment are polysymptomatic zombies after a few months in the clutches of an irresponsible, manipulative, abuse-obsessed therapist; if the clients weren't crazy before, they are now.

To attendees at the MPD conference, the scenes of egregious therapeutic malfeasance portrayed by FMSF are more like a parody of a Stephen King horror story than anything they recognize as good clinical practice. Many remember that early in their careers they had had little knowledge, training or experience in trauma-related and dissociative disorders. Before 1979, post-traumatic stress disorder wasn't even listed in the American Psychiatric Association's *Diagnostic and Statistical Manual* (DSM), childhood sex abuse was still a national family secret, and even now the relationship between early child abuse, amnesia, and dissociation remains controversial.

Far from seeking out or encouraging abuse disclosures, many therapists report that when they began treating survivors of overwhelming childhood trauma, they themselves often did not believe what they were hearing, did not understand the symptoms they were witnessing. Instead, they preferred to categorize their clients within more "acceptable" diagnostic limits—as borderlines, schizophrenics, hysterics, manic-depressives—rather than draw the conclusion that these people were in terrible shape because terrible things had been done to them. And many remember the first case they really "saw," however many they had missed before, the baptism by fire that shocked them into awareness.

The initial manifestations of dissociative disorders related to abuse, including MPD, are often far more dramatic than what seasoned and skeptical therapists experience from other clients. Joan Golston, a Seattle therapist who specializes in trauma recovery and dissociative disorders, remembers an early MPD case: a woman who complained vaguely about relationship difficulties and reported stroke-like symptoms following a recent physical assault. Golston saw the client for several months without much progress, feeling "as if there were some other communication going on in the room" that she could not define or pin down. She noticed that the woman used very graceful and eloquent hand gestures, so one day, without forethought, Golston began speaking in metaphors related to hands, using expressions lie "hand-in-hand," "handling things," and "handing over."

The woman left that day, and the next session began without apparent change. At one point in the session, however, the client got up from her chair as if to arrange something on a nearby table and turned away from Golston for a moment. Her body shook as if having a mild seizure. "Then, a voice I had never heard before said to me, 'I saw you see me last Thursday, and so I thought I should introduce myself.' " With that, the woman turned, stuck out her hand, and introduced herself as an alter personality, someone strikingly different in demeanor, voice, attitude, and expression. The woman eventually revealed a number of alters, and a history of extensive childhood abuse.

Even when survivors remember their abuse, they commonly dissociate the worst aspects of it in order to ward off the intense shame and self-hatred caused by trauma. Rolland Summit, community psychiatrist at Harbor UCLA Medical Center and associate professor of psychiatry at UCLA Medical School, remembers one client, a successful but depressed professional man, who had a memory of his uncle attempting to rape him as a child, and of himself escaping. In therapy, the man began talking about a feeling that haunted him, which he was sure nobody else experienced—the very real and uncanny sense of being inhabited by an alien part of himself, a little boy, of whom he was entirely conscious, but who nonetheless had a quite separate existence.

During the course of therapy, while visualizing the "little boy" escaping from the attempted rape, hiding behind a tree, and vowing never to let any such thing happen again, the man had the terrible realization that, in fact, he had *not* managed to escape from his uncle—the rape had actually occurred. At the time it was happening, however, he had created a kind of alter who in his mind did get away, ending the story the way he wanted it to end. He had been living with this fiction, in the dissociated form of a withdrawn, fearful, and morbidly depressed little boy hiding behind the tree, ever since.

Skeptics tend to harrumph at case histories like this and reduce them to manifestations of hysteria, picked up by the therapist and reinforced in the client. Therapists agree that severely abused and dissociative clients often show hysterical symptoms—self-dramatization, irrational angry outbursts, egocentricity, excessive demands, dependency, and manipulativeness—as do clients with many other disorders. But the severity and complexity of their pathology and the palpable quality of their pain makes an extraordinary impression on even initially skeptical therapists. Clients who have not been severely abused rarely show up in therapy with many different previous diagnoses, pervasive feelings of shame and self-disgust, a pattern of being sexually and physically abused in adulthood, and dissociative symptoms. As often as not, the bodies of these clients are covered with severe cuts, bruises, welts—either the result of chronic re-victimization or self-mutilation; they may also be alcoholic, drug-addicted, or bulimic.

Nor do therapists enjoy listening to horrible tales of abuse. "Four hours of therapy with [a severely abused patient] is like watching four hours of atrocity films," says Colin Ross, a leading researcher and prolific writer on MPD. "I don't know anyone who welcomes hearing about each new level of abuse," says Roland Summit. "Each new revelation is a kick in the ass; you try to resist it, hope it isn't really true, and once you are forced to believe it, your view of the world slips a little, your confidence in your former sense of reality is broken."

The unendurable and impossible-to-fake agony of the clients is the most powerful evidence for the truth of their experiences. During one workshop at the MPD conference, an audiotape is played in which a client relives the experience of being raped by her father when she was about 6 years old. During the session, she reexperiences the rape incident in the alter of the child she had been. She first exhibits the same dissociative phenomena that had allowed her to psychologically survive the trauma at the time. She again experiences the disembodied, depersonalized feeling of floating above the scene, while describing in a vague, dreamy, singsong voice what is happening to the little girl below. The therapist then suggests she try to reenter the little girl on the bed, and as the client does so, her voice registers increasing fear, then panic, terror, and horror. She starts to scream, "Daddy! Daddy! No, no, please! Daddy, Daddy! Why are you hurting me? I'll be good! I'll be good! Please stop, Daddy!"

There is, of course, no corroboration for such an event, no forensic evidence laid out before the disinterested eyes of a jury demonstrating empirically that this is anything other than a clever performance or a hysterical fit. And yet, so harrowing, so searing is the emotional force of this woman's voice—even through the secondhand presentation of a tape recorder—that an audience of experienced therapists is obviously deeply shaken. If the spoken tale of any human being can ever be believed at all, without a battery of forensic evidence to buttress it, then this woman is indeed telling a true story, whatever the "exact" details.

Furthermore, in contrast to a vision popular among FMSF members that clients read *The Courage to Heal* or watch John Bradshaw, then come into therapy and announce that they were abused in the crib at six months or two years, therapists report that survivors tend to underestimate or deny the damage that has been done to them, even while describing consciously remembered scenes of terrible trauma. Richard Loewenstein cites a typical scene from his own practice. "In a session, I asked a patient, 'Who did the disciplining in your family?' and he answered, 'I wasn't abused.' So I asked, 'Well, what's your definition of abuse?' and he said, 'Being abused is being beaten for something you didn't do. I got beat a lot, though. They beat me with boards and belts and coat hangers. Once, when I was 5, they beat me so hard I danced. They beat me all day.' Then I asked him, 'What did you do that time that made them beat you, do you remember?' 'Yes,' the patient answered. 'They said I gave my brother polio.' " Says Loewenstein, "That is much more typical of a clinical interview with someone who has been abused."

The tendency to minimalize severe trauma to oneself, or even accept blame for it, is apparently nearly universal, related to the intense shame trauma victims feel—that they must have been bad enough to deserve it. As Christine Courtois, clinical director of the Center for Abuse Recovery and Empowerment at the Psychiatric Institute of Washington, D.C., writes in her book, *Healing the Incest Wound*, "Their fearful belief is that no one could possibly view them as anything but contemptible and responsible." Paradoxically, taking on the blame also gives survivors a sense of meaning and control. To avoid feeling like inanimate, helpless things, it is preferable to believe they *did* something that logically caused the traumatic response.

According to Courtois, "Survivors who have memories don't want them; those who don't have memories are desperate to get them until they do get them, and then they don't want them anymore." Certainly, to a woman who has for years dissociated the experience of child abuse, the suggestion that she somehow "caught" her memories, like a flu bug, from a "contaminated" book or a John Bradshaw program, is simply lunatic. In the 1980s, for example, Margot Silk Forrest, now editor of *The Healing Woman*, a newsletter for abuse survivors, went on a month-long meditation retreat, returning home "feeling wonderful," she said. Three days later, however, she fell into the deepest depression she had ever known. "I didn't know what was wrong," she remembers, "but I just felt so much more terrible than the facts of my life would seem to warrant."

Without prompting from recovery literature or the therapist she was seeing for depression, she soon began to have terrible dreams of abuse, then gradually more vivid visual images, and finally knew with certainty that her father had assaulted her at least 100 times, beginning when she was 3. Even her mother believes her memories, says Forrest, but to this day she has difficulty emotionally accepting her past. "I would do anything to be able to say I made it up. These memories are absolutely shattering," she says. "They mean that I have lost my whole childhood. How do I reconcile the rapes with my memories of my Dad taking me blue-berry picking?"

Another survivor remembers the beginning stages of her long bout with MPD, when an alter personality came out during an acupuncture treatment she was getting to alleviate the sudden onset of severe exhaustion for which there was no apparent physical cause. In her mid-thirties at the time, she remembers suddenly *becoming*—not simply "feeling like"—a small, helpless, terrified 3-year-old child while in the acupuncturist's office, totally unable to understand or explain what was happening to her. Several times during the next few months, the shift into a 3-year-old self happened again, and she also began to have quick, intrusive, visual flashes of lying in a child's bed, and being hit extremely hard by an adult leaning over her with a blindingly bright light. Very soon, there were episodes of feeling more and more disoriented, doing odd, self-destructive things—she had begun cutting herself—meanwhile watching herself as if in a dream, unable to control anything that she was doing. Eventually, she was diagnosed as a multiple who had suffered extreme, extended, sadistic ritual abuse as a child, and began a long, grueling, but ultimately successful process of therapy.

Only after months in therapy could she even tolerate the memories and the renewed suffering they evoked. "The depth of the pain, the horror of being beaten and raped and cut, the unbearable feelings of hopelessness and loss when you see adults all around you watching what is happening to you and not one will help you—agony is too pale a word for it. It leaves a hole in your being that is unfillable," she says. "No therapist, nobody, could implant that."

In spite of the wrenchingly graphic and convincing testimony of such clients, the abuse stories sometimes seem bizarre, incredible, unreal, even to the therapists who are the staunchest allies and champions of the clients who tell them. Far from suggesting or leading patients into disclosing abuse or mimicking MPD symptoms, therapists frequently feel overwhelmed by what they witness in their offices, and inclined to disbelieve. An MPD conference attendee asks presenter Colin Ross if he believes everything he hears from his clients, particularly some of the more horrible stories of satanic ritual abuse. "If you believe that everything you are hearing is all literally true, you will go mad," Ross answers. The stories he hears from clients are so compelling and yet so frightful that he is "constantly unsure of what's going on, what is real and what is not. I'm always oscillating back and forth between belief and skepticism, which," he continues, "is where everybody should be."

Therapists who treat survivors of severe trauma, particularly satanic ritual abuse, recognize the inevitability of ambiguity in these cases.

"When I hear a client describe satanic ritual abuse, I feel in my own body the reality of what they are saying," says Maryland family therapist Terrence O'Connor. "The sense of their pain is quite excruciating, and I don't have to believe every detail to believe in their suffering. But when I look at the phenomena on a sociological level and wonder where the bodies are, I feel some skepticism. As a therapist and a citizen, I have to live with both those positions."

Toward the end of the MPD conference, one therapist emerges visibly distraught from a session about legal and ethical controversies in sex-abuse cases. "I don't know what I'm going to do," she says in a low, quivering voice, clutching a pad full of frantically scribbled notes. "I can't afford any more malpractice insurance, and I can't start video-taping all my sessions. I try not to 'lead' clients into saying anything, but you have to ask them direct questions sometimes, don't you? Do I have to get informed consent every time I use a visualization or relaxation technique? And I don't know now whether I should keep process notes or not—I guess I could be sued either way—and if a client asks me if I believe she was ritually abused, or if she has 'repressed memories,' what am I supposed to say so I don't lose my license or end up in court?" Another older, more experienced therapist soothes her, telling her she doesn't need to panic just yet, and suggests she go take a nice, long walk in the nearby nature preserve.

This alarmed therapist is not alone in her distress. A wave of anxiety has spread throughout much of the therapeutic community, which feels besieged and threatened by an unprecedented upsurge of negative publicity. Not that therapists, like lawyers and physicians and morticians, haven't often been the subjects of social grumbling—other people's pain is quite literally their gain. But lately, distrust of therapists shows signs of mutating into something far more toxic. "Therapists are now becoming society's scapegoats, blamed for bringing up these terrible things that nobody wants to see out in the open," says Christine Courtois. "I think it parallels the same displacement of guilt we see in the incestuous family, in which the victim is blamed for disclosing the abuse."

Why have the client's personal memories, however unsavory, never before of any particular concern to anybody except the two parties engaged in the very private task of therapy, now become the hot topic of a very public brawl? The answer lies in the twin American proclivities for litigation and legislation, the habit of seeking not only vengeance and redress for wrongdoing in courtrooms and legislatures, but social and public solutions to what were once considered private, "domestic" problems, as well.

This is not all bad. Many terrible social injustices have been cloaked in the veil of privacy. "Sexual abuse of children was once the perfect crime," Judith Herman pointed out at the recent American Psychiatric Association convention. "As a perpetrator, you were fairly guaranteed never to be caught or held accountable for your crime. Women, for the first time, have begun to use the courts to hold perpetrators accountable, and we see them fighting back."

Public fights in public forums, however, demand different standards of proof, different definitions of reality, than private meetings in private therapists' offices, and the black-and-white terms of the law are something other than the ambiguous, kaleidoscopic truths that emerge in therapy. Memories of terrible, long-term, and very real childhood trauma are often confused, contradictory, fragmented—specific times, dates, places, and even the identities of perpetrators are mixed up, forgotten, conflated with dream and fantasy.

Furthermore, survivors have been well taught by their abusers to distrust their own feelings and perceptions. Even when the evidence of the abuse is unmistakable and externally well corroborated, even while coming to believe and accept the reality of their memories, survivors of abuse have moments of doubting what they know. And the expression of doubt in others evokes the same sick, desolating sensation they had as abused children—that nobody believes, nobody understands, nobody accepts them. So how convincing can these survivors be as court witnesses when challenged by aggressive defense attorneys to come up with precise memories of events that happened to them as small children 20 or 30 years before?

The spongy narrative and symbolic truths of therapy—what the client subjectively *feels, remembers,* and *experiences,* as opposed to what can be objectively *known*—don't generally add up to a good foundation for building forensic cases. On the other hand, skeptics of the literal truth of retrieved memories sometimes seem bent on turning therapy with sex-abuse survivors into an interrogation, and therapists into police investigators. According to several FMSF supporters, including a number of forensic psychiatrists, the so-called prudent therapist presented with memories of sex abuse is ethically obligated to make a thorough, independent investigation, which includes intense interviews (with polygraph tests) of suspected family members, inquiries of friends and associates about the client's background, retrieval of the client's old medical, psychiatric, school, employment, and possible criminal records and probing examination of the patient's motives for making the accusations. In other words, what does the client expect to get from making the charges—an excuse for venting rage at parents, money from lawsuits, alibis for her irresponsibility or bad luck, a more glamorous identity as a "survivor," etc.?

Most therapists find this skeptical "show-me" attitude to clients antithetical to everything they hold dear, not to mention illegal according to current statutes protecting client confidentiality. "Forensic psychiatric investigations and individual psychotherapy are entirely different," says Lucy Berliner, director of research for the Harborview Sexual Assault Center at the University of Washington, and sole representative at the FMSF conference from the "other side" of the debate. "Certainly, if you required corroboration for all reports of sex abuse, the vast majority of victims could never be believed." In short, says Berliner, "you can't have therapy in a general climate in which nobody believes anything anybody says."

Yet, many therapists feel that this climate of unbelief *is* descending over their field like a new Ice Age, and that in some quarters therapists are beginning to regard their clients with the gimlet eye of a prosecuting attorney. "All this emphasis on caution can really inhibit therapy," says Wayne Reznick, a psychologist who, with his wife, directs the Center for Psychological Services in Alexandria, Virginia. "You have to be very careful not to lead or suggest anything to clients, to take very careful notes that say enough but don't go into too much detail, and indicate only that you are recording your client's apparent memories, which you cannot corroborate. If a client asks if I think she has been abused, the only statement I can make is that what she has told me is consistent with what we know about the pattern of abuse, though I cannot say for certain that she was actually abused."

On the other hand, a therapist who is too hesitant may also be in trouble. "We're between a rock and a hard place," says Christine Courtois (a phrase echoed in several interviews). "If we 'make suggestions' to clients, or appear to be 'too leading' in our interviews, we are liable to the charge of 'implanting' memories. On the other hand, if there are symptoms indicating an abuse history, but the patient doesn't mention abuse, and the therapist does not ask her about it specifically (to avoid the taint of 'leading'), and the patient actually *was* abused and does not get better because the issue is never raised, then the patient can sue the therapist. There have been a couple of successful lawsuits by MPD patients who didn't improve in therapy because the therapist allegedly 'missed' the diagnosis." In short, says Courtois, asking a client for detailed information about his or her background is just something a therapist *has* to do.

Beneath the putative argument over memory, repression, prevalence of sex abuse, and diagnostic categories may be an even more disquieting issue—a potentially revolutionary theory that undermines many standard assumptions about the origins of severe psychopathology. Numerous well-documented studies done since 1987 indicate that 50 to 60% of psychiatric inpatients, 40 to 60% of out-patients, and 70% of all psychiatric emergency room patients report childhood physical or sexual abuse, or both. To trauma researchers, this body of research suggests an intriguing new view of psychiatric etiology—that prolonged, severe childhood abuse may play a vastly underestimated role in the development of many serious psychopathologies now ascribed to biological factors, intrapsychic conflicts, or standard family-of-origin issues.

This surmise received an enormous boost recently in the astonishing data that unexpectedly emerged from field trials on post-traumatic stress disorder undertaken to refine the diagnosis for the upcoming *DSM-IV.* In a five-year research project with 528 trauma patients from five different hospital sites around the country, a team of researchers led by Bessel Van Der Kolk, professor at Harvard Medical School and chief of the trauma unit of Massachusetts General Hospital, gathered sufficient data to justify the creation of a new diagnosis—a much-elaborated and enlarged traumatic stress syndrome that they call DESNOS—disorders of extreme stress, not otherwise specified. This diagnosis correlates very closely with similar concepts of other trauma specialists, including Judith Herman, a colleague of Van Der Kolk's, who calls her formulation complex post-traumatic stress disorder; another, comparable diagnosis being considered by the International Classification of Diseases is named personality change from catastrophic experience.

Essentially, all these rather bulky new monikers reflect the belief among a growing body of clinicians that severe childhood trauma, adult dissociation, and a range of other psychiatric symptoms, which may or may not now be listed under PTSD, really should comprise a single, new diagnostic category. Van Der Kolk and his team found in their study—the largest, most comprehensive ever done on trauma patients—a range of symptoms in their patients that almost inevitably showed up together, and were well-correlated with prolonged, severe childhood sex abuse. These symptoms were the inability to regulate emotions like rage and terror, along with intense suicidal feelings; somatic disorders (mysterious but debilitating physical complaints); extremely negative self-perception (shame, guilt, helplessness, self-blame, strangeness); poor relationships; chronic feelings of isolation, despair, and hopelessness; and dissociation and amnesia. "They all go together," says Van Der Kolk at the MPD conference. "If you have one, you have the others—it's a package deal."

The implications are that real-world childhood sexual trauma may be responsible for many psychopathologies usually considered to have endogenous origins, including various kinds of phobic, depressive, anxiety, and eating disorders, not to mention borderline personality, antisocial personality, and multiple personality disorders. After all, 46% of the psychiatric patients studied by Van Der Kolk had every element of DESNOS, suggesting the possibility that at least half of all emotionally disturbed patients, whatever their formal diagnoses, are in fact survivors of childhood abuse—an astonishing thought.

As part of the study, Van Der Kolk also found that 100% of patients testing high on the standard test for dissociative disorders also reported having been sexually abused as children, compared with 7% whose test scores were very low. Patients with high dissociative scores almost all met formal criteria for depression as well, and every one met the criteria for the current diagnosis of PTSD.

Unfortunately, this massive, clinical detective story is, in the end, "a tragic tale," says Van Der Kolk. The study so overshot its original mandate, and its findings were deemed so disruptive to current diagnostic categories by the DSM authorities, that the new diagnosis was not even allowed space in the appendix. In spite of the massive size of the study and the 43-page bibliography Van Der Kolk sent to buttress it, the DSM hierarchy maintained that the new diagnosis "must be an accident," says Van Der Kolk, and therefore couldn't supplant the categories as they stood.

The new diagnosis, if it eventually flies, would represent something of a revolution in the dominant therapeutic worldview. "In 1975, mainstream psychiatric textbooks were still referring to incest as a one-in-a-million occurrence," says Colin Ross. "Since then, the widespread reality of childhood trauma has been forced from the outside on the psychiatric profession. [The growth of interest in] MPD is the thin edge of the wedge, compelling changes in the explanatory paradigm for a whole range of other diagnoses, for which the major contributor is probably severe trauma. There has been a lot of resistance to this."

Some trauma specialists believe this new paradigm would substantially alter the geography of psychiatric disorders. "If we could stop child abuse and neglect tomorrow," said John Briere in an interview for *The Healing Woman*, "two generations from now we'd only have organic disorders, schizophrenia, bipolar affective disorder, adult trauma reactions, and a couple of kinds of major depression. Or, at least, there would be so much less distress than now that the DSM would shrink down to a pamphlet."

It seems unlikely that the furious controversy over the question of retrieved memories can be resolved any time soon through dispassionate research and enlightened discourse. So incendiary has the issue become that involved parties seem irresistibly compelled to ask the same, bottom-line question: "Whom do you believe?" And yet, however compelling, this question seems far too crude, too simplistic to capture the elusive essence of what exactly is at stake.

Repeatedly, the FMSF insists they are not opposed to therapists or to the women's movement or to survivors. They reiterate that they know child abuse exists; that it is more common than once thought; that it is reprehensible; that perpetrators should be prosecuted; and that survivors should get the professional help they need for their recovery. Their organization, they say, simply wants to protect parents and children alike from the excesses of irresponsible therapists, stem what they believe is a growing tide of social hysteria and encourage the development of sound, scientific criteria for assessing the truth or falsehood of sex abuse allegations.

Therapists, for their part, have repeatedly stated that the issue is too complex and ambiguous to be reduced to simple black-and-white terms. They maintain that they know people can come to believe they were abused when they were not; that incompetent clinicians can misuse hypnotic techniques and misdiagnose child abuse; that normal memory is often unreliable, confused, and distorted by fantasy and belief; that there is not yet an incontestable body of scientific data on traumatic memory. They only want to ensure that real survivors receive the acceptance and therapeutic help they need; that the reality of child abuse not again be willfully obscured by society; and that the effects and treatment of trauma receive the scientific attention due any serious mental health problem.

Nevertheless, these legitimate points of view, cogently expressed, don't account for the extreme reactions on each side that seem more appropriate to a Manichaean struggle over absolute good and evil than to a debate about science and mental health policy. Surely, the truth must lie somewhere in the safe, sane middle.

But where is the middle? In this debate, every statement, every position, every example seems dogged by the shadow of its own contradiction. Every protestation of innocence by the FMSF parents, every sign of apparent "normality" in their lives, every emblem of their pleasant middle-class ordinariness seems in this eerie climate to be its opposite. Wouldn't a clever perpetrator tell his or her story with just this believable sincerity? Create just this plausible picture of happy, all-American family life, show just this rending grief about an estranged son or daughter? ("My father would have just loved coming to meetings like the FMSF conference," says one survivor of severe abuse.) Couldn't the FMSF recanters be, in fact, again dissociating, denying the memories of their abuse? Isn't it true that severely abused clients frequently veer back and forth between belief and acceptance? And yet, these people seem so nice, so honest, so truly devastated by what has happened to them, so eager to tell their stories.

On the other hand, how, in the absence of corroboration, do therapists specializing in childhood sex abuse know that their clients are telling the truth? Aren't some of these stories of recovered memories and some of these dissociative symptoms a little too melodramatic—a little, well, hysterical? Why do so many highly respected psychiatric authorities have doubts about the validity of the diagnosis and abuse etiology of MPD? Why do these abuse therapists believe the most outlandish stories of satanic ritual abuse when there is so little forensic evidence for it, and so many plausible, sensible arguments against it? And yet, the therapists seem so rational, so careful, so responsible, so intelligent, so knowledgeable. And the survivors seem so eloquent, so calmly certain, so truthful, so believable.

In this Twilight Zone between truth and reality, the question, "Whom do you believe?" however simplistic it may sound, acquires a powerful emotional urgency that demands a response. As one survivor put it, "You can believe me, or you can choose not to believe me, but you can't do both." At stake, from either perspective, is the question of loyalty, the terrible possibility that to make the wrong choice, to believe "the wrong side" is to collude in an outrage, to betray an innocent, grievously injured human being.

The question, "Whom do you believe?" strikes at the very heart of the American myth of innocence, our confidence in the fundamental goodness, fairness and justice of our civilization, our conviction that, for all our failings, we are a compassionate and honest people. How can we accept the possibility that hundreds of thousands, perhaps millions, of children have been and are being abused, tortured, even killed by the people most obligated to love and protect them? What does it mean to acknowledge that this is happening in virtually every American neighborhood by people who look and sound and dress exactly like *us*? They are our friends, our colleagues, our doctors, our lawyers, our politicians, our storekeepers, our plumbers. Perhaps they are our relatives, perhaps ourselves.

On the other hand, if these alleged child-abuse victims suffer only from the age-old psychological afflictions caused by varying combinations of characterological, intrapsychic and biological factors and current life stresses, then all of us are let off the hook. The child abuser remains that stock figure, the dangerous stranger, the unknown bogeyman lurking at the edges of playgrounds and schoolyards—nobody we know. We can go on believing that the vast majority of parents basically love and protect their children, that the family remains a cherished haven in a hard world. Where there are no victims, there are no perpetrators.

It is hard for most people to recognize evil, and almost impossible to fully accept it when it contradicts our dearest beliefs and most cherished values. Social psychologist Melvin Lerner writes that we all need so strongly to believe in a "just world"—one in which everybody mostly "gets what they deserve"—that if we cannot quickly and comfortably remedy a perceived injustice, we tend to deny it (this isn't as bad as it looks), blame the victim (she/he/they either made it all up, or they somehow deserved it) or simply flee the situation entirely. "The subject of child abuse is itself so passionate and so paradoxical that it provokes polarized dichotomies at every level," writes Rolland Summit in the journal *Psychiatric Clinics of North America,* "leaving indifference and avoidance as the only hope for serenity."

But if avoidance is a paltry and self-deluding defense against horror, then what Summit calls the "primitive need to take one side or the other and battle down the alien extreme" is not likely to resolve the impossible conundrum either. The excessive claims and counterclaims, the paradoxical human ability to experience, forget, inflict, and deny such terrible suffering, the bizarre social capacity for knowing and not knowing at the same time: like a fog permeating every crevice of the landscape, this controversy will not be throttled into neat categories labeled "fact" and "fantasy."

The truth doesn't lie somewhere in the mushy middle of the controversy, but all across the spectrum, from one extreme to the other. "There are examples of everything in the world," says Colin Ross. No possibility forecloses another contradictory possibility for somebody else. There could be innocent parents and guilty but amnesic parents and parents who engaged in some but not all of the abuse of which they are accused, and parents who are conscious perpetrators cynically using the controversy for their own ends. Similarly, there are adults who, in their own confusion and unhappiness, are remembering abuse that did not happen and adults who have truly suffered every form of sexual abuse from inappropriate looking and touching, to molestation, to the most sadistic, horrifying, long-term trauma imaginable and unimaginable.

Whatever the ultimate shakedown on the controversy, whatever the fate of the new mental health paradigm, it seems unlikely that as a society we can retreat to the pleasant, shared dream in which incest virtually never happened, sadistic abuse within the family was unthinkable, and American children were almost universally loved, protected, and spared any assault on their innocence. For most of human history, women and children were not believed when they told their stories about sexual abuse. That women now insist on being believed propels the issue of recovered memories into the maelstrom of politics as perhaps no other mental health issue ever has before.

Now, up to our necks in hot ash, with lava flowing all around us, we cannot pretend that the long-dormant volcano of sex abuse hasn't erupted in an explosion of revelations. The small voices once raised here and there to tell their tales of childhood savagely destroyed have swollen to a mighty chorus, and they won't be silenced easily, no matter how determined the opposition. Says one survivor, "Victims challenge everything we believe about ourselves and our world. People do not want to face the fact that their peers do horrendous things, but they're going to have to take reality as it is. I will be free, and I will do whatever is necessary to become free. Don't get in my way. People are shackled by fits, by silence, and I will not live in silence anymore."

3

THE SEDUCTIONS OF MEMORY

MICHAEL D. YAPKO

He told his wife that he simply couldn't deal with the memories of his horrible experiences in Vietnam. In the 20 years of their marriage, she had seen enough strange behavior from him to believe it. One night, he went berserk in an apparent reaction to the sneakers she happened to be wearing. After he calmed down, he told her that his Vietcong captors wore similar sneakers when they regularly dragged him out of his bamboo cage in order to beat and urinate on him. He told her he had been a prisoner for 15 days after a carrier-based F-4 jet fighter on which he was the navigator was shot down. He said he escaped after strangling a guard, who was also wearing the same kind of sneakers.

He went to see a therapist, who diagnosed him as suffering from post-traumatic stress syndrome and treated him for severe depression and explosive anger. He spent an inordinate amount of time obsessing about his experiences in Vietnam and was unable to make sense of what happened to him there. The therapist succeeded in getting him to talk more openly about the connection between his memories and his present mood swings, nightmares and irrational rages with his wife. Unfortunately, despite lengthy treatment, one day he committed suicide by inhaling carbon monoxide.

After his death, his wife attempted to get his name placed on the state Vietnam War Memorial, declaring him as much casualty of that war

This article first appeared in the *Family Therapy Networker* (September/October 1993): 31–37, and is copied here with permission.

as anyone who had actually died there. To support her effort, his therapist wrote a letter on his behalf, also requesting that his name be include among those of the other war dead. In response to their requests, his military background was extensively checked, but countless hours spent searching through Armed Forces files failed to turn up any record of the man's service in Vietnam. Much to the shock and dismay of both his wife and his therapist, it became inescapably clear that he had never been in Vietnam at all. The events that were so convincingly at the root of this disturbed man's deep unhappiness were entirely fictitious.

This is a true story involving one of my colleagues. This patient had suffered from excruciating symptoms of post-traumatic stress disorder, convincing his wife, his therapist and, apparently, himself that he was impaired by painful memories of events that had never actually happened. In his own mind, the memories were true, and he made them seem so real to others that anyone listening to him also believed they were true.

Now, imagine a variation on this story. Suppose the patient is a young woman who enters therapy complaining of terrifying nightmares, depression, and low self-esteem, and exhibiting a history of failed relationships with men. She has no memories of any particular childhood trauma that might explain her current misery but during the first session, her therapist tells her that her symptoms are classic indicators of repressed childhood sexual abuse and he suspects that this is what happened to her. At each successive session, he urges her to "think back, try and remember when it happened," and reassures her that her own failure to recall any incidents of abuse does not mean they did not occur.

During the fourth session, after convincing her that she will never be healed until she breaks through her denial and faces the past, the therapist guides her into hypnosis. During the trance, the woman has an image of a six-month-old baby girl having her diapers changed. The image is blurry and indistinct, but in response to her therapist's repeated questions, she finally says she thinks the baby "might be" herself and that the person diapering her is perhaps her father. Then her therapist throws a series of intense, driving questions at her: Why was her father diapering her? Was she alone with him? Where was he touching her? Where were his hands? His fingers? What was he doing to her?

The woman suddenly sits up in a panic, a vague but frightening image in her mind of someone (perhaps her father?) violating a small baby (perhaps her?). She bursts into sobs as she confesses this awful vision and asks her therapist if this means she has been abused. He nods knowingly and tells her that she has bravely taken the first step to recovery.

At the therapist's insistent questioning and encouragement in subsequent sessions, more images of abuse emerge, usually after she has been hypnotized. With each increasingly terrible image that she reports, her therapist praises her courage in "confronting the past" and exhorts her to remember more.

Eventually he tells her that the kind of abuse she suffered often takes place at the hands of a group of people, not just one or two. Sometimes, sexual and physical abuse is conducted as part of a ritual or ceremony he says. In an effort to be helpful, he asks more questions to stimulate her memory. Did there seem to be a number of people involved, perhaps as many as 13 or more? Did they appear to wear dark robe-like garments and engage in chanting? Were there lighted candles and ceremonial rituals of some kind? Were there dead, mutilated animals?

As horrific visions and images swirl in her mind, the woman becomes terrified, screams "No! No! No!" and faints. After a while she revives and asks what happened. The therapist tells her that some particularly powerful memories surfaced, giving her an even greater understanding of how extensive her abuse had really been. He explains to her that satanic ritual abuse is pervasive throughout the country, and that she is lucky to be alive and able to come to terms with what really happened to her.

What is the meaning of such a narrative? Not one of these events—from the alleged molestation by her father when she was six months old to the luridly gruesome details of satanic ritual abuse—were spontaneously remembered by the client; they emerged, presumably from unconscious memory, only with the strenuous efforts of her therapist.

In the comfortable world of informal therapeutic axioms, all reports of traumatic events, recovered through suggestive procedures or consciously remembered, are assumed to be literally true and are taken at face value. In other words, it is assumed without question that clients don't dream up past trauma, therapists cannot inadvertently implant it in clients' minds, and clinicians are ethically bound to believe whatever they hear. These two scenarios evoke uncomfortable questions regarding long-standing conventions about truth, memory and credibility: Can we believe in the validity of *every* allegation of abuse based on suddenly remembered repressed memories, particularly if the memories have been relentlessly elicited (or even just mildly implied) by the therapist and only emerge during therapy? Is it possible that memories of abuse can be inadvertently suggested by therapists who are convinced they "know" an unsuspecting client has been abused? Can these suggested memories then be integrated into the client's memory as if they were facts? How do we distinguish a real survivor from one who has unintentionally made up—"confabulated"—all or some of the details of past abuse? How dependable are repressed memories of long-past events, anyway?

During the last decade and a half, a remarkable shift has occurred in the way both the public and the mental health profession regard the incidence of child sexual abuse. Before the mid- to late-70s, childhood molestation, particularly incest, was considered a rare occurrence; accounts of adult survivors were more likely to be dismissed as the products of hysterical fantasy than accepted at face value as true. Now, sexual abuse is recognized as a disturbingly widespread phenomenon, and therapists are far more willing to take seriously clients' reports of their own abusive childhoods. Unfortunately, it seems the pendulum may have swung too far in the opposite direction: Some therapists unquestioningly accept even the vaguest allegations of abuse, based on the most ephemeral dreams, impressionistic flashbacks or suddenly revived but indistinct memories that have presumably been completely repressed for 20 or 30 years.

Revelations of child abuse can have severe and devastating effects on both clients and their families. Uncovered memories can overwhelm clients, rendering them deeply depressed, even suicidal; they can permanently tear families apart and engender economically ruinous legal battles when survivors decide to take accused parties to court. With such potentially catastrophic reverberations far from the safe confines of the therapy room, therapists cannot afford—for the sake of their clients, their clients' families, and their own professional integrity—to ignore the line between the narrative, clinical truth of what their clients feel and believe, and the literal, physical reality upon which their memories are supposedly based.

There is disturbing evidence that some therapists unintentionally insinuate into the minds of their clients memories of abuse that never happened. Therapists often find this hard to believe, because they underestimate the potent influence they can wield in the lives of clients and they certainly don't often *feel* powerful, pointing out that it is excruciatingly difficult to get their clients to make even the most meager changes. Nonetheless, the capacity to be therapeutic—to encourage, to soothe, to help shift world views, to change perceptions—is equally the capacity to be anti-therapeutic—to inculcate a mindset and a point of view, to project a vision of reality to the client that may not only be false, but ultimately damaging. Whether therapists like to admit it or not, they can convince people to adopt beliefs that might either help *or* harm them.

The controversy now unfolding around what are called *false memories*—recollections of abuse that later turn out to be gross exaggerations or complete fantasies—obscures the real issue, which is the suggestibility of human beings and their susceptibility to adopt false beliefs at the suggestion of or under the influence of somebody else. All too often, for example, a *belief* in abuse is first established—in therapy or in a survivor support group—before any *memory* has surfaced at all. The client, therapist and/or group members then go looking for evidence to confirm their already entrenched convictions—"I believe I was (or my client was) abused," the logic goes. "Help me find the memories to prove it."

Sometimes, clients steeped in self-help literature, recovery programs, and incest-survival groups come to therapy and announce that they are incest survivors—often without having recovered any memories of their abuse. They're in therapy because they want the therapist to troll for the memories they believe must be there, somewhere at the bottom of their psyches. Sometimes, clients come to therapy with what seem to be strong and vivid memories of abuse. In either case, therapists cannot always know what the literal truth is—perhaps they really were abused, or perhaps they are conflating fact and fantasy, or perhaps a very few are even lying outright. It really doesn't matter because, whether established by the therapist or present before the client comes into therapy, the belief that the incest occurred is rock solid—even if the memories are lacking and even if a *feeling* that they may have been abused is their only evidence. After all, these clients have read and been told countless times that the memories don't matter—only the feelings and the beliefs do.

This cavalier attitude toward conscious memory is often reinforced by therapists who apparently take literally the statements made in some of the recovery literature (including *The Courage to Heal* by Ellen Bass and Laura Davis) that since specific repressed memories of abuse may never surface, they don't necessarily matter. These therapists regard facts and external corroboration as a kind of insignificant epiphenomenon, much less important than the *real* therapeutic material *subjective feelings and beliefs*. Within this mindset, actual memories are somehow dispensable in the pursuit of healing. So therapy becomes a kind of *folie à deux*—in which both therapist and client tell each other that all that really matters are feelings and subjective interpretations of images and bodily sensations, which are the only confirmation required to demonstrate the literal truth of past abuse.

While many therapists recoil at the very idea of buttressing the internal emotional conviction of abuse with more prosaic and material evidence, other clinicians are not comfortable simply accepting, without question, whatever the client says. These more "insightful" therapists presume to know, long before their clients do and often in spite of their clients' fervent protestations, that abuse is behind their clients' troublesome symptoms. These therapists believe, without reservation, that it is their professional and personal duty to make clients, who describe these symptoms, accept for their own good the foreordained "truth" of their abuse.

Clients are not only encouraged to believe they were abused, but patiently exhorted to return again and again to whatever fragments of dream, imagination, or memory they can dig up, building a story and a case elaborate enough to satisfy the therapist. The client bold enough to reject the diagnosis of incest survivor is said to be "in denial," unwilling to confront the truth; the rejection of the diagnosis is *prima facie* evidence in its favor. In other words, if the client admits the abuse happened, it happened; if the client doesn't admit it happened, it *still* happened. Or, as Roseanne Arnold said recently on "The Oprah Winfrey Show," "When someone asks you, 'Were you sexually abused as a child?' there are only two answers: One of them is 'Yes,' and one of them is 'I don't know.' You can't say 'No.' "

More than most people, the client in a therapeutic relationship is particularly suggestible—needy and seeking answers, they are inclined to fall under the therapist's influence. Perceptions, even memories, can be fundamentally altered by the suggestions of a trusted and revered figure. Cult leaders, charismatic political ideologues, and totalitarian dictators can use a combination of seduction, pressure, and outright coercion to induce followers to believe almost anything, however malign or self-destructive. On a more benign plane, consider John Bradshaw, author of *Homecoming* and *Healing the Shame that Binds You*, who has persuaded millions of Americans that they have an "inner child" somewhere within themselves. People act as if this inner child were actually a tiny, vulnerable person within themselves; they literally talk to it, comfort it, give it a name and personality, defend it, indulge it and find ways to continually get to know it better. To millions of Americans, the existence of this little being is a concrete fact, as real as their own flesh-and-blood children— and often just as demanding. But, *there is no inner child—it is simply a metaphor!* If a television viewer can be moved to this extent by a media personality, imagine how much more suggestible a client is in the intense one-to-one relationship of therapy.

Few wrong diagnoses have more power to wreak destructive havoc in the life and family of a client than the attribution of childhood sexual abuse. And yet, some therapists appear to automatically diagnose past abuse without even a pretense of therapeutic caution or any knowledge of the client's history. Recently a woman called me to ask if I would hypnotize her in order to determine whether she had been molested as a child. She told me that she felt chronic, low self-esteem and had recently phoned another therapist to make a first appointment. The therapist, *never having met her*, said on the telephone that her problem with self-esteem meant that she must have been abused as a child, and she should be hypnotized to "recover" her repressed memories. This therapist obviously viewed hypnosis as a kind of truth serum or magical lie detector that could reliably uncover long-buried memories that, camera-like, had recorded the exact, objective, and complete truth of past events.

Even more shocking than such ignorance about suggestion and hypnosis, however, is the thought that a therapist working with as sensitive and potentially devastating material as child abuse would make an off-the-cuff diagnosis to a complete stranger and then be willing to dump her in someone else's office for a hit-and-run session involving investigative hypnosis. It is hard to imagine a more egregious disregard for good clinical judgment and ethical standards of practice. And yet, every day I get at least one phone call from a therapist asking me to spend a session hypnotizing a client to find out whether there was childhood abuse or not, as if the procedure of uncovering child abuse were as expeditious and unproblematic as getting dental x-rays.

Memories recovered through hypnosis are not *necessarily* inaccurate, but formal trancework, or even informal suggestion, can introduce misinformation that a client, eager to find substantial reasons for his or her symptoms, all too readily accepts as his or her own truth. A therapist can inadvertently collude in creating a skewed perspective on personal history that taints the client's own memories of the past. Most therapists already realize, for example, that severely depressed clients commonly revise their personal histories to correspond to their current dismal moods. Viewing their lives through the lens of depression, they selectively recall only long, unrelieved chronicles of pain and suffering.

By the same token, the presence of colorful detail and intensity of emotional affect in the memory are not evidence of reliability. Suggestive processes, like hypnosis, can produce amazingly vivid details and the expression of deep feelings, which seem very real. But cascades of sound and fury don't necessarily signify literal truth. After all, a person undergoing "past-life regression therapy" can produce the same dramatically convincing material while "reliving" the pain and suffering of being a deeply misunderstood Attila the Hun in the fifth century!

If some clients, after only a few therapy sessions, are bluntly or subtly told by their therapists that they are survivors of abuse, memories or no memories, why do they accept it? Why would a client agree, even reluctantly, and in the absence of any personal recollections of abuse, to a diagnosis that is likely to damage self-esteem and demolish family relationships? One explanation is that clients and therapists alike need to make sense of seemingly senseless symptomatic behavior, finding the origins and "root cause" of unhappiness—something that explains everything. They need to provide a framework for treatment and recovery. In some ways, the diagnosis of child abuse is an appealingly neat cause-and-effect proposition: "Believing I was abused explained so many things so quickly," said one client who eventually retracted her accusations. "I didn't have to search for reasons anymore."

Furthermore, the client's need for approval, which increases in close relationships, is amplified in the therapy context. Clients not only want to believe what their therapists tell them, they need the approval of their therapists, and the more confused and uncertain they are about what is wrong with them, the more likely they are to trust whatever the therapist says. Perhaps the most powerful explanation of all is the promise of a cure: "Believe this happened, work through the recovery process and you will be healed." To someone in deep distress, this promise is *very* tempting.

Even careful and painstaking therapists are often in a quandary about the nature and reliability of memory, and the role of therapist suggestion in determining client beliefs. In 1992, I surveyed nearly 1,000 practicing therapists about memory and suggestibility in clients. Many had little or no formal knowledge of the role and power of suggestion in therapy, or of the accumulated research data about memory. They held surprisingly naive and outmoded views about the mind's capacity to remember, believing, for example, that people can retrieve detailed and accurate memories of events from the first months of their lives, that the brain is like a computer, or a tape recorder, or a camera—objectively registering detailed images of past experiences. Contrary to these views, research data clearly indicate that memory is *not* always reliable, that it can be influenced by suggestion, and that it is a complex process often involving selective perception and the imaginative reconstruction of past events.

Even though most therapists in the survey seemed to believe that memory was something like an objective information-mirroring machine, they nonetheless acknowledged that they felt they could influence clients to believe things that were plausible, but not necessarily true. Also, surprisingly, hundreds of those surveyed revealed their doubts about the accuracy of their clients' allegations of abuse. Furthermore, almost all respondents confessed their inability to separate truth from fiction in their clients' reports of abuse. Unfortunately, most of the surveyed clinicians also indicated that precisely *because* they had no way of distinguishing false from true memories of abuse, they were inclined to accept noncritically whatever story the client told.

How are therapists to navigate the murky terrain between the obvious untruths and the undeniable reality that comprise so much of the practice of therapy? Suppose a client comes in and says, "I was hypnotized (or 'did imagery work' or 'guided meditation'), and the therapist uncovered some apparently repressed memories that indicate I was sexually abused as a child." Suppose, too, that, although the client did not suspect abuse until it was diagnosed, his or her symptoms make the diagnosis a reasonable possibility. How can a therapist be true to the client's needs and open to the possibility that there was sexual abuse, without colluding in a convenient diagnosis that may exhibit more evidence of suggestion than therapeutic observation and fact?

First and foremost, a therapist must not jump quickly to the conclusion that abuse occurred simply because it is plausible. Symptoms are not evidence for abuse. If the client has never mentioned being molested and has never previously identified him or herself as an abuse survivor, the therapist should generally *not* be the one to suggest it. There are, of course, times when a therapist has good reason to suspect abuse and deems it necessary to mention the possibility to the client. If there is resistance, however, the therapist should not pathologize it by interpreting it as "denial," but should strive instead to create an atmosphere in which the client may eventually decide for her- or himself whether the issue should be pursued.

A therapist should never simply assume that a client who cannot remember much from childhood is repressing traumatic memories or is in denial. Believe it or not, there *are* individuals with a here-and-now or future-oriented quality to their subjective experience, whose recollections about childhood are quite impoverished because they do not think or care very much about remembering it. Furthermore, accepting the theory of traumatically based amnesia as an explanation for the lack of memories from infancy or earliest childhood flies in the face of developmental research about cognitive maturation. Research consistently shows that memory is marginal at best before age two: before that age, children apparently do not have the mental structures to form long term coherent memories. While "body memory" is a convenient construct to maintain a belief in infant memory it is hardly objective.

In any case, no therapist should ever, either directly or indirectly, suggest abuse outside of a specific therapeutic context—certainly not to a client who is on the phone making a first appointment!

Nor should the therapist ask leading questions, which imply either a desired or correct answer. For example, don't ask questions like, "When were you abused? How did he/she/they molest you?" In the hypnotic context, such suggestive questions are based on what we call presuppositions—they presuppose that abuse did happen and all that needs to be determined is when and how. Presuppositions can be useful in therapy; asking a client "How will you feel when you discover you *can* have the kind of relationship you want?" engenders expectations of positive change in therapy. Presuppositions about the reality of abuse, on the other hand, can help create the very pathology that the therapist is presumably treating.

A client is most vulnerable to suggestion and the untoward influence of leading questions when therapy begins to delve into painful life situations from the past, particularly from childhood. At this point, the therapist is likely to ask, "How old were you? Where were you? What was going on? Was anyone around? What was said in the interaction between you and this person?" Such questions are necessary when they are asked to determine what the client has experienced, but therapists should be careful that they don't slide into more leading questions, like "Did you feel uncomfortable with the interaction? Can you recall how you were made to feel afraid and ashamed?"

Even if, after asking nonleading, neutral questions, the client does remember a formerly repressed memory of abuse, the therapist should be open to the possibility of other external sources of influence in the client's life. Has he or she, for example, read extensively in the incest-recovery literature, been pressured by a sibling, or been very active in a survivor group?

When planning to conduct a session aimed at uncovering sensitive information, including repressed memories of abuse, the therapist should consider videotaping or audiotaping the session, and even transcribing the questions that were asked. This kind of self monitoring enables the clinician to better determine whether or not he or she inadvertently suggested the possibility of abuse, thus provoking fictitious "memories" to emerge in a compliant or task-motivated client. Given the damage unsupported child abuse allegations can cause, therapists should perhaps infuse a bit of tolerance for ambiguity and what *really* happened into their practice, particularly when clients report that repressed memories have suddenly surfaced in abuse recovery groups, for example, or after reading recovery literature. In such ambiguous cases, it is probably wise to seek out corroboration of the abuse by obtaining medical and school records from the client's childhood, and interviewing family and friends about reported incidents—the more external evidence, the better.

Therapists also should be cautious about suggesting that clients cut off communication with their families. Among the most destructive aspects of the abuse epidemic is the splintering of families in the wake of allegations made by a son or daughter. Family members are not necessarily lying or in denial if they reject the accusations. The possibility shouldn't be dismissed out of hand that they are telling the truth, or experiencing heartfelt doubts and confusion themselves about what really happened. Certainly, doubt is inherent in the context, particularly for nonabusing family members. They *have* to wonder whether the abuse really happened or not; if it did, they can only come to accept the truth through open communication. Even if there has been abuse, it is irresponsible to frame predictable doubts and disbelief as toxic denial and precipitously insist that the client abandon his or her parents and siblings; unnecessarily tearing the family apart for the sake of "healing" is a bit like curing the disease but killing the patient.

Finally, therapists should reconsider the "no pain, no gain" philosophy of treatment. Much of the pressure to recover memories, whatever the cost, derives from a common belief that every gory detail of abuse must be remembered and worked through before the client can begin to get better. This theory does not work for everyone, especially not for all abuse survivors. Relentlessly doing memory work for long periods of time can actually make some clients worse—it forces them to bring up more of what they already feel unable to handle. Approaches that emphasize resource building rather than memory work can fare better and should be considered in formulating a treatment plan for a particular individual.

As therapists predisposed to like and believe our clients, to empathize with their pain, and to take their side, we may be too willing to let slide our critical faculties when it comes to the literal truth of what they are telling us. Because child abuse is so terrible, we do not want to be in the position of doubting people who may have suffered horribly because of it. At the same time, we cannot just dismiss the claims that false accusations are made simply because they go against the grain of our therapeutic inclinations, or because they are politically incorrect, particularly when the consequences of such allegations—true or false—are so dire.

As therapists, we like to think of ourselves as the good guys. We may assume that *some* therapists are harmful, but we have a hard time imagining that we may inadvertently hurt clients. Nonetheless, if, in our zeal to combat child abuse, we deny our own power to negatively influence clients and unintentionally create the very problem we intend to treat, we are betraying our mission. Nobody—not survivors of genuine abuse nor those who mistakenly believe they were abused, nor the families of either—is helped by therapists who abdicate their responsibility to think critically and who deny the need to make distinctions between truth and falsehood.

4

FACING THE TRUTH ABOUT FALSE MEMORY

DAVID CALOF

Tom, a 35-year-old mortgage broker, came to see me soon after his divorce. He had never been able to sustain a loving sexual relationship for more than a couple of months, and he felt like a failure because his career was stalled. We had hardly begun the first session when he said, "I suppose you're going to tell me that I was sexually abused as a child." Tom told me that in one of their first sessions, his previous therapist had jumped to this conclusion and he had quit treatment after a couple of weeks.

Later in the session, when I routinely asked about familial alcoholism, drug addiction, and sexual or physical abuse, Tom told me that while growing up, an older cousin had often beaten him, but neither the cousin nor anybody else had ever sexually abused him. And so our therapy began.

Over the months, as his trust in me grew, Tom confided that he occasionally had memory lapses and could not recall his whereabouts for hours. Sometimes, he heard voices, and he found personal checks written on his account—in his handwriting—that he could not remember writing. He found a marijuana pipe in his bedroom, even though he was a conservative man who condemned drug use, and he even found women's clothing in his closet, although he had no idea how these items had gotten there.

Five or six months into therapy, he began to have nightmares and

---

This article first appeared in the *Family Therapy Networker* (September/October 1993): 39–45, and is copied here with permission.

disturbing daydreams of forced, mutual masturbation with an older man. He could not see the man's face. When I asked him about these images, he put them down to an "overactive imagination."

The images stopped for several months and then returned more clearly and insistently. Sometimes, they were accompanied by a terrible pain or a feeling of fullness in his bowels. One day, he came into my office looking pale and drawn. He was afraid to sleep at night, and he told me he had been bleeding anally off and on since our last session.

Up until this point, Tom's case would seem to offer plenty of ammunition for critics of the way therapists handle cases in which the possibility of childhood abuse is raised. After all, even though Tom had no memories of sexual abuse, one therapist had suggested it to him early in therapy. Disturbing images involving sexual activity appeared only after he began seeing me. Perhaps they were an iatrogenic artifact of therapy. Clearly Tom had a fragmented sense of self and his bleeding was the kind of symptom that Freud once described as "hysterical." Many therapists would have considered Tom a "borderline" client whose tenuous sense of self made him highly suggestible, often inconsistent and occasionally dishonest. Perhaps, despite my best intentions, Tom had tried to please me by cooking up "memories" of sexual abuse, and perhaps he was looking for a single, simple explanation for his present difficulties.

Fearing his bleeding was caused by cancer, Tom went to his doctor. After an examination, he was told that he had a kind of severe anal scarring that often results from forced sex. The doctor's diagnosis crystallized something for Tom that had existed only in memory fragments at the edge of his consciousness before then. He began to remember being repeatedly sexually abused by his older cousin throughout his childhood.

Such cases are not rare. During the past 20 years, I have worked as a therapist and consultant with more than 400 people who were cruelly and repeatedly beaten or sexually abused as children. While some came into therapy with memories of relatively minor abuse, very few could recall severe abuse. Many of these clients did not begin therapy concerned with memories of abuse. They wanted to lose weight, or have better relationships; they were suicidal or insomniac, or were compulsively cutting themselves. They were prostitutes, business executives, paramedics, and therapists. Some had dangerous hobbies, such as mountain climbing, or they frequently had sex with strangers without using condoms. Others had eating disorders or failed marriages. They were all suspicious and self-deprecating.

But what stood out in many of these cases, apart from the initial presenting complaints, were symptoms common to other trauma victims, including survivors of such public horrors as the bombing of Dresden, the camps at Auschwitz, the massacred villages of Vietnam, Guatemala and Bosnia, the killing fields of Cambodia, and the torture chambers of Brazil. Like survivors of these public traumas, my clients had dissociative symptoms, such as sleepwalking and memory disturbances, as well as signs of post-traumatic stress, such as flashbacks, sleep disturbances, and nightmares. They wanted to be anonymous, or were socially withdrawn. They were depressed or had other mood disturbances. They often tended to minimize or rationalize painful present realities, and they suffered from feelings of numbness, emptiness and unreality.

Unlike the survivors of publicly acknowledged disasters, however, they did not know *why* they felt that way. Their memories of the traumas were often fragmented into bewildering mosaics or missing altogether. Often, they were veterans of intensely private wars that had taken place in barns, attics and suburban houses with the blinds drawn. Their wounds were never reported in newspapers or discussed with family members. There were rarely any witnesses other than the people who hurt them. Like most traumas, their childhood rapes and beatings were encoded into memory in fragments, in a state of terror, when their hearts and minds were flooded with adrenaline. They didn't remember them the way one remembers a walk in the park, and they doubted the fragments they did recall.

In the past two years—in response to an outpouring of uncertainty and horror generated by the stories some abuse survivors tell—believers in what has come to be called "false memory syndrome" have advanced the idea that patients who claim to recover repressed memories are the hapless victims of irresponsible therapists. According to this scenario, such therapists use hypnosis to implant memories where there are none, encourage so-called borderlines to believe their fantasies and urge adult survivors to confront and sue their parents.

In the past 20 years, I have supervised and consulted with many hundreds of therapists. In all that time, I've worked with perhaps a dozen who were doing the kind of bad therapy that has recently received so much media attention: therapists who hadn't resolved their rage about their own abuse and were sending their clients out as proxies to seek justice; others who had lost their boundaries and entered into a romantic relationship with a client, taken clients into their homes, given them money or hidden them from authorities and other family members. I have encountered far more therapists who do another kind of bad therapy by denying and minimizing their clients' experiences.

The false-memory critique treats extreme examples of bad therapy as if they were mainstream practice. It seems to arise from basic misunderstandings of what therapy is and what therapists do. It assumes there is some economic and emotional payoff for therapists in implanting memories of abuse when nothing of the sort has actually taken place. It ignores the fact that people who have been repeatedly abused tell their stories reluctantly and disbelieve themselves. Taking on the identity of a trauma survivor brings far more stigma than specialness.

Years ago, I started out with a hypnotherapy practice specializing in weight loss. I was not sexually or physically abused as a child, and I did not seek out these clients so much as they sought me out. The sometimes overwhelming stories my clients tell me are vicariously traumatic to me. Frankly, I would prefer to think they're false memories.

Treating adult survivors may mean a commitment of several hours a week over three to five years or longer. Most of them can't pay more than 25% of my usual fee. There are sometimes late-night phone calls and suicide attempts, hospitalizations, and threats of lawsuits—and worse—from other family members.

Lucy was a day-care worker in her early twenties when she began what was to be five years in therapy with me. She had absolutely no memory of abuse when we began. In the first year, she remembered that her father, an airline pilot, had raped her when she was six and then allowed two of his flying buddies to rape her. Her mother and sister both phoned and accused me of unduly influencing Lucy. Her sister told me about their wonderful family life; her mother informed me that if I didn't stop influencing Lucy to lie this way, she was going to sue.

Advocates of false memory often paint a picture of an idyllic family victimized by overzealous or unethical therapists and lying clients. They avoid discussing the possibility of lying, sociopathy, amnesia, dissociation, alcohol blackout, and other "false memories" in the families themselves. Yet, this is often the case. After five years of therapy, Lucy met with her mother and described being 11 years old and screaming while her father prepared to rape her in an upstairs bedroom. Her mother had opened the door and her father had said they were "just playing a game." As Lucy recounted her memory, her mother finally acknowledged seeing her daughter on the bed with her pants down and her father over her. "I didn't know, I didn't know," her mother said, crying. "He said you were just playing a game."

Let's take a look at some of the major misconceptions that underlie the current debate about false memory:

It is preposterous to think that someone could entirely forget repeated rape that occurred over years. Such "uncoverings" must be the mutual delusion of therapist and client.

Memory disturbance after shocking and horrifying events is so well-documented among survivors of other types of verified trauma that it is listed in the DSM-III-R. Bruno Bettelheim, for example, wrote eloquently of repressing his memories of Dachau and Buchenwald:

"A split was soon forced upon me, the split between the inner self that might be able to retain its integrity, and the rest of the personality that would have to submit and adjust for survival.

"Anything that had to do with the present hardships was so distressing that one wished to repress it, to forget it. Only what was unrelated to present suffering was emotionally neutral and could hence be remembered."

A study conducted in postwar Britain found that in times of public emergency 15% of all hospital psychiatric admissions were for psychogenic amnesia. Winnie Smith, a former army nurse and author of *American Daughter Gone to War*, writes that she forgot, for 16 years, whole segments of her traumatic experiences as a critical care nurse in Vietnam. Why, then, are we so suspicious about the years of self-protective forgetting those who were sexually abused?

If such memories were induced only by pesky therapists, survivors of childhood abuse would not spontaneously recover them outside therapy. But they do. According to Jack Kornfield, a well-known California psychologist and teacher of Buddhist meditation, women on month-long silent meditation retreats have spontaneously remembered long-forgotten incest. "I've known of many cases in which these women have gone back to their families and received confirmation," says Kornfield. After hearing a radio report about a pedophile priest arrested for molesting children, John Robitaille, a Providence, Rhode Island, public-relations man, suddenly recalled having been sexually abused at the age of 11 by the same priest. And in a *New York Times* article, Los Angeles attorney Shari Karney, who had never been in therapy, described recalling her incest experience in an overwhelming flashback while cross-examining a man accused of molesting his daughter.

Therapists believe that recovering traumatic memories will magically "cure" their patients.

The point is not to force memories of horrible things to the surface but to live free of the aftereffects of traumatic experiences. Tom, for example, needed to pay attention to his memories, not to persecute or blame his cousin but because he had a lifetime of practice at ignoring his own experience. He needed to learn to listen to intuitions and physical sensations in order to navigate effectively in his present world.

Like many adult survivors of unresolved childhood trauma, Tom minimized the damaging effects of ill treatment by others. Some women who were sexually abused as children, for instance, become so practiced at ignoring danger signals that they put themselves in harm's way and are raped again as adults. It is important for them to piece together their childhood experiences and to trust their present responses; otherwise, they may endlessly recreate the preconditions of trauma. Tom didn't trust his perceptions. When he disagreed with his boss over an important business decision, he found himself unable to make his point. Later, when the deal turned sour, his boss was furious that he had failed to alert him.

Therapists pressure clients to jump to the conclusion that they've been abused.

When I do my best work, I mirror back to my clients the things they put into the room and then disown—their dreams, body sensations, horrific drawings, writing, memories. At the same time, I try always to stay half a step behind them as they wrestle with the conflict between believing and not believing their memories. My job is not to advocate for any version of reality. It is to provide a forum where they may sit with all sides of their inner conflicts. I often ask, "What do these images or sensations mean to you?" I do not encourage clients to seek external validation, from me or anyone else; it's much more important that they stew in their ambivalence and uncertainty and decide for themselves what their memories mean.

Elise was 26 when she came into therapy because she was depressed, eating in trance-like binges, and having trouble in her relationships. She told me she had long periods of absent staring, feelings of being unreal, and an array of internal voices that she said had "ruled" her since she was a child.

In the second year of therapy, she began to have intrusive images of being beaten by her mother. For months, she denied that these images— and the mysterious bruises that appeared on her body—had any connection to what had actually happened to her. She often asked me whether I thought these images were memories. I said I thought they were a powerful communication from her unconscious, the meaning of which she needed to learn. I refused to take a position on whether they were true.

Her agonizing struggle continued, and I was sometimes tempted to take sides and stop her turmoil. She decided to quit therapy "to forget about them" and end her painful self-doubt. For the next two appointments, she came to my building but couldn't open my office door. On the morning of her next appointment, she woke to find herself covered with bruises that had no physical cause. Before her session, I found her just outside the door to my office frozen in a state of terror. By the time I led her inside, she had begun to have flashbacks of severe beatings by her alcoholic mother. By the end of that long session, she no longer denied what had happened to her.

For several more months, Elise worked on these memories and discussed confronting her mother, from whom she had been estranged for
many years. I discouraged this, because I felt she was still unsure about
what had happened and was looking for confirmation that she might not
get. A few months later, near the end of her therapy, when she no longer
needed anyone to validate her memories, she met with her mother. She
said she wanted "the experience of speaking the secret out loud."

Her mother, once an alcoholic, had been sober for many years and
was dying of cancer. Their conversation was brief. "I had a very difficult
life and I don't want to talk about it," her mother said. Elise turned the
conversation to an incident when she was eight years old and had broken
her wrist. Her mother had always told her she had fallen down the stairs,
and Elise, who had no memory of the accident, believed her for years.
But now Elise told her mother she remembered being thrown down the
stairs when her mother was in an alcoholic rage. Elise's mother tersely
admitted that she had been "a little hard on her," and had thrown her
downstairs. Then she refused to discuss it, or anything else, any further.

*Because of the ramifications in the world outside the therapy room,
therapists should get external verification before assuming that childhood
sexual abuse took place.*

I have no interest in such a task. I am a therapist, not a detective.
When clients come to me and genuinely risk disclosing and exploring
their life's issues, the therapeutic relationship must be, as it always has
been, a sanctuary—confidential, private, and safe.

I work in the aftermath of shattering experiences. I am less interested
in the pinpoint accuracy of every detail of clients' memories than I am in
the chronic, debilitating aftereffects. I am not piecing together legal evidence. It is well beyond the usual clinical covenant for therapists to enter
into their clients' lives as researchers, detectives, solicitors, or professional chroniclers.

I usually discourage abused clients from suing their perpetrators, and
over the years, only a handful have gone to court. Lawsuits usually take
more from the client than they are worth even if they prevail. Clients
who are at a deep therapeutic impasse sometimes prematurely try to
staunch their feelings of loss and try to validate their perceptions and
their suffering by involving the legal system.

Therapists using hypnosis often unwittingly suggest traumatic memories.

False-memory advocates set up a straw man, suggesting that hypno-
tists don't know how undependable hypnotically refreshed memory can
be. But, in fact, we know that hypnosis can distort memories by conflating them with present beliefs and feelings. I use hypnosis all the time,
but rarely to discover "what really happened." In fact, a patient may lose

the legal right to testify as a witness if his or her memories have been hypnotically refreshed. In the state of Washington, a victim who undergoes hypnosis as a part of post-traumatic intervention risks having all her recall from that point forward dismissed as evidence.

At one client's repeated insistence, I used adjunctive hypnotherapy successfully to recover memories (later corroborated) of childhood incest. She later considered suing me when she discovered that she had effectively lost her right to sue her perpetrator because she had been hypnotized. I now obtain consent before employing hypnotic techniques, and clearly indicate that clients may lose the right to testify in future legal proceedings.

There is a good reason for these legal safeguards. Hypnosis is not truth serum. The essence of its therapeutic value is that it can alter someone's attitude toward his or her traumatic memories and blend past impressions with present-day realities and beliefs. In this way, adult insights may be brought to bear on childhood perceptions. This complex interplay between memory and hypnosis can create memory distortion, and there is no way to distinguish this from true recall without corroboration. We do need to be careful. Clients under hypnosis are highly suggestible, and their "memories" can be altered by unwitting suggestions or leading questions. Clinicians must be cautious about suggesting content and use open-ended ways of providing empathy, support, and validation. If hypnosis is used for searching out memories at all, it is best to wait until the client has been able to accept some of his or her memories already, and is willing and committed to exploring for further traumatic content.

However, I frequently use hypnosis in other ways with trauma survivors. It has been recognized since at least World War I as a valuable adjunct treatment for trauma. With Tom, for example, hypnosis made the painful process of therapy easier on him. At the beginning of therapy, I used hypnosis to create positive expectations—saying, for example, "You'll find it easier to talk about things . . . this will be a place you experience some sense of discovery and expectancy, a place where you will learn to feel safe."

Later, when he was nearly overcome by memories and was having trouble sleeping and working, I used hypnosis to help him contain his pain by suggesting, "When you need to go to work, you can put these matters in the back of your mind and not be plagued by them as you work. When we work together, you can take them out again." While Tom was in trance, he put his memories in a time-lock vault and buried them under a tree between sessions.

Later, hypnosis was valuable in cognitive restructuring. Tom was able to correct his post-traumatic distortions, including the idea that he was a wimp who had failed to stop his cousin from abusing him, and would therefore fail at everything else. Otherwise, therapy might have simply condemned him to reliving his abusive memories endlessly.

That is how I usually use hypnosis—not to search out recalcitrant memories. My practice is to wait for traumatic content to bubble up, rather than go looking aggressively for it. I believe that clients want to remember and tell their stories. If I provide a supportive, consistent, caring, and empathic context, the client's story will eventually come into the room. If it doesn't, I look first at problems in our relationship and not to hypnosis.

As in other areas of clinical practice, there are few definitive research findings about the treatment of adult survivors. Like all therapists, clinicians who work with survivors must carefully look to their practices to test the validity of their methods and assumptions. The tough-minded questions we must ask ourselves are, "What are the effects of our assumptions and methods on our clients? Do they get better when we treat them as trauma survivors?"

Tom felt he had permission to explore his nightmares and body sensations only after a doctor told him he had been physically scarred. In therapy with me, he had found a place where he would be believed, supported, and not abandoned, no matter what memories or sensations he reported. I believe his memories emerged partly because I had helped him create a safe place for them. Soon after his visit to the doctor, Tom, in a nightmare, saw his older cousin forcing him to perform oral sex. After that, he had waking memories of his cousin raping him. With his parents' help, he tracked his cousin down and angrily confronted him on the phone. The man denied it all—denied even having beaten Tom— incidents that Tom had never forgotten. Knowing that, at least in one area, his cousin was either lying or had forgotten, Tom pressed on.

He called his cousin repeatedly, finally abandoning an accusatory tone and merely trying to talk about their childhoods. Finally, the cousin angrily shouted, "All right, all right, God dammit, we fooled around some! So what? Just leave me alone!" Tom continued to press on, naming places and times where the abuse occurred. Finally the cousin admitted that he had "abused" Tom, and though he could not remember any specifics, the cousin said it was "very possible" that there had been several acts of anal penetration.

When the time was right, Tom pieced together his traumatic memories and his life changed. Within a year, his nightmares, night terrors, and strange physical symptoms ended. For years, he had been impotent except during one-night stands with strangers. After therapy, that changed. He remarried, went back to school for an advanced degree, and moved up in his profession.

While Tom was able to get corroboration for his memories, many adult survivors do not. In most cases, this is simply not possible. What is important is not for clients to find external validations of these memories, but for them to learn to trust their perceptions and pay attention to the truth of their lives. The sanctuary of therapy is one place where many clients find they can confront their past instead of endlessly and numbly reenacting it. After two decades of working with abuse survivors, I know that listening to their stories and helping them explore the truth of their experiences has enabled many to turn their lives around. For now, that is the best—and the most satisfying—proof I can advance that the stories told me were true.

5

CHILDREN'S MEMORIES FOR STRESSFUL EVENTS

GAIL S. GOODMAN, JODI E. HIRSCHMAN, DEBRA HEPPS MCKEE, AND LESLIE RUDY

Children's memory for stressful events was investigated. Three- to 7-year-old children were videotaped while receiving venipuncture or inoculations as part of their health care at medical clinics. After delays of 2 to 3 days to as much as a year, the children's memory was tested. Correct free recall was not affected by age, but the ability to answer specific and misleading questions was age related. Accurate face recognition was inconsistently associated with age. Children's memory was not affected by stress until a very high level of distress was reached. At that point, stress had a beneficial effect on free recall and resistance to suggestion. The findings are discussed in relation to children's memory for nonstressful events, theories of the effects of stress on memory, methodological issues involved in this type of research, and concerns about the accuracy of children's testimony in legal proceedings.

Stressful events mar even the happiest of childhoods. The dread of an inoculation as the needle approaches, the sense of abandonment on the first day of school, or the pain of a dog bite on a too eager hand can leave enduring memories for children who otherwise experience uneventful youths. For less fortunate children—those who suffer victimization, death of a loved one, or hospitalization—traumatic memories may last a lifetime. A complete model of memory development must account for children's retention and possible distortion of personally sig-

Reprinted from *Merrill-Palmer Quarterly* 37, no. 1 (January 1991): 109–57 by permission of the Wayne State University Press. Copyright © 1991 by Wayne State University Press, Detroit, Michigan 48202.

nificant, aversive events. Moreover, an understanding of children's memory for stressful events is important for certain applied issues, such as predicting the accuracy of children's legal testimony.

The vast majority of memory development research has been conducted with nonstressful stimuli (e.g., unremarkable words, pictures, stories; see Flavell 1985; Kail 1989; and Mandler 1983; for reviews). Similarly, studies of memory for real-life events tend to focus on relatively mundane activities (e.g., eating at a restaurant; see Cohen 1989; and Nelson 1986; for reviews). Even research directly aimed at understanding children's testimony, which is often applied to the testimony of child victims of traumatic events, has typically concerned innocuous stimuli (e.g., Ceci, Ross, and Toglia 1987; Dent 1982; Goodman and Reed 1986; Saywitz 1987). Thus, we know surprisingly little about children's memory for stressful events and whether such memories differ in quality or quantity from memories of less stressful experiences.

Studies of memory for nonstressful events often uncover age differences, especially when children as young as 3 years are included (e.g., Brown and DeLoache 1978; Ceci et al. 1987; Goodman and Reed 1986; Perlmutter and Myers 1979). It is an open question whether age effects will be exaggerated, diminished, or unaffected when memory for a stressful event is tested. However, there is reason to believe that negative life events are given special status in children's minds. Miller and Sperry (1988), for example, found that the majority of young children's early conversational topics concern negative life experiences.

The importance of emotions, such as distress, as regulators of children's and adults' memory has been acknowledged for hundreds of years (see Rapaport 1942 for a historical review). Identifying the exact mechanisms involved or even the precise nature and direction of such effects has been surprisingly difficult, however. We will argue in the present paper that greater attention to the functions of discrete emotions, as opposed to a focus on general arousal, may lead to a more enlightened picture of the regulating role of emotion on memory. Before this argument is made, we review current research on stress and memory and present the findings of four studies.

STRESS AND MEMORY

Research on adults' memory for stressful events exists, but the finding are quite mixed (e.g., see Deffenbacher 1983 and Goodman and Hahn 1987 for reviews). The most common experimental design involves the comparison of an experimental (stressed) group and a control (nonstressed) group. Stress is varied by making the stimulus events differ slightly. For example, in a study by Lotus and Burns (1982), adults watched a film of a bank robbery. For half of the viewers, the film ended tragically with a young boy being shot in the face, whereas for the other half, the film ended on a less tragic note. Other experimental designs also have been successfully employed. For example, all of Brigham, Maass, Martinez, and Whittenberger's (1983) subjects were exposed to the same stimuli (i.e., a set of pictures) but only some subjects were concurrently exposed to aversive levels of electric shock.

Despite mixed findings, a number of influential writers have concluded that stress interferes with memory (Baddeley 1972; Deffenbacher 1983; Loftus 1979). The Yerkes-Dodson Law (Yerkes and Dodson 1908) and Easterbrook's (1959) expansion of it support this conclusion by providing a theoretical framework for interpreting adverse effects of stress on memory. Easterbrook proposed that arousal causes a reduction in the range of cues attended. Thus, as arousal increases, attention becomes focused on central details to the exclusion of peripheral details. As arousal increases past the optimum level, attention becomes so restricted as to exclude even central cues, thus leading to a decline in memory performance.

In contrast, some studies indicate that stress has no adverse, and at times even has beneficial, effects on memory (e.g., Bohannon 1988; Brown and Kulik 1977; Hosch and Cooper 1982; Ochsner and Zaragoza 1988; Warren-Leubecker, Bradley, and Hinton 1988). This benefit has been interpreted in terms of the adaptive value of retaining memories of aversive experiences. For example, Brown and Kulik (1977), in their discussion of "flashbulb" memories based on news of distressing events, argued that the human brain evolved to retain memories of information possessing high survival value (see also Goodman, Rudy, Bottoms, and Aman, in press; Pillemer 1984; but see Bohannon 1988; Neisser 1982; and McCloskey, Wible, and Cohen 1988). In support of Brown and Kulik's general contention, recent physiological studies indicate that adrenalin causes increased consolidation of memory (Gold 1987; McGaugh 1989; Kety 1970), thus providing a mechanism for heightened retention of stressful experiences.

Finally, others have proposed that stress has both positive and negative effects on memory. Baddeley (1982) entertained the possibility that stress may narrow attention, leading to poor memory for certain details, but might aid consolidation so that details attended are retained particularly well. Christianson and Loftus (1987) contend that memory of an event's occurrence is increased if the event is stressful, but that details of stressful events are retained less well than nonstressful events.

Inconsistent findings across studies may be the result of differences in memory tasks, stimuli, levels of distress reached, or other procedural variations. The effects of delay interval, repeated testing, and rehearsal have been focused upon as possible factors. Although both accuracy and completeness of report generally decline with delay, Erdelyi (1985) claims that memory for an arousing event can increase with time, especially given repeated testing (see also Butter 1970 and Kleinsmith and Kaplan 1963). Scrivner and Safer (1985) demonstrated hypermnesia for adult subjects who viewed a film of a burglary and violent shootings. It is possible that repeated testing of this sort serves as a form of rehearsal. Bohannon (1988) suggests that either emotion or rehearsal can maintain vivid memories over relatively short delays, but that both are needed to maintain vivid memories over long delays. Given that many factors, such as delay and rehearsal opportunity, vary across studies, inconsistent results are not surprising.

However, even if a consistent picture emerged from these studies, their findings may not generalize to memory for events that are not only stressful but that involve one's own body, such as when a person is badly hurt or becomes the victim of a criminal act. Although in many of these studies, the stressor (e.g., white noise) occurs concurrently with the to-be-remembered item (e.g., slides of faces), there is no causal link between the stressor and the to-be-remembered item, and the to-be-remembered item is itself neutral. Studies in which violent films or slides of disfigured faces are used as stimuli partially avoid this problem (e.g., Christianson and Nilsson 1984); however, the stimuli lack personal significance, subjects are not active participants in the events, and the events do not violate subjects' bodies. Numerous recent studies demonstrate that self-relevant information is retained with particular accuracy by both adults and children (e.g., Keenan and Baillet 1980; Pullyblank, Bisanz, Scott, and Champion 1985; Rogers, Kuiper, and Kirker 1977). Other studies indicate that participation in an event enhances memory (e.g., Paris and Lindauer 1976) and resistance to suggestion (Goodman et al., in press).

An important question that remains relatively unexplored concerns developmental differences in memory for stressful events. Unfortunately, there has been little in the way of theory concerning possible developmental differences in memory for stressful events to guide research (but see Case, Hayward, Lewis, and Hurst 1988; Fischer, Shaver, and Carnochan 1988). Most research concerning the effects of stress on children's memory consists of clinical reports (e.g., Pynoos and Eth 1984; Terr 1981, 1983, 1988). The absence of detailed objective records of the stressful events has made it difficult for clinical researchers to study memory with precision. Ethical constraints obviously preclude exposing children to traumatic events in the laboratory so that an objective record can be obtained and memory tested. Nevertheless, certain naturally stressful events occur in most children's lives, including events for which complete objective records can be obtained.

THE PRESENT STUDIES

The studies reported here constitute the first scientific research on children's memory for stressful events for which objective records are available. The stressful events were medical procedures, specifically venipuncture (blood drawing) and inoculations. Because these events occurred in medical settings, it was possible to obtain videotaped records of them. These medical procedures, particularly inoculations, were useful from a research standpoint for several reasons. First, because inoculations are required for school attendance, a sizable number of normal, healthy children could be solicited. Venipuncture seems to occur less often for healthy children but frequently enough to permit study. Second, inoculations and venipuncture are known to be stressful for many children and highly stressful for some. Children associate syringes with their least favorite part of visiting the doctor (Steward and Steward 1981). Third, the stress these procedures induce revolves around children's fears for personal safety. The events are therefore personally significant. At least to some degree, the fear induced by medical procedures may be similar to that experienced by victims of crime. Fourth, because children naturally vary in how much stress they experience from inoculations and venipuncture, it is possible to investigate the effect of different levels of stress on memory. Finally, these medical procedures are frequently experienced by children from 3 to 7 years of age, permitting us to examine age differences in memory. This age range was appropriate because children 7 years of age and younger are more emotional in response to medical procedures than are older children (Melamud 1976).

Several memory tests were included. Specific and misleading questions assessed memory for details about the person who administered the medical procedure, the room where it was given, and the actions involved. These questions were also categorized as pertaining to either central or peripheral information. This categorization permitted us to test Easterbrook's proposal that under arousing conditions peripheral information is not remembered as well as central information. Furthermore, a subset of the questions were of special interest in relation to child abuse cases. In addition to the specific and misleading questions, a face recognition test was also constructed to test age differences in children's ability to identify the "culprit" who gave the shots or drew the children's blood.

In Studies 1 and 3, children's memory for venipuncture or inoculations, respectively, was compared with children's memory for a less stressful event. In Study 2, we took advantage of natural variations in the stress children experienced and also studied the effects of short delays. In Study 4, we extended the delay interval to 1 year.[1]

Several predictions were made. First, it was predicted that age differences occur in children's memory for the events. Although it is possible that stressful events are retained with particular accuracy, it seemed unlikely that developmental differences would be eliminated, especially when memory for details of the experience was examined. Second, it was predicted that high levels of stress heighten rather than diminish memory. This prediction was based on the likelihood that stressful events have high personal significance to children and that, in general, it is adaptive to remember such events so that they can be avoided in the future. Previous experiments were unlikely to involve as high levels of stress as a subset of our children experienced, were unlikely to involve stress based on concern for personal safety, and thus may not have tapped memory for highly stressful, personally significant events. Finally, it was predicted that, despite the event's personal significance, memory for the event decreases over time (Christianson 1989; Harsch and Neisser 1989).

STUDY 1

In the first study, we examined children's memory for venipuncture. Children's memory for this event was compared to that of a group of control children who came to the same medical clinic but who experienced a less stressful event: having a design transferred to their arm.

Method

Subjects. Eighteen children participated, half in the experimental group and half in the control group. The children ranged in age from 3 years 2 months to 7 years 8 months (experimental group, $M = 4$ years 11 months, range = 3 years 2 months to 7 years 8 months; and control group, $M = 5$ years 0 months, range = 3 years 8 months to 7 years 3 months). Within each group, six of the children were boys, three were girls. Experimental group children were solicited from those who came to the Ambulatory Clinic at Children's Hospital for blood tests. Most parents who were approached and whose child qualified for the study (i.e., the child was not known to be ill at the time) agreed to participate. Control children were solicited from subject files maintained by the Department of Psychology. The children were mostly from middle-class socioeconomic backgrounds.

Children were screened to ensure that they did not have any currently known illnesses. Children in the experimental group were scheduled for blood tests for reasons such as candidacy for growth hormone treatment (i.e., they were short but not ill) or exposure to but no symptoms of hepatitis. Although it was possible that health status differences existed between the groups, children in the experimental group did not at the time of testing evidence symptoms of illnesses, had not been diagnosed for an illness, and, as demonstrated later, did not differ from children in the control group in memory ability on an independent memory test (i.e., digit span).

Three of the experimental children had been to the clinic once before. For two of these children the visit had occurred over 1 year earlier. For the other child, the visit occurred 5 to 6 months earlier. None of the control children had been to the clinic previously.

Children in the experimental and control groups were matched in terms of age (within 6 months), sex, race (all but one pair were Anglos), delay, laboratory technician seen (with two exceptions), and time in the room (within 60 s). One exception was caused by the laboratory assistant's unavailability when a control child arrived at the clinic. The second exception occurred because we intentionally balanced the mismatch in another pair.

Materials. The digit-span test, taken from the McCarthy (1972) scales, consisted of forward and backward series.

The questionnaire consisted of 24 questions that fell, eight each, into three categories: person questions, which concerned the technician's physical appearance; room questions (the content of the technicians' room was standardized across children); and action questions (the technicians' actions were highly scripted and similar across technicians). Six of the eight questions in each category were specific (i.e., not misleading). Two of the questions in each category were misleading (e.g., "What time did the clock on the wall say it was?" when in fact there was no clock on the wall). An approximately equal number of questions required a yes compared to a no response, and several questions required a more specific answer (see Appendix A).

Each question was categorized as to whether it tapped information that was central or peripheral to the episode. Six independent adult raters viewed videotapes of Session 1 and then rated each question's centrality on a scale from 1 (*very central*) to 4 (*very peripheral*). Questions that obtained an average rating of 2.5 or less were designated as central, and questions with an average rating above 2.5 were designated as peripheral. Questions concerning actions tended to be judged as central whereas questions concerning the room tended to be judged as peripheral. Questions concerning the person fell more evenly into the two categories.

For the face recognition test, three line-ups were constructed, one for each laboratory technician. Each line-up contained a color photograph of the technician along with five other women whose basic description matched the technician's. To ensure that the line-ups were unbiased, each was individually shown to 30 4- to 6-year-olds from local preschools. The children were asked to point to the person they thought was a nurse (for half of the children) or worked in a hospital (for the other half). We did not say *laboratory technician* because most children do not know that term.

The children's selections were analyzed using chi-square tests. The distribution of scores did not differ from chance for any of the line-ups, χ (5, $N = 30$) ≤ 8.88. For the one line-up in which the chi-square approached significance, the photograph most frequently chosen was not of the technician.

Procedure. In session 1 for the experimental group, children's parents were approached in the clinic waiting room. The study was described as involving children's reactions to medical procedures. After parental consent was obtained, the parent was asked to rate the child's current (prevenipuncture) stress on a 6-point scale, with 1 indicating *extremely happy* or *relaxed* and 6 indicating *extremely frightened* or *upset*.

The child and parent were then escorted to the venipuncture room, where the events were recorded by a concealed camera. The laboratory technician engaged the child and parent in conversation and then tightened a rubber tourniquet around the child's arm. The child was restrained if necessary, the needle inserted, and the child's blood drawn. At times, multiple needle insertions were required and multiple blood containers filled. The child was typically seated on a parent's lap.

The parent and child then returned to the waiting room. The parent was again asked to rate the child's level of stress using the same scale as before, but this time the rating reflected the child's feelings during venipuncture. Arrangements were made for the parent and child to come to the University for an interview concerning children's reactions to medical procedures.

In session 1 the procedure for the control children was identical to that described earlier, including being carried out at the same clinic, except that, instead of venipuncture, the technician gently rubbed an attractive design (e.g., a picture of flowers) onto the child's arm. Children were assured that they would not receive an inoculation or venipuncture, and syringes were out of view. Another exception was that parents of control children knew before coming to the clinic that two sessions would be required. However, the nature of the second session was described in the same ambiguous way for both sets of parents. Thus, neither group knew of the memory test until the start of session 2.

For session 2, the parent and child came to the University 3 to 4 days after session 1 ($M = 3.16$ days for both groups). At that time it was explained to the parent that the study concerned children's memory. The child was first given the digit-span test, and then asked to recall everything possible about his or her last visit to the doctor's office. The interviewer pointed to the child's arm and said, "Did someone do something to you here? Please tell me everything you can about that visit." Next the specific and misleading questions were asked, followed by the face recognition test. For the latter test, the child was asked if she or he saw the woman who administered the blood test and if so to point to her picture. The photographs were presented simultaneously, in random order across children. Children were given a small prize for participating. The entire session was videotaped.

Experimental and control group children were tested during an overlapping time period.

Results

Unless stated otherwise, all dependent measures were analyzed in a series of one-way analyses of variance, with group as a blocked variable, block defined as a pair of matched subjects. For the memory measures, analyses of variance were conducted including and excluding the three children who had been to the clinic before and their matched controls. The findings did not differ. The analyses reported include all of the children.

Exposure time. The difference in exposure time for the two groups was nonsignificant: experimental group, $M = 4$ min, 7 s, and control group, $M = 3$ min, 55 s.

Digit-span score. The digit-span test provided an independent assessment to ensure that the two groups did not differ in basic memory abilities. There was no significant difference in digit-span scores across the two groups: experimental, $M = 7.57$, and control, $M = 7.71$ (McCarthy scoring for forward and backward series totaled).[2]

Stress ratings. One rater scored the children's stress level during the medical procedure using the same 6-point scale as used by the parents. The correlation between the rater's scores and the parents' scores was

.68, $p < .001$, indicating adequate reliability. Parents' pre-venipuncture and venipuncture ratings were also significantly related, $r = .54$, $p < .05$.

The rater's judgments indicated that the experimental group, $M = 4.01$, experienced greater stress during the procedure than the control group, $M = 2.67$, $F(1, 8) = 17.61$, $p < .01$. Parents' ratings also indicated that the experimental group, $M = 3.67$, was more stressed than the control group, $M = 2.89$, during the procedure, although the difference fell short of statistical significance, $F(1, 8) = 2.02$. Stress was not reliable associated with age when the rater's judgments were considered, $r = -0.31$, or when the parents' judgments were considered (pre-venipuncture, $r = -.20$, and during venipuncture, $r = -.26$).

Free recall. Recall protocols were scored by two independent raters for correct and incorrect units of information. For example, if a child said, "She poked a needle in my leg," that child would receive three correct points (one for indicating the needle, one for indicating that the child was poked, and one for indicating the correct sex of the nurse) and one incorrect point for indicating that the needle had gone into his or her leg. The information scored had to be verifiable from the videotape of session 1 or from the clinic's layout. Proportion of agreement was .94.

The mean number of correct units of information recalled by the children did not differ significantly: experimental group, $M = 4.33$, and control group, $M = 3.89$, $F(1, 8) = 0.06$. Little incorrect information was recalled and these errors were evenly divided among the groups, both $Ms = 0.33$. The children's errors tended to be intrusions from other parts of the doctor's visit or of other recently experienced doctor visits (as verified by parents).

Specific questions. For each child, the proportion of specific questions answered correctly was entered into a 2(Group) × 3(Type of Information: person, room, action) analysis of variance, with both factors varying within subjects. The main effect of group was not significant, $F(1, 8) = 0.55$; experimental, $M = 0.71$, and control, $M = 0.67$. A significant main effect of type of information, $F(2, 16) = 10.77$, $p < .001$, reflected the trend for questions about actions, $M = 0.87$, to be answered with greater accuracy than questions about the person, $M = 0.55$, $F(1, 16) = 11.38$, $p < .001$, or the room, $M = 0.66$, $F(1, 16) = 4.90$, $p < .05$ (planned comparisons). Accuracy in answering the latter two types of questions did not reliably differ. There were no other significant effects.

In legal circles, many of our specific questions would be considered leading and thus relevant to the issue of children's suggestibility. Because both correct and "don't know" responses would indicate resistance to suggestion, an analysis identical to that described above was conducted in which both correct and don't know responses were combined. Again, the only significant finding was a main effect of type of information, $F(2, 16) = 3.66$, $p < .05$, with questions about actions, $M = 0.87$, answered with greater accuracy than questions about the person, $M = 0.69$, or the room, $M = 0.67$. Don't know responses mainly occurred in response to person questions.

Next, analyses of variance were conducted on answers to specific questions to determine if children in the experimental group were more likely to retain central information at the expense of peripheral information, as might be predicted by Easterbrook (1959). Proportion correct scores for each child were entered into a 2(Group) × 2(Centrality) analysis of variance with both factors varying within subjects. Both groups answered questions about central information better than peripheral information, $F(1, 8) = 18.67$, $p < .01$. Although the means were in the predicted direction, the Group × Centrality interaction was not significant, $F(1, 8) = 1.09$: experimental-central, $M = 0.81$; experimental-peripheral, $M = 0.49$; control-central, $M = 0.76$; and control-peripheral, $M = 0.56$. The interaction was also nonsignificant when correct plus don't know responses were considered.

Three of the specific questions were of special concern in relation to child abuse investigations. These questions were: "Did she touch you anywhere else?" "Did she put anything in your mouth?" and "Did she hit you?" All of the children answered these questions by saying no, except for one child who said "probably, maybe" in response to the question about being touched somewhere other than the arm.

Misleading questions. Answers to misleading questions were scored as correct if the child actively resisted the suggestion or said "I don't know." Each child's proportion of correct answers to the misleading questions was entered into a 2(Group) × 3(Type of Question) analysis of variance. The main effect of group was not significant, $F(1, 8) = 1.23$ (experimental group, $M = 0.60$, and control group, $M = 0.71$), and there were no other significant main effects or interactions.

It was also of interest to determine if the children in the two groups were more or less suggestible as a function of the centrality of the information. Proportion correct scores were entered into a 2(Group) × 2(Centrality) analysis of variance. Again, there were no significant main effects, and the Group × Centrality interaction was nonsignificant, $F(1, 8) = 2.66$: experimental-central, $M = 0.56$; experimental-peripheral, $M = 0.63$; control-central, $M = 0.78$; and control-peripheral, $M = 0.63$.

One of the misleading questions was of special relevance to child abuse cases. It was, "The nurse didn't touch you, did she?" Even though all of the children were touched on the arm, 11 children (61%) indicated they had not been touched. Thus, the children underreported rather than over-reported the touching that had occurred. Interestingly, a somewhat greater number of omission errors in response to this misleading question was made by the experimental children and largely accounted for the (nonsignificant) difference in the two groups' performance as reported above.

Face recognition. The control group, $M = 0.77$, was somewhat more likely than the experimental group to recognize the technician, $M = 0.55$, although the difference in these proportion-correct scores was not statistically significant. Only one child, a member of the control group, made a false identification. All of the other errors were omissions (i.e., saying the technician was not pictured in the display).

Age. Because relatively few children were tested, age effects were investigated through correlational analyses. Age was not significantly associated with the amount of correct or incorrect information recalled, answers to specific or misleading questions about the actions, answers to misleading questions about the room, or correct face recognition. In contrast, age was reliably associated with a number of other memory measures, with older children evidencing better performance: specific questions about the person, $r = .63$, room, $r = .57$, and central information $r = .53$; and misleading questions about the person, $r = .64$, and about central, $r = .62$, and peripheral, $r = .67$, information (all $ps < .05$, two tailed). The findings were the same when stress ratings were partialed out, except that age and correct answers to specific questions about peripheral information were now significantly related as well, $r = .49$, $p < .05$. Thus, with some important exceptions (e.g., correct and incorrect free recall and answering specific and misleading questions about the actions), older as compared to younger children were generally more accurate and less suggestible.

Discussion

Stress did not enhance or detract from the children's memory. However, the absence of statistical differences between the groups may be due in part to the relatively small number of children tested and the resulting lack of statistical power of our analyses.

Nevertheless, age differences emerged in the children's ability to answer questions about their experiences. These findings are generally consistent with the literature on children's memory for less stressful events. One exception concerned the lack of age differences in free recall. Age differences in free recall typically emerge across the 3- to 7-year age range (e.g., Goodman and Reed 1986; Nelson 1986). It was thus surprising they were not found here.

The children's memory for actions did not vary with age. Actions tend to be remembered relatively well by children (e.g., Davies, Tarrant, and Flin 1989; Fivush, Gray, and Fromhoff 1987; Jones, Swift, and Johnson 1988; Pear and Wyatt 1914), so the absence of an age difference was less surprising than it was for free recall. Although one might not expect children (or adults, for that matter) to remember much about the room, one might have expected better memory for the person than was evidenced by the children. However, part of the children's difficulty in answering the person questions might have resulted from a lack of conceptual understanding of standard units of measurement (e.g., years) rather than memory per se.

Age differences in face recognition are elusive (e.g., Flin 1980; Marin, Holmes, Guth, and Kovac 1979; see Chance and Goldstein 1984 for a review). The children's performance on the face recognition task as well as on the other memory measures will be discussed in greater detail once the findings of our other studies are presented.

In summary, although experimental-group children appeared nervous about the medical procedure, their distress did not reliably diminish their memory relative to a less stressed control group.

STUDY 2

Because we restricted our studies to healthy 3- to 7-year-olds with few previous visits to the clinic, a relatively small number of children qualified for Study 1. Moreover, the laboratory technicians were so proficient at calming children that extreme levels of stress were not reached. None of the experimental children, for example, received stress ratings of 6 by the research assistants and only one child received a stress rating of 6 by a parent. We therefore sought a different medical procedure, one that would permit us to test a larger number of children and one that was associated with greater stress. Based on doctors' advice, we chose inoculations.

By State law, children must be inoculated against diseases such as diphtheria, tetanus, and pertussis, as well as measles, mumps, and rubella, in order to enroll in school. Thus, during the late summer and early fall, many normal, healthy children receive inoculations.

In Study 1, the children's stress was varied by virtue of experiencing two different events. This approach is beneficial in assuring that a less stressed group of children is tested. The disadvantage of this approach is that different stimuli are necessarily involved (e.g., needles versus designs). Another tack is to examine memory for a stressful event only and then to take advantage of natural variation in the stress experienced. This was the approach taken in Study 2.

Because of our interest in children's testimony, we included in Study 2 several "competence" questions similar to those that might be asked in a court of law. One legal purpose of competence questions is to determine the child's understanding of the obligation to speak truthfully. Questions concerning truthfulness were included in the present study to investigate whether performance on such questions predicts children's eyewitness performance. Although competence examinations have been used for hundreds of years (*Rex* v. *Braddon and Speke*, 1684), in no studies to date have researchers investigated whether such examinations actually predict a child's testimonial capabilities.

Method

Subjects. Children were solicited from those who came to the Immunization Clinic of the State Department of Health and Hospitals to receive inoculations. A total of 48 children participated. The children were divided into two age groups: (a) 3- to 4-year-olds (*M* = 4 years, 1 month; range = 3 years, 0 months to 4 years, 9 months: *n* = 20, with 7 girls and 13 boys) and (b) 5- to 6-year-olds (*M* = 5 years, 7 months; range = 5 years, 0 months to 6 years, 9 months: *n* = 28, with 13 girls and 15 boys). Eleven children had been to the clinic before, but it had been more than a year since their previous visit. The ethnic and racial composition of the sample was quite diverse: 17 Hispanic, 20 Anglo, 7 Black, and 4 of other origins. Most of the children were from low-income families. To qualify for the study, children had to be healthy and fluent in the English language.

Most of the parents approached agreed to participate. However, of 69 families who agreed, seven families did not return for the second session, and two young children who did return refused to speak. In addition, 12 families either lacked transportation to return for the second session and/or a telephone number needed to arrange scheduling for a second session.

Materials. The digit-span test employed was the same as used in Study 1.

The questionnaires used consisted of 27 questions: 9 about the nurse who gave the children the inoculations, 9 about the room where the children received the inoculation, and 9 about the actions involved in giving the inoculation. One of the misleading questions about the actions was ambiguous and was eliminated from the analyses, leaving eight action questions. Eighteen of the questions were specific, and nine were misleading (see Appendix B).

In addition, each question was categorized as tapping central or peripheral information, which was determined by using the same proce-

Table 1. Mean Number of Correct and Incorrect Units of Information Recalled as a Function of Age and Delay: Study 2

	Time			
	Short Delay		*Long Delay*	
	Ages			
	3–4	5–6	3–4	5–6
	(8)	(12)	(13)	(15)
Correct	3.13	3.38	3.75	3.60
Incorrect	0.00	0.00	0.08	0.13

Note: The number of children in each Age × Delay group appears in parentheses.

dure as in Study 1 but based on ratings by five adults. Fifteen questions that received a mean rating of 1 to 2.50 were considered central; 11 questions that received a mean rating of 2.51 to 4 were considered peripheral. Some of the same questions were categorized differently in Studies 1 and 2; in some cases, this resulted from differences between the clinics. For example, the examination table in the venipuncture clinic was less centrally located than the one in the inoculation clinic. In other cases, the mean ratings of the questions fell on the boundaries of the categories. Because the site, people, and activities changed across the two studies, we felt it was necessary to base the categorizations on raters' judgments despite some inconsistencies.

For each of the six participating female nurses, a six-person photo line-up was constructed, consisting of color photographs of five women who matched the target nurse's general appearance, along with a color photograph of the target nurse herself. To ensure that the line-ups were not biased in favor of the nurses, each line-up was shown to 29 4- to 7-year-olds at a local preschool. On an individual basis, each child was presented with each of the six line-ups in random order and asked to point to the person in each line-up who looked most like a nurse. Chi-square values for the six line-ups ranged from 1.83 to 13.42 with 5 degrees of freedom and Ns of 29. Only one value reached statistical significance. However, it indicated that one of the alternative photos was selected significantly more often than the target nurse.

The competence questions concerned the child's ability to distinguish between the truth and a lie and the child's understanding of the ramifications of lying (see Appendix B). The questions were based on examples provided in legal texts (e.g., *American Jurisprudence* 1960).

Procedure. The session 1 procedure was identical to that of Study 1

Table 2. Mean Proportion of Correct Answers to Specific and Misleading Questions as a Function of Age Group, Delay, and Type of Question: Study 2

	Time				
	Short Delay		Long Delay		
	Years				
Question	3–4	5–6	3–4	5–6	Overall Mean
Specific					
Person	0.47	0.65	0.48	0.64	0.57
Room	0.69	0.78	0.67	0.77	0.73
Actions	0.85	0.79	0.68	0.79	0.77
Central	0.77	0.84	0.66	0.82	0.78
Peripheral	0.56	0.57	0.48	0.53	0.53
Misleading					
Person	0.42	0.90	0.50	0.62	0.61
Room	0.50	0.54	0.47	0.60	0.53
Actions	0.56	0.69	0.54	0.80	0.66
Central	0.46	0.76	0.47	0.67	0.60
Peripheral	0.48	0.67	0.50	0.65	0.59

Table 3. Children's Responses to the Abuse Questions Initially and After a One-Year Delay: Study 2 and Study 4

| | Time of Test | | | | | |
| | Time 1 (3 to 9 Days) | | | Time 2 (1 Year) | | |
Question	Percentage Correct	Percentage Omission	Percentage Commission	Percentage Correct	Percentage Omission	Percentage Commission
Did she hit you?	100	0	0	100	0	0
Did she kiss you?	96	0	4	95	0	0
Did she put anything in your mouth?	81	19	0	68	22	0
Did she touch you any place other than your arm/thigh?	50	50	0	50	22	14

Note: For each question at each time of test, all percentages add to 100% when don't know responses are included. *ns* Time 1 = 48, Time 2 = 22.

with the following exceptions. When the nurse was ready, she called the child and parent into the inoculation room. Although the child was almost always seated on a parent's lap, occasionally the child sat alone or reclined on an examination table with the parent standing alongside. The nurse proceeded to give the child an oral dose of polio vaccine (if needed), draw medicine into a syringe, and give the child one or two inoculations, usually on one or both arms but at times on the thigh.

While getting their shots, some of the children looked relatively relaxed and spontaneously said, "It didn't hurt." Others became nearly hysterical with fear. These children screamed and cried and had to be held down by as many as three adults. It was, of course, these latter children who received the highest stress ratings by the parents and research assistants. None of the children in Study 1 reacted with such extreme terror.

As in Study 1, we did not interfere with the nurses' usual practices, which were quite standardized across nurses. The contents of the room were also standardized. On average, the entire event lasted 3.5 min.

Occasionally, children saw the nurse before or after entering the inoculation room. For example, the nurse might walk by the child on the way to the front desk to get a form. Such exposure to the nurse was measured with a stop watch.

After the parent completed the inoculation stress rating, an appointment was made for the parent to bring the child to the University either 3 to 4 days (short delay) or 7 to 9 days (long delay) later for session 2. In a few cases, the second session took place in the children's homes. Children were assigned to delay conditions on a random basis, with the qualification that the session conform to the parents' schedules.

In session 2 the procedure was analogous to that described for Study 1, with the exceptions that, after the memory tests, the children were asked the competence questions and then parents (blind to their children's choices) were asked to identify the nurse. The second session lasted about 30 minutes. Parents were paid for their children's participation.

Results

Preliminary analyses indicated no significant effects associated with the children's race or sex. Therefore, the data were collapsed across these factors, except where indicated later. All analyses were conducted both excluding the 11 children who had been to the clinic before, and including them. The findings remained unchanged. Therefore, the analyses to be presented include all of the children. Finally, because preliminary analyses indicated that the children's memory did not differ as a function of the nurse seen, the data were collapsed across nurses.

Exposure time. It was important to determine whether differences occurred in children's exposure time to the nurse, because such differences could affect the results. For the four Age × Delay groups, the means for the exposure time in the inoculation room and exposure time outside of the inoculation room, respectively, were: 3- and 4-year-olds, short delay, *M*s = 3 min 34 s, and 28 s; 3- and 4-year-olds, long delay, *M*s = 4 min 3 s, and 2 min 17 s; 5- and 6-year-olds, short delay, *M*s = 3 min 1 s, and 75 s; 5- and 6-year-olds, long delay, *M*s = 2 min 54 s, and 1 min 55 s. The amount of time each child was exposed to the nurse in the inoculation room and outside of the inoculation room was entered into separate 2(Age) × 2(Delay) analyses of variance. There were no significant main effects or interactions.

Digit-span scores. Data from 45 children who completed the digit-span task were analyzed. As expected, the younger children's digit-span scores, *M* = 2.3, were lower than those of the older children, *M* = 6.7.[3]

Each child's digit-span score was entered into a 2(Age) × 2(Delay) analysis of variance with both factors varying between subjects. The only significant finding was a main effect of age, $F(1, 41) = 28.76$, $p < .001$.

Free recall. Two independent raters scored each child's free-recall protocol in terms of correct and incorrect units of information according the same system described for Study 1. Raters were highly reliable as determined by proportion of agreement scores (.87).

In Table 1, the mean numbers of correct and incorrect units of information recalled as a function of age and delay are presented. The two age groups performed equivalently and, although generally not providing detailed accounts of what happened, made very few false statements. The number of correct and incorrect statements made by each child was entered into separate 2(Age) × 2(Delay) analyses of variance. The main effects of age and delay were not significant in either analysis. There were no significant interactions.

Specific questions. Mean proportion of correct answers to the specific questions as a function of age, delay, and type of question are presented in Table 2. The proportion of correct answers provided by each child was entered into a 2(Age) × 2(Delay) × 3(Type of Information person, room, action) analysis of variance with type of information as the only within-subject factor. A main effect of age, $F(1, 44) = 6.56$, $p < .05$ and a main effect of type of information, $F(2, 88) = 20.33$, $p < .001$, were the only significant effects. Older children, *M* = 0.74, answered more specific questions correctly than younger children, *M* = 0.64. Regardless of age, questions about the person were answered more poorly than questions about the room, $F(1, 88) = 8.10$, $p < .001$, or about the actions, $F(1, 88)\ 16.90$, $p < .001$. The latter two means did not reliably differ, $F(1, 88) = 3.2$ (planned comparison). When correct plus don't know responses were considered, however, only a main effect of age emerged, $F(1, 44) = 5.43$, $p < .05$; older children, $M = 0.81$, and younger children, $M = 0.71$. As in Study 1, don't know responses mainly occurred for the person questions, raising that overall mean to 0.73.

For each child, proportion-correct scores were also entered into a 2(Age) × 2(Delay) × 2(Centrality: Central vs. Peripheral) analysis of variance with centrality as the only within-subject factor. A main effect on centrality emerged, $F(1, 44) = 60.55$, $p < .001$. Questions about central information were answered with greater accuracy than questions about peripheral information. The main effect of centrality was maintained when don't know responses were included, $F(1, 44) = 32.22$, $p < .001$; central, $M = 0.83$, and peripheral, $M = 0.67$.

As in Study 1, a subset of the questions was particularly relevant to children's testimony in child abuse cases. These questions were: "Did she hit you?" "Did she kiss you?" "Did she touch you anywhere other than your arm?" and "Did she put anything in your mouth?" If the children were to answer these questions with false affirmations, suspicion of abuse might arise. In general, the children provided very few false answers (Table 3). Specifically, the only commission errors were produced by small number of 3- to 4-year-olds who falsely agreed that they had been kissed.

Misleading questions. Children were judged to have resisted suggestion if they answered in opposition to the suggestion or said "I don't know." In Table 2, the mean number of correct answers to the misleading questions are presented as a function of age and type of question. Each child's proportion-correct score was entered into a 2(Age) × 2(Delay) × 3(Type of Information) analysis of variance with type of information as the only within-subject factor. There was a significant age effect, $F(1, 44) = 8.22$, $p < .01$, indicating that older children, $M = 0.69$, were less suggestible than younger children, $M = 0.51$. There was also a significant main effect of type of information, $F(2, 88) = 3.02$, $p < .05$. Planned comparisons revealed that the children were less able to resist suggestion about the room than about the actions, $F(1, 44) = 6.53$, $p < .05$, and the person, $F(1, 44) = 4.80$, $p < .05$, respectively. Children's ability to resist suggestion did not differ for the actions and the person, $F(1, 44) = 0.13$. The effect of delay was not significant, $F(1, 44) = 0.17$, and there were no significant interactions.

Each child's proportion correct score in response to the misleading questions was also entered into a 2(Age) × 2(Centrality) analysis of variance, with centrality as the only factor to vary within subjects. The main effect of age was again significant, $F(1, 44) = 12.25$, $p < .01$. The main effect of centrality was not significant, $F(1, 44) = 0.10$.

Table 4. Mean Accuracy on the Memory Measures as a Function of Stress Level: Study 2

| | Stress Level | | | |
Measure	3 (13)	4 (21)	5 (8)	6 (5)
Number correct recall	3.46	3.24	3.25	5.20
Number incorrect recall	0.00	0.09	0.13	0.00
Proportion correct to specific questions	0.70	0.69	0.66	0.70
Proportion correct to misleading questions	0.56	0.63	0.44	0.82
Proportion correct identification	0.62	0.33	0.25	0.40
Digit-span score	4.25	5.80	3.57	5.40
	(12)	(20)	(7)	(5)

Note: For all of the memory measures except digit span, the number of children at each stress level appears in parentheses directly below the stress level. There was missing data for one child. For the digit-span measure, the number of children at each stress level appears in parentheses under the children's scores at the bottom of the table.

Face recognition. Dichotomous scores reflecting the children's accuracy in identifying the nurse were entered into a 2(Age) × 2(Delay) analysis of variance with both factors varying between subjects. There were no significant main effects or interactions. However, the 3- and 4-year-olds' performance after the longer delay did not differ from chance, $M = 0.17$ $t(11) = 0.25$, whereas the older groups' performance did: 3- and 4-year-olds, short delay, $M = 0.50$, $t(7) = 2.00$, $p < .05$; 5- and 6-year-olds, short delay, M 0.54, $t(12) = 2.70$, $p < .01$; and 5- and 6-year-olds, long delay, M 0.53, $t(14) = 3.00$, $p < .01$.

Two types of errors were possible. The children could make an omission error, claiming the nurse was not among the alternatives or, worse from a legal perspective, a false identification. Dichotomous scores reflecting whether or not each child made a false identification were entered into a 2(Age) × 2(Delay) analysis of variance. The main effect of age approached significance, $F(1, 44) = 3.21$, $p < .10$. There were no significant effects. When the data were analyzed in a 2(Age) × 2(Sex) analysis of variance, the main effect of age was significant, $F(1, 44) = 4.21$, $p < .05$. Younger children, $M = 0.62$, made more false identifications than older children, $M = 0.31$. There were no other significant effects.

Although it is clear that the parents and children did not experience the same event (e.g., one was a witness, the other a "victim"), it was also of interest to compare the parents' and children's accuracy on the face recognition. A 2(Child's Age) × 2(Delay) × 2(Parent or Child) analysis of variance was performed on dichotomous (correct/incorrect) scores. Because two parents who had accompanied their children to the clinic were unavailable, the following analyses were based on 46 scores. The only significant effect to emerge was delay, $F(1, 42) = 5.63$, $p < 05$: short delay, $M = 0.80$, and long delay, $M = 0.37$. There were no other significant main effects or interactions. The mean proportion correct identifications for parents and children, as a function of the children's ages were: 3- and 4-year-olds, children, $M = 0.35$; 3- and 4-year-olds, parents, $M = 0.53$; 5- and 6-year-olds, children, $M = 0.51$; 5- and 6-year-olds, parents, $M = 0.47$. The overall means were: children, $M = 0.43$; parents, $M = 0.48$.

The same analysis was performed on the proportion of false identifications made by the parents and the children. This analysis revealed no significant main effects or interactions. The mean proportions of false identifications were: 3- and 4-year-olds, children, $M = 0.55$; 3- and 4-year-olds, parents, $M = 0.28$; 5- and 6-year-olds, children, $M = 0.51$; 5- and 6-year-olds, parents, $M = 0.36$. The overall means were: children, M = 0.43; parents, M = 0.33. Thus, although parents made somewhat fewer false identifications, they did not do so significantly less often. Overall, the parents' identification performance was comparable to that the 5- to 6-year-olds.

Because our subject sample as well as our group of volunteer nurses represented a variety of ethnic/racial groups, it was possible to determine if cross-racial identifications were inferior to same-race identifications as has been repeatedly reported in the adult face recognition literature (e.g., Brigham and Barkowitz 1978; Malpass and Kravitz 1969). The composition of the nursing staff included: three Anglos, two Blacks, and one Oriental. The children represented four ethnic/racial groups: Hispanic, Anglo, Black, and "other." Several sets of analyses were conducted in which these initial classifications were varied. One set focused on race in which Hispanic and Anglo children were combined into a single group whereas the Black and other children maintained separate classifications. Another focused on ethnicity. For this analysis, Hispanic and Anglo children treated as two separate groups as were the Black and other children. The nurses were similarly classified. Correct identifications and false identifications were analyzed separately in 2(Age) × 2(cross- vs. same-Race) analysis of variance with all factors varying between subjects. There were no significant main effects or interactions.

Stress ratings. As mentioned earlier, parents rated their children's pre-inoculation and inoculation stress. Two research assistants also rated

Table 5. Correlations Between Responses to the Legal Questions and Performance on Memory Tests for 3- and 4-Year-Olds (Not Underlined) and 5- and 6-Year-Olds (Underlined): Study 2

Questions	Correct Recall	Correct Answers to Specific Questions	Correct Answers to Misleading Questions	Photo ID Correct	False
1. Do you know the difference	−.05	.05	−.17	.08	.16
between the truth and a lie?	.21	.14	.16	.19	−.12
2. If you said the nurse					
kissed you, would that	.09	−.18	−.13	−.04	.05
be the truth or a lie?	.11	−.01	.02	.12	−.20
3. What happens if you tell	−.12	−.28	−.27	−.43	.42
a lie?	.44*	.61**	−.47*	.50**	−.53**
4a. Is everything you told me					
today the truth?	.14	−.14	−.17	−.05	.03
(scored *yes* vs. *no*)	.35	.08	−.10	−.23	.13
4b. Is everything you told					
me today the truth?					
(scored for accuracy	.19	−.17	−.31	.15	−.07
of the child's responses)	.02	.22	.25	.07	.07

*p < .05, **p < .01; two-tailed *t* tests.

the children's stress from videotapes of session 1. Based on viewing 15% of the children, the assistants obtained a .78 proportion of agreement. Each assistant then rated approximately half of the children remaining. Assistants were unaware of the experimental hypotheses. The ratings by parents and by research assistants were made using the same 6-point stress scale employed in Study 1.

Separate 2(Age) × 2(Delay) analyses of variance were conducted using first the parents' ratings of the children's stress during the inoculation and then the assistants' ratings. There were no significant main effect, or interactions. Across all of the children, the average parental inoculation stress rating was 3.81 and the average inoculation stress rating by the research assistants was 4.10.

The parents' ratings of the children's stress during the inoculation, correlated highly with the experimenters' ratings, $r = .72$, $p < .001$. Also the parents' pre-inoculation and inoculation stress ratings were significantly related, $r = .41$, $p < .01$. Experimenter ratings were employed for all analyses concerning the children's stress during the inoculations because, due to language difficulties, a few of the parents did not appear to understand the rating scale.

Separate one-way analyses of variance were conducted to determine the effects of stress on the children's performance, with stress rating, treated as an independent variable. Mean scores on the memory measures are presented in Table 4. As can be seen, children rated as the more stressed were the least suggestible and recalled the most about the event. The main effect of stress on suggestibility was significant, $F(3, 43)$ = 3.44, $p < .05$. Planned comparisons revealed that children who were rated the most stressed were less suggestible than children who received stress ratings of 3 or 5, $Fs(1, 43) \geq 14.70$, $ps < .001$. The planned comparison between children who received a rating of 6 and those who received a rating of 4 approached significance, $F(1, 43) = 3.17$, $p < .10$. The main effect of stress on correct recall was not significant in the overall analysis of variance, but was significant based on a planned comparison of the most stressed group compared with the less stressed groups, $F(1, 43) = 4.65$, $p < .05$. There were no significant effects of stress on the amount of incorrect information recalled, answers to specific questions, or photo identification.

Given that we could not randomly assign children to stress conditions, it was important to determine whether children who fell within each stress level significantly differed on an independent memory test. The digit-span test was used for this purpose. Each child's digit-span score was entered into a one-way analysis of variance with stress as the only factor. The main effect of stress was not significant.

Another possible confounding factor was the amount of time children spent in the inoculation room. Children who appeared to be the most highly stressed were in the room longer, $M = 4.32$ min, than children who were less stressed, $M = 3.13$ min. Analyses of covariance with time in the room entered as the covariate were performed. Children who obtained the highest stress level were still less suggestible than the less stressed children, $F(3, 42)$ 3.48, $p < .05$, and they recalled more correct information, $F(1, 42)$ 4.17, $p < .05$.

It also was possible that children who exhibited the greatest stress were disproportionally from the 5- to 6-year-old age group or from the 3-to 4-day delay group, either of which might have raised their average scores. This was not the case, however. The children whose stress level was rated 6 were, for example, no more likely to be older or tested sooner than were the children who received a stress rating of 5.

Finally, we explored whether children who were the most stressed during the inoculation evidenced more distress during a relatively neutral part of the interview. If so, one might suspect that dispositional factors contributed to the children's performance. Using the same 6-point scale employed for ratings of inoculation stress, two raters judged the level of stress evidenced by 20% of the children during the digit-span test. Proportion of agreement was .90, indicating high reliability. One of the raters, who was unaware of the experimental hypotheses, then completed judgments for the remaining children. When a one-way analysis of variance was conducted with inoculation stress level as the only factor, no significant differences emerged in the children's digit-span stress, $F(3, 36) = 2.18$.

The children's suggestibility as a function of stress level was also analyzed to determine if differences in suggestibility would emerge as a function of central versus peripheral information. Each child's proportion-correct score was entered into a 4(Stress) × 2(Centrality) analysis of variance, with centrality treated as a within-subject factor. A main effect of stress was the only significant finding, $F(3, 43) = 4.03$, $p < .05$. The children's answers to the specific questions were similarly analyzed. Again, stress did not differentially influence performance in relation to central or peripheral information.

In addition, children's pre-inoculation stress was also significantly related to performance, but only for identification of the nurse. Separate one-way analyses of variance were conducted on each of the main dependent measures. Because very few children received a stress rating of 5 or 6, these categories were collapsed with the next lowest category. Similarly, so few children received a rating of 1 that this category was collapsed with the next highest category. In the end, 16 children fell in the 1-to-2 stress category, 19 in the 3-stress category, and 12 in the 4-to-6 stress category. The only significant effect to emerge from this set of analyses was that children who were the most stressed before they received their shots were the most accurate in identifying the nurse, $F(2, 44) = 5.56$, $p < .01$. Planned comparisons revealed that the children who were the least stressed, $M = 0.13$, were less accurate in their identifications than were children in the higher stress groups: stress rating of 3, $M = 0.63$, and stress rating of 4 to 6, $M = 0.50$, $Fs \geq 4.67$, $ps \leq .05$. When each child's pre-inoculation stress was considered, children in each stress category did not significantly differ in digit-span scores, time in the inoculation room, exposure to the nurse outside of the inoculation room, or digit-span stress scores.

Competence questions. Answers to the competence questions were scored in terms of how the child's answer would likely be evaluated in a court of law (*American Jurisprudence* 1960; *American Law Reports* 1962). That is, if the child said that he or she did not know the difference between the truth and a lie, the response was scored as incorrect. A child who stated that he or she would get in trouble or be hit for telling a lie was scored as correct. Our interest was to determine if the competence questions would predict performance on our main memory measures (i.e., free recall, answers to specific and misleading questions, photo identification). When the children were considered as a group, there was only one significant correlation. Children who gave a legally acceptable answer to the question, "What happens if you tell a lie?" were more likely to answer the specific questions correctly, $r = .37$, $p < .05$.

As can be seen in Table 5, when the analyses were performed separately for the two age groups, there were no significant correlations for the 3- and 4-year-olds. However, for the 5- and 6-year-olds, correct answers to the question "What happens if you tell a lie?" predicted accuracy on each of the main measures.

Discussion

It was predicted that children who experienced a high degree of stress would perform better on the memory tests than children who were less stressed. On three of the tests, stress was associated with better memory. Children in the most highly stressed group were less suggestible and recalled more correct information than the less stressed children. Also, children who were more anxious before receiving their shots were more accurate in recognizing the nurse. It is likely that former studies of memory for stressful events have not involved events as stressful as the inoculations were for our most stressed children. Thus, beneficial effects of stress would have been missed, as they likely would have been here, had we combined all of the children in the inoculation group and compared them to children in a control group.

Also as predicted, older as compared to younger children were more accurate in answering specific questions and were also less suggestible. These findings are consistent with those of several researchers (e.g., Goodman and Reed 1986; King and Yuille 1987). As was true for Study 1, age differences in free recall were not found.

On the face recognition test, age differences emerged in the number of correct identifications, but only after a delay. However, recognition accuracy was relatively poor even among the children's parents. Apparently it is difficult for both children and adults to recognize people who are unfamiliar and briefly seen. Age differences were apparent in the number of false identifications made, with 5- and 6-year-olds producing fewer false identifications than 3- and 4-year-olds. This age difference could be as much a matter of willingness to guess as a matter of memory. Younger children may be more likely to point to an alternative on a photo lineup, whereas older children may more readily admit a memory lapse.

Contrary to findings with adults, there were no cross-racial effects in face recognition. In previous research on children, cross-racial effects also have not been found (Chance, Turner, and Goldstein 1982). Perhaps greater experience with the faces of the same race is needed before cross-racial effects emerge.

This was the first study in which the relationship between competence questions and accuracy on memory tasks has been investigated. Accuracy in answering only one of the competence questions predicted accuracy for the 5- and 6-year-olds, but none of the questions predicted accuracy for the 3- and 4-year-olds. Although the correlations for the older children were significant and accounted for a relatively sizable percentage of the variance (r^2 = .37 at most), reliance on these questions to screen child witnesses would result in many children being misclassified as potentially accurate or inaccurate witnesses. In fact, one of the most accurate children in our study, a 5-year-old who obtained an inoculation stress rating of 6, claimed that his nose would grow if he told a lie. He might well have failed a competence examination in a court of law despite his excellent memory.

STUDY 3

Study 3 was conducted as a partial replication of Study 1. Instead of venipuncture, inoculations constituted the stressful event. As in Study 1, a control group was included consisting of children who received a cheerful design on their arm or thigh instead of a shot.

Method

Subjects. Seventeen children (M = 5 years, 0 months; range = 3 years, 8 months to 6 years, 10 months) from Study 2 (the experimental group) and 17 children (M = 5 years, 0 months; range = 3 years, 7 months to 7 years, 0 months) solicited from local Head Start schools (the control group) participated. Head Start schools were selected for control-subject solicitation in order to include children from lower socio-economic families, comparable to many of those in our experimental group.

There were 10 males and 7 females in the experimental group and 11 males and 6 females in the control group. Overall, the subjects consisted of 29 Hispanics, 3 Anglo, and 2 Black children.

Each child in the control group was matched to a child from the the experimental group of Study 2 in terms of age, sex (with one exception), delay, exposure time, nurse seen, and race (with two exceptions in the later two cases). Analyses from Study 3 were conducted with and without these pairs of subjects and revealed no differences. Also, analyses from Study 2 indicated no significant effects of sex, race, or nurse. Therefore, these subjects were retained in the sample. The experimental children from Study 2 were chosen based on the availability of an acceptable match from the Head Start school.

Materials. The stimulus materials for Study 3 were identical to those of Study 2 except for the use of an attractive design in place of the inoculation and a "Slurpies" in place of the oral polio vaccine. Slurpies is a sweet drink that comes in a small wax tube. (The oral polo vaccine was concealed in a sweet liquid that was dripped into the child's mouth from a tube. The Slurpie was administered in the same manner.)

Procedure. The procedure in session 1 was identical to that of Study 2 with the following exceptions. Control children were scheduled to come to the Immunization Clinic individually to see the same nurse that their experimental match had seen. Children were told that they were to receive a design to be rubbed onto their arm or leg and not a shot. If the control child's match had received an oral polio vaccine, the control child was given the Slurpies drink. Then, instead of receiving an inoculation, the control children received the design. There were no syringes in view. Each control child received the same number of designs as the experimental child had inoculations, and had the design(s) placed in the same place as the inoculations(s) had been for the experimental child. In addition, the control child either sat on a parent's lap, sat alone in the chair, or received the design while on the examination table according to what the experimental child had experienced. Like experimental group families, control group families did not know of the memory test until session 2.

For session 2, the child and parent returned to the University either, 3 to 4 or 7 to 9 days later, according to the delay period the experimental child had experienced. The second session of Study 3 was identical to the second session of Study 2, with the exception that the wording of the questions was altered to coincide with the child's experience. Specifically, the word design was substituted for the word shot in all relevant questions. Although competence questions were asked in Studies 3 and 4, analyses of them are not presented here because of the relatively small number of children tested in the last two studies. Families were paid for participation. The control group was tested approximately 6 months after the experimental group.

Results

Preliminary analyses from Study 2 indicated that there were no significant effects of race, sex, nurse, or previous clinic visits, and few significant effects of delay. Therefore, these factors were collapsed across the control and experimental groups in the following analyses.

Exposure time. A one-way analysis of variance with group as a blocked variable revealed no significant differences between the mean exposure time in the room for the experimental children, M = 3 min 11 s, and the control children, M = 2 min 56 s, $F(1, 16)$ = 0.18. A one-way analysis of variance was also performed on exposure time to the nurse while in the waiting room. This also revealed no significant differences between the experimental children, M = 2 min 6 s, and the control children, M = 2 min 13 s, $F(1, 16)$ = 0.03.

Stress ratings. One of the same research assistants who scored the children's level of stress for Study 2 completed the stress ratings for Study 3, using the same 6-point scale. A one-way analysis of variance with group as a blocked variable was performed on the assistant's rating of each child's stress during the visit with the nurse. This analysis revealed a significant difference between the stress levels of experimental, M = 4.24, and control, M = 2.06, children $F(1, 16)$ = 78.23, $p < .001$. The same analysis was conducted on parents' ratings of their children's stress during the event at the clinic. A significant difference between level of stress for the control group, M = 2.00, and experimental group emerged, M = 3.75, $F(1, 16)$ = 15.04, $p < .01$. The parents' ratings of the children's inoculation stress correlated highly with the assistant's ratings of the children's stress, r = .80, $p < .001$.

Digit-span scores. A 2(Age) × 2(Group) analysis of variance was performed on the digit-span scores, with group treated as a blocked factor. The analysis revealed no significant effect of groups, and no significant interaction between age and group. A significant age effect emerged, $F(1, 30)$ = 14.35, $p < .001$; older children, M = 6.45, and younger children, M = 2.25.

Free recall. A new rater scored free-recall protocols for 25% of the experimental children from Study 2 who were not used in Study 3. Proportion of agreement scores between this rater and the two raters in Study 2 were .89 and .88, respectively. For Study 3, the new rater scored the free-recall protocols for the control children and rescored the free-recall protocols for the experimental children. A 2(Age) × 2(Group) analysis of variance was performed on the number of correct units of information recalled by each child. This analysis revealed no significant main effects of age (3- to 4-year olds, M 3.44, and 5- to 6-year-olds, M = 4.11) or group (experimental, M 3.41, and control, M = 4.18), and no significant interactions. An identical analysis of variance as that just described was performed on the mean number of incorrect units of information. There were no significant main effects of age, but there was

	Time of Test	
Measure	Time 1 (3 to 9 Days)	Time 2 (1 Year)

Table 6. Children's Performance One Year After Receiving Inoculations: Study 4

Measure	Time 1 (3 to 9 Days)	Time 2 (1 Year)
Number correct recall	3.50	2.32*
Number incorrect recall	.04	.27
Proportion specific questions		
answered correctly overall	.71	.67
Action questions	.87	.73*
Person questions	.57	.66
Room questions	.70	.61
Central questions	.82	.70*
Peripheral questions	.52	.58
Proportion misleading questions		
answered correctly overall	.64	.51*
Action questions	.75	.59*
Person questions	.62	.51
Room questions	.54	.44
Central questions	.68	.58
Peripheral questions	.57	.47
Identifications		
Correct	.50	.14**
False	.41	.32

$*p < .05. **p < .01.$

a significant main effect of group, $F(1, 15) = 6.37$, $p < .05$. Control children recalled more incorrect information, $M = 0.88$, than did experimental children, $M = 0.12$. The higher scores for the control children were due in part to a distracted 4-year-old boy who, when asked to recall the event, laughingly but insistently said that they beat up the nurse, cut her throat open, and had all gone to jail. (His mother had in fact gone to jail on a similar charge). However, even when this child's scores and those of his matched control were excluded from the analysis, the significant difference remained, $F(1, 14) = 6.17$, $p < .05$: experimental, $M = 0.13$, and control, $M = 0.63$.

Specific questions. A 2(Age) × 2(Group) × 3(Type of Information) analysis of variance was performed on each child's proportion of correct answers to the specific questions, with group as a blocked factor and type of information a within-subject factor. The main effect of group,

$F(1, 15) = 0.62$, was not significant. However, the main effect of type of information was significant, $F(2, 30) = 11.34$, $p < .001$ as was the Age × Type of Information interaction, $F(2, 30) = 3.67$, $p < .05$.

Simple effects analyses of this interaction revealed that older as compared with younger children were better able to answer specific question, about the person, $F(1, 32) = 6.47$, $p < .05$; $M = 0.66$ and $M = 0.47$ respectively. However, older children did not differ significantly from younger children on correct answers to room questions, $M = 0.72$ and $M = 0.67$, respectively, $F(1, 32) = 1.64$, or action questions, $M = 0.75$ and $M = 0.80$, respectively, $F(1, 32) = 0.97$. Simple effects analysis also revealed that older children did not differ in their ability to answer specific questions about the person, room, and actions, $F(2, 34) = 1.56$. However, younger children differed in their ability to answer the different types of questions, $F(2, 30) = 12.02$, $p < .001$. Planned comparisons indicated that younger children were more correct about the actions than about the room, $F(2, 30) = 5.0$, $p < .05$, or the person, $F(2, 30) = 24.20$, $p < .001$. Also, younger children were more correct about the room than about the person, $F(2, 30) = 7.20$, $p < .01$. However, when correct plus don't know responses were considered, only a significant effect of type of information emerged, $F(2, 30) = 3.49$, $p < .05$, again reflecting better memory for action, $M = 0.78$, than for room, $M = 0.71$, or person, $M = 0.67$, information.

A 2(Age) × 2(Group) × 2(Centrality) analysis of variance revealed that centrality of the question produced the only significant effect, $F(1, 30) = 45.79$, $p < .001$. All children answered specific questions about central information, $M = 0.75$, better than specific questions about peripheral information, $M = 0.50$, a pattern that was maintained when correct plus don't know responses were considered.

Misleading questions. Did the two groups differ in suggestibility? To answer this question, a 2(Age) × 2(Group) × 3(Type of Information) analysis of variance was performed on the proportion of correct answers provided by each child to the misleading questions, with group entered as a blocked factor and type of information as a within-subject factor. A correct response to a misleading question consisted of either a correct answer or a don't know response. The analysis revealed a significant main effect of age, $F(1, 15) = 7.44$, $p < .05$. Older children, $M = 0.61$ were less suggestible than younger children, $M = 0.46$. There was also a significant main effect of type of information, $F(2, 30) = 5.59$, $p < .01$. Planned comparisons revealed that children resisted suggestions about the actions more often than suggestions about the persons, $F(2, 30) = 4.83$, $p < .05$, or the room, $F(2, 30) = 10.87$, $p < .001$. However, there was no significant difference in their ability to resist suggestion about the person and the room, $F(2, 30) = 1.21$. The main effect of group was not significant, $F(1, 15) = 0.1\ 7$, and there were no significant interactions A 2(Age) × 2(Group) × 2(Centrality) analysis of variance was also performed on the proportion of correct responses made by each child to the misleading questions, with centrality as the only within-subject factor. A main effect of age, duplicating the one reported earlier, was the only significant effect, $F(1, 30) = 5.87$, $p < .05$.

Face recognition. A 2(Age) × 2(Group) analysis of variance was performed on the number of correct identifications. The main effect of age was significant, $F(1, 15) = 4.85$, $p < .05$; younger children, $M = 0.25$, and older children, $M = 0.56$. The main effect of group, $F(1, 15) = 0.43$ (experimental group, $M = 0.47$, and control group, $M = 0.35$) and the Age × Group interaction, $F(1, 15) = 0.33$, both failed to reach significance.

The same analysis was conducted on the number of false identifications. This analysis also failed to reveal significant main effects of age, $F(1, 15) = 2.22$: younger children, $M = 0.69$ and older children, $M = 0.45$; or group, $F(1, 15) = 0.07$, experimental group, $M = 0.53$, and control group, $M = 0.60$; or a significant Age × Group interaction, $F(1, 5) = 0.91$.

In addition, a 2(Age) × 2(Group) × 2(Parent or Child) analysis of variance was performed on the number of correct identifications made by children versus their parents. The analysis revealed no significant main effects or interactions. The means for the parents and the children, as a function of the children's age were: 3- and 4-year-olds, $M = 0.27$; 3- and 4-year-olds' parents, $M = 0.46$; 5- and 6-year-olds, $M = 0.60$; 5- and 6-year-olds' parents, $M = 0.35$. (The means for the children differ slightly from those reported earlier because two children were excluded from the analysis because their parents were unavailable to complete the task.) The overall means were: children, $M = 0.44$; parents, $M = 0.41$. The same analysis was conducted on the number of false identifications made by the children and their parents; this also failed to reveal any significant main effects or interactions. The means for the parents and the children were: 3- and 4-year-olds, $M = 0.69$; 3- and 4-year-olds' parents, $M = 0.38$; 5- and 6-year-olds, $M = 0.42$; 5- and 6-year-olds' parents, $M = 0.47$. The overall means were: children, $M = 0.55$; parents, $M = 0.42$.

Discussion

Study 3 was designed to examine further the effects of stress on children's memory by including a less stressed control group. The only difference as a function of group membership was in the amount of incorrect information recalled. That children in the control group recalled more incorrect information than children in the experimental group lends support to possible beneficial effects of stress on memory. The lack of difference between the groups' performance was much more striking than the one difference, however. These findings may seem inconsistent with those of Experiment 2 until it is realized that no children from Study 2 with a stress rating of 6 were included in Study 3. Given that it was only these children who evidenced the beneficial effects of stress on memory it is not surprising that few differences emerged.

Stress did not appear to affect differentially the memory of older and younger children, although, as in Study 2, main effects of age appeared. Five- and 6-year-olds were more accurate than 3- and 4-year-olds in answering specific and misleading questions. However, replicating the findings of Studies 1 and 2, there was no difference between the younger and older children on the amount of correct or incorrect information recalled. Age influenced the number of correct photo identifications made, with older children better able to recognize the nurse than younger children. However, older children and their parents did not significantly differ in face-recognition ability. The absence of significant differences may have occurred because of low statistical power of some of our tests, however.

On the specific questions, children were more accurate about central information than about peripheral information. However, this was not true for the misleading questions: Children were equally accurate on questions pertaining to central and peripheral information. It is likely that social factors (e.g., social influence) apart from memory played a role in producing age differences in suggestibility for central and peripheral information.

STUDY 4

It has been proposed that memory for emotional events may actually improve over time, especially with repeated questioning (e.g., Erdelyi 1985). Although effects of delay were not evident in Study 2, it is possible that with a longer delay and with a second memory test, hypermnesia could be found. In contrast, it is also possible that memory for aversive events declines over time as has so often been found for neutral events in laboratory studies.

To explore these possibilities, as many children as possible from Study 2 were retested after a 1-year delay. This delay was of interest for practical as well as theoretical reasons: When children testify in court there is often a long delay between the children's initial report and courtroom testimony (Goodman, Jones, Pyle, Prado, Port, England, Mason, and Rudy 1988).

Method

Subjects. Twenty-two children from Study 2 were tested, including 9 4- to 5-year-olds (M = 5 years 1 month; range 4 years 4 months to 5 years 8 months) and 13 6- to 7-year-olds (M = 6 years 8 months; range 6 years 0 months to 7 years 9 months). There were 8 females and 14 males. Three Black, 9 Anglo, and 8 Hispanic children were included, with the race/ethnicity of 2 children classified as "other." The group consisted of all children who could be contacted and whose parents agreed to participate. Analysis of variance confirmed that the 22 children tested after a year did not differ significantly from the 26 children who were not tested after this delay in terms of initial digit-span scores, parent- or experimenter-rated inoculation stress, or performance on the recall test, specific or misleading questions, or photo identification task in Study 2. In addition, subjects were screened to ensure they had not been to the inoculation clinic during the delay. Families had not been told previously that the children would be tested again.

Materials. The same questionnaire used in Study 2 was employed in this study. The only change was in the wording of the free recall question. Instead of asking about the visit that occurred a few days ago, children were asked about the last visit that occurred a long time ago.

Procedure. The procedure was identical to that of session 2 in Study 2.

Results

Children's performance at the time of original testing was compared to their performance at the 1-year delay. The main findings of the study are presented in Table 6.

Free recall. Free recall protocols for the 1-year data were scored by a new rater whose reliability had been established at .80 or above (proportion of agreement), based on free recall scoring in Study 2. For each child, the number of units of information correctly recalled was entered into a 2(Age) × 2(Time) analysis of variance with time as a within-subject factor. A main effect of time was the only significant finding, $F(1, 20) = 4.52$, $p = .05$, indicating that correct recall decreased over time. The number of incorrect units of information recalled was analyzed similarly, but there were no significant main effects or interactions. Interestingly, the younger children did not recall any incorrect information at time 1 or time 2, whereas the older children did. However, the older children's inaccuracies were primarily at time 2 ($M = 0.46$) as opposed to time 1 ($M = 0.08$), and consisted mainly of intrusions of general knowledge concerning doctor's visits or intrusions based on the merging of information from sessions 1 and 2 of the original study (e.g., that the nurse had given the children the toy prize we had actually given them).

Specific questions. The proportion of specific questions answered correctly by each child was entered into a 2(Age) $\times$ 2(Time) $\times$ 3(Type of information) analysis of variance, with time and type of information entered as within-subject factors. The main effects of age and time were not significant. Although the main effect of type of information, $F(2, 40) = 13.92$, $p < .001$, was significant, it was subsumed under a significant Type of Information $\times$ Time interaction, $F(2, 40) = 5.75$, $p < .01$. Analysis of simple effects revealed a significant decline in the ability to answer action questions correctly over time, $F(1, 21) = 8.46$, $p < .01$, but not person or room questions. Moreover, whereas a significant difference in the ability to answer action, person, and room specific questions existed at time 1, $F(2, 42) = 22.46$, $p < .001$, a significant difference did not exist at time 2, $F(2, 42) = 2.00$. Interestingly, when don't know responses were included in addition to correct responses, significant effects of time disappeared. Instead, the analysis produced significant main effects of age, $F(1, 20) = 5.65$, $p < .05$, older children, $M = 0.83$, and younger children, $M = 0.73$, and of type of information, $F(2, 40) = 4.49$, $p < .05$; action, $M = 0.85$, person, $M = 0.79$, and room, $M = 0.74$.

When the proportion of specific questions answered correctly by each child was entered into a 2(Time) $\times$ 2(Centrality) analysis of variance, a significant main effect of centrality, $F(1, 19) = 37.38$, $p < .001$, emerged, as well as a significant Time $\times$ Centrality interaction, $F(1, 19) = 11.66$, $p < .01$. There was a loss of central information, $F(1, 21) = 9.93$, $p < .01$, but not peripheral information between time 1 and time 2. Nevertheless, specific questions about central information were answered with greater accuracy at both time 1, $F(1, 2 1) = 80.86$, $p < .00 1$, and time 2, $F(1, 21) = 7.24$, $p < .05$. Because children were initially more accurate about central than peripheral information, their performance could drop further on the former than on the latter. Central information consisted, in large measure, of action questions, and the same pattern detected here held for the action questions, as described earlier.

The children's answers to the four questions of special interest in relation to child abuse cases were also examined. As can be seen in Table 3, the children's answers to these questions remained at about the same level of accuracy as for all of the children at time 1. Both at the original test and 1 year later, the children made few commission errors. The main exception was an increase in children who falsely affirmed that they had been touched somewhere other than their arm or thigh. Either spontaneously or in response to the probe question "Where?" the children incorrectly pointed to such places as their other arm, their wrist, or the top of their heads. The children did not provide responses indicative of sexual or physical abuse.

Misleading questions. The proportion of misleading questions answered correctly (including don't know responses) by each child was entered into a 2(Age) × 2(Time) × 3(Type of Information) analysis of variance, with time and type of information entered as within-subject factors. The main effect of time was significant, $F(1, 20) = 6.27, p < .05$. Children's suggestibility increased over the 1-year delay. Older children, $M = 0.67$, were again less suggestible than younger children, $M = 0.45$, $F(1, 20) = 7.44, p < .05$, but age did not interact with time. Overall, the children were less suggestible about the actions than about the room, $F(1, 20) = 4.18, p < .05$. Their suggestibility about the person did not differ significantly from the other two means. Although the children were least suggestible about the actions, over time they showed the greatest increase in suggestibility about the actions. A significant Age × Type of Information interaction, $F(2, 40) = 5.60, p < .01$, reflected that, regardless of time of test, older children were better able to resist suggestion about the actions, $M = 0.77$, and the person, $M = 0.73$, than were younger children, $M = 0.53$, $F(1, 20) = 6.27, p < .05$, and $M = 0.33$, $F(1, 20) = 14.05, p < .01$, respectively, whereas older children's suggestibility about the room, $M = 0.50$, was equivalent to that of the younger children, $M = 0.48$.

It was also of interest to determine if central information was retained better than peripheral information. A 2(Time) × 2(Centrality) analysis of variance on the proportion of misleading questions answered correctly by each child failed to produce any significant main effects or interactions.

Face recognition. Whether or not the children made a correct identification of the nurse was analyzed in a 2(Age) × 2(Time) analysis of variance. The effect of time was significant, $F(1, 20) = 14.52, p < .01$. Children were less able to identify the nurse after the 1-year delay.

Whether or not the children made a false identification was analyzed as described earlier for correct identifications. There were no significant main effects or interactions. If anything, the children made fewer false identifications with time, and surprisingly, younger children, $M = 0.32$, actually made somewhat fewer false identifications than older children, $M = 0.41$, though not significantly so.

Stress ratings. Of the 22 children retested after a year, 8 had originally been rated by the research assistants as at stress level 3, 10 as at stress level 4, 3 as at stress level 5, and 1 at stress level 6. To conduct valid analyses of variance, scores for children in stress levels 4, 5, and 6 were combined, resulting in only two levels of stress. There were no significant main effects or interactions from a series of 2(Stress) × 2(Time) analyses of variance performed on the main memory measures.

Discussion

After a 1-year delay, children's memory for a stressful event declined. Over time, children recalled less correct information, answered fewer specific questions about the actions accurately (although time did not affect accuracy on the action questions when don't know responses were included), were more suggestible in response to misleading questions, and made fewer correct identifications. Yet children did not show a significant increase in recall of incorrect information or in false identifications. There was no reliable evidence of a hypermnesia effect.

Unfortunately, too few children who were at the highest stress level in the original study returned for the 1-year delay test. In fact, only two stress levels could be tested. It is not surprising, therefore, that there were no significant effects of stress on memory.

GENERAL DISCUSSION

To our knowledge, the experiments described in this paper were the first scientific studies to examine children's memory for a stressful event for which objective records exist. Across the four studies, stress was never associated with a reliable negative effect on memory. In contrast, when stress was very high and children became nearly hysterical with fear, stress was associated with enhanced memory. This finding is consistent with recent physiological evidence that stress (specifically, the release of adrenalin that accompanies stress) aids consolidation of memory (e.g., Gold 1987).

Nevertheless, forgetting clearly occurred. Children's memory for the stressful event faded much as it might for a nonstressful event. The fate of the most highly stressed children's memory remains unknown, however, because so few of the most highly stressed children returned after the one-year delay. In general, however, our findings are consistent with those of Warren-Leubecker and Springfield (1987) who found that children's memory for the space shuttle Challenger disaster, an event that might be expected to produce a flashbulb memory for at least some children, also faded over time.

At the minimum, our findings counter the view that stress has a decremental effect on memory. We found little support for Easterbrook's (1959) proposal that central information would be retained at the loss of peripheral information as stress increased. Children remembered central information better than peripheral information regardless of stress. Although the Yerkes-Dodson law may apply to performance on certain tasks, it has rarely been tested on human memory for highly stressful, personally significant events that simulate bodily attack (but see Baddeley 1972).

Since we conducted our studies, a number of other researchers have examined children's memory for stressful events. Ochsner and Zaragoza (1988) report the same pattern of findings we report here, specifically, higher recall and reduced suggestibility in more highly stressed children. Warren-Leubecker et al. (1988) found that children who rated themselves as more emotional about the space shuttle disaster recalled more about the event than did less emotional children, even 2 years after the tragedy. In contrast, Peters (1987), reports several detrimental effects of stress on memory.

There are many methodological reasons why the findings of the present studies might differ from those of Peters (see Goodman, in press). Of more interest are conceptual reasons that can help explain discrepancies across studies generally. It has been popular in the past to think of emotion as arousal, a view reflected in the Yerkes-Dodson Law. In contrast, recent formulations consider the functional distinctiveness of different discrete emotions. This functional view emphasizes the adaptive nature of emotions and the organizing role they play in intrapsychic regulation (e.g., Bretherton, Fritz, Zahn-Waxler, and Ridgeway 1986; Campos, Barrett, Lamb, Goldsmith, and Stenberg 1983; Izard 1977). According to this view, emotions constitute guidance systems designed to appraise events and motivate appropriate action.

How should such guidance systems affect memory? We can speculate that discrete emotions guide attentional processing in the service of generally functional emotion-related goals (which Roseman 1984, in a similar analysis, called *emotivational* goals). When appraisal indicates that danger is imminent, the goal is to escape. Cognitive resources are allocated to accomplish that goal. This does not mean that there is necessarily a narrowing of attention but rather a redirection of it. If, before fear sets in, the organism's previous goal was exploration, then narrowing of attention may indeed result, assuming that narrowing of attention helps accomplish the goal of escape. That is only one of several possibilities, however. For example, if the previous goal were to solve a problem and, as a result, attention was highly focused, attention might not narrow further in response to the stressful event. Rather, it would be redirected in the service of the new goal.

According to this view, inconsistencies across studies may result from several factors. One is the nature of the comparison task (e.g., having a design rubbed onto a child's arm). The emotion and resulting goal involved in the comparison task will affect memory because the subject's attentional focus will be determined in large part by it. A second factor is the type of information tested. If memory tests primarily tap information relevant to an individual's major, emotion-determined goals, memory will appear to be enhanced by emotion. If the tests primarily tap information irrelevant to the main goals, memory may appear to be adversely affected by the emotion.

In a study reported by Peters (1989), a fire alarm (the stressor) went off while children's vital signs were read. At the same time, a woman entered the room, looked out the window, dropped something, and left. For control children, a radio (nonstressor) was turned on instead of a fire alarm. Later, the children's suggestibility was assessed by misleading questions. In these questions, events such as a woman wearing a yellow instead of a red sweater were suggested. Control children were found to be less suggestible than experimental children. Assuming that the fire alarm would be expected to direct attention toward self-protection and escape, it is not surprising that the children in Peters's experimental group had weaker memories and hence were more suggestible than children in the control group, given the kinds of information assessed in his memory tests.

In contrast, Ochsner and Zaragoza (1988) found that children in a stressful situation recalled more and were less suggestible than children in a nonstressful situation, a finding consistent with the results of our Study 2. Ochsner and Zaragoza's tests tapped information relevant to the stressor (i.e., characteristics of the actions and appearance of the man who stole a purse) and hence were goal-relevant.

Researchers have not paid sufficient attention to the relation between the emotions aroused in tasks, subjects' resulting goals, and the types of information tested. In terms of development, the complexity of the emotions aroused and the appraisal processes involved, as well as the actions that can be taken to obtain desired goals, would all be expected to change with consequent effects on memory.

The view we are espousing is consistent with the notion that strong emotions enhance consolidation of memory, but it predicts that different information will be consolidated as a function of the specific emotions involved and the relations between these emotions and various aspects of the situation. Thus, emotional events may be remembered better than nonemotional events (Christianson and Loftus 1987), but joyful events may be remembered as well as stressful events, although different goal-relevant features of the joyful and stressful events would be retained. Moreover, emotions are likely to play a regulating role in how often the event is rehearsed or told to others, factors that may be especially important for long-term retention. In sum, both the quality and the quantity of emotion play a role in regulating memory.

In addition to contributing to an emerging data base on children's memory for stressful events, our findings add to the literature on age differences in children's memory for real-life events. Surprisingly, across experiments we conducted, no age differences in free recall were found. The absence of age differences may have been due to a number of factors. One possibility is that it may be easier for younger children to retrieve information about a stressful than nonstressful event, thus eliminating age differences. If this were true, however, an Age × Group interaction should have been found in Study 3, and it was not. Moreover, one might expect that age differences in answers to specific questions would have been eliminated as well. Perhaps if a larger age span had been included, age differences would have emerged.

In any case, the results on the free-recall task support a previously documented conclusion: Although children report little information, what they do report is usually accurate (Dent and Stephenson 1979; Goodman and Reed 1986; Marin et al. 1979), barring motivation to lie. For some children, errors in free recall did appear, however. One young boy who had a traumatic past made up a wild story about attacking the nurse. Others, especially after a long delay, merged various events (e.g., other doctor visits) with the one of interest here. Thus, although errors tended to come from the children's actual life experiences, there were some inaccuracies on our free-recall tests.

Age differences were consistently found in the children's answers to specific and misleading questions, corroborating the findings of earlier studies (e.g., Goodman and Reed 1986; King and Yuille 1987; Zaragoza 1987). However, children tended to remember details about the actions particularly well and to be least suggestible about action details. These findings are consistent with the claim that memory for actions is superior to memory for other types of information (e.g., Fivush et al. 1987; Jones et al. 1988; Ochsner and Zaragoza 1988). As Jones et al. (1988) point out, retention of action information may be important for the establishment of scripts, which are needed to make the world predictable and understandable for children.

Results from the photo-identification task at times revealed age differences in the number of correct identifications made initially and over time, with younger as compared to older children more rapidly losing their ability to recognize the correct face. Moreover, younger children were more prone than older children to make false identifications, although this difference disappeared after a 1-year delay. Five- and 6-year-olds and parents did not differ in the number of correct and incorrect identifications made, however. Although the parents' and children's experiences were different (e.g., one was a bystander, the other a victim), the comparison suggests that recognition of a briefly seen stranger can be difficult across a large age range. This pattern of results matches that reported by Goodman and Reed (1986), who found poorer performance by 3-year-olds than 6-year-olds and adults on a photo identification task, but no differences between 6-year-olds and adults.

These studies were also the first to include questions of special relevance to child abuse cases (see, for example, Davies et al. 1989, and Goodman and Aman, in press, for more recent research in a similar vein). In general, the children were quite accurate in answering these questions, even a year after the event. They knew well that they had not been hit, for example, and sex-related answers (other than a few yes responses to the question about kissing) did not appear in response to our questions.

In interpreting our findings and those of other researchers, mention should be made of methodological difficulties in conducting research on stress and memory (see also Goodman, in press). One methodological difficulty is that no one generally accepted measure of stress exists, leaving open how to best capture the stress a child experiences (e.g., see Brigham et al. 1983; Weiner 1982). Another is that in the most typically used research design for studying stress and memory (e.g., Christianson and Nilsson 1984; Loftus and Burns 1982), control and experimental groups not only experience different levels of stress but slightly different events (as did the children in our Studies 1 and 3). It is difficult if not impossible to avoid such problems in this line of work. In regard to our own studies, the fact that the findings from Study 1 and Study 3 were consistent in combination with the findings of Study 2 supports the conclusion that stress had no adverse effects on the aspects of memory we tested.

However, an important caveat about our findings concerns the relatively small number of children in our experiments, and low statistical power to uncover significant differences. Had we tested more children, perhaps a greater number of statistically significant differences would have emerged (e.g., detrimental effects of stress on face recognition in Studies 1 and 2). Also, given that only five children in Study 2 reached the highest stress levels, replication of our findings is needed.

In summary, children's memory for a stressful event was similar to that for a nonstressful event, except when the highest levels of stress were reached then performance on selected tests was enhanced. Age differences in memory for the event appeared, but stress did not differentially affect memory as a function of age. However, the small number of children in the most highly stressed group limits conclusions about the interplay between age and stress. Future research is needed to identify the conditions under which stress has facilitating versus detrimental effects on children's memory, as well as how other emotions (e.g., joy, anger) serve to regulate memory and its development.

REFERENCES

American Jurisprudence Proof of Facts, vol. 6. San Francisco: Bancroft-Whitney.

American Law Reports. 1962. Rochester, N.Y.: Lawyers Cooperative Publishing.

Baddeley, A. D. 1972. Selective attention and performance in dangerous environments. *British Journal of Psychology* 63: 537–46.

———. 1982. *Your memory: A user's guide.* New York: Macmillan.

Bohannon, J. N. 1988. Flashbulb memories for the space shuttle disaster: A tale of two theories. *Cognition* 29: 179–96.

Bretherton, I., J. Fritz, C. Zahn-Waxler, and D. Ridgeway. 1986. Learning to talk about emotions: A functionalist perspective. *Child Development* 57: 529–48.

Brigham, J. C., and P. Barkowitz. 1978. Do "they all look alike"?: The effect of race, sex, experience, and attitudes on the ability to recognize faces. *Journal of Applied Psychology* 8: 306–18.

Brigham, J. C., A. Maass, D. Martinez, and Q. Whittenberger. 1983. The effect of arousal on facial recognition. *Basic and Applied Social Psychology* 4: 279–302.

Brown, A., and J. Deloache. 1978. Skills, plans, and self-regulation. In *Children's thinking: What develops?* ed. R. Siegler, 3–35. Hillsdale, N.J.: Erlbaum.

Brown, R., and J. Kulik. 1977. Flashbulb memories. *Cognition* 5: 73–99.

Butter, M. J. 1970. Differential recall of paired associations as a function of arousal and concreteness/imagery levels. *Journal of Experimental Psychology* 84: 252–56.

Campos, J. J., K. C. Barrett, M. E. Lamb, H. H. Goldsmith, and C. Stenber. 1983. Socioemotional development. In *Handbook of child psychology: Vol. 2. Infancy and developmental psychobiology,* 4th ed., ed. M. Haith and J. J. Campos, 783–915. New York: Wiley.

Case, R., S. Hayward, M. Lewis, and P. Hurst. 1988. Toward a Neo-Piagetian theory of cognitive and emotional development. *Developmental Review* 8: 1–51.

Ceci, S. I., D. F. Ross, and M. P. Toglia. 1987. Age differences in suggestibility: Narrowing the uncertainties. In *Children's eyewitness memory,* ed. S. J. Ceci, M. P. Toglia, and D. F. Ross, 79–91. New York: Springer-Verlag.

Chance, J. E., and A. G. Goldstein. 1984. Face-recognition memory: Implications for children's eyewitness testimony. *Journal of Social Issues* 40: 69–85.

Chance, J. E., A. L. Turner, and A. G. Goldstein. 1982. Development of differential recognition for own- and other-race faces. *Journal of Psychology* 112: 29–37.

Christianson, S. 1989. Flashbulb memories: Special, but not so special. *Memory and Cognition* 17: 435–43.

Christianson, S., and E. F. Loftus. 1987. Memory for traumatic events. *Applied Cognitive Psychology* 1: 225–39.

Christianson, S., and L. Nilsson. 1984. Functional amnesia as induced by psychological trauma. *Memory and Cognition* 12: 142–55.

Cohen, G. 1989. *Memory in the real world.* Hillsdale, N.J.: Erlbaum.

Davis, G., A. Tarrant, and R. Flin. 1989. Close encounters of the witness kind: Children's memory for a simulated health inspection. *British Journal of Psychology* 80: 415–29.

Deffenbacher, K. 1983. The influence of arousal on reliability of testimony. In *Evaluating eyewitness evidence,* ed. B. R. Clifford and S. Lloyd-Bostock, 235–51. Chichester, England: Wiley.

Dent, H. R. 1982. The effects of interviewing strategies on the results of interviews with child witnesses. In *Reconstructing the past,* ed. A. Trankell, 279–98. Deventer, Netherlands: Kluwer.

Dent, H. R., and G. M. Stephenson. 1979. An experimental study of the effectiveness of different techniques of questioning child witnesses. *British Journal of Social and Clinical Psychology* 18: 41–51.

Easterbrook, J. A. 1959. The effect of emotion on the utilization and organization of behavior. *Psychological Review* 66: 183–201.

Erdelyi, M. 1985. *Psychoanalysis: Freud's cognitive psychology.* New York: Freeman.

Fischer, K., P. Shaver, and P. Carnochan. 1988. From basic- to subordinate-category emotions: A skill approach to emotional development. In *Child development today and tomorrow: New directions for child development,* ed. W. Damon, 107–36. San Francisco: Jossey-Bass.

Fivush, R., J. Gray, and F. A. Fromhoff. 1987. Two-year-olds talk about the past. *Cognitive Development* 2: 393–409.

Flavell, J. H. 1985. *Cognitive development.* Englewood Cliffs, N.J.: Prentice-Hall.

Flin, R. H. 1980. Age effects in children's memory for unfamiliar faces. *Developmental Psychology* 16: 373–74.

Gold, P. E. 1987. Sweet memories. *American Scientist* 75: 151–55.

Goodman, G. S. 1984. Children's testimony in historical perspective. *Journal of Social Issues* 40: 931.

———. In press. Stress and accuracy in research on children's testimony: Commentary on Peters. In *The suggestibility of children's memory*, ed. J. Doris. Washington, D.C.: American Psychological Association.

Goodman, G. S., and C. Aman. In press. Children's use of anatomically detailed dolls to recount an event. *Child Development*.

Goodman, G. S., and A. Hahn. 1987. Evaluating eyewitness testimony. In *Handbook of forensic psychology*, ed. J. Weiner and A. Hess, 258–92. New York: Wiley.

Goodman, G. S., D. P. H. Jones, E. Pyle, L. Prado, L. P. Port, T. England, R. Mason, and L. Rudy. 1988. The child in court: A preliminary report on the emotional effects of criminal court testimony on child sexual assault victims. In *The child witness: Do the courts abuse children?: Issues in criminological and legal psychology*, ed. G. Davies and J. Drinkwater, 46–54. Leicester: British Psychological Association.

Goodman, G. S., and R. S. Reed. 1986. Age differences in eyewitness testimony. *Law and Human Behavior* 10: 317–32.

Goodman, G. S., L. Rudy, B. L. Bottoms, and C. Aman. In press. Children's concerns and memory: Issues of ecological validity in children's testimony. In *Knowing and remembering in children*, eds., R. Fivush and J. Hudson. New York: Cambridge University Press.

Harsch, N., and U. Neisser. 1989. *Substantial and irreversible errors in flashbulb memories of the Challenger explosion*. Paper presented at the meeting of the Psychonomic Society, Atlanta, Georgia, November.

Hosch H. M., and D. S. Cooper. 1982. Victimization as a determinant of eye-witness accuracy. *Journal of Applied Psychology* 67: 649–52.

Izard, C. 1978. *Human emotions*. New York: Plenum.

Jones, D. C., D. Swift, and M. A. Johnson. 1988. Nondeliberate memory for a novel event among preschoolers. *Developmental Psychology* 24: 641–45.

Kail, R. 1989. *The development of memory in children*, 3rd ed. New York: Freeman.

Keenan, J. M., and S. D. Baillet. 1980. Memory for personally and socially relevant events. In *Attention and performance*, ed. R. S. Nickerson, vol. 8, 651–69. Hillsdale, N.J.: Erlbaum.

Kety, S. D. 1970. The biogenic amines in the central nervous system: Their possible role in arousal, emotion, and learning. In *The neurosciences: Second study program*, ed. F. Schmitt. New York: Rockefeller University Press.

King, M. A., and J. C. Yuille. 1987. Suggestibility and the child witness. In *Children's eyewitness memory*, ed. S. J. Ceci, M. P. Toglia, and D. Ross, 24–35. New York: Springer-Verlag.

Kleinsmith, L. T., and S. Kaplan. 1963. Paired associate learning as a function of arousal and interpolated interval. *Journal of Experimental Psychology* 65: 190–93.

Loftus, E. F. 1979. *Eyewitness testimony*. Cambridge, Mass.: Harvard University Press.

Loftus, E. F., and T. E. Burns. 1982. Mental shock can produce retrograde amnesia. *Memory and Cognition* 10: 318–23.

Malpass, R. S., and J. Kravitz. 1969. Recognition of faces of own and other race. *Journal of Personality and Social Psychology* 13: 330–34.

Mandler, J. M. 1983. Representation. In *Handbook of child psychology: Vol. 3. Cognitive development,* 4th ed., ed. J. H. Flavell and E. Markman, 420–94. New York: Wiley.

Marin, B. V., D. L. Holmes, M. Guth, and P. Kovac. 1979. The potential of children as eyewitnesses. *Law and Human Behavior* 3: 295–306.

McCarthy, D. 1972. *Manual for the McCarthy scales of children's abilities.* New York: Psychological Corporation.

McCloskey, M., C. Wible, and N. Cohen. 1988. Is there a special flashbulb-memory mechanism? *Journal of Experimental Psychology: General* 117: 171–81.

McGaugh, J. L. 1989. Modulation of memory storage processes. In *Memory: Interdisciplinary approaches,* ed. P. R. Solomon, G. R. Goethals, C. M. Kelley, and B. R. Stephens, 33–64. New York: Springer-Verlag.

Melamud, B. G. 1976. Psychological preparations for hospitalizations. In *Contributions to medical psychology,* ed. S. Rachman, 43–74. Oxford: Pergamon Press.

Miller, P. I., and L. L. Sperry. 1988. Early talk about the past: The origins of conversational stories of personal experience. *Journal of Child Language* 15: 293–315.

Neisser, U. 1982. Snapshots or benchmarks? In *Memory observed: Remembering in natural contexts,* ed. U. Neisser, pp. 43–48. San Francisco: Freeman.

Nelson, K. 1986. *Event knowledge: Structure and function in development.* Hillsdale, N.J.: Erlbaum.

Ochsner, J. E., and M. S. Zaragoza. 1988. *The accuracy and suggestibility of children's memory for neutral and criminal eyewitness events.* Paper presented at the meeting of the American Psychology and Law Association, Miami, Florida, March.

Paris, S., and B. Lindaur. 1976. The role of inference in children's comprehension and memory for stories. *Cognitive Psychology* 8: 217–27.

Pear, T. H., and S. Wyatt. 1914. The testimony of normal and mentally defective children. *British Journal of Psychology* 3: 388–419.

Perlmutter, M., and N. A. Myers. 1979. Development of recall in two- to four-year-old children. *Developmental Psychology* 15: 73–83.

Peters, D. P. 1987. The impact of naturally occurring stress on children's memory. In *Children's eyewitness memory,* ed. S. J. Ceci, M. P. Toglia, and D. F. Ross, 122–41. New York: Springer-Verlag.

———. 1989. Stress and arousal effects on the child eyewitness. In C. Brainerd, chair, *Children's ability to remember witnessed events: Theoretical and in applied perspectives.* Paper presented at the meeting at the Society for Research in Child Development, Kansas City, Missouri, April.

Pillemer, D. 1984. Flashbulb memories of the assassination attempt on President Reagan. *Cognition* 16: 63–80.

Pullyblank, J., J. Bisanz, C. Scott, and M. A. Champion. 1985. Developmental invariance in the effects of functional self-knowledge on memory. *Child Development* 56: 1447–54.

Pynoos, R. S., and S. Eth. 1984. The child as criminal witness to homicide. *Journal of Social Issues* 40: 87–108.

Rapaport, D. 1942. *Emotions and memory.* Baltimore: Williams and Wilkins.

Rex v. Braddon and Speke, 9 How. Sr. 11 27, 1148 (1684).

Rogers, T. B., N. A. Kupier, and W. S. Kirker. 1977. Self-reference and the encoding of personal information. *Journal of Personality and Social Psychology* 35: 677–88.

Roseman, I. J. 1984. Cognitive determinants of emotions: A structural theory. In *Review of personality and social psychology,* ed. P. Shaver, vol. 5, 11–36. Beverly Hills, Calif.: Sage.

Saywitz, K. J. 1987. Children's testimony: Age-related patterns of memory errors. In *Children's eyewitness memory,* ed. S. J. Ceci, M. P. Toglia, and D. F. Ross, 36–52. New York: Springer-Verlag.

Scriver, E., and M. A. Safer. 1985. *Repeated testing of eyewitnesses.* Paper presented at the meeting of the American Psychological Association, Los Angeles, California, August.

Steward, M. S., and D. S. Steward. 1981. Children's conceptions of medical procedures. In *Children's conceptions of health, illness, and bodily functions: New directions for child development,* ed. R. Bibace and M. E. Walsh, 67–84. San Francisco: Jossey-Bass.

Terr L. C. 1981. Psychic trauma in children: Observations following the Chowchilla school-bus kidnapping. *American Journal of Psychiatry* 138: 14–19.

Terr L. C. 1983. Chowchilla revisited: The effects of psychic trauma four years after a school-bus kidnapping. *American Journal of Psychiatry* 140: 1543–50.

———. 1988. What happens to early memories of trauma? A study of twenty children under the age of five at the time of documented traumatic events. *Journal of the American Academy of Child and Adolescent Psychiatry* 27: 96–104.

Warren-Leubecker, A., C. Bradley, and I. Hinton. 1988. *Scripts and the development of flashbulb memories.* Paper presented at the Conference on Human Development, Charleston, South Carolina, March.

Warren-Leubecker, A. C., and M. Springfield. 1987. *Flashbulb memory revisited: Children recall the space shuttle accident.* Paper presented at the meeting of the Society for Research on Child Development, Baltimore, Maryland, April.

Weiner, G. A. 1982. A review and analysis of children's behavior in dental settings. *Child Development* 53: 1111–33.

Yerkes, R. M., and J. D. Dodson. 1908. The relation of strength of stimulus to rapidity of habit formation. *Journal of Comparative Neurology and Psychology* 18: 459–82.

Zaragoza, M. S. 1987. Memory, suggestibility, and eyewitness testimony in children and adults. In *Children's eyewitness memory,* ed. S. J. Ceci, M. P. Toglia, and D. F. Ross, 53–78. New York: Springer-Verlag.

APPENDIX A

Free Recall

Now I want you to think about your visit to the doctor's a few days ago. Did someone do something to you here? (*Interviewer points to child's arm.*) Please tell me everything you can remember about the visit. Anything else?

Now I'm going to ask you some questions about that visit.

Person Questions

Specific Questions

1. Was the person who took your blood (put the design on you) a man or a woman? (*c*)
2. What color hair did he/she have? (*p*)
3. Was she/he older or younger than I? Or the same age? (*c*)
4. Was he/she shorter or taller than I? Or the same height? (*p*)
5. Did you ever see him/her before that day? (*c*)
6. What color skin did that person have? (*c*)

Misleading Questions

1. His/her hair was this long, wasn't it? (Interviewer points to the middle of her back) (*c*)
2. What color was the scarf that she/he was wearing on her/his head? (*p*)

Room Questions

Specific Questions

1. Was there a bed in the room? (*p*)
2. How many doors were there in the room? (*p*)
3. Was there a T.V. set in the room? (*p*)
4. Was your mom or dad in the room with you? (*c*)
5. Were there any pictures or posters on the walls? (*p*)
6. Were there any toys in the room? (*p*)

Note: (*c*) = central and (*p*) = peripheral

Misleading Questions

1. There was only one chair in the room, wasn't there? (*p*)
2. What time did the clock on the wall say it was? (*p*)

Action Questions

Specific Questions

1. Did he/she know your name? (*c*)
2. Did he/she touch you anywhere else? (*c*)
3. Did he/she put something wet on your arm? (*c*)
4. When he/she took your blood (Put the design on your arm), were you standing or sitting or lying down? (*c*)
5. Did he/she put anything in your mouth? (*c*)
6. Did he/she hit you? (*c*)

Misleading Questions

1. The person didn't touch you, did he/she? (*c*)
2. What kind of candy did she/he give you? (*c*)

Photo Identification

I am now going to show you pictures of six women. Please look at each of them. Remember the woman who took your blood (put a design your arm)? Can you tell me if she is here, and if she is, can you point to her?

APPENDIX B

Free Recall

Now I want you to think about your visit to the doctor's office (nurse's office) a few days ago. Did someone do something to you here? (*Interviewer points to child's arm or thigh.*) Please tell me everything you can remember about what happened. Anything else?

Now I am going to ask you some questions about that visit.

Person Questions

Specific Questions

1. Was the person who gave you the shot a man or a woman? (*c*)
2. What color hair did she have? (*p*)
3. Was she older or younger than I? Or the same age? (*p*)
4. Was she shorter or taller than I? Or the same height? (*p*)
5. Did you ever see her before that day? (*c*)
6. What color skin did the person have? (*c*)

Misleading Questions

1. She wasn't an adult, was she? (*c*)
2. What color was the scarf that she was wearing on her head? (*p*)
3. Her hair was this long, wasn't it? (interviewer points to the middle of her back.) (*p*)

Room Questions

Specific Questions

Remember the room where she gave you the shot?
1. Was there a bed in the room? (*c*)
2. How many doors were in the room? (*p*)
3. Was there a TV set in the room? (*p*)
4. Was your mom or dad in the room with you? (*c*)
5. Were there any pictures or posters on the walls? (*p*)
6. Were there any toys in the room? (*c*)

Misleading Questions

1. What time did the clock on the desk say it was? (*p*)
2. There wasn't a refrigerator in the room, was there? (*p*)
3. There were only three chairs in the room, weren't there? (*p*)

Action Questions

Specific Questions

1. Did the person kiss you? (*c*)
2. Did she put something wet on your arm/thigh? (*c*)

3. When she gave you the shot (put the design on you), were you standing or sitting or lying down? (*c*)
4. Did she put anything in your mouth? (*c*)
5. Did she hit you? (*c*)
6. Did she touch you anywhere other than your arm/thigh? (*c*)

Misleading Questions

1. The person didn't touch you, did she? (*c*)
2. You didn't go in the room with the nurse, did you?*
3. What kind of toy did he/she give you? (*c*)

Photo Identification

I am now going to show you pictures of six women. Please look at each one of them, Remember the woman who gave you the shot at the clinic? Can you tell me if she is here, and if she is, can you point to her?

Legal Questions

1. Do you know the difference between the truth and a lie?
2. If you said the nurse kissed you, would that be the truth or a lie?
3. What happens if you tell a lie?
4. Is everything you told me today the truth?

NOTES

1. The studies reported as Studies 3 and 4 are, in an important sense, parts of Study 2; this is so because children from Study 2 are included in the latter two studies. The findings are presented separately to aid in exposition.

2. Four of the youngest children, two in the experimental group and two in the control group, did not know their numbers and were excluded from the digit-span analyses. Similarly, in Study 2, three young children did not know their numbers and were also excluded from the digit-span analyses.

3. The children's digit-span scores in Study 1 were noticeably higher than those in the other experiments. The differences appeared to be mainly due to the inclusion in Study 1 of several older children and children from a higher socioeconomic status.

---

*This question was placed in the action category because the technician had to say the child's name for a yes response to be scored as correct. Saying the child's name was considered an action.

PART TWO

REPRESSION AND AMNESIA

Despite the claims of innumerable clinicians that "repression" in the Freudian sense—i.e., the completely automatic, selective, and involuntary forgetting of material events that cause extreme psychological pain—is a proven and well-established psychological fact, there is little or no empirical evidence to support this claim. Holmes's paper makes this very clear.

The Pope and Hudson paper not only supports this view but from their examination of the four most-cited studies in support of repression, e.g., Herman and Schatzow, Briere and Conte, Loftus et al., and the Williams study, they concluded that "None of the four studies provide both clear confirmation of trauma and adequate documentation of amnesia."

Linda Williams, in her first paper (1994) of the interchange with Loftus, Garry, and Feldman, showed that in her clinical group 38% of the women did not recall the abuse documented seventeen years earlier. Williams concluded that "long periods with no memory of abuse should not be regarded as evidence that the abuse did not occur."

Loftus, Garry, and Feldman insist that Williams's findings "do not provide cogent support for the claim that a long stream of childhood traumas is routinely banished from conscious awareness and then can be reliably recovered later." Williams's findings, they maintain, only prove that many children can forget about a sexually abusive experience from their past. Although seldom mentioned, it is also possible—even probable—that some childhood sexual experiences were *not* traumatic.

Reisner's position, as the reader can see, is that *some* recovered memories of abuse and other trauma can be accurate and that there is enough experimental and corroborated anecdotal evidence to justify belief in the classical concept of repression. Reisner, nevertheless, firmly agrees that many false memories do occur—especially whenever hypnosis and hypnosis-like procedures are employed—and that such uncorroborated repressed memory evidence is hardly reliable enough for use in the courtroom. This position, at the moment, is certainly tenable and worthy of consideration until more evidence is in.

6

THE EVIDENCE
FOR REPRESSION:
AN EXAMINATION OF
SIXTY YEARS OF RESEARCH

DAVID S. HOLMES

At the outset, it might be helpful if I described briefly the role I played in the conference on "Repression, Dissociation, and the Warding off of Conflictual Cognitive Contents." When Jerome Singer called and invited me to participate, I was impressed with the topic and the participants, but I wondered, "Why invite me?" The question arose because some years earlier I had published a review in which I concluded that there was no reliable evidence for the existence of repression (Holmes 1974), and since then I had not seen anything new in the literature to change that conclusion. Singer replied that it was his hope to include within the conference the entire spectrum of points of view concerning repression and that my point of view was certainly "different" from those of most of the other participants. Furthermore, he suggested that it was important to have a critic at the conference. The role of "nonbeliever" and "critic" can be difficult, but it is one with which I had had some experience (e.g., Holmes 1968a, 1968b, 1974, 1978, 1981a, 1981b, 1983, 1984, 1985b). Indeed, a colleague once likened me to Diogenes, who walked through the night with a lantern looking for an honest man. I, he suggested, have walked through the dark night of psychology looking for a concept in which I could believe. My lantern has been a textbook on research methodology, and, unfortunately, it has often revealed more flaws than facts and more errors than insights. My

From *Repression and Dissociation: Implications for Personality Theory, Psychopathology, and Health*, edited by Jerome L. Singer (The University of Chicago Press, 1990), pp. 85–102. Copyright © 1990 by the University of Chicago. All rights reserved.

role in the conference, then, was to balance theory with data and to focus a critical light on the data.

DEFINITION

The definition of "repression" is of course essential to studying the phenomena. Unfortunately, defining "repression" presents a thorny problem because Freud used the term differently at different times, and Erdelyi has aptly demonstrated that, by referring to different citations, one can include or exclude almost any behavior from Freud's umbrella of repression. What is one to do in this situation? From my perspective, the most practical, pragmatic, and prudent thing to do is to use a definition of "repression" that matches as closely as possible the conventional use of the term. In other words, in the absence of an authoritative definition, we should use the definition held by most individuals. This may be heretical, but exactly what Freud did or did not mean by the term "repression" may be irrelevant now anyway. Arriving at the conventional usage is not a problem-free process, however, and my pen poised over a pile of texts and journals does not serve as an objective and infallible divining rod. However, examination of a variety of texts and the amalgam of laboratory research that has been published over the past sixty years does lead to what appears to be a widely held definition.

It is my belief that in its general use the concept of repression has three elements: (1) repression is the selective forgetting of materials that cause the individual pain; (2) repression is not under voluntary control; and (3) repressed material is not lost but instead is stored in the unconscious and can be returned to consciousness if the anxiety that is associated with the memory is removed (Freud [1915] 1957). The assertion that repression is not under voluntary control differentiates repression from suppression and denial, with which it is sometimes confused or which some theorists choose to consider as types of repression (Erdelyi). It should be noted that there are two types of repression. On the one hand, there is what Freud called "repression proper" or "after expulsion," in which an individual consciously recognizes something as threatening (anxiety provoking) and then represses the thought to avoid the anxiety (Freud [1915] 1957). On the other hand, there is "primary repression," in which threatening material is relegated to the unconscious before it is consciously recognized as stressful. Unless it is explicitly stated otherwise, in my discussion of repression I will focus on "after expulsion." Having defined "repression," we can now go on to consider the ways in which it has been traditionally studied in the laboratory.

APPROACHES TO STUDYING REPRESSION

Five approaches have been used to study repression in the laboratory, and in this section I will briefly consider the methods, findings, and weaknesses of each approach along with the conclusions that can be drawn.

Differential Recall of Pleasant and Unpleasant Experiences

In an early attempt to study repression, investigators asked subjects to make lists of their pleasant and unpleasant experiences. Later, the subjects were unexpectedly asked to recall the experiences they had recorded. The investigators then compared the two lists to determine whether subjects were less likely to recall (i.e., repress) unpleasant than pleasant experiences. In most studies, it was found that unpleasant experiences were less likely to be recalled, and the findings were taken as evidence for repression (e.g., Jerslid 1931; Meltzer 1931; Stagner 1931).

These results were initially appealing, but two sets of related findings raised questions about whether the differential recall was due to repression. First, subsequent investigators reported data demonstrating that the recall of personal experiences was due to the intensity of affect rather than the type of affect (pleasant vs. unpleasant) associated with the experiences (e.g., Menzies 1936; Waters and Leeper 1936). In other words, emotionally intense experiences were more likely to be recalled than less intense experiences regardless of whether they were pleasant or unpleasant.

The second set of findings stemmed from an attempt to reconcile the conflicting findings concerning the influence of intensity versus type of affect on recall. In 1970, I proposed that (a) the recall of experiences is determined by the intensity of affect associated with experiences at the time of recall, (b) the intensity of the affect associated with experiences declines over time, and (c) the affect associated with unpleasant experiences is more likely to decline or will decline faster than the affect associated with pleasant experiences (Holmes 1970). If the affect associated with unpleasant experiences showed more or faster declines, at the time of the second recall the unpleasant experiences would be less intense, and, if intensity determines recall, the unpleasant experiences would be less likely to be recalled. To test these hypotheses, college students were first asked to keep a diary of their pleasant and unpleasant experiences for seven days and to score each experience for pleasantness-unpleasantness on a nine-point scale. Each experience was recorded on a card, and the affect score for the experience was recorded on the back of the card. A week later, the subjects were unexpectedly asked to write down all the experiences they had recorded on their diary cards. When that task was

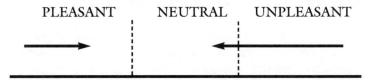

Fig. 1. Schematic representation of how the differential decline of the affective intensities associated with pleasant and unpleasant experiences influences subsequent recall of the experiences. Vertical lines represent intensity thresholds that determine whether an experience will be recalled. Evidence indicates that the affect associated with unpleasant experiences is more likely to decline to points below the threshold necessary for recall.

completed, the subjects were given their diary cards and asked to read each experience and to give the experience a score on a nine-point scale in terms of how pleasant-unpleasant it was at that time. (Note that the original scores for affect were on the backs of the cards and thus could not influence the subjects' second scoring.) With this procedure, it was possible to measure differential recall and to measure changes in affect for pleasant and unpleasant experiences that were and were not recalled. The results indicated that unpleasant experiences showed greater declines in affective intensity than pleasant experiences and as a consequence were less likely to be recalled. These results indicate that reduced recall of unpleasant experiences is due to a reduced affective intensity associated with the unpleasant experiences rather than to repression. These results are presented schematically in figure 1.

One caveat concerning these results must be noted. This investigation did not indicate why there were greater declines in the affective intensity associated with unpleasant than pleasant experiences. It could be argued that the declines were due to repression of the unpleasant affect, thus reintroducing repression as an explanation. There are, however, two alternative (and I think better) explanations for the decline in intensity of unpleasant experiences. First, given the lapse of time between the occurrence and the recall of the experiences, a subject may discover that the experience did not result in the dire consequences that were expected (failing a test in French is not the end of the world), or a subject may take some remediative action that alters the nature of the experience (studying harder may improve future performance in French). The absence of dire consequences or the use of remediative action could serve to reduce the original negativity of the experience and in turn reduce the likelihood of its recall. The second explanation is based on the findings that subjects think more about intense experiences than neutral experiences (D'Zurilla 1965; Menzies 1936; Waters and Leeper 1936) and that repeated exposure results in more positive attitudes toward stimuli (Zajonc 1968). It then may be that the attention given to unpleasant experiences results in their becoming less unpleasant and therefore less intense.

It might also be noted that, if the decline in affect or reduction in recall of unpleasant experiences was due to repression, it would be expected that individual differences in personality would be associated with the changes in affect/recall (e.g., it would be expected that "hysterics" would be more likely to show the effect than "nonhysterics"). To test that possibility, I conducted a second investigation using the same procedures, but I collected a wide variety of measures of personality from the subjects (Holmes 1973b). The results of that investigation replicated the earlier findings in terms of declines in affect and recall but failed to reveal any relation between declines in affect or recall and personality. Overall, then, it appears that the differential recall of pleasant and unpleasant experiences cannot be used to support the concept of repression.

I have dealt with these findings in some detail not only because they are interesting and relevant in terms of the laboratory research but also because they appear to be particularly relevant to nonlaboratory instances of forgetting that are interpreted as being due to repression. If a client were unable to recall an unpleasant experience, and if with some prompting the experience was recalled but stripped of its original negative affect, it is likely that this would be interpreted as an instance of repression or at least denial. However, there is no evidence for that interpretation, and the behavior can be more easily and parsimoniously accounted for in terms of the normal differential decline of affect associated with pleasant and unpleasant experiences and the effects those declines have on recall. Because this line of research does not provide evidence for repression, we must go on to consider the results generated by another approach.

Differential Recall of Completed and Incompleted Tasks

A second approach of studying repression involved having subjects work on a series of tasks that were constructed so that some tasks could be completed and others could not. Later, the subjects were asked to recall the completed and incompleted tasks. If incompletions are interpreted by subjects as stressful failures, it would be expected that incompletions would be more likely to be repressed and therefore recalled less well than completions.

Paradoxically, this line of research originally was begun to test the

Gestalt notion that incompletions create "tension systems" and thus will be *more* likely to be recalled (Butterfield 1964; Lewin 1940; Prentice 1944). In the early tests of that prediction, it was generally found that subjects recalled more incompletions than completions, but there were notable exceptions. These exceptions were sometimes explained by suggesting that "embarrassment" over failure to complete a task led the subject to repress the recall of the task (Lewis and Franklin 1944; Zeigarnik 1927). Experimenters then seized on the complete/incompleted task procedure as a technique for manipulating stress and testing for repression, and there followed a long series of experiments (Eriksen 1952a, 1952b; Forest 1959; Gilmore 1954; Glixman 1948; Green 1963, Rosenzweig 1943; Rosenzweig and Mason 1934; Sanford and Risser 1948; Smock 1957; Tudor and Holmes 1973). When testing for repression, the completable and incompletable tasks were usually represented as parts of an intelligence test so as to heighten the stress associated with incompletions.

In the six most methodologically refined experiments in this group, subjects participated under conditions of high stress (tasks were presented as an intelligence test) and low stress (no importance was attached to the tasks). It was predicted that under high stress fewer incompletions than completions would be recalled (i.e., incompletions would be repressed because they were threatening) and that under low stress there would not be a difference in the recall of incompletions and completions. This was found to be the case in all six experiments, thus apparently providing considerable evidence for the existence of repression (Eriksen 1952a, 1952b; Gilmore 1954; Glixman 1948; Lewis and Franklin 1944; Smock 1957; Tudor and Holmes 1973).

There is, however, an alternative explanation for the findings. Specifically, the differences in the recall of completed and incompleted tasks may be due to differences in the degree to which the tasks were originally learned. In other words, in these experiments differential learning may have been misinterpreted as differential forgetting (repression). Fortunately, data are available that enable us to disentangle differential learning from differential forgetting.

In one experiment (Caron and Wallach 1957), subjects in a "continued stress" condition were exposed to the completed and incompleted tasks under stress (they were led to believe that the task was an intelligence test), and then they were tested for recall under stress, as had been done in most of the research. In contrast, subjects in a "relief" condition were exposed to the tasks under the stress, were then debriefed concerning the deception so that the stress was eliminated, and then were tested for recall. If recall were influenced by repression, subjects in the continued stress group should recall fewer incompletions than subjects in the relief group because the stress had not been eliminated in the continued stress group and therefore the subjects in that group would still have reason to repress. On the other hand, if recall were a function of original learning, no differences in the recall of incompletions would be expected between the groups because the conditions under which they had learned the materials were identical. The results indicated that the subjects in the continued stress and relief groups did not differ in recall, and the authors concluded that "recall tendencies in the present study are due to a *selective learning* rather than a selective remembering mechanism" (Caron and Wallach 1957, 378 emphasis added). Similar results were produced in my laboratory (Holmes 1973a). It appears that what originally looked like repression was in fact differential learning. Overall, then, the differential recall of completed and incompleted tasks has not provided evidence for the concept of repression, and therefore we must go on to consider the results of yet another approach to studying repression.

Changes in Recall Associated with the Introduction and Elimination of Stress: Repression and the Return of the Repressed

In the third approach to studying repression in the laboratory, not only did investigators seek to demonstrate repression following a stress, but they also attempted to demonstrate that the repressed material could be returned to consciousness when the stress was removed (the "return of the repressed"). Furthermore, the investigators introduced procedures that ensured that the material for which recall was to be tested was equally learned by both experimental and control subjects prior to the experimental manipulation of stress, thereby eliminating the problem found in the differential recall of completions and incompletions.

In these experiments, subjects in the experimental and control conditions were first tested for their ability to recall a set of neutral materials (nonsense syllables, words, etc.). This was done to make sure that all the subjects actually knew the materials for which recall would be tested later. The subjects in the stress condition were then exposed to a stress (e.g., failure, negative personality feedback). The stress was associated with the materials to be recalled (e.g., the materials were part of a test that the subject was led to fail, or the stress occurred in the same situation in which the materials had been presented) so that the previously neutral materials were then "painful" or anxiety provoking. The subjects in the control condition were not exposed to the stress. After the exper-

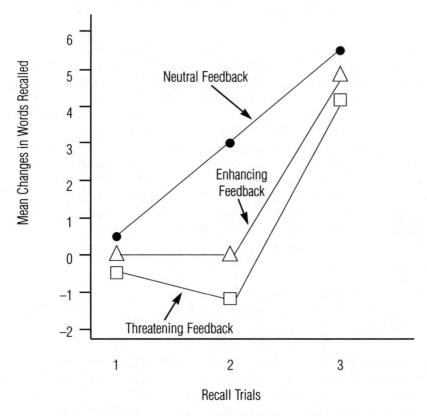

Fig. 2. Ego-enhancing personality feedback has the same deleterious effect on recall as does ego-threatening personality feedback, thus suggesting that declines in recall are due to interference rather than repression. (The differences between the "enhancing" and the "threatening" conditions in this figure are not statistically reliable.) When the deception is revealed and the interference is thereby eliminated, differences in recall among conditions are eliminated. Recall that trial 1 occurred before the stress/interference manipulation, trial 2 occurred after the stress/interference manipulation, and trial 3 occurred after the deception was revealed. (Figure adapted from Holmes 1970.)

imental manipulation of stress, the subjects were tested for recall. It was typically found that subjects in the stress condition recalled fewer of the previously neutral materials than subjects in the control condition, a finding that was interpreted as evidence for repression.

After stress had been manipulated and recall tested, the stress was eliminated so that the return of the repressed material could be tested. Stress was eliminated by exposing subjects to success (e.g., good performance on a test or positive personality feedback, depending on how stress had been induced), or the subjects were debriefed about the deception that was used to induce the stress. All the subjects were then tested again for their recall of the material. Typically, recall improved after the stress was eliminated ("return of the repressed"), and, consequently, there were no longer differences in recall between the stress and the control groups. This patterning of findings has been reported in numerous experiments, and in many cases it was concluded that the findings provided evidence for repression and the return of the repressed (Zeller 1950, experiments 1, 2; Zeller 1951; Merrill 1954; Flavell 1955; Holmes 1972; Holmes and Schallow 1969; Penn 1964; Aborn 1953; Truax 1957; D'Zurilla 1965). (Findings that are typical of this group of experiments are represented by the "neutral feedback" and "threatening feedback" conditions in fig. 2.)

These results were very impressive, and they were widely cited as evidence for repression. Unfortunately, however, there is a serious interpretative problem with this research. Although the performance of the subjects in these experiments is consistent with what would be expected on the basis of repression, most of these experiments did not offer evidence concerning the process that was responsible for the performance. It was assumed that the decrement in recall was due to repression, but it is also possible that the decrement in recall was due to the interfering effects of stress (Russell 1952; Truax 1957). As early as 1952, it was pointed out that "it is possible also that failure situations may produce a drive state (frustration, anxiety, or insecurity) which affects behavior in this case through the elicitation of *competing* responses" (Russell 1952, 214; emphasis added). Consistent with this possibility, post-experimental interviews revealed that subjects in the stress condition thought more about the stress to which they had been exposed than subjects in the control condition thought about the neutral experience to which they had been exposed (D'Zurilla 1965). This is exactly the opposite of what would be expected on the basis of repression and lends credence to the possibility that decrements in recall were due to stress-related interference rather than to repression.

To test the hypothesis that the decrements in recall following stress were due to interference rather than repression, I conducted two experiments in which subjects were exposed to either stressful, interfering, or neutral conditions (Holmes 1972; Holmes and Schallow 1969). In one experiment, the subjects first had their recall tested for a group of nouns. They then took a "multiple-choice Rorschach test" in which the words from the recall list were the response alternatives. During the test, the subjects in stress ("threatening feedback") condition received bogus feedback indicating that six of their ten responses were signs of serious pathology. Subjects in an interference ("enhancing feedback") condition received bogus feedback that their responses indicated that they were very creative and showed signs of leadership (i.e., something to think about that was not stressful). Finally, subjects in a control ("neutral feedback") condition received neutral personality feedback (Holmes 1972). After taking the bogus test, the subjects were again tested for their recall of the words. Finally, the subjects were debriefed concerning the deception, and their recall for the words was then tested again. The results indicated that, after the stress/interference manipulation, the subjects in the stress and interference conditions showed comparable levels of recall that were poorer than those of the subjects in the control condition. After being debriefed concerning the deception, the subjects in all the conditions showed comparable levels of recall. These results are presented in figure 2. From these results, it was concluded that decreased recall following stress was due to interference rather than to repression.

It could be argued that the comparable patterns of recall that were found in the stress and interference conditions were due to different processes. Specifically, it is possible that repression was operating in the stress condition and that interference was operating in the interference condition. It is impossible to demonstrate conclusively that identical processes were operating in the two conditions, but some data suggestive of that possibility are available (Holmes 1972). Specifically, if repression were operating, it would be expected that the decrement in recall would be greater for stimulus words that were directly associated with the stress (words used as responses that led to negative feedback) than for words that were not directly associated with the stress. That was not found to be the case; words that were not associated with the stress were just as likely to be forgotten as words that were associated with the stress. That effect could be accounted for better by interference than by repression. Once again, what originally appeared to be positive findings concerning repression were in fact due to another process, and therefore we must approach the study of repression in yet another way.

Individual Differences and the Search for Repression

Because there are numerous defense mechanisms (Holmes 1985a), it is not realistic to expect all individuals to use repression when exposed to stress. In some respects, that poses a problem for studying repression, but it also offers an opportunity because we can test for the existence of repression by comparing the recall patterns of individuals who are or are not expected to use repression. There are three lines of research in which this approach has been used. The most notable of these involves the use of the Repression-Sensitization Scale (R-S scale; Byrne, Barry, and Nelson 1963) to identify individuals who are expected to use repression. The R-S scale is made up of items from the Minnesota Multiphasic Personality Inventory (MMPI) that ask about the presence of symptoms. Individuals who do not acknowledge many symptoms are said to be "repressors," whereas individuals who acknowledge a high number of symptoms are said to be "sensitizers." This scale has been used in hundreds of studies of differential recall. Unfortunately, there is a very serious logical problem associated with the use of the R-S scale: there is no way to distinguish between individuals who actually have symptoms and do not report them ("repressors" or more likely deniers) and individuals who do not have symptoms and therefore cannot report them (nonrepressors). In other words, individuals without symptoms are falsely classified as repressors. Obviously, this scale cannot be used to support the notion that some individuals are more likely to use repression than others, and the use of the scale by researchers who did not consider the logic of the test has served only to add irrelevant data and erroneous conclusions to this body of literature.

The second line of research in which investigators attempted to link individual differences to the use of repression revolved around the complete/incomplete task recall paradigm (see the previous section). In this research, investigators examined the potential interaction between differential recall and personality factors such as ego strength, hysteria, hypnotizability, and need for achievement (Alper 1946, 1948, 1957; Atkinson 1953; Atkinson and Raphelson 1956; Caron and Wallach 1957, 1959; Coopersmith 1960; Eriksen 1954; Jourard 1954; Petrie 1948; Rosenzweig and Sarason 1942; Tamkin 1957; Tudor and Holmes 1973; Weiner 1965; Weiner, Johnson, and Mehrabian 1968). The only consistent finding in this line of research was that subjects with high need for achievement recalled more incompletions under high stress than low stress. It appears that, when subjects with high need for achievement were confronted with unsolvable problems in ego-involving situations, they persisted in working on or thinking about their failures rather than repressing them (Coopersmith 1960; Weiner 1965). Not only do these findings fail to provide support for the concept of repression, but they are the opposite to what would be predicted on the basis of repression.

The third line of research in this area was introduced by Schwartz, and it involves using measures of social desirability and anxiety (e.g., Davis and Schwartz 1987; Weinberger, Schwartz, and Davidson 1979; and see reviews by Davis and Weinberger). In these studies, subjects who had high scores on the Marlow-Crown Social Desirability Scale and low scores on the Taylor Manifest Anxiety Scale were identified as "repressors," and it was found that these subjects were less likely than other subjects to report stressful or unpleasant events. The problem is that individuals who are high on social desirability may be upset by and less willing to report undesirable events, but that does not mean that they are not aware of them. Indeed, the investigators reported that, although "repressors" did not report undesirable events, they showed higher physiological arousal than other subjects. If they had actually repressed the material and were unaware of it, they would not have been aroused. It is noteworthy that Schwartz and his colleagues were aware of the problem. In a footnote in one of their early articles, they wrote; "Although we propose retaining the term *repression* because of its use in the literature, the extent to which this defensive style is characterized by the use of repression relative to other defenses such as denial, negation and suppression is not currently known" (Weinberger, Schwartz, and Davidson 1979, 370). It is unfortunate that this important qualification concerning terminology was obscured in a footnote because many readers may have misinterpreted the evidence for denial as evidence for repression. Furthermore, Davis and Weinberger were aware of the problem I have raised before they wrote their reviews but unfortunately elected not to address the problem. Overall, then, this research provides interesting documentation concerning the use of denial, but it does not provide evidence for the existence of repression. Once again, we are left without evidence for repression.

Perceptual Defense

Thus far, this discussion has been focused on "repression proper" or "after expulsion," but, before concluding, some brief attention should be given to "primary repression."

Theoretically, with primary repression the stressful materials are relegated to the unconscious before the individual even becomes aware of their existence. In studying primary repression, investigators have generally sought to determine whether subjects were less likely to perceive stressful than nonstressful material (see the review in Eriksen and Pierce 1968). For example, stressful and nonstressful words were flashed on a screen for very short periods of time, and it was the subjects' task to read the words. In most of the early research, it was found that the stressful words had to be on the screen for longer periods of time than nonstressful words before the subjects were able to read them, and it was therefore concluded that the subjects were defending against (repressing) the recognition of the stressful words by simply not seeing them. Unfortunately, subsequent research indicated that the difference in the time required for recognition of the two types of words was due to factors other than repression. For example, it turned out that the stressful words were less familiar than the nonstressful words, and familiarity influences recognition. It was also found that subjects were less willing to say the stressful ("dirty") words until they were absolutely sure that it was those words that were being flashed and that hesitancy rather than lack of recognition influenced their reporting of words. When familiarity was equated across the two types of words, and when social constrains were eliminated from the situation, the perceptual defense or repression effect disappeared. About ten years ago, interest in perceptual defense was revived by Erdelyi, who proposed a variety of interesting cognitive theories to explain primary repression or perceptual defense (Erdelyi 1974; Erdelyi and Goldberg 1979). The problem is that, although Erdelyi offered explanations for the phenomenon, he did not provide controlled evidence that the phenomenon existed but instead relied on anecdotal clinical evidence. In other words, he offered an elegant and compelling explanation for a phenomenon that has not been demonstrated. Despite the lapse of over ten years, that situation has not changed, and therefore we are still without evidence supporting the existence of primary repression.

CONCLUSIONS

In conclusion, I want to make three points. First, I want to point out that, despite over sixty years of research involving numerous approaches by many thoughtful and clever investigators, at the present time there is no controlled laboratory evidence supporting the concept of repression. It is interesting to note that even most of the proponents of repression agree with that conclusion. However, they attempt to salvage the concept of repression by derogating the laboratory research, arguing that it is contrived, artificial, sterile, and irrelevant to the "dynamic processes" that occur in the "real world." That is an interesting argument, and I want to comment on it briefly before moving on.

With regard to its relevance, it is interesting to note that, when the laboratory research was initially published and appeared to provide support for repression, most theorists embraced the laboratory procedures as appropriate and cited the data as evidence for repression. Only when more refined research demonstrated that the data did not necessarily support repression did the advocates of repression turn their backs on the procedures. Note that the procedures had not changed, only the results. (It might be mentioned that Freud was a notable exception to the group that embraced the early laboratory demonstrations. When Rosenzweig wrote to him about his research on repression, Freud replied with disinterest, indicating that the concept did not need empirical support [see MacKinnon and Dukes 1964].)

Furthermore, by defining as irrelevant the many situations and stresses that have been employed in the laboratory investigations, the advocates of repression have severely limited the domain in which repression can supposedly operate. It is possible that we might someday find evidence for repression, but, because of the restrictions that have been imposed to protect the concept, it appears that the range of situations in which the concept can be applied will be so limited that it will be virtually useless.

After dismissing the laboratory research, the clinicians retreat to their consulting rooms for evidence for repression, but what evidence have they produced there? The "evidence" they offer consists only of impressionistic case studies, and, in view of the data concerning the reliability and validity of clinical judgments, those observations cannot be counted as anything more than unconfirmed clinical speculations—certainly not as "evidence" for repression. For a review of the reliability and validity of such clinical observations, I refer you to the excellent work of Mischel (1968). However, we need not go to that research because during this conference we had a dramatic demonstration of the unreliability of clinical judgments concerning repression when we watched the videotapes presented by Mardi J. Horowitz. The tapes were presented as a means of illustrating the use of repression by a client in therapy, but there was no agreement between the conferees concerning when, or even if, repression had occurred. Such unreliability is especially noteworthy in this group of individuals, who, by virtue of being invited to participate in this prestigious conference, must be defined as experts on repression. This is a serious blow to the clinical evidence.

It is important to note that my conclusion that there is no evidence for repression must not be interpreted as suggesting that repression does not exist because of course we cannot prove the null hypothesis. Those who choose to continue using the concept of repression may do so, but they must do so with the knowledge that, despite sixty years of research, there is no evidence for the concept. I think that our current regulations concerning "truth in packaging" and "protective product warnings" should be extended to the concept of repression. The use of the concept might be preceded by some such statement as, "Warning. The concept of repression has not been validated with experimental research and its use may be hazardous to the accurate interpretation of clinical behavior."

The second major point I wish to make is that, although there is no evidence for repression, it should not be concluded that there is not selectivity in perception and recall. Indeed, there is good evidence that transient and enduring factors such as cognitive sets, emotional states, and the availability of labels can influence what we perceive, store, and recall. The excellent work by Bower is clear testimony to the existence of such processes (Bower 1981). The important point here is that the processes underlying those effects are very different from the process of repression, and they lead to very different interpretations of the behavior.

It is important that we not misinterpret the evidence for those other processes as evidence for repression. The importance of making clear distinctions and discriminating between bodies of data is illustrated in the case of another defense mechanism, projection. For many years, evidence that individuals who were consciously aware of their traits and projected those traits onto others was mistakenly used as evidence for the projection of unconscious traits (see the reviews in Holmes 1968a, 1978, 1981a). The work of Schwartz and his colleagues has led to a parallel confusion in the area of repression (Davis and Schwartz 1987; Weinberger, Schwartz, and Davidson 1979). Their work on the influence of social desirability on recall and physiological responsiveness is fascinating and provides support for denial, but, as I pointed out earlier, it is not relevant to repression, and using it to support the concept of repression is erroneous and misleading.

In seeking evidence for repression, one could take the position of Humpty Dumpty, who pointed out, "When I use a word, it means just what I choose it to mean—neither more nor less" (Carroll 1960), and then simply define as "repression" the various processes that have been demonstrated to result in differential recall. That saves the term, but most of the important connotative features of the concept would have to be stripped away. It is better to keep the concept as it is but recognize that in its present form it is without empirical support.

Third, and finally, I would like to address briefly the question, Where do we go from here? It has been pointed out that in most cases "a theory is not overthrown by data but by a better theory" (Conant 1948). I agree, but I think that a distinction should be made between overthrowing a theory and abandoning a theory. We do not have another theory with which to overthrow repression, but despite numerous tests neither do we have data to support the theory, and therefore it might be appropriate to abandon the theory. From a practical standpoint, data provide the "bottom line." They are the test of the theory. If the data have been adequately collected but are inconsistent with what is predicted by the theory, then we must ask serious questions about the theory, elegant as it may be. The time has come to ask whether we should continue to pursue evidence for repression and whether we should now file the theory under "interesting but unsupported." The research on repression has been the preface to a larger area of research on factors that influence selective recall. From my perspective, the time has come to turn the page and begin focusing our attention and efforts on what may be more exciting and more productive lines of research related to information processing. One cannot prove the null hypothesis, and therefore we cannot conclude that repression does not exist, but, after sixty years of research has failed to reveal evidence for repression, it seems reasonable to question whether continued expenditure of effort on this topic is justified. Regardless of how fascinating the repression hypothesis is, the time may have come to move on. With regard to that possibility, a citation from Mischel is of interest. In his recent text, Mischel commented on Erdelyi's paper "Let's Not Sweep Repression under the Rug," which involves a defense of repression (Erdelyi and Goldberg 1979). However, Mischel "accidentally" cited the title as "Let's *Now* Sweep Repression under the Rug" (Mischel 1986, 534). That "Freudian slip" may very well have been prophetic. The time may very well have come for us to get repression behind us (or under the rug) so that we can move on.

REFERENCES

Aborn, M. 1953. The influence of experimentally induced failure on the retention of material acquired through set and incidental learning. *Journal of Experimental Psychology* 45: 225–31.

Alper, T. 1946. Memory for completed and incompleted tasks as a function of personality: An analysis of group data. *Journal of Abnormal and Social Psychology* 41: 403–20.

———. 1948. Memory for completed and incompleted tasks as a function of personality: Correlation between experimental and personality data. *Journal of Personality* 17: 104–37.

Alper, T. 1957. Predicting the direction of selective recall; its relation to ego strength and *N* achievement. *Journal of Abnormal and Social Psychology* 55: 149–65.

Atkinson, J. 1953. The achievement motive and recall of interrupted and completed tasks. *Journal of Experimental Psychology* 446: 381–90.

Atkinson, J., and A. Raphelson. 1956. Individual differences in motivation and behavior in particular situations. *Journal of Personality* 24: 349–63.

Bower, G. H. 1981. Mood and memory. *American Psychologist* 36: 129–48.

Butterfield. E. 1964. The interruption of tasks: Methodological, factual, and theoretical issues. *Psychological Bulletin* 62: 309–22.

Byrne, D., J. Barry, and D. Nelson. 1963. The revised repression-sensitization scale and its relationship to measures of self-description. *Psychological Reports* 13: 323–34.

Caron, A., and M. Wallach. 1957. Recall of interrupted tasks under stress: A phenomena of memory or learning? *Journal of Abnormal and Social Psychology* 55: 372–81.

———. 1959. Personality determinants of repressive and obsessive reactions to failure stress. *Journal of Abnormal and Social Psychology* 59: 236–45.

Carroll, L. 1960. *The annotated Alice: Alice's adventures in Wonderland and through the looking glass.* New York: Potter.

Conant, J. 1948. On understanding science: An historical approach. New Haven, Conn.: Yale University Press.

Coopersmith, S. 1960. Self-esteem and need achievement as determinants of selective recall and repetition. *Journal of Abnormal and Social Psychology* 60: 310–17.

Davis, P. J., and G. E. Schwartz. 1987. Repression and the inaccessibility of affective memories. *Journal of Personality and Social Psychology* 52: 155–62.

D'Zurilla, T. 1965. Recall efficiency and mediating cognitive events in "experimental repression." *Journal of Personality and Social Psychology* 3: 253–56.

Erdelyi, M. H. 1974. A new look at the new look: Perceptual defense and vigilance. *Psychological Review* 81: 1–25.

Erdelyi, M. H., and B. Goldberg. 1979. Let's not sweep repression under the rug: Toward a cognitive psychology of repression. In *Functional disorders of memory,* ed. J. F. Kihlstrom and F. J. Evans, 355–402. Hillsdale, N.J.: Erlbaum.

Eriksen, C. 1952a. Defense against ego threat in memory and perception. *Journal of Abnormal and Social Psychology* 47: 231–36.

———. 1952b. Individual differences in defensive forgetting. *Journal of Experimental Psychology* 44: 442–43.

———. 1954. Psychological defenses and "ego strength" in recall of completed and incompleted tasks. *Journal of Abnormal and Social Psychology* 49: 45–50.

Eriksen, C., and J. Pierce. 1968. Defense mechanisms. In *Handbook of personality theory and research,* ed. E. Borgatta and W. Lambert. Chicago: Rand McNally.

Flavell, J. 1955. Repression and the "return of the repressed." *Journal of Consulting Psychology* 19: 441–42.

Forest, D. 1959. The role of muscular tension in the recall of interrupted tasks. *Journal of Experimental Psychology* 58: 181–84.

Freud, S. [1915] 1957. Repression. In *The standard edition of the complete psychological works of Sigmund Freud,* vol. 14, ed. Jo Strachey. London: Hogarth.

Gilmore, J. 1954. Recall of success and failure as a function of subjects' threat interpretations. *Journal of Psychology* 38: 359–65.

Glixman, A. 1948. An analysis of the use of the interruption technique in experimental studies of repression. *Psychological Bulletin* 45: 491–506.

Green, D. 1963. Volunteering and the recall of interrupted tasks. *Journal of Abnormal and Social Psychology* 66: 392–401.

Holmes, D. S. 1968a. Dimensions of projection. *Psychological Bulletin* 69: 248–68.

———. 1968b. The search for closure in a visually perceived pattern. *Psychological Bulletin* 70: 296–312.

———. 1970. Differential change in affective intensity and the forgetting of unpleasant personal experiences. *Journal of Personality and Social Psychology* 15: 234–39.

———. 1972. Repression or interference: A further investigation. *Journal of Personality and Social Psychology* 22: 163–70.

———. 1973a. Differential recall of completed and incompleted tasks: Forgetting or learning. Psychology department, University of Kansas. Typescript.

———. 1973b. Differential recall of pleasant experiences and personality. Psychology department, University of Kansas. Typescript.

———. 1974. Investigations of repression: Differential recall of material experimentally or naturally associated with ego threat. *Psychological Bulletin* 81: 632–53.

———. 1978. Projection as a defense mechanism. *Psychological Bulletin* 85: 677–88.

———. 1981a. Existence of classical projection and the stress-reducing function of attributive projection: A reply to Sherwood. *Psychological Bulletin* 90: 460–66.

———. 1981b. The use of biofeedback for treating patients with migraine headaches, Raynaud's disease and hypertension: A critical evaluation. In *Medical psychology: A new perspective,* ed. L. Bradley and C. Prokop, 423–37. New York: Academic.

———. 1983. An alternative perspective concerning the differential physiological responsiveness of persons with Type A and Type B behavior patterns. *Journal of Research in Personality* 17: 40–47.

———. 1984. Meditation and somatic arousal reduction: A review of the experimental evidence. *American Psychologist* 39: 1–10.

———. 1985a. Defense mechanisms. In *Encyclopedia of psychology,* ed. R. J. Corsini, 347–50. New York: Wiley.

———. 1985b. Self-control of somatic arousal. An examination of meditation and biofeedback. *American Behavioral Scientist* 28: 486–96.

Holmes, D. S., and J. R. Schallow. Reduced recall after ego threat: Repression or response competition? *Journal of Personality and Social Psychology* 13: 145–52.

Jerslid, A. 1931. Memory for the pleasant as compared with the unpleasant. *Journal of Experimental Psychology* 14: 284–88.

Jourard, S. 1954. Ego strength and the recall of tasks. *Journal of Abnormal and Social Psychology* 49: 51–58.

Lewin, K. 1940. Formalization and progress in psychology: Studies in topological and vector psychology. *University of Iowa Studies, Studies in Child Welfare* 16: 9–44.

Lewis, H., and M. Franklin. 1944. An experimental study of the role of the ego in work. II. The significance of task-orientation in work. *Journal of Experimental Psychology* 34: 195–215.

MacKinnon, D., and W. Dukes. Repression. In *Psychology in the making,* ed. L. Postman. New York: Knopf.

Meltzer, H. 1931. Sex differences in forgetting pleasant and unpleasant experiences. *Journal of Abnormal Psychology* 25: 450–64.

Menzies, R. 1936. The comparative memory value of pleasant, unpleasant, and indifferent experiences. *Journal of Experimental Psychology* 18: 267–79.

Merrill, R. 1954. The effect of pre-experimental and experimental anxiety on recall efficiency. *Journal of Experimental Psychology* 48: 167–72.

Mischel. W. 1968. *Personality and assessment.* New York: Wiley.

———. 1986. *Introduction to personality,* 4th ed. New York: Holt, Rinehart and Winston.

Penn, N. 1964. Experimental improvements on an analogue of repression paradigm. *Psychological Record* 14: 185–96.

Petrie, A. 1948. Repression and suggestibility as related to temperament. *Journal of Personality* 16: 445–58.

Prentice, W. 1944. The interruption of tasks. *Psychological Review* 51: 329–40.

Rosenzweig, S. 1943. An experimental study of "repression" with special reference to need-persistive and ego-defensive reactions to frustration. *Journal of Experimental Psychology* 32: 64–74.

Rosenzweig, S., and G. Mason. 1934. An experimental study of memory in relation to the theory of repression. *British Journal of Psychology* 24: 247–65.

Rosenzweig, S., and S. Sarason. 1942. An experimental study of the triadic hypothesis: Reactions to frustration, ego-defense, and hypnotizability. I. Correlational approach. *Character and Personality* 11: 1–19.

Russell, W. 1952. Retention of verbal material as a function of motivating instructions and experimentally induced failure. *Journal of Experimental Psychology* 43: 207–16.

Sanford, R., and J. Risser. What are the conditions of self-defensive forgetting? *Journal of Personality* 17: 244–60.

Smock, C. 1957. Recall of interrupted or non-interrupted tasks as a function of experimentally induced anxiety and motivational relevance of the task stimuli. *Journal of Personality* 25: 589–99.

Stagner, R. 1931. The reintegration of pleasant and unpleasant experiences. *American Journal of Psychology* 43: 463–68.

Tamkin, A. 1957. Selective recall in schizophrenia and its relation to ego strength. *Journal of Abnormal and Social Psychology* 55: 345–49.

Truax, C. B. 1957. The repression response to implied failure as a function of the hysteria-psychasthenia index. *Journal of Abnormal and Social Psychology* 55: 188–93.

Tudor, T. G., and D. S. Holmes. Differential recall of successes and failures: Its relationship to defensiveness, achievement motivation, and anxiety. *Journal of Research in Personality* 7: 208–24.

Waters, R., and R. Leeper. 1936. The relation of affective tone to the retention of experiences in everyday life. *Journal of Experimental Psychology* 19: 203–15.

Weinberger, D. A., G. E. Schwartz, and R. J. Davidson. 1979. Low-anxious, high-anxious, and repressive coping styles: Psychometric patterns and behavioral and physiological responses to stress. *Journal of Abnormal Psychology* 88: 369–80.

Weiner, B. 1965. The effects of unsatisfied achievement motivation on persistence and subsequent performance. *Journal of Personality* 33: 428–42.

Weiner, B., P. Johnson, and A. Mehrabian. 1968. Achievement motivation and the recall of incompleted and completed examination questions. *Journal of Educational Psychology* 59: 181–85.

Zajonc, R. D. 1968. Attitudinal effects of mere exposure. *Journal of Personality and Social Psychology Monograph Supplement* 9: 2–27.

Zeigarnik, B. 1927. Uber das Behalten von erledigten und underledigten Handlungen. *Psychologische, Rorschung* 9: 1–85.

Zeller, A. 1950. An experimental analogue of repression. II. The effect of individual failure and success on memory measured by relearning. *Journal of Experimental Psychology* 40: 411–22.

Zeller, A. 1951. An experimental analogue of repression. III. The effect of induced failure and success on memory measured by recall. *Journal of Experimental Psychology* 42: 32–38.

7

CAN MEMORIES OF CHILDHOOD SEXUAL ABUSE BE REPRESSED?

HARRISON G. POPE JR. AND JAMES I. HUDSON

SYNOPSIS

We sought studies which have attempted to test whether memories of childhood sexual abuse can be repressed. Despite our broad search criteria, which excluded only unsystematic anecdotal reports, we found only four applicable studies. We then examined these studies to assess whether the investigators: (1) presented confirmatory evidence that abuse had actually occurred; and (2) demonstrated that their subjects had actually developed amnesia for the abuse. None of the four studies provided both clear confirmation of trauma and adequate documentation of amnesia in their subjects. Thus, present clinical evidence is insufficient to permit the conclusion that individuals can repress memories of childhood sexual abuse. This finding is surprising, since many writers have implied that hundreds of thousands, or even millions of persons harbor such repressed memories. In view of the widespread recent public and scientific interest in the areas of trauma and memory, it is important to investigate further whether memories of sexual abuse can be repressed.

From *Psychological Medicine* 25 (1995): 121–26. Copyright © 1995 Cambridge University Press. Reprinted with the permission of Cambridge University Press.

INTRODUCTION

Is it possible for victims of childhood sexual abuse to "repress" their memories? Many recent writers, both popular and scientific, have suggested that repression is common (Bass and Davis 1988; Blume 1990; Fredrickson 1992; Herman 1992). On the other hand, experimental evidence for the existence of repression is less convincing. In an extensive review, Holmes (1990) argues that laboratory studies have failed to produce clear evidence for repression, despite more than 60 years of attempts to do so.

Of course, even if repression cannot be induced in the laboratory, it might still occur in real life, such as in victims of childhood sexual abuse. And even if repression occurred in only a fraction of such victims, one would still expect to see many cases clinically, since childhood sexual abuse is common (Nash and West 1985; Wyatt 1985; Russell 1986: Bagley and Ramsay 1986; Finkelhor et al. 1990; Anderson et al. 1993). Specifically, using the conservative estimate that 10% of women and 5% of men have endured serious childhood sexual abuse, then 14,000,000 adults in the United States alone are former victims. If repression occurred in only 10% of these cases, at least 1,400,000 Americans, and millions more worldwide, now harbor such repressed memories. Given this huge pool of predicted cases, one might expect to find in the literature various published studies of patients exhibiting well-documented cases of repression.

In this paper we review this literature. We first discuss the criteria necessary for a satisfactory confirmation of the hypothesis that repression can occur, and then we examine the relevant studies.

CRITERIA FOR AN ACCEPTABLE STUDY

Evidence That the Traumatic Events Occurred

To demonstrate repression, one must first confirm that the traumatic events actually occurred. In many studies of trauma, such documentation is straightforward, because the events are a matter of historical record. Examples include a 4-year follow-up of 26 children kidnapped on a school bus (Terr 1979, 1983); a study of 16 children who witnessed a parent murdered (Malmquist 1986); an investigation of 113 elementary school children involved in a sniper's attack (Pynoos and Nader 1989); a 4-year follow-up of 34 survivors of a marine explosion (Leopold and Dillon 1963); an examination of 100 concentration camp survivors 12-20 years afterwards (Strom et al. 1962); and a follow-up of 23 victims of Nazi persecution, half of whom were age 19 or less at the onset of trauma (Chodoff 1963). Interestingly, although many of the subjects in these studies exhibited severe post-traumatic psychopathology, it appears that no subject in any of these studies developed amnesia. Indeed, many recalled the events in extraordinary detail.

Of course, sexual abuse is more difficult to document than kidnappings, murders, or war crimes. But there are various types of documentation that most investigators would accept: contemporaneous medical evidence of the abuse; photographs; reports from reliable and unbiased witnesses; or conformation by the perpetrator himself (or herself). Admittedly, many cases of alleged childhood sexual abuse can be neither definitely confirmed nor refuted, but given the large number of expected cases, there should still remain an adequate number sufficiently well-documented for study.

Evidence for "Psychogenic" Amnesia

The second requirement for a satisfactory test of repression is to demonstrate that the victim actually developed "psychogenic" amnesia for the trauma. To demonstrate amnesia, one must first exclude cases in which victims simply tried not to think about the events, pretended that the events never occurred, or appeared to derive secondary gain by merely claiming to have amnesia (i.e., to avoid embarrassment or to extend a legal statute of limitations).

Secondly, one must show that the failure of memory exceeds ordinary forgetfulness. Some experiences, though clearly meeting published research criteria for sexual abuse, may not be particularly memorable to a child (for examples, see Pope et al. 1994). Thus, a satisfactory test of the repression hypothesis must demonstrate amnesia for abuse sufficiently traumatic that no one would reasonably be expected to forget it.

Thirdly, to demonstrate "psychogenic" amnesia, one must exclude cases in which amnesia developed for some biological reason, such as seizures, alcohol and drug intoxication, or head trauma. This last factor figures strongly in war neuroses: in one study of 200 cases, 50% of the soldiers had lost consciousness and another 22% were "dazed" on the battlefield (Henderson and Moore 1944). A further biological source of amnesia is the immaturity of the developing central nervous system in young children. Children have nearly complete amnesia for events before the age of three, and substantial amnesia for events before the age of six (Fivush and Hudson 1990; Usher and Neisser 1993). Of course, it might be argued that some sexual abuse would be so traumatic that it ought to be remembered even by a child aged five or younger. But again, given the high predicted prevalence of repression, one should expect to find ample numbers of cases without having to rely on under-age-six examples.

Provided that the above exclusion criteria are met, the postulated mechanism of the amnesia—whether it be called "repression," "dissociation," or "traumatic amnesia"—is unimportant. It is sufficient that a study should simply exhibit individuals with complete amnesia for well-documented abuse that was too striking to be normally forgettable.

REVIEW OF THE EVIDENCE

In an attempt to find methodologically sound evidence for repression of memories of childhood sexual abuse, we searched the literature for studies that had examined this phenomenon in a series of patients. We included all reports that presented a group of patients analyzed in any quantitative manner; only unsystematic anecdotal reports were excluded. Despite this broad search, we found only four applicable studies in the literature (Herman and Schatzow 1987; Briere and Conte 1993; Loftus et al. 1994; Williams 1994). We review these studies below, using the criteria developed above.

The Herman and Schatzow Study

In the first attempt to document repression of memories of childhood sexual abuse, Herman and Schatzow (1987) reported on 53 women who they treated in time-limited group therapy for "incest survivors." The authors do not specify whether subjects were selected prospectively or retrospectively; it is also not clear whether they represented consecutive individuals or a chosen subsample.

Among the 53 patients, 14 (26%) were rated as having "severe" amnesia for the presumed incest, and might, therefore, represent examples of true repression. However, since the mean age of onset (± S.D.) of abuse in this group is reported as 4.9±2.4 years, abuse in some of these women apparently occurred during the period of normal childhood amnesia at age five or earlier. Thus, only a subset of the 14 women in the sample would meet the criterion of displaying full amnesia for events occurring at ages older than five.

But this subset shrinks further, or perhaps vanishes entirely, when we apply the second criterion: namely, the requirement that the abuse be confirmed. Only 21 (40%) of the 53 patients obtained "corroborating evidence" of the incest, and it is not clear whether these 21 cases include any of the women with "severe" amnesia described in the paragraph above. Admittedly, another 18 (34%) of the 53 patients were reported to have "discovered that another child, usually a sibling, had been abused by the same perpetrator." But the evidence that supported these latter discoveries is not specified, neither does it follow that abuse of a sibling, even if true, confirms abuse in the index case.

In short, it is not certain that any of the 3 subjects met both the criteria of clear amnesia and clear confirmation of trauma. Indeed, of the four case examples given, three do not meet the criteria (1 and 2 did not have amnesia, and 4 had virtually no confirmation). Case 3 apparently had at least partial amnesia, and good confirmatory evidence. But even this case, it appears, is not actually a real person, since the authors explain that "all examples cited are composites of several cases."

Parenthetically, it is curious that Herman (1981) hardly mentions repression or amnesia in her study, *Father-Daughter Incest*, published only 6 years earlier. In this book, all of the 40 women in the case series displayed apparently clear and lasting memories of their abuse.

The Briere and Conte Study

In the second study, Briere and Conte (1993) analyzed questionnaire responses of 450 patients "with self-reported histories of sexual abuse and who were currently in therapy." The questionnaire contained a single question regarding amnesia for sexual abuse: "During the period of time between when the first forced sexual experience happened and your eighteenth birthday was there ever a time when you could not remember the forced sexual experience?" A total of 267 (59%) of the 450 subjects answered "yes."

This result is open to several methodological questions. Subjects were "recruited by their therapists"; further details of the inclusion or exclusion criteria are not provided. It is not clear whether the abuse events were confirmed in any of the cases. Neither is it clear what portion of the subjects had experienced abuse sufficiently traumatic that they would reasonably be expected to remember it always. And, most importantly, a "yes" answer on this single question does not demonstrate clear repression of a traumatic memory. A subject answering "yes" might mean only that he or she gave no thought to the event during some period, or attempted to deny or minimize the event. No follow-up questions were asked to assess these possibilities.

Finally, some subjects may have been influenced by suggestion. All were in treatment with therapists who were part of an "informal sexual abuse treatment referral network," and who, therefore, may have communicated to their patients, explicitly or implicitly, that repression of traumatic experiences was to be expected. With this potential degree of expectation, and with therapists choosing which subjects would receive the questionnaire, it would not be surprising if many subjects answered "yes" to a question that asked if there was *ever* a time when they could not remember an abuse experience.

The Loftus, Polonsky, and Fullilove Study

Similar limitations affect the recent study of Loftus et al. (1994). In a design comparable to that of the Briere and Conte study, these authors interviewed 52 women with a history of abuse and asked whether they had forgotten the abuse "for a period of time and only later [had] the memory return." In contrast to the 59% rate found by Briere and Conte, only 10 (19%) of these 52 subjects reported a period of forgetfulness.

However, even the much lower 19% figure is subject to the same methodological questions as the previous study: none of the cases of abuse was independently confirmed, neither was the extent or nature of the "forgetfulness" investigated. In other words, the evidence does not show that any of the 10 women displayed lasting amnesia for documented events that would normally be expected to be unforgettable.

The Williams Study

In the most recent study, Williams (1994) has reported an investigation with a more rigorous design. She presents data from interviews of 129 women who, as children, had been brought to a city hospital emergency department in 1973–1975 for treatment and collection of forensic evidence after reported sexual abuse, even if no physical trauma occurred. The abuse was thus documented in medical records and interviews with research staff conducted at the time. The author notes that not all cases were extreme: about a third involved only touching and fondling (Williams 1992).

The women were aged 10 months to 12 years at the time of the abuse. They were contacted and interviewed approximately 17 years later, at age 18 to 31. They were told that their names had been "selected from the records of people who went to the city hospital in 1973–1975" for an "important follow-up study of the lives and health of women who during childhood received medical care at the city hospital." The interviewers asked detailed questions about each woman's history of sexual abuse, including questions about events that the patient herself perhaps did not define as abuse but which others had. The women were also asked if anyone in their families "ever got in trouble for his/her sexual activities." However, it appears that if the subjects still failed to report the known episode of abuse after these questions, they were not asked directly about their documented visit to the hospital to see whether they then acknowledged remembering it.

Forty-nine (38%) of the 129 women did not report the abuse event to the interviewer, and Williams speculates that most of these cases represent actual amnesia, rather than voluntary withholding of information. She supports this view by pointing out that many women gave detailed descriptions of other personal or embarrassing childhood events, including other experiences of sexual abuse, while still not acknowledging the index episode.

But it is hazardous to conclude that Williams's 49 "non-reporters" actually had amnesia. In considering this question, it is instructive to examine a similarly designed study by Femina and colleagues (1990). These investigators interviewed 69 young adults (mean age, 24 years) whose histories of abuse (primarily physical abuse) had been extensively documented years earlier during adolescence. On interview, 26 of the 69 subjects (also a proportion of 38%) gave responses discrepant with their previously documented histories. In particular, 18 of these 26 individuals were known to have been severely abused in childhood, yet they denied or minimized any experiences of abuse on interview as young adults.

Femina and colleagues then performed a second interview (which they called a "clarification interview") with eight of these 18 "deniers." When asked directly about their known abuse histories, it appears that all eight individuals admitted that they actually remembered, but had withheld the information during their first interview. For example, one woman, "whose mother had attempted to drown her in childhood and whose stepfather had sexually abused her, minimized any abuse at all on follow-up." But in the clarification interview, when presented with this history, she admitted, "I didn't say it cuz I wanted to forget. I wanted it to be private. I only cry when I think about it." Similarly, one man, who as a boy was frequently beaten by his father, also minimized any history of abuse on the first interview. When presented with the history in the clarification interview, he acknowledged the beatings but said, "My father is doing well now. If I told now, I think he would kill himself."

On the basis of these clarification interviews, Femina and colleagues list reasons for nonreporting of abuse as "embarrassment, a wish to protect parents, a sense of having deserved the abuse, a conscious wish to forget the past, and a lack of rapport with the interviewer." However, no case of non-reporting was ascribed to amnesia. Given this observation, it would be unwarranted to conclude that the 49 nonreporting subjects in

Williams's study actually had amnesia, since no clarification interviews were performed.

Indeed, the underreporting of life events on interview has been recognized and studied for several decades. For example, a study by the United States National Center for Health Statistics (1961) found that 28% of respondents when interviewed in detail by trained workers failed to report a one-day hospitalization that they were known to have undergone during the past year. Similar investigations have found that about 30% of individuals known to have been involved in an automobile accident (without recorded injury) did not report it on detailed interview 9-12 months later (National Center for Health Statistics 1972); 35% of another cohort did not report a visit that they had made to a doctor within the past 2 weeks (National Center for Health Statistics 1965); and 54% did not report a hospital admission that they had undergone 10-11 months prior to the date of interview (National Center for Health Statistics 1965). In light of these figures, it does not seem necessary to posit repression to explain Williams's 38% rate of non-reporting for events occurring 17 years earlier.

Williams's results may also reflect normal childhood amnesia: 25 (51%) of her 49 non-reporting subjects had experienced their index episode of abuse at age six or earlier. Indeed, the only case presented in detail in the paper is of a woman whose abuse (of unspecified severity) occurred at age four. And even among individuals who were older at the time of abuse, one must allow for ordinary forgetfulness for events not perceived as strikingly memorable, especially among the one-third of subjects who experienced only touching and fondling. Thus, Williams's 38% rate of non-reporting might be readily explained as a combination of cases of early childhood amnesia, cases of ordinary forgetfulness, and perhaps many cases of failure to report information actually remembered. Additional discussions of methodology of Williams's study, and some of the other studies analyzed above, may be found in other recent works (Loftus 1993; Ofshe and Singer 1994).

DESIGN OF FUTURE STUDIES

Williams's study provides a useful starting point for the design of a rigorous test of the repression hypothesis. First, one must seek a group of individuals unequivocally documented to have been traumatized, sexually or otherwise. For example, one might begin with a group of medical records, as Williams did, or one could trace all victims identified by a confessed perpetrator or a reliable witness. Opportunities of the latter type are uncommon, but may arise periodically in forensic settings. Secondly, one would select all individuals who were above the age of five at the time of abuse, and who were definitely known to have endured abuse too traumatic to be normally forgettable. Thirdly, one would locate and interview these individuals—with suitable ethical and therapeutic precautions—with regard to any past history of trauma. Fourthly, subjects who still denied abuse on this general interview would then receive a "clarification interview" in which they were asked directly about the known abuse event. If some subjects still reported amnesia even in response to the direct questions, this finding would suggest repression.

If one adhered to all aspects of this technique, a study with even a modest number of subjects might provide a useful test of the hypothesis that repression can occur. Indeed, even a series of several case reports, provided that they strictly met the criteria outlined above, could represent persuasive preliminary evidence for the existence, though not for the frequency, of repression.

CONCLUSION

Laboratory studies over the past 60 years have failed to demonstrate that individuals can "repress" memories. Clinical studies, which extrapolate from the laboratory to the study of real-life traumas, must consequently start with the null hypothesis: that repression does not occur.

To reject the null hypothesis, and show that repression of childhood abuse memories can occur clinically, one must meet two requirements. First, one must confirm that traumatic abuse actually occurred. Secondly, one must demonstrate that individuals actually developed amnesia, of non-biological origin (and after the age of five), for this abuse. We performed a literature search for studies that have attempted to document repression of memories of childhood sexual abuse. Despite our broad search criteria, which excluded only unsystematic case reports, we located only four such studies, which we then examined on the basis of the above two criteria. None of the four studies presents data that satisfy both of the two requirements.

It must be emphasized that these four studies are the only applicable studies that we were able to locate. In other words, this brief review does not present merely a selection of the most important studies, but the entirety of all published studies, which to our knowledge have systematically tested whether repression of memories of childhood sexual abuse can occur.

It might be argued that this dearth of studies is due to the difficulty of documenting trauma and demonstrating amnesia. But if repression affects even a small fraction of abused individuals, one would expect hundreds of thousands, if not millions, of current cases in the United States alone, and even larger numbers worldwide. Thus, the difficulties of documenting repression should be more than counterbalanced by the large pool of cases.

In summary, present evidence is insufficient to permit the conclusion that individuals can "repress" memories of childhood sexual abuse. This finding is surprising, since many writers have suggested that there is a high prevalence of repression in the population. Thus, this area of psychiatry begs further carefully designed studies to resolve one of its most critical questions.

REFERENCES

Anderson, J., J. Martin, P. Mullen, S. Romans, and P. Herbison. 1993. Prevalence of childhood sexual experiences in a community sample of women. *Journal of the American Academy of Child and Adolescent Psychiatry* 32: 911–19.

Bagley, C., and R. Ramsay. 1986. Sexual abuse in childhood: psychosocial outcomes and implications for social work practice. *Journal of Social Work and Human Sexuality* 4: 33–47.

Bass, E., and L. Davis. 1988. *The courage to heal*. New York: Harper & Row.

Blume, E. S. 1990. *Secret survivors*. New York: John Wiley and Sons.

Briere, J. and J. Conte. 1993. Self-reported amnesia for abuse in adults molested as children. *Journal of Traumatic Stress* 6: 21–31.

Chodoff, P. 1963. Late effects of the concentration camp syndrome. *Archives of General Psychiatry* 8: 323–33.

Femina, D. D., C. A. Yeager, and D. O. Lewis. 1990. Child abuse: adolescent records vs. adult recall. *Child Abuse and Neglect* 145: 227–31.

Finkelhor, D. 1980. Risk factors in the sexual victimization of children. *Child Abuse and Neglect* 4: 265–73.

Finkelhor, D., G. Hotaling, I. A. Lewis, and C. Smith. 1990. Sexual abuse in a national survey of adult men and women: prevalence, characteristics, and risk factors. *Child Abuse and Neglect* 14: 19–28.

Fivush, R. and J. A. Hudson, eds. 1990. *Knowing and remembering in young children*. New York: Cambridge University Press.

Fredrickson, R. 1992. *Repressed memories: A journey to recovery from sexual abuse*. New York: Simon and Schuster.

Henderson, J. L., and M. M. Moore. 1944. The psychoneuroses of war. *New England Journal of Medicine* 210: 273–78.

Herman, J. L. 1981. *Father-daughter incest*. Cambridge, Mass.: Harvard University Press.

Herman, J. L. 1992. *Trauma and recovery.* New York: Basic Books.

Herman, J. L., and E. Schatzow. 1987. Recovery and verification of memories of childhood sexual trauma. *Psychoanalytic Psychology* 4: 1–14.

Holmes, D. 1990. The evidence for repression: an examination of sixty years of research. In *Repression and dissociation: Implications for personality, theory, psychopathology, and health,* ed. J. Singer, 85–102. Chicago: University of Chicago Press.

Leopold, R. L., and H. Dillon. 1963. Psycho-anatomy of a disaster: a long term study of post-traumatic neuroses in survivors of a marine explosion. *American Journal of Psychiatry* 119: 913–21.

Loftus, E. F. 1993. The reality of repressed memory. *American Psychologist* 48: 518–7.

Loftus, E. F., S. Polonsky, and M. T. Fullilove. 1994. Memories of childhood sexual abuse: Remembering and repressing. *Psychology of Women Quarterly* 18: 67–84.

Malmquist, C. P. 1986. Children who witness parental murder: post-traumatic aspects. *Journal of the American Academy of Child Psychiatry* 25: 320–25.

Nash, C. L., and D. J. West. 1985. Sexual molestation of young girls: a retrospective study. In *Sexual victimization,* ed. D. J. West. Gower Aldershot.

National Center for Health Statistics. May 1961. Reporting of hospitalization in the Health Interview Survey: a methodological study of several factors affecting the reporting of hospital episodes. U.S. Dept. of Public Health, Education, and Welfare. Publication No. 584–D4: Washington.

———. July 1965: Health interview responses compared with medical records. Vital and Health Statistics. PHS Pub. No. 1000-Series 2-No. 7. Public Health Service. Washington: U.S. Government Printing Office: Washington.

———. April 1972. Optimum recall period for reporting persons injured in motor vehicle accidents. Vital and Health Statistics. Series 2-No. 50. DHEW Publ. No. (HSM) 72-1050. Health Services and Mental Health Administration. U.S. Government Printing Office: Washington.

Ofshe, R. J., and M. T. Singer. 1994. Recovered-memory therapy and robust repression: influence and pseudomemories. *International Journal of Clinical and Experimental Hypnosis* 42: 391–410.

Pope, H. G., Jr., B. Mangweth, A. B. Negrao, J. I. Hudson, and T. A. Cordas. In press. Childhood sexual abuse and bulimia nervosa: a comparison of American, Austrian, and Brazilian Women. *American Journal of Psychiatry.*

Pynoos, R. S., and K. Nader. 1989. Children's memory and proximity to violence. *Journal of the American Academy of Child Psychiatry* 28: 236–41.

Russell, D. E. H. 1986. *The secret trauma: Incest in the lives of girls and women.* New York: Basic Books.

Strom, A., S. B. Refsum, L. Eitinger, O. Gronvik, A. Lonnum, A. Engeset, K. Osvik, and B. Rogan. 1962. Examination of Norwegian ex-concentration camp prisoners. *Journal of Neuropsychiatry* 4: 43–62.

Terr, L. C. 1979. Children of Chowchilla. *Psychoanalytic Study of the Child* 34: 547–623.

Terr, L. C. 1983. Chowchilla revisited: the effects of psychic trauma four years after a school-bus kidnapping. *American Journal of Psychiatry* 140: 1543–50.

Usher, J. A., and V. Neisser. 1993. Childhood amnesia and the beginnings of memory for four early life events. *Journal of Experimental Psychology* 112: 155–65.

Williams, L. M. 1992. Adult memories of child sexual abuse: preliminary findings from a longitudinal study. *American Society for Prevention of Child Abuse Advisor* 5: 19–20.

———. (in press). Recall of childhood trauma. A prospective study of women's memories of child sexual abuse. *Journal of Consulting and Clinical Psychology.*

Wyatt, G. (1985). The sexual abuse of Afro-American and white American women in childhood. *Child Abuse and Neglect* 9: 507–19.

8

FORGETTING SEXUAL TRAUMA:
WHAT DOES IT MEAN WHEN 38% FORGET?

ELIZABETH F. LOFTUS, MARYANNE GARRY, AND JULIE FELDMAN

L. M. Williams (1994) has shown that many women who were sexually abused as children do not report the abuse when questioned two decades later. These findings do not support certain freely made claims about memory, but they do support other claims. The findings do not provide cogent support for the claim that a long stream of childhood sexual traumas is routinely banished from conscious awareness and then can be reliably recovered later. The findings do support the claim that many children can forget about a sexually abusive experience from their past. Extreme claims such as "if you were raped, you'd remember" are disproven by these findings.

Dale Akiki, a former Sunday school teacher, was accused in 1991 of sexually abusing, terrorizing, and kidnapping children in his care at Faith Chapel, a church near San Diego, California. Although the case lacked corroboration, the prosecution claimed that many victims had repressed their memories of these horrible incidents and recovered them in therapy. Akiki was acquitted of all charges in November 1993 after spending several years in jail (Sauer 1993). The trial lasted more than six months, but there was one short minute of testimony that captured the essence of a fundamental conflict between science and at least one testifying therapist in the case: Is therapy grounded in science?

From the *Journal of Consulting and Clinical Psychology* 62, no. 6 (1994): 1177–81.

One of Akiki's defense attorneys asked the therapist if a diagnosis in therapy needed to be based on research-verified science:

A: That's a different type of science . . . I think there's . . . there are different types of science. There's research science and . . .

Q: What type of science do you practice?

A: Artful science.

Q: O.K. So you're saying it's an art, it's not a science?

A: A little of both . . . I think there's a lot of counseling theory that has not necessarily been proven in scientific research.

The theory behind counseling, or all of psychotherapy for that matter, is best served if grounded in science. Williams's prospective study is an important empirical contribution to the much needed area of memory for childhood trauma. Ultimately, studies like this one will assist mental health professionals in doing as good a job with clients as they possibly can. It is important not only that the study be well done (which it is) but also that it not be misinterpreted (which, unfortunately, it already has been). This commentary focuses primarily on proper and improper ways to think about these novel findings.

WILLIAMS'S PRELIMINARY REPORT

Several years ago, Williams (1992) published a preliminary report of the study that is now reported more fully here. In the preliminary report, Williams told readers that she followed up 200 women who reported sexual abuse in the early 1970s. Her data were based on interviews with 100 of those women, primarily African Americans. All had, some 17 years earlier, been girls aged 10 months to 12 years old when they were brought to a city hospital emergency department for treatment and collection of forensic evidence after a sexual assault, even when there was no physical trauma present. The sexual abuse ranged from sexual intercourse (in about one-third of the cases) to fondling (also about one-third of the cases). The results showed that 38% did not recall the abuse or chose not to report it.

For several years before formal publication, the preliminary report found its way into the hands and minds of mental health professionals and journalists. Thus, here is a unique opportunity to observe how the study was being cited, and miscited, before it even formally appeared.

CITINGS OF THE WILLIAMS RESEARCH

Williams (1992) herself was fairly careful in her discussion of her own research. She summed it up this way: ". . . a large proportion of women do not recall childhood sexual victimization experiences" (21). Some characterizations of the findings have been reasonably careful as well. For example, Henderson (1993, p. 43) put it simply as follows: ". . . among childhood sexual abuse survivors whose abuse had been reported when it happened, 38% claimed no memory of it when questioned 17 years later."

Other writers have misstated the findings in small or even large ways, or they have drawn speculative or even unwarranted inferences. For example, one writer claimed that Williams found that "thirty-eight percent of this sample reported that they had not been abused, in spite of hospital records to the contrary" (Wylie 1993, 42–43). In fact, 38% did not say that had not been abused at all; rather, the majority of these women told about other abuse that they had experienced. Another writer claimed that Williams's study "supports Putnam's theory that traumatic events can be stored in the brain in a way that doesn't conform to the standard model of memory" (Wartik 1993, 65). In fact, the study says nothing about how traumatic events are stored in the brain differently from standard models of memory. Another scholar claimed that Williams, in her interviews 17 years after the abuse event, had found that "36% had no memory for that event including some of the people who were . . . 15, 16, 17 years of age" (Pezdek 1993). In fact, Williams's follow-up study only involved women who were ranged in age from 10 months to 12 years at the time of their abuse.

Other writers have claimed that the study supports "repression". One article called the study "one of the most systematic efforts to track memory repression" (Kandel and Kandel 1994, 34). Another used it as support for the claim that many "sexual-abuse victims repress memories for a period of time" (Horn 1993, 56). A third went even further: "This was repression or some other extreme 'forgetting' defense in action" (Terr 1994, 53). Although the study is often used to support the idea that repression of sex abuse memories is common, we argue later in this article that the findings actually do not constitute cogent support for anything like a repression mechanism of the sort originally speculated about by Freud.

THE REAL WILLIAMS STUDY

The analyses are based on interviews with 129 women who, as girls, reported sexual assault and were examined at the emergency room of a large urban general hospital in the early 1970s (McCahill, Meyer, and Fischman 1979). About 17 years later, when these women were interviewed, 38% failed to report the "index incident" that took them to the emergency room.[1]

WHAT THE DATA MEAN

Williams claims that it is "quite dramatic" that 38% of the women did not tell the interviewer about the child sexual abuse. However, for full appreciation of the drama of forgetting, it must be kept in mind that people can forget all kinds of things that might, at first thought, seem surprising. For example, people (over one quarter of those interviewed) have failed to recall automobile accidents 9 to 12 months after their occurrence, although someone else in the car had been injured (Cash and Moss 1972; see also Loftus 1982). People (over 20%) who, when they were 4 years old had a family member die have failed to recall a single detail about the death (Usher and Neisser 1993). People (over 15%) have failed to recall a hospitalization approximately 9 months after discharge (National Center for Health Statistics 1965; see also Loftus 1982). Patients have failed to recall visits to a health maintenance organization (HMO) that they made within the previous year for something that was serious or even very serious (Means and Loftus 1991). In light of figures such as these, it does not seem quite so dramatic that people might also fail to recall a sexual trauma that occurred to them 17 years earlier.

Do the Data Mean That the Women Have Completely Repressed Their Memories of Abuse?

When women do not recall an abusive incident from nearly 2 decades earlier, does this mean that they repressed their memories? Not necessarily; in establishing repression, it is necessary to show first that a memory existed in the first place. Perhaps some of the younger children who were examined, interviewed, or treated for sexual assault did not understand the meaning of their experience. It would be reasonable to assume that a parent might try to keep this knowledge from a young child to facilitate treatment or minimize damage to the child. If so, then some of these children never "knew" that they were traumatized and thus had nothing to repress. This is not simply speculation, as known cases exist of abused children who are interviewed by a psychotherapist but have no idea why they are being interviewed or are otherwise completely in the dark about the nature of their problem (Wagenaar, personal communication, March 28, 1994). It is important to remember that Williams herself reports that many of the girls did not allege assault themselves but were reported by others to have been assaulted.

Even if the event were understood and stored in memory, there are many reasons why it might not be recalled later on. Normal forgetting of all sorts of events is a fact of life, but is not thought to involve some special repression mechanism. Forgetting of all sorts of events happens, even significant events, even traumatic ones like hospitalizations, accidents, and deaths, but is not thought to involve a repression mechanism.

Others have opted to describe these data without using the term *repression*. Perhaps they do so because the meaning of repression depends on who is using it. Freud's use of the term evolved through several meanings, none of which were very well defined. What are some alternatives to the term "repression"? Herman and Harvey (1993) use the term *amnesia*. They describe the Williams (1992) study in the context of amnesia, referring to it immediately after this sentence: "Partial or even complete amnesia for childhood trauma is well documented" (p. 5).

One could, of course, say that the women whom Williams studied constitute cases of complete amnesia. Williams herself told a *Science News* reporter "I don't know exactly what psychological process causes the amnesia" (Bower 1993, 185). This would mean, however, that when we forget anything, it is an example of complete amnesia for that thing. It dilutes the meaning of the term "amnesia," which has often been reserved for discussing a pathological sort of forgetting. It is rather similar to using the word "assassination" to describe the squashing of a bug. Given the new broad-ranging definition of amnesia, how would we describe what happens to the person who goes into the supermarket specifically to get aspirin and leaves 10 minutes later with a Snickers bar, a magazine, a box of PopTarts, and no aspirin? Is this amnesia, or is it simply a case of forgetting? Amid all the arguing and rhetoric about real and suggested memories of abuse, what sometimes gets lost is this: Forgetting is an ordinary phenomenon. Remembering the past in detail can be considered the exception. Forgetting something is so utterly common that trying to puff it up with a scientific name to make it appear exotic is unnecessary and may, in fact, be an example of psychological "spin-doctoring," the merging of science and politics. Perhaps the best way to think about the 38% in Williams's sample who didn't remember is to say it simply: They don't remember.

What Do the Data Say About Remembering and Repressing Secretive Incestuous Abuse?

It is problematic to apply the current data to a prototypic case of incestuous abuse in which the child is threatened to keep the horrible secret to herself. It has been argued that some children repress their abuse memories because they cannot talk about their abuse. Their whole world is telling them that it didn't happen. The abuse experienced by the children in Williams's sample was generally not of this type. To enter the study in the first place, a female rape victim had to come to the hospital emergency room alleging rape (McCahill et al. 1979, 10). If they first went to the police, the police were instructed to take them to the hospital. If they first went to the hospital, in virtually all cases, the police were notified (p. 81). The pretreatment interviews were "extremely long" (p. 87), sometimes more than 3 hours. The police directive in effect at the time required that all victims under 18, although examined at the hospital, also be referred to a particular juvenile detention facility for a medical examination (p. 93). Then the victims were paid at least one visit and sometimes four visits by a social worker. In many cases the victims were involved in preliminary hearings and in trials. Thus, the typical victim talked with many individuals—hospital employees, law enforcement officers, social workers, district attorneys, and others. In some ways, this makes it even more surprising that the percentage who did not report the index abuse was as large as it was. Be that as it may, this study tells more about traumatic events that were not hidden than it does about events that were hidden away.

What Do the Data Say About Remembering and Repressing Repeated Episodes of Abuse?

The abuse experienced by these children was generally not of this type. The index abuse, when it happened, was typically a one-time event. At the time the initial data were collected, the victimized children were classified according to whether they had been sexually assaulted before by the same or a different offender (McCahill et al. 1979, 8); for the overall sample of 1,400, 80% were brought in because of a one-time assault. From the present analysis, it appears that 70% of the children in the sample were similarly brought in for a one-time assault. The only example of a child case described by McCahill et al. is clearly of this type: a 7-year-old girl who was raped by her babysitter's boyfriend a fortnight earlier—the "only such attack" (p. 148). The remaining 30% of the sample, at the time of their appearance at the hospital in the 1970s, had

had a previous experience by the same perpetrator or by someone else. We are not told how many of the 15 who did not remember had had a previous assault by a different person. We are not told, as the data were not collected, how many of the 15, if any, had been assaulted by the same offender on numerous previous occasions.

The number of critical events is important for a complete understanding of how these events might be remembered. Research on memory, with children and adults, suggests that people are more likely to forget an isolated incidence of abuse than a series of repeated events although the repeated events may become blended into a typical script (Lindsay and Read 1994; Means and Loftus 1991). Williams reported that 38% of women who had no previous experience of sexual abuse before the index event forgot the abuse, whereas 33% of women who had had a previous (possibly repeated) experience forgot. Although this difference was not significant, it is in the direction opposite to that posited by Terr's (1991) Type I–Type II trauma hypothesis. The Williams data are clear in showing that women often forget a single incident of sexual abuse. As Williams recognizes, they do not show that women who deny any experience of sexual abuse whatsoever were actually molested numerous times in childhood.

Do the Data Tell Us That People Repress Abuse, and Then Reliably Recover It Later?

The women in Williams's sample forgot their abuse. Even if one takes the position that it has been repressed, it is still the case that it has not been de-repressed. Perhaps that could be done. For example, it would be interesting to take her sample (or one similar to it) and randomly divide the sample into two treatments—one that gets "memory recovery" treatment and one that does not. Would the women in the memory recovery group later recover these memories? Before this type of study is undertaken, one would need to fully explore its ethics. Adequate research has not yet been done to show that digging out deeply repressed memories of molestation actually helps people get better. Potential investigators proposing such research would need to work through the consideration that such digging might make some of the women worse.

Have the Women Forgotten Their Abuse, or Have They Chosen Not to Report It?

Because many of the women were willing to report other sexual victimizations, although not the one in the hospital record, Williams believes that the bulk of the nonreports were due to women who actually did not remember.[2] Of course, another possibility is that some women may have been trying to report the index event, but their memory was sufficiently distorted that the researchers misclassified the woman as failing to remember the index event but remembering some other sexual abuse event. Misclassifications can arise because of the known difficulty of matching information from medical records to information obtained from people's memories (Loftus, Smith, Klinger, and Fiedler 1992).

To understand why women would report a different incident of abuse but not the index event, one should also examine when the various events happened relative to one another. If at the time of their appearance at the hospital in the 1970s 70% of the women had never before been sexually assaulted, then the "different" incident they were reporting to the researcher who interviewed them in the 1990s must have necessarily occurred more recently. Perhaps the more recent experiences were relatively salient in their minds, making the index events appear relatively less salient.

A related issue concerns how often the women have visited hospital emergency rooms in general and the particular hospital involved in the study. If some of them had been to the hospital on numerous occasions over their lifetime, one would expect that they may have some difficulty remembering the details of any one specific experience at the hospital.

Do the Data Mean That True Prevalence of Abuse Has Been Underestimated?

On the basis of her findings, Williams concluded that self-reports of childhood experiences of sexual victimization are likely to result in an underestimation of the true prevalence of such abuse. As Dawes (1994) has aptly noted, we cannot support this claim by looking only at the genuine memory errors. Dawes's claim can best be appreciated by first realizing that when people are asked about any event in the past there are two types of errors that are made: Some people experienced the event but didn't report it (false negatives), and some people did not experience the event but did report it (false positives). The balance between these two errors determines whether the reporting rate is an underestimation or an overestimation of the true rate. If the event in question is one that occurs in less than half of the population, the balancing test is particularly crucial, for false positives can easily equal or even outnumber false negatives.[3] Without an estimate for the proportion of nonabused people who erroneously remember abuse, this issue cannot be resolved.

Do These Data Justify Therapeutic Digging for Lost Memories of Childhood Sexual Abuse?

Although the data provide evidence of genuine memory failure, they do not eliminate concerns about the risks of using certain memory recovery techniques (Ceci, Loftus, Leichtman, and Bruck 1994, Lindsay and Read 1994; Loftus 1993; Loftus and Ketcham 1994). Although it may be tempting to argue that, because the rate of forgetting is so high (38%), it justifies the use of aggressive memory recovery techniques such as hypnotic age regression, sodium amytal interviewing, sexualized dream interpretation, creative imagination, and a host of other questionable procedures. However, first it must be shown that recovering such memories is therapeutically beneficial to clients. Even if the benefits for actual victims can be shown, therapists still face the same dilemma experienced by the doctor who has invented a new drug for diabetes. Assume that her drug is one that will help the patient who already has diabetes but will give the disease to the patient who did not initially have it. If the doctor does not know in advance the health status of the patient, should the new drug be prescribed?

CONCLUSION

Back in the 1970s, McCahill et al. (1979) said something that is as true today as it was then: "Rape hurts everyone" (p. 244). This study makes an important contribution to our understanding of how children might later remember or forget a significant childhood trauma. However, the study does not provide support for the notion that a long stream of childhood traumas is routinely banished from conscious awareness and then can later be reliably recovered. It must be kept in mind that the 49 women (38%) have forgotten but that they have not later reliably remembered. Some of them were so young when the abuse happened, it is exceedingly unlikely that they will ever be able to later genuinely remember, although conceivably they could be told about their abuse and construct a "true" memory of the experience. Others were abused when they were older, but their failure to remember the abuse can be understood as normal forgetting that follows the same laws as forgetting of all sorts of other life events.

Adapting an argument made by Pope and Hudson (1994), we are surprised that there are not more documented cases of total repression and reliable recovery later. If one conservatively estimates the number of Americans who have endured traumatic sexual abuse in the past, the figure could exceed 10 million. If repression occurred in only 10% of these cases, then at least 1 million adult Americans would presently harbor repressed memories of childhood sexual abuse. With these numbers, Pope and Hudson (1994) wonder why there are no published studies of groups of patients exhibiting well-documented cases of total repression and reliable recovery later. Williams's groundbreaking study gives us an idea of the kind of study that may provide evidence for this type of process. She has shown us how it is possible to go beyond the disputed cases that are based only on an alleged victim's de-repressed memory and an alleged perpetrator's denial-tragic as these cases may be. She has shown us that we need not relax the requirement that there be proof that the trauma occurred before we can study the forgetting and remembering of that trauma.

Not only does rape hurt everyone, but false memories of rape hurt everyone too. Hopefully, the important work of Williams will be used to help genuine victims heal from their past childhood traumas and will not be used to justify and rationalize the creation of new victims.

NOTES

1. The fact that the preliminary report claimed 38% of 100 women could not remember and the final report claimed that 38% of 129 women could not remember could be explained in at least two ways: (a) The preliminary report on 100 women was actually a report on roughly 100 women. (b) The data of an additional 29 women were included for the final report, and exactly 11 (38% of these) could not remember the abusive incident. The fact that the preliminary report 36% of cases involved sexual intercourse and the final report claimed that 60% involved sexual penetration could be due to different classification schemes.

2. In the preliminary report, Williams reported that 53% of women who failed to report the index event did report a different sexual abuse experience that occurred at some other time during their childhood. In the final report, Williams claims that 68% of those who did not recall the index event told about some other sexual abuse. The reason for this discrepancy is not immediately apparent but could be due to a change in the way responses were classified.

3. To appreciate Dawes's logic, assume that 24% of women are abused and one-quarter of these forget. This means that 6% of the total sample of women would be contributing to an underestimate. Now assume that 8% of the nonabused group erroneously reports abuse. This means that 6% of the total

sample of women (8% × 76% = 6%) would be contributing to an overestimate. The two errors would balance one another, and the prevalence estimates would then be accurate.

REFERENCES

Bower, B. 1993. Sudden recall. *Science News* 144: 184–86.

Cash, W. S., and A. J. Moss. 1972. *Optimum recall period for reporting persons injured in motor vehicle accidents*. National Center for Health Statistics. Vital and Health Statistics. Series 2, No. 50. DHEW Publication No. HSM 72–1050. Health Services and Mental Health Administration. Washington, D.C: U.S. Government Printing Office, April.

Ceci, S. J., E. F. Loftus, M. D. Leichtman, and M. Bruck. 1994. The role of source mis-attributions in the creation of false beliefs among preschoolers. *International Journal of Clinical and Experimental Hypnosis* 42: 304–20.

Dawes, R. M. 1994. *House of cards: Psychology and psychotherapy built on myth*. New York: Free Press.

Henderson, R. 1993. The tangled net of memory. *Common Boundary* 11: 38–45.

Herman, J. L., and M. R. Harvey. 1993. The false memory debate: Social science or social backlash? *Harvard Mental Health Letter* 4–6, April.

Horn, M. 1993. Memories lost and found. *U.S. News & World Report* (November 29): 52–56, 60–63.

Kandel, M., and E. Kandel. 1994. Flights of memory. *Discover* 15: 32–38.

Lindsay, S., and D. Read. 1994. *Applied cognitive psychology* 8: 281–338.

Loftus, E. F. 1982. Memory and its distortions. In *The G. Stanley Hall Lecture Series,* ed. A. G. Kraut, 123–54. Washington, D.C: American Psychological Association.

———. 1993. The reality of repressed memories. *American Psychologist* 48: 518–37.

Loftus, E. F., and K. Ketcham. 1994. *The myth of repressed memory*. New York: St. Martin's Press.

Loftus, E. F., K. D. Smith, M. R. Klinger, and J. Fiedler. 1992. Memory and mismemory for health events. In *Questions about questions: Inquiries into the cognitive psychology of surveys,* ed. J. M. Tanur, 102–37. New York: Sage.

McCahill, T., L. C. Meyer, and A. Fischman. 1979. *The aftermath of rape*. Lexington, Mass.: Lexington Books.

Means, B., and E. F. Loftus. 1991. When personal history repeats itself: Decomposing memories for recurring events. *Applied Cognitive Psychology* 5: 297–318.

National Center for Health Statistics. 1965. Reporting of hospitalization in the Health Interview Survey (Public Health Service, DHEW-HSM Publication No. 73–1261). Washington, D.C.: U.S. Government Printing Office, July.

Pezdek, K. 1993. Transcript of radio interview of Elizabeth Loftus on "The

Mike McConnell Show" of WLW Cincinnati. 1111 St. Gregory, Cincinnati, OH 45202, December 6.

Pope, H. G., and J. I. Hudson. 1994. *Can memories of childhood sexual abuse be repressed?* Unpublished manuscript, McLean Hospital, Harvard Medical School.

Sauer, M. 1993. Glad you're finally free. *The San Diego Union-Tribune* (November 21): A-1, A-21.

Terr, L. 1991. Child traumas: An outline and overview. *American Journal of Psychiatry* 148: 10–20.

———. 1994. *Unchained memories*. New York: Basic Books.

Usher, J. A., and U. Neisser. 1993. Childhood amnesia and the beginnings of memory for four early life events. *Journal of Experimental Psychology: General* 122: 155–65.

Wartik, N. 1993. A question of abuse. *American Health* (May): 62–67.

Williams, L. M. 1992. Adult memories of childhood abuse: Preliminary findings from a longitudinal study. *The Advisor* 5: 19–20.

———. 1994. Recall of childhood trauma: A prospective study of women's memories of child sexual abuse. *Journal of Consulting and Clinical Psychology* 62: 1167–76.

Wylie, M. S. 1993. Trauma and memory. *Family Therapy Network* 17: 42–43, September–October.

9

REPRESSED MEMORIES:
TRUE AND FALSE

ANDREW D. REISNER

ABSTRACT

The author establishes via literature review that recovered repressed memories of abuse can be accurate. Skeptics have provided important data and cogent arguments, yet the more extreme skeptical assertions, that repression itself may not exist, and that corroborated cases of recovered repressed memory do not exist, are not justified. Although the author maintains that recovered repressed memories can be valid, false memories can also occur. The author questions whether uncorroborated repressed memory evidence should be considered sufficiently reliable for use in litigation and criminal matters.

There seems to be agreement that child sexual abuse is common and that this abuse can have severe emotional consequences (Briere and Zaidi 1989; Finkelhor, Hotaling, Lewis, and Smith 1990; Grand and Alpert 1993; Loftus 1993). A national survey found that 27% of women and 16% of men reported having been sexually abused in childhood (Finkelhor et al. 1990). Briere and Zaidi (1989) found that 70% of women in their sample who presented at a psychiatric emergency room, reported, when specifically asked, that they had histories of sexual abuse. It was also found in this study that women who had been abused as children, as compared to those who had not been abused as children, were

From the *Psychological Record* 46 (1996): 563–79. Reprinted with permission of the author and publisher.

more likely to present in the emergency room with problems involving drug abuse, sex, suicidal ideation, suicide attempts, and severe personality disorder, especially Borderline Personality Disorder. Sexual abuse of children represents a significant problem in our society.

In recent years, however, concern has been raised over the validity of recovered repressed memories of abuse and the damages that can be done when false accusations of abuse result from false memories (Baker 1992a; Coleman 1990; Gray 1993; Jaroff 1993; Loftus 1993, 1995; Ofshe and Watters 1993; Pendergrast 1995; Steele 1994; Wakefield and Underwager 1992). Specialists in the area of sexual abuse investigation and treatment have been criticized for using methods which may be leading and which may result in false memories and false accusations (Coleman 1990; Gardner 1991; Hicks 1991; Ofshe and Matters 1993, 1994; Wakefield and Underwager 1992). Prosecution and imprisonment of possibly innocent people based largely upon evidence from questionable recovered repressed memories, or from leading, biased interviews with children have several authors comparing the current situation to the Salem Witch Trials. The term "witch hunt" is being used by some to describe the situation (Gardner 1991; Hicks 1991; Jaroff 1993; Sauer and Okerblom 1993; Loftus 1995).

Experimental and other empirical evidence indicates that long-term memory, rather than being a reliable tape recording, is a reconstruction which is subject to distortions based on later experience and influence (Baker 1992a; Loftus 1993; Spanos 1994; Yapko 1994). Questions have been raised as to whether the psychotherapy process, particularly when hypnosis is used, can result in false memories of such experiences as UFO abductions, past lives (Baker 1992a, 1992b; Ganaway 1989; Yapko 1994), and ritual satanic abuse (Hicks 1991; Mulhern 1991; Ofshe and Watters 1994; Spanos 1994). Similarly, misdiagnosis or the iatrogenic influence of therapy has been suspected in the creation of many, if not most, cases of Multiple Personality Disorder (Aldridge-Morris 1989; Freeland, Manchanda, Chiu, Sharma, and Merskey 1993; Merskey 1992a; Piper 1995; Reisner 1994; Simpson 1995; Spanos 1994; Spanos, Weekes, Menary, and Bertrand 1986). Such patients often report the most extreme and bizarre forms of abuse and are known to be highly suggestible and subject to memory distortions (Ganaway 1989; Mulhern 1991). The phenomenon of iatrogenesis, and the convincing evidence that false memories exist, raises questions as to the accuracy of reports of recovered repressed memories of more mundane varieties of abuse.

It has been established that the veracity of memories cannot be established either by the confidence of the subject in the reality of the memory or by the strength of the affect displayed (Baker 1992a; Yapko

1994). If this were not the case, we would have to accept the reality of abduction and abuse of humans by aliens in UFOs. These UFO abduction patients report high confidence in their recollections (often obtained under hypnosis) and, at times, display symptoms similar to Post Traumatic Stress Disorder (Hopkins, Jacobs, and Westrum 1992). The evidence for the reality of UFO abductions is exceedingly poor and alternate explanations have been offered (Baker 1992a, 1992b; Klass 1993; Reisner 1993; Sagan 1993; Stires 1993). The complexity of memory can create illusions which can deceive even those who should know better.

Although I am concerned about the impact of iatrogenesis on the lives of our patients and on the credibility of mental health practitioners, I am also concerned about some rather extreme and questionable statements being made by certain skeptics suggesting that repressed memories and repression may not exist at all. Please note the following:

> The notion of repression has never been more than an unsubstantiated speculation tied to other Freudian concepts and speculative mechanisms. (Ofshe and Watters 1993, 5)

> Repression cannot be said to be accepted in the scientific community except among analytically oriented therapists who base their beliefs on anecdotal reports and clinical case studies. (Wakefield and Underwager 1992, 491)

> I have not been able to find a publicly recorded example of an indubitably repressed memory which has been recovered and then proved correct. (Wakefield and Underwager review and criticize all the stock anecdotes.) (Steele 1994, 43)

> Here is the only guideline we need: The fact that a memory has been recovered after a period of alleged repression is sufficient to show that the so-called memory is worthless as evidence of any actual occurrence outside that person's mind or brain. (Steele 1994, 47)

> . . . there are no convincing data to indicate the existence of strong repression. (Pope 1994, 11)

> First, I want to point out that, despite over sixty years of research involving numerous approaches by many thoughtful and clever investigators, at the present time there is no controlled laboratory evidence supporting the concept of repression. (Holmes 1992, 96)

> The time has come to ask whether we should continue to pursue evidence for repression and whether we should now file the theory under "interesting but unsupported." (Holmes 1992, 98)

In addition to the above, Loftus (1993, 1994) notes that experimental evidence for repression and for the validity of recovered repressed memories is lacking. She notes that alternate explanations can often be found for case studies. One is left with the overall impression that Loftus considers the case for recovered repressed memories to be very weak.

EXPERIMENTAL EVIDENCE FOR REPRESSION

Critics of the concept of repression usually do not mention the well-established experimental paradigm involving perceptual defense and facilitation. It has been found that neurotic individuals who are judged to use repression and denial as primary defense mechanisms will take a longer time to perceive threatening words as compared to neutral words when the stimuli are tachistoscopically presented. Such individuals display "perceptual defense" (Bruner and Postman 1947) and are referred to as "Repressors." Neurotic individuals who primarily use intellectualization and rationalization, however, perceive threatening stimuli more readily than neutral stimuli. They are said to display perceptual facilitation and are referred to as "Sensitizers" (Eriksen 1954; Byrne 1961). In this experimental paradigm Hysterics are found to be "Repressors" and Obsessive-Compulsives are found to be "Sensitizers" (Byrne 1961; Lazarus, Eriksen, and Fonda 1951). Individuals who are high on the MMPI Hysteria Scale (Scale 3) are also high in perceptual defense (Mathews and Wertheimer 1958), and individuals who are high on measures of hysterical traits are also independently judged to be high in the defense mechanism of repression (Eriksen and Davids 1955). Hysterics are generally believed to use repression as a predominant defense (Blacker and Tupin 1991; Horowitz 1986; Mueller and Aniskiewicz 1986; Shapiro 1965). Repressors tend to block out emotionally threatening material whereas sensitizers seem to be hypervigilant for threatening stimuli.

Attempts to explain the phenomenon of perceptual defense generally make use of the concept of unconscious registration of stimuli. In Bruner and Postman's (1947) "Prerecognition Hypothesis" it is argued that with Repressors, threatening stimuli must first register unconsciously in order for the stimuli to be identified as threatening, and subsequently to be barred from entering consciousness. Eriksen (1954) suggested that threatening stimuli register unconsciously and create anxiety, and that the resulting anxiety is what blocks the perceptual processes. Also, differential ability to retrieve emotionally laden concepts from long-term memory may facilitate or impair the process of matching an incoming stimulus with similar internal concepts (Reisner 1985). In the later explanation, it is preexisting internal concepts that are "repressed" rather than the incoming stimulus itself.

A question might be raised as to whether the mechanism for perceptual defense would most closely resemble that for the defense mechanism of denial (keeping threatening external information from entering the conscious cognitive system) versus the defense mechanism of repression (banishing from consciousness information which has entered consciousness or which threatens to enter consciousness from the unconscious). To some extent this distinction may not be crucial because of the well-known paradox of denial: In order to be kept from entering consciousness, material to be "denied entry" must first be identified by the cognitive system as being threatening material. Thus, at some point, this threatening information *must* first enter the cognitive system (probably at an unconscious level) in order to later be "denied." Whether perceptual defense operates primarily via denial or primarily through repression, in either case information which has entered the system has been kept from consciousness.

A potential criticism of this theory involves the previously stated hypothesis that the incoming tachistoscopic stimulus may never be fully processed and "understood" by the repressive subject because of a failure to match the incoming stimulus with preexisting concepts in long-term memory. In this hypothesis, it is preexisting similar concepts that are repressed, preventing the incoming stimulus from ever being recognized (Reisner 1985).[1] There is evidence, however, that subliminal tachistoscopically presented stimuli are recognized at an unconscious level and do exert emotional affects (Silverman 1966, 1976; Silverman and Candell 1970). In Silverman's (1976) subliminal activation method, threatening stimuli are presented tachistoscopically below the level of conscious recognition. Subjects in various diagnostic groups have been found to respond emotionally to stimuli which they have not consciously recognized (Silverman 1976). Lazarus and McCleary (1951) also demonstrated emotional responsiveness to subliminal stimuli by evoking a galvanic skin response (GSR) to subliminally presented emotionally charged stimuli, and by failing to evoke a GSR to subliminally presented neutral stimuli. Shevrin and Fritzler (1986) demonstrated that subliminally presented material can affect the content on a later administered free association task. There *is* experimental support for the notion that stimuli can be recognized unconsciously.

Although Erdelyi (1974) and the current author consider the perceptual defense paradigm to be well established, Holmes (1992) reported that this paradigm was eventually found to be invalid when methodological faults were corrected. Specifically, he claims that threatening words used in these experiments were less familiar than the neutral words, and thus were not as readily perceived. Secondly, subjects may have perceived the threatening words but hesitated to report them, as they may have been seen as embarrassing and "dirty" words. This is the so-called "response suppression" effect. Although he cites no references in support of this claim (Holmes 1992), and did not cite such studies in an earlier review article (Holmes 1974), he stated, "When familiarity was equated across the two types of words, and when social constraints were eliminated from the situation, the defense or repression effect disappeared" (Holmes 1992, 96).

The investigators involved with the perceptual defense and perceptual facilitation experiments, however, were well aware of the criticisms involving word frequency and response suppression, and not only did they argue successfully against the criticisms (Eriksen 1954; Lazarus 1954), but they empirically demonstrated that the criticisms were essentially invalid (Aronfreed, Messick, and Diggory 1953; Kissin, Gottesfeld, and Dickes 1957; Mathews and Wertheimer 1958). In a review article, Eriksen (1954) points out that cases of perceptual defense have been demonstrated wherein subjects responded to neutral words that have been paired with frustration. In these cases, neither word frequency nor response suppression can account for the results. There would be no reason to consciously suppress the report of a neutral word.

There are several arguments against the word frequency criticism. One strong argument is the fact that Sensitizers perceive threatening words more readily than neutral words. How could this be if the threatening words are "low frequency" words, thus more difficult to perceive (Eriksen 1954)? Lazarus (1954) and Eriksen (1954) argue that the threatening words used in the studies were not low frequency words, and Eriksen (1954) establishes that a word must be of extremely low frequency to have an effect on a tachistoscopic task.

Mathews and Wertheimer (1958) matched their neutral and emotionally loaded words for length and word frequency using the Thorndike-Lorge General Word Count, and they also corrected for response suppression. Even after the response suppression effect was corrected for, they still obtained a perceptual defense effect. The subjects who demonstrated perceptual defense also scored high on the MMPI Hy scale, a scale associated with the use of denial and repression.

Loiselle (1966) repeatedly paired threatening visual stimuli with random two-digit numbers. Subjects took longer to perceive the emotionally charged numbers. There would be no reason for a subject to consciously suppress the report of a two-digit number. Also, in this experiment, the word frequency criticism could not apply. This experiment provides a clear demonstration of perceptual defense, free of contamination by either response suppression or by the word frequency effect.

To minimize the response suppression effect, Aronfreed et al. (1953) showed one group of subjects the types of threatening words to which they would be exposed so that they would feel more comfortable reporting them. With another group they did not similarly inform the subjects. Both the informed and uninformed groups displayed longer response times in reporting emotionally unpleasant stimuli as compared to neutral or pleasant stimuli. Women in the uninformed group did display longer response times for threatening stimuli than did women in the informed group, suggesting some degree of response suppression for the former group. There was no significant difference between men in the uninformed versus informed groups. Although the phenomenon of response suppression appears to exist, it probably does not account for the entire perceptual defense effect in this experiment.

Kissin et al. (1957) asked subjects in their study if they had delayed reporting of emotionally loaded words. The study found that half of the subjects delayed report of the first threatening word but did not delay report of subsequent emotionally loaded words. Overall, subjects reporting a deliberate delaying of their response was a "relatively rare occurrence" (p. 338). When they corrected for the response suppression effect, a robust perceptual defense effect remained. It was found that the degree of perceptual defense was related to the degree of personality inhibition and constriction as measured by projective tests.

Although the perceptual defense paradigm does not provide direct evidence for the repression of traumatic memories, it does provide a sort of construct validity for the concept of repression and for the differential operation of defense mechanisms in different types of neurosis. Lines of theoretical, clinical, and experimental evidence converge to support the concept of repression. As previously stated, Hysterics tend to heavily use repression and denial (Blacker and Tupin 1991; Eriksen and Davids 1955; Horowitz 1986; Mueller and Aniskiewicz 1986; Shapiro 1965), and Hysterics are high in perceptual defense (Byrne 1961; Lazarus et al. 1951; Mathews and Wertheimer 1958). Obsessive Compulsives tend to use rationalization, and tend to use less repression than do Hysterics, and Obsessive Compulsives tend to perceive tachistoscopically presented threatening stimuli more readily than neutral stimuli (Byrne 1961; Lazarus et al. 1951). At minimum, this paradigm establishes that different defensive and personality styles have an effect on perception of threatening stimuli. The experimental evidence presented is consistent with psychodynamic hypotheses concerning defense mechanisms, and the differential operation of unconscious and conscious thought processes. The evidence presented is also consistent with the operation of information processing at an unconscious level.

EMPIRICAL SUPPORT FOR REPRESSED MEMORIES

Surveys

There have been a few surveys of self-reported amnesia for sexual abuse. Briere and Conte (1993) found that among 450 adult self-reported sexual abuse cases, 59% reported that at some point prior to their eighteenth birthday they were not able to recall the abuse. This study was criticized by Loftus (1993) as the effect of therapy may have contaminated the subjects' responses. (The subjects could hypothetically have been misled by their therapists into believing that they were abused.) However, Loftus (1993) reported that in a study wherein she, herself, was a collaborator, it was found that 18% of their sample of self-reported sexual abuse victims reported a period of amnesia for the abuse. Wakefield and Underwager (1992) criticized this type of study, referring to an earlier survey report by Briere and Conte, because the reports of abuse were not corroborated.

Gold, Hughes, and Hohnecker (1994) reported that of 105 cases in their own study, 87% of whom were surveyed during an intake session, 30% reported that at some point they had completely blocked out their abuse, 9.5% reported that at some point they had a vague sense that they had been abused but had no memory, 14.3% had only partial memory, 16.2% remembered some but not all episodes of abuse, and 30% remembered all abuse. Loftus (1994) criticized this study because even though 87% were surveyed before this particular therapy began, there is no data indicating that the subjects did not have previous therapy which may have influenced their responses. This survey and that of Briere and Conte (1993) are also somewhat inconsistent with studies by Terr (1988) and Femina, Yeager, and Lewis (1990), who generally found that among verified cases of childhood trauma, the traumatic events tended to be remembered. Even so, it is difficult to believe that *all* of the respondents in the surveys who reported periods of amnesia for abuse were suffering from false memory syndrome.

A recent survey (Feldman-Summers and Pope 1994a) revealed that of 250 male and 250 female psychologists surveyed, 28.6% of the women and 17.9% of the men who responded reported having been abused.[2] Of the 79 cases reporting abuse, 32 (40.5%) reported a period during which they could not remember the abuse. Significantly, 46.9% of this group reported having some type of corroboration of the abuse. The abuser confessed in 5 cases (15.6%); someone else who knew of the abuse reported it to the subject in 7 cases (21.9%); the subject found their own forgotten diary recording the abuse in 2 cases (6.2%); someone else reported the same perpetrator for abuse in 5 cases (15.6%); and medical records were found documenting abuse in 2 cases (6.2%). This study is particularly important because *there was corroboration of the abuse for numerous cases wherein there had been a period of probable amnesia for the traumatic event.*

Case Studies

Herman and Schatzow (1987) reported on 57 cases of adult, female, alleged sexual abuse survivors who participated in group therapy. The authors encouraged the women to find verification for their abuse. The authors reported that of those clients who attempted to find verification only 6% were unable to find verification, and 11% did not attempt to find verification. The authors state (p. 10):

> The majority of patients (74%) were able to obtain confirmation of the sexual abuse from another source. Twenty-one women (40%) obtained corroborating evidence either from the perpetrator himself, from other family members, or from physical evidence such as diaries or photographs. Another 18 women (34%) discovered that another child, usually a sibling, had been abused by the same perpetrator. An additional 5 women (9%) reported statements from other family members indicating a strong likelihood that they had also been abused.

The overall findings of the study were that 64% of the women reported "some degree of amnesia" for the abuse (p. 10), and that 28% reported "severe memory deficits."

Wakefield and Underwager (1992), as well as Pope (1994), criticize the Herman and Schatzow (1987) study because the authors of the study did not specifically indicate that the women who had the most complete amnesia were also the same women who were able to obtain verification of the abuse. The study, however, cannot be dismissed based on this criticism, because as previously noted, 28% of the subjects reported "severe memory deficits," but only a total of 17% of the subjects were either unwilling or unable to find verification. Obviously, at least some of the women who suffered complete amnesia for the traumatic events were able to find some type of corroboration.

It is noted though, that in addition to the 17% who did not corroborate their abuse, there is another 9% whose "corroboration" might be considered questionable, as there was not a definite confirmation that the other family member was also abused. This would bring the total of "lacking or questionable" confirmations in the study to 26%. If, by chance, all of these questionable or lacking corroborations occurred in the "severe memory deficit group" (28% of the subjects), it would limit the significance of the study. Indeed, it would have been helpful had Herman and Schatzow (1987) specified the type of corroboration in relation to the type of amnesia (complete vs. partial amnesia). Nevertheless, the case examples presented provide strong indications of the validity of recovered repressed memories of abuse.

In an attempt to clarify some of the ambiguities of the Herman and Schatzow (1987) study, I wrote to the senior author requesting a response to several questions. Herman's response (personal communication, August 29, 1994) indicated that data were not available detailing the exact type of corroboration in relation to the extent of amnesia. However, Herman did indicate that a small number of women in each group did obtain the highest levels of corroboration, including physical evidence or perpetrator confession. Importantly, Herman reported that a few of the abused women who had been totally amnestic did obtain this type of clear and distinct corroboration.

Szanjnberg (1993) documents the case of a 12-year-old boy treated via psychoanalytic psychotherapy and later by psychoanalysis. In the course of treatment the boy uncovered a previously repressed memory of a strangulation attempt by his own mother. The mother reportedly confirmed to the therapist that she actually had tried to strangle her son. This case represents yet another example of a recovered repressed memory wherein corroboration was obtained.

Alpert (1991) provides some guidelines for working with possible cases of repressed memory; she cites cases in the literature wherein memories of sexual abuse were recovered in therapy. Review of some of the articles cited (Katan 1973; Williams 1987) revealed that although the recovered memories of abuse were plausible and were related to symptoms and therapy outcome, clear-cut corroboration of the abuse was not provided. Alpert (1991) also cites one of her own cases involving a patient who had recovered previously repressed memory fragments of sexual abuse, which "were validated from numerous sources" (p. 429). The author does not, however, present the case in sufficient detail to determine the nature of the validation.

Horn (1993) wrote an article concerning a 38-year-old ethics professor who experienced delayed recall of sexual abuse which reportedly occurred between ages 10 and 13 while attending a boys' camp. The professor phoned several other men who had attended the same camp when they were boys. He then heard similar stories about other molestations perpetrated by the same man, who had been the camp administrator. After this the professor reportedly phoned the perpetrator and obtained a confession. This case was presented as a corroborated case wherein sexual abuse was repressed and later remembered.

Pendergrast (1995), an investigative journalist who reportedly telephone-interviewed the ethics professor discussed above, accepts the reality of this man's molestation, but questions whether the memories were actually repressed versus simply being suppressed or forgotten for years. Pendergrast (1995, 102) writes that the ethics professor found the ongoing molestation experiences "not altogether unpleasant." He argues that because this man allegedly did not find the molestation to be particularly traumatic at the time, this case may be more a case of forgetting, as opposed to repression. Pendergrast (1995) noted that the professor had always remembered advances made by an Afro-American, male camp counselor. This counselor had reportedly kissed him on the lips, and the boy found these advances repugnant. Pendergrast reasons that if the future ethics professor did not repress the memory of these upsetting and objectionable advances made by the Afro-American counselor, why then would he repress memories of the seemingly less traumatic, ongoing molestation by the camp administrator?

Kaufman (1989) and Lewis (1992) suggest that shame may be a powerful force which motivates or even creates repression. In Tomkin's (1987, 1991) Affect Theory, upon which Kaufman's (1985, 1989) conceptualizations are based, guilt is seen as one manifestation of the affect of shame. Embarrassment has been conceptualized as being "shame before an audience" (Kaufman 1989, 24). Returning to the case of the ethics professor, one might speculate that he may have experienced a sense of shame if he did find some pleasurable aspects to the molestation. The subject's feelings about the ongoing molestation, upon his delayed recall, were described in terms of his feeling "visceral uneasiness" (Pendergrast 1995, 102) and embarrassment. There was also reportedly a sense of guilt associated with the incidents of molestation (Pendergrast 1995). As previously mentioned, both guilt and embarrassment can be conceptualized as being manifestations of shame. Essentially, this man may have repressed memory of the experience of ongoing molestation because of associated feelings of shame, but he may not have repressed memory of the one-time advances made by a different man because those advances were seen as entirely objectionable, thus, not as shame inducing.

The manner in which the professor remembered the earlier sexual abuse also suggests that an active process had been keeping the memories from consciousness. Initially he had received a phone call from his sister telling him that his nephew was going to join a boys' chorus. The camp wherein this man had been molested had been a camp for a boys' chorus. But the professor did not instantly remember that he had been molested in camp when he received the phone call. Rather, he felt "sickened by the news"—and gradually began sinking into a bewildering depression (Horn 1993, 52). For a time he did not know what was causing the depression, and he initially attributed it to other factors. It was not until he awoke one night with the beginnings of a memory of the man who molested him that he began to recover memories of what had happened to him as a boy (Horn 1993). What the above suggests, firstly, is that something which the client was unable to remember, after receiving the phone call in question, was apparently causing his depression. This tends to affirm the basic psychodynamic hypothesis that matters about which we are not presently aware can exert an emotional effect. It also suggests that some type of active, relatively unconscious process, was, for a time, keeping the memories out of consciousness. I would call this process repression.

TRAUMATIC AMNESIA
AND "COMBAT NEUROSIS"

Karon (1994) points out that during World War II there were numerous cases of trauma-induced amnesia. In the case of combat situations, corroboration of the traumatic events was not difficult to obtain, as compared to the case of sexual abuse, wherein the perpetrator of the trauma is motivated to conceal the truth. Karon states that accurate memories of battle-induced trauma were often recovered in therapy.

Fisher (1945), writing at the time of the World War II era, also notes that amnesia was a common result of battle-induced trauma. He cites literature indicating that 8.6% of 1000 cases of Anxiety Neurosis and Hysteria during the Africa campaign involved amnesia, as well as 5% of similar cases in the South Pacific. He does note, however, that 50% of persons in the latter cases also had been rendered unconscious during battle. Merskey (1992b), who recognizes the reality of psychologically induced amnesia in combat situations, also notes that at times the amnesia can result from physical trauma and have a neurological basis. Although this study suggests that there were numerous cases of emotionally induced amnesia during World War II, it is interesting to note that the frequency of amnesia among psychological casualties was rather low.[3] At issue in the current controversy, though, is whether psychologically induced repression of trauma exists at all. Evidence from the battlefield suggests that repression of traumatic memories does exist.

Fisher (1945) also presents several cases of psychogenic amnesia which accompanied fugue states and explains some of the dynamics of fugue in combat settings. In one case, a man developed amnesia and a fugue state after a Stuka dive bomber attack (wherein other soldiers were present), and the memory of the attack was restored under hypnosis. It was interesting that Fisher notes that this same patient had a "false memory" of the date of the dive bomber attack, confusing it with the date of his parent's death. Apparently Fisher, in 1945, was aware of false memory phenomena and the need for corroboration of recovered memories.

With regard to fugue states, Fisher (1945) suggests that a person is often in a situation wherein the need for safety and self-preservation is in conflict with his or her conscience or sense of military duty. The person unconsciously "decides" to forget and to temporarily take on a new identity and escape. It would appear that in these cases a sense of guilt (shame) over impulses to escape danger plays a role in the fugue and amnesia.

Spanos (1994), however, suggests that psychogenic amnesia may represent a conscious, voluntary, "goal-directed enactment" (p. 146). Indeed, malingering cannot be ruled out in cases where escape from combat is obtained via fugue and amnesia. Even though the concept of psychogenic amnesia is well established in the psychiatric literature (Classen, Koopman, and Spiegel 1993), the issue of combat-induced amnesia is not without its complications.

Discussion

Given the apparent validity of some repressed memory cases, should recovered memory evidence, lacking additional corroboration, constitute proof or decisive evidence that should hold up in a courtroom? I do not believe so. Alternate explanations are possible, including iatrogenesis stemming from therapist bias or biased evaluation of the validity of the recovered memory by the therapist. There is evidence, as previously noted, that some therapists and sexual abuse investigators conduct biased and leading interviews (Coleman 1990; Gardner 1991; Hicks 1991; Loftus 1993) and often recommend to their patients books which are biased and leading (Wakefield and Underwager 1992), which could potentially contaminate the subjects' memory. Memories of UFO abductions and past reincarnations, recovered in therapy sessions, stretch the bounds of credulity, and for some, represent a sort of reductio ad absurdum, casting doubt on the reliability of recovered repressed memories.

Given the existence of false memory phenomena, it is difficult to ascertain whether any specific uncorroborated recovered memory is true or false, or partly true and partly false. Although evidence exists for the existence of both true recovered repressed memories and false memories, there is inadequate data available concerning the relative frequency or prevalence of either type of memory. Because some recovered repressed memories are painfully real, the potential validity of any specific recovered memory cannot be dismissed on an a priori basis. However, people should not be going to prison, and huge sums of money should not exchange hands in lawsuits, based largely upon the assumed validity of an *uncorroborated* recovered repressed memory.

One might ask, however, what is the value of a theory that states that recovered repressed memories can be either true or false, as such a position may do little to clarify or simplify matters in the legal arena. Firstly, whether or not this position clarifies court cases, it is of scientific, theoretical, and psychotherapeutic importance to know whether or not repression exists and whether memories can be repressed in some cases. Secondly, this position *will* be of some assistance in legal matters. Specifically, if the position is accepted that repression of memory never happens, then any memory which emerges after a period of alleged repression can be claimed to be a false memory. Any claim which is made based on a repressed memory, thus, could be discounted on an a priori basis. Conversely, if it was widely held that recovered repressed memories were invariably accurate, or that a therapist can easily determine whether a recovered memory is true or false, then a wrongly accused party might suffer severe criminal and/or civil penalties many years after the alleged offense. Oversimplification of the repressed memory issue may lead to injustice.

SUMMARY

It is the author's contention that evidence supports the existence of reasonably accurately recovered repressed memories, but that recovered memories can also contain distortions or be entirely false. It is certainly true that evidence supporting the repressed memory hypothesis tends to come from case reports and surveys as opposed to controlled experimentation. Experimental research has been presented, however, which is, at minimum, consistent with the concepts of repression and denial as defense mechanisms, and which supports the concept of unconscious information processing.

There are significant limitations regarding the use of experimentation to determine the validity of repressed memories. Indeed, it would be unethical to deliberately traumatize one group of subjects and not traumatize a second group, and then subdivide these two groups into a "Therapy With Suggestion Condition," a "Therapy Without Suggestion Condition," and a "No Therapy Condition," to determine who would have true recovered memories and who would have false memories. Although less than optimal, case studies where corroboration has been established, as well as surveys, will have to play an important methodological role in the study of recovered memory phenomena. Critics, however, tend to devalue evidence from case studies and tend to prematurely dismiss cases where corroboration has actually been established.

There is a body of experimental evidence which suggests that people whose personality styles are "repressive," or who score high on the MMPI Hy scale, also tend to bar from consciousness or delay perception of threatening stimuli. Experimental evidence also generally supports the concept of unconscious information processing and unconsciously mediated selectivity in perception. The notion that people can, without conscious awareness, keep threatening information out of consciousness, is certainly consistent with the concept of repression. Although the repression of traumatic *memories* is not specifically supported by experimental research, there is experimental evidence which is highly consistent with the existence of the defense mechanisms of repression and denial. Given this, and the fact that corroborated cases of repressed memories have been documented in case studies and surveys, it is perhaps time to more seriously consider the strong possibility that, at times, memories can be repressed and later recovered.

NOTES

1. The author has changed his opinion regarding this hypothesis based upon the evidence which follows.

2. In an errata, Feldman and Pope (1994b) corrected these figures to reflect that 22.7% of the women and 16.5% of the men had reported abuse.

3. If, indeed, shame is a powerful motivator of repression (Kaufman 1989; Lewis 1992) this might partially account for the low incidence of combat-induced amnesia cases. Although soldiers may experience survival guilt, or shame involving other aspects of combat, I suspect that fear and constant stress account for many battlefield emotional casualties. Shame may be a more pervasive affect in sexual abuse cases as compared to combat stress cases. There may thus be a higher incidence of amnesia in sexual abuse cases as compared to combat stress cases. In a study of psychologists abused as children, 52.7% of those reporting sexual abuse by a relative had a period of "forgetting" some or all of the abuse (Feldman-Summers and Pope 1994a). In Briere and Conte's (1993) study 59%

of self-reported sexual abuse victims had a period wherein they were unable to remember the abuse. Fisher (1945), however, cited studies indicating that only 5 to 8.6% of combat psychological casualty cases suffered amnesia.

It would be of potential scientific merit to systematically study the affects aroused in sexual abuse victims as compared to combat stress victims (per Tomkin's [1991] classification system for the affects). Those who experience amnesia in both groups could be compared to those who did not experience amnesia to see if shame actually is a common element in repressed memory cases. One would also be able to determine to what extent sexual abuse victims experience more shame than do combat stress casualties.

REFERENCES

Aldridge-Morris, R. 1989. *Multiple personality: An exercise in deception.* London: Lawrence Erlbaum.

Alpert, J. L. 1991. Retrospective treatment of incest victims: Suggested analytic attitudes. *Psychoanalytic Review* 76 (3): 425–35.

Aronfreed, J., G. Messick, and J. Diggory. 1953. Reexamining emotionality and perceptual defense. *Journal of Personality* 21: 517–28.

Baker, R. A. 1992a. *Hidden memories: Voices and visions from within.* Amherst, N.Y.: Prometheus Books.

———. 1992b. *Alien abductions or human productions? Some not so unusual personal experiences.* Unpublished manuscript.

Blacker, K. H., and J. P. Tupin. 1991. Hysteria and hysterical structures: Developmental and social theories. In *Hysterical personality style and the histrionic personality disorder,* ed. M. J. Horowitz, rev. ed., 15–66. Northvale, N.J.: Aronson.

Briere, J., and J. Conte. 1993. Self-reported amnesia for abuse in adults molested as children. *Journal of Traumatic Stress* 6: 21–31.

Briere, J., and L. Zaidi. 1989. Sexual abuse histories and sequelae in female psychiatric emergency room patients. *American Journal of Psychiatry* 146 (12): 1602–1606.

Bruner, J., and L. Postman. 1947. Emotional selectivity in perception and reaction. *Journal of Personality* 15: 69–77.

Byrne, D. 1961. Repression-Sensitization Scale: Rationale, reliability, and validity. *Journal of Personality* 29: 334–49.

Classen, C., C. Koopman, and D. Spiegel. 1993. Trauma and dissociation. *Bulletin of the Menninger Clinic* 12 (2): 178–94.

Coleman, L. 1990. False accusations of sexual abuse: Psychiatry's latest reign of error. *Journal of Mind and Behavior* 11: 545–56.

Erdelyi, M. H. 1974. A new look at the new look: Perpetual defense and vigilance. *Psychological Review* 81: 1–25.

Eriksen, C. 1954. The case for perceptual defense. *Psychological Review* 61: 175–82.

Eriksen, C., and A. Davids. 1955. The meaning and clinical validity of the Taylor Anxiety Scale and the Hysteria-Psychesthenia Scales from the MMPI. *Journal of Abnormal and Social Psychology* 50: 135–37.

Feldman-Summers, S., and K. S. Pope. 1994a. The experience of "forgetting" childhood abuse: A national survey of psychologists. *Journal of Consulting and Clinical Psychology* 62 (3): 636–39.

———. 1994b. The experience of "forgetting" childhood abuse: A national survey of psychologists: Correction. *Journal of Consulting and Clinical Psychology* 62 (4): 800.

Femina, D. D., C. A. Yeager, and D. O. Lewis. 1990. Child abuse: Adolescent records vs. adult recall. *Child Abuse and Neglect* 11: 227–31.

Finkelhor, D., G. Hotaling, I. A. Lewis, and C. Smith. 1990. Sexual abuse in a national survey of adult men and women: Prevalence, characteristics, and risk factors. *Child Abuse and Neglect* 11: 19–28.

Fisher, C. 1945. Amnestic states in war neurosis: The psychogenesis of fugues. *The Psychoanalytic Quarterly* 14: 437–68.

Freeland, A., R. Manchanda, S. Chiu, V. Sharma, and H. Merskey. 1993. Four cases of supposed Multiple Personality Disorder: Evidence of unjustified diagnoses. *Canadian Journal of Psychiatry* 38: 245–47.

Ganaway, G. 1989. Historical versus narrative truth: Clarifying the role of exogenous trauma in the etiology of MPD and its variants. *Dissociation* 2 (4): 205–20.

Gardner, R. A. 1991. *Sex abuse hysteria: Salem witch trials revisited.* Cresskill, N.J.: Creative Therapeutics.

Gold, S. N., D. Hughes, and L. Hohnecker. 1994. Degrees of repression of sexual abuse memories. *American Psychologist* 49 (5): 441–42.

Grand, S., and J. L. Alpert. 1993. The core trauma of incest: An object relations view. *Professional Psychology: Research and Practice* 21 (3): 330–34.

Gray, P. 1993. The assault on Freud. *Time* (November 29): 47–51.

Herman, J. L., and E. Schatzow. 1987. Recovery and verification of memories of childhood sexual trauma. *Psychoanalytic Psychology* 4 (1): 1–14.

Hicks, R. D. 1991. *In pursuit of Satan: The police and the occult.* Amherst, N.Y.: Prometheus Books.

Holmes, D. S. 1973. Investigations of repression: Differential recall of material experimentally or naturally associated with ego threat. *Psychological Bulletin* 81 (10): 632–53.

———. 1992. The evidence for repression: An examination of sixty years of research. In *Repression and Dissociation,* ed. J. L. Singer, 85–102. Chicago: University of Chicago Press.

Hopkins, B., D. M. Jacobs, and R. Westrum. 1992. *Unusual personal experiences: An analysis of the data from three national surveys.* Bigelow Holding Corporation, 4640 South Eastern, Las Vegas, NV 89119.

Horn, M. 1993. Memories lost and found. *U.S. News & World Report* (November 29): 52–63.

Horowitz, M. J. 1986. *Stress Response Syndromes,* 2nd ed. Northvale, N.J.: Aronson.

Jaroff, L. 1993. Lies of the mind. *Time* (November 29): 52–59.

Karon, B.P. 1994. False memory syndrome [Letter to the editor]. *Skeptical Inquirer* 18 (2): 213.

Katan, A. 1973. Children who were raped. *Psychoanalytic Study of the Child* 28: 8–24.

Kaufman, G. 1985. *Shame: The power of caring.* Cambridge, Mass.: Schenkman Books.

——. 1989. *The psychology of shame: Theory and treatment of shame-based syndromes.* New York: Springer.

Kissin, B., H. Gottesfeld, and R. Dickes. 1957. Inhibition and tachistoscopic thresholds for sexually charged words. *The Journal of Psychology* 43: 333–39.

Klass, P. J. 1993. 3.7 million Americans kidnapped by aliens? Part 2: Additional comments about the "Unusual Personal Experiences" survey. *Skeptical Inquirer* 17: 145–46.

Lazarus, R. 1954. Is there a mechanism of perceptual defense?: A reply to Postman, Bronson, and Groper. *Journal of Abnormal and Social Psychology* 49: 396–98.

Lazarus, R., C. Eriksen, and P. Fonda. 1951. Personality dynamics and auditory perceptual recognition. *Journal of Personality* 19: 471–82.

Lewis, H. B. 1992. Shame, repression, field dependence, and psychopathology. In *Repression and Dissociation,* ed. J. L. Singer, 233–57. Chicago: University of Chicago Press.

Loftus, E. 1993. The reality of repressed memories. *American Psychologist* 41 (5): 518–37.

——. 1994. The repressed memory controversy. *American Psychologist* 11 (5): 443–45.

——. 1995. Remembering dangerously. *Skeptical Inquirer* 19 (2): 20–29.

Loiselle, R. H. 1966. A newer approach to perceptual defense. *Perceptual and Motor Skills* 21: 644.

Mathews, A., and M. Wertheimer. 1958. A "pure" measure of perceptual defense uncontaminated by response suppression. *Journal of Abnormal and Social Psychology* 57: 373–75.

Merskey, H. 1992a. The manufacture of personalities: The production of multiple personality disorder. *British Journal of Psychiatry* 160: 327–40.

——. 1992b. Psychiatric aspects of the neurology of trauma. *Neurological Clinics* 12 (4): 895–905.

Mueller, W. J., and A. S. Aniskiewicz. 1966. *Psychotherapeutic intervention in hysterical disorders.* Northvale, N.J.: Aronson.

Mulhern, S. 1991. [Letter to the editor]. *Child Abuse and Neglect* 15: 609–11.

Ofshe, R., and E. Watters. 1993. Making monsters. *Society* 1: 4–16.

——. 1994. *Making monsters: False memories, psychotherapy, and sexual hysteria.* New York: Charles Scribner's Sons.

Pendergrast, M. 1995. *Victims of memory: Incest accusations and shattered lives.* Hineburg, Vt.: Upper Access Books.

Piper, A. 1995. A skeptical look at multiple personality disorder. In *Dissociative*

Identity Disorder, ed. L. Cohen, J. Berzoff, and M. Elin, 135–74. Northvale, N.J.: Aronson.

Pope, H. G. 1994. "Recovered memories": Recent events and review of evidence. *Currents in Affective Illness* 13 (7): 5–12.

Reisner, A. D. 1985. *Some possible explanations for perceptual defense and facilitation.* Unpublished manuscript.

———. 1993. UFO-abduction "test" lacks validity [Letter to the editor]. *Skeptical Inquirer* 11 (4): 444–45.

———. 1994. Multiple personality disorder diagnosis: A house of cards? *American Journal of Psychiatry* 154 (4): 629.

Sagan, C. 1993. What's really going on? *Parade Magazine* (March 7): 4–7.

Sauer, M., and J. Okerblom. 1993. Trial by therapy. *National Review* (September): 30–39.

Shapiro, D. 1965. *Neurotic styles.* New York: Basic Books.

Shevrin, H., and D. E. Fritzler. 1968. Visual evoked response correlates of unconscious mental processes. *Science* 101: 295–98.

Silverman, L. 1966. A technique for the study of psychodynamic relationships: The effects of subliminally presented aggressive stimuli on the production of pathological thinking in a schizophrenic population. *Journal of Consulting Psychology* 10 (2): 103–11.

Silverman, L. 1976. Psychoanalytic theory: "The reports of my death are greatly exaggerated." *American Psychologist* 11 (9): 621–37.

Silverman, L., and V. Candell. 1970. On the relationship between aggressive activation, symbiotic merging, intactness of body boundaries, and manifest pathology in schizophrenics. *Journal of Nervous and Mental Disease* 150 (5): 387–99.

Simpson, M. A. 1995. Gullible's travels, or the importance of being multiple. In *Dissociative identity disorder,* ed. L. Cohen, J. Berzoff, and M. Elin, 87–134. Northvale, N.J.: Aronson.

Spanos, N. P. 1994. Multiple identity enactments and multiple personality disorder: A sociocognitive perspective. *Psychological Bulletin* 116 (1): 143–65.

Spanos, N. P., R. J. Weekes, E. Menary, and L. D. Bertrand. 1986. Hypnotic interview and age regression procedures in the elicitation of multiple personality symptoms: A simulation study. *Psychiatry* 49: 298–311.

Steele, D. R. 1994. Partial recall. *Liberty* 7 (3): 37–47.

Stires, L. 1993. 3.7 million Americans kidnapped by aliens? Part 1: Critiquing the "Unusual Personal Experiences" survey. *Skeptical Inquirer* 12: 142–44.

Szanjnberg, N. M. 1993. Recovery of a repressed memory and representational shift in an adolescent. *Journal of the American Psychoanalytic Association* 41 (3): 711–27.

Terr, L. 1988. What happens to early memories of trauma? A study of twenty children under age 5 at the time of documented traumatic events. *Journal of the Academy of Child and Adolescent Psychiatry* 21: 96–104.

Tomkins, S. 1987. Shame. In *The many faces of shame,* ed. D. L. Nathanson. New York: Guilford.

Tomkins, S. 1991. Affect, imagery, and consciousness, vol. 2. New York: Springer.

Wakefield, H., and R. Underwager. 1992. Recovered memories of sexual abuse: Lawsuits against parents. *Behavioral Sciences and the Law* 10: 483–507.

Williams, M. 1987. Reconstruction of an early seduction and its aftereffects. *Journal of the American Psychoanalytic* 145–63.

Yapko, M. D. 1994. *Suggestions of abuse*. New York: Simon & Schuster.

PART THREE

HYPNOSIS, SUGGESTION, AND IATROGENESIS

Yapko's discussion paper on the topic of false memories of sexual abuse engendered via the highly suggestive procedures used by psychotherapists in treating their patients is noteworthy in exposing the widespread amount of ignorance and misinformation currently existing among clinicians. Yapko found: "A significant number of psychotherapists erroneously believe, for example, that memories obtained through hypnosis are likely to be more accurate than those simply recalled, and that hypnosis can be used to recover accurate memories even from as far back as birth (54%)." Even more distressing is the fact that many (28%) believe in the reality of "past lives."

Ofshe and Watters's paper points out in graphic and disturbing detail how pervasive, dangerous, and damaging some recovered memory therapy can be. Not only do they agree with Yapko that a little knowledge can be a very dangerous thing but also that so much of psychotherapy as presently practiced can do much more harm than good. Far too much of recovered memory therapy is *iatrogenic* in nature, i.e., it is producing a psychopathology worse than the patient's initial presenting problem. Ofshe and Watters show, clearly and precisely, how this is done.

Tayloe, in a fascinating criminal case history, argues that extremely emotional events, interpreted as life-threatening on some level, can be actively repressed from conscious memory and then, under hypnosis, at a later date these memories can be accurately recalled. Despite Tayloe's arguments, there is good reason to question: (1) whether or not Bain's amnesia was genuine; and (2) whether or not the "hypnosis" was real. In Bain's case the arousal of intense emotion every time he was asked to recall the shooting may have made it difficult for him to vocalize and recount the sequence of events. With the excuse of "hypnosis" and the therapeutic suggestion that he is no longer involved in the past events and that he is merely an observer or bystander to the events taking place on a TV or a movie screen (a hypnotic technique frequently used to get traumatized witnesses to verbalize), Bain was then able to tell exactly and accurately what transpired. As for "hypnosis" per se, it is nothing more than relaxation, suggestion, and a turning on of one's imagination. It is not an altered state of consciousness that one "shifts" into and that permits the regurgitation of allegedly "repressed" material.

The Courtois contribution again relies heavily on the work of Terr, Herman, and Schatzow, and Briere and Conte but also discusses at length Braun's BASK model as well as specific clinical techniques for helping clients remember. Whether such procedures do more than enhance the recall of "false memories" remains to be seen. If one assumes, at the outset, that: (1) the client *has* been abused, (2) the client is in denial, (3) repression is a fact, and (4) sexual molestation trauma will not be healed until the memory of it is recovered and its associated affect soothed and eliminated—no other course of action is, obviously, possible!

10

SUGGESTIBILITY AND REPRESSED MEMORIES OF ABUSE:
A SURVEY OF PSYCHOTHERAPISTS' BELIEFS

MICHAEL D. YAPKO

The mental health field is deeply divided in its views regarding the possibility of creating false memories of sexual abuse through suggestive procedures. Psychotherapists in clinical practice were surveyed regarding their views on memory and hypnosis in order to assess how their perspectives might influence their clinical methods. Survey data regarding hypnosis and suggestibility indicate that while psychotherapists largely view hypnosis favorably, they often do so on the basis of misinformation. A significant number of psychotherapists erroneously believe, for example, that memories obtained through hypnosis are more likely to be accurate than those simply recalled, and that hypnosis can be used to recover accurate memories even from as far back as birth. Such misinformed views can lead to misapplications of hypnosis when attempting to actively recover memories of presumably repressed episodes of abuse, possibly resulting in the recovery of suggested rather than actual memories.

When someone asks you, "Were you sexually abused as a child?" there are only two answers: One of them is "Yes," and one of them is "I don't know." You can't say "No."
                              Roseanne Arnold, on "The Oprah Winfrey Show"
                                                              (Nathan 1992)

From the *American Journal of Clinical Hypnosis* 36, no. 3 (January 1994): 163–71. Reprinted with permission.

Consider a woman seeking psychotherapy who reports terrifying nightmares, an eating disorder, and difficulties in her interpersonal relationships, especially with men. She claims she has no idea what causes her symptoms, but her psychotherapist suggests to her directly that her symptoms indicate that she "must have been sexually abused and repressed the memories." She has no memories, or even hints of memories, for any such events. With the psychotherapist's help, though, she soon recovers some vague memories of sexual abuse occurring at a very early age. Did these episodes of abuse actually happen? Might they have been manufactured *unintentionally* in order to accommodate the expectations and suggestions of the psychotherapist? Is it possible to lead some to believe he or she was sexually abused when no such abuse ever actually occurred?

These difficult questions lie at the heart of one of the most heated controversies in the psychotherapy field today. On one side of the issue, we have those clinicians and researchers who believe that sexual abuse traumas that have been repressed can and should be readily identified from a known symptom checklist (Blume 1990; Fredrickson 1992). They further believe that treatment should involve first lifting the veil of repression with a variety of memory-recovery techniques, then working with the newly discovered traumatic material in order to help the patient reach new symptom-free resolutions. They are also concerned that perpetrators of sexual abuse will be given a new basis for evading responsibility for their actions by dismissing allegations of abuse as the product of false memories. And, finally, they believe that memories recovered in psychotherapy are essentially true, and need to be acknowledged as such before treatment can succeed. On the other side of the issue, we have those clinicians and researchers who are skeptical of anyone's professed ability to readily diagnose someone repressing memories of trauma on the basis of some symptom cluster that could be just as readily explained by other means (Ganaway 1991; Loftus 1993). After all, repression can not be studied directly; it can only be inferred. (One cannot ask someone, "Are you repressing memories of abuse?" If he or she knows about it, then it is not repressed.) These clinicians and researchers further believe that by reaching a conclusion that the patient has been abused and is repressing memories to that effect, psychotherapists can either intentionally or unintentionally influence the person to reach that same conclusion when it may not be true. They are concerned that innocent people will be falsely accused and their lives all but destroyed as a result. They recognize that people can be influenced, especially in some particularly vulnerable situations like psychotherapy, to believe damaging things that may have no basis in fact.

There has been increasing effort made to determine how responsive to suggestion memory might be. Studies by Laurence and Perry (1983), Orne (1979), Sheehan, Statham, and Jamieson (1991), Lynn, Milano, and Weekes (1992), and Loftus (1993) have all lent support to the recognition that memory is reconstructive, not reproductive. Thus, the accuracy of memory can be influenced by many factors, including suggestion and misinformation (Bower 1981; Loftus 1980). As another such factor, repression is an especially complicating variable because its influence on the accuracy of memory is not yet fully understood (Loftus and Yapko, in press). Specifically, it is not yet known how or even whether repression diminishes or enhances the accuracy of long-buried memories, and to what degree suggestive (hypnotic) procedures employed by psychotherapists to recover repressed memories might contaminate the memories derived from them (Laurence, Nadon, Nogrady, and Perry 1986; Loftus 1993).

Psychotherapists' hypnotic procedures for recovering presumably repressed memories are based on their views and understandings of the workings of both hypnosis and memory. What are the techniques psychotherapists employ to bring forth apparently repressed memories that are first *assumed* to be present? Are these methods valid—that is, do they bring forth actual repressed memories, or might they involve suggesting memories for events that never actually occurred, yet the patient comes to accept as genuine? It seems imperative to know how psychotherapists think about these matters in order to assess the relevance and appropriateness of their methods for working with such volatile issues as repressed memories of sexual abuse.

In 1992 I gathered data from over 860 psychotherapists from all over the United States about their ideas and practices regarding certain aspects of their patients who do and do not report a background of sexual abuse. These psychotherapists completed two different questionnaires about the roles of suggestion and memory in psychotherapy, especially as they relate to issues of repressed memories of sexual abuse. I wanted to find out whether psychotherapists were thinking critically and in an informed manner about the highly volatile issues that inevitably arise when a psychotherapist concludes, ". . . you must have been sexually abused and repressed it."

Consider the not uncommon scenario in which a patient is encouraged to recover a memory in a psychotherapy session, and the individual then has a single image come up, ostensibly from 6 months old, that involves some kind of abuse. Should it be considered authentic? Should the patient go home and allege abuse and tear apart the family on the basis of such an image? Those who already believe such early "memories" are valid will likely say yes, and those who do not will likely say no. This represents one of the main problems I intend to bring more attention to in this article: An individual's fate is placed in the hands of a psychotherapist's seemingly arbitrary beliefs about suggestion and memory (Yapko 1993).

BACKGROUND OF THE SURVEY

In order to assess psychotherapists' range of knowledge and beliefs about memory and hypnosis, I devised two survey instruments (questionnaires).* The first is called the *Memory Attitude Questionnaire* (MAQ); it involves a series of statements regarding various aspects of memory with which the respondent can agree strongly or slightly, or disagree strongly or slightly. The second questionnaire is called the *Hypnosis Attitude Questionnaire* (HAQ); it provides a series of statements regarding suggestibility and hypnosis in relation to memory with which the respondent can agree strongly or slightly, or disagree strongly or slightly. Key items of the HAQ are the subject of this article. (Complete data obtained from both instruments can be found in Yapko, in press.)

HYPNOSIS ATTITUDE QUESTIONNAIRE (HAQ)

Hypnosis, in one form or another (e.g., imagery, guided meditation, visualization), is commonly used as a tool for "uncovering" memories of abuse, as the leading self-help books suggest (Bass and Davis 1988; Fredrickson 1992). When psychotherapists employ methods like hypnosis to do memory work, they may do so without recognizing that they may contaminate the investigative process through suggestive questioning (Putnam 1979; Orne 1979; Lynn, Weekes, and Milano 1989). Do psychotherapists view hypnosis as a reliable, objective way to uncover repressed or hidden memories? Do psychotherapists recognize that they can sometimes unwittingly create the very problems they must then treat? The HAQ was designed to assess psychotherapists perspectives about the role of suggestibility in the psychotherapy process and how they typically view hypnosis as a tool for both retrieving and working with patients' memories.

---

*Both the MAQ and the HAQ are available from the author.

Table 1
Degrees of Respondents

HAQ

Degree	Number	Percent
Masters	560	64.4
Ph.D.	208	23.9
M.D.	34	3.9
B.A./B.S.	41	4.7
Other	17	2
No Answer	9	1
Total	869	100

DATA COLLECTION

The HAQ was presented to over one thousand psychotherapists all across the country during 1992. Approximately 90% of respondents were in attendance at national and international psychotherapy conventions. These included the annual meeting of the American Association of Marriage and Family Therapists, the Family Therapy Networker Symposium, a regional meeting of the American Society of Clinical Hypnosis, and the Fifth International Congress on Ericksonian Approaches to Hypnosis and Psychotherapy. The rest were in attendance at privately held workshops I conducted throughout the year on topics unrelated to the HAQ. The respondents returned 869 usable HAQs. This is objectively considered a statistically significant data base from which to realistically assess psychotherapists' attitudes and practices.

DEMOGRAPHICS OF RESPONDENTS

The average respondent was 44 years old, had formal education slightly (one year) beyond a master's degree, had been in clinical practice for over 11 years, and was most likely in private clinical practice. Forty-three percent of respondents said they had received formal training in hypnosis ("formal training" was not defined for respondents). Despite this figure, 53% said they use hypnosis in their work! Eight percent of respondents said they frequently use hypnosis to recover memories, while an additional 28% said they do so occasionally. The data describing the degrees of respondents are contained in Table 1.

Table 2
Responses to Key Items of the HAQ

	All Respondents			Trained		Untrained	
	Agree	Disagree	No Response	Agree	Disagree	Agree	Disagree
1. "worthwhile"	97.1	2.1	0.8	99.7	0.3	96.7	3.3
2. "cannot lie"	18	76.2	5.8	13.8	86.2	22.4	77.6
3. "greater faith"	46.8	48.5	4.7	45.5	54.5	52	48
4. "actually occurred"	30.7	64.7	4.6	26.6	73.4	36.1	63.9
5. "birth"	53.8	39.9	6.3	59.4	40.6	55.6	44.4
6. "past lives"	27.9	61.7	10.4	32.5	67.5	30.1	69.9
7. "false memories"	79.2	16.4	4.4	89.2	10.8	77.8	22.2
8. "trauma suggested"	18.9	75.4		27.3	72.7	14.2	85.8

RESPONSES TO SOME OF THE KEY ITEMS OF THE HAQ

It is beyond the scope of this article to include all of the data gathered from respondents completing the HAQ. Therefore, only responses to key items will be described in this section. These are summarized as percentages in Table 2. Tables 3 and 4 provide data regarding responses according to training in hypnosis and according to academic degree.

DISCUSSION OF RESULTS

Item 1: "Hypnosis is a worthwhile psychotherapy tool." The overwhelming majority of respondents, 97%, view hypnosis in a favorable light. Psychotherapists' positive appraisal is gratifying to those of us who work hard to create such a favorable attitude. However, it is clear from the misconceptions stated in other items of the HAQ that, for many psychotherapists, the positive appraisal may be based on misinformation.

Item 2: "People cannot lie when in hypnosis." Nearly one in five respondents (18%) agreed to some extent with an outright myth about hypnosis. Thus, these respondents are likely to accept whatever information is obtained hypnotically as true, even when it is the product of deception (whether deliberate or not) on the part of the patient.

Item 3: "Psychotherapists can have greater faith in details of a traumatic event when obtained hypnotically than otherwise." Nearly half (47%) of

Table 3
Percentage of Responses by Academic Degree

	M.A.		Ph.D.		M.D.		B.A.		Other	
Item	Agree	Disagree	Agree	Disagree	Agree	Disagree	Agree	Disagree	Agree	Disagree
1	98.6	1.4	98	2	94	6	95.1	4.9	94.1	5.9
2	19.8	80.2	12.8	87.2	16	84	35.9	64.1	33.3	66.7
3	50.7	49.3	41.5	58.5	54.5	45.5	55.2	44.8	65	35
4	34.1	65.9	23	77	33.3	66.7	40.5	59.5	58.8	41.2
5	58.5	41.5	48.2	51.8	63.6	36.4	70.2	29.8	80	20
6	33.3	66.7	22	78	28.1	71.9	36.8	63.2	62.5	37.5
7	83.8	16.2	86.2	13.8	81.2	18.8	72.5	27.5	50	50
8	18.3	81.7	27.3	72.7	18.7	81.3	13.5	86.5	5	95

respondents agreed to some extent with this item. Attributing greater accuracy of details to a memory of trauma recovered hypnotically is a distortion of fact with potentially hazardous consequences for the patient (Watkins 1989; Zelig and Beidelman 1981).

Item 4: "When someone has a memory of a trauma while in hypnosis, it objectively must actually have occurred." Does the mere fact of being hypnotized indicate the memory obtained is of a true event? Despite this being untrue (Dywan and Bowers 1983; Sheehan and Grigg 1985), nearly one in three respondents (31%) said they believe so.

Item 5: "Hypnosis can be used to recover memories of actual events as far back as birth." This statement reflects the notion that all memories, even those from the earliest stages of infancy, are stored and retrievable through special procedures like hypnosis. Nearly 54% of respondents agreed with this statement in principle, despite the available evidence that such early memories are not stored and available for recall (Kihlstrom and Evans 1979; Kihlstrom and Harackiewicz 1982).

Item 6: "Hypnosis can be used to recover accurate memories of past lives." As untenable as this clearly arbitrary belief might seem, more than one in four (28%) respondents professed an attitude of agreement.

Item 7: "It is possible to suggest false memories to someone who then incorporates them as true memories." This item represents the heart of this article by finding out whether psychotherapists generally recognize the possibility that some (unknown) percentage of previously repressed memories obtained during psychotherapy could be a product of suggestion and not a reflection of true events in the person's life. Nearly four out of five (79%) respondents agreed, to some extent, that untrue memories can be suggested to and integrated as genuine by some individuals.

Item 8: "Do you know of any cases where it seemed highly likely that a trauma victim's trauma was somehow suggested by a psychotherapist rather than a genuine experience?" This pivotal item asked whether psychotherapists are aware of the possibility that perhaps some, perhaps many, of the cases where sexual abuse has been alleged as a result of the influences of psychotherapy are questionable in terms of their authenticity. How pervasive is the problem of suggested abuse? No one knows for certain, but the HAQ may begin to provide some indication of just how widespread the problem of psychotherapist contamination may actually be.

Any "yes" answers to this question would have been too many. That is why it is especially distressing to find that almost one in five psychotherapists (19%) can point to cases where they believe other psychotherapists were a part of the patient's problem rather than a part of the solution.

CONCLUSION

When psychotherapists first suspect and then look intently for a history of abuse that has presumably been repressed in a particular patient, their beliefs about memory and their awareness (or lack thereof) of themselves as suggestive influences are directly involved in the "search and rescue" mission. Believing, for example, that one can accurately store and later remember memories of conversations and experiences from the very first moments of life leads to different psychotherapy techniques than if one has no such belief (Yapko 1990).

Unfortunately, many psychotherapists believe in past lives, the retrievability and accuracy of infantile memories, and the infallibility of hypnosis as a tool for recovering accurate memories. Many continue to maintain the rigid but unfounded belief that accurate memories of all experiences must be in there somewhere in one form or another and that all one needs is the right "key" to "unlock" them. False memories that are detailed and dramatic may be accepted as true simply because of the psychotherapist's preexisting beliefs (Scheflin and Shapiro 1989).

The survey data presented here suggest that too many psychotherapists treat their patients on the basis of their personal beliefs and philosophy, and *not* according to an objective consideration of the facts. This was generally true regardless of academic degree or whether or not someone had received formal training in hypnosis (as Tables 3 and 4 indicate). I am deeply concerned that psychotherapy patients will be led to believe destructive ideas that are untrue, recall memories of terrible events that never actually happened, jump to conclusions that are not warranted, and destroy the lives of innocent people—and even their own lives—in the process, all in the name of "psychotherapy." I am all too aware that the abuse of children is a huge problem growing to ever more sickening proportions. I am also aware that people can be led to believe things that are not true (Labelle, Laurence, Nadon, and Perry 1990; Loftus and Hoffman 1989; Sheehan et al. 1991). *Abuse happens, and so do false accusations.* The important task of mental health professionals is to methodically sort out which is which with a considerably greater degree of sophistication than is currently practiced. In order to do so, many questions will need to be researched and, hopefully, answered with precision. Some of these are presensed in the next section.

FURTHER RESEARCH NEEDED

Without objective corroborating evidence like a photograph or video-tape, how can one distinguish a real memory from a confabulation? This question goes right to the heart of the matter, and the answer is quite discouraging: No objectively reliable method for doing so currently exists. This conclusion represents the unanimous response of the many experts on both sides of the issue (see Yapko 1993, in press).

The mental health profession does not yet know very much about the repression of traumatic memories. In fact, some question repression's very existence (Holmes 1990). Clinicians do not yet know how common repression of childhood sexual abuse really is. We do not currently know the authenticity of memories that have been buried 20 or 30 years that suddenly and dramatically surface in response to a lecture, a self-help book, or a psychotherapy session. We do not know whether repressed memories always exist when symptoms are present, ever waiting to be uncovered as the source of that patient's problems, or whether the same kind of symptoms can exist independently of negative experiences that might have been repressed. We do not know how to characterize the differences between repression and merely forgetting. We do not know from what age repression is even possible. We do not know if trauma makes a repressed memory less or more accurate in a given individual. We do not know which techniques for recovering repressed memories will alter them in significant ways merely by using them. We do not know why some people repress a particular type of trauma and others do not. We do not know why some people never have traumatic memories surface in their awareness that are objectively known to exist in their backgrounds, while others have memories that eventually do return. These many unknowns all represent areas badly in need of further research.

When there is so much still to be learned, how can so many psychotherapists be so comfortable, even adamant, in their beliefs that what they are doing is objective, sound, and therapeutic? It can be very convincing for a patient plagued with doubt and uncertainty about his or her puzzling symptoms to be told with utmost confidence by the psychotherapist that "your symptoms clearly indicate you were abused." Can an uncertain patient be convinced by what appears to be (but is not) factual information presented in a confident manner by an authority? Decades of social psychological research indicate clearly that the answer is yes (Aronson 1992).

The issues are complex, and our knowledge about repression, trauma, and suggestibility is not yet great. It is vitally important that genuine abuse survivors are protected, and that innocent people are not wrongly accused because of some psychotherapist's arbitrary beliefs about symptoms and memories. Questioning the authenticity of repressed memories is *not* meant to imply skepticism about the terrible fact of widespread sexual abuse in this country. It is meant to highlight what is known to be true: When knowledge is scarce, the gaps in our understandings are inevitably filled in with confabulations (Loftus 1993; Loftus and Yapko, in press; Yapko 1990, 1993, in press). In those cases of repressed memories of abuse that surface in response to the suggestions of psychotherapists steeped in misconception, the confabulations can prove devastating on many levels. We must do as much as we can to prevent that from happening.

REFERENCES

Aronson, E. 1992. *The social animal,* 6th ed. San Francisco: W. H. Freeman and Co.

Bass, E., and L. Davis. 1988. *The courage to heal: Women healing from sexual abuse*. New York: Harper & Row.

Blume, E. 1990. *Secret survivors*. New York: Ballantine.

Bower, G. 1981. Mood and memory. *American Psychologist* 36: 129–48.

Dywan, J., and K. Bowers. 1983. The use of hypnosis to enhance recall. *Science* 222: 184–85.

Fredrickson, R. 1992. *Repressed memories*. New York: Fireside.

Ganaway, G. 1991. *Alternative hypotheses regarding satanic ritual abuse memories*. Paper presented at the 99th Annual Convention of the American Psychological Association, San Francisco, August.

Holmes, D. 1990. The evidence of repression: An examination of sixty years of research. In *Repression and dissociation: Implications for personality, theory, psychopathology and health*, ed. J. Singer, 85–102. Chicago: University of Chicago Press.

Kihlstrom, J., and F. Evans. 1979. Memory retrieval processes during post-hypnotic amnesia. In *Functional disorders of memory*, ed. J. Kihlstrom and F. Evans, 179– 218. Hillsdale, N.J.: Erlbaum.

Kihlstrom, J., and J. Harackiewicz. 1982. The earliest recollection: A new survey. *Journal of Personality* 50: 134–48.

Labelle, L., J-R. Laurence, R. Nadon, and C. Perry. 1990. Hypnotizability, preference for an imagic cognitive style and memory creation in hypnosis. *Journal of Abnormal Psychology* 99: 222–28.

Laurence, J-R., R. Nadon, H. Nogrady, and C. Perry. 1986. Duality, dissociation, and memory creation in highly hypnotizable subjects. *International Journal of Clinical and Experimental Hypnosis* 34 (4): 295–310.

Laurence, J-R., and C. Perry. 1983. Hypnotically created memory among highly hypnotizable subjects. *Science* 222: 523–24.

Loftus, E. 1980. *Memory*. Reading, Mass.: Addison-Wesley.

———. 1993. The reality of repressed memories. *American Psychologist* 48 (5): 518–37.

Loftus, E., and H. Hoffman. 1989. Misinformation and memory: The creation of new memories. *Journal of Experimental Psychology: General* 118: 100–104.

Loftus, E., and M. Yapko. In press. Psychotherapy and the recovery of repressed memories. In *Handbook of Allegations of Child Sexual Abuse*, ed. T. Ney. New York: Brunner/Mazel.

Lynn, S., J. Weekes, and M. Milano. 1989. Reality vs. suggestion: Pseudomemory in hypnotizable and simulating subjects. *Journal of Abnormal Psychology* 98: 137–44.

Lynn S., M. Milano, and J. Weekes. 1992. Pseudomemory and age regression: An exploratory study. *American Journal of Clinical Hypnosis* 35 (2): 129–37.

Nathan, D. 1992. Cry incest. *Playboy* (October): 162–64.

Orne, M. T. 1979. The use and misuse of hypnosis in court. *International Journal of Clinical and Experimental Hypnosis* 27: 311–41.

Putnam, W. 1979. Hypnosis and distortions in eyewitness memory. *International Journal of Clinical Hypnosis* 27: 437–48.

Scheflin, A., and J. Shapiro. 1989. *Trance on trial*. New York: Guilford.

Sheehan, P., and L. Grigg. 1985. Hypnosis, memory, and the acceptance of an implausible cognitive set. *British Journal of Clinical and Experimental Hypnosis* 3: 5–12.

Sheehan, P., D. Statham, and G. Jamieson. 1991. Pseudomemory effects over time in the hypnotic setting. *Journal of Abnormal Psychology* 100: 39–44.

Watkins, J. 1989. Hypnotic hypermnesia and forensic hypnosis: A cross-examination. *American Journal of Clinical Hypnosis* 32 (2): 71–83.

Yapko, M. 1990. *Trancework: An introduction to the practice of clinical hypnosis,* 2nd ed. New York: Brunner/Mazel.

———. 1993. The seductions of memory. *Family Therapy Networker* 17: 30–37.

———. In press. *Suggestions of abuse: True and false memories of childhood sexual trauma.* New York: Simon and Schuster.

Zelig, M. and W. Beidelman. 1981. The investigative use of hypnosis: A word of caution. *International Journal of Clinical and Experimental Hypnosis* 29: 401–12.

11

MAKING MONSTERS

RICHARD OFSHE AND ETHAN WATTERS

Practitioners on the fringes of the mental health professions periodically develop new miracle cures. Most of these therapies lean toward drama, if not theatricality, and are often marketed through pop-psych books and talk shows. Clients are led to undertake exotic techniques, such as screaming their way to happiness or submerging in sensory deprivation tanks. When the techniques prove ineffective, the damage is usually nothing worse than wasted time and money. Interest in the "cure" soon fades. But sometimes, a different breed of innovation emerges from the periphery—one that frequently causes considerable and often irreparable harm. Lobotomy and "re-parenting" are examples. Criticism from professionals and the public has, in the past, been able to persuade nearly all practitioners to abandon the damaging treatments.

With hindsight observers wonder how the professions that spawned these either frivolous or dangerous excesses could have tolerated such recklessness. How could practitioners who used them have been so foolish or so arrogant and cruel?

Recently, a new miracle "cure" has been promoted by some mental health professionals—recovered memory therapy. This treatment leads clients to see their parents as monsters who sexually abused them as children. Parents have to witness their adult children turn into monsters trying to destroy their reputations and lives. In less than ten years' time this therapy, in its various forms, has devastated thousands of lives. It has become a nationwide phenomenon—one that is becoming entrenched in our culture and the mental health professions with enormous speed.

The modus operandi of recovered memory therapy lies in uncovering supposed repressed memories from the client's past in order to cure their mental problems. According to practitioners, hundreds of thousands of adults, primarily women, suffer from the debilitating consequences of sexual abuse endured in childhood. Clients are told they have no knowledge of their abuse because their memories have been repressed. But full awareness of unrecognized abuse is the magic key to the client's return to mental health.

Practitioners of this type of therapy believe repression is a powerful psychological defense that causes one to lose all awareness of physically or sexually terrifying events. Not only is the event repressed but so are memories of the trauma's social context—that is, everything preceding and following it that would suggest to the victim that some trauma has occurred. According to the theory, virtually any mental disorder or symptom can result from repressed childhood abuse. Clients who respond to this therapy become convinced that they were ignorant of abuse which may have gone on for a decade or more. They may remain unaware of the trauma for perhaps thirty years, until they enter treatment where they discover their repressed memories. Once these memories are dredged up and accepted as real, practitioners encourage their clients to publicly accuse, confront, and perhaps sue those they believe to have been the perpetrators. These often turn out to be parents, siblings, grandparents, or sometimes groups of unidentified strangers. The inevitable result is the destruction of the families involved. Therapists feel obligated to do whatever is necessary to uncover their client's hidden traumatic history. The methods employed have generated profound controversies. Critics charge the therapy does not unearth real memories at all. Rather their origin is iatrogenic—therapist induced. Clients are essentially being tricked into believing that they are remembering events that never happened.

Two issues about this therapy should be considered. One is substantive, concerning the validity of the theories underlying recovered memory therapy. The other is an issue of policy. The substantive part of the controversy can be resolved by determining the answers to two questions: Does the repression mechanism exist and function as the therapy presumes? And are the techniques employed capable of producing false memories of abuse even if no abuse occurred?

The policy question lies in the mine field of political correctness. Sexual assault, particularly of children, has become starkly political in recent years. In the eyes of some, absolute belief in the accuracy and truthfulness of all charges is the only appropriate stance. In such a climate, one wonders if it matters if the therapy is valid or bogus? Because the therapy is becoming so rapidly institutionalized, it is questionable whether the conclusions from a reasoned analysis of it, or anything else is likely to affect its dissemination. Even if academics, researchers, and sophisticated clinicians were to conclude the therapy is harmful, would its use slow or stop?

REPRESSION AND MEMORY

The substantive controversy turns on the validity of the concept of repression, the central mechanism of the theory. Asked bluntly: Can the mind repress memories in the way these therapists claim? If repression is a valid concept, clients could be recovering long hidden memories of abuse. If invalid, repression is nothing more than a pseudo-scientific smoke screen for treatment techniques that create false memories. The concept of repression has been used in different ways in the mental health community for a hundred years. Freud employed the term to describe the mind's conscious and unconscious avoidance of unpleasant wishes, thoughts, or memories. Even under this conservative definition, the existence of repression has never been empirically demonstrated. Sixty years of experiments that would demonstrate the phenomenon have failed to produce any evidence of its existence. The notion of repression has never been more than an unsubstantiated speculation tied to other Freudian concepts and speculative mechanisms. The only support repression has ever had is anecdotal and contributed by psychoanalysts who presume the existence of the repression mechanism. Even leading psychoanalytic theoreticians recognize that the concept of repression is a meta-psychological principle rather than a testable hypothesis about human behavior.

In recovered memory therapy repression is the essential mechanism and the only acceptable explanation for a client's sudden report of abuse. Practitioners of the therapy have developed repression into a psychological phenomenon far more powerful than was ever suspected by Freud or anyone else until recently. Since 1980, the operational meaning of repression has been pumped up beyond all recognition.

In accordance with this robust repression concept, a person could, for example, banish awareness of the experience of having been brutally raped one or a hundred times during childhood. These distressing memories might be repressed serially, immediately following each event. Alternatively, all the memories might be collectively repressed at some time later, after the abuse had stopped. If the memory of rapes were serially repressed, a child could go from rape to rape ignorant of each previous assault. If memories were collectively repressed, the child could have retained awareness of the rapes throughout the years they were happening and repressed them as a group at some later moment. Whether serially or collectively repressed, the memories might not be "recovered" until years later under the influence of therapy. The only evidence supporting this concept is circumstantial and only comes out of the therapy sessions.

Modern memory research has demonstrated that normal recall of distant or even relatively recent events is subject to information loss and error for details. Recovered memory therapy's fundamental conception of how memory functions assumes that the human mind records and stores everything perceived. Under this assumption, it is reasonable to presume that minutely detailed recollections of the remote past are feasible. Freud's ideas about psychological processes influencing recall— what is remembered, distorted, forgotten, or repressed—all rely on this assumption. He also assumed that absent any adverse psychological influences, all information should be available to be accurately recalled— in present-day terms, it should be played back as if it had been recorded on a video camcorder.

Freud was mistaken. Scientific studies have revealed memory to be much more malleable than any recorder/playback analogy would suggest. Memory behaves in a reconstructionist fashion. Memories not only change over time but are influenced by the circumstances under which they are recalled. Memory is malleable for details, even for events that actually happened.

The properties of robust repression are dramatically different from those of accepted memory-related mental processes such as ordinary forgetting, intentional avoidance of a subject, and traumatic amnesia. While sharing certain superficial features with these phenomena, repression implies something distinct from each. By allowing repression to be confused with common memory phenomena, promoters of recovered memory therapy can more easily sell their theories to clients and the public. This confusion is important because it leads those being offered or told about recovered memory therapy to conclude that they comprehend what therapists mean by repression and mistake it for undisputed memory phenomena.

Everyone has experienced normal memory decay over time. Forgetting can include failing to remember an event or only recalling portions of it. Research demonstrates that the normal process of forgetting involves time-dependent memory decay. Repression, on the other hand, is an all or none phenomenon—now you see it, now you don't. Repression will cause the knowledge of the event to disappear entirely from awareness, perhaps only minutes after it happened. Someone who remembers only broad outlines of a distant, meaningful event is demonstrating normal memory. Simple failure of perfect recall or recall of only gross characteristics of distant events is not repression as the mechanism appears in recovered memory therapy.

It is also a common experience to remember an event after not having recalled it for years. The event may or may not be a distressing one. Consider a forty-five-year-old man who for the first time in twenty years thinks about the painful day of his father's funeral when he was eleven. For the first few years after the funeral the child may have periodically thought about that day, but with the passage of time he thought of it less often until eventually the gap lengthened to twenty years.

Not thinking about something for a long time is not the same as having repressed it. If the adult had repressed the memory in the manner suggested by promoters of recovered memory therapy, he would have become entirely ignorant of having attended the funeral and perhaps even of his father's death. If asked about the event, he would have said he was certain that there was none or absolutely sure that he did not attend. The person who simply had not thought about the funeral for twenty years would not have lost awareness of his father's death and, if probed, could have recalled the funeral. Due to normal memory decay, some details would likely be missing from his recollection.

A third common memory phenomenon is the motivated avoidance of a subject. In everybody's life there are moments or episodes one would prefer not to discuss or even think about because they were humiliating, guilt provoking, frightening, or emotionally painful. The twenty-year gap in conscious attention to one's father's funeral could very well have been caused by motivated avoidance. Avoiding a subject does not mean that its memory is buried in the unconscious and is inaccessible.

Amnesia induced through psychological trauma, that is, selective amnesia, is the memory phenomenon most easily mistaken for, or passed off as repression. Traumatic amnesia is the unusual but frequently reported phenomenon of becoming amnesiac for certain details or portions of a terrifying event. This mechanism describes, for instance, the inability of a teenage girl who endured a terrifying knife-point rape to recall many of its step-by-step events and her inability to give an accurate and complete narrative even shortly afterward. The most straightforward explanation for memory disruptions of this type is that the person became so terrified by the experience that the normal biological process underlying information storage was disrupted. The cause of traumatic amnesia may resemble what happens during an alcohol-induced "blackout." High levels of alcohol toxicity are known to cause a disruption in the biochemical process of memory. No information is stored in long-term memory during the period of the "blackout." A person experiencing an alcohol "blackout" will recall events up to the point at which long-term memory ceased to function. Later, the person knows that memory loss occurred.

Robust repression differs from traumatic amnesia in that repression supposedly leaves the person utterly unaware of the entire terrifying event and the circumstances that led up to and followed it. A woman unable to recall certain details of a life-threatening rape has not forgotten all that happened during the rape nor has she forgotten her terror. She remains painfully aware of the brutality of the assault, even if some of its elements can not be remembered.

Repressed memory therapists are not concerned with half-remembered events of trauma-induced amnesia and if a client clearly recalls instances of sexual exploitation, these practitioners remain uninterested. The only brutalization that truly matters to these therapists is abuse so devastating that it was repressed and is therefore entirely unknown and not even suspected when the client begins treatment. Any pre-therapy memories of childhood—painful, pleasant, or otherwise—are assumed to be nothing but facades hiding the truth. The accounts produced by recovered memory clients illustrate how the robust repression phenomenon differs from recognized memory processes and from the psychoanalytic concept of repression. Repression, in these accounts, turns out to be no less than psycho-magic.

A typical example is that of one thirty-eight-year-old woman who came to believe that she had accessed numerous repressed memories of being raped under a variety of circumstances. She was convinced that she remembered her knowledge of the rapes disappear at the conclusion of each event. In one account, she felt her awareness of having been raped pass into her unconscious as she climbed the stairs from the basement where the rape supposedly occurred. Because of the magical mechanism of repression, when she entered the kitchen at the top of the stairs, she appeared composed and normal to her family. All her accounts were arranged so that awareness was blocked from her consciousness at the conclusion of the traumatic scene as if a curtain descended over it. This pattern of repeated, instantaneous repression supposedly explained why her childhood seemed so placid to her siblings, parents, friends and in her own pre-therapy accounts. The accuracy of many of this woman's memories were verifiable because she saw her siblings also being raped in numerous hypnotically recovered scenes. Her siblings, who were not in therapy, denied that the rapes ever happened. Her siblings' denials forced the woman to claim that they had repressed their memories and only she knew the truth. The denials did not shake her confidence in her therapy.

In some instances, repression works in an entirely different fashion. Many clients of recovered memory therapists come to believe that they suffered strings of abusive acts, lasting years, and were aware of them throughout most of their childhood. In these scenarios the recalled abuse might start as early as shortly after birth and continue into their teens. Invariably, victims never confided the abuse to anyone. If groups were involved, no other victims ever told and perpetrators were never caught. At a certain age all knowledge disappeared from consciousness. Exactly why awareness of the abuse suddenly disappeared is unspecified or explained as somehow due to the activities of an evil group.

For these therapists the repression concept is all-powerful. In the end, repression does whatever therapists need it to do. For practitioners, repression rationalizes the existence of any therapy-elicited allegation, whether a single sexual act done to an infant or a toddler, incest continuing for a decade, multiple gang rapes, or ritual cannibalism and murders. The robust repression concept is devoid of either scientific corroboration or independent corroboration of clients' accounts. Once defined through its use in the therapy, robust repression appears to be science-fiction rather then science.

INFLUENCE OF PROCEDURES

To recover repressed memories, therapists employ various procedures such as hypnosis, guided fantasy, automatic writing, strategic use of support groups, suggestion, interpersonal pressure, and old-fashioned propaganda, that is, directing clients to seemingly authoritative books in which the therapist's theory is advertised. Recovered memory therapy is an example of the maxim that those who ignore history are doomed to repeat it. Early in his career Freud used some of the same techniques modern-day recovered memory therapists employ—specifically, hypnosis, interpersonal pressure, leading, and suggestion. He too produced accounts of early childhood sexual abuse. Patients never spontaneously told such tales nor did they ever tell complete stories without strong pressuring. In Freud's words, he could obtain these stories only "under the most energetic pressure of the analytical procedure, and against an enormous resistance." Almost perversely, Freud's confidence in the accounts grew in direct proportion to the amount of pressure he had to apply before patients provided him with tales of sexual abuse during the first years of their lives.

At first Freud was greatly impressed by the tales he obtained and quickly claimed a breakthrough for his psychoanalytic method of therapy. Eventually, however, he recognized that his methods were invariably yielding false statements from all of his patients. While he always maintained his confidence that some of his patients had actually been sexually abused during childhood, he realized that even these patients were confabulating accounts of early childhood sexual scenes. His realization that all eighteen of his patients invariably confabulated accounts of early childhood sexual abuse raised a serious question about the validity and value of his psychoanalytic treatment method. He needed a theory to support his already published claim that the new method was an important innovation. Only this would save his faltering career. As Freud put it, "Perhaps I persevered only because I had no longer any choice and could not then begin at anything else."

He then had to consider the possibility that his analytic method was causing patients to report false accounts of sexual scenes—that he was pressuring or suggesting these scenes in some way. Freud rejected this possibility out-of-hand and eventually concluded that his patients' accounts of sexual abuse stemmed from sexual instincts expressing themselves from within the unconscious. He convinced himself that the cause of all forms of mental illness (and many physical illnesses) was reflected in the patient's fantasy life. His psychoanalytic method would cure it all. This self-serving conclusion salvaged something of great significance of his new treatment method and became the basis for much of modern psychotherapy. Because Freud did not appreciate the danger of what is now known as "experimenter effects"—the influence of a researcher's expectations on a subject's behavior and the perception of that behavior—he could summarily reject the possibility that his treatment method was in essence causing the patients' fantasies.

In light of the moral and scientific paradigms prevalent in his time, Freud's conclusion that sexual deviance led to mental illness in some manner was not surprising. He shares his era's orienting moral perspective—essentially that sexual deviance was sure to be punished. Among the most seriously held ideas about mental illness in Freud's time were the notions that it was caused by either masturbation or coitus interruptus. In promoting his analytic method, Freud was merely seeking to distinguish himself from competitors for status and recognition. His writings about human psychology are shot through with assumptions about instinctual drives finding expression in human behavior and shaping it. Fighting against these drives will cause mental illness. It is quite likely that Freud communicated his strongly held assumptions and expectations about instinctual drives to his patients through questioning and interacting and that he unknowingly introduced and shaped the sexual contents of their fantasies. He was then correct to conclude that all of his patients were producing some fantasy material, but he failed to understand that his assumptions about human nature and the role of sex were causing the particular contents of their confabulated accounts of sexual abuse.

Freud's initial mistake of classifying pseudo-memories as factual accounts is chillingly similar to what is happening today in recovered memory therapy. Fortunately, examining the mechanisms of a contemporary phenomenon is much easier than conducting a retrospective analysis of Freud's techniques. Descriptions of the therapy's procedures are published in practitioners' books, articles, training tapes, and lectures on recovered memory therapy. In addition to the therapists' revelations, interviews with clients fill in important details of the picture of what transpires during treatment sessions and the pressures to which the clients are subjected. Therapists must first convince clients that they are in need of therapy. Early in the treatment they establish their special ability to identify the stigmata signaling repressed memories, which include classic symptoms of mental illness as well as a variety of commonplace physical symptoms, certain attitudes, and certain behaviors. In addition to obvious signs of major mental illness, "warning signs" of hidden abuse can include physical symptoms such as headaches, stomach pain, asthma, dizziness, and pelvic pain.

Lists of attitudes and behaviors that imply repressed memories are usually long and contain some quite exceptional statements, such as having a phobia about closing stall doors in bathrooms or awakening from sleep and attacking one's bed partner. Symptoms also include indications so general that they could apply to almost anyone—difficulty in maintaining a relationship, general feelings of dissatisfaction, liking sex too much, lack of career success, and fear of dentists. The presence of only a few symptoms is enough for someone to be considered a candidate for the therapy.

The first step in the cure is getting the trusting, unaware but possibly resistant, client to agree that brutalization probably did occur—most likely by a relative. Any shock or disbelief the client may express only confirms the reality of the abuse, the therapist tells them. The therapist's expectations predict the direction of the treatment. The client responds to techniques that encourage guesses, speculation, and confabulation. What starts as a guess about what type of abuse might have caused their present emotional problems, grows into guessing which relative committed the abuse. Repetitive retelling and reshaping of this account can transform a "perhaps" into a "for sure" and can thereby create a sense of certainty. The process may culminate in elaborate fantasies about schemes by parents, neighbors, teachers, or any other adults who were around during the client's childhood. It is now commonplace for clients to eventually arrive at the belief that they have repressed involvement in a satanic cult's rituals, involving murder of infants and cannibalism. Some therapists estimate that more than 15% of repressed memory therapy clients remember such brutal scenes. This estimate may well be very conservative.

Clients begin therapy with no awareness of the abuse that is supposedly at the root of their disorders. They are blank canvasses on which the therapists paint, using the techniques of the therapy. Studies have shown that people are most susceptible to suggestion when unsure about the matter at issue. New clients, being completely ignorant of what repressed memories their minds might contain, are exceedingly vulnerable to influence. Studies show that memories of details of actual events, even quite recent ones, are subject to gross distortion when pressure or subtle suggestion is used to change perceptions. Research also documents that entirely false memories can be created with minimal pressure or suggestion. For instance, subjects have "remembered" events from childhood that were made up by the researchers. Research into interrogations of crime suspects also shows that it is possible to lead psychiatrically normal suspects to "remember" committing a murder they did not commit. In both laboratory and field settings, once test subjects accept the premise that an event occurred, many confabulate appropriate details that make the memory seem real.

The process of recovered memory therapy is lengthy and offers the therapist innumerable opportunities to manipulate a client. The client/therapist relationship is ideal for influencing the attitudes and beliefs of the needy client. Even subtle pressure—signaling expectations or leading questions—can easily lead to conformity. It may take months to lead a client to the repressed memory root of the problem. A client may be told that recent dreams, or dreams remembered from childhood, are but tip-of-the-iceberg expressions of buried secrets.

A therapist may begin by focusing on a client's feeling, however vague, that someone made them uncomfortable in childhood or on an image of a silhouetted figure moving through their bedroom doorway. Any hostility the client may feel toward a parent may be explained as a sign that the parent did something to them far more terrible than the client presently knows. One or more of the pop-psychology books that report miraculous cures flowing from the "discovery" of such memories may be recommended by the therapist. In effect therapists prep these victims-in-training for key turning points in their therapy drama. Clients become sufficiently knowledgeable of the therapy's plot-line that they can improvise their way through the next scene. Often this prepping is done directly by the therapist or through books written by other practitioners of recovered memory therapy.

The training can also be done indirectly via victim-support groups in which long term clients pass on knowledge to newcomers. Knowledge of the expected twists and turns in the course of therapy can be acquired almost by osmosis just by being part of America's talk-show and tabloid culture in which stories of repressed memory discovery are told and retold.

The books recommended to victims-in-training prepare them to know among other things:

- How they should feel when a memory takes over;
- How to use vague and subtle sensations of uneasiness to license speculations about abuse;
- How mundane events can be triggers for memories, that is, serve as stimuli for engaging in fantasy;
- How "body memories"—literally, compelled physical reexperiencing of the pain of abuse—can be excepted to happen at certain points;
- How to use display of emotional suffering to legitimate reclassifying a guess, dream, or fantasy as a recovered memory.

Clients discover that playing the sexual abuse victim is a both demanding and engaging role. They do not realize that they have become involved in a living-theater psychodrama with their therapist, support groups, and family of orientation. In this exercise they eventually become committed to the role of victim and will emote. Whatever doubts they may have are subordinated to the therapist's judgment, the images they have fantasized, the stories they have confabulated, and the identity they have developed through participation in the course of this process.

In the repressed memory movement nothing is as pure and holy as a good cry or display of emotional pain. Clients who allow themselves to play the part of victim and describe an imagined rape scene set themselves up for strong feelings of distress. Allowing the release, that is, display, of the emotions appropriate to a rape increases confidence in the reality of the imagined event. Unaware of their ability to generate these emotions, clients use the display of emotion as proof of the truth of their fantasies.

Therapists also report that the memories their clients recover must be true because the emotions they display are so obviously real and powerful. These therapists are hardly unbiased observers. Even putting aside their commitment to repressed memory therapy, the proof of a therapist's skill and acumen rides on ability to elicit memories and provoke dramatic emotion. It is not surprising that therapists believe that these displays prove the existence of repressed abuse. In addition to showing appropriate emotion, clients can be expected to experience "body memories" at certain moments. Practitioners believe memories of abuse can be stored directly in muscle and skin tissue and that clients may reexperience the physical pain of the ancient abuse. Reports of body memories serve as added proof that the abuse happened.

As dramatic as these body memories may appear to be, research on the therapy's procedures shows why clients might experience pain for reasons other than budding repressed memories. The analgesic power of hypnosis, its ability to cause people to experience non-existent physical stimuli and to cause somatic charges, such as inhibiting perception of physical pain, has frequently been demonstrated. When hypnotized subjects are told they are about to be touched, perhaps even burned, with a hot object and then are actually touched with an ice cube, they will report feeling intense heat. Subjects can also be led to undergo somatic changes, such as raising skin wheels, altering body temperature, heart rate, and causing warts to disappear at the direction of the hypnotist.

Hypnotic procedures arm the therapist with a powerful tool for influencing perceptions and beliefs, procedures that play an important part in recovered memory therapy. Hypnotic trance can be accomplished either through formal induction procedures, which are obvious, or via indirect methods, such as guiding visualization or relaxation. Hypnosis has even greater dramatic power to create false memories than social influence. But like social influence, hypnosis induces subjects to confabulate additional details to fill in the gaps in their memory. Hypnosis can accomplish exceptional degrees of cognitive influence. The scientific literature documents that hypnotized subjects routinely accept as memories scenes that have been suggested and visualized in a state of trance. These pseudomemories help subjects develop confidence that these hypnotically generated fantasies are real.

In hypnotic settings, subjects prove sensitive to the social imperatives surrounding the hypnosis. Demand characteristics, as they are called, refer to the larger meaning and social structure that surrounds a hypnosis session. Clients engaged in past-life therapy, for example, bring into every therapeutic session their understanding of the assumptions underlying their treatment and knowledge of their position in a community of believers. Because of these demand characteristics, fantasies generated in past-life therapy predictably include costumes, props, and backdrops appropriate for earlier times. Clients of recovered memory therapy too understand the demand characteristics of their particular therapy and are influenced by them. At the beginning of each session, clients already know the goal is to search out childhood scenes of a sexually abusive father, mother, sibling, or neighbor. Any guidance, leading, or suggestion during the therapy session is affected by the overriding demand characteristics of recovered memory therapy. When a hypnotized client pictures the silhouette of a person standing in a doorway, a therapist might suggest letting the figure enter the room. When the figure enters, the demand characteristics of recovered memory therapy will influence a hypnotized client to imagine a relative intent on sexual assault.

The memories that result from such therapy sessions differ dramatically in quality and texture from normal recollections of long ago events and therefore must be regarded as highly suspect. The attributes of recovered memories match those of hypnotically induced pseudo-memories which can be so powerful and engaging that subjects sometimes volunteer that visualizing these scenes is "like watching a movie." With time and retelling, these visions tend to become highly detailed, in vivid color, and crystal clear. Details may include what people were wearing, what someone smelled like, and specific dialogue. Therapists take such vividness and detail as proof of the accuracy of the memory when it actually implies the opposite.

Recovered memory therapy seems to have been produced by a series of mistakes. Most obviously, practitioners manage to ignore research showing that their principal techniques, social influence, and hypnosis, cause false or grossly inaccurate memories. They refuse to acknowledge that three generations of researchers have tried and failed to confirm the existence of the repression phenomenon, in even its most conservative form. They ignore the fact that no evidence has been found to suggest that the human mind is capable of hiding from itself the kind of traumatic events elicited from clients in recovered memory therapy. Their assumptions about the way the human mind operates are known by specialists in memory to be nothing but prescientific folklore and myth. In short, these therapists are out of touch with modern research on the subjects on which the miracle cure depends. No one can doubt that recovered memory therapy is producing something quite significant—agreement with the therapist's expectations.

THERAPY IN SOCIAL CONTEXT

To a growing number of knowledgeable academic and clinical specialists in hypnosis, social influence, memory, clinical psychology, and psychiatry, it is obvious that the practitioners of repressed memory are misusing therapeutic techniques. Repressed memory therapy is a triumph of misapplied influence in which practitioners are demonstrating the power of their methods to create beliefs. Doubtless recovered memory clients are victims—victims not of their parents or their past, but of their therapists. While the outcome of the therapist's influence on the client is not always certain and many clients reject the suggestions, it has worked frequently enough to warrant recognition of its manipulative power and of the fact that recovered memory movement is evolving into one of the century's most intriguing quackeries masquerading as psychotherapy.

The distress some victims experience with the "discovery" of memories is only the first taste of pain to come. Because the memories implicate family and community members in horrible crimes, the trauma of this therapy radiates outward to involve often dozens of innocent people. The creation of two tiers of victims is one way in which this therapy differs from the usual quack cure. The primary victims are the therapists' clients, and the clients' parents and others who appear in the memories are the secondary victims.

As a result of this therapy, adult children eventually will come to hold their parents responsible for imagined betrayal and to detest them for it. As part of the cure many are urged to insult, revile, defame, humiliate and sometimes ruin the reputations and lives of those they believe have tormented them. Some are advised to sue their parents and grandparents as part of the cure. Thousands of families have already been shattered. The possibilities for fracturing family groups are all being realized: the accused spouse is divorced; siblings are forced to choose sides; grandparents are denied access to their grandchildren; grandchildren lose contact with their grandparents, and so on.

Practitioners of recovered memory therapy work the cure on both the unhappy and the seriously disturbed. Because the client learns to mimic the emotions of a brutally abused person, recovered memory therapy is exceptionally distressing. For those with serious disorders, the new cure is a needlessly painful and ineffective treatment. Recovered memory therapy diverts some seriously disturbed patients from effective treatments. In reality, most of these victims are probably caught up in a nightmare—an endless search for a not yet discovered cure for their actual disorder.

Those not suffering from major psychiatric disorders are likely to be relative newcomers to the psychotherapy industry. They do not realize that their therapists are primed to diagnose them in the current fashion and accept assurances that whatever their symptoms—anxiety, depression, anorexia, or malaise—their cause is repressed sexual abuse. Novices will believe that just because a practitioner is licensed, he has the expertise to help, knows what he is doing and that the treatment is based on proven methods.

Most victims of the new cure remain in treatment for years. Some former clients have realized they have been tricked into accepting the beliefs required by the cure. Many of those who have had the courage to reject their supposed healers are outraged at having been processed by this cookie-cutter therapy. Some who accused parents on the basis of their recovered memories now appreciate the damage done to their lives and the lives of those around them.

Even if well-intentioned, the therapists are like the physicians who once bled patients in order to cure them. But unlike those physicians, who were limited by the primitive state of medical knowledge of their time, the promoters of repressed memory therapy ignore reliable research, misuse their authority and techniques, and damage the lives of their clients and their clients' families.

In this dispute about recovered memory therapy, there is no room for a middle ground. The mind either functions in the way the therapy demands or it does not. The techniques either uncover repressed memories or they create pseudo-memories. For Ph.D.s and MDs on opposite sides of the controversy, the fight now starting may become the therapy world's gunfight at the OK Corral. Due to the extent to which the various forms of recovered memory therapy have infiltrated the mental health and social service professions, the seriousness of the allegations the therapies generate and the frequency with which damage occurs, if the therapy is invalid, the result of this shoot-out has far-reaching consequences for the future and respectability of clinical psychology and psychiatry.

FURTHER REACHES OF MEMORY THERAPY

Believing any number of events from a client's childhood could have been repressed, therapists often press for more and more memories. Like modern-day Don Quixotes, they are convinced of the purity of their mission and the essential evil of what they are fighting. Unrelenting pressure from the therapist encourages invention of ever more bizarre memories. The recovered memory movement is constantly expanding its boundaries to accommodate the progressively bizarre and difficult-to-believe abuses imagined by the clients. At the outer edges of recovered memory therapy lie multiple personality disorders (MPD) and satanic cults.

Despite the promises of its promoters, the therapy does not result in lasting relief from symptoms of schizophrenia, depression, anxiety, anorexia, or other serious disorders, nor does it turn unhappiness into joy. Indeed, life's problems appear to get worse rather than better after the clients become convinced that they were brutalized in childhood. Cutting themselves off from their family and unbelieving friends, they may restrict themselves to a social world filled only with true believers. The stress of the painful process of recovered memory therapy may exacerbate preexisting conditions or even precipitate disorders that had not previously been expressed.

Some long-term clients may be diagnosed as having multiple personality disorder (MPD). The frequency of this diagnosis has skyrocketed during the last decade. Often hospitalized, MPD sufferers find themselves subjected to a treatment regimen that is nothing less than spooky. They may be directed to host conversations among the various alter-personalities they have learned to role-play. Nondominant alter-personalities may communicate with the therapist via finger signals rather than through speech. Therapists have clients build dioramas in sand boxes with plastic figures of dead bodies, coffins, witches, and black-robed figures. Clients may be expected to respond to therapist's commands to call up computer-like programs installed in them by a satanic cult—programs the therapist then tries to erase by using secret instructions learned from other MPD clients.

The behavior and symptoms of the estimated 25,000 MPD patients diagnosed since 1980 bear little resemblance to the symptoms and behavior of the few people similarly diagnosed over the last century. Some specialists in dissociative disorders believe that MPD is being massively over-diagnosed. Others believe that it does not even exist as a distinctive psychiatric disorder. One recent study of the earliest MPD cases, reported before repressed memory therapy became trendy, concluded that in all likelihood the whole history of the MPD diagnosis is a mistake, springing from the influence of hypnosis and suggestion by physicians. Experimental research on the relationship between hypnosis and MPD has demonstrated that normal, nonsymptomatic subjects can be induced to display the behaviors and symptoms of MPD in response to hypnotic suggestion.

Once a client is diagnosed as having multiple personality disorder, the therapist no longer has the problem of explaining why the client is not getting better. The accepted prognosis for MPD is that virtually no one recovers fully. The other strategy for managing the embarrassing matter of long-term clients' failure to recover relies on the quintessential anti-Christian evil: the satanic cult. Therapists who occupy the point positions in the movement started this trend by reporting discoveries of satanic cults responsible for their clients' brutalization. The cults were also supposed to have induced the clients to repress their memories of the cults' activities. The satanic cults that exist in the recovered memories of clients' childhoods are an especially beastly bunch.

Unlike youth culture groups that develop an interest in the occult and paint graffiti on walls or mutilate animals, the satanic cults likely to be recalled by clients in recovered memory therapy seem to exist for the sole purpose of brutalizing children. Clients routinely tell sordid tales of childhoods entirely controlled by satanists who forced them to perform ritual sex, and who are involved in baby breeding, sacrifice of infants, and cannibalism. Some clients report having been programmed to kill their therapists in order to prevent them from exposing the existence of the cult or to kill themselves rather than disclose information about the cult. Like the term repression, "programmed" is a bit of word magic. It lacks, however, even the suspicion of respectability attached to repression. Programming, a concept invented to mystify and cover over a great hole in pseudo-scientific theories of how evil groups exercise absolute control over people's lives, has been incorporated into recovered memory theory. The term refers to a mysterious process that supposedly produces rigid patterns of behavior and Manchurian-candidate obedience.

In the mythology of the recovered memory movement, programming gives satanic cults powers of control that border on the miraculous. The true miracle is how convenient the supposed existence of such cults turns out to be as an explanation for the inexplicable scenes produced by the clients' fantasies. Hundreds of police investigations conducted throughout the country have failed to corroborate satanic cult memories. Kenneth Lanning, an FBI behavioral science specialist who has reviewed three hundred cases, makes the point in his book *Investigator's Guide to Allegations of "Ritual" Child Abuse* that it is now up to mental health professionals, not law enforcement officials, to explain why supposed victims are alleging things that do not seem to have happened.

The positions taken by the promoters of repressed memory therapy have gotten so bizarre, they nearly defy description. Take for example the recent report by Cory Hammond, Ph.D., one of the prominent figures in the movement. In a recent day-long training session for therapists, Hammond reported on cases of clients who were programmed as children by satanic cults and on the origins of the programming techniques that were used. From these clients, he learned that the programming techniques were invented by Nazi scientists who developed the procedures on death camp inmates. As it happened, the Nazi researchers were also satanists. These satanic scientists were captured by the CIA at the conclusion of the war and continued their "research" in the United States. The CIA code name for the programming project was Monarch.

According to Hammond, the key figure in the development and spread of satanic programming tn the United States is a Hasidic Jew and death-camp turncoat. As a young man he is supposed to have saved himself from extermination by being useful to his Nazi captors. Part of his appeal to the satanists was his knowledge of the Kaballah (a work of Jewish mysticism). Somehow, Jewish mysticism is supposed to integrate well with satanist beliefs. After the war, this man was also brought to the United States by the CIA to continue programming research. After graduating medical school, this Dr. Green, as he was called, began spreading his programming techniques throughout the satanic underground. Hammond warned that many other satanic programmers have also gone to medical school and are working as physicians in order to have easy access to children.

Hammond described clients' recovered memories of being programmed. They recalled being strapped to gurneys at age two or so and having electrodes inserted into their vaginas, vision disrupting goggles put over their eyes, and sound played into one ear. They were shocked and tortured in order to instill in them unreserved acceptance of the cult's commands. Hammond shared with his audience the particular instructions that would lead their clients to reveal the satanist-inserted programming and the verbal instructions for erasing these programs. Hammond went on to suggest that the *Illuminati* are the international network that controls all satanist activities. Satanists themselves, the *Illuminati* seek to take over the world, he said, and one of their goals is to produce an army of "Manchurian candidates" for use in the takeover.

It would be a mistake to write off Hammond's claims as coming from a lone voice in the wilderness. Other nouveau eminent figures in the intertwined recovered memory/ritual abuse/MPD tradition are prone to similar statements. Hammond revealed his discoveries to a large group of therapists eager to learn how to treat their recovered memory and MPD clients. Despite obvious ultra-right wing, lunatic left, and anti-Semitic elements, Hammond's account of an international satanic conspiracy was greeted with a standing ovation. The audience's ready acceptance of Hammond's intelligence briefing from the twilight zone is not explained by his eloquence or compelling evidence. Recovered memory therapists have been telling audiences about the satanic underpinnings of clients' problems for years.

The therapists who are creating these and other bizarre fantasies have painted themselves into a corner from which they have no escape. If they admit that even some recovered memories are inaccurate, their position crumbles because they have no independent way of distinguishing between truth and fantasy in the statements their methods elicit. They would be admitting to what research on hypnosis and social influence demonstrates, namely that truth and fiction blend together into an amalgam that no one, least of all the subject, can ever again reliably separate. The percentage of truth in a hypnotically or massively influenced story can run from zero on up and so can the percentage of fiction. What is valid recall and what is pseudomemory in the resulting story is unknowable without corroboration. Only pretherapy accounts of a person's history can be treated as a normal memory with only the ordinary component of error.

INSTITUTIONALIZATION AND LONGEVITY

It is unlikely that the therapy's practitioners will ever apologize for abusing their positions of trust, for failing to recognize the dangers of the techniques they are using and for neglecting to exercise appropriate care in the treatment of clients. This would be an admission that they have misled tens of thousands of people and convinced them that they have been horribly abused. It would be an admission that they have turned their clients against innocent parents and have caused enormous damage to the relations between their clients and their families. To do so would also be to admit that thousands of people have been hospitalized with the incorrect diagnosis of MPD—a condition that may not even exist. It would be an admission of massive malpractice for which they could be held accountable. Compared to other fringe psychology and psychiatric excesses the ghastly menage-à-trois—recovered memory therapy, multiple personality disorder, and satanic cult conspiracy—represents an exceptional problem. The robust, superpowerful repression mechanism and the therapy's methods are on the verge of being institutionalized and thereby exceeding the relatively short life expectancy of other psychological quackeries.

One reason for the recovered memory therapy's spread is that it possesses an organizational quality that distinguishes it from the typical exotic cure. Normally, clients quickly learn that the fad does not fix their symptoms, lose faith in self-proclaimed psychological geniuses, and withdraw. This prevents institutionalization of fads and hastens their decline. Victims of recovered memory therapy, however, are more likely to tolerate therapeutic failure for a longer time because they have concluded that something particular and identifiable has happened to them. Therapeutic failure is explained away because of the unanticipated seriousness of what the client and therapist are discovering together. New revelations of abuse account for continuing therapeutic failure—this failure, in turn, provokes suspicions of even more serious abuses, which is confirmed by new memories which, in turn, accounts for continuing therapeutic failure, and so it goes.

A therapy's success in developing an institutional basis ultimately depends on the political trends that contributed to its rise. Broad concerns about child protection and feminist thought have contributed to the interest in these therapeutic innovations and their ready acceptance. Unfortunately, movements promoting social change face the danger, if not the inevitability, of stimulating opportunistic, zealous, and simple-minded spin-offs.

The constituencies created by the larger social concerns provide the muscle behind the institutionalization of repression theory and the therapy's procedures. The most startling example of this institutionalization is legislation and/or recent court decisions in fifteen states that now permit litigation based on recently recovered repressed memories. The unsubstantiated repression hypothesis is thus elevated to the status of fact. The new laws are tantamount to official certification that the phenomenon exists.

The potential impact is staggering since it opens the door to thousands of civil and criminal complaints. By alleging negligence on the part of a nonperpetrator parent, it is possible to involve homeowner's insurance policies and create deep pockets for people of modest means. At least 300 such lawsuits are known to have been initiated on the basis of recovered repressed memories. Widespread attorney interest is predictable.

Developments in psychiatry and psychology and changing market conditions have made these professions fragile. They are vulnerable to the possibility of fracturing into interest-group coalitions held together in uneasy alliances under their respective professional banners. Given these volatile conditions and the customary unwillingness of professionals to make enemies by publicly accusing colleagues of quackery, it is unlikely that many will strongly object to recovered memory therapy no matter how absurd they might privately think it to be.

The change in psychiatry is coming from the fact that virtually all significant progress in ameliorating symptoms of major mental disorders has been made in the past forty years through scientific research in biopsychiatry. Genetic liability as a significant factor in vulnerability to major mental disorders is an established fact. This realization implies that valid treatment methods for major mental disorders will eventually emerge from laboratories and not from the insights of charismatic, engaging, self-proclaimed psychological geniuses. Although progress has not been without its false starts and errors, and success is far from near-at-hand, the treatment of major mental disorders is being re-absorbed into traditional medicine and demystified as fast as dependable treatment methods are developed. This trend, if it continues, should have a substantial effect on both altering the prognosis for persons afflicted and diminishing the stigma associated with mental illness.

Progress in biopsychiatry is causing a shift in the demand for psychiatric services away from talk-therapies and toward medical intervention in cases of major disorders. It is also forcing final realization of the uselessness of the dominant theoretical presumptions underpinning most modern psychotherapy—the role of the unconscious and the place of sexual instincts. Touted at first as a cure for all forms of mental illness, psychoanalysis, in the course of its history, has been in continuous retreat from the treatment of major mental disorders. The symptoms of major mental disorders have never been alleviated by talk-therapy. Psychoanalysis has devolved into a thinly disguised process of resocialization carried out under the label of medical or psychological treatment. The idea that the root of major mental disorders are found in interpersonal events in childhood is no longer supportable. The wish that discovering key events in childhood and releasing the supposedly pent-up emotions associated with them can be instrumental in curing major mental disorders also has become increasingly impossible to support in the face of the progress of biopsychiatry.

These changes have left some physicians, psychoanalysts, and therapy practitioners scrambling for customers. Therapists who claim to be able to make people happy by curing their symptoms through application of the same logic, of finding the event and bleeding off the emotional residue, are also being hard pressed. Despite the fact that clients frequently agree that the therapy is helping, there is little reason to believe that anything more than attitude change is happening. The attitude changes clients experience need not have anything to do with the theory the therapist claims to be using nor with long-term relief of symptoms.

Competition for clients has intensified due to the proliferation of numerous types of counselors, alternatively certificated practitioners and self-proclaimed therapists. Short-run client satisfaction with their therapy may have a great deal to do with the confidence the therapist has in the method employed. The more confidence the therapist has in the therapy, the more successful the therapist will be in manipulating a client's attitudes. This success need not have anything to do with the validity of the therapist's theory or treatment method.

If all that matters is customer satisfaction, that is, attitude toward the therapy, self-proclaimed geniuses and their off-the-wall therapies should and do compete quite well with traditionally certified and trained psychotherapists. Most often it makes no real difference which theory a therapist uses.

Recovered memory therapies are thinly disguised, politically correct, pumped-up versions of the core Freudian speculation. Apart from beefing-up the concept of repression, their real innovation is in their far more powerful persuasive tactics. Since they are based on Freudian speculation it is relatively painless for universities to embrace them as the "new truth." Responding to the competition for clients and the demands of students for trendy treatment methodologies, clinical psychology programs in universities are moving away from tradition and are rapidly embracing recovered memory theory.

Legitimation of recovered memory theory by academia is contributing to the institutionalization of the therapy. Speculative robust repression theory is being taught in university psychology graduate programs, education school psychology programs, psychiatric residence programs, doctoral programs in clinical psychology, and at schools of social work, as if it were fact. Practitioners who have completed their education are being exposed to the theory and methodology in continuing education programs, such as the one addressed by Cory Hammond. Producing believing followers is likely to gain this fad a lasting position among practitioners if for no other reason than the sheer numbers committed to it. Using the persuasive techniques of the therapy, each new therapist is likely to produce new crops of clients who will recover lots of lost memories.

Even if a professional consensus developed and the informed general public became convinced that arguments like those developed in this paper are correct, it would probably not markedly retard the spread of recovered memory therapy. The professional and societal mechanisms available to protect the public from this sort of quackery border on the nonexistent. The professions involved are too immature to have developed viable procedures for restraining excesses and have no way of prohibiting rank experimentation with humans.

In recent months the mass media has begun to report the other side of the repressed memory story, notably criticism by professionals and outrage by those who say they were falsely accused. If the media continues balanced coverage the most likely result is that therapists practicing the cure will become convinced that the world has misunderstood and rejected them. The elements of such a reaction are already evident.

In 1992 a grass roots organization, the False Memory Syndrome (FMS) Foundation, was formed in Philadelphia. It represents members of over 2,400 families who protest that they have been falsely accused. In the recovered memory movement the formation of FMS is classified as merely part of the backlash against women and children. Some leaders of the movement seem to regard anyone who questions their therapy as antifemale, antichild, probably stupid, or worse. Worse is that critics are, to use Hammond's description, "dirty"—meaning they are part of the satanist conspiracy. Many professionals who have voiced criticism of the movement have at one time or another been accused of being satanists or agents of satanists.

These responses signal the collective paranoia of a social movement turning inward. The steps to isolation include rejection of the opinions of nonbelievers and increased reliance on only those who validate the ideology and claims of persecution. Once people become committed to an ideology, even one that masquerades as a testable scientific theory, the fact that it has failed is not necessarily perceived or it is often discounted.

Making therapists responsible for the quality of the services they render and the damage they cause is the only measure likely to inhibit the practice of recovered memory therapy. If therapists who elicit recovered memories and convince clients of their truth were obligated to demonstrate the validity of these accounts, they would be unable to do so.

As long as practitioners are not accountable for what they lead their clients to believe and what they encourage them to do, they will remain reckless. They have no need to notice the power of their techniques and will continue to believe the damage they are causing is of benefit to their clients and the suffering they cause parents is a just punishment. Their refusal to acknowledge what the scientific literature demonstrates about their methods and to face the possibility that they are dreadfully wrong may be thought of as a defense mechanism that has deep psychological, professional, and economic meaning—it functions to protect therapists from full awareness of what they are doing. In the parlance of recovered memory therapy, they are in denial.

READINGS SUGGESTED BY THE AUTHORS

Hicks, R. 1991. *In pursuit of Satan: The police and the occult*. Amherst, N.Y.: Prometheus Books.

Loftus, E. 1992. *The reality of repressed memories*. Address to the American Psychological Association, Washington, D.C., August.

Mersky, H. 1992. The manufacture of personalities: The production of multiple personality disorders, *British Journal of Psychiatry* 160 (6).

Mulhern, S. 1991. Satanism and psychotherapy: A rumor in search of an inquisition. In *The satanism scare*, ed. J. T. Richardson, J. M. Best, and D. G. Bromley. San Francisco: Aldine de Gruyter.

12

THE VALIDITY OF REPRESSED MEMORIES AND THE ACCURACY OF THEIR RECALL THROUGH HYPNOSIS:
A CASE STUDY FROM THE COURTROOM

DONALD R. TAYLOE

For 100 years, repressed memories have remained an enigma and a defining point of conflict between various psychological disciplines. Since repressed memories are not readily available for conscious recall, the scientific proof of their existence remains elusive. At the present time, the only way to authenticate the existence of repressed memories is by a case report that documents the reality of the repressed event and then its recall after a period of amnesia. In the following case report, a subject on trial for murder had repressed the events surrounding the crime. Hypnosis was used to recover those memories. That information was then used to dramatically alter the outcome of the trial.

From the time Freud published "Studies on Hysteria" (Breuer and Freud 1955), the scientific community has agonized over questions of the validity of repressed memories and the accuracy of hypnosis to recall them. At the center of this debate have been concerns that false memories created through hypnosis by the therapist will be considered real and lead to false conclusions. The fact that false memories can be created through hypnosis has been known at least since 1884 when Bernheim demonstrated this dimension of hypnotic influence and called the phenomenon "Retroactive Hallucinations" (Bernheim 1884/1964).

Since Bernheim's observations there have been numerous published laboratory studies on the unreliability of hypnotically refreshed memories.

From the *American Journal of Clinical Hypnosis* 37, no. 3 (January 1995): 25–31. Reprinted with permission.

Orne and his colleagues reviewed many of these studies and used the results as a justification for their position that hypnosis should not be used prior to testimony in court (Orne, Soskis, Dinges, Orne, and Tonry 1985). The difficulty with this position is that none of the studies quoted by Orne included repressed memories in their research protocols. Therefore, one could argue that Orne's position should not be used to invalidate the use of hypnosis to uncover repressed memories in a forensic setting.

In addition to laboratory studies, there have been anecdotal reports on the misuse of hypnotic techniques during police investigations that have further confused the issue of repressed memories. Ofshe (1992) reported the case of a 43-year-old father who, after having false memories implanted in his mind through hypnosis (relaxation), falsely confessed to having participated for years in imagined satanic ritual abuse involving his two daughters. Ofshe stated that he "presumed" that the psychologist who questioned the defendant justified the use of relaxation techniques (hypnosis) as a means to uncover repressed memories. If that assumption was correct, then the psychologist was misguided, since Ofshe did not state that the defendant had neurotic symptoms that might be caused by repressed memories. Repression is a defense mechanism, and in most circumstances, a person who committed years of willful sexual abuse would not repress those memories.

That psychologically traumatic events can be repressed from conscious recall is incontrovertible. The weight of case histories describing verifiable repression is too heavy to support any other conclusion. For example, when Ross Cheit, a 38-year-old Brown University ethics professor, had recalled memories of childhood sexual abuse that had lain dormant for 25 years, he was able to verify his new-found memories with the very man who committed the abuse (Horn 1993). Rosen reported the case of a 27-year-old man with symptoms of depression, suicidal fantasies, and strange bodily sensations of "twisting" and "choking." During therapy, the patient was able to remember an episode, when he was 3 years old, of his mother attempting suicide by hanging. This memory was followed by an abreaction and amelioration of symptoms. The reality of his mother's suicide attempt was verified by the patient's father (Rosen 1955). Moreover, Herman and Schatzow reported on memory deficits in 53 patients undergoing group therapy for incest survivors. Twenty-eight percent had repressed memories of the abuse. The abuse in the women with repression started earlier in childhood and was more likely to include violence than in the patients with nonrepressed memories. Seventy-eight percent of the total group were able to eventually obtain confirmation of the abuse from another source (Herman and Schatzow 1987). One very recent case of repressed memory involved the conviction on November 30, 1990, of George Franklin Sr. for a murder he committed on September 22, 1969. The prosecution based its whole case on the recently recovered memories of the murder by Franklin's daughter Eileen (Terr 1994).

There have been several reports where hypnosis has been successfully used to uncover repressed memories in a forensic setting, (Mutter 1990; Kroger and Douce 1980). One case, *Rock* v. *Arkansas,* went all the way to the United States Supreme Court (Kuplicki 1988). A bare outline of the case is that during a domestic argument on the night of July 2, 1983, Frank Rock was shot and killed by a bullet fired from a gun that his wife, Vickie, picked up during the fight. Vickie was left with a poor recollection of events surrounding the crime. Prior to trial, on advice from her attorney, Vickie was hypnotized to refresh her memory. Posthypnotically she recalled that her finger was not on the trigger, and the gun discharged when Frank grabbed her arm. A weapons expert subsequently testified that the gun was defective and could be discharged without pulling the trigger (Kuplicki 1988).

The Arkansas State Court disallowed testimony derived from Vickie's posthypnotic memory, and Vickie was subsequently convicted of manslaughter. The Arkansas Supreme Court affirmed the conviction, holding that "the danger of admitting [hypnotically refreshed] testimony outweigh(s) whatever probative value it may have" (Kuplicki 1988). The case was appealed to the United States Supreme Court, which by a vote of five to four overturned the Arkansas ruling holding that, "Arkansas *per se* rule excluding all posthypnosis testimony infringes impermissibly on the right of a defendant to testify on his or her own behalf." Justice Blackmun, writing for the majority, also reasoned that it cannot be shown that "hypnotically enhanced testimony is always so untrustworthy and so immune to the traditional means of evaluating credibility that it should disable a defendant from presenting her version of the events for which she is on trial" (Kuplicki 1988).

Though the decision by the Supreme Court does not embrace witnesses for the prosecution, neither does it exclude them. Kuplicki argues that the decision should be used as a point of bifurcation, where hypnotically refreshed testimony by the defendant would be permissible, but excluded by the prosecution. This would preserve the constitutional rights of the defendant, but exclude tainted testimony by the prosecution (Kuplicki 1988). Orne changed his position and supports a bifurcated rule (Orne, Dinges, and Orne 1990). Udolf believes that the decision opens the door for hypnotically refreshed testimony by the prosecution if safeguards are followed and the testimony can be corroborated (Udolf 1990).

Clearly, there are many unanswered questions about the use of hypnosis in the forensic arena. The critical question is whether or not the concept of repressed memories is valid, and if the memories are valid, can they be accurately recalled through hypnosis. At the present time, we must rely on case histories to help us answer these questions. The following case report provides insight about the repression of memories as a defense mechanism and the use of hypnosis to uncover them.

CASE REPORT

On the morning of February 18, 1978, Mr. Marvin Bains Sr., a 50-year-old machinist who suspected his wife of 28 years of being unfaithful, discovered her sitting in her car with a male friend. Mr. Bains ordered his wife out of her car and drove her to their home. Shortly thereafter, Mr. Bains rang the doorbell of a neighbor. The neighbor, who had just heard what she thought were gunshots coming from the Bains's house, opened her door and discovered a remarkably composed Mr. Bains on her doorstep. The lower right side of Mr. Bains's jaw had been blown off. The neighbor called the police who found Mrs. Bains sitting in a kitchen chair with the top part of her head blown off by a shotgun. Mr. Bains was arrested and charged with murder. When questioning Mr. Bains, the police discovered that he had amnesia for the event in question.

Mr. Bains's amnesia appeared to be genuine. He was never caught "slipping up" by his defense team, by the police, or by anyone inside the jail. A psychiatrist consulting on the case also felt that Mr. Bains's amnesia was real. For the next 8 months, Mr. Bains's defense team, along with ballistics experts from the sheriff's office, the medical examiner, and the prosecutor's office, attempted to put together what had happened inside the Bains's home the day Mrs. Bains was killed.

Mr. Bains was charged with first-degree murder. With the trial date approaching and Mr. Bains unable to participate in his defense, his attorney requested a hypnotic evaluation to determine Mr. Bains's state of mind at the time of the killing.

On September 12, 1978, I met with the defense team and was told that Mr. Bains was accused of shooting his wife, had amnesia for the event, and had sustained a gunshot wound to his face that left him disfigured. No information about the physical evidence connected with the crime was provided. It was also disclosed that the Bains's home, where Mrs. Bains was killed, had been sold to pay for legal expenses and was unavailable for inspection.

The entire evaluation took place in Mr. Bains's cell in the Orange

County Jail in Santa Ana, California. First, Mr. Bains was interviewed alone in the "waking state" to take a complete history including a psychiatric evaluation. Mr. Bains had a clear waking memory right up to the time he stepped out of his car with his wife in front of his home, but from then on he remembered nothing until he regained his memory while riding to the hospital in the back of an ambulance. Mr. Bains was completely calm and seemed dissociated from what had happened to his wife. The events surrounding his wife's death appeared as if they were "surgically removed" from his memory, leaving intact his memory from both before and after her death.

Next, the defense team came back to the cell and videotaped the hypnotic interview. The method of induction was a combination of eye fixation and progressive relaxation. Mr. Bains was a good subject and easily slid into a hypnotic trance. Under hypnosis, Mr. Bains was age regressed back to just before the beginning of his amnesia. During the hypnotic interview Mr. Bains remained calm, spoke in a monotone, and still appeared dissociated from the killing. He proceeded to relate the story of Mrs. Bains's death.

Mr. Bains's story, as told under hypnosis, was that when he took his wife inside the kitchen, he told her that he was going to kill himself. She said "no, let's have coffee." While she fixed the coffee, he went into the bedroom and loaded his shotgun, brought it back to the kitchen, and laid it across the kitchen table between them. Intending to carry out his threat of suicide, he pulled the shotgun across the table to place the muzzle under his chin. In the process of pulling the shotgun back, it discharged and the blast struck his wife in the face. The recoil from the shotgun caused the gun to come back and hit him on the nose. The blast knocked off his wife's glasses. He reached down to the floor and put them back on the table. He then tried several times to shoot himself but failed. He went into the bathroom to check on his bleeding nose, then went and reloaded the shotgun, finally managing to blow off the right side of his jaw. At the end of the hypnotic session, Mr. Bains was given the suggestion, "You will be able to remember any of this story that is helpful to you, but will be unable to remember anything that is not helpful or would be harmful to you." After the session, it was clear that he still had amnesia, and remained composed. His story matched the facts of the case. Mrs. Bains was found sitting at the kitchen table. There was physical evidence of several shotgun blasts in the kitchen, and there was blood in the bathroom where he had inspected his bleeding nose. My report to the defense team was that the death was accidental.

When the trial started November 13, 1978 (*People* vs. *Bains* 1978), it was apparent that the prosecutor was going to press his case for first-degree murder on evidence that two shotgun blasts, and not one as related by Mr. Bains under hypnosis, had hit Mrs. Bains in the head. Since five spent shotgun shells were found at the scene of the crime, both sides agreed that the shotgun had been fired five times. The difficulty was that evidence for only four shots was found in the kitchen. The prosecutor was going to contend that the unaccounted-for shot must have struck Mrs. Bains. Wounds from two shots into Mrs. Bains would preclude accidental death as a defense.

Since Mr. Bains still had amnesia for the event, I was called back to rehypnotize him. This time I was told that all the shots could not be accounted for, and I was asked if Mr. Bains could, under hypnosis, relate the exact sequence of events and the placement of each shot. Under hypnosis, Mr. Bains was again age regressed back to the time just before his amnesia, and he was told to relate to us exactly what happened, with the additional instruction to count the shots as he fired the shotgun. The sequence of events was that Mr. Bains first loaded the shotgun with three shells. The first shell accidentally hit Mrs. Bains. Then he placed the muzzle under his chin, but since he had trouble reaching the trigger, the muzzle slipped off when he pushed the trigger, and the second shot went into the ceiling. He then repeated the maneuver, and again the shotgun slipped off his chin and another shell was fired into the ceiling. Mr. Bains then went back into his bedroom and reloaded with two more shells and went back into the kitchen. He tried again and was again unsuccessful, and the fourth shell went into the kitchen ceiling. Finally, on the fifth try he managed to shoot himself in the side of the face. So all five shots were accounted for.

As the trial went on, the county crimelab expert took the stand to give his explanation of the physical evidence. The top half of Mrs. Bains's head had been cleanly blown off, and there was a groove the size of a quarter down the middle of her skull. The DA theorized that the first shot took off the top of her head, and the second shot created the groove. The DA further theorized that Mr. Bains only missed himself twice since there were only two holes through the roof of the attic. He stated that the evidence was that two shots went inro the ceiling and out the roof of the attic, and one shot went into Mr. Bains's jaw, which left two shots for Mrs. Bains. The defense attorney theorized that the groove down the center of Mrs. Bains's skull may have been caused by the plastic-wad cup that holds the shot in each shotgun shell. The defense attorney was also convinced that Mr. Bains was telling the truth under hypnosis and that three shots had gone into the kitchen ceiling.

Armed with Mr. Bains's statements under hypnosis, the defense attorney, while court was in session and in front of the jury, challenged the expert witness to go back to the scene of the crime and to reexamine the physical evidence. It this point, the trial was stopped and a court order obtained to gain entrance to Mr. Bains's former home.

Both the defense attorney and the prosecution expert went back to the scene of the crime and climbed into the attic. The kitchen ceiling had been repaired, and the roof of the attic was patched. Just like the prosecution expert testified, there was evidence that only two shots came through the ceiling of the kitchen and out the roof of the attic. The defense attorney then put his hand down on the insulation covering the floor of the attic, and a splinter pierced his hand. The insulation was then pulled back to discover a cross beam that had been fully impacted by a shotgun blast. The beam had buckled but had not broken. It was clear that a third shot had hit the kitchen ceiling in the same general area as another shot and impacted the beam, which prevented the shot from going through the insulation and out the roof of the attic. Confusion about the number of shots hitting the ceiling existed because the pattern of two shots in the ceiling had merged together. At this point, the expert witness stated that he had been wrong and that three shots had gone into the kitchen ceiling, and that left only one shot for Mrs. Bains. The District Attorney then dismissed the murder count and Mr. Bains pled guilty to manslaughter.

Sometime after the second hypnotic session, Mr. Bains spontaneously regained his memory. He was in custody for 3 years. Six months after being released he completed the task that he had started in his kitchen and committed suicide by shooting himself.

DISCUSSION

Several questions can be raised regarding the authenticity of this case. Was the amnesia genuine? In this case, the setting lends credence to the creation of amnesia as a defense mechanism against severe emotional trauma. Mrs. Bains's death was an accident without premeditation or financial gain. There was no planning involved nor was there any complex series of maneuvers required to kill Mrs. Bains. Mr. Bains was not a devious person. He was a hardworking, blue-collar worker. There were no reports from third parties stating that they had heard Mr. Bains slip up and reveal that he did not have amnesia. Most importantly, he held the key to his own defense, since only he knew the placement of all the shots and would, therefore, have every reason to remember and no reason to fake amnesia.

Was the hypnosis real? If the amnesia was genuine, then the hypnosis was real, since only under hypnosis was he able to accurately recall the events surrounding Mrs. Bains's death. There were details about the crime that remained unknown to the investigators, which were provided by Mr. Bains's statements under hypnosis. Mr. Bains's testimony provided the first evidence of how blood came to be in the bathroom. Since his face was badly damaged, no thought had been given to other injuries. It was never disclosed that blood was found in the bathroom until after the first hypnotic session. However, the most crucial information provided by Mr. Bains was the information that three, not two, shots had been fired at the ceiling. It is easy to understand how the physical evidence was misinterpreted. It would be easy to assume that only two shots were fired at the ceiling, since only two exit holes were found in the roof of the attic. Clarification of the physical evidence provides proof that hypnotic testimony can be both accurate and helpful.

Moreover, if the amnesia was genuine, and the hypnosis real, can we equate Mr. Bains's amnesia to repression? If we define a repressed event as one so psychologically traumatic that the event is erased from memory only to surface later, more or less intact, then the killing of Mrs. Bains was repressed by Mr. Bains. It has been reported that, in some cases, amnesia can be a defense mechanism deployed against the threat of suicide (Gudjonsson and Haward 1982). In fact, one whole premise behind repressed memories is that they provide protection against a psychologically life-threatening event. At the time of the investigation, Mr. Bains had no waking memory of his suicide attempt; therefore, it could be hypothesized that had the amnesia continued, his suicide could have been prevented.

CONCLUSION

This case demonstrates that extremely emotional events, interpreted as life threatening on some level, can be actively repressed from conscious memory and that these memories can later be accurately recalled under hypnosis. This conclusion provides justification for using hypnosis in some legal cases.

REFERENCES

Bernheim, H. 1964. *Hypnosis and suggestion in psychotherapy.* New Hyde Park, N.Y.: University Books. (Original work published in 1884.)

Breuer, J., and S. Freud. 1955. Studies on hysteria. In *The standard edition of the complete psychological works of Sigmund Freud,* ed. J. Strachey. London: Hogarth Press Ltd., Vol. II. (Original work published in 1895.)

Gudjonsson, G. H., and L. R. C. Haward. 1982. Case report—Hysterical amnesia as an alternative to suicide. *Medical Science Law* 22 (1): 68–72.

Herman, J. L., and E. Schatzow. 1987. Recovery and Verification of memories of childhood sexual trauma. *Psychoanalytic Psychology* 4 (1): 1–14.

Horn, M. 1993. Memories lost and found. *U.S. News & World Report* (November 29): 2–63.

Kroger, W. S., and R. G. Douce. 1980. Forensic uses of hypnosis. *American Journal of Clinical Hypnosis* 23 (2): 86–92.

Kuplicki, F. P. 1988. Fifth, sixth, and fourteenth amendments—A constitutional paradigm for determining the admissibility of hypnotically refreshed testimony. *Journal of Criminal Law & Criminology* 78: 853–76.

Mutter, C. B. 1990. Hypnosis with defendants: Does it really work? *American Journal of Clinical Hypnosis* 32: 257–62.

Ofshe, R. J. 1992. Inadvertent hypnosis during interrogation: False confession due to dissociative state; mis-identified multiple personality and the satanic cult hypothesis. *International Journal of Clinical & Experimental Hypnosis* 40: 125–56.

Orne, M. T., D. F. Dinges, and E. C. Orne. 1990. *Rock* v. *Arkansas*: Hypnosis, the defendant's privilege. *International Journal of Clinical & Experimental Hypnosis* 38: 250–65.

Orne, M. T., D. A. Soskis, D. F. Dinges, E. C. Orne, and M. H. Tonry. 1985. *Hypnotically refreshed testimony: Enhanced memory or tampering with evidence? Issues and practices in criminal justice.* Washington, D.C.: National Institute of Justice.

People v. *Bains,* No. C-40058 (Super. Ct., Orange Co., CA, June 6, 1978).

Rosen, V. 1955. The reconstruction of a traumatic childhood event in a case of derealization. *Journal of the American Psychoanalytic Association* 3: 211–21.

Terr, L. 1994. *Unchained memories.* New York: Basic Books.

Udolf, R. 1990. *Rock* v. *Arkansas*: A critique. *International Journal of Clinical & Experimental Hypnosis* 38: 239–49.

13

THE MEMORY RETRIEVAL PROCESS IN INCEST SURVIVOR THERAPY

CHRISTINE A. COURTOIS

The resolution of sexual abuse trauma requires the retrieval of memory and the working through of associated affect. This article provides information about amnesia, repression, and dissociation in the aftermath of childhood trauma and about the storage and retrieval of memory, including the necessary conditions for retrieval. Specific strategies are suggested for use according to the phase of the traumatic stress response and according to the needs and defenses of the individual survivor.

A paradox exists regarding the memories of abuse available to adult survivors of incest and other forms of childhood trauma: Those with access to memory usually wish to forget, repress, or minimize what they know. Those with absent, hazy, or fragmented memory are usually desperate to remember, until memory returns. They then move to the position of survivors with memory: they want to forget. Additionally, many survivors hold the belief that "If I don't remember it, it did not happen." Herman and Schatzow (1987) have observed that "Survivors often know more than they know that they know," and Meiselman (1990) has noted their propensity to re-repress memories after their retrieval. In a similar vein, many survivors who access memories of non-response by caretakers along with the particulars of the actual abuse often disbelieve what they remember or that the events actually occurred. This disavowal protects them from the pain and the loss inherent in the acceptance of both the abuse and the lack of protection.

Copyright © 1992 The Haworth Press, Inc., Binghamton, NY. *Journal of Child Sexual Abuse* 1, no. 1 (1992): 15–31. Reprinted with permission.

Although remembering is but one goal of retrospective incest therapy (Bass and Davis 1988; Blume 1990; Briere 1989; Courtois 1988; Dolan 1991; Gil 1988; Olio 1989; Poston and Lison 1989), memory retrieval is obviously an important component of the process. While it is not necessary for survivors to recover every incident of abuse in absolute detail, representative abuse memories must be captured with enough associated affect to process the trauma in some detail and to work it through (Dolan 1991; McCann and Pearlman 1990; Olio 1989; Steele 1989; Watkins 1980).

Memory deficits, amnesia, and dissociation are quite characteristic of trauma response (Horowitz 1986; Speigel 1989; van der Kolk 1987) and are utilized in the interest of defense and protection. This is an essential point for the clinician to understand in working on trauma resolution in general and memory retrieval in particular. Other defenses and coping strategies (i.e., minimization, disbelief, rationalization, addictions/compulsions, disavowal) also work against memory retrieval. Defenses and protective strategies should be seen as having once been functional and as therefore understandable in the context of the trauma. They should not be pathologized nor should they only be seen as the client's "resistance" in a pejorative sense, according to Summit (1983). Such defenses usually become so ingrained that they function in a semi- or wholly autonomous fashion and may be largely unconscious. They must be lessened slowly and with care rather than precipitously in order that the client not be left defenseless, overwhelmed, or both.

Memory retrieval is idiosyncratic and varies quite dramatically between individuals according to psychological defenses, ego strength, and other personal resources, internal and/or environmental cues, and the phase of treatment. Therapy is geared not only to the retrieval of autobiographical memory, but toward the integration of affect with recall to achieve resolution of the trauma (Courtois 1988; Horowitz 1986; Meiselman 1990).

The goals of this article are threefold: (1) to provide general information regarding the memory deficits, amnesia, repression, and dissociation characteristic of the traumatic stress response to incest; (2) to discuss ways the therapist and the client can create an environment which facilitates remembering; and, (3) to discuss the variety of ways in which memories return and to suggest specific triggers and strategies conducive to memory retrieval.

MEMORY LOSS AND DISCONTINUITY IN RESPONSE TO INCEST TRAUMA

Incest has numerous characteristics and dynamics which make it traumatic for the victim both in childhood and later in adulthood (Armsworth 1984;

Blume 1990; Briere 1989; Courtois 1988; Herman 1981; Russell 1986; Summit 1983; Terr 1991). A number of studies have identified that incest has high traumatic potential and results in a traumatic stress response with phasic alternations of intrusive symptoms and then numbing (Armsworth 1984; Donaldson and Gardner 1985; Lindberg and Distad 1985). Incestuously abused children often suffer untreated Post-traumatic Stress Disorder which may follow several different courses: it remits naturally over time, it lies dormant for years emerging in delayed form in reaction to life events and triggers, or it impacts continuously over the lifespan (frequently without conscious awareness on the part of the survivor).

In this article, the focus is on the denial-numbing phase of the post-trauma response in terms of memory loss and on the intrusive-repetitive phase in terms of memory retrieval. These phases are found whether the trauma response is acute and short-term or whether it is long-term or delayed (van der Kolk 1987). In fact, one or the other phase may contribute to the type and duration of the trauma response. For example, many adult incest survivors have lost memory for the childhood trauma due to being predominantly or exclusively in the denial-numbing phase for a period of years. In the case of incest, the denial-numbing response is reinforced by the dynamics of secrecy, shame, and lack of validation that occur in the family. Incest dynamics clearly support not remembering and not telling, making disclosure and recall quite arduous tasks for many survivors, especially if threats were made to enforce secrecy.

The numbing-denial phase encompasses many different mechanisms and behaviors, among them: repression, dissociation, partial, selective, or total amnesia (discontinuous memory), emotional constriction, self-anesthesia, self-hypnosis, emotional and social withdrawal, anhedonia, and an avoidance of emotions or situations related to the trauma. Intrusive/reliving phase mechanisms and behaviors include many forms of psychological and physiological arousal: hyperreactivity and hypervigilance, startle responses, intrusive recollections in the form of flashbacks and other perceptual disturbances, repetition compulsions and reenactments, aggressive discharge toward the self or others, and/or social and emotional withdrawal (Courtois 1988; Meiselman 1990; Terr 1991; van der Kolk 1987).

Most incest does not involve physical force but includes manipulation and misrepresentation of the activity. Abusers commonly misuse their authority and relationship to the child as they prey upon the child's immaturity and dependence. In some cases, physical force and/or threats and coercion are essential components of the incest. Whether the abuse is physically violent or not, it constitutes emotional blackmail of the child and therefore is considered a form of violence (Courtois 1988).

The abuser almost always tries to get the child to keep the activity secret. The very nature of the secrecy conveys that the activity is wrong and bad. This, in turn, leaves many a child feeling ashamed and, by extension, deserving of the abuse. This internalization is reinforced when disclosed or overt abuse is disbelieved or otherwise denied or discounted (Sgroi 1982; Summit 1983). Lack of response leaves the child isolated and at risk for further abuse. Over time, the child learns to keep the incest secret and to not tell anyone for fear of being blamed, hurt, rejected or abandoned, to protect other family members, or even to please or keep favor with the abuser. The pressure for secrecy contributes to protective blocking or forgetting of abuse memories.

Two studies have been conducted on memory in incest survivors with findings that are remarkably consistent. Herman and Schatzow (1987) found that of a clinical sample of 53 women participating in time-limited group treatment for incest, 64% did not have full recall of the abuse and reported some degree of amnesia and 28% reported severe memory deficits. Several variables of the abuse were most related to repression: (1) abuse which occurred at an early age. *Mild to moderate* memory deficits were reported for abuse that began in latency and ended by early adolescence. *No memory deficits* were reported when abuse had begun or continued into adolescence. *Marked memory deficits* were associated with abuse that began early in childhood (often preschool years) and ended before adolescence. (2) The greater the degree of sadistic or violent abuse, the greater the memory deficits. In addition, differences were observed in the adaptive styles and symptoms of these patients: Those with *full recall* wished they could repress the memories and relied heavily on dissociation and isolation of affect to ward off feelings. When the dissociation failed, they relied on more maladaptive coping strategies such as somatization and drug use. Those with *mild to moderate memory disturbance* recaptured memories with the stimulus of group participation, which led to periods of increased anxiety. Those with severe memory deficits had almost complete amnesia for childhood but recurrent intrusive images associated with extreme anxiety. They had obsessive doubt about the reality of abuse (i.e., "If I don't remember it, it's not real and did not happen"). Some had flooding of memories and affect in response to a trigger event, leading to the symptoms of severe Post-traumatic Stress Disorder which were further upsetting and anxiety-provoking in their own right.

Briere and Conte (1989) reported that approximately 60% of a clinical sample of 468 subjects reported some amnesia for abuse which occurred before age 18. The variables of abuse most related to repression were: (1) occurrence at an early age; (2) the number of psychological symptoms; and, (3) the degree of violence associated with the abuse.

Although the findings of these two studies should be considered preliminary, they have strong face validity due to their high degree of concurrence. They are also in agreement with the observations of many clinicians conducting retrospective incest treatment. Interestingly, they are consistent with research conducted on other forms of childhood trauma. Terr (1991) has extensively studied the effects of different types of childhood trauma and has recently published a theoretical article about her findings. She postulates two types of childhood trauma, Type I which involves one sudden crisis and Type II which consists of prolonged, repealed ordeals. Of note: children suffering from "single-blow" Type I traumas retain full, detailed memories while those whose trauma was of the Type II variety do not.

With the new data being generated about incest, it is becoming apparent that amnesia does not only affect a clinical population. Blume (1990) identifies amnesia as the most common feature of the post-incest syndrome and that perhaps half of all survivors do not remember the abuse. Her observation corresponds to the findings discussed above and to clinicians' descriptions of the "disguised presentation" for therapy made by "secret survivors" (Blume 1990; Courtois 1988; Gelinas 1983; Meiselman 1990). A pattern of common presenting symptoms has been identified by which the clinician can suspect incest/child sexual abuse in the patient's background without direct knowledge or disclosure.

The disguised presentation contains clues to the abuse history including such relationship patterns in the family as role reversal between parent and child, chronic family discord, secrecy and denial, and alcoholism or other addictive/compulsive problems. Patients often present with a characterological depression with atypical impulsive and dissociative elements and often with personality disturbances and gross polarities of attitudes and behaviors. Anxiety disorders are frequent as are low self-esteem and self-deprecation. Relationships are often conflictual, marked by mistrust and ambivalence, patterns brought into the therapeutic relationship. Very often, sexual dysfunction accompanies these relationship difficulties. Hidden survivors have histories of suicidal ideation and gestures as well as other self-destructive and self-mutilative behaviors. They often have repeat episodes of victimization which exacerbate existing problems of mistrust, helplessness, shame, and negative self-worth. Finally, many hidden survivors describe feeling "crazy," different, stigmatized, and unlike "normal people" because their symptoms are disconnected from any memory of the abuse (Blume 1990; Briere 1989; Courtois 1988; Gelinas 1983; Meiselman 1990).

Adult survivors commonly have an alternating and diagnostically confusing spectrum of intrusive and/or constrictive symptoms associated with undiagnosed chronic or delayed PTSD. Clinicians used to believe that treatment was sought due to the greater discomfort associated with intrusive symptoms. It is becoming more obvious that constrictive/numbing symptoms such as depersonalization, derealization, patterns of amnesia and selective memory, lost time, and the creation of alternate parts or selves, cause discomfort of a different sort and frequency lead to the request for treatment. These symptoms are as important as intrusive symptoms but are more often overlooked because they are not as observable or dramatic (Speigel 1989), or the clinician has not been trained to assess for them in the standard mental status examination or intake interview (Ross 1989).

STORAGE AND THE RETURN OF THE REPRESSED MEMORIES

Gil (1988) describes three concepts regarding memory that are useful to the clinician working on the retrieval of the traumatic material: (1) that the events were perceived and stored by a young child, possibly one who was preverbal at the time of the abuse; (2) that visual (imaginal) and other sensory cues can stimulate the retrieval of memory; and, (3) that memories were stored during experience(s) that produced arousal and helplessness; therefore, the client may have to re-experience painful emotion in order to remember and may "resist"/protect the self against remembering in an attempt to ward off the pain. Olio (1989) further discusses some of the difficulties of retrospective reconstruction. She writes that memory is not like a stored camera image nor does it preserve an exact record which can be retrieved in its entirety. Rather, the work of Loftus and her colleagues (Loftus and Loftus 1980) documented that the original form of memory is altered by intervening experiences and differing external sources, a process labeled updating. The process is therefore dynamic rather than static (Bonnano 1990).

Olio goes on to discuss the process of *memory condensation* as another factor relevant to understanding the process of recalling traumatic memories. Through this process, a description of an early scene may be an amalgam of experience rather than a single episode. The clinician must understand that memories return in disorganized, occluded, fragmented, and condensed fashion and should not disavow or dismiss the patient's account if it lacks coherence.

Braun (1988a, b) has developed the BASK Model of dissociation to account for the memory disturbance of individuals who suffer violent and prolonged abuse of the sort which is inconsistently interspersed with loving attention by a caretaker. This model posits that an individual's main stream of consciousness is made up of four domains (Behavior, Affect, Sensation, and Knowledge) within a time continuum which are split off or separated from each other by the process of dissociation in the interest of making the trauma bearable. Thus, the overwhelming experience is defensively fragmented and disorganized and emerges in disjointed form. In treatment, the dissociated individual is assisted to access all four domains for the information they contain about the trauma. The information is then reintegrated into consciousness in its totality.

Using information regarding modes of memory representation, the therapist can ask not only about *what* is remembered but *how* it is remembered, imaginally and visually as well as through the other senses (Bonnano 1990; McCann and Pearlman 1990; Olio 1989). It should be assumed that, in keeping with other individuals suffering from amnesia, survivors "may not have lost their memory but rather their awareness of the knowledge" (Olio 1989, 95). Specific techniques therefore can be used to bring material back into awareness.

The Role of Triggers and Memory Cues

A good guideline about triggers (or cues to memory retrieval) is that virtually anything can be a trigger for anyone at any time. Cues or triggers are associational, causing what was previously dissociated to be reassociated. They occur in any of the four domains described by Braun's BASK Model (1988a, b). While it is not completely clear why a reaction is triggered at one point in time and not another by the very same stimulus, conditions favoring remembering and de-repression are becoming more evident. For example, Meiselman (1990) has found that when life events are somehow associated with the trauma and when defenses are lowered due to life stress and triggers, associated material from the past often surfaces in fragmented form. An atmosphere of support and validation is also conducive to memory and, in and of itself, is often a memory retrieval cue. In therapy, the development of safety, trust, and pacing assist the survivor in maintaining positive control.

Olio (1989) was one of the first authors to identify triggers to memory retrieval in incest survivors. Courtois (1988, 1990) organized triggers (or associational cues) for recall and reaction into five categories: (1) normative developmental events or developmental crises of an incremental type (such as the development of an intimate relationship or the birth of a child) or decremental type (such as the death of the perpetrator or other significant kin); (2) exposure to events which symbolize or resemble the original trauma (such as a specific person, body type, sound, smell, body position or movement, childhood picture, media account, phrase or image, anniversary reaction, medical or denial procedure, and sexual activity or sexual event); (3) crises associated with recollection, disclosure, confrontation, reporting, and criminal justice concerning the client's personal abuse experience or the abuse of other family members or acquaintances; (4) issues within the therapy (such as support, trust, and validation, the encouragement to associate and disclose) and, (5) life stages or cumulative life events (such as the "empty nest syndrome" or mid-life crisis of the middle-aged woman, and "hitting bottom" and/or achieving sobriety or another form of recovery from a substance or process addiction/compulsion). Group therapy with other survivors and involvement with self-help groups often cause a chaining of associated memory. Triggers/associational cues vary from those that are quite specific to the trauma to those which are more general or subtle.

Ways Memory Returns

Remembering occurs in numerous ways and, as mentioned above, often in fragmented and disconnected fashion. Memory can return *physiologically*, through body memories and perceptions. The survivor might retrieve colors, specific visions or images, hear sounds, experience smells, odors, and taste sensations. His or her body might react in pain reminiscent of the abuse and might even evidence physical stigmata as the memory of a particular abuse experience is retrieved and worked through (Calof 1987; Ellenson 1986). Other physiological reactions include the stress responses of fight, night, or freeze to particular stimuli, states of hyperreactivity and arousal (including sexual), anxiety, temperature change, and age regression. Memories might also occur *somatically* through pain, illness (often without medical diagnosis), nausea, and conversion symptoms such as paralysis and numbing.

Memories can also return *affectively* or emotionally. The survivor may have sudden, intense feelings or vague, more subtle affect shifts. Memories sometimes recur through flashbacks, sensory and image flashes that some survivors describe as feeling as intense as the original experience and as very disconcerting, especially when their onset is sudden. Memories might also return via dreams and nightmares, perceptual disturbances, and skewed reactions to events or people. The *schemata* (or beliefs) the survivor holds about self and others give clues to memories (Bonnano 1990; McCann and Pearlman 1990) as do transference and countertransference reactions in the therapy. *Self-perception* marked predominantly by shame, stigma, self-hatred, self-estrangement, and feelings of worthlessness and despair may be forms of memory.

CREATING A THERAPEUTIC ENVIRONMENT CONDUCIVE TO REMEMBERING

This is about memory. A kind of memory that a great many of us have fiercely repressed. A kind of memory that we have no awareness of. That profoundly shapes our intimate lives without our understanding. Without our assent. It has no relationship to formal education or "remember when. . . ." This memory is the interface (inner face) of a self-induced amnesia. . . . It has to do with being victimized, usually an invisible victimization. No witnesses. No visible scars.

So why seek out this memory? Why not leave "well enough" alone? So, you've happened to build your house on top of a toxic waste deposit: just don't dig around, stir things up, or plant a garden. Sell and don't tell. Not possible. (Client's Voice: Betsy Warland in Laidlaw, Malmo and Associates [1990], 215–16)

This passage eloquently describes the memory loss and discontinuity experienced by this incest survivor. The goal of therapy (expanding her metaphor) is to assist her to dig out and shore up her foundation in order to achieve a sense of wholeness and a continuity to her life experience. Remembering allows the survivor to recapture lost parts of self, to experience the self more fully than previously possible, and to loosen vitality and energy in the interest of comfort with the self and in intimacy with others. Obviously, remembering and recollecting parts of the self are important components of this therapeutic goal (Blume 1990; Briere 1989; Courtois 1988; Dolan 1991; McCann and Pearlman 1990; Meiselman 1990).

The alliance between therapist and survivor must be strong enough to provide the psychological security necessary for memory work. The importance of the alliance is repeatedly stressed in the writings of clinicians working with this population (Briere 1989; Courtois 1988; Gil 1988; Herman 1981; McCann and Pearlman 1990; Meiselman 1990). Meiselman (1990) summarizes these recommendations in the principle and subprinciples of what she has termed reintegration therapy. "The establishment and maintenance of the client-therapist relationship is central to work on incest-related disturbances" (p. 95). She also makes the following recommendations: the bond between client and therapist should gradually develop into a special relationship in which the therapist feels genuinely caring toward the client; the therapist should be explicit about the limits and boundaries of the therapeutic relationship and should guard against any form of dual relationship; the therapist should be predictable and reliable; the therapist should be sensitive to the power aspects of the relationship; the therapist should guard against role reversal; and, the therapist should recognize the client's right to leave and to return. Additionally, the therapist must be prepared to be a witness to the survivor's traumatic history and must sometimes serve as an alter ego, expressing and labeling emotional reactions when the survivor is numb or otherwise dissociated or blocked.

Josephson and Fong-Beyette (1987) found that certain therapist behaviors and characteristics assist survivors in disclosing their abuse history (and so can be expected to assist in the remembering process): a calm, accepting, soothing, and nonjudgmental manner; the provision of information and education about abuse; direct and indirect questioning conducted in a matter-of-fact manner conveying empathy and respect, and reassurance, encouragement, and validation. The therapist must be cognizant of the fact that individuals suffering human-induced traumatization are notoriously difficult to ally with because of the interpersonal damage they suffered (Chu 1988; Courtois 1988). The therapist must therefore guard against distancing from the client during times of transference or countertransference crises, during memory retrieval and/or reliving (abreacting) with its attendant discharge of intense affect (such as rage, terror, despair, or sadness). The therapist should also anticipate resistances to remembering and the necessity at times to re-forget or re-repress aspects of the trauma (Dolan 1991; Meiselman 1990).

The therapist further assists the client by explaining the traumatic stress syndrome and, in particular, normative postsexual abuse reactions. The therapy and remembering process must also be described in detail. These explanations (or psycho-educational interventions) serve to demystify reactions and processes. They assist the survivor to anticipate stages of recovery and to recognize indicators and symptoms of memory retrieval. The therapist must remain acutely aware of and educate the client about the importance of pacing in the recapturing of memory. The unplanned emotional flooding of the survivor is to be avoided as it has the potential to revictimize or retraumatize rather than heal. At times, however, a flooding technique (abreaction, implosion, amytal interview) is deliberately employed to bypass defenses and to process the trauma.

It is generally advisable to reassure the survivor that defenses will not be dismantled wholesale and without regard to their necessity and that informed consent will be sought for such a technique. Otherwise, it is recommended that the survivor's psychological defenses and ego strength be assessed and strengthened before proceeding with memory retrieval. McCann and Pearlman (1990) are most emphatic on this point and stress "self work before memory work" as an important sequencing guideline. It is in line with general recommendations regarding sequencing outlined by Courtois (in press).

In addition to the iatrogenic reinforcement of trauma due to mis-pacing and the subsequent emotional flooding of the survivor, therapists may engage in behaviors which discourage disclosure due to counter-transference responses or other difficulties (Courtois 1988; McCann and Pearlman 1990; Meiselman 1990). These include responses of denial, pity, blame, distancing, rescuing, the premature assuaging of guilt and shame responses, premature resolution through forgiveness, and probing solely for the verbal and cognitive aspects of the trauma response.

It is helpful for the therapist to determine with the client what memory is available along with reactions to what is remembered. The expectations the client holds about remembering must be determined with the goal of making them realistic and achievable. At this stage, the survivor can be cautioned about the counterproductivity of working "too hard" or too compulsively on recall. This problem has been mentioned by Bass and Davis (1988), Blume (1990), Meiselman (1990), and other clinicians who have stressed the "internal wisdom" of intrapsychic defenses and that memories "return in *their own* good time."

Therapist and survivor together explore and work through defenses and fears which impede the remembering process. Some defenses are resolved in a rather simple and straightforward process while others need more extensive assessment and interpretation. Abandonment fears as well as fears of being disbelieved, blamed, further shamed, or rejected by the therapist are especially salient concerns which require direct discussion and reassurance. Real losses and abandonments in the past support these fears. Particularly poignant questions to pose to survivors at this juncture are: "What do you have to give up to remember? What do you lose?" In response to these queries, survivors often become tearful as they describe giving up their fantasies and desires for attachment to their parents and other family members. They correctly intuit that remembering involves additional losses, not the least of which is the loss of fantasized parental love, protection, and relationship potential. In articulating their fears and losses, survivors confront and defy the rules (especially denial, distortion, and dissociation) by which the family functioned and covered the incest. They also engage in mourning for past, present, and anticipated losses.

The remembering process may be harrowing for therapist and survivor alike. The readiness and energy level of each must be assessed prior to engaging in formal memory work. The survivor must have safety and support resources in place (see Dolan 1991, and McCann and Pearlman 1990 for more extended discussion of safety strategies), and must have the ego resources and strength to proceed. Likewise, the therapist should be in a position to provide increased support throughout the recalling, reliving, and resolving of memory and its associated affect.

Education precedes formal recall strategies to insure the survivor a cognitive framework within which to process emotions which accompany recall. Cognitive strategies legitimize the approach—avoid tendencies associated with trauma and its management (Roth and Newman 1991). Ambivalence is to be expected and respected—the therapist actually assists the survivor by empathizing with the wish to avoid but must not contribute permanently to a stance of denial/avoidance (Dolan 1991; Gil 1988). A related strategy is to explore what memories and clues are available and to "play Columbo" or private investigator. Disparate, fragmented evidence often must be pieced together, much like completing a giant jigsaw puzzle (a useful metaphor for the memory retrieval process). At times, it may be necessary for the therapist to put the pieces together and speculate about the emerging picture and its significance; however, at no time is it appropriate or ethical for the therapist to conclusively inform the client of specific abuse experiences unless irrefutable evidence supports such a finding.

STRATEGIES AND TECHNIQUES TO ASSIST RECALL

Many therapeutic strategies are available for memory retrieval.[1] Horowitz (1986) has articulated guidelines for choice of strategy according to the phase of the trauma response (denial-numbing or intrusive-repetitive) which assist in the pacing of the therapy process. The clinician should keep in mind that information is contained in both response phases but is expressed or contained differently; therefore, it is imperative to carefully assess each phase for the information it conveys either directly or indirectly. For example, memories often return overtly or in symbolic form via intrusive-repetitive processes such as flashbacks, body memories, nightmares/dreams, etc. Memories conveyed in denial-numbing symptoms such as dissociation are more covert but offer important clues. The clinician can investigate what the client is blocking or denying in order to understand the trauma of the past. Gil (1988) gives the example of a woman who spontaneously dissociated when her partner fondled her breast. Through "backtracking," identifying and labeling the behavior and its traumatic significance, the survivor was able to recall fondling abuse she had previously repressed but expressed symptomatically through her spontaneous dissociation.

Whatever trauma response phase the survivor expresses, the therapist must offer support and encouragement. S/he must remain cognizant that traumatic material is being evoked and that remembering may be terrifying and even life-threatening (Courtois 1988). As the concealment of the past gives way to memory and expression, it contradicts the injunctions or threats to not tell and/or to not remember.

The Denial-Numbing Phase

It is when the client/survivor is in the denial-numbing stage that evocative, elicitive strategies are the most useful. The survivor is encouraged to "take the plunge" and to move away from avoidance but in a deliberately paced manner. Uncontrolled, unpaced abreaction and catharsis are to be avoided as they put the survivor out of control and thus have the potential to retraumatize. Courtois (1988) has listed a number of experiential/expressive-cathartic techniques including hypnosis, guided imagery, writing, drawing, guided movement, body work, and those drawn from the schools of Gestalt therapy and psychodrama as well as exploratory/psychodynamic techniques to assist in memory retrieval. Detailed recommendations for the safe application of solution-focused and hypnotherapeutic techniques are to be found in Dolan (1991) and McCann and Pearlman (1990).

Both therapist and client can deliberately and selectively introduce triggers during this treatment phase. These include but are not limited to such associational cues as writing an autobiography, making a family genogram, constructing a lifeline, drawing the floorplan of the childhood home, using assessment tools such as the Dissociative Experiences Scale (Putnam 1989), the Dissociative Disorders Interview Schedule (Ross 1989), the Incest History Questionnaire (Courtois 1988), selectively interviewing family members and childhood associates, and bringing in family pictures or other memorabilia of childhood (toys, report cards, diaries, etc.). Group therapy also functions as a memory stimulus and should be considered as a very important adjunct in this stage of the treatment if not contraindicated for the particular client (see Courtois 1988 for a description of group contraindications). Herman and Schatzow (1987) have provided a detailed description of this process.

When using techniques of the type for this treatment phase, the clinician should prepare the survivor for the inevitable and normal aftershocks of recall and should have containment/support strategies in place. Finally, the clinician must take care that the survivor is not left in the middle of a traumatic episode at the end of a session. Memory work should be done in the early to mid-phases of a therapeutic session with adequate time left for closing down. Many clinicians have found it beneficial to extend the average 50-minute session to one of 75 minutes when memories are being stimulated.

The Intrusive-Repetitive Phase

During the intrusive/repetitive phase, containment strategies are best employed to prevent uncontrolled flooding of memory and affect. It is in this stage that triggers and environmental stimuli are deliberately removed and that the client is encouraged to reconstruct and work through what has been remembered. The client is supported in cognitively and emotionally processing the retrieved material to achieve resolution through the development of new understanding and new meaning (Courtois 1988; Donaldson and Gardner 1985; McCann and Pearlman 1990; Silver, Boon and Stones 1983).

Cognitive-behavioral and stress/coping techniques are most effectively utilized during this phase to assist the survivor in self-soothing strategies and to provide structure and perspective. Horowitz (1986) provided a listing of treatment strategies including reducing environmental demands; decreasing environmental stimuli conducive to recall; offering support and encouraging appropriate rest and relaxation; offering temporary management of overwhelming emotions (e.g., the selective use of antianxiety agents. work leave, or hospitalization); and shifting the focus back and forth on the traumatic material. In a similar vein, McCann and Pearlman (1990) discuss taking planned vacations from memory work for respite. Roth and Newman (1991) have demonstrated that approach/avoidance characterizes trauma response and that the judicious application of such a strategy can maximize safety in retrospective trauma work.

Group therapy can be useful if it provides the survivor with safety, support, and understanding. Groups are very powerful in eliciting memories since survivors associate or "chain" to each others' recollections and feelings. The group therapist must carefully monitor and pace the group process so that members are not continuously emotionally overwhelmed.

NOTE

1. The strategies described here are for use with the survivor *not* diagnosed as Dissociative Disorder, Not Otherwise Specified or Multiple Personality Disorder. With these dissociative disorders, it is necessary for the clinician to modify these strategies to access individual ego states or personalities created to retain the traumatic material and hence which hold individual memories. Therapy for major dissociative disorders follows the principles articulated for incest treatment in general (Briere 1989; Courtois 1988; Meiselman 1990) but must be further refined in order to access memories (Putnam 1989; Ross 1989).

REFERENCES

Armsworth, M. W. 1984. *Posttraumatic stress responses in women who experienced incest as children and adolescents.* Unpublished doctoral dissertation, University of Cincinnati, Cincinnati, Ohio.

Bass, E., and L. Davis. 1988. *The courage to heal.* New York: Harper & Row.

Blume, E. S. 1990. *Secret survivors: Uncovering incest and its aftereffects in women.* New York: John Wiley and Sons.

Bonnano, G. 1990. Remembering and psychotherapy. *Psychotherapy* 27 (2): 175–86.

Braun, B. 1988a. The BASK model of dissociation. *Dissociation* 1: 4–15.

———. 1988b. The BASK model of dissociation, part II: Treatment. *Dissociation* 1: 16–23.

Briere, J. 1989. *Therapy with adults molested as children: Beyond survival.* New York: Springer.

Briere, J., and J. Conte. 1989. Amnesia in adults molested as children: Testing theories of repression. Paper presented at the annual meeting of the American Psychological Association, New Orleans, Louisiana.

Calof, D. 1987. *Treating adult survivors of incest and child abuse.* Workshop presented at The Family Network Symposium, Washington, D.C.

Chu, I. 1988. Ten traps for therapists in the treatment of trauma survivors. *Dissociation* 1: 24–32.

Courtois, C. 1988. *Healing the incest wound: Adult survivors in therapy.* New York: W. W. Norton and Co.

———. 1990. Adult survivors of incest and molestation. In *Crisis intervention book 2: The practitioner's sourcebook for brief therapy,* ed. H. J. Parad and L. Parad. Milwaukee, Wisc.: Family Service America

———. In press. Theory, sequencing, and strategy in treating adult survivors. In *Child sexual abuse: Clinical implications,* ed. J. Briere. San Francisco: Jossey-Bass.

Dolan, Y. 1991. *Resolving sexual abuse: Solution-focused therapy and Ericksonian hypnosis for adult survivors.* New York: W. W. Norton and Co.

Donaldson, M. A., and R. Gardner. 1985. Diagnosis and treatment of traumatic stress among women after childhood incest. In *Trauma and its wake: The study of post-traumatic stress disorder,* ed. C. R. Figley. New York: Brunner/Mazel.

Ellenson, G. S. 1986. Disturbances of perception in adult female incest survivors. *Social Casework: The Journal of Contemporary Social Work* 67: 149–59.

Gelinas, D. 1983. The persisting negative effects of incest. *Psychiatry* 46: 313.

Gil, E. 1988. *Treatment of adult survivors of childhood abuse.* Walnut Creek, Calif.: Launch Press.

Herman, J. 1981. *Father-daughter incest.* Cambridge, Mass.: Harvard University Press.

Herman, J., and E. Schatzow. 1987. Recovery and verification of memories of childhood sexual trauma. *Psychoanalytic Psychology* 4: 1–14.

Horowitz, M. J. 1986. *Stress response syndromes,* 2nd ed. Northvale, N.J.: Aaronson.

Josephson, G., and M. L. Fong-Beyette. 1987. Factors assisting female clients' disclosure of incest during counseling. *Journal of Counseling and Development* 65: 475–78.

Laidlaw, T., C. Malmo, and Associates. 1990. *Healing voices: Feminist approaches to therapy with women.* San Francisco: Jossey-Bass.

Lindberg, F. H., and L. J. Distad. 1985. Post-traumatic stress disorders in women who experienced childhood incest. *Child Abuse and Neglect* 9: 521–26.

Loftus, E., and G. Loftus. 1980. On the permanence of stored information in the human brain. *The American Psychologist* 35: 409–20.

McCann, L., and L. Pearlman. 1990. *Psychological trauma and the adult survivor: Theory therapy and transformation.* New York: Brunner/Mazel.

Meiselman, K. 1990. *Resolving the trauma of incest: Reintegration therapy with survivors.* San Francisco: Jossey-Bass.

Olio, K. A. 1989. Memory retrieval in the treatment of adult survivors of sexual abuse. *Transactional Analysis Journal* 19: 93–100.

Poston, C., and K. Lison. 1989. *Reclaiming our lives: Hope for adult survivors of incest.* Boston: Little, Brown.

Putnam, F. 1989. *Diagnosis and treatment of multiple personality disorder.* New York: Guilford.

Ross, C. 1989. *Multiple personality disorder: Diagnosis, clinical features, and treatment.* New York: John Wiley and Sons.

Roth, S., and E. Newman. 1991. The process of coping with sexual trauma. *Journal of Traumatic Stress* 4: 279–98.

Russell, D. 1986. *The secret trauma: Incest in the lives of girls and women.* New York: Basic Books.

Sgroi, S., ed. 1982. *Handbook of clinical intervention in child sexual abuse.* Lexington, Mass.: D.C. Heath.

Silver, R. L., C. Boon, and M. H. Stones. 1983. Searching for meaning in misfortune: Making sense of incest. *Journal of Social Issues* 39: 81–102.

Speigel, D. 1989. Hypnosis in the treatment of victims of sexual abuse. *Psychiatric Clinics of North America* 12: 295–305.

Steele, K. 1989. A model for abreaction with MPD and other dissociative disorders. *Dissociation* 2: 151–59.

Summit, R. 1983. The child sexual abuse accommodation syndrome. *Child Abuse and Neglect* 7: 177–93.

Terr, L. C. 1991. Childhood traumas: An outline and overview. *American Journal of Psychiatry* 148: 10–20.

van der Kolk, B. 1987. *Psychological trauma.* Washington, D.C.: American Psychiatric Press.

Watkins, H. 1980. The silent abreaction. *The International Journal of Clinical and Experimental Hypnosis* 28: 101–12.

PART FOUR

PROFESSIONAL PROBLEMS AND ETHICAL ISSUES

Fincham et al. raise a number of troublesome problems that plague all of those whose profession it is to deal formally with the sexual abuse of children. Major problems now facing all those working in child protection services (CPS) include the fact that "judgments about sexual abuse allegations upon which subsequent action depends, are often more intuitive than objective." Moreover, independent of false accusations is the fact that the investigation itself may have a negative impact on the child. Further, assumptions that abuse did, in fact, occur may cause unabused children and innocent adults to suffer needlessly. Intervention should never be more harmful than the abuse it protects against. An even more serious problem is the fact that many CPS workers are overburdened and inadequately trained. More troublesome is another fact: the fact that most child abuse cases are not clear-cut and the research base necessary to make certain detection and proof of abuse does not exist.

Fallacious notions such as "children never lie," or "all childhood reports of abuse are sexual fantasies," or "all children who were abused need psychological treatment" should not be tolerated. All cases of childhood sexual abuse are not equivalent although they are too often treated this way. Even more distressing is the realization that, here and now, we still have no idea of the extent of child sexual abuse, since the figures we get from the various surveys and studies vary widely. From the information we do have we must also face the fact that some 70% of the allegations, i.e., reports of suspected sexual abuse, are not substantiated. In addition, large numbers of children are investigated annually where no credible evidence of sexual abuse is found. In 1993, for example, 700,000 were investigated and no useful evidence, i.e., proof of abuse, was found. It may or may not have occurred. Also noteworthy is the fact that the first 1981 National Incidence Survey showed that 53% of the CPS-substantiated cases failed to meet the definition of abuse used in the survey. How does one separate the "true" from the "false" at the outset? Either underreporting or overreporting is a problem.

One reason why overreporting occurs is the knowledge that if the investigation is wrong in assuming abuse has occurred nothing serious results and the CPS worker's job isn't threatened. Failing to report or investigate and a subsequent death or injury could cost the CPS investigator his job.

Fincham et al. not only argue that the reinforcement contingencies currently shaping professional behavior need to be changed, but also those influencing legislators and policy makers—as well as litigants in divorce disputes—also need to be changed. In other words, everyone involved in cases of sexual abuse needs to be held more accountable for their professional behavior and should not be granted legal—either partial or complete—immunity.

Finally, the authors make some important suggestions for research, e.g., improving our understanding of the impact of sexual abuse, and showing how individual researchers and practitioners can act to improve the welfare of the abused. They also suggest that practitioners should know their legal responsibilities and the limits of their expertise, and they should keep up with current research in this area—particularly with work in the area of children's memory.

This suggestion is followed up by the work of Ceci and Bruck, who summarize clearly and concisely the complexity of the interrelationship of the factors affecting children's suggestibility. They also note that "there is no 'Pinocchio' test that can be used by even the most qualified investigators to definitely ascertain whether or not abuse occurred." It is also noteworthy that Ceci and Bruck recognize and appreciate the sanity and wisdom of Fincham et al. in their analysis and recommendations.

Unfortunately, Pezdek, in her article "Empty Promises," sees that the position of Fincham et al. is fallacious and his crusade only of use in a "perfect world." Pezdek argues that false negative errors are more harmful than false positive errors but offers no evidence to support this position. Faulconer also feels that children are being harmed much more than falsely accused adults and that many of Fincham's suggestions would not serve the best interests of children in any way. Faulconer's position is that debates over the reliability of children's memories also detract from the needed research on exactly why abuse occurs in the first place. What we need, she avers, is to develop ways and means of stopping it cold!

Fincham et al. respond to these comments by arguing the necessity and importance of finding common ground so that everyone can work together and do what is best for children. Haverkamp and Daniluk close out this section by listing a number of serious and perplexing ethical problems facing any therapist working in this emotional and ethical minefield. First of all they indicate that behavior may be ethical yet illegal, unethical and illegal, or unethical yet outside of legal jurisdiction and "in cases where law and ethics suggest contradictory action, the therapist must choose between two conflicting, yet legitimate loyalties." Unfortunately, while existing ethical codes of conduct are helpful, they are usually inadequate in providing specific and sufficient direction in cases of child sexual abuse. Particularly difficult issues in such cases involve: (1) informed consent and disclosure, (2) legally mandated reporting of abuse, and (3) the therapeutic treatment of abuse. Haverkamp and Daniluk conclude that the therapist's awareness of the metaethical principles involved in working with families where sexual abuse may have occurred can help him or her arrive at not only a satisfactory but also a defensible and ethically sound decision.

14

THE PROFESSIONAL RESPONSE
TO CHILD SEXUAL ABUSE:
WHOSE INTERESTS ARE SERVED?

FRANK D. FINCHAM,
STEVEN R. H. BEACH,
THOM MOORE, AND CAROL DIENER

This article examines the professional response to child sexual abuse by posing three questions: Are there problems with current practice and research? What maintains current professional behavior? Can individual professionals improve children's welfare? Numerous professional practices that may harm children are documented. Analysis of the contingencies that shape professional behavior suggests that it will be difficult to change current practices. Several ways in which individual professionals can promote children's welfare in allegations of sexual abuse are highlighted.

Few images are more painful to us today than those of the sexual molestation of innocent children. So painful, in fact, that such injury has in modern times evoked a most primitive defense mechanism—denial (cf. Olafson, Corwin, and Summit 1993). Fortunately, over the last two decades this coping strategy has become less viable with increasing awareness of child abuse. For example, child abuse reporting laws were passed in every state between 1963 and 1967; Congress passed the landmark Child Abuse and Treatment Act in 1973 establishing, among other things, the National Center on Child Abuse and Neglect and the current child protective system; and media coverage of child abuse is at a historic high (45 million viewers watched "Scared

From *Family Relations* 43, no. 3 (July 1994): 244–54. Copyrighted © 1994 by the National Council on Family Relations, 3989 Central Ave. NE, Suite 550, Minneapolis, MN 55421. Reprinted by permission.

Silent" on September 4, 1992, the first non-news event covered simultaneously in prime time by different networks [Rowe 1992]). Across relevant professions, interest in child maltreatment has skyrocketed—a recent search of a data base in psychology (PSYCHLIT) for the past 6 years yielded 1,193 journal articles under the descriptor *child sexual abuse*. Combined with numerous books, conference papers, professional seminars, and so on, the professional response to this particular form of child abuse is overwhelming to the neophyte. These developments suggest that the harsh reality of child sexual abuse has been at last recognized and that a broad coalition has formed to address this problem.

Although the end of our denial of child sexual abuse is overdue, it would be premature to celebrate the results of our fledgling efforts to "do something" about child sexual abuse. Unfortunately, the same discomfort that led to denial of the problem in previous years may lead to premature acceptance of current responses and remedies. That is, we are now in danger of uncritically embracing whatever is offered as a remedy, even though it is not at all clear that we should be comforted by the "something" that is being done about this tragic phenomenon. On the contrary, the major premise of this article is that there is cause for considerable concern in regard to the professional response to child sexual abuse at both the applied, especially child protection services (CPS), and research levels. This article therefore raises numerous disquieting issues regarding the potential for harm resulting from the professional response to child sexual abuse. Although the images that result are sometimes as painful as the images of abused children, we must not fall victim to a new denial that allows us to participate in the (unwitting) disservice to and even harming of children and families by professionals. The paucity of inquiry on the potential harm-doing of professionals in the prodigious child maltreatment literature suggests that one form of denial may have been replaced by another.

This article begins by offering a brief sketch of some problems in the current state of professional practice and research. Following this sketch, we ask what maintains current practice and identify reinforcement contingencies that shape professional behavior and impede change in the professional response to child sexual abuse. In the final major section, we identify some actions that individual researchers and practitioners can take to make a difference in this field. The article concludes by calling for an end to our denial and for critical self-scrutiny of our professional actions.

IS THERE A PROBLEM? A SNAPSHOT

The overview provided in this section is necessarily incomplete, as the complexity of the topic cannot be done justice with such a brief sketch. Moreover, this sketch attempts to provide a counterpoint to the dominant view in the literature by providing a perspective seldom found in it. By attempting to introduce more balance into the literature, it is not our intent to deny or diminish positive contributions made by professionals in responding to child sexual abuse, but to facilitate much needed critical self-scrutiny.

Problems in Professional Practice

A practitioner guidebook, written by respected experts on child abuse, advises practitioners to report suspected child abuse to CPS workers in the knowledge that if there is no abuse "no harm will come to the family or child" (Walker, Bonner, and Kaufman 1988, 18). Although this is certainly comforting to professionals who hope that their actions carry no potential for harm, a moment of reflection shows that this is at best wishful thinking.

First, there is little reason to think that CPS personnel are any more immune from error than other human beings. In point of fact, the potential for error in this difficult and emotionally taxing area would seem to be quite high. As Jackson and Nuttall (1993) note, "judgments about sexual abuse allegations, upon which subsequent action depends, are often more intuitive than objective" (p. 127). Unfortunately, intuitive judgments tend to yield conclusions that are unreliable and overly dominated by potentially misleading heuristics. In fact, even basic definitional problems regarding abuse may be so profound as to leave families "at the mercy of their accusers' interpretation of these terms" (Giovannoni and Becerra 1979, 8). It seems clear to us that we must acknowledge openly the possibility of error and mitigate the harm that might result from such error, including the possibility of harm resulting not only from false negatives but also false positives.

Second, current practice may have a negative impact on children independently of error. At a minimum, children in such cases will undergo a medical examination (including genital examination), interviews (which often will be stressful, repetitive, and unsettling for the child and will sometimes entail threats, harassment, and so on), and be separated from the alleged perpetrator (usually a parent), most often by being placed in foster care. As Goldstein, Freud, and Solnit (1973) note, children "react to even temporary infringement of parental autonomy with anxiety, diminishing trust, loosening of emotional ties, or an increasing tendency to be out of control" (p. 9). Even in cases where all would agree that investigation is necessary, we need to acknowledge that the process is unlikely to be entirely benign from the child's vantage point.

Third, as alluded to earlier, there appears to be widespread use of heuristics or short cuts in child sexual abuse investigations. The most commonplace heuristic in sex abuse investigations is to pursue the idea that abuse has indeed occurred to the exclusion of other possibilities. Thus, clinical professionals persist in acting as if abuse occurred when children deny it (e.g., Bass and Davis 1988). Because some sexually abused children deny abuse, it is not uncommon for denial of abuse to be viewed as evidence of its occurrence. Thus, children who accurately report that they have not been abused are sometimes in the curious position of not being believed by professionals who adhere to simple heuristics like "children never lie." In such cases, children may be harassed, bribed, and so on to admit to the occurrence of abuse (for examples, see brief on behalf of amicus developmental, social, and psychological researchers, social scientists, and scholars filed in *State of New Jersey* v. *Kelly Michaels 1993*). This situation emphasizes the problems that occur when overly simplistic rules are used.

Adoption of the heuristic that abuse has occurred to the exclusion of other possibilities represents a clear choice, for as Lloyd notes, "By design, the clinical approach provides no method for a therapist or other investigator to confirm that no abuse occurred . . . investigators maintain that this approach serves the best interests of children and protects them from further abuse" (1992, 111). Indeed, the stated job of CPS workers, as reflected in an official handbook, is to "aid the prosecution to establish a case against the perpetrator" (Charlier and Downing 1988, 15; see Wexler 1990 for further examples). Not surprisingly, after examining 120 official records of child abuse. Margolin (1992) concluded that in all cases the accused was assumed to be guilty and that the "goal is not to determine 'who did what to whom,' since that information is presumed at the outset, but rather, to document that agency rules have been followed, and that the investigation was conducted in a rational impersonal manner" (p. 64).

The use of such heuristics has the effect of inflating the number of substantiated cases and therefore reassuring us that we are doing our best to apprehend child molesters. Unfortunately, it is difficult to document just how widely this heuristic is used, owing to the confidential nature of investigations. Moreover, even when families waive their rights to confidentiality, CPS agencies have been unwilling to disclose information, leading some to question whether such confidentiality is used to protect agencies rather than families (see Hechler 1993).

The use of heuristics might be less troubling if there were no costs associated with them. However, the costs to children and families are real. Just as the media have for a long time reported cases of abuse where CPS agencies failed to protect children, there are now a growing number of media reports in which CPS intervention has seriously harmed children and their families. Many more anecdotal reports do not make it into the media, suggesting that the harm done to children is not limited to the sensational cases reported in the media (for examples of cases see Hechler 1993; Mikkelsen, Gutheil, and Emens 1992; Wexler 1990). Nonetheless, the dominant professional response is to assert of such cases "that there is no evidence that these are widespread" as a justification to advocate continued use of current practices (Finkelhor 1993a, 279). Without access to materials from CPS agencies and family courts it is virtually impossible to document harm done by professional intervention. In any event, this position provides little reassurance, because there is no evidence to show that such miscarriages are indeed rare. Such a circumstance might be less troublesome were it not for the awesome power invested in CPS workers, including the right to strip-search children without a warrant (accused rapists and murderers have retained Fourth Amendment rights), remove them from their home, and so on (for extended discussion of the resulting problems, see Wexler 1990). Although well motivated, the secrecy involved in this area makes it impossible to document in a systematic manner error and harmdoing to children and promotes denial of any culpability on the part of professionals.

In sum, the conclusion of an official investigation of case reports in Philadelphia that noted "each individual worker had adhered to his or her own, often inconsistent criteria for assessing family function and children at risk" (cited in Wexler 1990, 117) may well characterize much practice. In a similar vein, judges presented with the same cases made rulings that agreed less than half the time, as "Each judge seemed to use his own unique value system" (Aber 1980, 166–67). Runyan (1993) summarizes the situation well by noting that even a cursory exposure to the CPS system shows that "social workers are overloaded, the mental health treatment of children is haphazard or unavailable, foster care may be overused or even hazardous to children's health, and crowded court dockets and procedural rules minimize the likelihood that a timely and just determination of the truth will occur" (p. 263). Not surprisingly, the newly appointed Inspector-General of the Department of Child and Family services in Illinois has concluded that in Illinois the child protection system "does not work" (p. 1), with 54 employees being suspended over the preceding 34 months for actions that harmed children (Kane 1994).

Lest it appear otherwise, the above analysis is not an argument against intervention to protect children, but rather an attempt to highlight the costs of such intervention for children. It reminds us of the need to ensure that our intervention is not worse than the abuse it protects against. However, it can be argued that investigation of alleged sexual abuse necessarily entails some costs, and that these costs have to be weighed against those of not protecting children. Given such a choice, it is not difficult to find cases in which all reasonable persons would agree that investigation and intervention are warranted, even in the face of unavoidable risk of harming the child(ren) involved. This position is a sound one, provided the costs of investigation and intervention are minimized. Unfortunately, we preclude a rational approach to the minimization of costs if we protect ourselves as professionals by denying or minimizing the possibility of error and of harm resulting from our actions. Protecting ourselves in this way is likely to result in greater victimization of children by the investigative process than is necessary.

Notwithstanding the above qualification, it is likely that some colleagues will quickly dismiss our analysis, arguing that we do a disservice to the field to raise these issues, potentially harm efforts to bring child molesters to justice, and that we show bias against hardworking health professionals who are trying to help the victims of sexual abuse. This would be an unfortunate response, as the polarization of the field has done little to advance the welfare of children. Those who seem to require near perfect knowledge before sanctioning intervention would force us back into denying that child sexual abuse is a serious societal problem. On the other hand, those who leave no room for questioning the effectiveness or accuracy of the current approach to child sexual abuse or who believe that any change that decreases the number of substantiated cases is automatically a change for the worse, force us to adopt the new denial. We believe that the underlying motivation for these positions, serving the best interests of children, will be realized by working toward more accurate forms of detection, by better validation of methods for substantiating cases, and by optimizing the benefit/cost ratio for children. Thus, far from being a call to reduce the effectiveness of professionals' response to child sexual abuse, the current analysis suggests the importance of redressing the structural problems inherent in a system that is chronically underfunded and overburdened and depends on a labor force that is given insufficient training and insufficient time to adequately handle cases. The existence of "blind spots" and extreme positions also seems to characterize research, an area to which we now turn.

Problems in Research

As in many areas in the helping professions, the gap between re-
search/theory and practice appears to be vast in the area of child abuse,
but this gap has received remarkably little attention. Because of the
importance of legal issues in this area, it is also noteworthy that judicial
and legislative branches of government are not "well-known for their
intensive use of data" (Reppucci and Aber 1992, 263). It appears that
simply doing something about child sexual abuse may have taken precedence over drawing on available knowledge to do something that
ensures children's best interests are served by our actions.

But is there a knowledge base upon which we can base such action?
Unfortunately, the answer to this critical question is not as straightforward as it might be; simply becoming familiar with the impressively large
literature on child sexual abuse, let alone related areas of inquiry, represents a major challenge. There are certainly pockets of research that can
inform practice and legislative and judicial reform. For example, research
on children's memory and their suggestibility (e.g., Ceci and Bruck
1993a; Doris 1991; Goodman and Bottoms 1993) has obvious implications for interviewing children and helping them give testimony that is
both credible and more likely to provide accurate information; this
research appears to have had almost no impact on police and CPS investigators to date (e.g., Brief on behalf of amicus developmental, social,
and psychological researchers, social scientists, and scholars filed in *State
of New Jersey* v. *Kelly Michaels* 1993). However, when it comes to evaluating the overall progress made in research and theory, the outcome is
less sanguine.

The National Research Council (a council administered by the
National Academy of Sciences, National Academy of Engineering, and
the Institute of Medicine) recently convened a panel of experts to provide "a comprehensive examination of the theoretical and pragmatic
research needs in the area of child maltreatment" (National Research
Council 1993, 3). The panel position is summarized in the observation,
"we still lack a solid base of research information that can guide and
enhance society's efforts to intervene and prevent child abuse and
neglect" (National Research Council 1993, vi).

The reasons for this state of affairs are numerous and include the one
explored in this article, the denial of professionals possibly inflicting
harm on children and the subsequent failure to examine in an even-
handed manner the professional response to child abuse. Another, however, is so fundamental to understanding the current state of practice
that it must be briefly noted. According to the panel, "little progress has

been made in constructing clear, reliable, valid, and useful definitions of child abuse and neglect" (National Research Council 1993, 5). This does not preclude consensus on clear-cut cases of abuse: The presence of a sexually transmitted disease in a young child, pornographic pictures, and so on leave little doubt about the occurrence of abuse (though they do not identify the perpetrator). However, the vast majority of child sexual abuse cases are not clear-cut. Scientists are therefore left with an ill-defined phenomenon to study that is not easily measured reliably, conditions that make the lack of progress understandable.

Although current research is not yet at a level that allows clear guidance for practitioners or legislators in all critical areas, the available research does provide direct answers to some questions and offers tentative guidance on many others. It is therefore worth noting that despite its conclusions, the panel also applauded the progress made in research over the last three decades. Clearly, knowledge is fragmented and lacks cohesion in this area, but this does not mean that the fragments are uninformative. Most importantly, knowledge of research will inoculate us against accepting the extreme, sometimes contradictory, and often quite erroneous positions found in writings on child sexual abuse (e.g., "children never lie," "children's reports of abuse are sexual fantasies," "all children who have been sexually abused need treatment").

How is it possible for professionals to tolerate, let alone participate in, the state of affairs outlined? This question is a reasonable one, but is perhaps not the most appropriate, for it assumes awareness of the problems sketched, an assumption that is not easily supported by examination of the professional literature. It seems more appropriate to ask how professionals have managed to actively deny or avoid confronting the problems outlined. One suspects that, like the preceding form of denial in this area, the current form of denial is tenaciously held because it serves an important purpose. It is quite uncomfortable to imagine that our current response to child sexual abuse has not solved the problem and that much child sexual abuse remains undetected. Hence, anything that creates the illusion that we are responding adequately is likely to be welcome. Even more uncomfortable is the possibility that our best efforts may, in some cases, have done more harm than good, or even have victimized some children who were in no danger before coming to the attention of professionals. However, we need to free ourselves of denial in order to make progress.

In the remainder of this section we elaborate on the professional response to child sexual abuse by examining how our use of language and of numbers blinds us to the problems sketched in our analysis of professional practice and research.

Problems in Language Use:
The Pen Is Mightier Than the Sword

Language use is important because of its power to influence thought processes and thereby shape reality. In emotionally charged areas, the probability of examining assumptions underlying our use of words is likely to drop, giving words even greater power. This is demonstrated by examining a few of the words used in the area of child sexual abuse.

Investigators of allegations are frequently called *validators* (cf. Gardner 1992), and it is not uncommon for even the most sophisticated researchers who are sensitive to the complex issues in this area to refer to "assessment and *validation* procedures" (emphasis added; Ceci and Bruck 1993b, 21). The language used here implies that the sole purpose is to confirm or validate abuse rather than to adopt the more balanced position of investigating an allegation. Such language supports the investigative heuristic outlined earlier whereby only evidence consistent with the occurrence of abuse is sought.

In a similar vein, the use of the word *perpetrator* is telling. Investigative case reports show that the suspect is "routinely identified as the 'perpetrator' " (e.g, "3/26 interview with detective J at Police station with CPI [child protection investigator] and child. Perpetrator arrested," Margolin 1992, 64), reflecting the agency's official handbook guidelines regarding the collection of information from "perpetrators," not "suspects" (see Margolin 1992, 64). In scholarly articles, it is not uncommon to find similar use of language or to find an initial reference to the *alleged perpetrator* only to find later references in which the word *alleged* is dropped. Even in one of the most prestigious scholarly journals, reference is made to the "acquittal of the perpetrator" (Kendall-Tackett, Williams, and Finkelhor 1993, 172), showing that—despite contrary legal findings—suspects are still viewed as perpetrating abuse.

The bias inherent in language use is omnipresent in scholarly writings and in research. So, for example, the epidemiological literature is oriented toward "documenting the widespread nature of the problem" (Finkelhor 1993b, 67). This purpose, as compared to "documenting the extent of the problem," (or "documenting how widespread the problem is") shows a subtle prejudgment reminiscent of the heuristic used by CPS workers. Similarly, the first National Incidence Study was guided by the concept that cases known to CPS authorities are only the "tip of the iceberg" (National Research Council 1993, 80), an image that similarly presumes, at least in broad terms, the nature of the outcome of the investigation. The outcome may be consistent with the image, but it does not justify its a priori use. The intent here is not to split hairs, but to emphasize that biased language is also frequently found in "objective" research.

These examples highlight how the language of professionals sustains the state of affairs described earlier and shapes the reality of child sexual abuse (rather than, say *illegal sexual activity with children*). Indeed, the term *child sexual abuse* is itself problematic. By making no reference to the activities involved (e.g., noncontact exposure of sex organs, fondling, penetration, masturbation), it facilitates the belief that all cases are equivalent and display equal need for treatment, does not encourage a sensitive approach to clinical interviewing and assessment, and confuses research and treatment literatures.

The current use of language appears to serve our own interests by justifying behavior that is all too often quite arbitrary. Our vigorous actions may make us feel better, but they may not always be in the best interests of the child, especially when they reflect an overwhelming preoccupation with reprimanding an alleged perpetrator.

Problems in the Use of Statistics: Paint by Numbers

In this section we highlight some problems in the use of statistics and the arguments offered that perpetuate these problems. We begin by asking a simple question: What, exactly, is the extent of child sexual abuse? This question is actually far more difficult to answer than it seems. Before offering figures, it is important to note, "much of the methodology for prevalence and incidence research in the area of child abuse and neglect is seriously flawed" (National Research Council 1993, 93), and hence we need to treat such figures with caution. Figures have been obtained from a variety of sources, including community surveys, congressionally mandated maltreatment reports, and college student samples. Depending on the source used and the definition employed, lifetime rates of sexual abuse based on responses of adults to questions about their childhood history yield estimates from 6% (Siegel, Sorenson, Golding, Burnam, and Stein 1987) to 62% (Wyatt 1985) for females and 3% to 31% for males (Peters, Wyatt, and Finkelhor 1986). Although the validity of recalled incidents of child abuse in adults is quite controversial (see Loftus 1993), the major source of variability in these rates comes from different definitions of abuse (National Research Council 1993).

Perhaps the most widely used data come from the two National Incidence Surveys (1979–80 and 1986; National Center for Child Abuse and Neglect 1981, 1988) and the more recent National Child Abuse and Neglect Data System (National Center for Child Abuse and Neglect 1993). The second National Incidence Survey showed the incidence of sexual abuse to be 2.1 per 1,000 children in 1986, using the least restrictive definition employed in the survey (Sedlak 1990); this indicates a 300% increase from 1980 to 1986. Most recently, of the 2.7 million reports of suspected abuse and neglect in 1991 (involving over 3 million children), 123,697 were substantiated cases of sex abuse. *Substantiated* usually means that CPS officials judged there was *some credible evidence* of abuse; only 12 states use the least stringent legal standard for determining guilt, the *preponderance of evidence,* for deciding whether a case is substantiated (National Center for Child Abuse and Neglect 1993).

Figures on the extent of child sexual abuse dominate the statistics offered in professional writings. Whatever the deficiencies of these figures, there is little doubt that sexual abuse is a major societal problem that deserves our full attention. However, the figures cited do not paint a complete picture, thereby doing a disservice to children. Approximately 16% of suspected maltreatment reports are sexual in nature, and hence we also need to consider that in 1991 the 123,697 substantiated cases of sexual abuse were accompanied by approximately 300,000— some 70% of the allegations—reports of suspected sexual abuse that were not substantiated. It is not known whether this group includes all 4% to 10% of sex abuse allegations that are knowingly falsely made (Berliner 1988; Pearson and Thoennes 1988). Reports should not be confused with cases, but even so it is clear that large numbers of children are investigated where no credible evidence of sexual abuse is found; Besharov (1993) notes that 700,000 families are investigated annually for child abuse allegations that are determined "unfounded." Of course this does not mean that abuse did not occur, but it also does not mean that abuse did occur—and just turned out to be too difficult to document—a position that pervades much professional writing. Indeed, with the vagueness of the child abuse laws, the minimal standard used for finding a case substantiated and the immense power of investigators it is truly amazing that the percentage of substantiated cases is not higher. Finally, it bears noting that the first National Incidence Survey showed that 53% of CPS substantiated cases failed to meet the definition of abuse used in the survey (National Center for Child Abuse and Neglect 1981).

The large number of unsubstantiated reports is a problem for at least two reasons. First, the overwhelming number of cases strains CPS resources and impairs our ability to protect abused children. This makes understandable the fact that 25% to 50% of child abuse deaths are those of children who already have been reported to authorities (Besharov 1988). Unfortunately, attention to overreporting is infrequent and tends to be viewed in terms of the rights of parents versus the rights (protection) of children, a false dichotomy. The large number of unsubstantiated cases, like underreporting, is a problem for *children's* welfare as the system collapses under its sheer weight.

Second, determining that a report is unsubstantiated usually occurs "after an unavoidably traumatic investigation" (Besharov 1993, 264). Many professionals challenge such a claim. For example, Finkelhor (1993a) argues, "according to child protection officials" typical investigations involve talking to the parents and the child to reach a decision. He characterizes such investigations as "benign." The facts flatly contradict such a simplification. For instance, in the first author's county, children are routinely placed in foster care following a sex abuse allegation, and proper investigation of cases often requires talking to relevant persons outside of the nuclear family (e.g., teachers, neighbors). Unfounded cases can and do sometimes leave behind parents whose employment has been terminated, children with a parent who has committed suicide, children who have been traumatized by foster care, children abused in foster care (e.g., 21% of abuse and neglect cases in Louisiana involved foster homes; in Kansas City 25% and in Baltimore 28% of children in foster care were abused by foster parents; see Wexler 1990, 198), traumatized children and families for whom no services are provided and so on (for examples, see Wexler 1990). At a minimum, those investigated must live with the community's "tendency to assume that parents are abusive because they have been investigated by protective services" (Reppucci and Aber 1992, 263). As noted earlier, it is impossible to systematically document these cases, making another of Finkelhor's (1993a) arguments against the traumatic nature of investigations that the "intrusiveness" (read "damage done by") of investigations is unknown, somewhat meaningless. It is, however, important to recognize that the quality of investigations varies across investigators, CPS jurisdictions, and states. Therefore, not all families have the same experience, though anyone who is exposed to investigated families soon learns that the investigative experience is often quite traumatic.

Finkelhor (1993a) also claims that the number of unsubstantiated cases is not a problem because many of them are simply plea bargains, where actual abuse did occur; in exchange for parents admitting to abuse and agreeing to remedial action, workers record the case as unsubstantiated. Although it would be difficult to document systematically what happens in plea bargains between CPS workers and families, it cannot be assumed that this increases the rate of unsubstantiated cases. Indeed, plea bargains may increase the rate of substantiated cases. With children removed from the home, vague laws (e.g., undefined terms such as *injurious environment* are criteria for rulings) and hints (sometimes blatant threats) by CPS workers that parents "will never see their children again" if they do not admit abuse, some lawyers advise innocent clients that the quickest way to regain custody of their children is to *stipulate,* or admit abuse.

Finally, Finkelhor argues that the number of unsubstantiated cases compares favorably to the efficiency of the criminal justice system, a comparison that is misleading at best. To claim that the report-to-substantiation rate in the child abuse area is similar to the arrest-to-conviction ratio in the criminal justice system is a hollow victory. With the earlier noted exception of 12 states, substantiated cases do not even meet the lowest legal standard, preponderance of the evidence, and cases are not decided by an impartial third party. In contrast, the criminal justice system employs the highest standard of proof ("beyond a reasonable doubt"), includes presentation of both sides of the case, and involves a judicial decision. In effect, that comparison does the opposite of what it intended—it serves once again to highlight the poor quality of our efforts to protect children.

It appears that both underreporting and overreporting of suspected cases pose problems for the optimal protection of children (Besharov 1993). Rather than examine rationally such problems and how best to deal with them, raising the problem of overreporting is characterized as "alarmist" and as reflecting the view "that addressing child abuse is not worth it" (Finkelhor 1993a, 283). The tendency to label those who question the picture painted in the professional literature as uninterested in protecting children, and by implication pro child molestation, serves to show just how much personal factors pervade scientific writings (Finkelhor 1993a, characterizes the founding Director of the National Center on Child Abuse and Neglect in this manner!). In short, we should always examine very carefully any figures presented (and those omitted) on child sexual abuse to ensure we obtain a balanced and realistic picture.

Coda

In offering this sketch there is no intention to discount the pain of children who are sexually abused, the need to allocate adequate resources to protect children from such abuse, or the fact that many abused children have been rescued from damaging situations through the efforts of committed CPS workers. Indeed, it should be clear that it is largely through the allocation of greater resources for research, training, and child protective services that progress can be made. Rather, the sketch is motivated by confidence that unbiased research and appropriate, informed investigation of sex abuse allegations will ensure that sorely needed resources become more available for protecting children from such violence, and that children brought into the CPS system (nonabused and abused) will suffer less from the process.

WHAT MAINTAINS CURRENT PRACTICES? CONTINGENCIES SHAPE BEHAVIOR

Clearly, we believe that there are serious problems in the professional response to child sexual abuse. But what maintains current professional responses? In addition to the denial discussed in the last section, one set of issues to consider in understanding the current state of practice and research is the reinforcement contingencies that shape professional behavior. Understanding these contingencies provides insight into powerful forces that maintain current practices and impede needed change in this area. In highlighting some of these contingencies, it is important to note that the American public wants more to be done about child abuse (Finkelhor 1993a). In this the public is much in agreement with professionals. Having given up the complacency of denying the problem of child sexual abuse, the urgency to do something to fix the problem is considerable. In addition, this is a welcome change from what has historically been the case. However, it is quite conceivable that, in an attempt to right past wrongs, the pendulum has swung to the opposite extreme. Indeed, the central thesis of this article is that we need to pay less attention now to doing something and more attention to the quality of what we do, lest we inadvertently find ourselves doing more harm than good. Because professionals operate in a broader societal climate, we begin our analysis of contingencies by considering briefly their operation on legislation and litigation.

Contingencies for Legislators

Given the public mood that reinforces intervention regardless of its quality, it is not surprising to find that single tragic cases tend to drive legislation and social policy. For example, following a case in which two girls were left behind while their parents vacationed, Illinois legislators hastily passed legislation pertaining to such situations, even though many legislators acknowledged that the statutes were technically poor and might actually make the situation worse. The intent here is not to diminish the need for action, but rather to demonstrate the tremendous pressure to do something that too often overshadows careful deliberation to ensure that the "something" is optimal. As Wexler (1990) reminds us, with such clear-cut villains and heroes, the issue of child abuse provides powerful opportunities for politicians to express what is known as *no-cost rectitude* (expressions of wrongful omission that are unlikely to lose votes); he notes that of 236 relevant bills introduced into state legislatures, most dealt with toughening laws, thus allowing easier convictions, and only 25 even addressed the problems that cause child abuse.

Contingencies for Litigants

In this climate, it is not surprising to find that allegations of sexual abuse (and child abuse in general) have become powerful weapons in disputes. This is particularly evident in divorce disputes, which can drag on through the courts for extended periods. However, an allegation of sex abuse will ensure that the case will be in court within days, and so it is becoming increasingly common to find sex abuse allegations in such cases, with estimates of false allegations ranging from 36% (Green 1986) to 55% (Benedek and Schetky 1984, cited in Everson and Boat 1989). However, the power of this conflict tactic can also be found in adolescent-parent conflicts, conflicts between neighbors, and tenant-landlord disputes (for a typology of false allegations, see Mikkelsen et al. 1992). This misuse of CPS resources makes it all the more important to approach sexual abuse allegations with an open mind.

Contingencies for Practitioners

It is difficult for professionals to maintain a neutral stance in this climate. The contingencies they face are powerful and are perhaps best summarized by the aphorism "better safe than sorry." Such contingencies promote certain kinds of errors over others. A CPS investigator who concludes that abuse did not occur or that abuse will not recur takes a serious risk: if she or he is wrong and the child is subsequently harmed, the public outcry could easily lead to the loss of his or her job. The worker would also no doubt experience considerable guilt for not "rescuing" the child. False negatives have real consequences.

In contrast, identifying abuse is a relatively safe course of action with minimal, if any, potential adverse consequences for the investigator; if the investigator is wrong (false positive), there is absolutely no threat to his or her livelihood. Most states grant some form of immunity to professionals involved in child abuse allegations, and where parents have tried through the courts to make professionals accountable for their actions they have not been very successful (Meyers 1992). For example, it is virtually impossible to prove that the professional acted with "malicious intent," and it would be a rare professional who acted with such intent. Hence, J. L. Aber's (cited in Wexler 1990) assertion that for every false negative there is at least one false positive (a wrongly substantiated case of abuse) is likely to be a very conservative estimate. Finally, in the absence of professional belief and hard research data indicating the harmful effects of wrongly identifying abuse, the CPS worker also experiences no pangs of conscience.

The above reinforcement contingencies are particularly troublesome when one recalls the intolerably high caseloads carried by CPS investigators. As the American Civil Liberties Union argued in its Illinois lawsuit against strip searches of children without a warrant, "Simple common sense leads to the conclusion that workers in these circumstances will conduct searches as a matter of expedience, whether or not searches relate in any way to the state's protective goals" (cited in Wexler 1990, 113). Similarly, Margolin's (1992) finding that workers are more intent on showing that they have followed agency procedures than in determining whether or not abuse occurred, becomes more understandable. We should not be surprised at such actions, for professionals involved in child abuse cases are, after all, only human. Why should we expect their behavior to transcend the reinforcement contingencies they face? Why should CPS investigators with their awesome powers not be subject to Lord Acton's dictum, "power tends to corrupt, absolute power absolutely"? In a nation that prides itself on checks and balances, it is worrisome that so few meaningful checks and balances exist in this area.

Contingencies for Researchers

Can research help change the contingencies? It is important not to underestimate the industry that has grown up in the area of child sexual abuse. This industry provides a living for many people, ranging from large numbers of "experts" to publishers who meet the current demand for self-help books for "incest survivors." Also, for a variety of reasons, experts in an area may resist evidence that appears to contradict cherished precepts. It would be naive to believe that there are no vested interests in the scholarly and research communities. Those few who question the dominant ideology of sex abuse research are marginalized by subtly being portrayed as anti-child protection (and, by implication, pro-child molestation). Indeed, as was recently observed on the Family Science Network (an electronic bulletin board), a simple request for research articles on *false memory syndrome* can evoke hostile, ad hominem responses involving the gender and disciplinary affiliation of the person who made the request and those who offered scholarly references. Apparently, only certain possibilities (e.g., *child abuse accommo-*

dation syndrome) consistent with the dominant professional viewpoint can be the subject of scholarly inquiry, even though they have no different epistemological status than those that are rejected (e.g., false memory syndrome).

In sum, if professionals are to act more effectively in response to the phenomenon of child abuse, the current contingencies clearly need to be changed. At the level of practice, all those involved in cases of child sexual abuse need to be held more accountable for their professional behaviors and not be granted legal (partial or complete) immunity. Similarly, scholars and researchers need to be reinforced for the quality of their work, however uncomfortable we feel about the questions addressed. Such changes will most likely require changes in the broader culture, but the responsible professional cannot wait for such changes to be effected. Consequently, we turn in the next section to consider whether individual researchers and practitioners can make a difference.

CAN INDIVIDUALS MAKE A DIFFERENCE?

In this article we have offered a serious critique of both practice and research in the professional response to child sexual abuse. However, we do not have the luxury of offering a critique without raising the issue of alternatives. This would be tantamount to sanctioning the continued victimization of children by those adults who are closest to them, or by the professionals who are entrusted with safeguarding their well-being. Neither alternative is acceptable. What is required to facilitate a more effective response to child sexual abuse is a series of initiatives mounted at multiple levels, including professional practice as well as research, legislation, judicial reform, social policy, and public education.

The goal of this article, however, is not to outline comprehensive solutions to the problems we identify, but, rather, to bring an end to our denial and to open discussion on problems with the professional response to child sexual abuse. Nonetheless, we are mindful that in addressing problems with the professional response to child sexual abuse there is the danger of individuals feeling overwhelmed by the enormity of the problems and by a feeling of powerlessness to effect needed changes. Therefore, in the remainder of the article, we consider actions that individual researchers and practitioners can take to advance the successful investigation of child sexual abuse and improve the welfare of children suspected of being victims of sexual abuse. These suggestions are not intended to be exhaustive or sufficient to address fully the problems outlined earlier. Rather, our goal in this section is to empower individuals committed to responsible professional behavior by illustrating the kind of contributions each of us can make to ensure that we are not contributing unwittingly to harming children.

Research

In light of the observations made thus far, it is not surprising to find that some critical questions for advancing our knowledge of child sexual abuse have received little or no attention. Before offering examples, it is worth noting that the very existence of these omissions provides additional support for our concerns regarding the professional response to child sexual abuse. This section briefly highlights some of these questions. Rather than wait for funding initiatives to address such questions, we believe that individual researchers can begin to investigate them.

Improve the understanding of the impact of sexual abuse. The literature on the effects of sexual abuse is prodigious (for reviews see Beitchman, Zucker, Hood, daCosta, and Akman 1991; Beitchman et al. 1992; Kendall-Tackett et al. 1993). What emerges is that just about any worrisome childhood behavior has been associated with child sexual abuse. It appears that there is no specific syndrome or pattern of symptoms associated with sexual abuse.

The nature of the comparisons made to determine the correlates of abuse and the foci of research efforts will be used to illustrate the blinders worn by researchers. Typically, children who have been abused (usually identified by CPS records) are compared to nonabused children, although comparisons to a clinical group have recently been included. However, we were not able to find a single study that compares abused children to children reported to CPS but whose cases turned out to be unfounded. This comparison is critical in separating the possible impact of abuse from the potential impact of professionals' response to the abuse. The importance of research that disentangles correlates of abuse from correlates of experiences that follow the allegation of abuse is emphasized by the small number of studies documenting the negative impact of court involvement on children (e.g., Goodman et al. 1992; Runyan, Everson, Edelsohn, Hunter, and Coulter 1988). In the most authoritative recent review of the impact of child sexual abuse, this critical issue of disentangling effects receives half a sentence (Kendall-Tackett et al. 1993).

Few studies have focused on whether individual children who have been sexually abused are symptomatic at all, as most research has attempted to document symptoms correlated with abuse by examining mean level of symptoms in abused and comparison groups. A small number of investigators have, however, shown that a sizable proportion of children are symptom free (49%, Caffaro-Rouget, Lang, and vanSantem 1989; 31%, Mannarino and Cohen 1986; 21%, Conte and Schuerman 1987). Such findings may reflect many factors, including CPS misclassification of children (a factor that tends not to be mentioned), and the possibility that symptoms vary as a function of the severity of abuse. Again, however, comparatively little attention has been paid to the issue of abuse severity, although extant research does show that the frequency and duration of abuse and the presence of penetration (oral, anal, and vaginal) is associated with increased symptoms (see Kendall-Tackett et al. 1993). The findings are consistent with the view that we need to stop talking about child sexual abuse in general and instead talk about specific activities. It seems unlikely that noncontact abuse (exposure to parents' sexual intercourse), a single incident of fondling with all clothes on, repeated penetration over a long period of time, and so on are equivalent.

Even these few cursory observations show the misleading nature of the widespread assertion that the impact of sexual abuse is serious. Such global claims can potentially lead to harm as "any sweeping generalization is certain to be fallacious . . . undue emphasis on the worst possible prognoses is not always in the victim's best interests . . . excessive and over-hasty intervention may satisfy feelings of outrage at the cost of further damage to the victims" (West 1991). Like the numbers game, the generalizations found in the literature depict only part of the truth. By lumping together all cases of abuse and failing to examine the impact of our responses to disclosures, we again do a disservice to children most in need of intervention.

Understanding children's experience of sex abuse investigations. In view of our efforts to act in children's best interests, one might have expected to find a great deal of research that examined children's experience of child abuse investigations. Such research would have allowed us to ensure that our actions minimized children's distress. For instance, in suspected sexual abuse the need for genital examinations is unquestionable, and the potential stress of such examinations calls for an understanding of children's experience of them. Recommendations made for such examinations emphasize the potential stress for children. For example, a leading expert recommends,

> To clarify the boy's definition of the sexual acts, the physician can perform a rectal examination that includes the penetration of the boy's anus by the physician's gloved and lubricated examining finger . . . This allows the boy to compare that sensation with the sensation of abuse. (Levitt 1990, 236)

One can only imagine the outcry at such an approach being used for vaginal examinations of rape victims. For some children, these examinations will comprise the only sexual abuse they experience.

Surprisingly, very little is known about children's experience of genital examinations, a circumstance that may reflect the fact "It is not uncommon to hear physicians state that children are not upset by current sexual abuse evaluation procedures" (Berson, Herman-Giddens, and Frothingham 1993, 42). However, Money and Lamacz (1987) conclude from their study that "Some children do, indeed, subjectively experience the physical examination . . . as an equivalent of sexual assault" (p. 713). Similarly, Berson et al. (1993) state that their findings from 514 evaluations challenge erroneous beliefs of medical examiners "regarding the sensitivity and gentleness with which examinations are conducted" (p. 43).

The minimal data available suggest that children can experience even this single aspect of the investigation as stressful. Little data exist on the impact of foster care (cf. Runyan 1993) and the impact of court appearances (cf Goodman et al. 1992), and no data were found on children's experiences of the interviews to which they are subjected. It is amazing that well-meaning professionals acting in children's interests have chosen to all but ignore children's experience of their actions. Moreover, the earlier noted claims that investigations are benign is quite incorrigible.

Exorcising questionable foundations for claims of expertise. An important thread in child abuse research concerns the problems of prosecuting suspected offenders (Howitt 1992). The generation of large numbers of experts knowledgeable about abuse is therefore not surprising. In view of the consequence of experts' judgments for children, it may be surprising to find a virtual absence of research on the validity of expert judgments. This omission is emphasized by the minimal data that do exist. Ceci and Bruck (1993b) report that they presented to 1,000 experts videotapes of children who had and had not been induced to make errors (including those involving perceptual details) in reporting an experience. The experts were to determine which events reported were accurate and to rate the credibility of the child. The majority of experts were inaccurate, despite showing considerable confidence in their judgments. Most disturbing was the finding that children making the least accurate reports were rated as the most credible!

The need for research on expert judgment is further emphasized by Mason's (1991) analysis of 122 appellate court cases involving child sexual abuse. She found that testimony was frequently internally inconsistent and that contradictory facts were cited as evidence of abuse by differing experts (e.g., consistent accounts of abuse *and* inconsistent accounts of abuse were offered as evidence of abuse). Because the courts tended to accept expert testimony at face value and rarely questioned the credentials of the expert or whether the testimony is accepted in the scientific community, this state of affairs does a disservice to our children. Finally, it is worrisome to know that some forms of expert testimony (e.g., to rehabilitate the credibility of a child witness) can be given by a CPS worker "with six months on the job and knowledge of three or four pertinent articles" (Meyers 1993, 177). It takes a great deal more knowledge of the literature to know that many of the behaviors associated with sexual abuse (e.g., delayed reporting, retraction of allegation, inappropriate knowledge of sexual behavior, inconsistent accounts) are frequently found in nonabused children who have been exposed to suggestive influences (Ceci and Bruck 1993b).

The purpose of this section was not to document exhaustively research needs. Rather, it was to identify a few examples of omissions that reflect our failure to consider whose interests are best served by the professional response to child sexual abuse. Clearly, there are many more that could be identified. Once identified, researchers can take steps to remedy these lacuna. Many of these omissions are not easy topics to research, owing to the ethical and practical difficulties of conducting studies on them. Although such difficulties have no doubt contributed to the lack of research, they cannot justify continued neglect of these topics. Anything less than rigorous, open-minded research will ultimately result in a disservice to our children, for the most effective response will be informed by such research.

Practice

Notwithstanding the powerful forces that shape professional behavior, individual practitioners can make a difference if they engage in critical self-scrutiny. Such scrutiny may be uncomfortable, but its importance for assuring the well-being of children should far outweigh its costs. This section therefore offers some guidelines to facilitate such self-scrutiny.

Know your legal responsibilities. Citizens have the responsibility to know whether they are *mandated* reporters of suspected child abuse. Mandated reporters are legally required to make reports of suspected child maltreatment. However, one does not have to be a mandated reporter to call the state hotline to report a suspected case of abuse. In view of the overwhelming number of hotline calls made to CPS agencies, a starting point for each professional is to be thoroughly acquainted with reporting laws. A deep understanding of these laws can ensure that CPS services are used efficiently with minimal effort being used to investigate inappropriate calls. Such understanding is likely to require knowledge of local CPS practice to determine the criteria used to operationalize the language used in reporting laws (e.g., how is *cause to believe* understood?). It is also a good idea to consult with an informed colleague whenever the issue of suspected sex abuse arises.

Know the limits of your expertise. Effective professional action in the child sexual abuse area requires specialized training and knowledge. Too many practitioners tend to believe that their general qualifications and license to practice are sufficient credentials for involvement in sexual abuse cases. Most applied disciplines have ethical guidelines that enjoin professionals not to practice outside of their domain of expertise and to regularly update their knowledge through continuing education. It is also important to realize that professionals qualified to offer one form of expert testimony are not necessarily qualified to offer other types of expert testimony (see Meyers 1992).

Be informed by the latest research. Being informed by the latest research is particularly important in the current domain, as major changes are occurring in some areas, with profound implications for practice. This will be illustrated using two examples, research on children's memory and the use of anatomically detailed dolls. Each has important implications for interviewing children in suspected cases of child sexual abuse.

Children's memory. Become acquainted with available research on children's memory. As recently as 5 years ago, research on children's memory was dominated by studies that assessed memory following exposure to a trivial incident irrelevant to the child. However, more recent research has begun to examine children's memories for personally relevant events under conditions that more closely approximate those of CPS investigations. The results are dramatic. As they have recently been summarized in an excellent review (Ceci and Bruck 1993a; see also Ceci and Bruck 1993b), only the conclusions are briefly described.

First, there are age differences in suggestibility, with preschoolers being most vulnerable to suggestion. This suggestibility occurs even for "crucial, personally experienced, central events" (Ceci and Bruck 1993a, p. 432). For example, children can be led to falsely report that they have been kissed while being bathed, and a substantial minority (32% of 3-year-olds, 24% of 5-year-olds) gave false answers when asked questions such as, "Did he touch your private parts" (see Goodman, Rudy, Bottoms, and Aman 1990). There is some evidence to suggest that suggestibility effects can give rise to very strong illusory beliefs that are resistant to change, especially when the suggestions are strong.

Second, a number of interviewing practices can adversely influence the accuracy of children's statements about events, including repeating the same (especially yes/no) question, introducing misinformation during questioning (especially when it is repeated across interviews), setting an accusatory emotional tone for the interview (with children more likely to fabricate reports when an accusatory tone is set), subjecting children to peer pressure by telling that others have made disclosures, being interviewed by someone of high status (e.g., a uniformed police officer), and introducing stereotypes about the suspect (e.g., "Mary does naughty things," "John is a bad person"). Finally, children's reports can be shaped to conform with interviewer beliefs (biases), and this is most likely to occur when interviewers pursue a single hypothesis about what happened.

Third, inaccurate reporting can occur in a subtle manner when children and adults make errors by mistaking the source of the information they report. Thus, children may inaccurately report as remembered aspects of the event material communicated to them by others (including the interviewer).

Fourth, children sometimes embellish the information that they incorporate into their memories, providing vivid and detailed accounts of events that never occurred.

Fifth, individual differences exist in children's susceptibility to the influences mentioned; some children are extremely resistant to such influences.

Sixth, children sometimes lie when the "motivational structure is tilted toward lying" (Ceci and Bruck 1993a, 433).

Finally, the above observations should not blind us to the fact that even very young children are *capable* of recalling information accurately when interviewed under appropriate conditions.

In sum, it is clear that the simple question of children lying versus telling the truth is another of the false dichotomies that pervade this area. Children can provide untruthful statements without any attempt to deceive. Indeed, they may adamantly believe in the truthfulness of their statements, even when they are completely fabricated. Reports from children are more likely to be reliable to the extent that they are made by older children, made in a nonthreatening and nonsuggestible atmosphere, do not follow multiple interviews, occur in the absence of exposure to adults invested in a particular outcome (which can result in relentless and suggestive interviewing and sometimes outright coaching), and if the child's original report remains largely consistent over time.

Anatomically detailed dolls. Become acquainted with the research on anatomically detailed dolls. The use of anatomically detailed, also known as *anatomically correct* dolls, is widespread among professionals (90%,

Boat and Everson 1988). In some cases, the dolls are the only toys made available to the child. Not surprisingly, their use has been criticized for encouraging children to engage in sexual play. For instance, the novelty of dolls with genitalia may lead a child to insert a finger into a vagina in line with what is known as the *affordance phenomenon*. According to this phenomenon, children will afford themselves of the opportunities provided by novel stimuli and so, for example, may insert their finger in the hole of a doughnut when they are given one. Such exploratory play can have devastating effects when it facilitates an incorrect conclusion regarding the occurrence of sexual abuse.

More important in the present context is the existence of research that questions the use of these dolls for assessment purposes. After reviewing this research, Wolfner, Faust, and Dawes (1993) noted that doll play "cannot be validly used as a component [of an evaluation], however, unless it provides incremental validity, and there is virtually no evidence that it does" (p. 9). Similarly, Skinner and Berry (1993) from their review of the literature note that the "use of dolls in validation interviews fails to meet scientific test criteria . . . [and] should not be used as the basis for expert opinions or conclusions" (p. 418). Yet as Mason's (1991) analysis shows, expert testimony is often based on children's use of such dolls, and professional organizations continue to encourage their use.

These continued practices are particularly disturbing in the light of recent research showing that, for young children, doll use results in *less* accurate reports than assessments that do not use anatomically detailed dolls. For example. DeLoache (in press) showed that 2.5- and 3-year-old children gave fuller and more accurate accounts of where they had been touched by an experimenter without the dolls than with them. These results are consistent with prior ret search showing no advantage of using a doll in questioning young children (e.g., Goodman and Aman 1990) and with other emerging studies showing that doll use may impede and/or distort children's statements (e.g., Bruck, Ceci, Francouer, and Barr, in press).

Thus, the informed professional would, at a minimum, cease routine use of anatomically detailed dolls in the knowledge that not only do they fail to provide unique information but may actually provide less information than straightforward, neutral questioning designed to explore various hypotheses about the child's experience. In short, the use of dolls may actually impede our efforts to protect children, yet many professionals persist in using them. Unfortunately, the continued use of flawed procedures in sexual abuse cases is not limited to anatomically detailed dolls; despite their well-known deficiencies, polygraph and phallometric assessments are also widely used (Becker and Quinsey 1993).

The chasm between research and practice must be bridged in order to serve our children's interests optimally. Unfortunately, at least one well-known case (*State of New Jersey* v. *Kelly Michaels* 1993) shows that the value of research has lain more in demonstrating the faulty and abusive nature of interviews than in improving practice. Indeed, the authors of a recent Amicus Brief stated that they "will be permanently disturbed that children were interviewed in such abusive circumstances" (p. 59, Brief on behalf of amicus developmental, social, and psychological researchers' social scientists, and scholars filed in *State of New Jersey* v. *Kelly Michaels* 1993). The tragedy is further compounded by the fact that such interviewing makes it impossible to determine whether abuse occurred.

Keep magnetic records whenever possible. Keeping video or audio tape records has several advantages. Foremost among these is that such records can contribute to children's well-being. By the time children see a professional, they have been asked to tell their story a mean of 2.3 times (Conte, Sorenson, Fogarty, and Rosa 1991). They may then go on to be interviewed numerous times by a variety of professionals (e.g., CPS investigator, caseworker, pediatrician, therapist, law enforcement official, and state's attorney). The existence of magnetic records has the potential to obviate some of this duplication. They may be particularly important for the first professional to interview the child, especially if the child's account should change.

A second advantage of magnetic records is that they allow one to engage in continued self-examination to increase expertise. With such records, the practitioner can watch tapes of his or her behavior, and, after gaining appropriate consent, obtain consultation from colleagues. The need for continuing education in any area of practice is important, but is particularly necessary in an area progressing as fast as this one. As new knowledge emerges, it is important to ensure that such knowledge is translated into appropriate action. Each professional has the potential to do this by examining his or her actions, provided records are kept to make this possible.

Although we offer these initiatives in good faith, it would be naive to believe that they will be embraced enthusiastically. It should be evident that there are powerful forces that shape professional behavior in the area of child sexual abuse. If we are to enhance the welfare of children and families, it is important to acknowledge that even the kinds of steps outlined in this article will require commitment and courage on the part of individual professionals who follow them.

CONCLUSION

This article presents a perspective that is rarely found in the child maltreatment literature. The goal has been to introduce more balance in this area, without any intention to diminish the reality of the tragedy of child sexual abuse, its prevalence, or the important strides made to deal with this serious societal problem. The hope is that honest examination of professionals' responses to this problem will facilitate more effective action to deal with child sex abuse. Continued failure to examine ourselves merely replaces one form of denial (that sexual abuse of children does not occur) with another (that professionals always act in the best interests of children and do not harm them). Consequently, many painful observations were offered about the professional response to child sexual abuse.

The horror of child sexual abuse propels us to action and to want to be assured that we are doing our best to protect children from such experiences. This is understandable, and there is little doubt that every professional response documented in this article is well-intended. However, good intentions are not sufficient. They need to be accompanied by effective action. Effective action, in turn, requires us to be brutally honest with ourselves and engage in continual self-examination. It may also require that we spend less time as a field in staking out extreme positions and more time in working to improve the results we achieve. Anything less is a disservice to the children in whose name we act.

REFERENCES

Aber, J. L. 1980. The involuntary placement decision: Solomon's dilemma revised. In *Child abuse: An agenda for action,* ed. G. Gerber, C. J. Ross, and E. Zigler, 156–70. New York: Oxford University Press.

Bass, E., and L. Davis. 1988. *The courage to heal.* New York: Harper & Row.

Becker, J. V., and V. L. Quinsey. 1993. Assessing suspected child molesters. *Child Abuse and Neglect* 17: 169–74.

Beitchman, J. H., K. J. Zucker, J. E. Hood, G. A. daCosta, and D. Akman. 1991. Review of the short-term effects of child sexual abuse. *Child Abuse and Neglect* 15: 537–56.

Beitchman, J. H., K. J. Zucker, J. E. Hood, G. A. daCosta, D. Akman, and E. Cassavia. 1992. Review of the long-term effects of child sexual abuse. *Child Abuse and Neglect* 16: 101–18.

Berliner, L. 1988. Deciding whether a child has been sexually abused. In *Sexual abuse allegations in custody and visitation cases,* ed. B. Nicholson, 48–69. Washington, D.C.: American Bar Association.

Berson, N. L., M. A. Herman-Giddens, and T. E. Frothingham. 1993. Children's perceptions of genital examinations during sexual abuse evaluations. *Child Welfare* 72: 41–49.

Besharov, D. J., ed. 1988. *Protecting children from abuse and neglect: Policy and practice.* Springfield, Ill.: Charles C. Thomas.

———. 1993. Overreporting and underreporting are twin problems. In *Current controversies on family violence,* ed. R. J. Gelles and D. R. Loeske, 257–72. Newbury Park, Calif.: Sage.

Boat, B. W., and M. D. Everson. 1988. The use of anatomical dolls among professionals in child abuse investigations. *Child Abuse and Neglect* 12: 171–86.

Bruck, M., S. Cecil, E. Francouer, and R. Barr. In press. "I hardly cried when I got my shot!": Influencing children's response about a visit to their pediatrician. *Child Development.*

Caffaro-Rouget, A., R. A. Lang, and V. vanSantem. 1989. The impact of child sexual abuse. *Annals of Sex Research* 2: 29–47.

Ceci, S. J., and M. Bruck. 1993a. Child witnesses: Translating research into social policy. *Social Policy Report* 8 (3): 1–30.

———. 1993b. The suggestibility of the child witness. *Psychological Bulletin* 113: 403–39.

Charlier, T., and S. Downing. 1988. Justice abused: A 1980s witch hunt. (Memphis, Tenn.) *Commercial Appeal* (January 15): 15.

Conte J., and J. Schuerman. 1980. The effects of sexual abuse on children: A multidimensional view. *Journal of Interpersonal Violence* 2: 380–90.

Conte, J. R., E. Sorenson, L. Fogarty, and J. D. Rost. 1991. Evaluating children's reports of sexual abuse. Results from a survey of professionals. *American Journal of Orthopsychiatry* 78: 428–32.

DeLoache, J. S. In press. The use of dolls in interviewing young children. In *Memory and testimony in the child witness,* ed. M. S. Zangoza, J. R. Graham, G. C. N. Hall, R. Hirschman, and Y. S. Ben-Porath. Newbury Park, Calif.: Sage.

Doris, J. L., ed. 1991. *The suggestibility of children's recollections.* Washington, D.C.: American Psychological Association.

Everson, M. D., and B. W. Boat. 1989. False allegations of sexual abuse by children and adolescents. *Journal of the American Academy of Child and Adolescent Psychiatry* 282: 230–35.

Finkelhor, D. 1993a. The main problem is still underreporting, not overreporting. In *Current controversies on family violence,* ed. R. J. Gelles and D. R. Loeske, 273–87. Newbury Park, Calif.: Sage.

———. 1993b. Epidemiological factors in the clinical identification of child sexual abuse. *Child Abuse and Neglect* 17: 67–70.

Gardner, R. A. 1992. *True and false accusations of child sexual abuse.* Cresskill, N.J.: Creative Therapeutics.

Giovannoni, J., and R. Becerra. 1979. *Defining child abuse.* New York: Free Press.

Goldstein, J., A. Freud, and A. J. Solnit. 1973. *Beyond the best interests of the child*. New York: Free Press.

Goodman, G. S., and C. J. Aman. 1990. Children's use of anatomically detailed dolls to recount an event. *Child Development* 61: 1859–71.

Goodman, G. S., and B. L. Bottoms, eds. 1993. *Child victims, child witnesses*. New York: Guilford.

Goodman, G. S., L. Rudy, B. Bottoms, and C. Aman. 1990. Children's concerns and memory issues of ecological validity in the study of children's eyewitness testimony. In *Knowing and remembering in young children*, ed. R. Fivush and J. Hudson, 249–84. New York: Cambridge University Press.

Goodman, G. S., E. P. Taub, D. P. H. Jones, P. England, L. K. Port, L. Rudy, and L. Prado. 1992. Testifying in criminal court: Emotional effects on child assault in adult victims. *Monographs of the Society for Research on Child Development* 57 (5, Serial No. 229).

Green, A. H. 1986. True and false allegations of sexual abuse in child custody disputes. *Journal of the American Academy of Child Psychiatry* 4: 449–56.

Hechler, D. 1993. Damage control. *Child Abuse and Neglect* 17: 169–74.

Howitt, D. 1992. *Child abuse errors: When good intentions go wrong*. New Brunswick, N.J.: Rutgers University Press.

Jackson, H., and R. Nuttal. 1993. Clinician response to sexual abuse allegations. *Child Abuse and Neglect* 17: 127–43.

Kane, D. 1994. DCFS report focuses on employee conduct. (Champaign-Urbana, Ill.) *News-Gazette* (January 12): 1.

Kendall-Tackett, K. A., L. M. Williams, and D. Finkelhor. 1990. Impact of sexual abuse on children: A review and synthesis of recent empirical studies. *Psychological Bulletin* 113: 164–80.

Levitt, C. 1990. Sexual abuse of boys: A medical perspective. In *The sexually abused male*, ed. M. Hunter, vol 1, 227–40. Lexington, Va.: Lexington Books.

Lloyd, R. M. 1992. Negotiating child sexual abuse: The interactional character of investigative practices. *Social Problems* 39: 109–24.

Loftus, E. F. 1993. The reality of repressed memories. *American Psychologist* 48: 518–37.

Mannarino, A. P., and J. A. Cohen. 1985. A clinical demographic study of sexually abused children. *Child Abuse and Neglect* 10: 17–23.

Margolin, L. 1992. Deviance on record: Techniques for labeling child abusers in official documents. *Social Problems* 39: 58–70.

Mason, M. A. 1991. A judicial dilemma: Expert witness testimony in child sex abuse cases. *Psychiatry and Law* 42: 185–219.

Mikkelsen, E. J., T. G. Gutheil, and M. Emens. 1992. False sexual abuse allegations by children and adolescents: Contextual factors and clinical subtypes. *American Journal of Psychotherapy* 46: 556–70.

Money, J., and M. Lamacz. 1987. Genital examinations and exposure experienced as nosocomial sexual abuse in childhood. *Journal of Nervous and Mental Disease* 175: 713–21.

Meyers, J. E. B. 1990. Expert testimony regarding child sexual abuse. *Child Abuse and Neglect* 17: 175–85.

———. 1992. *Legal issues in child abuse and neglect.* Newbury Park, Calif.: Sage.

National Center for Child Abuse and Neglect. 1981. *National study of the incidence and severity of child abuse and neglect.* (Document No. 81-30325). Washington, D.C.: U.S. Department of Health and Human Services. [NIS I]

———. 1988. *Study findings: Study of national incidence and prevalence of child abuse and neglect.* Washington, D.C.: U.S. Department of Health and Human Services [NIS 2]

———. 1993. *National child abuse and neglect data systems, 1991. Summary data component.* Gaithersburg, Md.: U.S. Department of Health and Human Services.

National Research Council. 1993. *Understanding child abuse and neglect.* Washington, D.C.: National Academy Press.

Olafson, E., D. L. Corwin, and R. C. Summit. 1993. Modern history of child sexual abuse awareness: Cycles of discovery and suppression. *Child Abuse and Neglect* 17: 7–24.

Pearson, J., and N. Thoennes. 1988. Difficult dilemma: Responding to sexual abuse allegations in custody and visitation disputes. In *Protecting children from abuse and neglect: Policy and practice,* ed. D. Beshiutv, 91–112. Springfield, Ill.: Charles C. Thomas.

Peters, D. D., G. E. Wyatt, and D. Finkelhor. 1986. Prevalence. In *A sourcebook on child sexual abuse,* ed. D. Finkelhor, 15–59. Newbury Park, Calif.: Sage.

Reppucci, N. D., and M. S. Aber. 1992. Child maltreatment prevention and the legal system. In *Prevention of child maltreatment,* ed. D. J. Willis, 249–66. New York: Wiley.

Rowe, P. 1992. Child abuse telecast floods national hotline. *Children Today* 21: 11.

Runyan, D. K. 1993. The emotional impact of societal intervention into child abuse. In *Child victims, child witnesses,* ed. G. S. Goodman and B. L. Bottoms, 263–78. New York: Guilford.

Runyan, D. K., M. D. Everson, G. A. Edelsohn, W. M. Hunter, and M. L. Coulter. 1988. Impact of legal intervention on sexually abused children. *Journal of Pediatrics* 113: 647–53.

Sedlak, A. J. 1990. *Technical amendments to the study findings—national incidence and prevalence of child abuse and neglect [NIS 2] 1988.* Rockville, Md.: Westate Inc.

Siegel, J. M., S. B. Sorenson, J. M. Golding, M. A. Burnam, and J. A. Stein. 1987. The prevalence of childhood sexual assault: The Los Angeles epidemiological catchment area project. *American Journal of Epidemiology* 126: 1141–53.

Skinner, L. J., and K. K. Berry. 1993. Anatomically detailed dolls and the evaluation of child sexual abuse allegations: Psychometric considerations. *Law and Human Behavior* 17: 399–422.

State of New Jersey v. *Kelly Michaels* 264 N.J. Super 579 (1993).

Walker, C. E., B. L. Bonner, and K. L. Kaufman. 1988. *The physically and sexually abused child.* New York: Pergamon.

West, D. J. 1991. The effects of sex offenses. In *Clinical approaches to sex offenders and their victims,* ed. C. R. Hollin and K. Howells, 55–73. Chichester, England: Wiley.

Wexler, R. 1990. *Wounded innocents: The real victims of the war against child abuse.* Amherst, N.Y.: Prometheus Books.

Woffner, G., D. Faust, and R. Dawes. 1993. The use of anatomical dolls in sex abuse evaluations: The state of the science. *Applied and Preventive Psychology* 2: 1–11.

Wyatt, G. E. 1985. The sexual abuse of Afro-American and White women in childhood. *Childhood Abuse and Neglect* 9: 507–19.

15

HOW RELIABLE ARE CHILDREN'S STATEMENTS? . . . IT DEPENDS

STEPHEN J. CECI AND MAGGIE BRUCK

How accurate are very young children's recollections about events, people, and places from their distant past? How likely is their testimony to be biased about such matters if interviewers use leading questions or suggestive therapeutic techniques (e.g., hypnosis, role playing, visually guided imagery, fantasy play)? How important is it for interviewers to test explicitly at least one alternative hypothesis during an investigation? Does the use of anatomical dolls facilitate the accuracy of young children's reports? And, finally, can experienced interviewers tell when a child provides an erroneous report, particularly if the child has been exposed to persistently suggestive interviews?

These are not only theoretically interesting questions for researchers, but also important practical questions. Each year, tens of thousands of children enter America's courtrooms to testify about their recollections of events. The cases may involve charges such as sexual abuse, custody disputes, or domestic violence, or the children are testifying in civil suits such as product liability (Ceci and Bruck 1993a). What can research tell us about children's recollections in such cases?

Fincham, Beach, Moore, and Diener (1994) have provided a provocative and thoughtful approach to answer these questions. Because we agree with most of their assertions, we confine ourselves here to an elab-

From *Family Relations* 43, no. 3 (July 1994): 255–57. Copyrighted © 1994 by the National Council on Family Relations, 3989 Central Ave. NE, Suite 550, Minneapolis, MN 55421. Reprinted by permission.

oration of several of their points that we, as researchers in this area, believe to be important, and yet are often unknown to front-line workers and therapists. In our commentary, we shall address the reliability risks raised by Fincham et al. about interviewer's confirmatory bias, the use of anatomical dolls, and the ability of clinicians and other professionals to discriminate between accurate and inaccurate statements of children.

CONFIRMATORY BIAS

In warning interviewers to take care when eliciting statements from young children, Fincham et al. (1994) briefly glanced into the "jaw" of the problem known among researchers as *confirmatory bias*. Here, we put teeth to it. Ample research evidence indicates that interviewers do not come to an interview tabula rasa. Rather, they come with preexisting ideas about what may have transpired (see Kayne and Alloy 1988; Maddux 1993). Any time preexisting ideas impede the interviewer's ability to test an alternative hunch, then there is a risk for serious misreporting on the part of the child, especially if the witness is a young preschooler.

At its core, science is "proof by disproof" (Ceci and Bronfenbrenner 1991), meaning that a common hallmark of all scientific endeavors is that scientists attempt to disprove a hypothesis by giving alternative hypotheses a fair chance to be confirmed while simultaneously giving their pet hypothesis a fair chance to be falsified. Although not all scientists attempt to test alternative hypotheses all of the time, they nevertheless acknowledge the benefit of doing so, and recognize that any lapse into a confirmatory bias may result in weaker science (Boyd 1981; Popper 1962). Simply put, scientists try to arrive at the truth by ruling out rival hypotheses—particularly, the most reasonable rivals—and by falsifying their favored hypothesis (see Dawes 1992). In well-worked fields of scholarship, if scientists do not attempt to disconfirm their hypothesis, others can be counted on to do the job for them. Unfortunately, in clinical and forensic interviews, it is not always the case that others can be counted on to test alternative hypotheses if front-line professionals fail to do so.

The earliest recorded evidence of the dangers of interviewer confirmatory bias was reported by Rice (1929). He examined 12 experienced interviewers from various social service agencies in New York City who were assigned, in what was for all practical purposes a random manner, to interview approximately 2,000 homeless men to ascertain the causes of their destitution. Rice was struck by the manner in which the interviewers' beliefs influenced the contents of the reports they obtained. The most obvious example of this came in the case of two interviewers who differed in their social orientations, one being known by coworkers as a "socialist," the other as an ardent "prohibitionist." Rice found that the socialist was nearly three times more likely to conclude that the men's destitution was due to industrial causes beyond their control (e.g., lay-offs, plant closings, seasonal labor), while the prohibitionist was nearly three times more likely to report that the basis of their destitution was alcohol and drug abuse. Not only were the conclusions of the two inter-viewers consistent with their pet hypotheses, but the homeless men themselves seemed to have incorporated the interviewers' biases into their own answers. Recent research demonstrates biases among mental health professionals that are similar to those found by Rice (e.g., Alloy and Tabachnik 1984; Brehm and Smith 1986, 1984; Maddux 1993).

There is some evidence that those charged with interviewing young children do not follow training instructions, and that they frequently pursue a single hypothesis to the exclusion of alternatives. For example. Pettit and her colleagues (cited in Ceci and Bruck 1993b) instructed interviewers to obtain full reports from preschoolers who had experi-enced an unusual event in their classroom. These interviewers were told to avoid the use of leading questions. Before conducting these inter-views, the interviewers were deliberately misinformed about some of the actual events that had occurred in the classroom. Pettit et al. discovered that despite their instructions to avoid leading questions, 34% of inter-viewers' questions could be categorized as leading, and many inter-viewers pursued a single hypothesis. Interviewers who were misled about the event managed to elicit from children significantly more errors in their reports than did non-misled interviewers. So, children often ended up corroborating interviewers' erroneous hypotheses.

Interviewers, like scientists, should also attempt to rule out rival hy-potheses instead of exclusively attempting to confirm their favored hypothesis, because the failure to test a rival hypothesis can result in var-ious types of errors (e.g., suggestibility effects, misattributions, source confusions). We have conducted studies in which interviewers are given erroneous hypotheses about what may have happened during some orchestrated event. When this happens, interviewers tend to get the chil-dren to assent to events that never occurred but that are consistent with their false hypothesis.

For example, in one study, we told a social worker that children had played a game one month earlier during which they may have licked an adult's elbow and put something in her ear. Neither of these things hap-pened, yet the social worker, who was led to hypothesize that such events may have occurred, managed to get some of the children to assent to them. One month later, a second interviewer, using the social worker's notes as a guide for her second interview, managed to get these children to elaborate on their inaccurate reports elicited by the social worker one month earlier (Ceci and Bruck 1993a)

In a related study (Ceci, unpublished raw data), we asked parents to watch a video that their preschool child watched in an adjoining room and to interview their child to determine what he or she could remember from the video. Unbeknownst to the parents, their children watched a different video than the one the parents had watched. Nevertheless, these parents managed to get some of their children to "remember" watching things that had only occurred on the parents' video.

ANATOMICAL DOLL-BASED INTERVIEWS

Elsewhere, we have written at length about the uses and abuses of doll-centered assessments (Ceci and Bruck 1993a, 1993b). Our argument is essentially similar to that of Fincham et al. (1994), with a few differences that we need not delve into here. Suffice to say that the question of *incremental validity* (how much the dolls add unique variance to the prediction of abuse) has not been answered; indeed, it has not even been addressed by those who advocate the use of the dolls. Although there is some indication that the dolls may be somewhat helpful for older preschoolers (see Gordon et al. 1993), or at least not an impediment to them (Goodman and Aman 1990), there is a growing suspicion that they are highly suggestive with younger preschoolers (Ceci and Bruck 1993a). In our work with three-year-olds, we have found that approximately half of these children can be led with the dolls to falsely indicate genital and anal insertions. While we attach no confidence to the exact percentages obtained in our study and believe that they will fluctuate somewhat depending on the conditions of the interviews, we do assert that no one should use these dolls with three-year-olds unless they are able to make a compelling case against their suggestiveness. We simply must find better ways than the use of the dolls to minimize young children's linguistic limitations and feelings of embarrassment (the two main reasons offered in support of doll use). No one would want to plant a false accusation in a three-year-old by asking the child to show on a doll where someone had touched him or her; it is possibly harmful to the child (for it alters his or her biography) and it is certainly harmful to whomever is falsely accused.

CAN ADULTS DISCRIMINATE BETWEEN ACCURATE AND INACCURATE REPORTS?

Although children's reports may be highly influenced by a number of suggestive influences, this does not necessarily mean that the children will appear credible when they parrot interviewers' erroneous suggestions. Of particular concern is whether a juror, or a child development researcher, or a child therapist, can differentiate children whose reports are accurate from those whose reports are a product of suggestive interviews. The existing evidence suggests that even highly trained professionals cannot tell the difference between these two kinds of children.

In some of our studies we have asked experts to judge the credibility of our subjects after they have been subjected to a series of suggestive interviews. In one study, videotapes of the children were shown to approximately one thousand researchers and clinicians who work on children's testimonial issues (Leichtman and Ceci, in press). These researchers and clinicians were asked to decide which of the events reported by the children actually had transpired and then to rate the overall credibility of each child. The majority of the professionals were highly inaccurate. Experts who conduct research on the credibility of children's reports, who provide therapy to children suspected of having been abused, and who carry out law enforcement interviews with children generally failed to detect which of the children's claims were accurate and which were not, despite being confident in the judgments (for similar results in other studies, see Ceci, Crotteau, Smith, and Loftus, in press; Ceci, Loftus, Leichtman, and Bruck, in press). In this case, the highly credible yet inaccurate reports obtained from the children may have resulted from a combination of repeated interviews with persistent and intense suggestions that built on a set of prior stereotypes. Similarly, it may become difficult to separate credibility from accuracy when child witnesses, after repeated interviews, give a formal videotaped interview or testify in court.

One might argue that the content of the children's narrations in these studies is quite different from that of children who report sexual abuse. Perhaps well-trained professionals can reliably differentiate between true and false reports of sexual abuse. Unfortunately, the existing literature suggests that there is little consistency among these professionals' judgments. There are two programs of research to illustrate this point.

Realmuto, Jensen, and Wesco (1990) asked a highly trained child psychiatrist to interview children and then to determine which of the children had been sexually abused. Next, videotapes of these assessments were shown to 14 professionals (pediatricians, psychiatrists, social workers, psychologists, attorneys), each with more than 10 years of experience in the field of child sexual abuse. The professionals were asked to classify the children as abused or nonabused. Although there was high concordance between the interviewer and the raters in terms of which children they classified as abused and nonabused, the overall rates of accurate classification were low. The interviewing psychiatrist correctly identified 33% of the abused children and 67% of the nonabused children. The group of professionals correctly classified 23% of the abused children and 85% of the nonabused children.

Homer, Guyer, and Kalter (1993a, 1993b) presented an actual case of alleged sexual abuse of a three-year-old to mental health specialists. These clinicians heard a detailed presentation of the court-appointed clinician's findings, which included parent interviews and videotaped child-parent interaction sequences. The case presentation lasted approximately two hours, during which time the participants questioned the clinician who evaluated the child and her family. After the presentation, the clinicians estimated the likelihood of sexual molestation. The range of estimated probabilities of abuse was extreme—many clinicians were confident that abuse did not take place, and others were just as confident that abuse had occurred. The same patterns were obtained when the analyses were restricted to a smaller group of experts who were uniquely qualified to assess child sexual abuse.

Although surprising to some, these results are depressing to all. They suggest that when allegations of child sexual abuse are made in many cases, there is no "Pinocchio" test that can be used even by the most qualified investigators to definitively ascertain whether or not abuse occurred.

THE SUGGESTIBILITY OF CHILDREN

In our previous work we have made the following three general comments about the suggestibility of young children. First, there are reliable age effects in children's suggestibility, with preschoolers being more vulnerable than older children to a variety of factors that contribute to unreliable reports. Second, the important question is not whether children can provide credible testimony, but rather, what are the conditions that both facilitate and obstruct children's ability to remember and report? The answer to this is first and foremost an empirical question, one that awaits future research. But for now, we can state with confidence that children's report accuracy is maximized when interviewers are not attached to a single hypothesis, refrain from using persistently suggestive techniques (e.g., leading questions, hypnosis, visually guided imagery, fantasy inductions, role playing), and avoid the use of dolls. The violation of any one or combination of these conditions raises the possibility that young children can be led to make an inaccurate disclosure that experts find impossible to discriminate from accurate ones.

Third, it is important to appreciate the complexity of the interrelationships of the factors affecting children's suggestibility. As in most areas of social science, effects are rarely as straightforward as one might wish. Even though suggestibility effects may be robust, the effects are not universal. Results vary between studies, and children's behavior varies within studies. Thus, even in studies with pronounced suggestibility effects, there are always some children who are highly resistant to suggestion. We have seen this in our own studies as well as in the transcripts of many forensic and therapeutic interviews: In some cases, no matter how much an interviewer may try to suggest that an event occurred, some children will consistently resist and not incorporate the interviewer's suggestion or point of view. On the other hand, although suggestibility effects tend to be most dramatic after prolonged and repeated interviewing, some children incorporate suggestions quickly, even after one short interview.

CONCLUSION

In concluding, we want to commend Fincham et al. (1994) for the professional manner in which they presented their arguments. In this emotionally charged area, it is rare to come across professionals who present their arguments dispassionately. To their credit, Fincham et al. do not follow a common stream of attack: They do not marginalize their opponents by casting personal aspersions about their values, about their feelings for children, and about their profit motives. It is refreshing to see how fairly these authors deal with their opponents. It is too much to hope that everyone will agree with the arguments of Fincham et al., but it is not too much to hope that those who disagree will espouse their views with the same equanimity that these authors have shown. We sincerely believe that the interests of children are best served when all parties agree that ideas are to be attacked, not the persons who endorse them. Too much mean-spirited, self-righteous zealotry has been promulgated by extremists on both sides of this debate. Fincham and his colleagues have refrained from dipping into this trough of opponent vilification, and for that the entire field ought to thank them.

REFERENCES

Alloy, L. B., and N. Tabachnik. 1984. Assessment of covariation by humans and animals: The joint influence of prior expectations and current situational information. *Psychological Review* 91: 112–49.

Boyd, R. 1951. Scientific realism and naturalistic epistemology. In *PSA*, vol. 2, ed. P. D. Asquith and R. N. Giere, 613–62. East Lansing, Mich.: Philosophy of Science Association.

Brehm, S. S., and T. W. Smith. 1986. Social psychological approaches to psychotherapy and behavior change. In *Handbook of psychotherapy and behavior change*, 3rd ed., ed. S. L. Garfield and A. Bergin, 69–116. New York: Wiley.

Ceci, S. J., and U. Bronfenbrenner. 1991. On the demise of everyday memory: Rumors of my death are greatly exaggerated. *American Psychologist* 46: 27–31.

Ceci, S. J., and M. Bruck. 1993a. Child witnesses: Translating research into policy. *Social Policy Report: Society for Research in Child Development* 8 (3): 1–30.

———. 1993b. The suggestibility of the child witness. *Psychological Bulletin* 113: 403–39.

Ceci, S. J., M. Crotteau, E. Smith, and E. W. Loftus. In press. Repeatedly thinking about nonevents. *Consciousness and Cognition*.

Ceci, S. J., E. W. Loftus, M. Leichtman, and M. Bruck. In press. The role of source misattributions in the creation of false beliefs among preschoolers. *International Journal of Clinical and Experimental Hypnosis*.

Dawes, R. 1992. The importance of alternative hypothesis and hypothetical counterfactuals in general social science. *The General Psychologist* (Spring): 2–7.

Fincham, F. D., S. R. H. Beach, T. Moore, and C. Diener. 1994. The professional response to child sexual abuse: Whose interests are served? *Family Relations* 43: 244–54.

Goodman, G., and C. Aman. 1990. Children's use of anatomically detailed dolls to recount an event. *Child Development* 61: 1859–71.

Gordon, B., P. A. Ornstein, R. Nida, A. Fodmer, C. Creshaw, and G. Alben. 1993. Does the use of dolls facilitate children's memory of visits to the doctor? *Applied Cognitive Psychology* 7: 459–74.

Horner, T. M., M. J. Guyer, and N. M. Kalter. 1993a. Clinical expertise and the assessment of child sexual abuse. *Journal of the American Academy of Child and Adolescent Psychiatry* 32: 925–31.

———. 1993b. The biases of child sexual abuse experts: Believing is seeing. *Bulletin of the American Academy of Psychiatry and Law* 21: 281–92.

Kayne, N. T., and L. B. Alloy. 1988. Clinician and patient as aberrant actuaries: Expectation-based distortions in assessment of covariation. In *Social cognition and clinical psychology: A synthesis*, ed. L. Y. Abramson, 295–365. New York: Guilford.

Leichtman, M. D., and S. J. Ceci. In press. The effect of stereotypes and suggestions on preschoolers' reports. *Developmental Psychology*.

Maddux, J. E. 1993. The mythology of psychopathology: A social cognitive view of deviance, difference, and disorder. *General Psychologist* 29: 34–45

Popper, K. R. 1962. *Conjectures and reflections.* New York: Basic Books.

Realmuto, G., J. Jensen, and S. Wescoe. 1990. Specificity and sensitivity of sexually anatomically correct dolls in substantiating abuse: A pilot study. *Journal of the American Academy of Child and Adolescent Psychiatry* 29: 743–46.

Rice, S. A. 1929. Interviewer bias as a contagion. *American Journal of Sociology* 35: 421–23.

16

AVOIDING FALSE CLAIMS OF CHILD SEXUAL ABUSE:
EMPTY PROMISES

KATHY PEZDEK

This article provides a commentary to the piece, "The Professional Response to Child Sexual Abuse: Whose Interests are Served?" by Fincham, Beach, Moore, and Diener (1994). In that article, it is argued that in their zeal to "do something" about child abuse, practitioners who work in child protective services may have adopted ineffective procedures that are unwittingly harmful to children. The major source of harm addressed is that resulting from pursuing claims of sexual abuse that in fact are false. This commentary focuses on one point—the importance of recognizing that any attempts to reduce the probability of false claims of child abuse (Type II error) would necessarily result in increasing the probability of missing true claims of child abuse (Type I error). The hypothesis-testing framework is offered as a useful heuristic for conceptualizing the tradeoffs between these two types of errors.

The job of separating real from false instances of child sexual abuse is often a truly ambiguous task. It involves decision making in the face of uncertainty, in a highly emotional situation, with dire consequences for errors. Fincham et al. (1994) have identified numerous problems that might result from current practices in responding to child abuse allegations. It is hard to argue with their position that practitioners must be careful to avoid "merely replacing one form of denial (that sexual abuse

From *Family Relations* 43, no. 3 (July 1994): 258–60. Copyrighted © 1994 by the National Council on Family Relations, 3989 Central Ave. NE, Suite 550, Minneapolis, MN 55421. Reprinted by permission.

of children does not occur) with another (that professionals always act in the best interests of children and do not harm them)" (p. 253). And, few professionals would disagree that there is room for improvement in the methods of (a) identifying child abuse when it occurs and (b) effectively dealing with the child and the perpetrator. However, *the over-arching logic of the position of Fincham et al. is fallacious.*

THE HYPOTHESIS-TESTING FRAMEWORK

In a perfect world, one could easily jump on the crusade proposed by Fincham et al. (1994) and join in the battle cry to reduce or eliminate false claims of child abuse. But the world is not perfect. Fincham et al. make an empty promise by failing to recognize the fact that any attempts to reduce the probability of false claims of child abuse would necessarily result in increasing the probability of missing true claims of child abuse. I suggest that the hypothesis-testing framework offers a useful heuristic for conceptualizing the tradeoffs between reducing false claims and missing true claims of child abuse. Figure 1 presents the hypothetical probability distributions for two populations: The distribution on the left represents the distribution of the amount of evidence of abuse for the population in which abuse did not occur; the distribution on the right represents the distribution of the amount of evidence of abuse for the population in which abuse did occur.

The point in presenting these two distributions in this way is that it captures several characteristics of the reality of the situation. First, the amount of evidence of abuse is a continuous variable that ranges from little evidence on the left to much evidence on the right. The evidence of abuse is not an all-or-none phenomenon: it is not useful to think of the evidence of abuse as either present or absent. Second, each population distribution spans the full range along the horizontal axis from the minimum to the maximum amounts of evidence of abuse. This reflects the ambiguity in the situation—even if there is minimal evidence of child abuse, it may be that the abuse really did occur, and even if there is a great deal of evidence of child abuse, it may be that the abuse did not really occur. However, because it is assumed that these are normal distributions, the probability of these extreme cases is quite small.

Third, the most important point in characterizing the problem of detecting child abuse according to the hypothesis-testing framework is that it clarifies the fact that there is an overlap between these distributions in terms of the amount of evidence for abuse that might exist. That is, one may not be able to discriminate between many abusive and non-

Figure 1. **Hypothetical Probability Distributions for Cases in Which Abuse Occurred and Cases in Which Abuse Did Not Occur**

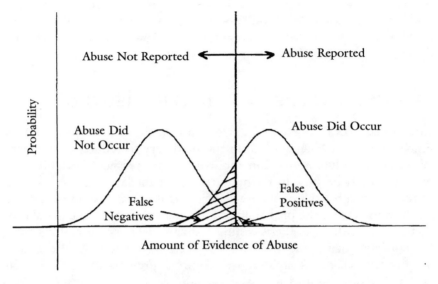

Note. The distribution of the amount of evidence of abuse for the population in which abuse did not occur (on the left) and the population in which abuse did occur (on the right). The decision criterion (the vertical line) is positioned such that abuse is not reported in cases that fall to the left of the criterion, and abuse is reported in cases that fall to the right of the criterion. Accordingly, the probability of false positives (Type I error) and false negatives (Type II error) are indicated.

---

abusive cases, as the amount of evidence for abuse could be similar for both types of cases. These more ambiguous cases exist in the overlap of the distributions in Figure 1.

Given the ambiguity in this situation, how does one make a decision for individual cases, regarding whether abuse occurred or not? Another way of framing this question is to ask, "Where does one place the decision criterion?" The criterion will be placed at some point along the horizontal axis, such that if in an individual case, the amount of evidence of abuse is greater than the criterion (to the right of the criterion in Figure 1), the case will be reported as one suspected of abuse, and if in an individual case, the amount of evidence of abuse is less than the criterion (to the left of the criterion in Figure 1), the case will be reported as one in which abuse is not suspected. The vertical line in the middle of Figure 1 represents one possible placement of the decision criterion. Generally speaking, the criterion in Figure 1 is positioned at a reasonable point; most of the cases where abuse did occur would correctly be reported as abuse, and most of the cases where abuse did not occur would correctly be reported as not abusive.

The above framework also elucidates two inevitable errors in making decisions about the occurrence of abuse. One error focused on by Fincham et al. (1994) is that a false accusation might be made. This would be a false positive error or Type I error. Referring to Figure 1, the probability of a false positive error corresponds to the shaded area to the right of the criterion, under the distribution representing the population in which abuse did not occur. That is, abuse did not occur, but it is erroneously decided that abuse did occur. The other type of error is a false negative or Type II error. Referring to Figure 1, the probability of a false negative error corresponds to the shaded area to the left of the criterion, under the distribution representing the population in which abuse did occur. That is, abuse did occur, but it is erroneously decided that abuse did not occur.

Now, to illustrate the thesis of this commentary, the inevitable tradeoff between false positive error and false negative error can be seen by observing what happens to the size of the area of the curve corresponding to the false positive error rate and the false negative error rate as the criterion is shifted to the right and then to the left. Referring to Figure 1, if one wants to reduce the incidence of false positives, the criterion should be raised (i.e., shifted to the right), but in so doing, the incidence of false negatives would increase. If one wants to reduce the incidence of false negatives, the criterion should be lowered (i.e., shifted to the left), but an increase in false positives would correspondingly result. The point not made in the article by Fincham et al. (1994) is that there is a price to be paid for reducing the number of false claims of child sexual abuse: *it is impossible to reduce the incidence of false positives without a corresponding increase in false negatives.*

EVALUATING THE COSTS OF FALSE NEGATIVE ERRORS AND FALSE POSITIVE ERRORS

So how do practitioners in the field decide where hypothetically to place the criterion in terms of how much evidence will be required prior to pursuing a claim of child sexual abuse? Ordinarily, the statistical standard is to place the criterion such that the rate of false positives (also called alpha error) is limited to .05. However, in any domain, the decision regarding where the criterion should be placed depends on weighing the costs of false positives against the costs of false negatives. Surely we must agree with Fincham et al. (1994) that it is incorrect to assume that "if there is no abuse no harm will come to the family or child"(Walker, Bonner, and Kaufman 1988, 18). Some awkwardness, if not psychological harm, is surely caused by taking a child or a parent from the home for some period of time, by subjecting a child to an unnecessary physical examination, and by raising suspicions in the school and in the neighborhood. These would be the costs of a false positive error, that is, pursuing a claim of child sexual abuse when no abuse in fact occurred.

On the other hand, what would be the costs of a false negative error? If sexual abuse is occurring and nothing is done to prevent its recurrence, a child could be subjected to a childhood of frequent sexual abuse. Although Fincham et al. (1994) argue, "the widespread assertion that the impact of sexual abuse is serious" is "misleading" (p. 251), I think that most people would be appalled by this position. I recently heard someone argue at a public forum that what makes incest so bad for children is the unnecessary fuss made about it by society. This view does not seem a far cry from the position taken on this issue in the target piece. Fincham et al. propose that more research is necessary to determine how serious the consequences of child sexual abuse are. In particular, it is argued that studies are necessary to compare "abused children to children reported to CPS [Child Protective Services] but whose cases are unfounded" (p. 250), to separate out the effects of the abuse from the effects of the professionals' response to the abuse. Although from a logical positivist point of view I agree that such a study is necessary to isolate the effects of these two variables, I can only imagine Senator Proxmire's delight in bestowing the "Golden Fleece Award" on such a research enterprise.

I have difficulty even imagining a convincing argument supporting the view that the severity of the consequences of raising false accusations of sexual abuse even approaches the severity of the consequences of leaving a child in a situation where he or she will be repeatedly abused. Fincham et al. (1994) demean the motivation of child protective services practitioners by implying that it is their zeal to simply do something that may be generating a very large false positive rate. It is more likely their astute awareness of the dire consequences of leaving a child in an abusive situation that has motivated them to set their decision criterion high to minimize false negative errors.

Fincham et al. (1994) refer to a very thorough review of the literature on the impact of sexual abuse on children by Kendall-Tackett, Williams, and Finkelhor (1993), in which it is reported that there does not appear to be a single pattern of symptoms associated with sexual abuse. Although Fincham et al. interpret this finding as minimizing the seriousness of the effects of child abuse ("just about any worrisome childhood behavior has been associated with child sexual abuse," p. 250), this was not at all the tenor of the conclusions reported by Kendall-Tackett et al. Kendall-Tackett et al. reported that the absence of a single pattern of symptoms associated with sexual abuse is an indication of the complexity of the dynamics of sexual violation of children. The consequences of sexual abuse appear to depend on the type and severity of the abuse, the relationship between the perpetrator and the victim, and a range of situational variables and person-specific variables. But that there are serious consequences of child sexual abuse is not questioned by Kendall-Tackett et al.

SUGGESTIBILITY AS A SOURCE OF FALSE POSITIVE ERRORS

Fincham et al. (1994) emphasize the importance of becoming acquainted with the available research on children's memory. The implication here is that because children are usually the only witnesses in child abuse cases, it is important to understand the conditions that affect the accuracy of children's memory. And, because suggestibility is often implicated as a major culprit at the source of false positive errors, it is also important to understand the conditions under which children's memory is vulnerable to suggestibility. However, the summary of the research offered by Fincham et al. utilizes too broad a brush to be considered truly accurate.

Fincham et al. (1994) state, "There is some evidence to suggest that suggestibility effects can give rise to very strong illusory beliefs that are resistant to change, especially when the suggestions are strong" (p. 252). Although there is some evidence supporting this view, Fincham et al. belie their objectivity by failing to report that there is significant disagreement about this point in the research literature. For example, although Bruck, Ceci, Francouer, and Barr (in press) and Ceci, Crotteau, Smith, and Loftus (in press) reported that misleading questions can plant memories for events that did not occur, Baker-Ward, Gordon, Ornstein, Larus, and Clubb (1993); Rudy and Goodman (1991); and Saywitz, Goodman, Nichols, and Moan (1991) reported very weak evidence for planting memories for events that did not occur, and Pezdek and Roe (in press) reported that ten-year-old children are highly resistant to having information planted in memory. With such notable inconsistencies in the conclusions reached among these apparently similar studies, it would be premature to draw any conclusions from the literature currently available regarding the probability of suggestively planting memories for events that did not occur.

Several other points reported by Fincham et al. (1994) in the section on children's memory are not consistent with the conclusions reached from a thorough literature review. These points are especially suspect, as no original source material was referenced for each. Rather than providing a detailed critique and review of the relevant research in this commentary, I simply want to point out that the following are among the conclusions reponed by Fincham et al. that are inaccurate by virtue of being deceivingly global (the italics were added for emphasis):

> "children *may* inaccurately report as remembered aspects of the event material communicated to them by others" (p. 252),

> "children *sometimes* embellish the information that they incorporate into their memories, providing vivid and detailed accounts of events that never occurred" (p. 252),

> "individual differences exist in children's susceptibility to the influences mentioned; *some* children are extremely resistant to such influences" (p. 252),

> "children *sometimes* lie when the 'motivational structure is tilted toward lying' " (p. 252).

A review of the research literature on the suggestibility of children's memory would lead to the qualified conclusion that, at present, there is no evidence that illusory memories for sexual abuse are a widespread phenomenon.

IMPLICATIONS OF THE HYPOTHESIS-TESTING FRAMEWORK FOR FUTURE RESEARCH

One interesting research suggestion follows from using the hypothesis-testing approach to frame the issue of separating real versus false claims of sexual abuse. There is one change that would simultaneously decrease the rate of false negative errors and false positive errors, and that is, decreasing the variance within the two distributions. Referring to Figure 1, if the means of the two distributions remained constant (there is no way to move these distributions farther apart), and the criterion remained fixed, reducing the variance within the two distributions (i.e., making both distributions taller and skinnier) would decrease both types of error. The variance of these two distributions would be decreased if we had less measurement error, that is, a more sensitive and precise technique for assessing the amount of evidence of abuse. If we had a better understanding of the critical indicators of child sexual abuse, there would be less overlap in the two distributions in Figure 1, indicating less uncertainty regarding whether sexual abuse is evident or not in any particular situation. This argues for the need for research focused on developing a battery of measures that more accurately predicts when abuse has occurred. Application of the hypothesis-testing framework to the issue of child sexual abuse thus has clear implications for conceptually framing the tradeoffs between false positive errors and false negative errors, and suggests productive avenues for future research.

CONCLUSION

I am certainly not arguing in this commentary that false accusations of child sexual abuse are trivial, nor that they should be ignored. Rather, I am using the hypothesis-testing framework to illustrate the fact that the rate of false accusations cannot be reduced without increasing the rate of false negatives. And, given the consequences of leaving a child in a situation where he or she is likely to be repeatedly sexually abused, the costs of false negatives are substantially greater than the costs of false positives.

REFERENCES

Baker-Ward, L., B. N. Gordon, P. A. Ornstein, D. M. Larus, and P. A. Clubb. 1993. Young children's long-term retention of a pediatric examination. *Child Development* 64: 1517–33.

Bruck, M., S. J. Ceci, E. Francouer, and R Barr. In press. "I hardly cried when I got my shot!": Influencing children's reports about a visit to their pediatrician. *Child Development*.

Ceci, S. J., M. L. Crotteau, E. Smith, and E. F. Loftus. In press. Recalling nonevents: An experimental investigation of source misattribution errors. *Consciousness and Cognition*.

Fincham, F. D., S. R. H. Beach, T. Moore, and C. Diener. 1994. The professional response to child abuse: Whose interests are served? *Family Relations* 43: 244–54.

Kendall-Tackett, K. A., L. M. Williams, and D. Finkelhor. 1993. Impact of sexual abuse on children: A review and synthesis of recent empirical studies. *Psychological Bulletin* 113: 164–80.

Pezdek, K., and C. Roe. In press. Memory for childhood events: How suggestible is it? *Consciousness and Cognition*.

Rudy, L., and C. S. Goodman. 1991. Effects of participation on children's reports: Implications for children's testimony. *Developmental Psychology* 27: 527–38.

Saywitz, K. J., G. S. Goodman, E. Nichols, and S. F. Moan. 1991. Children's memories of a physical examination involving genital touch: Implications for reports of child sexual abuse. *Journal of Consulting and Clinical Psychology* 59: 682–91.

Walker, C. E., B. L. Bonner, and K. L. Kaufman. 1988. *The physically and sexually abused child*. New York: Pergamon.

17

CHILD SEXUAL ABUSE:
FINDING COMMON GROUND

FRANK D. FINCHAM,
STEVEN R. H. BEACH, THOM MOORE,
AND CAROL DIENER

> Mundus vult decipi: the world wants to be deceived. The truth is too complex and frightening.
>
> Walter Kaufman (1970, 9)

The field of child sexual abuse is increasingly characterized by the competing and contradictory claims of polarized factions. One reaction to the sometimes vitriolic exchanges in the literature is to despair of progress in a field so mired in anger and hyperbole. An alternative reaction is to ask how we might harness the tension that exists in this area to propel the field forward and best serve the interests of children. By adopting the position that many, if not all, of the competing claims pertaining to child sexual abuse ultimately boil down to empirical claims that can be investigated and discussed by persons with initially divergent positions, we create an opportunity to increase consensus in the field. Accordingly, we respond to those aspects of the commentaries that concern empirical issues and do not engage rhetoric, question authors' objectivity, or speculate on decisions about the Golden Fleece Awards.

From *Family Relations* 43, no. 3 (July 1994): 264–66. Copyrighted © 1994 by the National Council on Family Relations, 3989 Central Ave. NE, Suite 550, Minneapolis, MN 55421. Reprinted by permission.

THE CORE ARGUMENT

Before addressing specific issues, we restate the core argument we offered in our original article (Fincham, Beach, Moore, and Diener 1994) to ensure that it is clearly understood. This will allow the reader to better evaluate the extent to which concerns expressed in this exchange represent differences among the authors.

The core argument was that children's well-being should determine all professional action, no matter how painful this may be for the professional. Thus, our article was an exercise in self-scrutiny that attempted to transcend the new denial about child sexual abuse by identifying viewpoints and practices that have the potential to unnecessarily harm children who come to the attention of professionals. We discussed potential harm-doing in relation to children who have not been sexually victimized because virtually no attention has been paid to such children and because the contingencies in the field overwhelmingly favor false positive errors (finding children to have been abused when no such abuse had occurred). However, we did not limit ourselves exclusively to such cases. Many of the concerns we expressed and the suggestions we made apply equally to decreasing the rates of false positives *and* false negatives, are relevant to gaining greater resources and credibility for child protective services (CPS), and were designed to improve the lot of *all* children who come to the attention of professionals, regardless of whether their case is ultimately determined to be founded or not.

It follows from our argument that we did not adopt, nor do we accept, the view that suffering caused by one type of error (false positive, false negative) is more acceptable than suffering caused by another type of error, and we consider inexcusable any unnecessary continuation of practices harmful to children (abused and nonabused) that were documented in our article. In addition, our arguments and our concerns have clearly centered on the well-being of children. To the extent that parenting responsibilities are unnecessarily disrupted, we are concerned about adults as well, but primarily because of the impact on children's well-being. Any implication that our argument is predicated on the need to protect the rights of adult suspects at the expense of children's well-being is false.

COMMON GROUND

Perhaps the greatest disservice to children documented in our original article is the adoption of assumptions that are elevated to the status of "truth" without either considering alternative viewpoints or examining data that bear on the assumptions. The commentators do not appear to differ much from us in this regard as, to varying degrees, all three cite empirical research in their commentaries. They deserve to be commended for acknowledging the importance of data. Such acknowledgment from authors representing seemingly divergent perspectives has the potential to move us forward—while we may not always agree in our interpretation of the data, appeals to data have the potential to be self-correcting and therefore ultimately to build consensus.

In light of our common acceptance of data as the appropriate basis for resolving differences of opinion, we highlight a most curious omission. The commentators who take issue with our questioning current CPS practices offer no data to show that victims of sexual abuse who experience CPS interventions are better off than those who do not come to the attention of CPS professionals. This is simply to ask the basic question that any psychotherapeutic intervention is currently expected to answer. Are current methods of intervention better than nothing? It is the failure to ask such obvious questions, and taking issue with those who do ask these questions, that we find most disturbing. At the risk of making an obvious point, if involvement with CPS does not produce reliably better outcomes than noninvolvement, this situation would not imply that we should stop intervening to prevent child sexual abuse. It would, however, strongly suggest that current CPS approaches need to be reviewed carefully to see what steps might be taken to achieve better outcomes.

A similar logic applies to comparing true victims of abuse reported to CPS with those whose cases are unfounded. It is indeed ironic, and quite irrational, to claim concern about the welfare of children but to be unwilling to evaluate possible adverse effects of one's attempts to help them. Without such evaluation how can services be improved? Resistance to such evaluation is consistent with the field's failure to consider children's views of their experiences, a viewpoint that Faulconer (1994) argues should be considered. We agree, and hope that children's perspectives of the abuse they have suffered and their view of the professional response to their experience will be taken more seriously by professionals interested in children's welfare. Mindful of the fact that children are not asked to consent to the services to which they are subject, we consider such a perspective critical to improving the services delivered to them.

EVALUATING THE COSTS OF ERRORS

We are similarly perplexed by Faulconer's (1994) and Pezdek's (1994) failure to offer any data bearing on a major source of concern they raise, the cost of false positive and false negative errors. Both commentators adopt the position that false negative errors are more harm than false positive errors, but do not offer any evidence for this empirical claim. Instead, Pezdek rejects the possibility that a false positive case can ever approach the severity of consequences found in a false negative case. Several points need to be considered here.

First, our goal was not to trade off one form of suffering against another, but rather to argue for improving the quality of practice and research. Such improvement would decrease suffering in all child abuse investigations regardless of outcome and would reduce both types of error because testing various hypotheses would likely result in more accurate findings. Thus, mindful of the problems created by the confirmatory bias detailed by Ceci and Bruck (1994), we addressed the issue of unnecessary measurement error in child abuse investigations by calling for hypothesis testing by CPS investigators. In this regard, we agree fully with Pezdek's (1994) call for methods to increase the validity and decrease the error in assessment procedures—such rationality is a vast improvement over the irrational, but understandable, current use of confirmatory heuristics. These changes should improve the quality of the evidence of abuse and thereby decrease the variance within the distributions (making them taller and skinnier) in Pezdek's figure. We are not suggesting that such improvements will produce nonoverlapping distributions, but we are arguing that currently there is unnecessary overlap due to incompetent and biased investigation that produces false negative, and particularly false positive, errors. Thus, there is considerable room for decreasing both types of errors before we need to trade off one type of error against the other.

Second, it is easy to contrast the extreme consequences in some cases of abuse that go undetected (false negatives) against the supposedly mild consequences (Pezdek uses the descriptor *awkwardness* to describe these) caused by false positive errors. However, it is completely erroneous to conclude from such idiosyncratic contrasts that the cost of false negatives is always, or even usually, greater than the cost of false positives. This error in logic is widespread in the literature and reflects two common misconceptions that ignore existing data.

The first of these misconceptions is addressed in our original article and concerns the impact of child sexual abuse. Data reviewed by Kendall-Tackett, Williams, and Finkelhor (1993) show that the impact of sexual abuse can be devastating—surely this is not in dispute. However, as Pezdek (1994) points out "the consequences of sexual abuse appear to depend on the type of and severity of the abuse, the relationship between the perpetrator and the victim and a range of situational variables and person-specific variables" (pp. 259–60). We agree, and that is why it is quite misleading, and irresponsible, to simply assert that the impact of sexual abuse is serious and leave it at that. It is far more accurate to state that the impact of sexual abuse varies from apparently minor consequences to very severe consequences. This is perhaps not surprising when one recalls the variability of behavior that is included under the title of sexual abuse. With some 21% to 49% of victims apparently being symptom free (see Kendall-Tackett et al. 1993), we surely need to understand better the variability in impact by examining more closely the very factors that Pezdek identifies. By opposing our call for research to better understand the impact of abuse, Pezdek appears to be abandoning her commitment to science in favor of a priori assumptions.

The second misconception concerns the impact of professional intervention on children and underlines why simply asserting that false negatives are more harmful than false positives is quite irresponsible. Just as one can contrast severe and devastating cases of abuse with the awkwardness of interventions for nonabused children, so also can one contrast devastating cases of intervention with cases of sexual abuse (e.g., a single incident of noncontact abuse, overhearing parents having intercourse) that leave the child feeling "awkward" but symptom free. One cannot imagine a more devastating impact than the loss of life, yet there are documented cases where children removed from their homes by the state have died unnecessarily while in protective custody. In addition, there are documented cases where the state has simply "lost" children in its care and cannot locate them any longer, where they have been sexually abused by foster parents, been physically abused by foster parents, received inadequate nutrition, received no or adequate medical attention, and been exposed to safety hazards, infection hazards, and so on (see Benker and Rempel 1989; Wexler 1990). The cases are not simply isolated, rare events—the state of Illinois is currently under a federal court order because of such problems in its child protective system. Indeed, it is a supreme irony that the case that gave rise to the modern child protection movement, the case of Mary Ellen Wilson, involved abuse and neglect while Mary Ellen was in the custody of the state (Antler and Antler 1979). Anyone who cares to look into this area will soon learn that placing a child in protective custody is not only traumatic for the child but can also carry additional risks for the physical and mental well-being of the child.

In view of these two misconceptions, simply concluding that false negative errors are more costly than false positive errors is clearly naive and not in the best interests of the child. Equally, it should not be concluded that false positive errors are inevitably more costly than false negative errors. It seems most reasonable, on the basis of available information, to conclude that each kind of error can be devastating, depending on the circumstances in which it occurs.

CHILDREN'S MEMORY

Finally, we would like to address comments raised about the suggestibility of children. In our original article, we offered a number of conclusions about children's memory. The conclusions were not our own—they were those reached in the most thorough and scholarly review of the literature available (Ceci and Bruck 1993), and in an analysis presented by 45 "concerned developmental, social, and psychological researchers, social scientists and scholars" in the form of an Amicus Brief (filed in *State of New Jersey* v. *Kelly Michaels* 1993). If, as Pezdek (1994) asserts, we cannot draw any conclusions from the substantial literature on this topic, then we must also not draw any conclusions from the literature on the impact of sexual abuse on children. In both sets of literature one can find studies that are not consistent with the conclusions drawn. Rather than eschew all data, we chose to be careful in presenting the conclusions on children's memories by including the qualifications and subtleties of existing knowledge (e.g., "children *may* inaccurately report, *some* children are extremely resistant, children *sometimes* embellish").

The manner in which we handled the literature on children's memory is consistent with a major theme of our original article, namely, that simple, unqualified generalizations in the area of child sexual abuse are most likely to be erroneous, or at least misleading. We do not regret exercising such care but, rather, believe it is integral to good scholarship, and, ultimately, in the best interests of children. The temptation to adopt simple rules, sweeping generalizations, and easy solutions is indeed great, but has to be resisted if we are to better serve children's needs. A major theme in our original article was that such rules and heuristics seem better suited to meeting the needs of professionals than to advancing children's welfare.

CONCLUSION

Understanding and responding to the phenomenon of child sexual abuse is more complex than it seems. The responses to our original article begin to acknowledge such complexity and demonstrate that empirical data provide common ground for those approaching child sexual abuse from differing perspectives. Because we agree that child sexual abuse, its consequences, and efforts to intervene reflect a complex reality, we are happy to see exchanges like the current one. It seems likely that by discussing candidly our differing perspectives and the different experiences they articulate, we will come to a view of child sexual abuse that is a more adequate representation of the complex reality and a more useful framework for guiding efforts at child protection.

Everyone wants what is best for children, and all are disturbed by harm done to them. We believe that only self-protective denial could lead to the argument that harm done by professionals is somehow less painful than harm done by parents. Unfortunately, a recent City Health Report produced by the Public Interest Health Consortium for New York City concludes,

> we are permitting two entirely different standards of justice. When parents act in a manner to harm or risk harm to their children, they are charged with abuse and neglect. But when government officials persistently, willfully, and unnecessarily harm children . . . these officials are not held accountable. (Benker and Rempel 1989, 33–34)

The truth is indeed complex and frightening. We applaud the respondents for joining us in addressing this reality. Despite our differences, we remain convinced that it is only through finding common ground that we will be able to adequately meet the needs of children.

REFERENCES

Antler, S., and J. Antler. 1979. From child rescue to family protection: The evolution of the child protective movement in the United States. *Children and Youth Services Review* 1: 178–95.

Benker, K., and J. Rempel. 1989. Inexcusable harm. City Health Report, Public Interest Health Consortium for New York City, 490 Riverside Drive, Room 243, New York, NY 10027.

Ceci, S. J., and M. Bruck. 1993. The suggestibility of the child witness. *Psychological Bulletin* 113: 403–39.

Ceci, S. J., and M. Bruck. 1994. How reliable are children's statements? . . . It depends. *Family Relations* 43: 255–57.

Faulconer, L. A. 1994. In the best interests of children? *Family Relations* 43: 261–63.

Fincham, F. D., S. R. H. Beach, T. Moore, and C. Diener. 1994. The professional response to child abuse: Whose interests are served? *Family Relations* 43: 244–54.

Kaufman, W. 1970. *I and thou: A new translation, with a prologue and notes.* New York: Charles Scribner's Sons.

Kendall-Tackett, K. A., L. M. Williams, and D. Finkelhor. 1993. Impact of sexual abuse on children: A review and synthesis of recent empirical studies. *Psychological Bulletin* 113: 164–80.

Pezdek, K. 1994. Avoiding false claims of child sexual abuse: Empty promises. *Family Relations* 43: 258–60.

State of New Jersey v. *Kelly Michaels,* 264 N.J. Super 579 (1993).

Wexler, R. 1990. *Wounded innocents: The real victims of the war against child abuse.* Amherst, N.Y.: Prometheus Books.

18

CHILD SEXUAL ABUSE:
ETHICAL ISSUES FOR THE FAMILY THERAPIST

BETH HAVERKAMP
AND JUDITH C. DANILUK

Marital and family therapists working with families where child sexual abuse is disclosed or suspected face ethical confusion that may not be clearly addressed by professional codes of conduct or legal statutes. Ethical dilemmas commonly encountered in family sexual abuse cases are discussed and recommendations for ethical decision making and action are provided.

Estimates of the incidence of childhood sexual abuse range from 15% to 22% for female children and 3% to 8% for male children (Briere and Runtz 1988; Browne and Finkelhor 1986), or higher, depending on the definition of abuse and the method of data collection (Bagley and King 1990). Most marital and family therapists will be required to assist victims and their families in dealing with the far-reaching consequences of childhood sexual abuse. The therapist may be guided by the considerable amount of recent literature aimed at helping to mediate the impact of sexual abuse and rebuilding the lives of those affected by this trauma (e.g., Courtois 1988; Russell 1986; Trepper and Barrett 1989). However, it may be difficult for therapists to negotiate the many thorny ethical dilemmas inherent in working with these families, especially when individual or family needs and ethical principles appear to conflict.

From *Family Relations* 42, no. 2 (April 1993): 134–39. Copyrighted © 1993 by the National Council on Family Relations, 3989 Central Ave. NE, Suite 550, Minneapolis, MN 55421. Reprinted by permission.

Melton and Limber (1989) point out that child maltreatment cases invite violations of implicit therapeutic contracts simply because there are inherent ambiguities as to roles, responsibilities, and allegiances. Because of the far-reaching consequences of childhood sexual abuse, and the fact that such abuse often occurs within the context of complex familial interactions, alliances, and loyalties, few treatment areas are as rife with ethical dilemmas and concerns.

In this paper, the primary ethical problems faced by marital and family therapists working with families in which child sexual abuse is suspected or has occurred are examined. The sexual abuse of children is most frequently perpetrated by males upon females, with stepfather or biological father/daughter molestation being the most commonly reported form of abuse (Bagley and King 1990; Courtois 1988; Koss and Burkhart 1989; Marshall, Laws, and Barbaree 1990; Russell 1983; Trepper and Barrett 1989; Wyatt 1985). As such, the primary focus of this discussion will be paternal incestuous abuse, with the recognition that siblings, extended family, and stepparents may also be perpetrators (Valentich and Anderson 1989).

REASONS FOR DILEMMAS

According to Thompson (1990), ethical dilemmas arise for several reasons. Behavior may be ethical and yet illegal (e.g., choosing not to report suspected child abuse due to the risk of physical reprisal for the child), unethical and illegal (e.g., failure to report or pursue suspected child abuse, based on a lack of knowledge regarding reporting procedures), or unethical yet outside of legal jurisdiction (e.g., working with families in which abuse has occurred, without specific training and/or supervision in sexual abuse intervention). In cases where law and ethics suggest contradictory action, the therapist must choose between two conflicting, yet legitimate, loyalties.

While existing ethical codes of conduct are helpful (e.g., Code of Ethical Principles of Marriage and Family Therapists, American Association for Marriage and Family Therapy [AAMFT] 1985), they may be inadequate in providing sufficient direction to practitioners in cases of child sexual abuse. Professional ethical codes may be criticized for a lade of comprehensiveness, but their major limitation lies in their inherent ambiguity (Green and Hansen 1986, 1989; Margolin 1986). In the area of child sexual abuse, where therapist values are likely to be strongly held, the needs of various family members may appear to conflict, and issues of morality, legality, and ethics intertwine.

ETHICAL PRINCIPLES

Kitchener (1984) distinguishes between two levels of moral decision making that may be employed by therapists in determining the most ethical course of action: the intuitive level and the critical-evaluative level. She argues convincingly that while the intuitive level of moral reasoning (the level which includes knowledge of professional codes of conduct) is important, it is not sufficient. The critical-evaluative level of reasoning is necessary to guide ethical practice based on reasoned judgments and evaluation. To facilitate these judgments, Kitchener (1984) and Thompson (1990) suggest that the practitioner turn to the following six general ethical principles to guide ethical decision making: *autonomy, fidelity, justice, beneficence, nonmaleficence, and self-interest*. These ethical principles are implicit in most professional codes of conduct and provide a framework for considering the specific ethical dilemmas encountered by family therapists who are confronted with child sexual abuse.

Promoting client autonomy is a central goal of psychotherapy, as it implies "the maximization of the individual's ability to choose freely and competently how to conduct his or her life" (Thompson 1990, 13). Elements of practice which are relevant to client autonomy include informed consent, privacy, cooperative working alliances between the therapist and the family, and avoidance of coercive techniques. Autonomy is most dearly embedded in Section 1 of the AAMFT (1985) code.

Fidelity is implicit in the therapeutic contract and involves loyalty, faithfulness, and promise keeping. The therapist promises to assist the family, protect family interests, maintain confidentiality, and do no harm. The therapist, as a member of a psychotherapeutic profession, also owes fidelity to the larger society, an obligation which is incorporated in laws on the limits of confidentiality and the duty to warn. Fidelity is most clearly embedded in Sections 1, 4, and 7 of the AAMFT (1985) code.

The principle of justice implies fairness and equality in treatment (Kitchener 1984; Thompson 1990). The notion of justice also extends to the fair distribution of benefits and burdens (Beauchamp and Childress 1983). Justice is particularly relevant when the therapist is attempting to decide who in the family is to receive services and whether they are to be comparable to the services received by other family members. The doctrine of distributive justice directs a therapist to be fair in response to individual members of a family and to avoid discriminatory practice. However, in situations where inequality exists, the principle of justice would suggest that nonequal persons, in this case children, have a right to be treated differently if the inequality is relevant to the issue in question, as in the case of incestuous abuse. Justice is most clearly embedded in Sections 1 and 6 of the AAMFT (1985) code.

Beneficence, or doing good, is the core principle which underlies the actions of all helping professionals toward clients (Thompson 1990). This principle is central to all professional codes of conduct (Kitchener 1984). The mandate to provide competent services is central to this principle, and is clearly embedded in Sections 3 and 4 of the AAMFT (1985) code.

The principle of nonmaleficence can be paraphrased as above all, do no harm, and has been identified by some as the primary ethical responsibility in applied psychology (Kitchener 1984; Rosenbaum 1982; Thompson 1990). The therapist has a responsibility to anticipate possible harm and to prevent, reduce, or remove the risk of harmful acts. Many ethicists have concluded that, other factors being equal, the obligation to avoid harm overrides the principle of beneficence (e.g., Kitchener 1984; Thompson 1990). Nonmaleficence is clearly embedded in Sessions 3 and 4 of the AAMFT (1985) code.

The principle of self-interest reflects the moral and ethical responsibility of self-knowledge, self-improvement, self-protection, and self-care. When therapists fail to attend to their own legitimate interests or are unaware of their beliefs and limitations, their needs and values may indirectly interfere with their treatment decisions. Ethical decision making is enhanced when therapists are explicitly aware of their personal needs and motivations. Owing a duty to self is an extension of the imposition of all ethical duties and is embedded in Section 3 of the AAMFT (1985) code.

ETHICAL ISSUES AND DILEMMAS

In the following discussion, the primary ethical issues which arise in treating families experiencing child sexual abuse are identified. Particularly difficult issues include informed consent and disclosure, legally mandated reporting, and specific treatment issues. Ethical dilemmas faced by the marriage and family therapist are highlighted, and recommendations for action are illustrated for each. The meta-ethical principles are cited to explain how dilemmas present ethical conflicts and to illustrate the rationale for the proposed recommendations.

Informed Consent and Disclosure

Informed consent requires the therapist to share information about the limits to confidentiality and about the likely risks and benefits of engaging in treatment. It is a means of "respecting the rights of those persons seeking assistance" (Principle 1.0, AAMFT 1985). Offering informed consent to multiple family members embodies autonomy, in that each member is free to make independent decisions about the level of participation and disclosure. Fidelity is implicated because the act of offering informed consent creates an implicit promise that clients will be consulted about therapeutic actions which affect them. Informed consent embodies beneficence in equalizing the power imbalance inherent in the therapist-client relationship (Hare-Muslin, Marecek, Kaplan, and Liss-Levinson 1979).

Two major dilemmas. The requirement of informed consent creates two major dilemmas when child sexual abuse is suspected. The first is common to family therapy in general and revolves around the fact that multiple family members are making individual consent decisions. The consequences of therapy and confidentiality may be different for each family member, and each will differ in the ability to give informed consent. The second dilemma implicates the principle of nonmaleficence. The therapist's full disclosure of information about the mandatory reporting of abuse invites each member to monitor disclosures, with the result that information about current harm to children may remain hidden, thereby preventing the therapist from acting to avoid harm. Consequently, the therapist is faced with two dilemmas: (a) who in the family should give informed consent, and (b) what response is appropriate when members differ in their willingness or ability to do so.

The therapist can obtain some guidance for the first dilemma, who should give consent, from the legal understanding of consent. Legally, informed consent contains three elements: adequate comprehension of information, the capacity to make rational decisions, and voluntariness and freedom from coercion (Bray, Shepherd, and Hays 1985). Meeting each of these criteria requires a minimum level of cognitive sophistication and emotional integration (Kitchener 1984; Thompson 1990). The exercise of each is problematic in families experiencing sexual abuse. Age is particularly relevant in terms of competence, since limited cognitive development results in limited competence. Power differentials within the family will also impair autonomous decision making. The therapists must ascertain the level at which each family member is competent to make autonomous and informed consent decisions. A determination must be made as to how to proceed when one or more of the three criteria listed above are not met.

The first criterion, adequate comprehension of information, includes an awareness of consequences and is reflected in Principle 1.4 of the AAMFT (1985) code, which requires the therapist to "respect the rights of clients to make decisions and help them understand the consequences of those decisions." Disclosure of sexual abuse impacts all members of the family system and is certain to permanently alter the structure of the family (Alexander 1992; Briere 1989; Gavey, Florence, Pezaro, and Tan 1990; Herman 1981; Russell 1986). The therapist's challenge is to balance the clients' rights to consent with the mandate of preventing harm, reflected in the principle of nonmaleficence.

These conflicting mandates can be balanced through an early discussion of the limits of confidentiality, introduced as part of obtaining informed consent for treatment. From a legal and ethical standpoint, it is recommended that a written statement of the limits of confidentiality and the necessity for mandatory reporting in the event of disclosure, suspicion, or high potential of abuse be provided at the outset of therapy, and signed by the therapist and all family members who are considered competent (Bray et al. 1985; Courtois 1988; Kitchener 1984; Stadler 1989; Thompson 1990). In this way, clients are alerted to their choices but the limits of the promise of confidentiality are also made clear. If harm is suspected, the therapist acts on the principle of nonmaleficence without betraying fidelity, since the promise has been clarified. It is also recommended that any discussion of mandated reporting be framed as a social commitment to respecting and protecting the rights of all family members.

Considering children's rights. The additional legal requirements in informed consent, the capacity to make rational decisions and freedom from coercion, are particularly relevant in family therapy. The therapist must decide how to offer informed consent to children in the family and must determine whether parents are competent to give consent on the children's behalf. The therapist's key responsibility is to insure that offering informed consent for the adults does not create additional risks for the children; the rights of the child victim must be considered primary (Keith-Speigel and Koocher 1985; Koocher 1976).

Age alone should not be construed as justification for denying the child's right to choose what to share or disclose. Research suggests that anyone aged 15 years or older, who is not developmentally impaired, is generally capable of comprehending the implications of participating in treatment and of making rational decisions (Belter and Grisso 1984; Gustafson and McNamara 1987). However, coercion or fear of retribution may impair the ability to freely consent. The issue is even more complex for young children, because their ability to comprehend the scope and consequences of disclosure is limited. Young children are particularly vulnerable to coercion, given the potential for increased risk upon disclosure of sexual abuse. Also, the parents' difficulties may disqualify them as competent to consent for the child (Kitchener 1984).

When families present for treatment for incestuous abuse, it is recommended that children be initially interviewed without the parents, in an attempt to inform and support their decision making and to lessen the direct effects of parental coercion. When abuse is suspected after treatment has begun, mandated reporting laws require that the therapist act to promote the child's autonomy and to ensure that greater harm is not incurred by nondisclosure. All members of a family have the right to individual safety and personhood (Valentich and Anderson 1989), and the children's right to safety and protection from possible harm must be taken into consideration by the therapist in attempting to limit possible coercion by adult family members.

Mandated Reporting of Abuse

Therapists are often faced with families who present with issues unrelated to incest but who provide clues during treatment that suggest that abuse may be occurring. The difficulty arises because there is no clear definition of when a clinical hunch or intuition becomes suspicion, with its attendant legal requirements. Given the disruptive and potentially dangerous consequences for all family members of reporting abuse to the child protection authorities (Courtois 1988; Herman 1981), therapists are faced with the ethical dilemma of deciding how to proceed with ascertaining whether these dues warrant suspicion of incestuous abuse. Autonomy is also implicated, because families have not explicitly consented to pursue this issue. Justice is clearly implicated, in that the therapist's decision to report may be perceived as discriminating against one or more members of the family. The question of what therapeutic actions are appropriate when cues consistent with abuse are noted involves the principles of nonmaleficence, fidelity, and autonomy.

Pursuing possible abuse. The therapist may feel that the principle of autonomy is being breached in further pursuing the possibility of abuse when families have not given explicit consent to this therapeutic agenda. However, not to pursue an intuition of abuse would violate the principle of nonmaleficence which, all else being equal, should take precedence in directing ethical practice (Beauchamp and Childress 1983; Kitchener 1984; Thompson 1990). Consistent with the principle of nonmaleficence, it is recommended that the therapist thoroughly pursue any clues that might lead to a suspicion of abuse (Melton and Limber 1989; Thompson 1990).

Therapists can feel more confident in giving client autonomy secondary importance in pursuing their hunches of abuse, if they are familiar with client or family characteristics which are commonly associated with incestuous abuse. The importance of therapist knowledge and competence is critical. In particular, therapists should be alert to possible abuse in families characterized by minimal cohesion and high levels of conflict and violence (Alexander 1992; Courtois 1988). Similarly, a parental history of child sexual abuse should prompt an examination of possible sexual offenses within the present family constellation (Briere 1989; Courtois 1988; Russell 1983). The importance of therapist knowledge and competence is critical in the thorough assessment of clues that may be indicative of possible sexual abuse. If, after pursuing the possibility that abuse is occurring, the therapist is still very uncertain as to the validity of his or her intuitions, peer consultation with a colleague knowledgeable in the assessment of child sexual abuse is highly recommended.

Reporting abuse. Once enough clues have been presented to warrant suspicion of sexual abuse, or a disclosure of abuse has been made, the therapist is faced with another critical issue. The laws in all states and provinces require that a report be filed with the appropriate legal and social service authorities. The dilemma is that this action, while legal, may cause harm which would be unethical (Keith-Speigel and Koocher 1985; Thompson 1990), as in cases where a report results in retaliation against a child. Evidence that family therapists are aware of this dilemma can be found in surveys (Kalichman, Craig, and Follingstad 1989; Pope and Bajit 1988) which document that 57% to 60% of therapists have indicated situations in which they have made decisions not to report abuse.

Ethically, the therapist is bound by the principle of nonmaleficence, and the avoidance and/or prevention of harm to the child (Keith-Speigel and Koocher 1985; Kitchener 1984; Thompson 1990). The experience of sexual abuse causes severe and protracted harm for the child, and the child's rights to protection are clearly violated by not taking action (Briere and Runtz 1988; Browne and Finkelhor 1986; Russell 1986; Valentich and Anderson 1989). However, the intervention of authorities must result in serious physical, financial, and emotional disruption and injury for all family members (Melton and Limber 1989; Stadler 1989). Herman (1981) notes that disclosure of sexual abuse "disrupts whatever fragile equilibrium that has been maintained, jeopardizes the functioning of all family members, increases the likelihood of violent and desperate behavior and places everyone, but particularly the [child] at risk for retaliation" (p. 131).

Although reporting is the appropriate action in the majority of cases, it the possibility of precipitating greater harm which creates the major dilemma. Under circumstances where ethical responsibilities clearly conflict with legal requirements, it is recommended that therapists weigh "the potential value of forced intervention against its potential harm" (Thompson 1990, 189). Areas of potential harm that need to be evaluated include the likely negative consequences for the child and the family of not reporting and the potential negative consequences to both that may be precipitated by reporting.

Herman (1981) suggests "any approach which fails to report incest to the legally designated authority, creates more problems than it solves" (p. 134). The negative consequences of not reporting suspected or disclosed abuse most obviously include the likelihood of continued victimization of the child, which cannot be considered an acceptable outcome (Valentich and Anderson 1989). For parents who were also child victims, failure to report may reinforce a belief that societal rules cannot protect individuals from abusive behavior and may interfere with their own healing (Van Eenwyk 1990). Reporting also communicates to the family the therapist's lack of willingness to collude in ongoing abuse and in the maintenance of the incest secret (Courtois 1988).

It is recommended that the therapist view the needs of the family from the perspective of short- and long-term outcomes, balancing the short-term disruption of the family and its members against the long-term outcome of prolonged sexual victimization and the maintenance of this family secret. If the abuse is not addressed, the abuser will not be provided with the opportunity to change his behavior, the family will never function in a manner that serves to nurture and protect the health and development of all its members, and the abused child will be faced with the consequences of invalidation and further victimization (Butz 1985; Conte 1986; Courtois 1988; Valentich and Anderson 1989). While the immediate consequence of reporting may be experienced by some family members as negative, the long-term outcomes of not addressing abuse are clearly destructive to all family members (Courtois 1988; Haman 1981).

Limiting harm due to reporting. Once a need to report is determined, a proactive attempt to limit harm can provide a compromise between preventing harm to the child, to the family as a unit, and to ongoing treatment. Having clearly informed the family regarding the limitations of confidentiality at the outset of treatment, the therapist will have a starting point from which to explain the situation to the family (Butz 1985). If the limits of confidentiality have been explained at the outset, fidelity is not compromised when abuse is reported.

Families also benefit from being kept informed of the procedures that will follow a report of abuse. It is recommended that the therapist fully inform the family of the policies and procedures involved in the investigation of reports of child sexual abuse within their districts. Given the overburdened nature of most child protection services, it is also recommended that the therapist fully inform the child protection workers of the potential risks of retaliation within this particular family constellation, and assist as much as possible in helping to diminish the potential negative consequences for all family members. From the initial report through investigation and action, it is recommended that therapists work as cooperatively as possible with the police and social service personnel involved in managing these cases (Courtois 1988; Serrano and Gunzburger 1983), undertaking the least destructive approach to maintaining "an effective helping relationship with clients while conforming to the reporting laws" (Butz 1985, 90).

Child protection services may request that the therapist maintain involvement with the family in terms of conducting a formal assessment of sexual abuse, or in terms of sexual abuse treatment. However, the therapist may not have the specialized skills that are required for a thorough assessment or treatment of sexual abuse. In such cases it is recommended that the therapist refer the family to a colleague who has specialized training in working with families in which sexual abuse has occurred. Therapists who work outside their areas of competence are in violation of the AAMFT (1985) code's mandate "not to attempt to diagnose, treat or advise on problems" which exceed their competence (Principle 3.6). Such behavior also violates Principle 1.2, which directs the therapist to "avoid exploiting the trust and dependency of such persons." Families facing the pain and upheaval resulting from allegations of abuse have a right to expect that the principle of fidelity, in the implicit promise of therapist competence, will be honored.

If the therapist is convinced that reporting will result in severe retaliation to family members by the abuser, reporting may need to be timed in such a way as to ensure the safety of the family members who are at risk. Also, in all situations of suspected abuse, it is highly recommended that the therapist consult with one or more respected colleagues for support and supervision (Kitchener 1984; Serrano and Gunzburger 1983; Thompson 1990).

In exceptional circumstances a therapist may decide not to report because of ethical concerns, but must recognize that this is a choice to break the law. As with other illegal acts of conscience, the therapist must be prepared to accept the personal consequences of such action, as well as the consequences to the children of continued sexual violation (Valentich and Anderson 1989). The profession cannot generally condone such violations of the law.

Therapeutic Treatment of Abuse

Therapist competence is of critical ethical importance in working with families in which sexual abuse is occurring. Consideration of the assumptions and interventions associated with different theoretical approaches is also important, as is awareness of the therapist's personal and emotional limits. While many of the meta-ethical principles are implicated, beneficence and self-interest are clearly relevant.

Therapists are clearly directed in the AAMFT (1985) code not to practice outside their areas of competence (Principle 3.6). However, therapists may not be aware of what constitutes adequate competence in the area of sexual abuse or may feel ethically conflicted in making a referral to another professional after a strong therapeutic relationship has been established with a family. In answer to both dilemmas, and in accordance with the AAMFT (1985) code, it is recommended that sexual abuse treatment with these families not be undertaken without specialized training and supervision (Principle 1.6). The therapist may need to refer the family, a process that can be facilitated by helping the clients understand that this action affirms the therapeutic promise to promote their welfare. If a referral is not possible, the therapist should not proceed with sexual abuse treatment without direct supervision from a trained professional.

Adequate training needed. However well-intentioned, the family therapist who fails to be of help to the family based on a lack of skill, knowledge, or expertise in the treatment of sexual abuse is clearly acting in an unethical manner. Adequate training that is critical to ethical practice must include techniques in the assessment of suspected abuse (Courtois 1988; Melton and Limber 1989), knowledge of the contextual and familial variables commonly associated with abuse (Alexander 1992; Cole and Putnam 1992), knowledge of the short- and long-term sequelae and characteristic indicators of child sexual abuse (Briere and Runtz 1990; Browne and Finkelhor 1986; Courtois 1988), and knowledge of the state laws and local child protection service procedures involved in cases of child sexual abuse (Butz 1985; Courtois 1988; Serrano and Gunzburger 1983; Thompson 1990). Additionally, the therapist must have ongoing training and supervision in effective therapeutic interventions for working with families in which sexual abuse has occurred or is occurring (Barrett and Trepper 1992; Gavey et al. 1990; Markowitz 1992; Schwartz 1992; Taggart 1985; Willbach 1989). The AAMFT (1985) code mandates that therapists, even those previously trained in sexual abuse treatment, "remain abreast of new developments in family therapy knowledge and practice" (Principle 3.4).

Using appropriate theoretical approaches. The second major area of ethical decision making within the treatment of sexual abuse concerns the assumptions and interventions associated with varied theoretical approaches. The potential dilemma faced by the therapist is that the theoretical orientation the therapist prefers and is trained in may be ethically inappropriate for sexual abuse treatment. There are several theoretical approaches to and assumptions regarding problem conceptualization and treatment that may become problematic in families where sexual abuse is disclosed or suspected (Valentich and Anderson 1989). Consistent with the principles of beneficence, nonmaleficence, and autonomy, intervention strategies must be assessed for their appropriateness within the dynamic context of child sexual abuse. Specific issues which merit evaluation include questions of conflicting needs and agendas of individual family members versus the family system, the position of neutrality, and systemic attributions of responsibility for the abuse, such as circular causality.

One area where ethical dilemmas may arise is the therapist's position on the value of maintaining an intact family structure. The decision the therapist faces is whether disruption of the family can ever be considered a successful or ethical outcome of therapy. There is a broad consensus that the primary principle of ethical treatment is nonmaleficence, particularly for children (Koocher 1976). Most evidence would suggest that sexually abused children are placed at risk of further victimization (Courtois 1988; Taggart 1985; Willbach 1989) when the family structure is maintained. Theoretical flexibility informed by knowledge of treatment efficacy is recommended, with nonmaleficence for the children taking precedence over both the autonomy of the abuser and maintenance of the family system.

Another area where the therapist's theoretical stance may conflict with ethical requirements is in the use of particular techniques or therapeutic postures that are fundamental to many systemic approaches to family therapy. For example, therapist neutrality is based on the belief that problems are situated between, not within, individuals (Willbach 1989). This posture may be viewed as being consistent with the principle of justice. In cases of child abuse, however, the therapist's primary responsibility must be to the child(ren) most at risk in the family (Koocher 1976). Thompson (1990) argues that such neutrality is an ideal that may be pursued but which is impossible to obtain. Ethical concerns have also been raised in response to the use of certain commonly used family therapy notions, such as circular causality, that may actually serve to obscure power imbalances within the family, deflect individual responsibility for violent and unethical behavior, and fail to acknowledge the larger sociopolitical contest of families (Alexander 1992; Gavey et al. 1990; Taggart 1985).

The therapist is faced with the dilemma of whether to implement therapeutic techniques, based on a clear theoretical rationale or treatment posture, that may conflict with legal requirements and ethical principles. If faced with this dilemma, it is recommended that ethical principles take precedence over theoretical purity, with particular attention to nonmaleficence and autonomy (informed consent) in the selection of all therapeutic interventions. In such cases, flexible utilization of different techniques and approaches may be necessary. Amelioration of the longterm effects of sexual abuse for the child and the other family members is likely to require acknowledgment of power imbalances within the family and the abuser's responsibility for his actions.

Consistent with the principle of therapist self-interest, for all treatment issues discussed above, the therapist must be willing to examine the ethical implications of his/her theoretical stance; "this will result, not only in an appropriate treatment plan, but a more integrated, consistent, sincere and spontaneous sense of self for the therapist" (Willbach 1989, 50).

Protecting the therapist. A final treatment issue that has ethical implications is that of therapist self-interest and its relationship to beneficence toward clients. While all therapists face the task of balancing client needs and personal needs, many clinicians have elaborated on the emotional turmoil and physical exhaustion that often accompanies a heavy case load of sexual abuse counseling (e.g., Courtois 1988; Russell 1983). Therapists cannot adequately meet the needs of their clients if they are emotionally exhausted. It is recommended that therapists act on their ethical obligation to their clients, their families, and themselves, in protecting themselves from burnout. Therapist autonomy and self-care in such cases may extend to the issues of referring clients, obtaining peer support and supervision, placing limits on the provision of services, exercising control over scheduling, maintaining a health-promoting lifestyle, and seeking personal counseling if necessary (Thompson 1990). This is echoed in AAMFT (1985) Principle 3.2, which directs therapists to "seek appropriate professional assistance for their own personal problems and conflicts."

In addition, team approaches to treatment, commonly used in many family therapy settings, offer protection to both therapists and clients. Teams are an excellent source of peer supervision and may serve the valuable function of identifying possible blind spots or biases on the part of the therapist. Whether through individual efforts or reliance on a therapy team, therapists who adhere to the principle of self-interest in providing for their own self-care also serve to promote beneficence for their clients.

CONCLUSION

In conclusion, therapist awareness or suspicion of child sexual abuse in a client family presents immediate, multiple ethical dilemmas. Awareness of the meta-ethical principles involved in working with these families can help to identify where principles may conflict. Knowledge of these principles and their application to the ethical dilemmas inherent in working with these families may enable the therapist to weigh competing family and individual needs in arriving at a defensible ethical decision.

REFERENCES

Alexander, P. 1992. Application of attachment theory to the study of sexual abuse. *Journal of Consulting and Clinical Psychology* 60: 185–95.

American Association for Marriage and Family Therapy. 1985. *Code of ethical principles for marriage and family therapists.* Washington, D.C.: Author.

Bagley, C., and I. King. 1990. *Child sexual abuse: The search for healing.* New York: Tavistock Routledge.

Barrett, M. J., and T. S. Trepper. 1992. Unmasking the incestuous family. *Family Therapy Networker* (May/June): 39–46.

Belter, R. W., and T. Grisso. 1984. Children's recognition of rights violations in counseling. *Professional Psychology: Research and Practice* 15: 899–910.

Beauchamp, T. L., and J. F. Childress. 1983. *Principles of biomedical ethics,* 2d ed. Oxford: Oxford University Press.

Bray, J. G., J. N. Shepherd, and J. R. Hays. 1985. Legal and ethical issues in informed consent to psychotherapy. *The American Journal of Family Therapy* 13: 50–60.

Briere, J. 1989. *Therapy for adults molested as children: Beyond survival.* New York: Springer.

Briere, J., and M. Runtz. 1988. Symptomatology associated with childhood sexual victimization in a nonclinical adult sample. *Child Abuse and Neglect* 12: 51–59.

———. 1990. Differential adult symptomatology associated with three types of child abuse histories. *Child Abuse and Neglect* 14: 357–64.

Browne, A., and D. Finkelhor. 1986. Impact of child sexual abuse: A review of the research. *Psychological Bulletin* 99: 66–77.

Butz, R. A. 1985. Reporting child abuse and confidentiality in counseling. *Social Casework: The Journal of Contemporary Social Work* 66: 83–90.

Cole, P., and F. Putnam. 1992. Effect of incest on self and social functioning: A developmental psychopathology perspective. *Journal of Consulting and Clinical Psychology* 60: 174–84.

Conte, J. 1986. Failure to report sexual victimization of children: The context of professional behavior. In *Proceedings of Symposium on Professional Ethics and Child Abuse.* Rockville, Md.: National Institute of Mental Health.

Courtois, C. 1988. *Healing the incest wound: Adult survivors in therapy.* New York: Norton.

Gavey, N., J. Florence, S. Pezaro, and J. Tan. 1990. Mother-blaming, the perfect alibi: Family therapy and the mothers of incest survivors. *Journal of Feminist Family Therapy* 2: 1–25.

Green, S. L., and J. C. Hansen. 1986. Ethical dilemmas in family therapy. *Journal of Marital and Family Therapy* 12: 225–30.

———. 1989. Ethical dilemmas faced by family therapists. *Journal of Marriage and the Family* 15: 149–58.

Gustafson, K. E., and J. R. McNamara. 1987. Confidentiality with minor clients: Issues and guidelines for therapists. *Professional Psychology: Research and Practice* 18: 503–508.

Hare-Mustin, R. T., J. Marecek, A. G. Kaplan, and N. Liss-Levinson. 1979. Rights of clients, responsibilities of therapists. *American Psychologist* 34: 3–16.

Herman, J. L. 1981. *Father-daughter incest.* Cambridge, Msss.: Harvard University Press.

Kalichman, S. C., M. Craig, and D. Follingstad. 1989. Factors influencing the reporting of father-child sexual abuse: Study of licensed practicing psychologists. *Professional Psychology: Research and Practice* 20: 84–89.

Keith-Spiegel, P., and G. P. Koocher. 1985. *Ethics in psychology: Professional standards and cases.* New York: Erlbaum.

Kitchener, K. S. 1984. Intuition, critical evaluation and ethical principles: The foundation for ethical decisions in counseling psychology. *The Counseling Psychologist* 12: 43–55.

Koocher, G. P. 1976. A bill of rights for children in psychotherapy. In *Children's rights and the mental health professions,* ed. G. P. Koocher. New York: Wiley.

Koss, M., and B. Burkhart. 1989. A conceptual analysis of rape victimization. *Psychology of Women Quarterly* 13: 27–40.

Margolin, G. 1986. Ethical issues in marital therapy. In *Clinical handbook of marital therapy,* ed. N. S. Jacobson and A. S. Gurman, 621–38. New York: Guilford.

Markowitz, L. M. 1992. Reclaiming the light. *Family Therapy Networker* (May/June): 17–25.

Marshall, W., D. Laws, and H. Barbaree. 1990. *Handbook of sexual assault.* New York: Plenum.

Melton, G. B., and S. Limber. 1989. Psychologists' involvement in cases of child maltreatment: Limits of role and expertise. *American Psychologist* 44: 1225–33.

Pope, K. S., and T. R. Bajit. 1988. When laws and values conflict: A dilemma for psychologists. *American Psychologist* 43: 828–29.

Rosenbaum, M. 1982. *Ethics and values in psychotherapy.* New York: Free Press.

Russell, D. E. 1983. The incidence and prevalence of intrafamilial and extrafamilial sexual abuse of female children. *Child Abuse and Neglect* 7: 133–46.

———. 1986. *The secret trauma: Incest in the lives of girls and women.* New York: Basic Books.

Schwartz, R. 1992. Rescuing the exiles. *Family Therapy Networker* (May/June): 33–37.

Serrano, A. C., and D. W. Gunzburger. 1983. Incest and professional boundaries: Confidentiality versus mandatory reporting. *International Journal of Family Therapy* 5: 145–49.

Stadler, H. A. 1989. Balancing ethical responsibilities: Reporting child abuse and neglect. *The Counseling Psychologist* 1: 102–10.

Taggart, M. 1985. The feminist critique in epistemological perspective: Questions of context in family therapy. *Journal of Marital and Family Therapy* 11: 113–26.

Thompson, A. 1990. *Guide to ethical practice in psychotherapy.* New York: Wiley and Sons.

Trepper, T., and M. Barrett. 1989. *Systematic treatment of incest: A therapeutic handbook.* New York: Brunner/Mazel.

Valentich, M., and C. Anderson. 1989. The rights of individuals in family treatment of child sexual abuse. *Journal of Feminist Family Therapy* 1: 51–65.

Van Eenwyk, J. R. 1990. When laws and values conflict: Comment on Pope and Bajit. *American Psychologist* 45: 399–400.

Willbach, D. 1989. Ethics and family therapy: The case management of family violence. *Journal of Marital and Family Therapy* 15: 43–52.

Wyatt, G. E. 1985. The sexual abuse of Afro-American and White-American women in childhood. *Child Abuse and Neglect* 9: 507–19.

PART FIVE

RESEARCH, NEEDED RESEARCH, AND LEGAL IMPLICATIONS

I n this, perhaps the most important section of the book, the Browne and Finkelhor review of what is known about the impact of child sexual abuse is noteworthy for pointing out how infirm our knowledge base really is. Clearly, the initial effects of abuse produce "reactions of fear, anxiety, and depression, anger, hostility and inappropriate sexual behavior." Even so, the authors caution, these effects may not be representative of all children. As for long-term effects, the empirical work also confirms clinical reports in that adults "victimized as children are more likely to show depression, self-destructive behavior, anxiety, feelings of isolation and stigma, poor self-esteem, a tendency toward revictimization and substance abuse." Avoidance of sexual activity has also been reported. Summarizing, one-fifth to two-fifths of abused children seen by clinicians show pathological disturbances and, as adults, the victims as a group demonstrate impairment, but less than one-fifth show serious psychopathology. Finally, it seems that abuse by adults and by fathers and stepfathers has more of a negative impact than abuse by others. Also experiences involving force and genital contact are more serious than other sorts of sexual abuse and abuse by others. The authors warn that this research has only just begun.

The Ceci and Bruck article about child witnesses argues that, in general, research in this area has been of little use in affecting practice and policy. Recognizing the tremendously difficult task CPS workers face, i.e., providing for the child's mental health needs while simultaneously protecting the legal rights of the accused, we cannot tolerate any situa-

tion in which therapists and forensic interviewers "change the fundamental nature of children's emotionally salient autobiographical memories." Nor is it in any way defensible when so-called experts go beyond
what current scientific findings seem to warrant. Expert testimony must
be evaluated for its scientific merit and all so-called experts must be
aware of current research findings. The authors also urge that the present gulf between the scientific community and the judiciary be healed,
that the research and clinical practice come closer together, and that the
professional organizations play a stronger role as ethical gatekeepers.

According to many practicing attorneys, the sort of research that
would be forensically relevant and valuable to lawyers involved in child
abuse litigation is seldom done. Since modern criminal trials are
grounded in the adversary model, and "victory" rather than "truth" is
the goal, all clients are entitled to zealous representation, and if justice is
not served then—then too bad for justice! Thus, while defense attorneys
do not attack a child's credibility, the defense attorney's duty and
responsibility to his client is to do so. Therefore, many feel society is justified in asking children to testify, and despite its stressful nature children
"weather the storm" and "bounce back." Yet, the finding from
Goodman et al. (*Testifying in Criminal Court,* Monograph Society for
Research in Child Development 57, no. 5 [1992]) shows that face-to-
face confrontations impair children's ability to communicate demands
and that testimony via closed circuit TV, allowing supportive adults to
accompany the child as he or she testifies, seeing that the child avoids eye
contact with the defendant, and changing the courtroom to make the
child witnesses more comfortable, and so forth seems highly desirable.
The unified family court concept may also keep the child from having to
testify many times or multiple times. As for research, a great deal of past
and present child development research is not only highly relevant but
very useful in the forensic context. Unfortunately, it rarely falls into the
hands of judges and attorneys. Research focused specifically on
improving both the accuracy and the completeness of children's testimony (e.g, Goodman's work) must be continued. Also, more research
focused directly on the reliability of children's hearsay statements, on
methods that can be used to maintain children's accuracy in reporting
facts and reducing their factual inconsistency, and helping children testify more effectively with less stress is also an important research goal, as
is the development of forensically defensible interview techniques. It
would also be a good idea to get attorneys who have been involved in
child abuse cases involved in the planning and conduct of upcoming psychological research.

The Wakefield and Underwager report is particularly valuable in stressing that "claims of repressed memories of childhood sexual abuse recovered in the course of therapy are unlikely to be supported by empirical data." Their Recovered Memory Questionnaire Project carried out in conjunction with the False Memory Syndrome Foundation certainly deserves to be better known. Their review of all of the major issues and controversies discussed in this volume also provides a superb review and summary. Their discussion of Multiple Personality Disorder, allegations of ritual and satanic abuse, and their criteria and guidelines for dealing with accusations and allegations are excellent. They are also highly useful for anyone working daily in these areas of controversy and litigation.

Recently, a number of clinicians have seriously questioned the argument that so many pseudomemories can be produced in therapy. They have asked, "Where is the scientific data to back up these claims?" Indeed, there is little in the way of carefully conducted experimental studies of memory performance or suggestibility effects in therapy in the literature. Nevertheless, the absence of definitive research into improper therapeutic practices in no way allows us to ignore the "real life–real world" consequences of therapeutic incompetence and the horribly destructive results of their unwarranted accusations and actions. Cases like those of Kelly Michaels, George Franklin, the Edentown North Carolina case, and others will not go away and the damage done to those falsely accused will not be eased or excused by any amount of "additional research." Though some clinicians have argued that traumatic memory processing is neurologically different from normal memory processing, this claim remains a hypothesis, not a fact. While it is true that laboratory simulation may not be relevant to real-life traumatization, no one would ever seriously entertain producing such trauma just so it could be "studied." One possible population source for research on trauma and pseudomemory and one that is growing larger every day is the rapidly increasing number of psychotherapy victims and the iatrogenically impaired.

Before concerning ourselves with protecting incompetent therapists, we should show an equal concern not only for victims of child sexual abuse but also for the growing number of victims of therapeutic abuse. It is always desirable to end a volume such as this on a hopeful note. Most encouraging is the fact that many jurists are not only well informed about the many complex issues involved in cases of sexual abuse and recovered memory, the process of psychotherapy, the pseudophenomenon of repressed memory, and the facts of hypnosis, but they are equally well informed as to the new standards governing the admissibility of scientific evidence.

19

THE IMPACT OF CHILD SEXUAL ABUSE:
A REVIEW OF THE RESEARCH

ANGELA BROWNE
AND DAVID FINKELHOR

This article reviews studies that have tried to confirm empirically the effects of child sexual abuse cited in the clinical literature. In regard to initial effects, empirical studies have indicated reactions—in at least some portion of the victim population—of fear, anxiety, depression, anger and hostility, aggression, and sexually inappropriate behavior. Frequently reported long-term effects include depression and self-destructive behavior, anxiety, feelings of isolation and stigma, poor self-esteem, difficulty in trusting others, a tendency toward revictimization, substance abuse, and sexual maladjustment. The kinds of abuse that appear to be most damaging, according to the empirical studies, are experiences involving father figures, genital contact, and force. The controversy over the impact of child sexual abuse is discussed, and recommendations for future research efforts are suggested.

Although clinical literature suggests that sexual abuse during childhood plays a role in the development of other problems ranging from anorexia nervosa to prostitution, empirical evidence about its annual effects is sparse. In this article we review the expanding empirical literature on the effects of child sexual abuse, discuss its initial and long-term effects, review studies on the impact of different kinds of abuse, and conclude with a critique of the current literature and some suggestions for future research.

From *Psychological Bulletin* 99, no. 1 (1986): 66–77. Copyright © 1986 by the American Psychological Association. Reprinted with permission.

Child sexual abuse consists of two overlapping but distinguishable types of interaction: (a) forced or coerced sexual behavior imposed on a child, and (b) sexual activity between a child and a much older person, whether or not obvious coercion is involved (a common definition of "much older" is 5 or more years). As might be expected, not all studies relevant to our purposes share these parameters. Some have focused on experiences with older partners only, excluding coerced sexual experiences with peers. Others have looked only at sexual abuse that was perpetrated by family members. Such differences in samples make comparisons among these studies difficult. However, we include all the studies that looked at some portion of the range of experiences that are bounded by these two criteria. (See Table 1 for a breakdown of sample composition of the studies reviewed.)

Two areas of the literature are not included in our review. A small number of studies on the effects of incest (e.g., Farrell 1982; Nelson 1981), as well as one review of the effects of child sexual experiences (Constantine 1980), combine data on consensual peer experiences with data that involve either coercion or age disparity. Because we were unable to isolate sexual abuse in these studies, we had to exclude them. Secondly, we decided to limit our review to female victims. Few clinical, and even fewer empirical, studies have been done on male victims (for exceptions, see Finkelhor 1979; Rogers and Terry 1984; Sandfort 1981; Woods and Dean 1984), and it seems premature to draw conclusions at this point.[1] Under "empirical" studies, we include any research that attempted to quantify the extent to which a sequelae to sexual abuse appeared in a specific population. Some of these studies used objective measures, whereas others were based primarily on the judgments of clinicians.

INITIAL EFFECTS

By initial effects, we mean those reactions occurring within 2 years of the termination of abuse. These early reactions often called *short-term* effects in the literature. We prefer the term *initial* effects, however, because "short-term" implies that the reactions do not persist—an assumption that has yet to be substantiated.

Emotional Reactions and Self-Perceptions

Although several empirical studies have given support to clinical observations of generally negative emotional effects resulting from childhood sexual abuse, only two used standardized measures and compared sub-

TABLE 1: STUDIES OF EFFECTS OF SEXUAL ABUSE

Study	Source of sample	N	Gender	Age of respondents	Focus of study	Comparison group
Anderson, Bach, & Griffith 1981	Sexual assault center	227	F = 155 M = 72	Ad	I, E	No
Bagley & Ramsay 1985	Random sample	679	F = 401 M = 278	A	I, E	Yes
Benward & Densen-Gerber 1975	Drug treatment center	118	F = 118	Ad, A	I	No
Briere 1984	Community health center	153	F = 153	A	I, E	Yes
Briere & Runtz 1985	College students	278	F = 278	Ad, A	I, E	Yes
Courtois 1979	Ads and mental health agencies	31	F = 31	A	I	No
DeFrancis 1969	Court cases	250	F = 217 M = 33	C, Ad	I, E	No
DeYoung 1982	College students, therapy patients, and others	80	F = 72 M = 8	C, Ad, A	I	No
Fields 1981	Prostitutes recruited after arrest	85	F = 85	A	I	Yes
Finkelhor 1979	College students	796	F = 530 M = 266	Ad, A	I, E	Yes
Friedrich, Urguiza, & Beilke, in press	Sexual assault center, group therapy	64	F = 49 M = 15	C	I, E	No
Fromuth 1983	College students	482	F = 482	Ad, A	I, E	Yes
Harrison, Lumry, & Claypatch 1984	Dual disorder treatment program	62	F = 62	A	I, E	Yes
Herman 1981	Clients in therapy	60	F = 60	Ad, A	I,	Yes
James & Meyerding 1977	Prostitutes selected from arrest records					
Study 1		92	F = 92	Ad, A	I, E	No
Study 2		136	F = 136	A	I, E	No
Landis 1956	College students	950	F = 726 M = 224	A	I, E	Yes
Langmade 1983	Mental health centers, private clinics	68	F = 68	A	I	Yes
Meiselman 1978	Clinical records, psychiatric clinic	108	F = 97 M = 11	C, Ad, A	I	Yes
Peters, J., 1976	Rape crisis center	100	—	C	I	No
Peters, S., 1984	Follow-up, community random sample	119	F = 119	A	I, E	Yes
Russell, in press	Random sample	930	F = 930	A	I, E	Yes
Sedney & Brooks 1984	College students	301	F = 301	Ad, A	I, E	Yes
Seidner & Calhoun 1984	College students	152	F = 118 M = 34	A	I, E	Yes
Silbert & Pines 1981	Prostitutes recruited by ads	200	F = 200	Ad, A	I, E	No
Tsai, Feldman-Summers, & Edgar 1979	Ads	90	F = 90	A	I, E	Yes
Tufts study 1984	Clinical referrals	156	F = 122 M = 34	C, Ad	I, E	No

Note, F = female and M = male. C = child, Ad = adolescent, and A = adult. I = intrafamilial and E = extrafamilial.

jects' scores to general population norms. In an early study of the effects of sexual abuse on children, DeFrancis (1969) reported that 66% of the victims were emotionally disturbed by the molestation: 52% mildly to moderately disturbed, and 14% seriously disturbed. Only 24% were judged to be emotionally stable after the abuse. However, because this sample was drawn from court cases known to Prevention of Cruelty to Children services or to the police, and because the subjects came primarily from low income and multiple-problem families who were on public assistance, these findings may have little generalizability.

In investigating a different type of special population, Anderson, Bach, and Griffith (1981) reviewed clinical charts of 155 female adolescent sexual assault victims who had been treated at the Harborview Medical Center in Washington and reported complications in 63% of them. Reports of "internalized psychosocial sequelae" (e.g., sleep and eating disturbance fears and phobias, depression, guilt, shame, and anger) were noted in 67% of female victims when the abuse was intrafamilial and 49% when the offender was not a family member. "Externalized sequelae" (including school problems and running away) were noted in 66% of intrafamilial victims and 21% of extrafamilial victims. However, no standardized outcome measures were used, so the judgments of these effects may be subjective.

In what is probably the best study to date, researchers affiliated with the Division of Child Psychiatry at the Tufts New England Medical Center gathered data on families involved in a treatment program restricted to those children who had been victimized or revealed their victimization in the prior 6 months. Standardized self-report measures— the Louisville Behavior Checklist (LBC), the Piers-Harris Self-Concept Scale, the Purdue Self-Concept Scale, and the Gottschalk Glesser Content Analysis Scales (GGCA)—with published norms and test validation data were used, so that characteristics of sexually abused children could be contrasted with norms for general and psychiatric populations. Subjects ranged in age from infancy to 18 years and were divided into preschool, latency, and adolescence age groups. Data were gathered on four areas: overt behavior, somaticized reactions, internalized emotional states, and self-esteem.

In evaluating the initial psychological effects of child sexual abuse, Tufts (1984) researchers found differences in the amount of pathology reported for different age groups. Seventeen percent of 4- to 6-year-olds in the study met the criteria for "clinically significant pathology," demonstrating more overall disturbance than a normal population but less than the norms for other children their age who were in psychiatric care. The highest incidence of psychopathology was found in the 7- to 13-year-old age group, with 40% scoring in the seriously disturbed range. Interestingly, few of the adolescent victims exhibited severe psychopathology, except on a measure of neuroticism.

Friedrich, Urguiza, and Beilke (in press) also used a standardized measure in their study of 61 sexually abused girls. Subjects were referred by a local sexual assault center for evaluation or by the outpatient department of a local hospital. Children in this sample had been abused within a 24-month period prior to the study. Using the Child Behavior Check List (CBCL; see Achenbach and Edelbrock 1983, for a description of this measure), Friedrich et al. reported that 46% of their subjects had significantly elevated scores on its Internalizing scale (including fearful, inhibited, depressed, and overcontrolled behaviors) and 39% had elevated scores on its Externalizing scale (aggressive, antisocial, and undercontrolled behaviors). This was compared with only 2% of the normative sample who would be expected to score in this range. Younger children (up to age 5) demonstrated a tendency to score high on the Internalizing scale, whereas older children (ages 6–12) were more likely to have elevated scores on the Externalizing scale.

Breaking down emotional impact into specific reactions, we find that the most common initial effect noted in empirical studies, similar to reports in the clinical literature, is that of fear. However, exact proportions vary from a high of 83% reported by DeFrancis (1969) to 40% reported by Anderson et al. (1981). Because of its use of standardized measures, we would give the most credence to the Tufts (1984) study, which found that 45% of the 7- to 13-year-olds manifested severe fears as measured by the LBCs, compared with 13% of the 4- to 6-year-olds. On the adolescent version of the LBC, 36% of the 14- to 18-year-olds had elevated scores on "ambivalent hostility," or the fear of being harmed.

Another initial effect in children is reactions of anger and hostility. Tufts (1984) researchers found that 45% to 50% of the 7- to 13-year-olds showed hostility levels that were substantially elevated on measures of aggression and antisocial behavior (LBC), as did 35% on the measure of hostility directed outward (GGCA). Thirteen percent to 17% of 4- to 6-year-olds scored above the norms on aggression and antisocial behavior (LBC), whereas 25% of 4- to 6-year-olds and 23% of the adolescents had elevated scores on hostility directed outward (GGCA). In his study of court cases, DeFrancis (1969) noted that 55% of the children showed behavioral disturbances such as active defiance, disruptive behavior within the family, and quarreling or fighting with siblings or classmates. DeFrancis's sample might have been thought to overselect for hostile reactions; however, these findings are not very different from findings of the Tufts study for school-age children.

Guilt and shame are other frequently observed reactions to child sexual abuse, but few studies give clear percentages DeFrancis (1969) observed that 64% of his sample expressed guilt, although this was more about the problems created by disclosure than about the molestation itself. Anderson et al. (1981) reported guilt reactions in 25% of the victims Similarly, depression is frequently reported in the clinical literature, but here too, specific figures are rarely given. Anderson et al. (1981) found that 25% of female sexual assault victims were depressed after the abuse.

Sexual abuse is also cited as having an effect on self-esteem, but this effect has not yet been established by empirical studies. Fifty-eight percent of the victims in the DeFrancis (1969) study expressed feelings of inferiority or lack of worth as a result of having been victimized. However in a surprising finding, Tufts (1984) researchers, using the Purdue Self-Concept Scale, found no evidence that sexually abused children in any of the age groups had consistently lower self-esteem than a normal population of children.

Physical Consequences and Somatic Complaints

Physical symptoms indicative of anxiety and distress are noted in the empirical literature as well as in clinical reports. In their chart review of female adolescent victims, Anderson et al. (1981) found that 17% had experienced sleep disturbances and 5%-7% showed changes in eating habits after the victimization. J. Peters (1976), in a study of child victims of intrafamilial sexual abuse, reported that 31% had difficulty sleeping and 20% experienced eating disturbances. However, without a comparison group, it is hard to know if this is seriously pathological for any group of children, or for clinical populations in particular. Adolescent pregnancy is another physical consequence sometimes mentioned in empirical literature. DeFrancis (1969) reported that 11% of the child victims in his study became pregnant as a result of the sexual offense; however, this figure seems far too high for a temporary sample. Meiselman (1978), in analyzing records from a Los Angeles psychiatric clinic, found only 1 out of 47 incest cases in which a victim was impregnated by her father.

Effects of Sexuality

Reactions of inappropriate sexual behavior in child victims have been confirmed by two studies using standardized measures (Friedrich et al., in press; Tufts 1984). In the Tufts (1984) study, 27% of 4- to 6-year-old children scored significantly above clinical and general population norms on a sexual behavior scale that included having had sexual relations (possibly a confounding variable in these findings), open masturbation, excessive sexual curiosity, and frequent exposure of the genitals. Thirty-six percent of the 7- to 13-year-olds also demonstrated high levels of disturbance on the sexual behavior measure when contrasted to norms for either general or clinical school-age populations. Similarly, Friedrich et al. (in press), losing the CBCL to evaluate 3- to 12-year-olds, found that 70% of the boys and 44% of the girls scored at least one sexual deviation above a normal population of that age group on the scale measuring sexual problems. Interestingly, sexual problems were most common among the younger girls and the older boys.

Effects on Social Functioning

Other aftereffects of child sexual abuse mentioned in the literature include difficulties at school, truancy, running away from home, and early marriages by adolescent victims. Herman (1981) interviewed 40 patients in therapy who had been victims of father-daughter incest and compared their reports with those from a group of 20 therapy clients with seductive, but not incestuous, fathers. Of the incest victims, 33% attempted to run away as adolescents, compared with 5% of the comparison group. Similarly, Meiselman (1978) found that 50% of the incest victims in her sample had left home before the age of 18, compared with 20% of women in a comparison group of nonvictimized female patients. Younger children often went to a relative, whereas older daughters ran away or eloped, sometimes making early marriages in order to escape the abuse. Two studies, neither with comparison groups, mentioned school problems and truancy. Ten percent of the child victims in J. Peters's (1976) study quit school, although all of his subjects were under the age of 12 at the time. Anderson et al. found that 20% of the girls in their sample experienced problems at school, including truancy or dropping out.

A connection between sexual abuse, running away, and delinquency is also suggested by several studies of children in special treatment or delinquency programs. Reich and Gutierres (1979) reported that 55% of the children in Maricopa County, Arizona, who were charged with running away, truancy, or listed as missing persons were incest victims. In addition, in a study of female juvenile offenders in Wisconsin (1982), researchers found that 32% had been sexually abused by a relative or other person close to them.

Summary of Initial Effects of Child Sexual Abuse

The empirical literature on child sexual abuse, then, does suggest the presence—in some portion of the victim population—of many of the initial effects reported in the clinical literature, especially reactions of fear, anxiety, depression, anger and hostility, and inappropriate sexual behavior. However, because many of the studies lacked standardized outcome measures and adequate comparison groups, it is not clear that these findings reflect the experience of all child victims of sexual abuse or are even representative of those children currently being seen in clinical settings. At this point, the empirical literature on the initial effects of child sexual abuse would have to be considered sketchy.

LONG-TERM EFFECTS

Emotional Reactions and Self-Perceptions

In the clinical literature, depression is the symptom most commonly reported among adults molested as children, and empirical findings seem to confirm this. Two excellent community studies are indicative of this. Bagley and Ramsay (1985), in a community mental health study in Calgary utilizing a random sample of 387 women, found that subjects with a history of child sexual abuse scored more depressed on the Centre for Environmental Studies Depression Scale (CES-D) than did nonabused women (17% vs. 9% with clinical symptoms of depression in the last week), as well as on the Middlesex Hospital Questionnaire's measure of depression (15% vs. 7%). S. Peters (1984), in a community study in Los Angeles also based on a random sample, interviewed 119 women and found that sexual abuse in which there was physical contact was associated with a higher incidence of depression and a greater number of depressive episodes over time, and that women who had been sexually abused were more likely to have been hospitalized for depression than nonvictims. In a multiple regression that included both sexual abuse and family background factors (e.g, a poor relationship with the mother), the variable of child sexual abuse made an independent contribution to depression.

The link between child sexual abuse and depression has been confirmed in other nonclinical samples as well. Sedney and Brooks (1984), in a study of 301 college women, found a greater likelihood for subjects with childhood sexual experiences to report symptoms of depression (65% vs. 43% of the control group) and to have been hospitalized for it (18% of those depressed in the childhood experience group vs. 4% of women in the control group). These positive findings are surprising, in that the researchers used an overly inclusive definition of sexual experiences that may not have screened out some consensual experiences with peers. Their results are consistent, however, with those from a carefully controlled survey of 278 undergraduate women by Briere and Runtz (1985) using 72 items of the Hopkins Symptom Checklist, which indicated that sexual abuse victims reported that they experienced more depressive symptoms during the 12 months prior to the study than did nonabused subjects.

Studies based on clinical samples (Herman 1981; Meiselman 1978) have not shown such clear differences in depression between victims and nonvictims. For example, although Herman (1981) noted major depressive symptoms in 60% of the incest victims in her study, 55% of the comparison group also reported depression. Meiselman (1978) reported depressive symptoms in 35% of the incest victims whose psychiatric records she reviewed, compared with 23% of the comparison group; again, this difference was not significant.

Both clinical and nonclinical samples have shown victims of child sexual abuse to be more self-destructive, however. In an extensive study of 153 "walk-ins" to a community health counseling center. Briere (1984) reported that 51% of the sexual abuse victims, versus 34% of nonabused clients, had a history of suicide attempts. Thirty-one percent of victims, compared with 19% of nonabused clients, exhibited a desire to hurt themselves. A high incidence of suicide attempts among victims of child sexual abuse has been found by other clinical researchers as well (e.g., Harrison, Lumry, and Claypatch 1984; Herman 1981). Bagley and Ramsay (1985), in their community study, noted an association between childhood sexual abuse and suicide ideation or deliberate attempts at self-harm. And Sedney and Brooks (1984) found that 39% of their college student sample with child sexual experiences reported having thoughts of hurting themselves, compared with 16% of the control group. Sixteen percent of these respondents had made at least one suicide attempt (vs. 6% of their peers).

Another reaction observed in adults who were sexually victimized as children is symptoms of anxiety or tension. Briere (1984) reported that 54% of the sexual abuse victims in his clinical sample experienced anxiety attacks (compared with 28% of the nonvictims), 54% reported nightmares (vs. 23%), and 72% had difficulty sleeping (compared with 55% of the nonvictims). In their college sample, Sedney and Brooks (1984) found 59% with symptoms indicating nervousness and anxiety (compared with 41% of the controls); 41% indicated extreme tension (vs. 29% of the controls), and 51% had trouble sleeping (compared with 29% of the controls). These findings are supported by results from community samples, with Bagley and Ramsay (1985) noting that 19% of their subjects who had experienced child sexual abuse reported symptoms indicating somatic anxiety on the Middlesex Hospital Questionnaire, compared with 9% of the nonabused subjects.

The idea that sexual abuse victims continue to feel isolated and stigmatized as adults also has some support in the empirical literature, although these findings come only from the clinical populations. Sixty-four percent of the victimized women in Briere's (1984) study reported feelings of isolation, compared with 49% of the controls. With incest victims the figures are even higher Herman (1981) reported that all of the women who had experienced father-daughter incest in her clinical sample had a sense of being branded, marked, or stigmatized by the victimization. Even in a community sample of incest victims, Courtois (1979) found that 73% reported they still suffered from moderate to severe feelings of isolation and alienation.

Although a negative self-concept was not confirmed as an initial effect, evidence for it as a long-term effect is much stronger. Bagley and Ramsay (1985) found that 19% of the child sexual abuse victims in their random sample scored in the "very poor" category on the Coopersmith self-esteem inventory (vs. 5% of the control group), whereas only 9% of the victims demonstrated "very good" levels of self-esteem (compared with 20% of the controls). Women with very poor self-esteem were nearly four times as likely to report a history of child sexual abuse as were the other subjects. As might be expected, self-esteem problems among clinical samples of incest victims tended to be much greater. Eighty-seven percent of Courtois's (1979) community sample reported that their sense of self had been moderately to severely affected by the experience of sexual abuse from a family member. Similarly, Herman (1981) found that 60% of the incest victims in her clinical sample were reported to have a "predominantly negative self-image," as compared with 10% of the comparison group with seductive but not incestuous fathers.

Impact on Interpersonal Relating

Women who have been sexually victimized as children report problems in relating both to women and men, continuing problems with their parents, and difficulty in parenting and responding to their own children. In DeYoung's (1982) sample, 79% of the incest victims had predominantly hostile feelings toward their mothers, whereas 52% were hostile toward the abuser. Meiselman (1978) found that 60% of the incest victims in her psychotherapy sample disliked their mothers and 40% continued to experience strong negative feelings toward their fathers. Herman (1981) also noted that the rage of incest victims in her sample was often directed toward the mother and observed that they seemed to regard all women, including themselves, with contempt.

In addition, victims reported difficulty trusting others that included reactions of fear, hostility, and a sense of betrayal. Briere (1984) noted fear of men in 48% of his clinical subjects (vs. 15% of the nonvictims), and fear of women in 12% (vs. 4% of those who had not been sexually victimized). Incest victims seem especially likely to experience difficulty in close relationships. Sixty-four percent of the victims in Meiselman's (1978) clinical study, compared with 40% of the control group, complained of conflict with or fear of their husbands or sex partners, and 39% of the sample had never married. These results are supported by findings from Courtois's (1979) sample, in which 79% of the incest victims experienced moderate or severe problems in relating to men, and 40% had never married.

There is at least one empirical study that lends support to the idea that childhood sexual abuse also affects later parenting. Goodwin, McCarthy, and Divasto (1981) found that 24% of mothers in the child abusing families they studied reported incest experiences in their childhoods, compared with 3% of a nonabusive control group. They suggested that difficulty in parenting results when closeness and affection is endowed with a sexual meaning, and observed that these mothers maintained an emotional and physical distance from their children, thus potentially setting the stage for abuse.

Another effect on which the empirical literature agrees is the apparent vulnerability of women who have been sexually abused as children to be revictimized later in life. Russell (in press), in her probability sample of 930 women, found that between 33% and 68% of the sexual abuse victims (depending on the seriousness of the abuse they suffered) were raped later on, compared with 17% of women who were not childhood victims. Fromuth (1983), in surveying 482 female college students, found evidence that women who had been sexually abused before the age of 13 were especially likely to later become victims of nonconsensual sexual experiences. Further evidence of a tendency toward revictimization comes from a study conducted at the University of New Mexico School of Medicine on 341 sexual assault admittances (Miller et al. 1978). In comparing women who had been raped on more than one occasion with those who were reporting a first-time rape, researchers found that 18% of the repeat victims had incest histories, compared with only 4% of first-time victims.

In addition to rape, victims of child sexual abuse also seem more likely to be abused later by husbands or other adult partners Russell (in press) found that between 38% and 48% of the child sexual abuse victims in her community sample had physically violent husbands, compared with 17% of women who were not victims; in addition, between 40% and 62% of the abused women had later been sexually assaulted by their husbands, compared with 21% of nonvictims. Similarly, Briere (1984) noted that 49% of his clinical sexual abuse sample reported being battered in adult relationships, compared with 18% of the nonvictim group.

Effects on Sexuality

One of the areas receiving the most attention to thee empirical literature on long-term effects concerns the impact of early sexual abuse on later sexual functioning. Almost all clinically based studies show later sexual problems among child sexual abuse victims, particularly among the victims of incest. However, there have not yet been community-based studies on the sexual functioning of adults molested as children, as there have been of other mental health areas such as depression.

Of the clinical studies, Meiselman (1978) found the highest percentage of incest victims reporting problems with sexual adjustment. Eighty-seven percent of her sample were classified as having had a serious problem with sexual adjustment at some time since the molestation, compared with 20% of the comparison group (women who had been in therapy at the same clinic, but had not been sexually victimized as children). Results from Herman's (1981) study are somewhat less extreme: Fifty-five percent of the incest victims reported later sexual problems, although they were not significantly different from women with seductive fathers on this measure. Langmade (1983) compared a group of women in therapy who had been incest victims with a matched control group of nonvictimized women and found that the incest victims were more sexually anxious, experienced more sexual guilt, and reported greater dissatisfaction with their sexual relationship than the controls. In his study of a walk-in sample to a community health clinic, Briere (1984) found that 45% of women who had been sexually abused as children reported difficulties with sexual adjustment as adults, compared with 15% of the control group. Briere also noted a decreased sex drive in 42% of the victims studied, versus 29% of the nonvictims.

Two nonclinical studies show effects on sexual functioning as well. Courtois noted that 80% of the former incest victims in her sample reported an inability to relax and enjoy sexual activity, avoidance of or abstention from sex, or, conversely, a compulsive desire for sex. Finkelhor (1979), studying college students, developed a measure of sexual self-esteem and found that child sexual abuse victims reported significantly lower levels of sexual self-esteem than their nonabused classmates. However, Fromuth (1983), in a similar study also with a college student sample, found no correlation between sexual abuse and sexual self-esteem, desire for intercourse, or students' self-ratings of their sexual adjustment. Virtually all (96%) of Fromuth's respondents were unmarried and their average age was 19, so it is possible that some of the long-term sexual adjustment problems reported by women in the clinical and community samples were not yet in evidence in this younger population. Still, this does not explain the discrepancy from the Finkelhor findings.

In another study, Tsai, Feldman-Summers, and Edgar (1979) compared three groups of women on sexual adjustment measures: sexual abuse victims seeking therapy, sexual abuse victims who considered themselves well-adjusted and had not sought therapy, and a nonvictimized matched control group. Results indicated that the "well-adjusted" victims were not significantly different from the control group on measures of overall and sexual adjustment, but the victims seeking therapy did show a difference. They experienced orgasm less often, reported themselves to be less sexually responsive, obtained less satisfaction from their sexual relationships, were less satisfied with the quality of their close relationships with men, and reported a greater number of sexual partners. It is hard to know how to interpret findings from a group of victims solicited on the basis of feeling "well-adjusted." This seems far different from a comparison group of victims who were not in therapy, and thus these results are questionable.

A long-term effect of child sexual abuse that has also received a great deal of attention in the literature is an increased level of sexual behavior among victims, usually called promiscuity (e.g., Courtois 1979; DeYoung 1982; Herman 1981; Meiselman 1978). Herman noted that 35% of the incest victims in her sample reported promiscuity and observed that some victims seemed to have a "repertoire of sexually stylized behavior" that they used as a way of getting affection and attention (p. 40). DeYoung (1982) reported that 28% of the victims in her sample had engaged in activities that could be considered promiscuous; Meiselman (1978) found 25%. However, in her study of 482 female college students, Fromuth (1983) found no differences in this variable and observed that having experienced child sexual abuse only predicted whether subjects would describe themselves as promiscuous, not their actual number of partners. This potentially very important finding suggests that the "promiscuity" of sexual abuse victims may be more a function of their negative self-attributions, already well documented in the empirical literature, than their actual sexual behavior; thus researchers should be careful to combine objective behavioral measures with this type of self-report.

Another question that has received comment but little empirical confirmation concerns the possibility that sexual abuse may be associated with later homosexuality in victims. Although one study of lesbians found molestation in their backgrounds (Gundlach 1977), Bell and Weinberg (1981), in a large-scale, sophisticated study of the origin of sexual preference, found no such association. Studies from the sexual abuse literature have also found little connection (Finkelhor 1984; Fromuth 1983; Meiselman 1978).

Effects on Social Functioning

Several studies of special populations suggest a connection between child sexual abuse and later prostitution. James and Meyerding (1977) interviewed 136 prostitutes and found that 55% had been sexually abused as children by someone 10 or more years older, prior to their first intercourse. Among adolescents in the sample, 65% had been forced into sexual activity before they were 16 years old. Similarly, Silbert and Pines (1981) found that 60% of the prostitutes they interviewed had been sexually abused before the age of 16 by an average of two people for an average of 20 months. (The mean age of these children at the time of their first victimization was 10.) They concluded that, "The evidence linking juvenile sexual abuse to prostitution is overwhelming" (p. 410). However, Fields (1981) noted that, although 45% of the prostitutes in her sample had been sexually abused as children, this did not differentiate them from a comparison group of nonprostitutes matched on age, race, and education, of which 37% had been abused. Although there was no difference in prevalence between the two groups, Fields did find that the prostitutes were sexually abused at a younger age—14.5 versus 16.5—and were more apt to have been physically forced.

An association between child sexual abuse and later substance abuse has also received empirical support. S. Peters (1984), in a carefully controlled community study, found that 17% of the victimized women had symptoms of alcohol abuse (vs. 4% of nonvictimized women), and 27% abused at least one type of drug (compared with 12% of nonvictimized women). Herman (1981) noted that 35% of the women in her clinical sample with incestuous fathers abused drugs and alcohol (vs. 5% of the women with seductive fathers). Similarly, Briere (1984), in his walk-in sample from a community health center, found that 27% of the childhood sexual abuse victims had a history of alcoholism (compared with 11% of nonvictims), and 21% had a history of drug addiction (vs. 2% of the nonvictims). College student samples appear more homogeneous: Sedney and Brooks (1984) found a surprisingly low reported incidence of substance abuse, and no significant differences between groups.

Summary of Long-Term Effects

Empirical studies with adults confirm many of the long-term effects of sexual abuse mentioned in the clinical literature. Adult women victimized as children are more likely to manifest depression, self-destructive behavior, anxiety, feelings of isolation and stigma, poor self-esteem, a tendency toward revictimization, and substance abuse. Difficulty in trusting others and sexual maladjustment in such areas as sexual dysphoria, sexual dysfunction, impaired sexual self-esteem, and avoidance of or abstention from sexual activity have also been reported by empirical researchers; although agreement between studies is less consistent for the variables on sexual functioning.

IMPACT OF SEXUAL ABUSE

In light of the studies just reviewed, it is appropriate to evaluate the persistent controversy over the impact of sexual abuse on victims. It has been the continuing view of some that sexual abuse is not traumatic or that its traumatic impact has been greatly overstated (Constantine 1977; Henderson 1983; Ramey 1979). Proponents of this view contend that the evidence for trauma is meager and based on inadequate samples and unwarranted inferences. Because of the general lack of research in this field, clinicians have only recently been able to substantiate their impressions that sexual abuse is traumatic with evidence from strong scientific studies. However, as evidence now accumulates, it conveys a clear suggestion that sexual abuse is a serious mental health problem, consistently associated with very disturbing subsequent problems in some important portion of its victims.

Findings of long-term impact are especially persuasive. Eight non-clinical studies of adults (Bagley and Ramsay 1985; Briere and Runtz 1985; Finkelhor 1979; Fromuth 1983; S. Peters 1984; Russell, in press; Sedney and Brooks 1984; Seidner and Calhoun 1984), including three random sample community surveys, found that child sexual abuse victims in the "normal" population had identifiable degrees of impairment when compared with nonvictims. Although impairments in these nonclinical victims are not necessarily severe, all the studies that have looked for long-term impairment have found it, with the exception of one (Tsai et al. 1979).

These findings are particularly noteworthy in that the studies were identifying differences associated with an event that occurred from 5 to 25 years previously. Moreover, all these studies used fairly broad definitions of sexual abuse that included single episodes, experiences in which no actual physical contact occurred and experiences with individuals who were not related to or emotionally close to the subjects. In all four studies that used multivariate analyses (Bagley and Ramsay 1985; Finkelhor 1984; Fromuth 1983; S. Peters 1984), differences in the victimized group remained after a variety of background and other factors had been controlled. The implication of these studies is that a history of childhood sexual abuse is associated with greater risk for mental health and adjustment problems in adulthood.

Unfortunately, although the studies indicate higher risk, they are not so informative about the annual extent of impairment. In terms of simple self-assessments, 53% of intrafamilial sexual abuse victims in Russell's (in press) community survey reported that the experience resulted in "some" or "great" long-term effects on their lives. Assessments with standardized clinical measures show a more modest incidence of impairment. In Bagley and Ramsay's (1985) community survey, 17% of sexual abuse victims were clinically depressed as measured by the CES-D, and 18% were seriously psychoneurotic. Thus, most sexual abuse victims in the community, when evaluated in surveys, show up as slightly impaired or normal. It is possible, however, that some of the impairment associated with childhood molestation is not tapped by these survey evaluations.

Summarizing, then, from studies of clinical and nonclinical populations, the findings concerning the trauma of child sexual abuse appear to be as follows: In the immediate aftermath of sexual abuse, from one-fifth to two-fifths of abused children seen by clinicians manifest pathological disturbance (Tufts 1984). When studied as adults, victims as a group demonstrate impairment when compared with their nonvictimized counterparts, but under one-fifth evidence serious psychopathology. These findings give reassurance to victims that extreme long-term effects are not inevitable. Nonetheless, they also suggest that the risk of initial and long-term mental health impairment for victims of child sexual abuse should be taken very seriously.

EFFECTS BY TYPE OF ABUSE

Although the foregoing sections have been concerned with the various effects of abuse, there are also important research questions concerning the effects of various kinds of abuse. These have usually appeared in the form of speculation about what types of abuse have the most serious impact on victims. Groth (1978), for example, on the basis of his clinical experience, contented that the greatest trauma occurs in sexual abuse that (a) continues for a longer period of time, (b) occurs with a more closely related person, (c) involves penetration, and (d) is accompanied by aggression. To that list, MacFarlane (1978) added experiences in which (e) the child participates to some degree, (f) the parents have an unsupportive reaction to disclosure of the abuse, and (g) the child is older and thus cognizant of the cultural taboos that have been violated. Such speculations offer fruitful directions for research. Unfortunately, however, only a few studies on the effects of sexual abuse have had enough cases and been sophisticated enough methodologically to look at these questions empirically. Furthermore, the studies addressing these issues have reached little consensus in their findings.

Duration and Frequency of Abuse

Although many clinicians take for granted that the longer an experience goes on, the more traumatic it is, this conclusion is not clearly supported by the available studies. Of nine studies, only four found duration associated with greater trauma. (We are treating duration and frequency synonymously here because they tend to be so highly correlated.) Three found no relation, and two even found some evidence that longer duration is associated with less trauma.

Russell's (in press) study reported the clearest association: In her survey of adult women, 73% of sexual abuse that lasted for more than 5 years was self-rated as extremely or considerably traumatic by the victims, compared with 62% of abuse lasting 1 week to 5 years and 46% of abuse occurring only once. Tsai et al. (1979) found duration and frequency associated with greater negative effects, when measured with the Minnesota Multiphasic Personality Inventory and a problems checklist, at least in their group of adult sexual abuse victims who sought counseling. Bagley and Ramsay (1985) found that the general mental health status of adult victims—measured by a composite of indicators concerning depression, psychoneurosis, suicidal ideation, psychiatric consultation, and self-concept—was worse for longer lasting experiences. Finally, Friedrich, Urguiza, and Beilke (in press), studying children, found that both duration and frequency predicted disturbances measured by the CBCL, even in multivariate analysis.

However, other studies have not found such relations. Finkelhor (1979), in a retrospective survey of college students, used a self-rating of how negative the experience was in retrospect and found no association with duration. Langmade (1983) reported that adult women seeking treatment who had had long or short duration experiences did not differ on measures of sexual anxiety, sexual guilt, or sexual dissatisfaction. In addition, the Tufts (1984) study, looking at child victims with more comprehensive measures than Friedrich et al. (in press), could find no association between duration of abuse and measures of distress, using the Louisville Behavior Checklist and the Purdue Self-Concept Scale, as well as other measures.

Finally, some studies indicated a completely reversed relation. Courtois (1979), surprisingly, found that adult victims with the longest lasting experiences reported the least trauma. In addition, in their college student sample, Seidner and Calhoun (1984) reported that a high frequency of abuse was associated with higher self-acceptance (but lower social maturity) scores on the California Psychological Inventory.

In summary, then, the available studies reach quite contradictory conclusions about the relation between duration and trauma. However, duration is closely related to other aspects of the abuse experience—e.g., age at onset, a family relationship between victim and offender, and the nature of the sexual activity. Some of the contradictions may be cleared up when we have better studies with well-defined multivariate analyses that can accurately assess the independent effect of duration.

Relationship to the Offender

Popular and clinical wisdom holds that sexual abuse by a close relative is more traumatic than abuse by someone outside the family. Empirical findings suggest that this may be the case, at least for some types of family abuse. Three studies have found more trauma resulting from abuse by relatives than by nonrelatives: Landis (1956), in an early study asking students about how they had recovered; Anderson et al. (1981), in a chart review of adolescents in a hospital treatment setting; and Friedrich et al. (in press), in their evaluation of young victims. However, other researchers (Finkelhor 1979; Russell, in press; Seidner and Calhoun 1984; Tufts 1984) found no difference in the impact of abuse by family members versus abuse by others.

It must be kept in mind that how closely related a victim is to the offender does not necessarily reflect how much betrayal is involved in the abuse. Abuse by a trusted neighbor may be more devastating than abuse by a distant uncle or grandfather. Also, whereas abuse by a trusted person involves betrayal, abuse by a stranger or more distant person may involve more fear, and thus be rated more negatively. These factors may help explain why the relative-nonrelative distinction is not necessarily a consistent predictor of trauma.

What has been more consistently reported is greater trauma from experiences involving fathers or father figures compared with all other types of perpetrators, when these have been separated out. Russell (in press) and Finkelhor (1979) both found that abuse by a father or step-father was significantly more traumatic for victims than other abuse occurring either inside or outside the family. The Tufts (1984) study also reported that children abused by stepfathers showed more distress, but for some reason it did not find the same elevated level of distress among victims abused by natural fathers. Bagley and Ramsay (1985) found a small but nonsignificantly greater amount of impairment in women molested by fathers and stepfathers.

Type of Sexual Act

Results of empirical studies generally suggest, with a couple of important exceptions, that the type of sexual activity is related to the degree of trauma in victims. Russell's findings on longterm effects in adult women are the most clear-cut: Fifty-nine percent of those reporting completed or attempted intercourse, fellatio, cunnilingus, analingus, or anal intercourse said they were extremely traumatized, compared with only 36% of those who experienced manual touching of unclothed breasts or genitals and 22% of those who reported unwanted kissing or touching of clothed parts of the body. The community study by Bagley and Ramsay (1985) confirms this, in a multivariate analysis that found penetration to be the single most powerful variable explaining severity of mental health impairment, using a composite of standardized instruments.

Moreover, four other studies confirm the relation between type of sexual contact and subsequent effects by demonstrating that the least serious forms of sexual contact are associated with less trauma (Landis 1956; S. Peters 1984; Seidner and Calhoun 1984; Tufts 1984). However, some of these studies did not find the clear differentiation that Russell and Bagley and Ramsay did between intercourse and genital touching. The Tufts (1984) study, for example, using measures of children's anxiety, found children who had been fondled without penetration to be more anxious than those who actually suffered penetration. Moreover, there are three additional studies (Anderson et al. 1981; Finkelhor 1979; Fromuth 1983) that do not show any consistent relation between type of sexual activity and effect. Thus, a number of studies concur that molestation involving more intimate contact is more traumatic than less intimate contact. However, there is some disagreement about whether intercourse and penetration are demonstrably more serious than simple manual contact.

Force and Aggression

Five studies, three of which had difficulty finding expected associations between trauma and many other variables, did find an association between trauma and the presence of force. With Finkelhor's (1979) student samples, use of force by an abuser explained more of a victim's negative reactions than any other variable, and this finding held up in multivariate analysis. Fromuth (1983), in a replication of the Finkelhor study, found similar results. In Russell's (in press) study 71% of the victims of force rated themselves as extremely or considerably traumatized, compared with 47% of the other victims.

The Tufts (1984) study found force to be one of the few variables associated with children's initial reactions: Children subjected to coercive experiences showed greater hostility and were more fearful of aggressive behavior in others. Tufts researchers reported that physical injury (i.e., the consequence of force) was the aspect of sexual abuse that was most consistently related to the degree of behavioral disturbances manifested in the child, as indicated by the LBC and other measures. Similarly, Friedrich et al. (in press) found the use of physical force to be strongly correlated with both internalizing and externalizing symptoms on the CBCL.

Three other studies present dissenting findings, however. Anderson et al. (1981), in studying initial effects, concluded that, "the degree of force or coercion used did not appear to be related to presence or absence of psychosocial sequelae" in the adolescents they evaluated (p. 7). Seidner and Calhoun (1984), in an ambiguous finding, noted that force was associated with lower social maturity but higher self-acceptance. In addition, Bagley and Ramsay (1985) found that force was associated with greater impairment, but this association diminished to just below the significance level in multivariate analysis. Despite these findings, we are inclined to give credence to the studies showing force to be a major traumagenic influence, especially given the strong relation found by Finkelhor, Friedrich et al., Fromuth, Russell, and the Tufts study. Although some have argued that victims of forced abuse should suffer less long-term trauma because they could more easily attribute blame for abuse to the abuser (MacFarlane 1978), empirical studies do not seem to provide support for this supposition.

Age of Onset

There has been a continuing controversy in the literature about how a child's age might affect his or her reactions to a sexually abusive experience. Some have contended that younger children are more vulnerable to trauma because of their impressionability. Others have felt that their naivete may protect them from some negative effects, especially if they are ignorant of the social stigma surrounding the kind of victimization they have suffered. Unfortunately, findings from the available studies do not resolve this dispute.

Two studies of long-term effects do suggest that younger children are somewhat more vulnerable to trauma Meiselman (1978), in her chart review of adults in treatment, found that 37% of those who experienced incest prior to puberty were seriously disturbed, compared with only 17% of those who were victimized after puberty. Similarly, Courtois (1979), in her community sample, assessed the impact of child sexual abuse on long-term relationships with men and the women's sense of self, and also found more effects from prepubertal experiences.

However, four other studies found no significant relation between age at onset and impact. Finkelhor (1979), in a multivariate analysis, found a small but nonsignificant tendency for younger age to be associated with trauma. Russell (in press) also found a small but nonsignificant trend for experiences before age 9 to be associated with more long-term trauma. Langmade (1983) could find no difference in sexual anxiety, sexual guilt, or sexual dissatisfaction in adults related to the age at which they were abused. Bagley and Ramsay (1985) found an association between younger age and trauma, but that association dropped out in multivariate analysis, especially when controlling for acts involving penetration.

The Tufts (1984) study gave particular attention to children's reactions to abuse at different ages. Tufts researchers concluded that age at onset bore no systematic relation to the degree of disturbance. They did note that latency-age children were the most disturbed, but this finding appeared more related to the age at which the children were evaluated than the age at which they were first abused. They concluded that the age at which abuse begins may be less important than the stages of development through which the abuse persists.

In summary, studies tend to show little clear relation between age of onset and trauma, especially when they control for other factors. If there is a trend, it is for abuse at younger ages to be more traumatic. Both of the initial hypotheses about age of onset may have some validity, however: Some younger children may be protected by naivete, whereas others are more seriously traumatized by impressionability. However, age interacts with other factors like relationship to offender, and until more sophisticated analytical studies are done, we cannot say whether these current findings of a weak relation mean that age has little independent effect or is simply still masked in complexity.

Sex of Offender

Perhaps because there are so few female offenders (Finkelhor and Russell 1984), very few studies have looked at impact according to the sex of the offender. Two studies that did (Finkelhor 1984; Russell, in press) both found that adults rated experiences with male perpetrators as being much more traumatic than those with female perpetrators. A third study (Seidner and Calhoun 1984) found male perpetrators linked with lower self-acceptance, but higher social maturity, in college-age victims.

Adolescent and Adult Perpetrators

There are also very few studies that have looked at the question of whether age of the perpetrator makes any difference in the impact of sexual abuse on victim. However, two studies using college student samples (Finkelhor 1979; Fromuth 1983) found that victims felt significantly more traumatized when abused by older perpetrators. In Finkelhor's multivariate analysis (which controlled for other factors such as force, sex of perpetrator, type of sex act, and age of the offender), age of the offender was the second most important factor predicting trauma. Fromuth (1983) replicated these findings. Russell (in press), with a community sample, reported consistent, but qualifying, results. In her survey, lower levels of trauma were reported for abuse with perpetrators who were younger than 26 or older than 50. The conclusion that experiences with adolescent perpetrators are less traumatic seems supported by all three studies.

Telling or Not Telling

There is a general clinical assumption that children who feel compelled to keep the abuse a secret in the aftermath suffer greater psychic distress as a result. However, studies have not confirmed this theory. Bagley and Ramsay (1985) did find a simple zero-order relation between not telling and a composite measure of impairment based on depression, suicidal ideas, psychiatric consultation, and self-esteem. However, the association became nonsignificant when controlled for other factors. Finkelhor (1979), in a multivariate analysis, also found that telling or not telling was essentially unrelated to a self-rated sense of trauma. Further, the Tufts (1984) researchers, evaluating child subjects, reported that the children who had taken a long time to disclose the abuse had the least anxiety and the least hostility. Undoubtedly, the decision to disclose is related to many factors about the experience, which prevents a clear assessment of its effects alone. For example, although silence may cause suffering for a child, social reactions to disclosure may be less intense if the event is past. Moreover, the conditions for disclosure may be substantially different for the current generation than they were for past generations. Thus, any good empirical evaluation of the effects of disclosure versus secrecy needs to take into account the possibility of many interrelationships.

Parental Reaction

Only two studies have looked at children's trauma as a function of parental reaction, even though this is often hypothesized to be related to trauma. The Tufts (1984) study found that when mothers reacted to disclosure with anger and punishment, children manifested more behavioral disturbances. However, the same study did not find that positive responses by mothers were systematically related to better adjustment. Negative responses seemed to aggravate, but positive responses did not ameliorate, the trauma. Anderson et al. (1981) found similar results: They noted 2.6 times the number of symptoms in the children who had encountered negative reactions from their parents. Thus, although only based on two studies of initial effects, the available evidence indicates that negative parental reactions aggravate trauma in sexually abused children.

Institutional Response

There is a great deal of interest in how institutional response may affect children's reactions to abuse, but little research has been done. Tufts (1984) researchers found that children removed from their homes following sexual abuse exhibited more overall behavior problems, particularly aggression, than children who remained with their families. However, the children who were removed in the Tufts study were also children who had experienced negative reactions from their mothers, so this result may be confounded with other factors related to the home environment.

Summary of Contributing Factors

From this review of empirical studies, it would appear that there is no contributing factor that all studies agree on as being consistently associated with a worse prognosis. However, there are trends in the findings. The preponderance of studies indicate that abuse by fathers or stepfathers has a more negative impact than abuse by other perpetrators. Experiences involving genital contact seem to be more serious. Presence of force seems to result in more trauma for the victim. In addition, when the perpetrators are men rather than women, and adults rather than teenagers, the effects of sexual abuse appear to be more disturbing. These findings should be considered tentative, however, being based on only two studies apiece. When families are unsupportive of the victims, and/or victims are removed from their homes, the prognosis has also been shown to be worse; again, these findings are based on only two studies.

Concerning the age of onset, the more sophisticated studies found no significant relation, especially when controlling for other factors; however, the relation between age and trauma is especially complex and has not yet been carefully studied. In regard to the impact of revealing the abuse, as opposed to the child keeping it a secret, current studies also suggest no simple relation. Of all these areas, there is the least consensus on the effect of duration of abuse on impact.

DISCUSSION

Conclusions from the foregoing review must be tempered by the fact that they are based on a body of research that is still in its infancy. Most of the available studies have sample, design, and measurement problems that could invalidate their findings. The study of the sexual abuse of children would greatly benefit from some basic methodological improvements.

Samples. Many of the available studies are based on samples of either adult women seeking treatment or children whose molestation has been reported. These subjects may be very self-selected. Especially if sexual abuse is so stigmatizing that only the most serious cases are discovered and only the most seriously affected victims seek help, such samples could distort our sense of the pathology most victims experience as a result of this abuse. New studies should take pains to expand the size and diversity of their samples, and particularly to study victims who have not sought treatment or been reported. Advertising in the media for "well-adjusted" victims, as Tsai et al. (1979) did, however, does not seem an adequate solution, as this injects a different selection bias into the study.

We favor sampling for sexual abuse victims within the general population, using whole communities—as in Russell's (in press), S. Peters's (1984) and Bagley and Ramsay's (1985) designs—or other natural collectivities (high school students, college students, persons belonging to a health plan, etc.). Obtaining such samples may be easier with adult than with child victims. If identified child victims must be used, care should be taken to sample from all such identified children, not just the ones that get referred for clinical assessment and treatment and who may therefore represent the most traumatized group.

Control groups. Some of the empirical studies cited here did not have comparison groups of any sort. Such a control is obviously important, even if it is only a group of other persons in treatment who were not sexually victimized (e.g., Briere 1984; Meiselman 1978). In some respects, however, this control procedure may actually underestimate the types and severities of pathology associated with sexual abuse, because problems that sexual abuse victims share with other clinical populations will not show up as distinctive effects. An as yet untried, but we believe fruitful, approach is to match victims from clinical sources with other persons who grew up with them: that is, schoolmates, relatives, or even unvictimized siblings.

Measurement. Most of the studies we reviewed used fairly subjective measures of the outcome variables in question (e.g., guilt feelings, fears, etc.). We are encouraged by the appearance of studies such as the Tufts study and Bagley and Ramsay's survey, which used batteries of objective measures. However, empirical investigations need to go even further. To test for the specific and diverse sequelae that have been associated with child sexual abuse, it would appear that special sexual abuse outcome instruments now need to be developed. Instruments designed specifically to measure the aftereffects noted by clinicians might be more successful at showing the true extent of pathology related to the experience of sexual abuse in childhood.

Sexual abuse in deviant subpopulations. Some of the studies purporting to show effects of child sexual abuse are actually reports of prevalence among specialized populations, such as prostitutes (James and Meyerding 1977; Silbert and Pines 1981), sex offenders (Groth and Burgess 1979), or psychiatric patients (Carmen, Rieker, and Mills 1984). To conclude from high rates of abuse in deviant populations that sexual abuse causes the deviance can be a misleading inference. Care needs to be taken to demonstrate that the discovered rate of sexual abuse in the deviant group is actually greater than in a relevant comparison group. In at least one study of sex offenders, for example, although abuse was frequent in their backgrounds, even higher rates of prior abuse were found for prisoners who had not committed sex crimes (Gebhard, Gagnon, Pomeroy, and Christenson 1965). It is important to recognize that such data do not indicate that sexual abuse caused the deviance, only that many such offenders have abuse in their backgrounds.

Developmentally specific effects. In studying the initial and long-term effects of sexual abuse, researchers must also keep in mind that some effects of the molestation may be delayed. Although no sexual difficulties may be manifest in a group of college student victims (as in Fromuth 1983), such effects may be yet to appear and may manifest themselves in studies of older groups. Similarly, developmentally specific effects may be seen among children that do not persist into adulthood, or that may assume a different form as an individual matures. The Tufts (1984) study clearly demonstrated the usefulness of looking at effects by defined age groupings.

Disentangling sources of trauma. One of the most imposing challenges for researchers is to explore the sources of trauma in sexual abuse. Some of the apparent effects of sexual abuse may be due to premorbid conditions, such as family conflict or emotional neglect, that actually contributed to a vulnerability to abuse and exacerbated later trauma. Other effects may be due less to the experience itself than to later social reactions to disclosure. Such questions need to be approached using careful multivariate analyses in large and diverse samples or in small studies that match cases of sexual abuse that are similar except for one or two factors. Unfortunately, these questions are difficult to address in retrospective long-term impact studies, as it may be difficult or impossible to get accurate information about some of the key variables (e.g., how much family pathology predated the abuse).

Preoccupation with long-term effects. Finally, there is an unfortunate tendency in interpreting the effects of sexual abuse (as well as in studies of other childhood trauma) to overemphasize long-term impact as the ultimate criterion. Effects seem to be considered less "serious" if their impact is transient and disappears in the course of development. However, this tendency to assess everything in terms of its long-term effect betrays an "adulto-centric" bias. Adult traumas such as rape are not assessed ultimately in terms of whether they will have an impact on old age: They are acknowledged to be painful and alarming events, whether their impact lasts 1 year or 10. Similarly, childhood traumas should not be dismissed because no "long-term effects" can be demonstrated. Child sexual abuse needs to be recognized as a serious problem of childhood, if only for the immediate pain, confusion, and upset that can ensue.

NOTE

1. The whole literature on sexual abuse poses problems for differentiating according to gender of victims. As Table 1 shows, many studies contain a small number of men included in a larger sample of women. Unfortunately, many of these studies do not specifically mention which effects apply to men, so it is possible that some of the sequelae described apply only to the men. However, we believe that most of the sequelae described relate primarily to women.

REFERENCES

Achenbach, T. M., and C. Edelbrock. 1983. *Manual for the child behavior checklist*. Burlington: University of Vermont.

Anderson, S. C., C. M. Bach, and S. Griffith. 1981. *Psychosocial sequelae in intrafamilial victims of sexual assault and abuse*. Paper presented at the Third International Conference on Child Abuse and Neglect, Amsterdam, The Netherlands, April.

Bagley, C., and R. Ramsay. 1985. *Disrupted childhood and vulnerability to sexual assault: Long term sequels with implications for counselling*. Paper presented at the Conference on Counselling the Sexual Abuse Survivor, Winnipeg, Canada, February.

Bell, A., and M. Weinberg. 1981. *Sexual preference: Its development among men and women*. Bloomington: Indiana University Press.

Benward, J., and J. Densen-Gerber. 1975. *Incest as a causative factor in antisocial behavior: An exploratory study*. Paper presented at the meeting of the American Academy of Forensic Science, Chicago, February.

Briere, J. 1984. *The effects of childhood sexual abuse in later psychological functioning: Defining a "post-sexual-abuse syndrome."* Paper presented at the Third National Conference on Sexual Victimization of Children, Washington, D.C., April.

Briere, J., and M. Runtz. 1985. *Symptomatology associated with prior sexual abuse in a non-clinical sample*. Paper presented at the meeting of the American Psychological Association, Los Angeles, August.

Carmen, E., P. P. Rieker, and T. Mills. 1984. Victims of violence and psychiatric illness. *American Journal of Psychiatry* 141: 378–83.

Constantine, L. 1977. *The sexual rights of children: Implications of a radical perspective*. Paper presented at the International Conference on Love and Attraction, Swansea, Wales.

———. 1980. Effects of early sexual experience: A review of synthesis of research. In *Children and sex*, ed. L. Constantine and F. M. Martinson, 217–44. Boston: Little, Brown.

Courtois, C. 1979. The incest experience and its aftermath. *Victimology: An International Journal* 4: 337–47.

DeFrancis, V. 1969. *Protecting the child victim of sex crimes committed by adults*. Denver: American Human Association.

DeYoung, M. 1982. *The sexual victimization of children*. Jefferson, N.C.: McFarland.

Farrell, W. W. 1982. *Myths of incest: Implications for the helping professional*. Paper presented at the International Symposium on Family Sexuality, Minneapolis, Minnesota.

Fields, P. J. 1981. Parent-child relationships, childhood sexual abuse, and adult interpersonal behavior in female prostitutes. *Dissertation Abstracts International* 42: 2053B, November.

Finkelhor, D. 1979. *Sexually victimized children*. New York: Free Press

Finkelhor, D. 1984. *Child sexual abuse: New theory and research.* New York: Free Press.

Finkelhor, D., and D. Russell. 1984. Women as perpetrators of sexual abuse: Review of the evidence. In *Child sexual abuse: New theory and research,* ed. D. Finkelhor, 171–87. New York: Free Press

Friedrich, W. N., A. J. Urguiza, and R. Beilke. In press. Behavioral problems in sexually abused young children. *Journal of Pediatric Psychology.*

Fromuth, M. E. 1983. The long term psychological impact of childhood sexual abuse. Unpublished doctoral dissertation, Auburn University, Auburn, Alabama, August.

Gebhard, P., J. Gagnon, W. Pomeroy, and C. Christenson. 1965. *Sex offenders: An analysis of types.* New York: Harper & Row.

Goodwin, J., T. McCarthy, and P. Divasto. 1981. Prior incest in mothers of abused children. *Child Abuse and Neglect* 5: 87–96.

Groth, N. A. 1978. Guidelines for assessment and management of the offender. In *Sexual assault of children and adolescents,* ed. A. Burgess, N. Groth, S. Holmstrom, and S. Sgroi, 25–42. Lexington, Mass.: Lexington Books.

Groth, N. A., and A. W. Burgess. 1979. Sexual trauma in the life histories of rapists and child molesters. *Victimology: An International Journal* 4: 10–16.

Gundlach, R. 1977. Sexual molestation and rape reported by homosexual and heterosexual women. *Journal of Homosexuality* 2: 367–84.

Harrison, P. A., A. E. Lumry, and C. Claypatch. 1984. *Female sexual abuse victims: Perspectives on family dysfunction, substance use and psychiatric disorders.* Paper presented at the Second National Conference for Family Violence Researchers, Durham, New Hampshire, August.

Henderson, J. 1983. Is incest harmful? *Canadian Journal of Psychiatry* 28: 34–39.

Herman, J. L. 1981. *Father-daughter incest.* Cambridge, Mass.: Harvard University Press.

James, J., and J. Meyerding. 1977. Early sexual experiences and prostitution. *American Journal of Psychiatry* 134: 1381–85.

Landis, J. 1956. Experiences of 500 children with adult sexual deviation. *Psychiatric Quarterly Supplement* 30: 91-109.

Langmade, C. J. 1983. The impact of pre- and postpubertal onset of incest experiences in adult woman as measured by sex anxiety, sex guilt, sexual satisfaction and sexual behavior. *Dissertation Abstracts International* 44: 917B (University Microfilms No. 3592).

MacFarlane, K. 1978. Sexual abuse of children. In *The victimization of women,* ed. J. R. Chapman and M. Gates, 81–109. Beverly Hills, Calif.: Sage.

Meiselman, K. 1978. *Incest.* San Francisco: Jossey-Bass.

Miller, J., D. Moeller, A. Kaufman, R. Divasto, R. Fitzsimmons, D. Pather, and J. Christy. 1978. Recidivism among sexual assault victims. *American Journal of Psychiatry* 135: 1103–1104.

Nelson, J. 1981. The impact of incest: Factors in self-evaluation. In *Children and sex,* ed. L. Zakus and E Mahlon, 163–74. Boston: Little, Brown.

Peters, J. J. 1976. Children who are victims of sexual assault and the psychology of offenders. *American Journal of Psychotherapy* 30: 398–421.

Peters, S. D. 1984. The relationship between childhood sexual victimization and adult depression among Afro-American and white women. Unpublished doctoral dissertation, University of California, Los Angeles.

Ramey, J. 1979. Dealing with the last taboo. *Sex Information and Education Council of the United States* 7: 1–2, 6–7.

Reich, J. W., and S. E. Gutierres. 1979. Escape/aggression incidence in sexually abused juvenile delinquents. *Criminal Justice and Behavior* 6: 239–43.

Rogers, C. M., and T. Terry. 1984. Clinical intervention with boy victims of sexual abuse. In *Victims of Sexual Aggression,* ed. I. Stewart and I. Greer, 1–104. New York: Van Nostrand, Reinhold.

Russell, D. E. H. In press. *The secret trauma: Incest in the lives of girls and women.* New York: Basic Books.

Sandfort, T. 1981. *The sexual aspect of paedophile relations.* Amsterdam: Pan/Spartacus.

Sedney, M. A., and B. Brooks. 1984. Factors associated with a history of childhood sexual experience in a nonclinical female population. *Journal of the American Academy of Child Psychiatry* 23: 215, 218.

Seidner, A., and K. S. Calhoun. 1984. *Childhood sexual abuse: Factors related to differential adult adjustment.* Paper presented at the Second National Conference for Family Violence Researchers, Durham, New Hampshire, August.

Silbert, M. H., and A. M. Pines. 1981. Sexual child abuse as an antecedent to prostitution. *Child Abuse and Neglect* 5: 407–11.

Tsai, M., S. Feldman-Summers, and M. Edgar. 1979. Childhood molestation: Variables related to differential impact of psychosexual functioning in adult women. *Journal of Abnormal Psychology* 88: 407–17.

Tufts' New England Medical Center, Division of Child Psychiatry. 1984. *Sexually exploited children: Service and research project.* Final report for the Office of Juvenile Justice and Delinquency Prevention. Washington, D.C.: U.S. Department of Justice.

Wisconsin Female Juvenile Offender Study. 1982. *Sex abuse among juvenile offenders and runaways.* Summary report. Madison, Wisc.: Author.

Woods, S. C., and K. S. Dean. 1984. *Final report: Sexual abuse of males research project* (Contract No. 90 CA/812). Washington, D.C.: National Center on Child Abuse and Neglect.

20

CHILD WITNESSES:
TRANSLATING RESEARCH INTO POLICY

STEPHEN J. CECI AND MAGGIE BRUCK

On August 12, 1983, Judy Johnson, the mother of a toddler at a prestigious nursery school in Manhattan Beach, California, told police that her 2-year-old son had been molested by Raymond Buckey, a teacher and the grandson of the school's founder, Virginia McMartin. Buckey was arrested but subsequently released for lack of evidence. On March 22, 1984, he was indicted by a grand jury and rearrested along with six female teachers, including his mother, Peggy McMartin Buckey. He was held without bail until 1989.

In August 1984, the first of many preliminary hearings had begun for the seven McMartin Preschool defendants. Fourteen former students at the nursery school took the witness stand at this hearing and described a series of bizarre events involving sexual abuse, satanic rituals, and animal mutilation that allegedly occurred at their preschool. Based on these children's testimony, the defendants were accused of 115 counts of abuse, later expanded to 321 counts, including rape, sodomy, fondling, oral copulation, and drugging, and photographing of at least 100 children in the nude.

In January 1986, after 17 months of preliminary hearings in which each child witness was cross-examined by each of seven different defense attorneys, charges against five of the six women were dropped because of insufficient evidence. Only 26-year-old Raymond Buckey and his 58-

From *Social Policy Report* (Society for Research in Child Development) 7, no. 3 (Fall 1993): 1–30. Reprinted by permission of the authors.

year-old mother, Peggy McMartin Buckey, remained as defendants. After spending 2 years in jail, Peggy McMartin Buckey's bail was set at $500,000 in 1986, while her son remained remanded without bail in a proceeding that would last an additional 4 years.

In the ensuing years of legal proceedings, the major issue before the court was whether or not to believe the children. On the one hand, it was argued that the children's reports were authentic and that their bizarre and chilling accounts of events, which were well beyond the realm of most preschoolers' knowledge and experience, only served to substantiate the fact that the children had actually participated in them. On the other hand, it was argued that the children's reports were the product of repeated suggestive interviews by parents, law enforcement officials, and therapists, and that the children were only reporting events suggested to them during these interviews.

In January 1990, following a 33-month trial and 9 weeks of deliberation, the jury in the McMartin Preschool sexual abuse case returned "not guilty" verdicts on 52 of the 65 counts. The jury deadlocked on 12 molestation charges against Raymond Buckey and on 1 count of conspiracy against his mother. Judge William Pounders dismissed the conspiracy charge.

In response to the acquittals, the children's parents railed at the way the case had been handled and at the jury's verdicts. The children themselves appeared on nationally televised talk shows, weeping over the jury's seeming refusal to believe their claims of ritualistic abuse. Newspapers and magazines across the nation ran headlines such as: "Doubt the children and jail the parents!"

During a postverdict press conference, many jurors claimed that they believed that some of the children had been abused, but were unable to reach a guilty verdict because of the suggestive way the children had been interviewed. These jurors claimed that the social workers prevented the children from speaking in their own language and thus diminished their credibility.[1]

By January 1990, the prosecution announced Buckey would be retried on the remaining 12 charges on which the jurors had been deadlocked. Although this trial was shorter, the jury again deadlocked. When the judge declared a mistrial, the prosecution did not retry the case.

The McMartin case made legal history. In sheer magnitude, it was without parallel, lasting 7 years from the time of its inception to the final verdicts, producing hundreds of thousands of pages of transcript, and costing the State of California over $16 million. From the very start, the McMartin case captured the attention of the national media, with regular accounts of the children's allegations appearing on television (e.g., ABC

News *Nightline* April 20, 1984), in newspapers (e.g., Charlier and Downing 1988; Shaw 1990) and in magazine articles (e.g., Fischer 1988).

The McMartin case is not a singular happening. There have been many similar cases in North America and Europe, some of which have received extensive media attention.[2] For the most part, these cases share the following elements: First, the witnesses were preschoolers at the time of the alleged abuse. Second, the disclosures were not made immediately following the alleged event, but after a long delay. Third, the disclosures often were preceded by intensive interviewing of the children by various professionals (e.g., child protective service workers, law enforcement) and nonprofessionals (e.g., parents, grandparents). Fourth, the children were the only witnesses to these alleged events, and corroborative physical evidence was lacking. Fifth, none of the defendants ever made a confession; all maintained their innocence, even after some co-defendants were convicted. Finally, the major issue before the jury in all of these cases was whether to believe the children.

Researchers in child development have served as witnesses or consultants for the defense and/or the prosecution in all of these trials. More importantly, these cases have changed the course of our research and thinking on children's memory development. They have encouraged researchers to tackle new issues, to develop innovative experimental paradigms, and to challenge and elaborate previous research on the reliability of young children's statements.

In this *Social Policy Report* we provide a glimpse into the social science research that has accumulated on the aspect of children's testimony that figured so prominently in the McMartin case and hundreds of others like it,[3] namely, preschoolers' presumed suggestibility. We then present some tentative thoughts about the policy implications of this research, by addressing the questions: What can (and should) researchers and mental health professionals tell courts when they are called upon to serve as expert witnesses and consultants? What is the proper role for professional organizations to play in overseeing expert testimony? First, however, we provide some background information about the problem of child sexual abuse in the U.S. and about the history of children providing courtroom testimony.

PREVALENCE OF ABUSE AND COURT INVOLVEMENT

Crime statistics reflecting the sexual abuse of children are of great social concern. These statistics come from two major sources: one is based on annual rates of "substantiated" or "indicated" reports of child abuse,[4] and the other is based on adults' reports of abusive events during their own childhoods. The first source thus provides estimates of *incidence*, whereas the second provides estimates of *prevalence*.

According to the most recent incidence figures (based on data from 45 states), there were 2.7 million reports of suspected child maltreatment in 1991 (National Center for Child Abuse and Neglect 1993); 129,697 of these were substantiated or indicated cases that were sexual in nature, indicating an incidence of childhood sexual abuse of less than 1% of children for that year. The accuracy of these rates has been challenged, (e.g., Besharov 1991; Robin 1991). On the one hand, these figures may overestimate the extent of child sexual abuse because they include indicated and substantiated cases which are not validated. Others, however, argue that these rates may underestimate the incidence of child sexual abuse, because many cases of actual child sexual abuse end up being classified "unsubstantiated," or significant numbers of cases of abuse are never reported to authorities. It seems plausible that while some substantiated cases are actually false, many more unsubstantiated and unreported cases are real. Thus, the national data likely underestimate the true incidence, although no one can say by how much.

Random samples of adults, asked about their childhood history, yield highly variable estimates of childhood sexual abuse, ranging, for females, from 6.8% (Siegel, Sorenson, Golding, Burnam, and Stein 1987) to 62% (Wyatt 1985); and for males, from 3% to 31% (see Peters, Wyatt, and Finkelhor 1986). A number of methodological factors may account for these discrepant figures, but review of these is beyond the scope of this article. Our point is that even if the lowest prevalence rates are the most accurate, and even if the incidence of child sexual abuse in 1991 was 1%, this still represents a serious societal problem.

As a result of society's reaction to these dramatic figures, and particularly in reaction to the ineffective prosecution of child abuse cases, the legal system has been forced to change some of its rules concerning the admissibility and treatment of child witnesses. For example, until recently courts of law in all English-speaking countries were reluctant to accept the uncorroborated statements of child witnesses (Chadbourn 1978). This reluctance was reflected in competency hearings, corroboration requirements, and cautionary instructions that some judges gave to juries concerning the risk of convictions based solely on the testimony of child witnesses (Andrews 1964; Cohen 1975). During the 1980s, however, all but a few states dropped their corroboration requirement for children in sexual abuse cases, a crime that by its nature lacks corroboration. Seventeen states now allow children to testify regardless of the nature of the crime, permitting the jury to determine how much weight to give to the child's testimony. With the continued adoption by states of Federal Rules of Evidence, the number of child witnesses is likely to expand.

As more and more children have been admitted as witnesses in the courtroom, legal and courtroom procedures have been modified. For example, some courts have instituted shield laws which permit a child witness to testify either behind a one-way screen or over closed-circuit television, to occlude the child's view of the defendant but not the defendant's view of the child. Hearsay exceptions are also allowed, whereby therapists, pediatricians, and others describe what children have said to them. These measures serve to assist child witnesses who otherwise might be "psychologically unavailable" to testify in open court (McGough, in press; Montoya 1992, 1993).

In light of claims that many of these modifications challenge the constitutional rights of defendants (*Maryland* v. *Craig* 1990; *Coy* v. *Iowa* 1988), it is important to determine whether such procedures do, in fact, facilitate the accuracy of children's testimony (Montoya 1993). This is particularly important in light of the fact that recent court decisions regarding the treatment of child witnesses have not been predicated exclusively on humane issues (i.e., reducing the stress placed on child witnesses), but also on the presumption that courtroom modifications will increase testimonial accuracy (Harvard Law Review Notes 1985; Montoya 1992). No scientific data addressing these issues are yet available, although some data on the costs and benefits of courtroom innovations on children's courtroom behavior have been gathered (Batterman-Faunce and Goodman 1993; Flin 1993).

There are, however, no reliable national data on the impact of these changes on the number of children who actually end up participating in family court or criminal justice proceedings. Gray's recent analysis (1993) of eight jurisdictions suggests that 3% to 10% of all cases of sexual abuse that are eventually filed with police result in a trial. Based on the National Center on Child Abuse and Neglect (1993) statistics cited above, this would suggest that, in the 45 states reporting, up to 13,000 children testified in sexual abuse trials that year. For various reasons, however, the actual incidence of court involvement may be considerably higher. The majority of cases that end in pleas still require the child to be deposed even if the child does not testify in a court trial. Second, these figures do not include data from five states, one of which is New York, where as many as 3,150 children had formal court involvement in sexual abuse cases in 1990 (Doris 1993). Finally, if nonsexual types of abuse and nonabuse cases involving children serving as witnesses are included (e.g., cases of domestic violence, custody disputes, accidents, playground injuries), then the estimate of children's participation in the legal system rises considerably, possibly to over 100,000 cases annually. We must emphasize, however, that this is, at best, an educated guess.

One final point about children's court involvement is in order. It appears that preschoolers are disproportionately more likely to be abused and more likely to have their cases come to trial. In an analysis of a sample of nearly 800 alleged victims of child sexual abuse in New York, preschoolers (ages 6 and younger) accounted for nearly 40% of the official sexual abuse cases, and 28% were aged 5 and younger (Doris 1993). In Gray's recent analysis (1993), children below the age of 8 accounted for 45% of sexual abuse cases, and 18% were 5 years old or younger; 31% of the cases involving 5- to 6-year-old children went to trial, and 24% of cases involving 3- to 4-year-olds went to trial, whereas only 10% of the cases involving 13- to 14-year-olds went to trial.

Despite modifications in the judicial system resulting in the greater court involvement of children, both jurists and social scientists continue to raise fundamental questions about whether these changes actually facilitate the accuracy of children's testimony (Montoya 1992, 1993) and, more broadly, whether the testimony that children do give is accurate. Next, we discuss the research that has been carried out on one important aspect of the accuracy of children's reports: the degree to which very young children are disproportionately prone to suggestion.

RESEARCH ON CHILDREN'S SUGGESTIBILITY: PAST AND PRESENT TRENDS

The scientific research on the suggestibility of children's recollections is both contradictory and confusing. A review of 20th-century studies of children's suggestibility can be found in Ceci and Bruck 1993. Our purpose in this report is not to recap that analysis but to highlight some of the salient conclusions of these studies and to focus on the different experimental approaches used in investigating children's suggestibility.

Early Studies of Suggestibility

Early studies of children's suggestibility, with few exceptions, led to a jaundiced portrayal of children's proneness to suggestibility. Beginning with the early experiments of Binet and his European colleagues (Binet 1900; Lipmann 1911; Stern 1910; Varendonck 1911), and concluding with empirical studies in the 1920s and 1930s (Messerschmidt 1933;

Otis 1924; Sherman 1925), early researchers viewed children as extremely susceptible to leading questions and unable to resist an interviewer's suggestions. M. R. Brown (1926), a legal scholar, wrote:

> Create, if you will, an idea of what the child is to hear or see, and the child is very likely to see or hear what you desire. (p. 133)

Although the conclusions of these early researchers were confirmed by studies conducted right up until the 1980s, modern researchers have been ambivalent about generalizing these results to the forensic arena for several reasons. First, despite the fact that there is great concern currently about the reliability of preschoolers' reports, not one study in the first 80 years of this century included preschoolers. More recent research has begun to fill this void; since 1980, over 20 studies relevant to the issues of children's suggestibility have included a preschool sample.

A second and more important concern was that most of the previous studies involved children's recall of events that were forensically irrelevant. In most of this earlier literature, researchers examined the influences of a single misleading suggestion or a leading question on children's reports of neutral, nonscripted, and often uninteresting events that occurred in a laboratory setting. Although these results may be of importance for theoretical conceptualizations of the mechanisms that underlie suggestibility effects and memory processes, they have limited practical and legal relevance to the reliability of the child witness. In many court cases, the allegations involve the child as participant and not as bystander; they involve the child's recall of salient, rather than peripheral, events; they often involve repeated interviews which are highly suggestive; and they frequently involve emotionally charged and highly stressful events, such as sexual molestation. The earlier experiments of this century provide no clues as to the testimonial accuracy of children in such circumstances.

But how does a researcher conduct an ethically acceptable experiment that mirrors the many conditions that are characteristic of the child victim-witness? It would be unacceptable, for example, to determine whether an interviewer can successfully suggest to children with substantiated histories of abuse that the abuse had never taken place. Similarly, it would be unacceptable to determine if nonabused children will make allegations of sexual abuse after a highly suggestive interview. It is ethically impermissible to alter such fundamental aspects of young children's autobiography.

MODERN STUDIES OF CHILDREN'S SUGGESTIBILITY

In the past several years, a number of researchers have attempted to deal with these issues by developing new paradigms which admittedly do not mirror all of the conditions that bring children to court, but which do contain some important elements of the child witness's experiences. This section describes three major lines of recent research, each of which illustrates a different paradigm: (1) increasing the salience of the experienced events about which children will be interviewed, (2) increasing the dynamics of the interview situation, and (3) adding anatomically correct dolls to the interviewing context.

Increasing the salience of events. As discussed above, earlier studies were criticized as not forensically relevant because they did not examine how children respond to questions about events that involved their own body, or about other salient events that occurred in personally experienced and stressful situations. In response, a number of researchers have designed studies in which children are asked misleading questions about being touched. In some studies, children are questioned about their previous interactions with an experimenter in a laboratory (e.g., Rudy and Goodman 1991). In other studies, children are questioned about an inoculation (Goodman, Hirschman, Hepps, and Rudy 1991) or a genital examination (Saywitz, Goodman, Nicholas, and Moan 1991).

For example, Saywitz and her colleagues (Saywitz et al. 1991) examined 5- and 7-year-old girls' memories of a medical examination. Half of each age group had a scoliosis exam (for curvature of the spine), and the other children had a genital exam. When children were interviewed either 1 or 4 weeks later, they were asked suggestive and nonsuggestive questions that were abuse-related (e.g., "How many times did the doctor kiss you?") or nonabuse-related (e.g., "Didn't the doctor look at your feet first?"). Although the older children were initially more accurate than the younger children on most questions, some of these age differences disappeared after the 4-week delay. Most importantly, although there were age differences in response to the suggestive abuse questions, very few children of either age gave incorrect responses; the 7-year-old children never made a false report of abuse, and the 5-year-olds did so only 4 times, although they were given 215 opportunities.

Saywitz and her colleagues point out specific patterns of results in this study. They conclude the children's inaccurate reports involved mainly errors of omission rather than commission. The majority of children in the genital examination condition did not disclose genital contact unless specifically asked to do so. This latter opportunity was only provided with the direct (leading) question format ("Did the doctor touch you here?"). In the scoliosis condition, when children were asked these direct questions, 2.86% of the children falsely affirmed vaginal touch and 5.56% falsely affirmed anal touch.[5] In reviewing this study, Goodman and Clarke-Stewart (1991) conclude that:

> . . . obtaining accurate testimony about sexual abuse from young children is a complex task. Part of the complexity rests in the fact that there are dangers as well as benefits in the use of leading questions with children. The benefits appear in the finding . . . that leading questions were often necessary to elicit information from children about actual events they had experienced (genital touching). . . . The children . . . were generally accurate in reporting specific and personal things that had happened to them. If these results can be generalized to investigations of abuse, they suggest that normal children are unlikely to make up details of sexual acts when nothing abusive happened. They suggest that children will not easily yield to an interviewer's suggestion that something sexual occurred when in fact it did not, especially if nonintimidating interviewers ask questions children can comprehend. (pp. 102–103)

Thus, according to this group of researchers, earlier studies of children's suggestibility may have overestimated the extent to which they are suggestible. For example:

> There is now no real question that the law and many developmentalists were wrong in their assumption that children are highly vulnerable to suggestion, at least in regard to salient details. Although some developmentalists may be challenged to find developmental differences in suggestibility in increasingly arcane circumstances, as a practical matter who really cares whether 3-year-old children are less suggestible about peripheral details in events that they witnessed than are 4-year-old children? Perhaps the question has some significance for developmental theory, but surely it has little or no meaning for policy and practice in child protection and law. (Melton 1992, 154)

It is important, however, to point out that not all data on children's reports of medical procedures are consistent with these conclusions. Ornstein and his colleagues (Baker-Ward, Gordon, Ornstein, Larus, and Clubb, in press; Ornstein, Gordon, and Larus 1992) found that when children were later questioned about their memories of the visit to the pediatrician, 3-year-olds were more prone than 6-year-olds to make false claims in response to suggestive questions about silly events involving body contact (e.g., "Did the nurse lick your knee?"). Oates and

Shrimpton (1991) also found that preschoolers were more suggestible than older children about previously experienced events that involved body touching. In contrast to the Saywitz et al. findings that false reports in response to suggestive questions are relatively infrequent, the younger children in these latter studies provided a substantial number of false reports in response to suggestive questions. Until recently, however, only a few studies have included explicit questions about sexual touching. Recent research by us and our colleagues has yielded different results, which will be reported in greater detail later when we describe our study of a pediatric examination.

Increasing the dynamics of the interview. A second major innovative theme in the current research on children's suggestibility involves examining the effects of various interviewing techniques on children's reports. This focus has arisen in response to the concern that the interviewing procedures of earlier studies were less intense than those that bring children to court—so much so as to result in a potential *underestimation* of children's suggestibility (Raskin and Esplin 1991; Steller 1991).

The interviewing procedures used in traditional laboratory studies and those used in the forensic arena differ in several ways. First, it is frequently the case that children who come to court are questioned weeks, months, or even years after the occurrence of an event, as opposed to minutes or days later. Suggestibility effects may be more salient after long delays, because the original memory trace has faded sufficiently to allow the suggestion to intrude more readily than might occur after shorter delays.

Second, child witnesses are rarely interviewed only one time, by one interviewer, or under nonstressful conditions. The modal child witness has been interviewed between 4 and 11 times prior to the first courtroom appearance; sometimes children are interviewed weekly for years about the same event—in therapy sessions, for instance. Leichtman and Ceci (1993) have suggested that the incessant use of leading questions and suggestions in these repeated interviews may result in a qualitatively different type of report distortion than that which arises from a single misleading question in a single postevent interview.

Third, an examination of the interviews of some child witnesses reveals that the label "suggestive interview" may describe more than the use of misleading questions. Rather, implicit and explicit suggestions can be woven into the fabric of the interview through the use of bribes, threats, repetitions of certain questions, and the induction of stereotypes and expectancies (Ceci and Bruck 1993).

Finally, the questioning of child witnesses is typically conducted by parents, therapists, and legal officials, all of whom represent status and power in the eyes of the child; children may thus be more likely to comply with the suggestions of these interviewers than with those of the neutral interviewers employed in most research studies.

Although it is very difficult to create experimental conditions that simulate the confluence of the conditions present in child witness interviews (stressful episodes, with repeated and suggestive questioning over prolonged periods of time), researchers are beginning to examine how children's reports are influenced by the repetition of suggestions in multiple interviews prior to and following the occurrence of an event. In addition, researchers have focused on the interviewer and the potential effects that a particular interviewer's bias may have on the reports elicited from young children. We confine our discussion here to three studies recently carried out with our colleagues at Cornell and McGill universities, as they were designed specifically to address these issues (see Ceci and Bruck [1993], for discussion of additional studies). In focusing on our own studies, we necessarily present a particularized view, inspired by our own hypotheses, assumptions, and values, but the studies are designed to build on and challenge extant research.

In these studies, we patterned our experimental manipulations after materials collected over the past decade from court transcripts and from therapy sessions and law enforcement interviews involving children in cases similar to the McMartin case where there was a strong suspicion of abuse (see transcripts in Ceci, in press; Ceci and Bruck 1993). These materials reveal that a child's first "disclosure" about abuse commonly occurs when an interviewer pursues a single hypothesis about the basis of the child's difficulties, which entails leading and suggestive interviews, often with fantasy inductions and "self-empowerment" techniques—the techniques themselves being potentially suggestive and stereotype inducing. Such disclosures are then pursued in law enforcement, child protective service, or therapeutic interviews.

Study 1: The effect of interviewer bias on children's reports

Ideally a forensic interview should be guided by a hypothesis-testing framework. Just as scientists try to arrive at the truth by ruling out rival hypotheses or by falsifying a favored hypothesis (Ceci and Bronfenbrenner 1991; Dawes 1992; Popper 1962), interviewers should, in similar manner, attempt to rule out rival hypotheses, rather than exclusively attempting to confirm their favored one. However, because of situational pressures (e.g., caseworkers must sometimes make immediate determinations of potential danger to a child), it is not feasible that interviewers generate and test every conceivable hypothesis or, conversely, that they be "blind" to obviously relevant information pertaining to a main hypothesis that abuse is indeed present. Failure to recognize relevant information provided by the child could result in crucial missed opportunities.[6] But, as the following study shows, failure to test a rival hypothesis can result in reporting errors.

In this study (Ceci, Leichtman, and White, in press), we examined how an interviewer's hypothesis can influence the accuracy of young children's reports. Preschoolers were exposed to a game-like event and then interviewed 1 month later. The interviewer was given some information about events that might have occurred; some of the information was accurate and some of it was inaccurate. The interviewer was told to interview each child and to use whatever strategies she felt necessary to elicit the most factually accurate report from the child. The information we provided influenced the interviewer's hypotheses about what had transpired in this game, which, in turn, appeared to exercise a powerful influence on the dynamics of the interview, with the interviewer eventually shaping some of the children's reports to be consistent with her hypothesis about what had happened. When the interviewer was accurately informed, she got children to recall correctly 93% of the events that had transpired. It is important to note that the children made no false accusations when the interviewer was correctly informed, that is, they only made "errors of omission." However, when the interviewer was misinformed, 34% of the 3- to 4-year-olds and 18% of the 5- to 6-year-olds corroborated one or more false events that the interviewer erroneously believed had transpired. Thus, in the misinformed condition, the children made "errors of commission." Finally, the children seemingly became more credible as the interview unfolded. Many children initially stated details inconsistently, or with reluctance or even denial, but as the interviewer persisted in asking about nonevents, some abandoned their hesitancy and denials.

Because the interviewers were trained professionals (one was an experienced social worker, the other a nursery school teacher), we feel that the types of interactions observed in this study may be similar to those that occur in interviews between young children and parents, teachers, and professionals who are not given explicit training in how to generate and test alternative hypotheses. Our review of the materials from some publicized cases, such as McMartin, reveals that professional interviewers often steadfastly stick with one line of inquiry even when children continue to deny that the questioned events ever occurred (for examples see Ceci, in press).

Study 2: The effects of stereotype induction and repeated suggestions on young children's reports

A stranger named Sam Stone paid a 2-minute visit to preschoolers (aged 3 to 6) in their day-care center (Leichtman and Ceci, in press). Following Sam Stone's visit, the children were asked for details about the visit on four different occasions over a 10-week period. On each occasion, the interviewer refrained from using suggestive questions; she simply encouraged children to describe Sam Stone's visit in as much detail as possible. One month later, the children were interviewed a fifth time by a new interviewer, who first elicited a free narrative about the visit. Then, using probes, she asked about two "nonevents" which involved Sam Stone doing something to a teddy bear and a book. In reality, he never touched either item.

When asked in the fifth interview, "Did Sam Stone do anything to a book or a teddy bear?" most children accurately replied, "No." Only 10% of the youngest (3- to 4-year-old) children's answers contained claims that Sam Stone did anything to a book or teddy bear. When asked if they actually saw him do anything to the book or teddy bear, as opposed to "thinking they saw him do something," or "hearing he did something," now only 5% of their answers contained claims that anything occurred. Finally, when these 5% were gently challenged ("You didn't really see him do anything to the book/the teddy bear, did you?") only 2.5% still insisted on the reality of the fictional event. None of the older (5- to 6-year-old) children reported that they had seen Sam Stone do either of the fictional actions.

Another group of preschoolers was presented with a stereotype of Sam Stone before he ever visited their school. We did this to mimic the sort of stereotypes that some child witnesses have acquired about actual defendants. (In actual cases, for example, some children have been told repeatedly that the defendant did "bad things.") Each week, beginning a month prior to the visit, the children in our study were told a new Sam Stone story in which he was depicted as very clumsy. For example:

> You'll never guess who visited me last night. [pause] That's right. Sam Stone! And guess what he did this time? He asked to borrow my Barbie and when he was carrying her down the stairs, he tripped and fell and broke her arm. That Sam Stone is always getting into accidents and breaking things!

Following Sam Stone's visit, these children were interviewed four times over a 10-week period. These four interviews contained erroneous

suggestions (e.g., "When Sam Stone ripped that book, was he being silly or was he angry?"). At the fifth interview, these children were asked for a free narrative about Sam's visit and were then asked probing questions about the two nonevents.

In this last interview, 72% of the youngest preschoolers claimed that Sam Stone did one or both misdeeds, a figure that dropped to 44% when they were asked if they actually saw him do these things. Importantly, 21% continued to insist that they saw him do these things, even when gently challenged. The older preschoolers, though more accurate, included 11% of children who insisted they saw him do the misdeeds.[7]

Some researchers have opined that the presence of perceptual details in reports is one of the indicators of an actual memory, as opposed to a confabulated one (Raskin and Yuille 1989; Schooler, Gerhard, and Loftus 1986). In this study, however, the presence of perceptual details was no assurance that the report was accurate. In fact, children in the stereotype plus suggestion condition produced a surprising number of fabricated perceptual details to embellish their false accounts of nonevents (e.g., claiming that Sam Stone took the teddy bear into a bathroom and soaked it in hot water before smearing it with a crayon). The difference in the quality of reports obtained in this study compared to others in the suggestibility literature may reflect the conditions under which the reports were obtained. As mentioned earlier, in most past studies, children's erroneous reports were in response to a single misleading question, posed after a brief delay following the event in question. In contrast, in the present study, children's false reports were a product of repeated erroneous suggestions over a relatively long period of time, coupled with a stereotype that was consistent with these suggestions.

It is one thing to demonstrate that children can be induced to make errors and include perceptual details in their reports, but it is another matter to show that their faulty reports are convincing to others. To examine the believability of the children's reports, we showed videotapes of their final interview to approximately 1,000 researchers and clinicians who work on children's testimonial issues. These researchers and clinicians were told that all the children observed Sam Stone's visit to their day-care centers. They were asked to decide which of the events reported by the children actually transpired and then to rate the overall credibility of each child.

The majority of the professionals were inaccurate. Analyses indicated that these experts—who conduct research on the credibility of children's reports, provide therapy to children suspected of having been abused, or carry out law enforcement interviews with children—generally failed to detect which of the children's claims were accurate, despite being confident in their judgments. Since so many of the children claimed that Sam

Stone ripped the book and/or soiled the bear, it is understandable that many of the experts reasoned that these events must have transpired. But their overall credibility ratings of individual children were also highly inaccurate, with the very children who were least accurate being rated as most accurate. We believe that the highly credible yet inaccurate reports obtained from the children resulted from a combination of repeated interviews with persistent and intense suggestions that built on a set of prior expectations (i.e., a stereotype). In a similar way, it may become difficult to separate credibility from accuracy when children, after repeated interviews, give a formal videotaped interview or testify in court.

Study 3: Influencing children's reports of a pediatric visit

It could be argued that the Sam Stone Study is not relevant to evaluating the reliability of a child witness who reports personally experienced events involving his or her own body, especially when the experience involves some degree of distress. Furthermore, some might argue that the Sam Stone data are not germane to testimony about highly predictable and scripted events. In cases where the event involves a child's own body, is somewhat stressful, and is predictable, it is often thought that children may be less prone to suggestion.

To determine if children could be misled under such circumstances, we examined the influence of postevent suggestions on children's reports about a pediatric visit where they were examined (Ceci, Leichtman, and Bruck, in press). The study had two phases. In the first phase, 5-year-old children visited their pediatrician for an annual check-up. A male pediatrician examined the child. Then the child met a female research assistant who talked about a poster that was hanging on the wall in the examining room. Next, the pediatrician gave the child an oral polio vaccine and a DPT inoculation. Then the research assistant gave the child one of three types of feedback about how the child had acted when receiving the inoculation. One group was given pain-affirming feedback; they were told that it seemed as though the shot really hurt them, but shots hurt even big kids (hurt condition). A second group was given pain-denying information; these children were told that they acted like the shot did not hurt much, and that they were really brave (no-hurt condition). Finally, a third group was merely told that the shot was over (neutral condition). After the feedback, the research assistant gave each child a treat and then read the child a story. One week later, a different assistant visited the children and asked each one to indicate through the use of various rating scales how much he or she had cried during the shot and how much the shot hurt.

The children's reports did not differ as a function of feedback condition. Thus, we found that children could not be influenced to make inaccurate reports concerning significant and stressful procedures involving their own bodies. These results are similar in spirit to those of Saywitz et al. (1991) who also provided children with suggestions about stressful, personally experienced events in a single interview and discovered that children can be quite resistant to erroneous suggestions.

In the second phase of our study, we reinterviewed the children three more times, approximately 1 year after the shot. During these interviews, children were provided with repeated suggestions about how they had acted when they received their inoculations. Thus, as in the first phase of the study, some children were told that they were brave when they got their shot, whereas other children were not given any feedback. (For ethical reasons, we provided only "no-hurt" and "neutral" feedback in this phase of the study. We felt that providing "hurt" feedback might induce false or unpleasant memories about visiting the doctor.) When the children were visited for a fourth time and asked to rate how much the shot had hurt and how much they had cried, there were large suggestibility effects. Those who had been repeatedly told that they had acted brave when they had received their inoculation a year earlier reported significantly less crying and less hurt than children who were given no feedback. Thus, these data indicate that children's reports of stressful events involving their own bodies can be distorted under certain circumstances.

In the second phase of this study, we also tried to mislead children about the people who performed various actions during the original inoculation visit. Some children were falsely reminded on three occasions that the pediatrician gave them treats, showed them the poster, and read them a story. Some children were falsely reminded on three occasions that the research assistant gave them the inoculation and the oral vaccine. Control children were merely reminded that "someone" did these things. Based on the conclusions of other researchers (e.g., Fivush 1993; Melton 1992), it was hypothesized that children should not be suggestible about such important events and that they should be particularly immune to suggestions that incorporate shifts of gender. The male pediatrician had never given them treats or read them a story, and the female research assistant had never performed any medical procedures.

Contrary to these predictions, the children were misled. In the fourth interview, when asked about their doctor's visit in the previous year, 67% of the children (versus 27% of the control children) who were given misleading information about the pediatrician reported that the pediatrician showed them the poster, gave them treats, or read them a story. For children who were falsely told that the research assistant had given them the shot and the vaccine, 50% (versus 16% of the control children) fell sway to at least one of these two suggestions. Interestingly, 38% of the children who were given misleading information that the research assistant gave them the oral vaccine and the inoculation also said that the research assistant had performed other scripted events that not only had never occurred but also had never been suggested (e.g., reporting that the research assistant checked their ears and nose). None of the control children made such inaccurate reports. Thus, our suggestions influenced not only children's reports of personally experienced, salient events, but also their reports for nonsuggested scripted events that were related to the suggested events.

These data indicate that under certain circumstances children's reports concerning stressful events involving their own bodies can be influenced. The two factors that were most critical to this pattern of results were the intensity of the suggestions (i.e., repeating the suggestions over multiple interviews) and their timing (i.e., the long delay between the original event and interview about the event). These same two factors are characteristic of the conditions under which children made allegations of sexual abuse in many of the cases described at the beginning of this report.

The results of this study are consistent with the Sam Stone study even though the nature of the events about which children were misled were different. In the Sam Stone study, repeated suggestions and stereotypes led to convincing fabrications of nonoccurring events. In the pediatrician study, misleading information given in repeated interviews after a long delay following a target event influenced children's reports of personally experienced, salient events.

The suggestibility of anatomically correct dolls. Anatomically correct dolls are frequently used by professionals, including child therapists, police, child protection workers, and attorneys, in interviewing children about suspected sexual abuse. According to recent surveys, 90% of field professionals use anatomical dolls at least occasionally in their investigative interviews with children suspected of having been sexually abused (Boat and Everson 1988; Conte, Sorenson, Fogarty, and Rosa 1991). Although no national figures are available, it appears that expert testimony is often based on observations of children's interactions with such dolls (Mason 1991). We include a discussion here of anatomical dolls, because a number of commentators have raised questions about whether the dolls are suggestive (e.g., McGough, in press; Moss 1988; Raskin and Yuille 1989).

One rationale for the use of anatomical dolls is that they allow children to manipulate objects reminiscent of a sexual event, thereby cuing recall and overcoming language and memory problems. Another rationale is that their use is thought to overcome embarrassment and shyness. The dolls have also been used as projective tests. Some claim that if a child actively avoids these dolls, shows distress if they are undressed, or shows unusual preoccupation with their genitalia, this is consistent with the hypothesis that the child has been abused (see Mason 1991).

The use of anatomically correct dolls has raised skepticism, however, among researchers and professionals alike. Two related arguments are frequently invoked against their use. The first is that the dolls are suggestive, that they encourage the child to engage in sexual play even if the child has not been sexually abused (e.g., Gardner 1989; Terr 1988). A child may insert a finger into a doll's genitalia, for instance, simply because of its novelty or "affordance," much the way a child may insert a finger into the hole in a doughnut. Another criticism is that it is impossible to make firm judgments about children's abuse status on the basis of their doll play because there are no normative data on nonabused children's doll play.

In several studies, researchers have compared the doll play of sexually abused and nonabused children. In addition, there have been a score of studies examining the doll play of nonabused children. Reviews of this literature (Berry and Skinner 1993; Ceci and Bruck 1993; Wolfner, Faust, and Dawes 1993) indicate that many of the studies are methodologically inadequate and do not allow for firm interpretations about the potential usefulness or risks of using dolls. Furthermore, some data indicate that some of the play patterns thought to be characteristic of abused children, such as playing with the dolls in a suggestive or explicit sexual manner, or showing reticence or avoidance when presented with the dolls, also occur in samples of nonabused children (see Bruck and Ceci [1993] for a review). Finally, other data indicate that the dolls, though not suggestive, do not improve reporting—particularly among younger children (e.g., Goodman and Aman 1990).

We have recently completed a study of 3-year-old children's interactions with anatomically correct dolls that highlights each of these results (Bruck, Ceci, Francoeur, and Renick, in press). The children in this study visited their pediatrician for their annual check-up. The pediatrician conducted genital examinations with half the children; the remaining children did not receive genital exams. Immediately after the examination, the child was interviewed by a research assistant. Pointing to the buttocks and then to the genital areas of an anatomically correct doll, the assistant asked each child, "Did the doctor touch you here?" Later in the interview, the child was asked to use the doll to show how the doctor had touched his or her buttocks and genitals.

Children were quite inaccurate across all conditions. Only 45% of the children who received genital examinations correctly answered "Yes" to the questions "Did the doctor touch you here [on buttocks or genitals]?" Only 50% of the children who did not receive genital exams correctly replied "No" to these questions. Further, the children's accuracy did not improve when they were given the dolls and asked to show how the doctor had touched them. Only 25% of the children who had received genital examinations correctly showed how the pediatrician had touched their genitals and buttocks. (A significant number of female subjects in this condition were inaccurate, because they inserted their fingers into the anal or genital cavities of the dolls—which the pediatrician never did.) Only 45% of the children who did not receive genital examinations were accurate in not showing any touching; that is, 55% of the children who did not receive genital examinations falsely showed either genital or anal touching when given the dolls, a pattern most prevalent among the females in this group; 75% of the females who did not receive a genital examination falsely showed that the pediatrician touched their genitals or their buttocks.

With the data on the potential usefulness of dolls equivocal at best, we feel that an important confound in the literature deserves mention: the context for the presentation of the dolls in these research settings is very different from that of actual forensic and clinical settings. Transcripts of therapy sessions with children suspected of having been sexually abused reveal interviewers employing various practices: naming the dolls after defendants; berating the dolls for alleged abuses against the child (e.g., shaking a finger at the male doll who has been named after the defendant and yelling, "You are naughty for hurting Jennifer!"); assuming the role of fantasy characters in doll play; and creating a persistent atmosphere of accusation. In the research settings in which the use of anatomical dolls has been studied, nonabused children were never subjected to such highly suggestive experiences prior to being interviewed with the dolls; they were not given prior motivation to play with the dolls suggestively or aggressively. On the other hand, children who were alleged to have been abused were sometimes exposed to the dolls repeatedly prior to coming to the research setting; perhaps these interviews had involved repeated suggestions from parents and interviewers about various sexual themes. That their play with the dolls differed from that of nonabused children who lacked this prior experience could be attributed to the abused children's prior therapeutic or investigatory experiences, rather than to any inherent way in which they might be expected to play with the dolls.

Unfortunately, no study has examined the suggestive attributes of anatomical dolls, controlling for the preexperimental experience as a potentially serious confound. We simply do not know how nonabused children would behave with the dolls were they to have suggestive experiences prior to the experimental interview.[8] Conversely, we also do not know how abused children play with the dolls in their *first* investigatory interview, since the children in these studies have often been interviewed more than once and some have been exposed to the dolls at least once, prior to the experimental interview.

On the basis of our literature review (Ceci and Bruck 1993), we concluded that the inconsistent findings point to the need for additional research and to the need for the development of explicit procedures to govern the use of anatomically correct dolls by interviewers. Until such research is available, the dolls ought to be used with great caution. Recently, Berry, and Skinner (1993) and Wolfner and his colleagues (1993) were even less supportive of doll use:

> . . . we are left with the conclusion that there is simply no scientific evidence available that would justify clinical or forensic diagnosis of abuse on the basis of the dolls. The common counter is that such play is "just one component" in reaching such a diagnosis based on a "full clinical" picture. . . . [Doll] play cannot be validly used as a component, however, unless it provides incremental validity, and there is virtually no evidence that it does." (Wolfner et al., 9)

Summary of current literature. The studies reviewed here highlight the different paradigms that researchers are now employing to examine children's suggestibility. In our review of this literature (Ceci and Bruck 1993), we found that results of the most recent studies, in contrast to older ones, are somewhat more contradictory about the reliability of children's reports. One can locate studies claiming that young children are as immune to suggestion as older children (e.g., Marin, Holmes, Guth, and Kovac 1979; Saywitz, et al. 1991), and studies claiming that younger children are more suggestible (Ceci, Ross, and Toglia 1987; Cohen and Harnick 1980; King and Yuille 1987). Such mixed results have led to a confusing juxtaposition of headlines: "Study shows children are credible as witnesses." Or, "Research shows child witnesses unable to distinguish reality from fantasy."

A careful reading of the literature suggests, however, that there *are* reliable age differences in suggestibility, with preschoolers' reports more influenced by erroneous suggestions than older children's. In our review of the suggestibility literature, we found 18 studies that compared preschoolers to older children or to adults; in 15 of 18 of these studies, suggestibility was greater among preschoolers than older children or adults (see Table 2 in Ceci and Bruck 1993). To be sure, some researchers attach various caveats to this conclusion. For example, some have claimed that age differences in suggestibility are evident mainly for nonparticipant children, i.e., bystanders (Rudy and Goodman 1991); end for peripheral, nonsalient events (Fivush 1993). And some researchers find that although young children may make some errors in response to suggestive questions with a sexual theme, on the whole they are highly resistant to such questions (e.g., Saywitz et al. 1991; Goodman et al. 1991). Still others have found larger age differences in suggestibility for questions with sexual themes (e.g., Baker-Ward et al., in press; Goodman, Rudy, Bottoms, and Aman 1990) and for questions about salient events (e.g., Cassel and Bjorklund 1993).

Although preschoolers are usually depicted as being the most suggestible, it is important to point out that older children and adults are also suggestible. For example, as described above, 7-year-olds' reports, after 1 year, of their visits to the pediatrician could be quite easily altered through suggestion. Clarke-Stewart, Thompson, and Lepore (reported in Goodman and Clarke Stewart 1991) also found that 7-year-old children's reports and interpretations of a recently experienced event could be easily manipulated through suggestion. Also, Goodman, Wilson, Hazan, and Reed (1989) found that a substantial number of 7- to 10-year-old children incorrectly agreed with interviewers' suggestions about details of an event that occurred 4 years earlier. Many of these misleading suggestions had sexual themes. Finally, suggestions can alter some fundamental aspects of adults' autobiographical memories (Loftus 1993). Thus, we cannot conclude that older children and adults are not suggestible, only that their level of suggestibility is less than that of preschoolers.

We reiterate, however, that the conditions created in these studies differ markedly from those that occur in actual therapy or in law enforcement investigations: these latter two contexts are seldom as sanitized of affect and free of motives as those in the research setting. The real life situation may entail high levels of stress, assaults to the child's body, and loss of control. In some cases, children are interviewed and reinterviewed under emotionally charged circumstances, entailing the use of bribes and threats, and often in the presence of highly distressed parents; under such conditions some children may finally utter reports that are simply consistent with the interviewer's expectations. In the McMartin case, interviewers were alleged to have coerced children's statements by praising them when they reported events that were consistent with the interviewer's beliefs and criticizing them for failing to do so (e.g., calling them "dumb"). Interviewers in both this case and other day-care cases also told children that other children had already disclosed the details of the abuse, thus creating added pressure to assent to suggestions of abuse. Not surprisingly, interviewers in the McMartin case managed to elicit statements of abuse from 369 of nearly 400 children they interviewed (Sauer 1993), although only one child had made claims of abuse prior to the interviews. (This girl's accusations were so bizarre that the prosecution dropped them from the case [Sauer 1993]).

Elsewhere we and others have used more emotionally laden events to examine issues related to the role of affect and bodily touching in producing misinformation effects, including suggestions about being kissed while naked, witnessing parents violate norms, or hurting others to protect loved ones (see Ceci, Leichtman, Putnick, and Nightingale 1993), and experiencing painful and/or embarrassing medical procedures (e.g., Goodman 1993; Ornstein, Baker-Ward, Gordon, and Merritt 1993). Although children's resistance to suggestions are sensitive to all of these factors (and others), no study has attempted to incorporate all of them into a single experiment.

It is highly unlikely, however, that we will ever mimic the assaultive nature of some acts or interviews perpetrated on child victims and witnesses. Thus we are far from being able to provide a definitive conclusion about the reliability of all child witnesses' reports. It is safe to conclude, though, that past pronouncements by some rather extreme advocates on both sides of the bench are simply unfounded. Children are neither as hypersuggestible and coachable as some prodefense advocates have alleged, nor as resistant to suggestions about their own bodies as some proprosecution advocates have claimed. They can be led, under certain conditions, to incorporate false suggestions into their accounts of even intimate bodily touching, but they can also be amazingly resistant to false suggestions and able to provide highly detailed and accurate reports of events that transpired weeks or months ago (e.g., Baker-Ward et al., in press). This mix of suggestibility and resistance to suggestion underscores the need for great caution in accepting the claims of those who would put either a prodefense or proprosecution "spin" on the data.

POLICY IMPLICATIONS

Expert Witnesses

When a child comes to court to testify, this is often because he or she is the sole witness to a crime; this is particularly likely to be the situation in sexual abuse cases where the child is not only the sole witness, but there may be no physical evidence of abuse. The problem of uncorroborated testimony is compounded by the fact that the testimony of children may at times seem to lack credibility. As a result, both the prosecution and defense may call physicians, mental health professionals, and social scientists to serve as expert witnesses. In this section, we discuss the qualifications and roles of mental health professionals and social scientists who serve as expert witnesses in cases involving child witnesses, particularly in cases of alleged sexual abuse.

According to legal views (see Mason 1991; Myers 1993), these expert witnesses can be classified into two categories. (1) The first type, usually a mental health professional, is asked either to provide a generic description of the behavioral symptoms associated with sexual abuse, or to provide an opinion as to whether or not a particular child was abused. In the latter instance, the expert may have formulated his or her opinion based on therapy with the child or an assessment of a child's behavior; in some cases, the expert witness may have had no contact with the child in question. This type of expert is also frequently called upon to rehabilitate the credibility of a child witness who has been attacked by the defense, e.g., for delayed reporting. In this situation, the expert witness explains that, though such behaviors are not themselves diagnostic of abuse, it is not unusual for abused children to display a range of behaviors, such as recantation, delay of reporting, and inconsistent reporting. (2) The second type of expert witness is called to review the scientific literature on issues relevant to the credibility of child witnesses. This expert may cover various topics, including the literature on suggestibility as well as that on cognitive, emotional, and social development.

Although one might conclude that the research on children's suggestibility, discussed in this report, has policy implications for only the second type of witness, we argue that knowledge of this research is relevant to the professional qualifications and testimony of the first type of expert witness as well. The mental health professional who testifies on the diagnosis of sexual abuse or who describes to a court the symptoms associated with sexual abuse must also take into consideration competing hypotheses that might explain why the child in question, or children in general, demonstrate particular symptoms or make allegations of sexual abuse. One of the alternative hypotheses to be considered is that the particular child's allegations or symptoms have resulted from suggestive influences of the sort described above. It is important for the expert to consider such an alternative, because those same symptoms associated with sexual abuse (delayed reporting, retraction of the allegation, inconsistent accounts, inappropriate knowledge of sexual behavior, or unusual play with anatomically correct dolls) have been observed in nonabused children who have been exposed to suggestive influences (see Berliner and Conte 1993; Kendall-Tackett, Williams, and Finkelhor 1993, for recent reviews of the literature).

Diagnosing child sexual abuse is thus a complex task requiring experience with sexually abused children and knowledge of both the clinical and the suggestibility and developmental literature. Experts who testify on such matters should be well-versed in these domains (Myers 1993).

Some legal scholars have pointed out, however, that little experience and training is required of expert witnesses who provide testimony to rehabilitate the child witness. Myers (1993) writes that because this type of testimony is thought straightforward and simple, "a child protection services worker with six months on the job and knowledge of three or four pertinent articles is qualified to provide rehabilitative testimony on recantation and delayed reporting" (p. 177). We argue that this witness should have a more thorough knowledge of the scientific literature on both the indicators of child sexual abuse and the literature on suggestibility.

The second type of expert witness, those who testify about the scientific literature on suggestibility and child development, does not require clinical experience. However, this expert must have a thorough knowledge of the research literature germane to his or her testimony.

What the expert witness on children's suggestibility should tell the court. We come now to the question that has vexed any social scientist who ever dreamed (or had nightmares) of being called upon to serve as an expert witness or to prepare an amicus brief for an appellate court on children's testimony, namely, what does our present state of scientific knowledge permit us to say about the reliability of the testimony of the child witness? Having acknowledged the complexities of the research, we hold that expert witnesses, regardless of whether they are testifying for the prosecution or for the defense, should cover several points based on the literature:

1. There are reliable age effects in children's suggestibility, with preschoolers being more vulnerable than older children to a variety of factors that contribute to unreliable reports.

2. Although young children are often accurate reporters, some do make mistakes—particularly when they undergo suggestive interviews: and these errors can relate not only to peripheral details, but also to salient, predictable events that involve their own bodies.

3. Measures can be taken to lessen the risk of suggestibility effects. To date, the factors that we know most about concern the nature of the interview itself—its frequency, degree of suggestiveness, and demand characteristics.

- A child's report is less likely to be distorted, for example, after one interview than after several interviews (the term "interviews" here includes informal conversations between parents and child about the target events).
- Interviewers who ask nonleading questions, who do not have a confirmatory bias (i.e., an attachment to a single hypothesis), and who do not repeat close-ended, yes/no questions within or across interviews, are more likely to obtain accurate reports from children.
- Interviewers who are patient, nonjudgmental, and who do not attempt to create demand characteristics (e.g., by providing subtle rewards for certain responses) are likely to elicit the best quality reports from young children.

Thus, at one extreme we can have more confidence in a child's spontaneous statements made prior to any attempt by an adult to elicit what they suspect may be the truth. At the other extreme, we are more likely to be concerned when a child has made a statement after prolonged, repeated, suggestive interviews. Unfortunately, most cases lie between these extremes and require a case-by-case analysis.

4. Finally, it is also important that the court appreciate the complexity of the interrelationships of the factors affecting children's suggestibility. As in most areas of social science, effects are rarely as straightforward as one might wish. Even though suggestibility effects may be robust, the effects are not universal. Results vary between studies, and children's behavior varies within studies. Thus, even in studies with pronounced suggestibility effects, there are always some children who are highly resistant to suggestion. Some studies may show reliable age differences in suggestibility even though the majority of both younger and older children did not succumb to suggestion. We have seen this in our own studies as well as in transcripts of forensic and therapeutic interviews: in some cases, no matter how much an interviewer may try to suggest that an event occurred, some children will consistently resist and not incorporate the interviewer's suggestion or point of view. On the other side, although suggestibility effects tend to be most dramatic after prolonged and repeated interviewing, some children incorporate suggestions quickly, even after one short interview (e.g., Clarke-Stewart et al. 1989, as reported in Goodman and Clarke-Stewart 1991). No facile conclusion can be presented to courts on this matter.

Ideal vs. Actual Expert Witnesses. The "model" expert witness who comes forward to testify on issues related to children's suggestibility should be someone who has thoroughly reviewed the pertinent literature and who can present the relevant facts in a balanced manner to the triers of fact. This requirement is not an easy one to meet: this research area is developing rapidly and is riddled with a host of complex issues that necessitate a broad understanding of design, statistics, and theory not likely possessed by someone outside the research community.

Unfortunately, many who serve as expert witnesses do not have this breadth of knowledge. We have reviewed many examples of testimony by so-called experts that appeared to have been based on incomplete and at times dubious knowledge. Nowhere in their testimony is there any hint of the complexities that ought to have tamed the witness's statements to the jury. In the worst cases, the testimony was actually opposite to what we know to be the best evidence from systematic research. All too often such an expert appears in court strictly because his or her opinion is consistent with that of the defense or the prosecution, rather than because the witness is truly knowledgeable about the field. Such testimony can be a disservice to the aims of justice, not to mention to the professions these expert witnesses represent.

Although the above discussion pertains mainly to the social scientist who testifies about children's suggestibility, our review of case material and the literature suggests that these same criticisms can be made of some experts who testify about the behavioral symptoms associated with sexual abuse. Mason (1991) analyzed 122 civil and criminal appellate court cases in which expert witnesses testified about child sexual abuse. She found that experts frequently presented testimony that was either internally inconsistent or contradicted by other experts. For example, 14 experts cited age-inappropriate knowledge of sex and sexual preoccupations as characteristics of an abused child, whereas 6 experts asserted that naivete and aversion to sexual matters characterized the sexually abused child. Some experts maintained that consistent accounts of events were important indicators of sexual abuse, whereas others maintained the opposite, that sexually abused children are characterized by their inconsistent accounts. Mason also reported that appellate courts tend to take expert testimony at face value; that they rarely raise questions about the testimony's acceptance by the scientific community, or about the credentials of the mental health professional presenting expert testimony.

The response of the courts in this study reveals that there is a critical gulf between the scientific community and the judiciary. Judges are not willing and probably not able to critically evaluate the reliability of the testimony offered (Mason 1991, p. 205).

An example of the unscientific nature of some experts' testimony is illustrated by *State of New Jersey* v. *Kelly Michaels*. Michaels was a preschool teacher convicted on 115 counts of sexual offenses involving

20 children, and sentenced to 47 years in prison. The expert witness for the prosecution testified that conduct of all but one of the child witnesses was consistent with having been sexually abused. She did not seriously consider the possible effects of numerous suggestive influences on the children's testimony, which had included persistent, aggressive, and suggestive interviews with children who initially denied that anything had happened. In this case, the appellate court did challenge the testimony of the expert witness, reversing Michael's conviction (after she had spent 5 years in prison), in part because the expert's testimony concerning the child behavioral indicators of abuse did not have acceptance within the relevant scientific community.

Problems with expert testimony are endemic to our legal system and to those of other countries whose codes have been derived from common law. As far back as one can check, jurists and laypersons alike have viewed expert witnesses as untrustworthy, as inclined to put a "spin" on interpretations of the data toward the side that hired them:

> Perhaps the testimony which least deserves credit with a jury is that of skilled witnesses. . . . It is often quite surprising to see with what facility, and to what extent, their views can be made to correspond with the wishes and interests of the parties who call them. (Judge John Pitt Taylor, 1858, p. 65–69, as quoted in Gross 1991)

These views continue to be expressed by American jurists:

> To put it bluntly, in many professions service as an expert witness is not generally considered honest work. . . . Experts in fields see lawyers as unprincipled manipulators of their disciplines, and lawyers and experts alike see expert witnesses—those members of the learned professions who will consort with lawyers—as whores. (Gross 1991, 1115)

And by British jurists:

> Expert evidence is sometimes given by people whose level of knowledge seems lamentably low. A number of the recent, and best known scandals show this. . . . How does this come about? In the first place, I think it is because our present system provides no systematic quality control. Broadly speaking, anyone can be an expert witness, provided they have some relevant knowledge, and nothing whatever is done to see that only the best people are used. To be allowed to give expert evidence, witnesses must satisfy the judge that they have some practical experience, or some professional qualifications; but that is all. No minimum standards are laid down. The only test is opposing counsel's

cross-examination; and, in a jury trial, this may be designed to score clever points, rather than to test whether they (i.e., the experts) are really good at their job. (Spencer 1992, 216–17)

The Relationship of Research to Clinical Practice

That the judicial community is unwilling or unable to evaluate critically the testimony of social science experts and mental health professionals reflects to some degree an incomplete or inaccurate understanding of the relevant knowledge base, but it also reflects, in the case of the reliability of children's reports, a gulf between clinical practice and social science research. As a result, in those cases where clinical practice is not informed by research findings, clinicians and social scientists may present diametrically opposite expert testimony on the very same topic. Two examples illustrate this breach between the two perspectives.

The first involves a survey of 212 mental health professionals about their assessment and validation procedures in sexual abuse cases (Conte et al. 1991). Of relevance to the present report, it was found that children had already been asked to tell their story an average of 2.3 times before talking to the professional respondent; only 27% of respondents indicated that they were the first person to talk with the child about the abuse. In discussing these findings, however, the authors do not seriously consider the impact of such interviewing practices:

> Little is currently known about the effects of such prior interviewing on the child's willingness to engage with yet another adult or on the quality of information obtained from the child. While some professionals are likely to make much of the possible "contamination" that these prior interviewers have on the child's reports, there are virtually no data currently available suggesting that adults have the power through interviewing techniques to alter fundamentally a child's understanding of and ability to describe what events did or did not take place. (433)

We hope that this report will begin to inform professionals that such data are available.

A second example that illustrates the gulf between practice and research concerns the use of anatomically correct dolls. Many professionals have no formal training or experience in the use of the dolls (Boat and Everson 1988) and may view some interactions of children with the dolls (e.g., placing a finger in the doll's anal cavity, tugging on its penis, or avoiding the dolls altogether) as indicative of sexual abuse, even though there is no scientific support that such interactions are diagnostic of abuse. In a recent survey, for example, only 16% of mental health and law professionals stated that avoidance of the dolls was normal, while 80% rated digital penetration as abnormal (Kendall-Tackett 1991). Yet, as reviewed above, such behaviors are commonly observed in nonabused children.

Of more concern, perhaps, is the American Psychological Association's (1991) current position on the use of the dolls. The following statement was issued by APA's Council of Representatives:

> Neither the dolls nor their use are standardized or accompanied by normative data. . . . We urge continued research in quest of more and better data regarding the stimulus properties of such dolls and normative behavior of abused and nonabused children. . . . Nevertheless, doll-centered assessment of children, when used as part of a psychological evaluation and interpreted by experienced and competent examiners, may be the best available practical solution for a pressing and frequent clinical problem. (APA 1991, 1)

The APA's policy position seems contradictory in its noting first that there are no standardized methods for doll interviews or normative data on nonabused or abused children's doll play, but then asserting that experienced interviewers may nevertheless find doll-centered assessment the best available method for evaluating children suspected of having been sexually abuse. Even if one assumes that experienced examiners can avoid making false inferences from children's doll play, and that such doll play can provide important clinical insights not obtainable from other sources, the APA should nevertheless codify this expert knowledge in such a way that researchers can accurately assess the incremental validity of doll-based assessments. Our reading of the literature is that at present such knowledge is more illusory than real (see Wolfner et al.'s criticism [1993] of the lack of incremental validity of doll-based assessments). Even if anatomical dolls are used as just one part of an assessment, other aspects of so-called "developmentally sensitive assessments" (e.g., play therapy, role playing, techniques that induce visually-guided imagery, self-empowerment training) may interact with the doll use to produce false positive assertions of abuse. Because the appropriate research has yet to be done, it is shortsighted to assume (as some experts have testified in court) that the dolls do not present reliability risks. Although it could be the case that the use of dolls does provide important information, it could also be the case that this method leads to unacceptable levels of false positive reports. Only research will tell.

The fact remains that clinicians and mental health professionals face many dilemmas and choices in providing for children who may have been sexually abused. Often the favored choice may conflict with forensic procedures. Let us consider one scenario: a child has been removed from her home as a result of a report of sexual abuse and has been placed in emergency foster care, separated from her family, friends, and school. The child is greatly distressed and in need of immediate counseling. The forensic interviews will not be completed for several months. In light of some research findings that children's reports are likely to be more accurate if interviews (which include therapy sessions) concerning the alleged abuse are held to a minimum until after the forensic interview takes place, when should the mental health professional begin therapy with the child? How can we avoid the twin dangers of, on the one hand, putting the child's emotional needs on hold until after the forensic interviews and, on the other hand, providing counseling that can be potentially damaging to the veracity of the child's report? We know of no easy answers.

Given the pressing needs of both sides in a criminal dispute to prepare, investigate, and often reinterview, no amount of child-friendly court procedures can totally alleviate some of the problems associated with children's testimony. Yet, perhaps there are ways of providing therapeutic support that lessen the likelihood of tainting the child's report. Therapeutic procedures that involve visually-guided imagery in the context of the abuse-related allegations might be avoided, as might forms of therapy that make contact with the abusive scenario (e.g., self-empowerment training, role playing, doll use, hypnosis).

Although some might argue that it would be too restrictive and ultimately damaging to a child's development were therapists to avoid potentially suggestive techniques, it could also be argued that employing such interventions simply constitutes too great a risk. On the one hand, if the defendant is innocent, such techniques could promote and reinforce false allegations. On the other hand, if the defendant is guilty, these interventions may end up discrediting the child's testimony, with defense attorneys arguing that the child's reports are the product of highly suggestive therapeutic techniques. Finally, on the empirical side, we are unaware of any persuasive treatment-outcome validity research indicating that suggestive techniques are necessary in therapy to achieve a positive mental health outcome for children suspected of being abused. Given this state of knowledge, clinicians might consider limiting interventions to nonsuggestive techniques in therapy until young clients have given sworn statements; such an approach may afford minimal danger to the child.

Professional Organizations as Ethical Gatekeepers

Professional organizations could help resolve some of the problems we have been discussing by making ethics codes for expert witnesses more explicit. Existing codes for expert witnesses of the organizations that represent various constituencies (psychology, social work, pediatrics) tend to be weak and ill-defined—in part because "expert witness" is an ill-defined legal concept.[9] The Federal Rules of Evidence 702 states that if scientific, technical, or other specialized knowledge will assist a fact finder in understanding evidence, then a witness may be regarded as an expert by virtue of his or her knowledge, skill, experience, training, or education. This rule construes expertise broadly enough to cover all fields, including emerging areas within fields, and is constrained by two other Federal Rules of Evidence (401 and 403), which specify that the expert testimony must be relevant. Together, these Federal Rules allow virtually anyone who possesses an advanced degree, or who has some clinical experience, to offer expert testimony on children's credibility, even though the expert may have scant knowledge of the current scientific findings. As a result, experts testifying in child sexual abuse cases have offered totally opposite interpretations of children's behavior and testimony (see Mason [1991] above).

To some extent, weak ethics codes also reflect the ascendancy of guild interests. Because no constituency wants to be excluded from activities that involve service to others (at times for financial gain), its representatives ensure that its members' role is not diminished by ethics code language. Ethics codes tend to be explicit about matters that are relatively benign to the group as a whole (e.g., rules for preparing reports, or statements regarding generic conflicts of interest), but vague about matters that could adversely affect the entire membership (e.g., defining precisely what an expert should know in order to testify about children's suggestibility, or what it means to conduct a good interview). Thus, for example, when psychologists look to their own specialty guidelines and general ethics codes for guidance about the credentials or conduct of an expert witness, they find little help other than enjoinders to act responsibly, to be informed, and to aspire to the norms that guide a professional toward the highest ideals. Consider some of the sections of the most recent APA code of ethics revision (Ethical Principles 1992) relevant to forensic services:

- Psychologists appropriately take into account the ways in which a prior relationship might affect their professional objectivity or opinions and disclose potential conflict to the parties. (Section 705)

- Psychologists who engage in . . . professional activities maintain a reasonable level of awareness of scientific and professional information in their fields. (General Standards 1.5)
- Psychologists rely on scientifically and professionally derived knowledge when making scientific or professional judgments. (General Standards 1.6)
- In addition, psychologists base their forensic work on appropriate knowledge of a competence in the areas underlying such work. (General Standards 7.1)
- In forensic testimony and reports, psychologists . . . describe fairly the bases for their testimony and conclusions [and] whenever necessary to avoid misleading, acknowledge the limits of their data or conclusions. (General Standards 7.4).

However well intended, these statements taken together lend themselves to ambiguous interpretation. For example, can a psychologist, in testifying about children's suggestibility, rely on *either* research knowledge *or* clinical experience? Can a therapist be expected to avoid a conflict of interest and maintain sufficient objectivity to serve as an expert witness when he or she has had extended contact with the child? (Apparently so. Mason's analysis [1991] showed that many expert witnesses who testified in abuse cases were often the child's therapist, and only 13% of all experts had no prior relationship with the child.)

Missing from ethics codes and specialty guidelines for expert witnesses (e.g., Committee on Ethical Guidelines 1991) is language that would specify that they bring to court more than an advanced degree, a supervised internship which had brought them into contact with sexually abused children, or other clinical experience whereby they had occasionally seen sexually abused clients in their practice. An expert testifying on children's suggestibility, and more generally on the credibility of child witnesses' should be intimately familiar with the systematic scholarship on the topic. Although it is not necessary for this expert to be a researcher, he or she needs to be at least a critical consumer of the research literature.

The failure of professional organizations to constitute and then to enforce principled guidelines has serious consequences. First, it can undermine the judicial system's confidence in the capacity of professionals to offer reliable testimony. More important, in criminal proceedings where the defendant faces incarceration, or in civil proceedings where the future placement of the child is at stake, the legitimacy of the expert's testimony can be critical to preserving the rights of both the child and the defendant.

To conclude, enforcement mechanisms are needed to ensure that expert testimony can be evaluated for its scientific merit. Until such mechanisms are openly advertised to all consumers of legal services, enjoinders to "stay informed" will probably do little to ebb the sorts of abuses reported by Mason (1991) and Spencer (1992). Because of their vagueness, professional ethics codes will be implemented more often in the breach than in the letter.

CONCLUSION

We have argued that the investigation of child sexual abuse allegations and expert testimony addressing such investigations are fraught with problems. Scientists have begun to contribute important insights to these problems, though clearly more research is needed. We have provided some troubling examples of how research has failed to inform practice, and how experts often go beyond what current scientific findings seem to warrant.

To be sure, those charged with investigating, reporting, and treating suspected child maltreatment face immense obstacles. These professionals are deeply aware of the pervasiveness of child sexual abuse, and the all too frequent ineffectiveness of prosecution. They know better than most the emotionally wrenching sequelae of abuse, especially intrafamilial abuse. And they are keenly aware that the evidence from research must always be tempered by real-world considerations, no matter what the "significance level" or "effect size" of a finding. Thus, many pressing, unresolved issues concerning the interviewing and treatment of individual children remain.

We presented a scenario highlighting the difficult task faced by many professionals on a daily basis—how to promote two goals that often conflict: how to provide for the child's mental health needs while simultaneously protecting the legal rights of the accused. While we must strive to uncover abuse, we must eschew interview processes that may promote false beliefs, fantasies, or fabrications—regardless of the nature of the initiating event. Just as we have argued above that it is unethical for social scientists to institute experimental manipulations that might change the fundamental nature of children's emotionally salient autobiographical memories, it is equally indefensible for therapists or forensic interviewers to cause such changes. The results of persistent erroneous suggestions and of failures to test alternative hypotheses can be lasting, as evidenced by the experiences and reactions of the child witnesses in the McMartin trials, described at the beginning of this report:

> No one who saw them will soon forget the frenzied faces of . . . former McMartin pupils (who) had spent their last six years—fully half their lives—instructed in the faith that they had been subjected, at ages 4 and 5, to unspeakable sexual horrors; this belief they had come to hold as the defining truth of their lives and identities. It is not surprising that these children should have wept and raved when the verdict was handed down denying all that they believed in. (Rabinowitz 1990, 63)

NOTES

1. In view of the public outcry against the seeming refusal by jurors to believe the children, posttrial statements by these same jurors about believing some of the children's claims may have been self-serving. One close observer of the trial suggested this possibility to us.

2. Several have been the focus of books. The Wee Care case involving Kelly Michaels was the source for several books, including *Naptime* (Manshel 1990) and *Not My Child* (Crowley 1990). Other cases have been detailed in television documentaries (e.g., the Little Rascals case involving Bob Kelly and five other defendants, which was the focus of three "Frontline" documentaries, e.g., *Loss of Innocence*); movies (e.g., the Country Walk day-care case in Miami, which was the basis of the movie *Unspeakable Acts*); and magazine and newspaper articles (e.g., Nathan 1987; Rabinowitz 1990).

3. Although this report focuses on the interviewing of alleged child sexual abuse victims, the literature reviewed is equally important to nonabuse cases that involve the child witness. Sexual abuse is of special interest, because this category of complaints appears to represent the single largest class of actions that eventuate in criminal court testimony (as opposed to neglect cases or custody disputes which are largely litigated in juvenile and family court systems). Our discussion centers on nursery school cases, because, although these cases represent only a small proportion of sexual abuse complaints, in absolute numbers they involve a large number of children (in the McMartin case, for instance, interviewers under contract to the State of California alleged the abuse of 369 children [Sauer 1993]); moreover, day-care cases are relevant to the more general testimonial issues found in many nondaycare cases (i.e., repeated suggestive questioning, interviewer stereotypes, failure to test alternative hypotheses). Finally, because of their visibility, daycare cases are often more extensively documented.

4. Cases are classified as *substantiated* or *indicated* based on how consistent the evidence from an investigation is with abuse; in most states this is a matter of case worker judgment. States usually have a two-tiered system of classifying investigations as either substantiated/founded, on the one hand, or unsubstantiated/not founded, on the other. Some states use a third tier that is interme-

diate between substantiated and unsubstantiated, namely, "indicated." This term is given to cases in which the agency doing the investigation may have "reason to suspect" that abuse occurred, but the level of evidence does not rise to the level required for the designation "substantiated." The lowest level of evidence needed to substantiate a case is "some credible evidence," which is used by 18 states, while the highest level of evidence needed is "preponderance of evidence," which is used by 12 states. An intermediate level of evidence is used by an additional 12 states, and the remaining states use idiosyncratic terminology (see Figure 5 of National Center of Child Abuse and Neglect 1993, 28). Thus, lower levels of evidence increase the possibility that, upon further investigation, a subsequent determination may be made that insufficient evidence exists to designate the presence of abuse. For these reasons it is important not to use the terms "substantiation," "indication," and "validation" interchangeably.

5. Some have suggested that these two figures be summed to 8%. This assumes, however, that there were different children in the two categories, which is not clear from the published report. The breakdown reported here is that reported by Saywitz et al. (1990).

6. Courts have taken notice of the need to distinguish between an interviewer whose view reflects a strongly held expectation versus the interviewer who possesses relevant background information. For example, in *Idaho* v. *Wright* the Court accepted the argument contained in an amicus brief that "there is an important distinction between preconceptions that can cloud judgment, and background information that is needed for thorough evaluation of sexual abuse" (Amicus Brief to the Supreme Court in *Idaho* v. *Wright,* No. 89-260, p. 96).

7. These data reveal an interesting disjunction with the reasoning that when children retract earlier claims of sexual abuse, this is indicative, if not diagnostic, of a truthful original report (Sgroi 1982; Summit 1983). In this study, it was often the case that children originally made false allegations, which they then, with gentle persuasion, recanted. Were this finding applicable to situations that are abuse-related—and we make no such claim here—it could be suggested that retraction might also be consistent with an erroneous original report.

8. Pilot data from one subject addresses this question. A $3\frac{1}{2}$-year-old nonabused girl was examined by a pediatrician. She was not given a genital examination. Immediately after the examination, when interviewed by the experimenter, she correctly said that the doctor had not touched her genitals or buttocks. Furthermore, when shown an anatomically correct doll and told to show how the doctor had touched her genitals and buttocks, she correctly stated that he had not touched her. Three days later, the same child was shown the anatomically correct doll and asked to show all the things that the doctor did to her in her previous visit. This time, she inserted a stick into the vagina of the doll. Upon further questioning, however, she said that the doctor did not do this. Three more days later, the child was asked to use the anatomically correct doll to show her father everything that had happened at the examination. This time, she hammered a stick into the doll's vagina and then inserted a toy earscope into the doll's anus. When asked if this really happened, she said "Yes

it did." When her father and the experimenter both tried to debrief her with such statements as, "Your doctor doesn't do those things to little girls. You were just fooling. We know he didn't do those things," the subject clung tenaciously to her claims. Thus, for this one subject, repeated exposure to the doll, with minimal suggestions, resulted in highly sexualized play. It is critical that such a finding be replicated with a large, diverse sample to determine if this child's response is representative of nonabused children.

9. For example, most courts disallow expert testimony that speaks directly to the *ultimate question,* that is, the defendant's guilt or innocence. In some courts, however, expert witnesses are permitted to testify as to whether they believe the child was abused (see Myers 1992). One would think that an expert's opinion that a particular child was abused might have the same effect as speaking to the child's credibility. This leads to confusion even among the legal scholars whom we have consulted. with one remarking that the courts' thinking regarding this issue is little more than "wordplay."

REFERENCES

American Psychological Association. 1991. *Statement on the use of anatomically detailed dolls in forensic evaluations.* Washington, D.C.: APA Council of Representatives.

Andrews, J. A. 1964. The evidence of children. *Criminal Law Review* 64: 769–77.

Baker-Ward, L., B. Gordon, P. A. Ornstein, D. Larus, and P. Clubb. In press. Young children's long-term retention of a pediatric examination. *Child Development.*

Batterman-Faunce, J. M., and G. S. Goodman. 1993. Effects of context on the accuracy and suggestibility of child witnesses. In *Child victims and child witnesses: Understanding and improving testimony,* ed. G. S. Goodman and B. L. Bottoms, 301–30. New York: Guilford.

Berliner, L., and J. R. Conte. 1993. Sexual abuse evaluations: Conceptual and empirical obstacles. *Child Abuse and Neglect* 17: 111–25.

Berry, K., and L. G. Skinner. 1993. Anatomically detailed dolls and the evaluations of child sexual abuse allegations: Psychometric considerations. *Law and Human Behavior* 17: 399–422.

Besharov, D. 1991. Child abuse and neglect reporting and investigation: Policy guidelines for decision making. *Child and Youth Services* 15: 35–50.

Binet, A. 1900. *La suggestibilité.* Paris: Schleicher Freres.

Boat, B., and M. Everson. 1988. The use of anatomical dolls among professionals in sexual abuse evaluations. *Child Abuse and Neglect* 12: 171–86.

Brown, M. R. 1926. *Legal psychology.* Indianapolis: Bobbs Merrill.

Bruck, M., S. J. Ceci, E. Francoeur, and R. Barr. In press. "I hardly cried when I got my shot!": Influencing children's response about a visit to their pediatrician. *Child Development.*

Cassel, W. S., and D. F. Bjorklund. 1993. *Tell me about. . . . Don't you remember . . . ? Isn't it true that . . . ? Developmental patterns of eyewitness responses to increasingly suggestive questions.* Unpublished manuscript, Florida Atlantic University, Boca Raton, Florida.

Ceci, S. J. In press. Cognitive and social factors in children's testimony. In *APA Master Lectures: Psychology and the Law,* ed. B. Sales and G. VandenBos. Washington, D.C.: American Psychological Association.

Ceci, S. J., and U. Bronfenbrenner. 1991. On the demise of everyday memory: The rumors of my death are greatly exaggerated. *American Psychologist* 46: 27–31.

Ceci, S. J., and M. Bruck. 1993. The suggestibility of the child witness. *Psychological Bulletin* 113: 403–39.

Ceci, S. J., M. Leichtman, M. Putnick, and N. Nightingale. 1993. Age differences in suggestibility. In *Child witnesses, child abuse, and public policy,* ed. D. Cicchetti and S. Toth, 117–38. Norwood, N.J.: Ablex.

Ceci, S. J., M. D. Leichtman, and M. Bruck. In press. The suggestibility of children's eyewitness reports: Methodological issues. In *Memory development: State of the art and future directions,* ed. F. Weinert and W. Schneider. Englewood Cliffs, N.J.: Erlbaum.

Ceci, S. J., M. Leichtman, and T. White. In press. Interviewing preschoolers: Remembrance of things planted. In *The child witness in context: Cognitive, social, and legal perspectives,* ed. D. P. Peters. Holland: Kluwer.

Ceci, S. J., D. Ross, and M. Toglia. 1987. Age differences in suggestibility: Psycholegal implications. *Journal of Experimental Psychology: General* 117: 38–49.

Chadbourn, J. 1978. *Wigmore on evidence.* Boston: Little, Brown.

Charlier, T., and S. Downing. 1988. Justice abused: A 1980's witch hunt. *Memphis Commercial Appeal,* January 17-22.

Clarke-Stewart, A., W. Thompson, and S. Lepore. 1989. *Manipulating children's interpretations through interrogation.* Paper presented at the biennial meeting of the Society for Research in Child Development, Kansas City, April.

Cohen, R. L. 1975. Children's testimony and hearsay evidence. *Law Reform Commission of Canada. Report on evidence.* Ottawa: Information Canada.

Cohen, R. L., and M. A. Harnick. 1980. The susceptibility of child witnesses to suggestion. *Law and Human Behavior* 4: 201–10.

Committee on Ethical Guidelines for Forensic Psychologists. 1991. Specialty guidelines for forensic psychologists. *Law and Human Behavior* 15: 655–65.

Conte, J. R., E. Sorenson, L. Fogarty, and J. D. Rosa. 1991. Evaluating children's reports of sexual abuse: Results from a survey of professionals. *Journal of Orthopsychiatry* 78: 428–32.

Coy v. *Iowa,* 108 S. Ct. 2798 (1988).

Crowley, P. 1990. *Not my child: A mother confronts her child's sexual abuse.* New York: Doubleday.

Daro, D., and L. Mitchel. 1990. *Current trends in child abuse reporting and fatalities: The results of the 1989 annual 50 states survey.* Washington, D.C.: National Commission for the Prevention of Child Abuse.

Dawes, R. 1992. The importance of alternative hypothesis and hypothetical counterfactuals in gene social science. *The General Psychologist* (Spring): 2–7.

Doris, J. 1993. Child witness conference. Supplemental RFP Children's Justice and Assistance Act funds. Submitted by the Family Life Development Center, Cornell University.

Ethical principles of psychologists and code of conduct. 1992. *American Psychologist* 47: 1597–1611.

Federal Rules of Evidence, Rule 702.

Fischer, M. A. 1988. Flip-flop: Why four years later the press is taking a strikingly different approach to the McMartin preschool scandal. *Los Angeles Magazine* 33: 85–94.

Fivush, R. 1993. Developmental perspectives on autobiographical recall. In *Child victims and child witnesses: Understanding and improving testimony,* ed. G. S. Goodman and B. L. Bottoms, 1–24. New York: Guilford.

Flin, R. 1993. Hearing and testing children's evidence. In *Child victims and child witnesses: Understanding and improving testimony,* ed. G. S. Goodman and B. L. Bottoms, 279–300. New York: Guilford.

Gardner, R. 1989. *Sex abuse hysteria: Salem witch trials revisited.* Longwood, N.J.: Creative Therapeutics Press.

Glaser, D., and C. Collins. 1989. The response of young, non-sexually abused children to anatomically correct dolls. *Journal of Child Psychology and Psychiatry* 30: 547–60.

Goodman, G. S. 1993. *Children's memory for stressful events: Theoretical and developmental considerations.* Paper presented at the biennial meeting of the Society for Research in Child Development, New Orleans, March.

Goodman, G. S., and C. Aman. 1990. Children's use of anatomically detailed dolls to recount an event. *Child Development* 61: 1859–71.

Goodman, G. S., and A. Clarke-Stewart. 1991. Suggestibility in children's testimony: Implications for child sexual abuse investigations. In *The suggestibility of children's recollections,* ed. J. L. Doris, 92–105. Washington, D.C.: American Psychological Association.

Goodman, G. S., J. E. Hirschman, D. Hepps, and L. Rudy. 1991. Children's memory for stressful events. *Merrill Palmer Quarterly* 37: 109–58.

Goodman, G. S., L. Rudy, B. Bottoms, and C. Aman. 1990. Children's concerns and memory: Issues of ecological validity in the study of children's eyewitness testimony. In *Knowing and remembering in young children,* ed. R. Fivush and J. Hudson, 249–84. New York: Cambridge University Press.

Goodman, G. S., M. E. Wilson, C. Hazan, and R. S. Reed. 1989. *Children's testimony nearly four years after an event.* Paper presented at the annual meeting of the Eastern Psychological Association, Boston, April.

Gray, E. 1993. *Unequal justice: The prosecution of child sexual abuse.* New York: Macmillan.

Gross, S. R. 1991. Expert evidence. *Wisconsin Law Review* 1113, 1114–1231.

Harvard Law Review Notes. 1985. The testimony of child sex abuse victims in sex abuse prosecutions: Two legislative innovations. *Harvard Law Review* 98: 806–27.

Idaho v. *Wright,* 110 S. Ct. 3139 (1990).

Kendall-Tackett, K. 1991. *Professionals' standards of "normal" behavior with anatomical dolls and factors that influence these standards.* Paper presented at the biennial meeting of the Society for Research in Child Development, Seattle, April.

Kendall-Tackett, K. A., L. M. Williams, and D. Finkelhor. 1993. Impact of sexual abuse on children: A review and synthesis of recent empirical studies. *Psychological Bulletin* 113: 164–80.

King, M., and J. Yuille. 1987. Suggestibility and the child witness. In *Children's eyewitness memory,* ed. S. J. Ceci, M. Toglia, and D. Ross, 24–35. New York: Springer-Verlag.

Leichtman, M. D., and S. J. Ceci. Revision under review. The effect of stereotypes and suggestions on preschoolers' reports. *Developmental Psychology.*

Lipmann, O. 1911. Pedagogical psychology of report. *Journal of Educational Psychology* 2: 253–61.

Loftus, E. F. 1993. The reality of repressed memories. *American Psychologist* 48: 518–37.

Manshel, L. 1990. *Nap time.* New York: Kensington.

Marin, B. V., D. L. Holmes, M. Guth, and P. Kovac. 1979. The potential of children as eyewitnesses. *Law and Human Behavior* 3: 295–305.

Maryland v. *Craig,* 110 S. Ct. 3157 (1990).

Mason, M. A. 1991. A judicial dilemma: expert witness testimony in child sex abuse cases. *Psychiatry and Law* (Winter-Fall): 185–219.

McGough, L. In press. *Fragile voices: The child witness in American courts.* New Haven, Conn.: Yale University Press.

Melton, G. 1992. Children as partners for justice: Next steps for developmentalists. *Monographs of the Society for Research in Child Development* 57 (Serial No. 229), 153–59.

Messerschmidt, R. 1933. The suggestibility of boys and girls between the ages of six and sixteen. *Journal of Genetic Psychology* 43: 422–37.

Montoya, J. 1992. On truth and shielding in child abuse trials. *Hastings Law Journal* 43: 1259–1319.

———. 1993. *When fragile voices intersect with a fragile process: Pretrial interrogation of child witnesses.* Unpublished monograph. University of San Diego School of Law.

Moss, D. C. 1988. "Real" dolls too suggestive: Do anatomically correct dolls lead to false abuse charges? *American Bar Association Journal* 24: 24–25.

Myers, J. E. 1992. *Legal issues in child abuse and neglect.* Newbury Park, Calif.: Sage.

———. 1993. Expert testimony regarding child sexual abuse. *Child Abuse and Neglect* 17: 175–85.

Nathan, D. 1987. The making of a modern witch trial. *The Village Voice* 33: 19–32.

National Center for Child Abuse and Neglect. 1988. *Study of national incidence and prevalence of child abuse and neglect: 1988.* Gaithersburg, Md.: U.S. Department of Health and Human Services.

———. 1993. *National Child Abuse and Neglect Data System, 1991: Summary data component.* Gaithersburg, Md.: U.S. Department of Health and Human Services.

New Jersey v. Michaels (1993). 264 N.J. super (AppDiv) 579.

Oates, K., and S. Shrimpton. 1991. Children's memories for stressful and non-stressful events. *Medicine, Science, and the Law* 31: 4–10.

Ornstein, P. A., L. Baker-Ward, B. Gordon, and K. Merritt. 1993. *Children's memory for medical procedures.* Paper presented at the biennial meeting of the Society for Research in Child Development, New Orleans.

Ornstein, P. A., B. N. Gordon, and D. Larus. 1992. Children's memory for a personally experienced event: Implications for testimony. *Applied Cognitive Psychology* 6: 49–60.

Otis, M. 1924. A study of suggestibility in children. *Archives of Psychology* 11: 5–108.

Peters, D. D., G. E. Wyatt, and D. Finkelhor. 1986. Prevalence. In *A sourcebook on child sexual abuse,* ed. D. Finkelhor. Beverly Hills, Calif.: Sage.

Popper, K. R. 1962. *Conjectures and reflections.* New York: Basic Books.

Rabinowitz, D. 1990. From the mouths of babes to a jail cell: Child abuse and the abuse of justice. *Harper's Magazine* (May): 52–63.

Raskin, D., and P. Esplin. 1991. Assessment of children's statements of sexual abuse. In *The suggestibility of children's recollections,* ed. J. L. Doris, 153–64. Washington, D.C.: American Psychological Association.

Raskin, D., and J. Yuille. 1989. Problems in evaluating interviews of children in sexual abuse cases. In *Adults' perceptions of children's testimony,* ed. S. J. Ceci, M. P. Toglia, and D. F. Ross, 184–207. New York: Springer Verlag.

Robin, M. 1991. The social construction of child abuse and "false allegations." *Child and Youth Services* 15: 1–34.

Rudy, L., and G. S. Goodman. 1991. Effects of participation on children's reports: Implications for children's testimony. *Developmental Psychology* 27: 527–38.

Sauer, M. 1993. Decade of accusations. *San Diego Union Tribune* (August 29): D1-D3.

Saywitz, K. J., G. S. Goodman, E. Nicholas, and S. F. Moan. 1991. Children's memories of a physical examination involving genital touch: Implications for reports of child sexual abuse. *Journal of Consulting and Clinical Psychology* 59: 682–91.

Schooler, J. W., D. Gerhard, and E. F. Loftus. 1986. Qualities of the unreal. *Journal of Experimental Psychology: Learning, Memory, and Cognition* 12: 171–81.

Sgroi, S. M. 1982. *Handbook of clinical intervention in child sexual abuse.* Lexington, Mass.: Lexington Books.

Shaw, D. 1990. McMartin verdict: Not guilty. *Los Angeles Times,* January 19–22, Series.

Sherman, J. 1925. The suggestibility of normal and mentally defective children. *Comparative Psychology Monographs* 2.

Siegel, J. M., S. B. Sorenson, J. M. Golding, M. A. Burnam, and J. A. Stein. 1987. The prevalence of childhood sexual assault: The Los Angeles epidemiologic catchment area project. *American Journal of Epidemiology* 126: 1141–53.

Spencer, J. R. 1992. Court experts and expert witnesses. In *Current legal problems,* ed. R. W. Rideout and B. Hepple, vol. 45, 214–36. London: Oxford University Press.

Steller, M. 1991. Commentary: Rehabilitation of the child witness. In *The suggestibility of children's recollections,* ed. L. Doris, 106–109. Washington, D.C.: American Psychological Association.

Stern, W. 1910. Abstracts of lectures on the psychology of testimony and on the study of individuality. *American Journal of Psychology* 21: 270–82.

Summit, R. 1983. The child sexual abuse accommodation syndrome. *Child Abuse and Neglect* 7: 177–93.

Taylor, J. P. (cited in S. R. Gross) 1858. *Treatise on the law of evidence,* 3rd ed. §§ 45–50, 65–69.

Terr, L. 1988. Anatomically correct dolls: Should they be used as a basis for expert testimony? *Journal of the American Academy of Child and Adolescent Psychiatry* 27: 254–57.

Varendonck, I. 1911. Les témoignages d'enfants dans un proces retentissant [The testimony of children in a famous trial]. *Archives de psychologie* 11: 129–71.

Wolfner, G., D. Faust, and R. Dawes. 1993. The use of anatomical dolls in sexual abuse evaluations: The state of the science. *Applied and Preventative Psychology* 2: 111.

Wyatt, G. E. 1985. The sexual abuse of Afro-American and white American women in childhood. *Child Abuse and Neglect* 9: 507–19.

21

RECOVERED MEMORIES OF ALLEGED SEXUAL ABUSE:
LAWSUITS AGAINST PARENTS

HOLLIDA WAKEFIELD
AND RALPH UNDERWAGER

Recently there has been increased civil litigation by adults suing parents and others for sexual abuse following the recovering of memories of the abuse through therapy. The memories are recovered with the help of therapists who use concepts such as repression and dissociation to account for the lack of memories and who then use techniques such as hypnosis and survivors' groups. However, the claims of repressed memories of childhood sexual abuse recovered in the course of therapy are unlikely to be supported by empirical data.

A dults claiming to have recovered repressed memories of childhood abuse appear in the media regularly. The abuse supposedly is "repressed" until, with the help of a therapist, it is remembered. Although most of the claims allege parental abuse, recently recalled abuse by teachers, priests, relatives, and others has also appeared. Some accounts are widely publicized (Arnold 1991; Heller 1991; Kennedy 1991; Monaghan 1990; Sifford 1991; Toufexis 1991; Van Derbur Atler 1991). "Survivors" with "recovered memories" appear on Geraldo Rivera, Oprah Winfrey, and other TV talk shows. The claims include childhood ritual, satanic abuse, multiple personality disorder, and participation in murder, sacrifice, cannibalism, orgiastic rites, and other bizarre actions.

Civil litigation by adults claiming recovered memory has increased sharply in recent years (Colaneri and Johnson 1992; Kaza 1991; Wares

From *Behavioral Sciences and the Law* 10 (1992): 483–507. Copyright © 1992 John Wiley & Sons, Limited. Reproduced by permission of John Wiley & Sons, Limited.

1991). The increase follows changes in statutes of limitation, parental immunity laws, redefinition of the term "negligence," and the differentiation between "intentional infliction of injury" and "intentional act" (Colaneri and Johnson 1992).

Several states have now extended the statutory period of limitation in civil cases until several years after abuse is remembered and/or after it is understood there was damage done by the abuse (Colaneri and Johnson 1992; Geffner 1991; Hendrix 1989; Kaza 1991; Loftus and Kaufman, in press). If the discovery rule states that a cause of action does not accrue until a person discovers, or should have discovered the injury, the alleged abuser may be sued many years after the alleged event. This is significant if the survivor claims no awareness of injury until the statute of limitations period has passed. When the adult child claims memories of abuse were blocked out until therapy opened them up, the limitation period does not begin until the abuse is remembered. Another claim may be that the survivor did not realize the abuse had caused injury until therapy identified it.

These laws therefore accord a special status to one type of memory of abuse but not to others. If memory for abuse was "repressed," civil action is possible, but if the memory was always there nothing can be done (Loftus and Kaufman, in press).

Survivors' groups encourage civil lawsuits to help the victim heal (Crnich and Crnich 1992; Nohlgren 1991). A widely distributed survivor book, *Courage to Heal* (Bass and Davis 1988), not only describes how to file civil suits, but contains a list of attorneys who take such cases. It maintains lawsuits are psychologically beneficial for survivors and the settlements can be collected from homeowners insurance and from the defendant if he has money. In Texas, a recent ruling established that homeowner's insurance policies may be tapped in such cases. The result in Texas has been a sudden, dramatic increase in the number of such actions (Hull 1991).

HOW ARE MEMORIES "RECOVERED"?

A growing network of professionals who believe in recovered repressed memories are encouraging alleged survivors. Summit (1990), for example, refers to the victims "we don't know about, those who don't disclose." He claims that memory of abuse is buried within a conscious memory of a happy childhood. He also asserts that half of all women were sexually abused in childhood but many do not remember the abuse.

Others make similar claims. Maltz (1990) believes that half of all incest survivors suffer from some form of memory loss. She gives a long list of physical and psychological problems she maintains are caused by sexual abuse and recommends helping patients with no memories of abuse to validate their experiences and set the stage for the hidden memories of incest to surface. Paxton (1991) states that half of all incest survivors do not remember that abuse occurred, that many incest survivors have only vague bits and pieces of memories and/or awareness, and that some will never remember the actual abuse.

Treatment programs use a variety of techniques to help patients recover memories of sexual abuse. Summit (Roan 1990) recommends using therapy methods that are "invasive and intrusive." Such techniques include direct questioning, hypnosis, reading books, attending survivors' groups, age regression, and dream analysis. A typical example is Lundberg-Love's treatment program at the University of Texas at Tyler (1989 and updated). Here, the first goal of treatment is to work on memory retrieval. After the woman can develop memories of the abuse and talk about what happened, she is encouraged to express her rage by throwing darts at pictures of the perpetrator and writing him angry letters. Her feelings of shame are dealt with through art and music, and by taking bubble baths to eliminate dirty feelings. The description of this program contains no outcome data.

Grand, Alpert, Safer, and Milden (1991) have described how to help a patient uncover memories of sexual abuse. They stress that the role of the therapist is to help the patient become convinced of the historical reality of the abuse, even when there is no verification and the patient herself doubts that the memory is real.

The book *The Courage to Heal* (Bass and Davis 1988) is used by many therapists. This book contains statements such as "If you are unable to remember any specific instances . . . but still have a feeling that something abusive happened to you, it probably did" (p. 21); "If you think you were abused and your life shows the symptoms, then you were" (p. 22); and "If you don't remember your abuse you are not alone. Many women don't have memories, and some never get memories. This doesn't mean they weren't abused" (p. 81). Demands for details or corroboration are seen as unreasonable: "You are not responsible for proving that you were abused" (p. 137). The book encourages revenge, anger, fantasies of murder or castration, and deathbed confrontations. The veracity of the recovered memories is never questioned—one section uncritically presents an account of ritual abuse by a satanic cult of town leaders and church officials that included sexual abuse, murder, pornography, drugs, electric shock, and forcible impregnation of breeders to produce babies for sacrifice.

Individuals are frequently referred to survivors' support groups or self-help groups such as those for adult children of alcoholics. Price (1992) describes her experience in such a survivors' therapy group where there was continual encouragement for uncovering memories of increasingly intrusive and deviant abuse. She also describes the suggestibility and group influence where, after one woman would suddenly recall a new abusive event, others would soon recall similar events. Galanter (1990) describes how self-help groups can exercise an intense group influence toward conformity to the shared belief. In many survivors' groups the normative belief is that group members were abused whether or not they remember it, and that the task of therapy is to uncover the hidden memories. Great attention and reinforcement are given to members as they report newly uncovered memories.

THE RECOVERED MEMORY QUESTIONNAIRE PROJECT

In conjunction with Pamela Freyd from the False Memory Syndrome Foundation[1] we are engaged in an ongoing project in which 26-page questionnaires are being sent to people whose adult children have accused them of recently recovered memories of repressed childhood sexual abuse. Subjects are people who responded to newspaper articles or other media presentations in several cities about the FMS (False Memory Syndrome) Foundation, a tax-exempt research and educational institution formed in early 1992. The newspaper articles contained an 800 number to call for information. In its first 6 months of existence, the foundation received calls from approximately 600 families. Questionnaires are being sent to callers who reported that their adult child had recently recovered a memory of repressed sexual abuse which the caller denies. Although most respondents come from the geographical areas in which the articles or television show appeared, there are people from four-fifths of the states in the U.S.

The cut-off date for mailing the initial 260 surveys was April 1992. To date, 133 surveys have been returned. Of those not returned, 18 were later determined to have been inappropriately sent. Therefore, the return rate to date, based on 242 questionnaires and 133 returns, is 54%. This is expected to be higher as more questionnaires are returned.

The respondents are not a random sample and the information comes from the accused parents, not the accusing child. Despite these limitations, these are the first data available regarding families, parents, and adult children where there are allegations of recovered memories of sexual abuse.

The preliminary result suggest several unusual and some unexpected characteristics of this sample. It was anticipated that most families would be dysfunctional and that the adult child would have a history of significant disturbance. However, the picture emerging from the preliminary questionnaire data is one of functional, intact, successful families. The annual median family income is $60,000–69,000. Four-fifths of the parents are still married and four-fifths of these judge their marriages to be happy. The parents are well educated—two-thirds of the fathers and half of the mothers have an undergraduate or graduate degree. The majority of the parents report routinely eating dinner together as a family, going on family vacations, and being actively involved with their children when the child was growing up.

The accusing adult children, 90% of whom are females, are also highly educated—only one-fifth have just a high school degree. Over one-fourth have a graduate degree and the rest have a B.A. or some college. Although it was hypothesized that the accusing child would have a long history of psychological problems, in only one-third of the cases did the individual have psychological or psychiatric treatment prior to adulthood.

The feature common to the sample appears to be the therapy received by the adult children. Although many of the parents know little about the therapist or type of therapy provided, those who do report similar information. The memories were recovered in therapy in all but a few cases. In almost all cases where the parents had knowledge of the therapy program, the book, *Courage to Heal,* was used along with other survivor or self-help books. Hypnotherapy, dream interpretation, and survivor and other groups are frequently reported. A variety of fringe therapy techniques were also reported, such as prayer, meditation, age regression, neurolinguistic programming, reflexology, channeling, psychodrama, casting out demons, yoga, trance writing, and primal scream therapy. The therapists, approximately three-fourths of whom were females, are identified as social workers (24%), psychologists (33%), psychiatrists (8%), and "counselors" (33%). Over half of the female therapists were between age 30-39, while the majority of the male therapists were over 40.

In one-third of the cases, mothers were accused along with the fathers. In one-third of the cases, a variety of other people were accused, most often along with the parents. The abuse typically was said to have begun at a very young age—1% at age 2 or younger, and 38% at age 3 to 5. In only 21% of the cases was the abuse said to have begun at age 6 and older. The years the memory was "repressed" ranged from 8 to 51 with a median of 25 years.

One-third of the respondents did not have much idea as to what they were supposed to have done. When this information was known, the allegations tended to be of extremely deviant and intrusive behaviors.

Only a few were of fondling alone. Repeated physical violence or forced anal or vaginal penetration was alleged in almost half of the cases. Witnesses to the abuse were reported in one-third of the cases and in 18% the allegations were of satanic, ritual abuse.

In some cases, siblings also eventually made allegations of abuse. However, in most (86%) cases siblings did not make allegations and in three-fourths of the cases, siblings did not believe that the allegations made by the accusing child were true.

The typical reaction described by the accused parents were shock and devastation. Few had any warning that anything was wrong prior to being told suddenly by a phone call, letter, or announcement at a holiday or family reunion. The parents report having great difficulty getting specific information as to what they were supposed to have done. Typical responses to their inquiries were "You know!" "You are an abuser," or "You incested me." For over half of the parents, civil lawsuits are a serious concern and for almost a fifth, lawsuits have already been filed.

THE SCIENTIFIC BASIS OF THE CLAIMS OF RECOVERED MEMORY

Claims of repressed memories of childhood abuse recovered in the course of therapy are not supported by credible scientific data. The scientific and popular literature in this area seems dominated by believing therapists who simply repeat clinical anecdotes, state subjective speculation, and make unsupported assertions about repressed abuse.

Claims of Repressed Memory in the Literature

A report by Briere and Conte (1989) on a sample of 468 adults who reported childhood sexual abuse is typical of the literature supporting the concept of repressed memories. The authors state that 60% of their subjects reported some period before the age 18 when they could not recall their first abuse experience and concluded that "repression (partial or otherwise) appears to be a common phenomenon among clinical sexual abuse survivors" (p. 4). They then use this conclusion as support for the contention that "some significant proportion" of psychotherapy clients who deny a history of sexual abuse have, nevertheless, been abused. Nowhere in their article, however, is there any information concerning verification of the claimed abuse. It is simply assumed that a client who recovers the memory under the guidance of a therapist is reporting an actual event.

Herman and Schatzow (1987) state that three out of four of 53 women in an incest survivor group were able to "validate their memories by obtaining corroborating evidence from other sources" (p. 1). They also note that the survivor group was a "powerful stimulus for recovery of previously repressed traumatic memories" (p. 1). However, most of their sample was of women who had either full or partial recall of the abuse prior to therapy; only a minority had no recall before entering the survivor group. But in discussing the corroboration, no distinction was made between women who had always remembered the abuse and those who didn't recall it until entering therapy. Also, the details of the corroboration were vague and depended upon the reports of the women in group therapy.

Briere (1990) justifies the acceptance of clients' reports in a study by Briere and Zaidi (1989) by noting that (1) the abuse rate was comparable to rates found in other studies; (2) aspects of the clients' victimization correlated with symptoms that made intuitive sense and that had been reported by other authors; and (3) the clinical experience of the authors suggested that the disclosures were accompanied by distress, shame, and fear of stigma, as opposed to enjoyment. None of these criteria meets acceptable standards for establishing the veracity of the reports, especially when the reports are of memories uncovered only in the course of therapy.

Briere (1992) maintains that some adults, by virtue of a need to avoid painful abuse memories, may be amnesic for some or all of their childhood victimization. He asserts that the problem of repressed memories in retrospective research on sexual abuse effects is a "significant concern" because the abuse is therefore not reported (p. 197). However, he acknowledges that there is no satisfactory way to ensure the validity of subjects' recollections of childhood sexual abuse and states that the accuracy of sexual reports cannot be assured in terms of ruling out either false positives or false negatives. In speculating upon the reasons for false positives, he briefly mentions fantasies, delusions, or intentional misrepresentations for secondary gain. However he shows no awareness that clients may develop accounts of abuse through the influence of therapists who believe that much abuse is repressed.

The Nature of Memory

The fact that memory is reconstruction rather than recall is generally accepted in the scientific community (Goodman and Hahn 1987). Although people introspectively believe that their memories are a process of dredging up what actually happened, in reality memories are largely determined by current beliefs and feelings (Loftus, Korf, and Schooler 1989). Dawes (1988) notes:

> Our recall is often organized in ways that "make sense" of the present—thus reinforcing our belief in the conclusion we have reached about how the past has determined the present. We quite literally "make up stories" about our lives, the world, and reality in general. The fit between our memories and the stories enhances our belief in them. Often, however, it is the story that creates the memory, rather than vice versa (p. 107).

Loftus describes the reconstruction process and notes that through it, people can believe firmly in events that never happened:

> Truth and reality, when seen through the filter of our memories, are not objective facts but subjective, interpretative realities. We interpret the past, correcting ourselves, adding bits and pieces, deleting uncomplimentary or disturbing recollections, sweeping, dusting, tidying things up. Thus our representation of the past takes on a living, shifting reality; it is not fixed and immutable, not a place way back there that is preserved in stone, but a living thing that changes shape, expands, shrinks, and expands again, an amoebalike creature with powers to make us laugh, and cry, and clench our fists. Enormous powers—powers even to make us believe in something that never happened (Loftus and Ketcham 1991, 20).

The concept of recovered memories rests on a Freudian model in which the brain stores all experiences and therapy is seen as a process of uncovering lost or repressed memories and thus freeing patients from their autonomous and sublimated influence. Psychoanalytic therapists rely upon unearthed unconscious memories with little regard for empirical verification.

But the Freudian brain model is not accurate. In fact, the process of therapy increases the probability that the material "remembered" is not historically true. The process of verbally describing memories, which is what happens in therapy, appears to make it even more difficult to distinguish between memories for real and imagined events (Suengas and Johnson 1988). Also, eyewitness research indicates that the misleading effect is greater when the misleading information is provided by an expert. Since the psychotherapist is viewed as an expert, the patient's recollections during therapy will be affected by the questions the therapist asks, the interpretation given, and the reinforcement of the answers.

Bonanno (1990) notes that rather than uncovering historical truth, therapy results "in the production of an articulated narrative understanding or narrative truth" (p. 176). This narrative truth is a product of the communication between the therapist and the patient. The task of the therapist is not to help the patient retrieve lost memories, but to help the patient revise the life story. Greenwald (1980) notes that the cognitive biases found in the human self result in fabrication and revision of personal history.

Ganaway (1991) observes:

> The analogy of an intrapsychic videotape machine recording traumatic memories in all their exquisite detail and storing them away in the unconscious until retrieved via "flashback" or abreaction during the interview situation is slick, simplistic and attractive, but not consistent with a hundred years of empirical evidence. Reconstructed memories may incorporate fantasy, distortion, displacement, condensation, symbolism, and other mental mechanisms that make their sum factual reliability highly questionable. When suggestibility, high hypnotizability, and fantasy-proneness are added to the equation, the result is a potential for such a potpourri of facts, fantasy, distortion, and confabulation as to confound even the most astute investigator to separate the wheat from the chaff (p. 5).

Infantile Amnesia

Adults and older children do not usually remember incidents from their lives that happen prior to age three to four. The basic question is whether the lack of early memories implies that the memory system itself is different in early years or whether other factors, such as changes in cognitive organization, are responsible for the effect.

Nelson and Ross (1980) report a series of studies demonstrating that memory development proceeds from a single novel experience to fused representations to differentiated representations that are capable of being recalled and shared in the absence of external cues and notes, "Prior to the achievement of the last two steps, individual autobiographical memories will not be remembered as such" (p. 100). Thus the phenomenon of infantile amnesia is not a function of lack of memories or repression but rather the normal process of growth and development.

Eisenburg (1985) reports a study of children showing that a concept of the past does not emerge in children's dialogues until after age three. Fivush and Hamond (1990) show that young children's memories are very inconsistent with different information appearing in separate recollections. They also tend to recall routine events rather than novel events and require more questions from adults to produce memories. Early memories are more fragmented and more difficult to produce later in the developmental process. Nelson (1989) reports an analysis of recorded monologues and observes that the memories of young children are impossible to separate from fantasy.

In sum, the information about infant amnesia does not support claims of recovered memory from very young ages, such as the recent claim of a prominent actress that she can now remember being sexually abused by her mother at 6 months of age.

Repression

The concept of repression, used in different ways by different researchers and theorists (Singer and Sincoff 1990), is a key concept in Freudian psychodynamic theory (Erdelyi 1990; Singer 1990; Weinert and Perlmutter 1988). The theory is that a considerable portion of human thought, communication, social behavior, or psychological symptomatology involves efforts to ward off from consciousness a variety of threatening cognitions or emotional reactions. Freud believed that nothing, once formed in mental life, could perish; everything is somehow preserved. Human frustration and conflicts arise from memories that are not conscious. Freud therefore focused on forgotten memories. The individual could be cured of ills by uncovering the unconscious strata of experience. Psychoanalysis was his method of reviving memories and thereby curing individuals.

Traditional analytically orientated therapists are concerned with the patient's current perceptions of reality, rather than the historical truthfulness of these perceptions (Wakefield 1992). Although they deal with childhood recollections, they do not use the material uncovered in therapy as a way to determine historical truth. They would not insist, in the face of a patient's skepticism, that the memories uncovered are the actual events.

The difficulty with the concept of repression is that there is no empirical quantifiable evidence to support it. Over the years, there have been hundreds of studies testing the concept of repression (Hoch 1982; Holmes 1990; Hornstein 1992). In 1974 Holmes published a review in which he concluded that there was no reliable evidence for repression. In 1990, he stated that he has not seen anything new in the literature to change this conclusion. In addition to reviewing the literature, Holmes conducted experiments which found alternative explanations for research that claims to support repression. The only "evidence" for repression comes from impressionistic case studies and anecdotal reports.

Holmes (1990) concludes: "despite over 60 years of research involving numerous approaches by many thoughtful and clever investigators, at the present time there is no controlled laboratory evidence supporting the concept of repression" (p. 96). . . . "We do not have another theory with which to overthrow repression, but despite numerous tests neither do we have data to support the theory, and therefore it might be appropriate to abandon the theory" (p. 98).

Bower (1990) discusses the concept of repression and recovery of forgotten memories. He observes that procedures in therapy, such as associations, can be successful in slowly retrieving lost memories. But a problem lies in ascertaining the accuracy and veracity of the memory that is retrieved. He states:

> Memories of remote events are notoriously subject to all manners of distortion. To mention just the common memory distortion: we may mislocate where or when an event occurred; we may confuse and fuse together aspects from two different events; we may confuse a heard-of or imagined event with an actual witnessed event; we may fill in its gaps by completing the story fragment in a conventional, schematized way; and our memory is often "self-serving," assigning ourselves greater power and responsibility than we deserve for good outcomes and less blame than we deserve for bad outcomes. . . . Given such possibility for distortions, the analyst who recovers an "alleged" memory should be cautious in claiming its veracity, no matter what effect is attached to the memory (pp. 222–23).

In sum, the construct of repression has been subjected to much criticism (Weinert and Perlmutter 1988) and efforts to investigate repression experimentally have failed. Repression cannot be said to be accepted in the scientific community except among analytically oriented therapists, who base their beliefs on anecdotal reports and clinical case studies. Even if accepted as a concept, there is nothing in the repression literature supporting the assertion that it is common for repeated episodes of sexual abuse to be repressed and inaccessible to memory and to be remembered only years later in bits and pieces.

Dissociation

Another concept hypothesized to account for the lack of memory for childhood abuse is dissociation. Dissociation is seen as a process that alters the person's thoughts, feelings, or actions so that certain information is not associated with or integrated with other information. It is defined in the DSM-III-R (American Psychiatric Association 1987) as "a disturbance or alteration in the normally integrative functions of identity, memory, or consciousness" (p. 269). A dissociated memory is seen as distinctly different from one that is simply forgotten (Spiegel 1991). Dissociation forms a continuum ranging from minor and commonly experienced forms, such as becoming lost in a television program or book or "spacing out" while driving, to pathological forms such as depersonalization, amnesia, or multiple personality disorder (Putnam 1991a).

The assumption is that the individual dissociates the childhood experiences of sexual abuse so that they are not available to memory. A "state-dependent" effect is posited in which amnesia results when the traumatic events are encoded during an altered state resulting in limited conscious access to these memories during the ordinary state (Loewenstein 1991). The amnesias for these events are therefore seen as a type of state-dependent memory retrieval. Therefore, retrieval is accomplished through an altered state of consciousness such as hypnosis or age regression.

Individuals differ in their dissociability, and children are believed to have a greater capacity to dissociate than do adults (Bernstein and Putnam 1986; Putnam 1991a). Dissociation is seen as a protective response in the face of extreme trauma and childhood trauma is believed to enhance dissociativity. Childhood trauma is thought to enhance or preserve into adulthood the child's normatively elevated ability to dissociate, and childhood sexual abuse is believed to result in dissociative disorders (Putnam 1991a).

Just what constitutes psychopathology in children is not at all clear. It does appear that any system designed for diagnosis of adults is not transferable to children. Anna Freud (1965) advances this point and maintains that only one aspect of a child's behavior can demonstrate pathology—blockage of the developmental process. Achenbach (1980) argues the same point and concludes that since most major adult disorders have no clear counterpart in children, it is an error to apply indiscriminately adult-oriented diagnosis constructs to children. His 20-year plus effort to build a taxonomy of childhood disorders using factor analytic studies of large numbers of children has not produced clusters of behaviors which look like dissociative disorders.

If, indeed, the frequency of repression of memories of childhood abuse approaches anywhere near the claimed one-quarter of the population of women and this is supposed to occur through a process of dissociation, the behaviors and symptoms of dissociation occurring in childhood should have been evident somewhere in the massive, lengthy study of children's psychopathology. It does not seem likely that behavior with such a high antecedent probability would have been missed so thoroughly. The reasonable conclusion is that it is best to be extremely cautious about any clinical anecdote, clinical judgments, or case studies used to support the construct of dissociation in children as the cause of repressed memories which are then recovered by adults in therapy unless there is an unambiguous corroboration of dissociation symptomatology during childhood.

The dissociation mechanism postulated to account for the lack of memory for the childhood abuse is psychogenic amnesia. The DSM-III-R (American Psychiatric Association 1987) notes that the essential feature of psychogenic amnesia is a sudden inability to recall important personal information. Loewenstein (1991) broadens the definition of psychogenic amnesia to a "reversible memory impairment in which groups of memories for personal experience that would ordinarily be available for recall to the conscious mind cannot be retrieved or retained in a verbal form" (p. 191). The assumption is that sexual abuse forms a category of events for which the individual has amnesia. Dissociated memories show up in disguised forms such as conversion symptoms, nightmares, and somatoform symptoms. The amnesia symptoms are found not only in patients with multiple personality disorder but in patients with other dissociative symptoms. There is, however, no research supporting this conception of psychogenic amnesia.

The clinical case studies of amnesia reported in the literature describe a history of severe life stresses in the patients. They are seen as having experienced extremely traumatic childhoods or later highly traumatic events, such as torture, confinement in concentration camps, or combat. Such highly traumatic events should be able to be independently verified. Without verification that an event has occurred, one cannot talk about amnesia for the event.

This is a major difficulty in using the formulation of dissociation and/or psychogenic amnesia to account for the fact that the memory of the abuse is said to be buried within a conscious memory of a happy childhood. There must be verification of the reported childhood trauma in order to conclude that there is amnesia for the trauma. However, in most of the cases in the above-described questionnaire project, the parents and siblings do not corroborate the trauma. The majority of the parents in the project report functional families, intact, happy marriages and high interest and nurturance of the children.

In the literature reporting on psychogenic amnesia, almost all information comes from anecdotal descriptions or clinical observations. The same is true of multiple personality amnesia. Although there is research on neurologically based amnesia, most information about psychogenic amnesia comes from clinical descriptions of patients rather than from experimental research. Since there is a lack of systematic studies, there is a corresponding absence of well-established facts. The clinical observations of therapists who have helped patients recover memories of abuse do not meet the standard for establishing facts. Claims of amnesia show up frequently in a variety of legal situations, including criminal trials, disability and Social Security hearings, and personal injury suits. Although some researchers believe that clinical detection of malingering can be accomplished by noting inconsistencies among verbal statements or behavior (Kiersch 1962; Power 1977), the consensus is that it is difficult to distinguish real and simulated amnesia. There is no evidence that experts (psychologists and psychiatrists) can reliably distinguish between them (Brandt 1988; Schacter 1986; Wiggins and Brandt 1988). Surprisingly little research has specifically examined whether normal individuals can successfully feign clinical memory deficits.

The diagnosis of Post-traumatic Stress Disorder (PTSD) is frequently found in cases of child sexual abuse, including recovered memory cases. Patients diagnosed with dissociative disorders are believed to often meet criteria for PTSD (Loewenstein 1991). The DSM-III-R (American Psychiatric Association 1987) defines PTSD as the development of characteristic symptoms following a psychologically distressing event that is outside the range of usual human experience. The stressor would be disturbing to almost anyone, and is usually experienced with intense fear, terror, and helplessness. The characteristic symptoms involve reexperiencing the traumatic event, avoidance of stimuli association with the event or numbing of general responsiveness, and increased arousal.

The criteria for PTSD mention numbing and efforts to avoid thoughts or feelings along with psychogenic amnesia for an important aspect of the event, but not total amnesia for the whole event. Nor do these criteria mention complete selective amnesia for repeated events. Also, there must be a known stressor in order to make this diagnosis, a concern demonstrated by the experience with PTSD diagnoses in Vietnam veterans who later were found not to have been in combat.

Spiegel (1991) reviews a number of studies on the reactions of people subjected to documented severe trauma, such as fires, airplane crashes, automobile accidents, and being held hostage. Many people showed a variety of symptoms including depersonalization, hallucinations, flashbacks, out-of-body experiences, and some sort of memory impairment. However, total amnesia for the entire event was not mentioned as a common response.

In summary, psychogenic amnesia is for a specific critical event. It is not for a category of events stretching across several years at different times and under different circumstances in differing environments. Although Loewenstein (1991) has attempted to broaden the definition to refer to a group of events, there are no data supporting this and it cannot be said to be generally supported in the scientific community.

Multiple Personality Disorder

Individuals who allegedly recover memories of child sexual abuse are often diagnosed as suffering from multiple personality disorder, particularly when the abuse alleged is violent and extreme, such as ritual satanic abuse. The DSM-III-R (American Psychiatric Association 1987) defines multiple personality disorder (MPD) as the existence within the person of two or more distinct personalities or personality states. The disorder is thought to develop early in life, typically between the ages of 4 and 8, and symptoms usually can be documented from adolescence through adulthood. Most people diagnosed with MPD are women.

Multiple personality disorder is claimed to be a syndrome which follows child abuse, and case reports suggest that most individuals diagnosed with MPD were abused as children (Kluft 1987, 1991; Putnam, Guroff, Silberman, Barban, and Post 1986). Clinically, MPD patients frequency report that they first dissociated when the abuse began. A "protector" personality is said to emerge and take over the patient, who therefore is allowed to escape psychologically from the abuse (Spiegel 1991). There is, however, no empirical quantified research to support this theory since the hypothesized connection is based on case reports. In a recent review of the literature on the longterm effects of child sexual abuse, Beitchman, Zucker, Hood, daCosta, and Akman (1991) concluded that as yet there is insufficient evidence to confirm a relationship between childhood sexual abuse and multiple personality disorder.

Also, despite its inclusion in DSM-III-R, MPD itself is controversial. Aldridge-Morris (1989) notes that a few therapists are seeing most of the MPD cases, and that the vast majority of them are in the United States. Practitioners who are convinced of the reality of multiple personality often belong to a professional subculture which favors hypnotherapeutic techniques, have an analytical orientation, and see their patients over long periods of time. Aldridge-Morris maintains that even if MPD should pass muster as a psychiatric syndrome, it has been grossly over-diagnosed. There is little empirical evidence supporting it and it is heavily dependent upon cultural influences for both its emergence and its diagnosis. Most thinking about MPD has been through oral traditions of workshops and communication between therapists. Aldridge-Morris (1989) hypothesizes that MPD is a variant of a hysterical psychosis which occurs in highly suggestible persons.

Others are also skeptical about the recent dramatic increase in MPD cases. Fahy (1988) suggests that MPD is a hysterical symptom and that there is little evidence that it represents a distinct psychiatric disorder. Thigpen and Cleckley (1954, 1984), who described the case of the three faces of Eve, later became extremely concerned over the overdiagnosis of MPD.

Spanos has developed a social psychological conception of MPD (Spanos 1991; Spanos, Weekes, and Bertrand 1985). He observes that most psychotherapists never see a case of MPD in their entire career while others report dealing with over 50. From 1920–1971 there were 12 cases of MPD in the literature. There were thousands after 1974. He notes that relatively few patients show clear signs of a multiple personality at the beginning of therapy. People learn to enact the role of the multiple personality patient and psychotherapists often play an important part in the generation and maintenance of this role enactment. Since knowledge concerning the multiple personality role is widespread, some patients combine their general knowledge of the role with the information gleaned from their therapeutic interactions to enact the "symptoms" of multiple personality.

Spanos and his colleagues (Spanos 1991; Spanos, Weekes, and Bertrand 1985), in role-playing experiments, used a regression-to-past-lives hypnotic technique. Half of the subjects reported a past life. After the hypnosis was over, some subjects still believed they really did have a past life. The degree to which subjects were imaginative did *not* predict whether they believed it afterwards. In another experiment, the authors gave false information to some of the subjects about what to expect in the past life. These subjects incorporated the suggestions into their description of past lives. Child abuse suggestions were given to some subjects, who later reported much more severe abuse in their past lives. Subjects given neutral suggestions about abuse reported only spanking.

Children and Memories for Documented Trauma

Although there is a lack of corroborating evidence to verify the alleged abuse in uncovered memory cases, research with traumatized children provides independent verification of the trauma. Terr (1985, 1988, 1990), for example, describes several cases of children with documented trauma. She notes that children over the ages of 3 or 4 do not become partly or fully amnesic for the trauma or employ massive repression or denial. She reports that although ordinary memory may be distorted and changed by later input, traumatic memories are clearer and detailed with little chance of gradual wipeout. Children over 3 or 4 clearly remember their trauma and, although they may deny parts of the aftermath and the effect on them, do not deny the event.

Terr (1988, 1990) reports on a study of 20 children under 5 at the time of documented traumatic events. The children were evaluated from 5 months to 12 years after the event. Only two of the 11 children under 3 (they were ages 28 months and 34 months) had full verbal recall. The nine children over 3 had full verbal recall or extensive spot memories. Terr reports that repeated traumatic events are less accurately remembered than a single traumatic event. However, although the memories may have been inaccurate and fragmented, only one child (28 months old) forgot everything. Terr concludes that although children under 3 or 4 forget the trauma because of their age, they will show the memories afterwards through reenactment in play. There is no evidence in her study that it is common for memories of childhood trauma to be completely repressed. Terr found no children over 28 to 36 months who entirely forgot the traumatic event.

Femina, Yeager, and Lewis (1990) report on the follow-up study of 69 subjects who were interviewed during young adulthood. On follow-up 26 gave histories discrepant with those obtained from records and interviews conducted in adolescence. Eighteen denied or minimized abuse when it was in their records and 8 claimed abuse although there was none in the records. Clarification interviews were conducted with 11 of these subjects—8 who denied abuse although their records indicated abuse, and 3 who reported abuse when abuse was not in the records. The authors concluded from the interviews that all 11 had, in fact, been abused. However, in the clarification interviews, none of the subjects who had originally denied or minimized had forgotten or "repressed" their childhood abuse. All acknowledged it in the second interview and gave reasons such as embarrassment, a wish to protect the parents, and a desire to forget, for their previous denial or minimization.

These studies are important because abuse was documented. They do not provide support for the assumption that actual abuse is repressed and not remembered until years later.

In addition, if it were true that many children are sexually abused, but have dissociated and therefore have no memories of the abuse, adults would see a variety of dissociative disorders in these children. They would be commonly encountered by clinicians. However, several recent review articles (Lahey and Kazdin 1988, 1989, 1990) on childhood disorders do not even mention dissociative disorders and the DSM-III-R lists no dissociative disorders under childhood disorders. Steinberg (1991) reports that there are only a few instances of depersonalization in children and this disorder is thought to begin in adolescence.

Hypnosis

Hidden memories of childhood sexual abuse are often recovered with hypnosis (sometimes with narcosynthesis). This raises serious questions about the veracity of the resulting memory. There is agreement and empirical verification regarding several aspects of hypnosis (Cardena and Spiegel 1991; Orne, Soskis, Dinges, Orne, and Tonry 1985; Putnam 1991a; Spanos, Quigley, Gwynn, Glatt, and Perlini 1991):

1. In hypnosis, there is an increase in the vividness and conviction of imaginal experiences;
2. MPD patients and those with PTSD appear to have high hypnotizability;
3. People who are highly hypnotizable agree more with a persuasive communication.
4. The central characteristics of a laboratory-induced traumatic event are likely to be retained in memory.
5. Under hypnosis, people are more suggestible.
6. Both laboratory and forensic investigations have shown a number of serious problems with the accuracy and validity of memories recovered through hypnosis.
7. Hypnosis fails to improve accuracy but does enhance confidence.
8. Hypnotized subjects experience the memories as real, which may increase their assurance and persuasiveness.

Ganaway (1991) notes that individuals with severe dissociative disorders, including MPD, are highly hypnotizable, highly suggestible, and fantasy prone. They may spontaneously enter autohypnotic trance states, particularly during stressful interview situations. Memories retrieved in a hypnotic trance are likely to contain a combination of both fact and fantasy in a mixture that cannot be accurately determined without external corroboration. Hypnosis increases the person's confidence in the veracity of both correct and incorrect recall material. Therefore, the hypnotist should be very cautious about reinforcing the truthfulness of any memories which are elicited through hypnosis. These memories should never be assumed to be totally factual detailed accounts of actual occurrences without outside corroboration.

ALLEGATIONS OF RITUALISTIC AND SATANIC ABUSE

Many recovered memory cases, including ones that result in civil law suits, contain allegations of ritual satanic abuse. The American Bar Association is conducting a survey of local prosecutors to obtain an estimate of the national incidence of different types of cases of child abuse. The survey is not yet finished, but as of early 1991 the preliminary data indicate that about one-third of local prosecutors have handled cases involving "ritualistic or satanic abuse" (Victor 1991a, 1991b).

The allegations of ritual abuse come from two sources—adult survivors and day care cases. The survivors uncover memories of bizarre satanic ritual abuse ceremonies during the course of therapy. The day care cases involve children who have allegedly been ritualistically abused at day care centers; the McMartin case is the best known example.

Survivors generally first uncover memories of these experiences during psychotherapy. Techniques such as hypnosis, dream analysis, age regression and survivors' groups are commonly used, and the survivors are often diagnosed as suffering from multiple personality disorder. Survivors often allege memories of bizarre events, including ritual murder and torture, cannibalism, and baby breeding. A few therapists seem to be finding almost all of the survivors and the allegations have not been independently verified.

Young, Sachs, Braun, and Watkins (1991) report on 37 alleged satanic cult survivors found among dissociative disorder patients, but there is no convincing corroborating evidence supporting these reports. Although the author claims corroboration through some physical findings such as scars on the back, a distorted nipple, a satanic tattoo on the scalp and a breast scar on one patient, they provide no information of detailed medical workups or photographs of these alleged physical markings. Other evidence of physical findings include three women with endometriosis diagnosed before age 16, one with pelvic inflammatory disease at age 15, and one whose school performance dropped from age 7 to 10 during the years she supposedly was in the cult until the family moved. These findings are all completely nonspecific.

Mulhern (1991) has spoken to one of the authors and strongly criticizes this report. She notes that since the 1980s, repeated law enforcement investigations have found no corroborating evidence of criminal satanists as described by these patients. Also, since all 37 were in treatment for dissociative disorder, they are highly suggestible patients who move in and out of altered states of consciousness, have significant gaps in autobiographical memory retrieval, suffer from source amnesia, are particularly vulnerable to trance logic, and compulsively seek to discover and conform to even the most subtle expectations of their therapists. Their reports of ritual abuse are basically rarefied memory narratives assembled in therapy over time out of bits of images and affect which emerged when the patients were abreacting, dreaming, experiencing flashbacks, experiencing dissociated states, or responding to explicit questioning during hypnotic interviews. Old body scars and a satanic scalp tattoo, which have been incorporated into memory narratives by highly hypnotizable patients, cannot reliably be endorsed as corroborative evidence.

The allegations of ritual abuse in day care centers first attained national attention in the McMartin Preschool case. Soon after the McMartin case attracted national attention, similar accusations of ritual sexual abuse swept across the country (Charlier and Downing 1988;

Nathan 1991; Underwager and Wakefield 1991). As in the survivors' accounts, there has been no evidence found to support the ritual abuse allegations. The allegations come from the way the children are interviewed in these cases: by interviewers who believe the abuse is real, who attend the same workshops and conferences, who consult with one another, and who then interview children with suggestive and leading questions (Wakefield and Underwager 1992).

No one disputes that there are sadistic and disturbed people who abuse and brutalize children. Some of these people may abuse a child in what looks like or is interpreted as a satanic ritual, a possibility that becomes more probable given the current media attention and publicity. However, there is no evidence of an organized conspiracy of satanists who abuse and sacrifice children. Lanning (1991) notes that there are many meanings given to the terms ritualistic and/or satanic abuse and the lack of a consensus makes investigation more difficult. However, despite hundreds of investigations by the FBI and police, there is no independent evidence of ritual abuse, animal and human sacrifice, murder, and cannibalism of hundreds of children by a conspiracy of apparently normal adults who are functional and organized enough to leave no trace of their activities (Hicks 1991; Lanning 1991, 1992; Putnam 1991b; Richardson, Best, and Bromley 1991; Victor 1991a, 1991b, and in press).

If there is no independent evidence of the satanic ritual abuse allegations, why do some professionals believe in them? Victor (in press) maintains that the belief in satanic cults is a form of collective behavior which arises from deep-seated frustrations and anxieties by people about modern society. Cognitive dissonance theory predicts that people who hold a strong belief will continue to believe, despite disconfirming evidence (Aronson 1988; Festinger, Riecken, and Schachter 1956). Underwager and Wakefield (1991) speculate that the believers may have personality characteristics which predispose them to believe. Dawes (1992) maintains that the beliefs arise from a trust in authorities who have attested to the existence of widespread satanic cults, consensual validation from interacting with other believers, and a tendency for people to accept memories as valid. Also, the believers simply do not understand the problems with the disclosures by either adults or young children.

CRITERIA FOR JUDGING AN ALLEGATION

When a psychologist or ocher mental health professional becomes involved in a case of recovered memories of repressed sexual abuse, it is essential to get as much information as possible about the circumstances surrounding the disclosure and accusations. Daly and Pacifico (1991) note that investigating an allegation of sexual abuse that allegedly occurred years earlier requires new investigative techniques that have not yet been perfected. Important information in assessing such allegations include:

1. All medical, psychiatric, and school records of the person claiming abuse from childhood to the present.
2. Any information concerning relationships with peers, siblings and parents, or any childhood behavior problems of the person claiming abuse.
3. Any information concerning the sexual history of the person claiming abuse, including rapes, other childhood sexual abuse, abortions, etc.
4. The nature and origin of the disclosure, in as much detail and specificity as possible.
5. Information about any current problems or stresses in the life of the person claiming abuse.
6. The nature of any current therapy, e.g., whether techniques such as hypnosis and survivors' groups were used, the training and background of the therapist, and whether he or she specializes in treating MPD or "recovered" abuse.
7. Any books, television shows, or workshops about sexual abuse or rape to which the person claiming abuse may have been exposed.
8. Any exposure to recovered memory cases through a highly publicized case in the media or through friends who may have reported that this happened to them.
9. The work history of the person claiming abuse, including any problems with supervisors or coworkers, especially any allegations of sexual harassment.
10. The psychological characteristics and social and family history of the accused adult(s), including any drug or alcohol use, sexual history, family relationships, and job history.
11. Any criminal record or prior behaviors in the accused adult which would support or undermine the credibility of the allegations.
12. A detailed description of the behaviors alleged to have occurred.
13. Possible ways by which the person making the accusation might benefit from or receive reinforcement from making the accusation (e.g., a civil law suit, an explanation for why life has gone well, the expression of anger for perceived childhood injustices, power over a dominant parent, attention, acceptance, new friends [in survivor group], etc.).

Despite the lack of empirical research, the following are suggested as provisional criteria for assessing the probability or improbability of an allegation of recent remembered abuse:

1. When there is no corroborating evidence, and the alleged behaviors are highly improbable, it is unlikely that the abuse actually happened.

Knowledge of the behavior of actual abusers is important in evaluating an allegation in cases where the accused denies the allegation and there is no corroborating evidence. If the alleged behaviors are extremely improbable, then it is less likely that the allegation is true.

For example, Tollison and Adams (1979) describe the general behaviors engaged in by the pedophile as follows:

> Pedophiliac behavior may involve caressing a child's body, manipulating a child's genitals, or inducing a child to manipulate an adult's genitals. Occasionally, the behaviors also include penile penetration (partial or complete—vaginal or anal), oral sex, and any practice utilizing the sexual parts or organs of a child so as to bring the person in contact with the child's body in any sexual manner. Pedophiliac acts may be homosexual or heterosexual in nature and may include touching, caressing, masturbation, oral-genital contact, and intercourse, as well as pedophiliac exhibitionism, voyeurism, rape, sadism, and masochism. . . Physical violence to the child occurs in only 2% of instances. . . (p. 326).

Erickson (1985) and Erickson, Walbek and Seely (1988) examined data from verified and admitted child sex abusers and report that vaginal and anal penetration is very rare in young children, is extremely painful, and results in injuries and laceration. Bribery is more common than threat. Most child victims of sexual abuse are girls (estimates range from two girls to one boy to five girls to one boy). Aggression and violence are not usually part of the behavior.

In a recent retrospective study, Kendall-Tackett and Simon (1992) report on 365 adults reporting childhood molestation. Fondling was common for all victims and approximately half were subjected to oral intercourse. Anal intercourse occurred for 30% of the males but only 7% of the females.

Thus, when the sexual abuse allegations include extreme behaviors, such as rape, physical violence, vaginal or anal penetration of a very young child, bestiality, and ritual abuse with several people involved, the allegations are not likely to be true.

2. If the alleged events are highly deviant and the accused is psychologically normal, the allegations are less likely to be true.

Assessment of allegations requires knowledge of the personality characteristics of actual child sexual abusers. Although there are few satisfactory psychological studies on traits peculiar to child sexual abusers, there is some agreement about their psychological characteristics.

Several claims about sexual abusers are not supported by the literature. While some have postulated a distinction between "fixated" and "regressed" pedophiles, research does not support the existence of this typology (Conte 1990; Knight 1989; Knight, Carter, and Prentky 1989; Simon, Sales, Kaszniak, and Kahn 1992).

It is often claimed that abusers were themselves abused as children. For example, the DSM III-R (American Psychiatric Association 1987) states that childhood abuse is a predisposing factor in pedophilia. However, the empirical evidence does not support this belief (Garland and Dougher 1990; Langevin and Lang 1985; Widom 1989a, 1989b, 1989c; RiveraandWidom 1990).

Many researchers report that pedophiles are inadequate, immature individuals with low self-esteem and poor social skills, although this hypothesis is based upon not much more than clinical inference. Contradictory traits have been used to describe incest fathers. They are seen as tyrannical, domineering, and behaving without regard for other family members. But some are described as shy, inhibited, and ineffectual in social relations. They are seen as feeling inadequate as males, angry at women, hostile, aggressive, psychopathic, and violent (Langevin 1983). But all of these features are clinically inferred since systematically controlled studies are almost nonexistent.

Child sexual abusers generally do not have normal MMPI profiles. The more aberrant the behavior of the abuser, the more likely it is that he will have a pathological MMPI. Although sex offenders are heterogeneous in personality characteristics, they tend to have difficulties which are reflected in the MMPI. The pathology is most likely to be seen in the elevation of the scales which reflect poor impulse control, antisocial behavior, poor judgment, a history of acting out, lack of self-esteem, feelings of inadequacy, a schizoid social adjustment, much time spent in fantasies, and/or thought disorders and confusion. Still, some sex offenders produce within normal limits MMPIs. Erickson, Luxenberg, Walbek, and Seeley (1987) report that 19% of their convicted sex offenders had profiles that were within normal limits.

If it cannot be demonstrated that an accused person has pathology associated with child sexual abusers, the likelihood of a false accusation increases. However, a "normal" personality based on an MMPI or other assessment techniques does not mean that the individual could not be a sexual abuser. Consideration of the personality characteristics of the accused becomes more useful as the alleged abusive behaviors become more bizarre and deviant. It is highly unlikely that a psychologically normal individual would engage in sadistic and violent sexual behaviors.

3. When a woman is accused of sexually abusing the child, the allegations are less likely to be true.

In a third of the questionnaire cases described earlier, the mother was also accused of sexually abusing the adult child. Awareness of women perpetrators of sexual abuse has greatly increased in recent years. However, sexual contact between children and women represents a minority of child-adult sexual contacts and the traditional view of child sexual abuse as a primarily male problem is correct (Wakefield and Underwager 1991).

Finkelhor and his colleagues (Finkelhor, Williams, and Burns 1988; Finkelhor, Williams, Burns, and Kalinowski 1988), in a national study of 270 day cases, report that 40% of the perpetrators were women. These women tended to be intelligent, educated, highly regarded in their communities, and not likely to have a history of known deviant behavior. Many of these apparently normal women were alleged to have engaged in extremely deviant, low frequency behavior, including oral-genital penetration, urolagia, coprophagia, and ritualistic mass abuse.

This study has received both popular and professional attention and it is already being cited as evidence that apparently ordinary women are sexually abusing children. However, there are significant difficulties with the methodology of this study. Although the authors require the abuse to be "substantiated," their definition of substantiation was simply that any one of the individuals assigned to investigate the report believed that abuse was real, regardless of what anyone else may have thought. Therefore, their sample includes many cases in which there were never criminal charges and other cases which ended in dismissals, acquittals, or convictions that were later reversed. For example, the McMartin case, which later ended in dropped charges and acquittals, is included.

4. If the recovered memory is for abuse that occurred at a very young age, such as abuse during diaper changing when the person was an infant, the memory is not likely to be true.

Tollison and Adams (1979) found that the average age of female sexual abuse victims is 6 to 12; male victims are somewhat older. Kendall-Tackett and Simon (1992) report that the average age of the beginning of the abuse was the 7.6 years for females and the 7.65 for males. These figures are comparable to what is generally reported. Abuse alleged to have started at a very young age is therefore less likely to be true. In addition, data on infant amnesia make it highly unlikely that events reported to have occurred before the ages of 3 or 4 will be accurately recalled.

5. When the accusing adult is claiming "repression" or "amnesia" and has only recently "remembered" the abuse, it is less likely to be true than if she maintains that she had always remembered the abuse, but only now is disclosing.

Childhood abuse is often not disclosed until years later. Patients often tell a therapist about childhood sexual abuse which was never previously mentioned. This is very different from the situation in which the individual originally has no memories of abuse but develops them after engaging in a course of therapy designed to recover memories.

6. If there are allegations of a series of abusive incidents across time in different places and situations, the abuse is less likely to be true than if it is for a single incident.

The literature on dissociation and psychogenic amnesia indicates that, although rare, an individual can develop amnesia for a highly traumatic event. However, this information comes from anecdotal or clinical descriptions of amnesia for a specific traumatic episode. With the exception of MPD, there is nothing in the literature on psychogenic amnesia that describes selective amnesia for a series of traumatic events which occur at different ages and at different times and environments.

7. If the accusations emerge only after reading Courage to Heal, *hypnosis, survivors' groups participation, or dream analysis, they are likely to be the result of the influence of the therapy.*

8. Any claims that the individual must have been abused because of problems in her life should be viewed cautiously.

When there are multiple causes for problems such as eating disorders, sexual dysfunction, or depression, the existence of one or more of these problems cannot be used to support the probability of abuse. Beitchman et al. (1991) concluded that as yet there is insufficient evidence to confirm a relationship between childhood sexual abuse and borderline or multiple personality disorder. Pope and Hudson (1992) reviewed studies on bulimia and sexual abuse and concluded that these studies did not find that bulimic patients show a higher prevalence of childhood sexual abuse than control subjects. Nevertheless, the existence of such problems is often used as support for the belief that the person was, in fact, sexually abused.

9. When the progression of the allegations across time is from innocuous, relatively innocent behaviors to even more intrusive, abusive, and highly improbable behaviors, there is a strong possibility that the growth and embellishment of the allegations are products of suggestions and reinforcement in therapy.

10. The subjective certainty of the reality of the abuse is not a useful way for judging whether the abuse is probable or improbable.

Many therapists believe that they must affirm the reality of abuse if the patient expresses doubts, and may therefore persuade the patient to move towards subjective certainty. Learned and suggested memories can be as vivid and real to the individual as are memories for actual events (Loftus and Kaufman, in press). This is also true of memories developed under hypnosis.

While there is value in attending to the subjective reality of the patient, there is no therapeutic benefit to the clinician abandoning rational thinking and incorporating error into the process of psychotherapy (Gambrill 1990). The therapist who erroneously supports the development of recovered, repressed memories of abuse, leads a patient to develop an attributional view of the world that cannot be adaptive or helpful.

11. When there is a history of emotional disturbance, diagnosis, and treatment in the life of the adult raising an accusation, pathological factors in the person's personality may contribute to the development of a false accusation.

12. Corroborating evidence, such as a childhood diary with unambiguous entries or pornographic photographs, makes the allegations much more likely to be true.

At the same time, ambiguous evidence, such as a childhood story or drawings now reinterpreted in light of the believed-in abuse cannot be used as evidence that the abuse actually occurred. For example, Kluft (1987) describes a case that he maintains was "corroborated." The woman claimed to be active in satanic rituals and was going to bear a child for use in a ritualistic sacrifice. Kluft states that this was corroborated by her boyfriend and best friend, but all they witnessed were her nocturnal absences. They tried to follow her, without success. The police were contacted, but they too were unable to trace her movements.

13. Allegations of ritual abuse by intergenerational satanic cults are highly unlikely to be true.

Although this seems to be self-evident, 18% of the cases in the questionnaire project described earlier involve such allegations.

CONCLUSIONS

The clinical decision about claims of recovered repressed memories of childhood sexual abuse is a question of base-rates. On the one hand is a complex, multi-faceted chain of assumptions, speculations, inferred internal states, and mental processes for which there is, at best, very limited credible scientific support. For many of the claims, there are no corroborating data. Such memories, if they are accurate, are a truly low base-rate event. To believe in the reality of these memories often requires suspension of critical reasoning and a leap of blind faith.

On the other hand are the known credible scientific data on social influence, expectancy effects, the nature of memory, the malleability of memory, the problems in diagnosis and concepts of disorder, and the power of a psychotherapeutic relationship to produce conformity in the patient, together with quantifiable data on sexual abuse.

The costs of belief in such memories are devastating to families, society, and the social contract we need to continue our civilization. The anguish and pain generated by these claims is devastating to those accused. The cost to persons believing in the memories is substitution of unknowns for their family relationships. Children may grow up without grandparents. Families may be bankrupted by legal expenses. In some instances criminal charges may be filed. The costs may well include very practical realities such as a trebling of home owner insurance rates for every citizen. The benefit may be a transient, ephemeral lift in mood when it becomes possible to attribute problems and failures to other people and external factors, but this is the attributional bias described by Nisbett and Ross (1980) that may lead to "harmful and damaging judgments" (p. 252) because it is simply wrong. It is not likely to produce long-term benefits to anyone.

The most reasonable response at this stage of knowledge is to choose the high base-rate explanation and control the potential for iatrogenic damage. This choice may include attending to Meehl's (1989) suggestion about providing accurate information to the society about the limits and provisional nature of psychological constructs of low and doubtful validity.

NOTE

1. The False Memory Syndrome Foundation, a tax-exempt institute, is located at 3508 Market Street, Suite 128, Philadelphia, PA 19104, (215) 387-1865.

REFERENCES

Achenbach, T. M. 1980. DSM-III in light of empirical research on the classification of child psychopathology. *Journal of the American Academy of Child Psychiatry* 19: 395–412.

Aldridge-Morris, R. 1989. *Multiple personality: An exercise in deception.* East Sussex, United Kingdom: Lawrence Erlbaum Associates.

American Psychiatric Association. 1987. *Diagnostic and statistical manual of mental disorders-revised (DSM-R).* Washington, D.C.: Author.

Arnold, R. 1991. A star cries incest. *People* (October 7): 84–88.

Aronson, E. 1988. *The social animal,* 5th ed. New York: W. H. Freeman and Co.

Bass, E., and L. Davis. 1988. *Courage to heal.* New York: Harper & Row.

Beitchman, J. H., K. J. Zucker, J. E. Hood, G. A. daCosta, and D. Akman. 1991. A review of the short-term effects of child sexual abuse. *Child Abuse and Neglect* 15 537–56.

Bernstein, E., and F. W. Putnam. 1991. Development, reliability, and validity of a dissociation scale. *Journal of Nervous and Mental Disorders* 174: 727–35.

Bonanno, G. A. 1990. Remembering and psychotherapy. *Psychotherapy* 27 (2): 175–86.

Bower, G. H. 1990. Awareness, the unconscious, and repression: An experimental psychologist's perspective. In *Repression and dissociation,* ed. J. L. Singer, 209–31. Chicago: University of Chicago Press.

Brandt, J. 1988. Malingered amnesia. In *Clinical assessment of malingering and deception,* ed. R. Rogers, 65–83. New York: Guilford.

Briere, J. 1990. Letter to the editor. *American Journal of Psychiatry* 147: 1389–90.

———. 1992. Methodological issues in the study of sexual abuse effects. *Journal of Consulting and Clinical Psychology* 60: 196–203.

Briere, J., and J. Conte. 1989. *Amnesia in adults molested as children: Testing theories of repression.* Paper presented at the annual meeting of the American Psychological Association, New Orleans, August.

Briere, J., and L. Y. Zaidi. 1989. Sexual abuse histories and sequelae in female psychiatric emergency room patients. *American Journal of Psychiatry* 146: 1602–1606.

Cardena, E., and D. Spiegel. 1991. Suggestibility, absorption, and dissociation. In *Human suggestibility,* ed. J. F. Schumaker, 93–107. New York: Routledge.

Charlier, T., and S. Downing. 1988. Facts, fantasies caught in tangled web. *The Commercial Appeal,* Memphis, Tennessee (January): 1A-26A.

Colaneri, J. K., and D. R. Johnson. 1992. Coverage for parents' sexual abuse. *For the Defense* (March): 2–5.

Conte, J. R. 1990. The incest offender: An overview and introduction. In *The incest perpetrator: A family member no one wants to treat,* ed. A. L. Horton, B. L. Johnson, L. M. Roundy, and D. Williams, 15-28. Newbury Park, Calif.: Sage.

Crnich, J. E., and K. A. Crnich. 1992. *Shifting the burden of truth: Suing child sexual abusers: A legal guide for survivors and their supporters.* Lake Oswego, Ore.: Recollex.

Daly, L. W., and J. F. Pacifico. 1991. Opening the doors to the past: Decade delayed disclosure of memories of years gone by. *The Champion* (December): 42–47.

Dawes, R. M. 1988. Biases of retrospection. In *Rational choice in an uncertain world.* San Diego: Harcourt Brace Jovanovich.

———. 1992. *Why believe that for which there is no good evidence?* Paper presented at the Fourth Annual Convention of the American Psychological Society, San Diego, June 20.

Eisenberg, A. R. 1985. Learning to describe past experiences in conversation. *Discourse Processes* 8: 177–204.

Erdelyi, M. H. 1990. Repression, reconstruction, and defense: History and integration of the psychoanalytic and experimental frameworks. In *Repression and dissociation,* ed. J. L. Singer, 1–31. Chicago: University of Chicago Press.

Erickson, W. D. 1985. Unpublished manuscript.

Erickson, W. D., M. G. Luxenberg, N. H. Walbek, and R. K. Seeley. 1987. Frequency of MMPI two-point code types among sex offenders. *Journal of Consulting and Clinical Psychology* 55 (4): 566–70.

Erickson, W. D., N. H. Walbek, and R. K Seeley. 1988. Behavioral patterns of child molesters. *Archives of Sexual Behavior* 17: 77–86.

Fahy, T. A. 1988. The diagnosis of multiple personality disorder: A critical review. *British Journal of Psychiatry* 153: 597–606.

Femina, D. D., C. A. Yeager, and D. O. Lewis. 1990. Child abuse: Adolescent records vs. adult recall. *Child Abuse and Neglect* 14: 227–31.

Festinger, L, H. W. Riecken, and S. Schachter, 1956. *When prophecy fails.* Minneapolis: University of Minnesota Press.

Finkelhor, D., L. M. Williams, N. Burns. 1988. *Nursery crimes: Sexual abuse in day care*. Newbury Park, Calif.: Sage.

Finkelhor, D., L. M. Williams, N. Burns, and M. Kalinowski. 1988. *Sexual abuse in day care: A national study*. Study prepared under grant 90-CA-1155 from the National Center on Child Abuse and Neglect. University of New Hampshire: Family Research Laboratory.

Fivush, R., and N. R. Hamond. 1990. Autobiographical memory across the preschool years: Towards reconceptualizing childhood amnesia. In *Knowing and remembering in young children,* ed. R. Fivush and J. A. Hudson, 223–48. New York: Cambridge University Press.

Freud, A. 1965. *Normality and pathology in childhood*. New York: International University Press.

Galanter, M. 1990. Cults and zealous self-help movements: A psychiatric perspective. *American Journal of Psychiatry* 147: 543–51.

Gambrill, E. 1990. *Critical thinking in clinical practice*. San Francisco: Josey-Bass.

Ganaway, G. K. 1991. *Alternative hypotheses regarding satanic ritual abuse memories*. Presented at the 99th Annual Convention of the American Psychological Association, San Francisco, August 19.

Garland, R. J., and M. J. Dougher. 1990. The abused/abuser hypothesis of child sexual abuse: A critical review of theory and research. In *Pedophilia: Biosocial dimensions,* ed. J. R. Feierman, 488–509. New York: Springer-Verlag.

Geffner, B. 1991. Editor's comments. *Family Violence Bulletin* 7 (1): 1.

Goodman, G. S., and A. Hahn. 1987. Evaluating eyewitness testimony. In *Handbook of forensic psychology,* ed. I. B. Weiner and A. K. Hess, 258–92. New York: John Wiley and Sons.

Grand, S., J. L. Alpert, J. M. Safer, and R. Milden. 1991. Symposium: Incest and amnesia—How do we know what really happened. Presentation at the 99th Annual Convention of the American Psychological Association, San Francisco, August 17.

Greenwald, A. G. 1980. The totalitarian ego: Fabrication and revision of personal history. *American Psychologist* 35: 603–18.

Heller, K. 1991. Dirty little secrets, courtesy of the stars. *Philadelphia Inquirer* (October 6): 3G.

Hendrix, K. 1989. Challenge to child abuse. *Los Angeles Times* (December 29): E1, E16–E18.

Herman, J. L., and E. Schatzow. 1987. Recovery and verification of memories of childhood sexual trauma. *Psychoanalytic Psychology* 4 (1): 114.

Hicks, R. D. 1991. *In pursuit of Satan*. Amherst, N.Y.: Prometheus Books.

Hoch, E. L. 1982. Perspective on experimental contributions to clinical research. In *Handbook of research methods in clinical psychology,* ed. P. C. Kendall and J. N. Butcher, 13–57. New York: John Wiley and Sons.

Holmes, D. S. 1974. Investigations of repression: Differential recall of material experimentally or naturally associated with ego threat. *Psychological Bulletin* 81: 632–53.

Holmes, D. S. 1990. The evidence for repression: An examination of sixty years of research. In *Repression and dissociation,* ed. J. L. Singer, 85–102. Chicago: University of Chicago Press.

Hornstein, G. A. 1992. The return of the repressed: Psychology's problematic relations with psychoanalysis, 1909–1960. *American Psychologist* 47: 254–63.

Hull, M. 1991. Family secrets. *Texas Lawyer* (September 16): 1, 34, 35.

Kaza, C. 1991. Victims of childhood sexual abuse are hiding no more. *The Flint Journal* (December 29): A1, A10.

Kendall-Tackett, K. A., and A. F. Simon. 1992. A comparison of the abuse-experiences of male and female adults molested as children. *Journal of Family Violence* 7 (1): 57–72.

Kennedy, E. 1991. Suit accuses parents of incest. *Philadelphia Inquirer* (September 3): 1B, 4B.

Kiersch, T. A. 1962. Amnesia: A clinical study of ninety-eight cases. *American Journal of Psychiatry* 119: 57-60.

Kluft, R. P. 1987. The parental fitness of mothers with multiple personality disorder: A preliminary study. *Child Abuse and Neglect* 11: 273–80.

———. 1991. Multiple personality disorder. In *Review of psychiatry,* ed. A. Tasman and S. M. Goldfinger, 161–88. Washington, D.C.: American Psychiatric Press.

Knight, R. A. 1989. An assessment of the concurrent validity of a child molester typology. *Journal of Interpersonal Violence* 4: 131–50.

Knight, R. A., D. L. Carter, and R. A. Prentky. 1989. A system for the classification of child molesters. *Journal of Interpersonal Violence* 4: 3–23.

Lahey, B. B., and A. E. Kazdin. 1988. *Advances in clinical child psychology,* vol. 11. New York: Plenum Press.

———. 1989. *Advances in clinical child psychology,* vol. 12. New York: Plenum Press.

———. 1990. *Advances in clinical child psychology,* vol. 13. New York: Plenum Press.

Langevin, R. 1983. *Sexual strands: Understanding and treating sexual anomalies in men.* Hillsdale, N.J.: Lawrence Erlbaum Associates.

Langevin, R., and R. Lang. 1985. Psychological treatment of pedophiles. *Behavioral Sciences and the Law* 3: 403–17.

Lanning, K. V. 1991. Ritual abuse: A law enforcement view or perspective. *Child Abuse and Neglect* 15: 171–73.

———. 1992. *Investigator's guide to allegations of "ritual" abuse.* National Center for the Analysis of Violent Crime: Quantico, Va.

Loewenstein, R. J. 1991. Psychogenic amnesia and psychogenic fugue: A comprehensive review. In *Review of psychiatry,* ed. A. Tasman and S. M. Goldfinger, 189–221. Washington, D.C.: American Psychiatric Press.

Loftus, E. F., and L. Kaufman. In press. Why do traumatic experiences sometimes produce good memory (flashbulbs) and sometimes no memory (repression)? In *Affect and accuracy in recall: The problem of "flashbulb" memories,* ed. E. Winograd and U. Neisser. New York: Cambridge University Press.

Loftus, E. F., and K. Ketcham. 1991. *Witness for the defense.* New York: St. Martin's Press.

Loftus, E. F., N. L. Korf, and J. W. Schooler. 1989. Misguided memories: Sincere distortion of reality. In *Credibility assessment,* ed. J. C. Yuille, 155–74. Dordrecht, The Netherlands: Kluwer Academic Publishers.

Lundberg-Love, P. 1989. *Research and treatment issues concerning adult incest survivors.* Paper presented as part of a symposium titled "Treating incest victims and offenders: Applying recent research" at the 97th Annual Meeting of the American Psychological Association, New Orleans, August 11–15.

Lundberg-Love, P. J. (Undated). *Treatment of adult survivors of incest.* Unpublished manuscript.

Maltz, W. 1990. Adult survivors of incest: How to help them overcome the trauma. *Medical Aspects of Human Sexuality* (December): 42–47.

Meehl, P. E. 1989. Law and the fireside inductions (with postscript): Some reflections of a clinical psychologist. *Behavioral Sciences and the Law* 7: 521–50.

Monaghan, G. 1990. Writing book helped her come to grips with memories of sexual abuse as child. *Star Tribune* (March 12): 1E, 9E.

Mulhern, S. 1991. [Letter to the editor]. *Child Abuse and Neglect* 15: 609–10.

Nathan, D. 1991. Satanism and child molestation: Constructing the ritual abuse scare. In *The Satanism scare,* ed. J. Richardson, J. Best, and D. Bromley, 75–94. New York: Aldine de Gruyter.

Nelson, K. 1989. *Narratives from the crib.* Cambridge, Mass: Harvard University Press.

Nelson, K., and G. Ross. 1980. The generalities and specifics of long-term memory in infants and young children. *New Directions for Child Development* 10: 87–100.

Nisbett, R., and L. Ross. 1980. *Human inference: Strategies and shortcomings of social judgment.* Englewood Cliffs, N.J.: Prentice-Hall.

Nohlgren, S. 1991. Making a case to punish incest. *St. Petersburg Times* (April 28): 1B, 5B.

Orne, M. T., D. A. Soskis, D. F. Dinges, E. C. Orne, and M. H. Tonry. 1985. *Hypnotically refreshed testimony: Enhanced memory or tampering with evidence?* Washington, D.C.: U.S. Dept. of Justice, National Institute of Justice.

Paxton, C. 1991. A bridge to healing: Responding to disclosures of childhood sexual abuse. *Health Values* 15 (5): 49–56.

Pope, H. G., and J. I. Hudson. 1992. Is childhood sexual abuse a risk factor for bulimia nervosa? *American Journal of Psychiatry* 149: 45–46.

Power, D. J. 1977. Memory, identification, and crime. *Medicine, Science, and the Law* 17: 132–39.

Price, L. 1992. Presentation at the Midwest Regional FMS Foundation Meeting, Benton Harbor, Michigan, April 20.

Putnam, F. W. 1991a. Dissociative phenomena. In *Review of psychiatry,* ed. A.

Tasman and S. M. Goldfinger, 145-160. Washington, D.C.: American Psychiatric Press.

Putnam, F. W. 1991b. The satanic ritual abuse controversy. *Child Abuse and Neglect* 15: 175–79.

Putnam, F. W., J. J. Guroff, E. K. Silberman, L. Barban, and R. M. Post. 1986. The clinical phenomenology of multiple personality disorder: Review of 100 recent cases. *Journal of Clinical Psychiatry* 47 (6): 285–93.

Richardson, J. T., J. Best, and D. G. Bromley, eds. 1991. *The Satanism scare.* New York: Aldine de Gruyter.

Rivera, B., and C. S. Widom. 1990. Childhood victimization and violent offending. *Violence and Victims* 5, no. 1 (Spring): 19–35.

Roan, S. 1990. Experts see adult effects of molestation. *Los Angeles Times* (August 7): E1, E11, E12, .

Schacter, D. L 1986. On the relation between genuine and simulated amnesia. *Behavioral Sciences and the Law* 4: 47–64.

Sifford, D. 1991. Accusations of sex abuse, years later. *The Philadelphia Inquirer* (November 24): 1F, 5F.

Simon, L. M. J., B. Sales, A. Kaszniak, and M. Kahn. 1992. Characteristics of child molesters: Implications for the fixated-regressed dichotomy. *Journal of Interpersonal Violence* 7: 211–25.

Singer, J. L. 1990. Preface. In *Repression and dissociation,* ed. J. L. Singer, xi–xxi. Chicago: University of Chicago Press.

Singer, J. L., and J. B. Sincoff. 1990. Summary: Beyond repression and the defenses. In *Repression and dissociation,* ed. J. L. Singer, 471–96. Chicago: University of Chicago Press.

Spanos, N. P. 1991. *Hypnosis, suggestion, and creation of false memories and secondary personalities.* Presentation at the 99th Annual Convention of the American Psychological Association, San Francisco, August.

Spanos, N. P., C. A. Quigley, M. I. Gwynn, R. L. Glatt, and A. H. Perlini. 1991. Hypnotic interrogation, pretrial preparation, and witness testimony during direct and cross examination. *Law and Human Behavior* 15: 639–53.

Spanos, N. P., J. R. Weekes, and L. D. Bertrand. 1985. Multiple personality: A social psychological perspective. *Journal of Abnormal Psychology* 94: 362–76.

Spiegel, D. 1991. Dissociation and trauma. In *Review of psychiatry,* ed. A. Tasman and S. M. Goldfinger, 261–75. Washington D.C.: American Psychiatric Press.

Steinberg, M. 1991. The spectrum of depersonalization: Assessment and treatment. In *Review of psychiatry,* ed. A. Tasman and S. M. Goldfinger, 223–47. Washington, D.C.: American Psychiatric Press.

Suengas, A. G., and M. K. Johnson. 1988. Qualitative effects of rehearsal of memories for perceived and imagined events. *Journal of Experimental Psychology: General* 117: 377–89.

Summit, R. 1990. Reaching the unreachable. Midwest Conference on Child Abuse and Neglect, Madison, Wisconsin, October 29-November 1.

Terr, L. C. 1985. Children traumatized in small groups. In *Post-traumatic stress disorder in children,* ed. E. Eth and R. S. Pynoos, 45-70. Washington, D.C.: American Psychiatric Press.

———. 1988. What happens to early memories of trauma? A study of twenty children under age five at the time of documented events. *Journal of the American Academy of Child and Adolescent Psychiatry* 27 (1): 96–104.

———. 1990. *Too scared to cry.* New York: Harper & Row.

Thigpen, C. H., and H. M. Cleckley. 1954. *The three faces of Eve.* New York: McGraw Hill.

———. 1984. On the incidence of multiple personality disorder. *International Journal of Clinical and Experimental Hypnosis* 32: 63–66.

Tollison, C. D., and H. E. Adams. 1979. *Sexual disorders: Treatment, theory, and research.* New York: Gardner Press.

Toufexis, A. 1991. When can memories be trusted? *Time* (October 28): 86–88.

Underwager, R., and H. Wakefield. 1991. Cur Allii, Prae Aliis? (Why some and not others? *Issues in Child Abuse Accusations* 3: 178–93.

Van Derbur Atler, M. 1991. The darkest secret. *People* (June 10): 89–92, 94.

Victor, J. S. 1991a. The dynamics of rumor-panics about satanic cults. In *The Satanic scare,* ed. J. T. Richardson, J. Best, and D. G. Bromley, 221–36. New York: Aldine de Gruyter.

———. 1991b. The satanic cult scare and allegations of ritual child abuse. *Issues in Child Abuse Accusations* 3: 135–43.

———. In press. *Rumors of evil: The Satanic cult scare and the creation of imaginary deviance.* Peru, Ill.: Open Court Publishing Company.

Wakefield, H., and R. Underwager. 1992. Assessing credibility of children's testimony in ritual abuse allegations. *Issues in Child Abuse Accusations* 4: 32–44.

———. 1991. Female child sexual abusers: A critical review of the literature. *American Journal of Forensic Psychology* 9 (4): 43–69.

Wakefield, J. 1992. *Recovered memories of alleged sexual abuse: Memory as production and reproduction.* Paper presented at the Fourth Annual Convention of the American Psychological Society, San Diego, June 20.

Wares, D. 1991. The unleashing of memory. *California Lawyer,* pp. 19–20.

Weinert, F. E., and M. Perlmutter. 1988. *Memory development: Universal changes and individual differences.* Hillsdale, N.J.: Erlbaum Associates.

Widom, C. S. 1989a. Child abuse, neglect, and adult behavior: Research design and findings on criminality, violence, and child abuse. *American Journal of Orthopsychiatry* 59: 355–67.

———. 1989b. Does violence beget violence? A critical examination of the literature. *Psychological Bulletin* 106: 3–28.

———. 1989c. The cycle of violence. *Science* 244: 160–66.

Wiggins, E. C., and J. Bandt. 1988. The detection of simulated amnesia. *Law and Human Behavior* 12: 57–78.

Young, W. C., R. G. Sachs, B. G. Braun, and R. T. Watkins. 1991. Patients reporting ritual abuse in childhood: A clinical syndrome. Report of 37 cases. *Child Abuse and Neglect* 15: 181–89.

PART SIX

SUMMARY AND CONCLUSIONS

22

WHERE DO WE GO FROM HERE?

ROBERT A. BAKER

In the heated debate over these highly emotional issues it is important that we keep our perspective. Like every airliner crash, every case of child sexual molestation is a disaster. But, like the airplane crash, the case of abuse is significant because of its rarity. And, in spite of the appalling numbers, child sexual abuse is still, thank heaven, uncommon, infrequent, and rare. Millions of children are brought up happily and unscathed by billions of healthy, well-adjusted, loving, and caring parents. The abused child is, gratefully, a very small minority when compared with the uncountable numbers of children who are loved and protected. *We must not forget this fact!* Yet, every case of abuse and mistreatment, unfortunately, has deep, painful, and far-reaching social repercussions affecting many different people. There is certainly enough pain and tragedy here already without creating more in our misguided efforts to help the alleged victims. We must not add insult to injury by falsely creating cases of sexual abuse where they never existed.

As we have seen in many of the preceding essays, far too many CPS workers, psychiatrists, psychologists, psychotherapists et al., in their good-intentioned zeal to help their alleged victims obtain revenge and dispense justice have, instead, done considerable harm and have created even worse problems than the original one they were supposed to solve. *This must not be allowed to continue.* We simply cannot afford or tolerate therapeutic incompetence.

Neither can we any longer countenance or tolerate "ignorant experts" and "legal incompetence" when our molestation cases reach the

461

courts. In a truly groundbreaking paper published in 1993, "A Paradigm Shift for Expert Witnesses" (*Issues in Child Abuse Accusations* 5, no. 3: 156–67), Underwager and Wakefield called attention to the Supreme Court decision in the *Daubert* v. *Merrell Dow* case which has dramatically changed the criteria by which scientific testimony is admitted as evidence in court. The Supreme Court's unanimous decision states that "the criterion of the scientific status of a theory is its falsifiability, refutability, or testability." By replacing the Frye test, this ruling renders inadmissible all testimony based on such concepts and theories as the child sexual abuse accommodation syndrome and claims that childhood sexual abuse has been repressed. In fact, as Underwager and Wakefield indicate, in the past in case after case, testimony offered and presented as "science" or "scientific" would no longer be admitted because of its unfalsifiability. Examples would be whenever:

- The child makes any statement which may be broadly interpreted to imply abuse. Since children cannot lie about abuse and cannot talk about things they have not directly experienced, all such statements must be taken at face value, regardless of their face validity or incredibility.

- The child initially denies abuse but later discloses after "disclosure therapy." The child will initially deny because the child needs time to overcome shame and embarrassment, develop a trusting relationship with the therapist, and then feel safe enough to disclose the abuse. In the interval, it is perfectly proper to use leading and suggestive questioning, coercion, persuasion, and any other methods of social influence, to assist the child in disclosing the terrible secret.

- The child initially acknowledges some abuse, but then recants or retracts earlier statements. Though recanted or retracted, the abuse allegation is still true because the child is under pressure from the perpetrator or the family to recant and is scared. Recantation is described as typical of children who have been abused and, therefore, cannot disprove abuse.

- The child "discloses" abuse years after the period encompassed by the allegation. Even given demonstrable adult social influence triggering the disclosure, the assumption is that it is typical of abused children that they will delay disclosure.

- The child "discloses" abuse immediately after the period encompassed by the allegation. The child is viewed as overwhelmed by the abuse, or is too fearful to maintain the secret, or has found him/herself in a "safe" situation within which to disclose the abuse.

- The medical examination finds genital "trauma" indicative of sexual abuse. Medical findings of genital "trauma" may or may not take into consideration the baseline rates of similar genital findings in nonabused children.

- The medical examination finds no genital "trauma" which, given the frequency of fondling and nonpenetrative sexual contact as the predominate act of sexual abuse, is consistent with the child having been abused.

- The child is calm and cooperative during a genital examination. Such a child is viewed as experienced in having the genitals touched and examined by virtue of the abusive experience (i.e., has been desensitized to genital contact).

- The child struggles and resists the genital examination, or becomes emotionally distraught by the exam. Such a child has previously been traumatized by sexual abuse leading to reluctance to having anyone else touch or examine the genitals.

- In the absence of physical findings, the adult accompanying the child to the medical exam, informs the physician of the abuse history. The physician, though finding no physical evidence of sexual abuse, renders the conclusion, "abuse by history," as a result of the report of abuse by the accompanying adult.

(Underwager and Wakefield 1993, 160)

On the other side, in interpreting the behavior of the accused, abuse is supported when:

- The accused proclaims innocence. Such individuals are in denial regarding the abuse.

- The accused passes the polygraph or penile plethysmograph. Such individuals are in even greater denial regarding the abuse.

- The accused shows little or no emotion when being confronted or questioned about the abuse. The accused is thus either in denial, is sociopathic, or is a master manipulator and has little concern for society's mores and values.

- The accused becomes emotional or tearful when confronted or questioned about the abuse. The accused is overwhelmed by guilt and disgust over his behavior.

- The accused becomes angry or defiant when confronted or questioned about abuse. The accused is defending against his actions by projecting blame and responsibility onto others.

- The accused requests to speak to an attorney before questioning. If the accused had nothing to hide, an attorney would not be needed.

- The accused cooperates with the interrogator and, in attempting to identify the source of the abuse accusation, talks about innocuous or ambiguous behavior. The statements of the accused are viewed as confessions as he is struggling to admit the true nature of the abusive acts.

(Underwager and Wakefield 1993, 161)

As Underwager and Wakefield stress, "almost any circumstance, behavior, or observation can be rationalized as supporting the conclusion that sexual abuse occurred ". . . in fact there is no circumstance, behavior, or observation which could be used to conclude that abuse did not occur." In sum, there is no way that anyone can prove the underlying theory false.

As a society we must also learn to use restraint and reason and avoid a panicked "rush to judgment" when the media bombards us with stories having a paranormal or occult tinge or with tales that go against the grain of common sense as in the persistent reports of satanic cults and ritualistic child abuse. The massive, intense, and nationwide investigation carried out by Dr. Gail Goodman and her colleagues and sponsored by the National Center on Child Abuse and Neglect finally was able to substitute truth and reason for rumor and superstition. In Goodman's final report published in 1994 she stated:

Results indicated that the purported evidence for claims of ritualistic abuse, especially in cases involving alleged adult survivors of satanic cult activity, is questionable. In contrast, convincing evidence was available for a variety of types of religion-related abuse (e.g., withholding of medical care, abuse by religious officials such as priests . . .). Reports of repressed memory of ritualistic abuse made by adult-survivors were found to be particularly extreme, especially when the adult survivor claimed to be both a victim and perpetrator of abuse.

(Abstract, Final Report to NCCAN, Gail Goodman et al., Department of Psychology, University of California, Davis, 1994)

Here, it is important to remember, abuse can take varied forms. A particularly poignant and telling phrase taken from Goodman et al.'s conclusion is worth repeating:

Our research leads us to believe that there are many more children being abused in the name of God than in the name of Satan. Ironically, while the public concerns itself with passing laws to punish satanic child abuse, laws already exist that protect parents whose particular variants of belief in God deny their children life-saving medical care. The freedom to choose religions and to practice them will, and should, always be protected by our constitution, but the freedom to abuse children in the course of these practices ought to be curtailed.

(Abstract, Final Report 1994, cited above)

We must also conclude, based on the weight of the evidence, that psychotherapeutic and clinical practice must be improved. It is urgent that therapists keep up with current research in all areas bearing on the issue of sexual molestation and abuse, i.e., children's memory, children's testimony, and child developmental findings as well as what is currently known about hypnosis and hypnosislike procedures which create confabulated memories, i.e., fantasies that are indistinguishable from reality. Obviously, research must continue on the nature of and effects of trauma on both memory and behavior.

To further improve therapists' behavior and to increase their responsibility to their clients, state legislators should give serious consideration to the enactment of the Truth and Responsibility in Mental Health Practices Act (or some modified version of it) currently being sponsored by Dr. R. C. Barden in Minnesota and that is currently being considered in a number of states including New Hampshire, Missouri, Texas, Illinois, and Kentucky. Some form of such legislation would go a very long way toward not only putting psychotherapy and clinical practice on a scientific footing but it would also effectively counter and eliminate most of the current recovered-memory miscarriages of justice.

Finally, it is highly unlikely that cases of sexual molestation of children will ever be totally and entirely eliminated from modern civilization. It may, however, be "possible" in the future to effectively reduce its occurrence. We say *possible* instead of *probable* simply because our society has never, thus far, been ready, willing, or able to behave in a sane, coordinated, cooperative, and rational manner when facing such vast social dilemmas as crime, punishment, drugs, poverty, mental health, or education. Sexual molestation is another such "unsolvable" social problem. Those in any position to take positive, remedial steps do not have either the popular support or the political courage to act alone. Moreover, there are too many experts at cross-purposes who have let their emotions color their judgments and who have amassed armies and ammunition to cripple and maim those who disagree. The result is clear: nothing is done to ease or affect the problem. All efforts in this area—as well as our struggles with the war on drugs—more and more resemble the sucking quagmire of Yugoslavia.

Be that as it may, socially and politically we may not—at our current level of civilized progress—be able to affect the rate of or the causes of child abuse. What we can do if we are willing to act forcibly against the organized opposition and to make a few entrenched individuals with strong vested interests "mad" is to bring to an end *all* or at least *most* of the injustices created by "recovered-memory" therapy.

It is also conceivable that it is possible, sometime in the future, to improve family life by reducing economic pressures and by raising the standard of living of the average family simply by improving health care and increasing income. Also by improving education in child care and by providing stress-reduction training, marital counseling, and emotional, i.e., mental health education and reeducation—those tension storms and emotional explosions that lead directly or indirectly to child molestation might be averted. It is even possible that nurturance can be taught. No one knows, however, until someone tries. In any event, prevention in the form of positive steps to head off abuse before it happens is something that needs exploring. A step in this direction is a model program that has been very successful in Hawaii called Healthy Start. Its approach is to intervene early and help new parents raise healthy and happy children. The program was started in 1985 and has been copied extensively on a nationwide basis with approximately twenty different states now having such a program in development. Sponsored and supported by the National Committee to Prevent Child Abuse, Anne C. Donnelly, executive director of NCPCA, says that program employees visit new parents at the hospital shortly after their child is born and, with parental consent, the program workers talk to the parents about their current situation and their past history. If danger signs or signals exist, then program workers make home visits and serve as confidants, advocates, and catalysts to help with any and all problems in living. Healthy Start's annual budget is now only $8 million and it costs the state about $2,500 per family. Thus far, all such programs are showing positive results. In the families who have made use of Healthy Start since its inception there is less than a 1% incidence of child abuse as compared with the national average of 4.7% (Margery Stein, "We're Breaking the Cycle of Abuse," *Parade Magazine*, July 23, 1995, p. 8). Preventive programs such as these can certainly use all of our existing crop of social workers, psychotherapists, CPS employees, child development workers, and teachers who could and would serve admirably in such a role.

Unfortunately, with the current political tide turned against doing anything positive to help the poor, unfortunate, downtrodden, disabled, old, incompetent, and hapless or even going so far as to provide universal health care, it is most unlikely that anything on a large social scale capable of having any long-run or lasting consequences will ever be done. When simple, workable, tested, and proved programs like Head Start are tossed in the trash bin, what hope is there for anything in the way of social progress or help for the coming generations of children? At the moment, we have no political leaders with either the vision or human concern to make such expensive or unpopular causes any part of their political agenda. It is highly unlikely that any such champion will ever emerge, and if and when they do their chance for political survival would most likely be slim. Like most of our citizens, when faced with such social issues as child sexual abuse, they avert their eyes and minds and pray the problem will go away. Thus far, at least, such prayers have fallen on deaf ears and into the laps of the powerless. Mere prayer, we are convinced, is a waste of time. Something much more powerful and effective is needed.

Of course, if one cares enough and is concerned enough one doesn't have to wait for our leaders and politicians to act. A few individuals can join forces at the grass-roots level and, on their own as did the people in Hawaii who formed Healthy Start, make a difference child by child, family by family. This, in the long run, might be infinitely more effective and productive than any political action or inane and ineffective legislative war such as our "war on crime," "war on drugs," "war on poverty," and so on and on ad infinitum and ad nauseam. For as we all know, the one sure way *not* to change human behavior is to pass a law forbidding it.

RECOMMENDED READINGS

OVERVIEWS

Fredickson, R. 1992. *Repressed memories: A journey to recovery from sexual abuse.* New York: Simon and Schuster.

Goldstein, Eleanor, and Kevin Farmer. 1992. *Confabulations: Creating false memories destroying families.* Boca Raton, Fla.: Upton Books.

———. 1993. *True stories of false memories.* Boca Raton, Fla.: Upton Books.

Loftus, Elizabeth F., and K. Ketcham. 1994. *The myth of repressed memory.* New York: St. Martin's Press.

Nathan, Debbie, and Michael Snedeker. 1995. *Satan's silence: Ritual abuse and the making of a modern American witch hunt.* New York: Basic Books (HarperCollins).

Ofshe, Richard, and Ethan Watters. 1994. *Making monsters: False memories, psychotherapy and sexual hysteria.* New York: Scribner's.

Pendergast, Mark. 1995. *Victims of memory: Incest accusations and shattered lives.* Hinesburg, Vt.: Upper Access Books.

Pope, Kenneth S., and Laura S. Brown. 1996. *Recovered memories of abuse: Assessment, therapy, forensics.* Washington, D.C.: American Psychological Association.

Wakefield, Hollida, and Ralph Underwager. 1994. *Return of the furies: An investigation into recovered memory therapy.* Chicago & La Salle, Ill.: Open Court.

Wassil-Grimm, Claudette. 1995. *Diagnosis for disaster: The devastating truth about false memory syndrome and its impact on accusers and families.* Woodstock. N.Y.: The Overlook Press.

Yapko, Michael. 1994. *Suggestions of abuse.* New York: Simon and Schuster.

HYPNOSIS

Baker, Robert A. 1990. *They call it hypnosis.* Amherst, N.Y.: Prometheus Books.

SEXUAL ABUSE TRAUMA

Briere, John N. 1992. *Child abuse trauma: Theory and treatment of the lasting effects.* Newbury Park, Calif.: Sage.
Herman, Judith. 1992. *Trauma and recovery.* New York: Basic Books
Terr, Leonore. 1990. *Too scared to cry.* New York: Harper & Row.
———. 1994. *Unchallenged memories.* New York: Basic Books

CHILDREN'S TESTIMONY

Ceci, Stephen, and Maggie Bruck. 1995. *Jeopardy in the courtroom: A scientific analysis of children's testimony.* Hyattsville, Md.: American Psychological Association.
Doris, John, ed. 1991. *The suggestibility of children's recollections.* Hyattsville, Md.: American Psychological Association.
Goodman, Gail S. 1992. Testifying in criminal court: Emotional effects on child sexual assault victims. *Monograph of Society for Research in Child Development* 57 (5): 229.
Myers, John E. B. 1993. The competence of young children to testify in legal proceedings. *Behavioral Science and the Law* 11: 121–33.

PSYCHOTHERAPY

Baker, Robert A. 1996. *Mind games.* Amherst, N.Y.: Prometheus Books.
Campbell, Terence W. 1994. *Beware the talking cure: Psychotherapy may be hazardous to your health.* Boca Raton, Fla.: Upton Books.
Journal of Psychohistory. 1995. Special issue: Backlash against psychotherapy. Vol. 22, no. 3 (Winter 1995). New York.

SEXUAL ABUSE (GENERAL)

Courtois, Christine. 1988. *Healing the incest wound: Adult survivors in therapy.* New York: W. W. Norton & Company.
Deaton, Wendy, et al. 1995. *The child sexual abuse custody dispute annotated bibliography.* Thousand Oaks, Calif.: Sage.
Journal of Psychohistory. 1991. Special issue: The sexual abuse of children. Vol. 19, no. 2 (Fall 1991).

LEGAL ISSUES

Bulkley, Josephine A., and M. J. Horowitz. 1994. Adults sexually abused as children: Legal actions and issues. *Behavioral Sciences and the Law* 12: 65–87.

Rogers, Martha L. 1994. Factors to consider in assessing adult litigant's complaints of childhood sexual abuse. *Behavioral Sciences and the Law* 12: 279–98.

RESEARCH ISSUES

Brown, Daniel. 1995. Pseudomemories: The standard of science and the standard of care in trauma treatment. *American Journal of Clinical Hypnosis* 37, no. 3 (January): 1–24.

Myers, John E. B. 1991. Commentary: Steps toward forensically relevant research. In *Children's memory for stressful events,* edited by G. S. Goodman, J. E. Hirschman, D. Hepps, and L. Rudy. *Merrill-Palmer Quarterly* 37: 109–98.

Pope, Kenneth S. 1996. Memory, abuse, and science: Questioning claims about the false memory syndrome epidemic. *American Psychologist* 51 (9): 957–74.

ORGANIZATIONS

False Memory Syndrome Foundation: 3401 Market Street, Suite 130, Philadelphia, PA 19104 PHONE: 215-387-1865.

National Resource Center on Child Sexual Abuse: 2204 Whitesburg Drive, Suite 200, Huntsville, AL 35801 PHONE: 205-534-6868.

CONTRIBUTORS

Robert A. Baker, Ph.D., is professor emeritus in psychology, University of Kentucky, Lexington, Kentucky.

Dr. Steven R. H. Beach is associate professor of psychology at the University of Georgia, Athens.

Dr. Barry L. Beyerstein is professor of psychology at Simon Fraser University, Burnaby, B.C., Canada.

Dr. Angela Browne is at the Better Homes Fund, Newton Centre, Massachusetts.

Dr. Maggie Bruck is a professor in the department of psychology, McGill University, Montreal, Quebec, Canada, and coauthor (with Stephen J. Ceci) of *Jeopardy in the Courtroom* (Washington, D.C.: American Psychological Association, 1995).

Dr. David Calof is a family therapist in private practice in Seattle and editor of *Treating Abuse Today,* a newsletter for clinicians working with sexually abused clients.

Dr. Stephen J. Ceci is a professor in the department of family studies and human development at Cornell University, Ithaca, New York, and coauthor (with Maggie Bruck) of *Jeopardy in the Courtroom* (Washington, D.C.: American Psychological Association, 1995).

Dr. Christine A. Courtois is clinical director of the Center for Abuse Recovery and Empowerment at the Psychiatric Institute, Washington,

473

D.C., and a psychologist in private practice. She is also the author of *Healing the Incest Wound* (W. W. Norton Co., 1988).

Dr. Judith C. Daniluk is assistant professor of counseling psychology at the University of British Columbia, Vancouver, Canada.

Dr. Carol Diener is director of the mental health worker program at the University of Illinois, Champaign.

Julie Feldman is professor of psychology at the University of Washington in Seattle.

Dr. Frank D. Fincham is at the School of Psychology, University of Wales, Cardiff.

Dr. David Finklehor is a member of the Family Research Laboratory and the Family Violence Research Program at the University of New Hampshire, Durham.

Maryanne Garry is professor of psychology at the University of Washington in Seattle.

Dr. Gail S. Goodman is professor of psychology at the University of California, Davis.

Dr. Beth Haverkamp is assistant professor of counseling psychology at the University of British Columbia, Vancouver, Canada.

Jodi E. Hirschman is the Attorney-In-Charge of the Bronx trial office of the Legal Aid Society, Juvenile Rights Division.

Dr. David S. Holmes is professor of psychology at the University of Kansas, Lawrence.

James I. Hudson, M.D., is a psychiatrist at the McLean Hospital, Belmont, Massachusetts, and the department of psychiatry, Harvard Medical School, Cambridge, Massachusetts.

Dr. Elizabeth F. Loftus, another memory expert, is professor of psychology at the University of Washington in Seattle.

Debra Hepps McKee is a clinical psychologist.

Dr. Thom Moore is director of the Psychological Services Center, University of Illinois at Urbana-Champaign.

Dr. Richard Ofshe is professor of sociology at the University of California in Berkeley, California, and coauthor (with Ethan Watters) of *Making Monsters* (Scribners, 1994).

Dr. James R. P. Ogloff is professor of psychology at Simon Fraser University, Burnaby, B.C., Canada.

Dr. Kathy Pezdek is professor of psychology at the Center for Organizational and Behavioral Sciences, Claremont Graduate University, Claremont, California.

Harrison G. Pope Jr., M.D., is a psychiatrist at McLean Hospital, Belmont, Massachusetts, and the department of psychiatry, Harvard Medical School, Cambridge, Massachusetts.

Dr. Andrew D. Reisner, Psy.D., is a clinical psychologist with Community Counseling Services in Gallon, Ohio.

Leslie Rudy, Ph.D., is a clinical researcher associated with the Columbus Family & Child Guidance Centers.

Donald R. Tayloe, M.D., is at the department of veterans affairs in Fresno, California, and the University of California, San Francisco.

Dr. Ralph Underwager is a psychologist associated with the Institute for Psychological Therapies in Northfield, Minnesota. He is the coauthor (with Hollida Wakefield, M.A.) of *Return of the Furies: An Investigation into Recovered Memory Therapy* (Chicago and La Salle, Ill.: Open Court, 1994).

Hollida Wakefield, M.A., is a psychologist associated with The Institute for Psychological Therapies in Northfield, Minnesota. She is the coauthor (with Dr. Ralph Underwager) of *Return of the Furies: An Investigation into Recovered Memory Therapy* (Chicago and La Salle, Ill.: Open Court, 1994).

Ethan Watters is a freelance journalist and coauthor (with Richard Ofshe) of *Making Monsters* (Scribners, 1994).

Dr. Mary Sykes Wylie is senior editor of *The Family Therapy Network*, published by the Family Therapy Network of Washington, D.C.

Dr. Michael D. Yapko is a clinical psychologist in private practice in Leucadia, California, and author of *Suggestions of Abuse* (Simon & Schuster, 1994).

Addiction and Recovery, 54
Alcock, James, 21
alien abduction, 17, 47n. 1
allegations, criteria for judging accuracy of, 444–51
American Association for Marriage and Family Therapy (AAMFT) code of ethical principles, 336–40, 345, 347
American Civil Liberties Union (ACLU), 294
anatomically correct dolls, 301–302
  use in investigations, 312, 401–403, 411–12, 418–19n. 8
Arnold, Roseanne, 81, 215

Bains, Marvin, 253–56
Baker, Robert, 22
Barden, R. C., 465
Bartlett, Frederick, 18
Bass, Ellen, 16, 28, 52, 80
Berliner, Lucy, 69
Bernheim, H., 250
biopsychiatry, 246–47
Bowers, Kenneth, 22
Bradshaw, John, 52, 64, 65, 81

Briere, John, 61, 71
Buckey, Raymond, 384–94

Canada, sexual abuse in, 15
Ceci, Stephen, 23
child protection services (CPS), 280–81, 282, 322, 328–29, 461, 466
child sexual abuse. *See* sexual abuse
child witnesses, credibility, 384–424
childhood amnesia, 32, 98–145, 194, 433–34
children's rights, 340–41
Clinical Psychiatry News, 61
confirmatory bias, 310–12
Country Walk day-care case, 417n. 2
Courage to Heal, 16, 35, 52, 59, 64, 80, 427, 429, 449
Courtois, Christine, 65, 67, 69
credibility of child witnesses. *See* child witnesses, credibility
cryptomnesia, 20–21

Daubert v. *Merrell Dow*, 462
Davis, Laura, 16, 28, 52, 80
DeMause, Lloyd, 13
depression, 449

DESNOS (disorders of extreme stress, not otherwise specified), 70–71
Diagnostic and Statistical Manual (DSM), 62, 70, 91, 447
Discover, 41
dissociation, 21, 72, 89, 260, 264–65, 425, 435–38
Donnelly, Anne C., 466
dream interpretation, 429

error in child abuse investigations, 330–32
evidence, levels of, 417–18n. 4

False Memory Syndrome Foundation (FMSF), 23, 50–75 passim, 248, 428, 452n. 1
Federal Rules of Evidence, 414
Forrest, Margot Silk, 65
Freud, Sigmund, 150, 229, 233–35, 250, 432
Frye test of evidence, 462

Ganaway, George, 32, 61
Gardner, Richard, 56–57
Georgia Skeptic, 28
Goodman, Gail S., 464
Gottman, John, 45–46
group therapy, 272
guided imagery, 34
Guze, Samuel, 61

Hammond, Cory, 243, 248
Healing the Incest Wound, 65
Healing Woman, The, 65, 71
Healthy Start, 467
Herman, Judith, 60, 68
Hilgard, Ernest, 22
Hirschman, Jodi E., 97
Hoult v. *Hoult*, 42–44
hypnosis. *See* hypnotherapy
hypnosis attitude questionnaire (HAQ), 218–23
hypnotherapy, 82, 90, 93–95, 215–

26, 233, 238–41, 244, 251, 252, 256–57, 427, 429, 441–42, 465

Idaho v. *Wright*, 418n. 6
incest, 13, 260–62
    effects, 355–83
infantile amnesia. *See* childhood amnesia
Issues in Child Abuse Accusations, 57, 462

Journal of Psychohistory, 13

Kelly, Bob, 417n. 2
Kluft, Richard, 61
Kornfield, Jack, 91

Lerner, Melvin, 74
Lief, Harold, 17–18, 54
Little Rascals case, 417n. 2
Loewenstein, Richard, 60, 65
Loftus, Elizabeth, 11, 19, 28

Mack, John, 47n. 1
McKee, Debra Hepps, 97
McMartin Preschool case, 384–94, 405, 417n. 3, 443
memory. *See also* suggestibility of children
    accuracy, 90, 91, 193–212, 309–10, 313
    children's, 300–302, 332–33, 465
    confabulated (false), 465
    criteria for judging accuracy of, 444–51
    retrieval techniques, 270, 425–58, 466
    theories, 18–19, 431–33
Michaels, Kelly, 409–10, 417n. 2. *See also State of New Jersey* v. *Kelly Michaels*
Mother Jones, 43
multiple personality disorder (MPD), 62, 66, 69, 73, 241–42, 245, 425, 438–40, 449

National Center on Child Abuse and Neglect (NCCAN), 464
National Child Abuse and Neglect Data System, 288
National Committee to Prevent Child Abuse (NCPCA), 466
National Incidence Surveys, 288–89

Ofshe, Richard, 22–23, 54, 55, 251
"Oprah Winfrey Show," 81, 215
Orne, Martin, 22, 23

Parade Magazine, 466
Penfield, Wilder, 19
Piaget, Jean, 21
post-traumatic stress disorder, 62, 70, 71, 76–77, 89, 262
Project Monarch, 243
Psychiatric Clinics of North America, 74
psychoanalysis, 247
Putnam, Frank, M.D., 9

Rational Enquirer, 28
recanters, 58
reincarnation, 20
repression, 11, 16, 21–22, 38, 149–214, 223–24, 228, 229–33, 251, 264–65, 425, 434–35, 464, definition, 150
Reznick, Wayne, 69
ritual satanic abuse. *See* satanic ritual abuse
Rock v. *Arkansas*, 252
Ross, Colin, 64, 66, 71, 74
Rudy, Leslie, 97

satanic cults, 241–43, 244, 427
satanic ritual abuse, 31–32, 67, 78, 384–85, 425, 427, 442–51, 464–65
sexual abuse

accusations, criteria for judging, 444–51
accusations, false, 325, 330–32
Canada, 15
children's experience of investigations, 297–99
definition, 288
effects, 9, 296, 355–83
ethical dilemmas, 335–53
extent, 12–14, 79, 280–84, 465–67
mandated reporting, 341–44
research, 296–99
therapy, 344–47
sexual dysfunction, 449
Skeptical Inquirer, 17
Smith, Winnie, 91
Spanos, Nicholas, 22, 28
State of New Jersey v. *Kelly Michaels*, 282, 285, 303, 332, 409–10
suggestibility, 428
of children, 314–15, 323–24, 332, 389–411, 418–19n. 8
Summit, Rolland, 63, 64, 74

testimony, expert, 410–11, 414–17, 461–62
of children, 384–424, 465
trauma, 440–41. *See also* post-traumatic stress disorder
triggers, 265–66, 271
Truth and Responsibility in Mental Health Practices Act, 465

United States Supreme Court, 462
Unspeakable Acts, 417n. 2

Van Der Kolk, Bessel, 70, 71
Victor, Jeffrey, 59

Wee Care case, 409–10, 417n. 2
witches, 38–40
witnesses, expert. *See* testimony, expert